FRIENDLY FIRE

THE UNTOLD STORY OF THE U.S. BOMBING THAT KILLED
FOUR CANADIAN SOLDIERS IN AFGHANISTAN

MICHAEL FRISCOLANTI

WILEY

John Wiley & Sons Canada, Ltd.

National Library of Canada Cataloguing in Publication Data

Friscolanti, Michael, 1976–
    Friendly fire : the untold story of the U.S. bombing that killed four Canadian soldiers in Afghanistan / Michael Friscolanti.

Includes bibliographical references and index.

ISBN-13 978-0-470-83686-6
ISBN 10 0-470-83686-5

    1. Friendly fire (Military science)—Afghanistan. 2. Afghan War, 2001–
—Aerial operations, American. 3. Canada—Armed forces—Afghanistan.
4. Canada. Canadian Armed Forces. Princess Patricia's Canadian Light
Infantry. 5. Canada—Military relations—United States. 6. United
States—Military relations—Canada. I. Title.

DS371.4.F75 2005   958.104'7   C2005-905482-4

Production Credits:
Cover & Interior text design: Mike Chan

Printer: Tri-Graphic Printing Ltd.

John Wiley & Sons Canada, Ltd.
6045 Freemont Blvd.
Mississauga, Ontario
L5R 4J3

Printed in Canada

10 9 8 7 6 5 4 3 2 1

TABLE OF CONTENTS

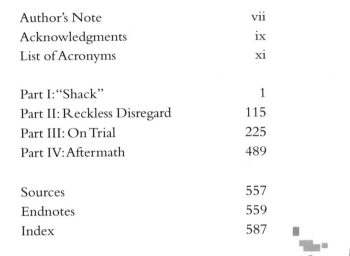

Author's Note

On April 17, 2002, an American F-16 pilot flying over Afghanistan dropped a bomb on what he thought was the enemy. He was wrong. Four Canadian soldiers died. Eight others were wounded. This book is the story of that mistake.

Nine months ago, I began this project with what seemed like a simple goal: recreate the events of that night and the years since through the eyes and opinions of those who lived it. Tell the story, and let the readers draw their own conclusions. At the time, I figured I knew the saga as well as anybody. As a journalist at the *National Post*, I was among the many reporters who covered this case from day one, sifting through the spin and the sensation in search of the next day's headline. Only years later, when I started to piece together this book, did I realize just how much of this story has yet to be told.

As part of my research, I met and interviewed dozens of the people most closely connected to this incident. Soldiers. Pilots. Relatives. Lawyers. Investigators. I also reviewed thousands of pages of sworn testimony and exhibits, much of it classified until now. The end result is a complex story, as technical as it is emotional. Readers looking for an academic study on the phenomenon of friendly fire will not find it here. This book offers no simple answers, no solutions. It is a narrative, the most complete account yet of what happened at Tarnak Farm, and what happened after.

For clarity's sake, the book unfolds in chronological order, split into four distinct sections. Section I recalls the night of the attack and the horror and heroics that followed. Section II takes readers inside the official investigations, including access to closed-door conversations that, to this day, are still considered secret by the United States Air Force and the Canadian Department of National Defence. Section III chronicles the pre-trial hearing of Major Harry Schmidt and Major Bill Umbach, the Illinois pilots who were charged in connection with the bombing. The final section provides a glimpse into the current lives of many of the main characters, and what some continue to endure.

Much of the dialogue in this book is taken directly from official transcripts, logbooks and tape-recorded radio calls. The symbol ⌣ indicates a break in ongoing interviews or testimony of an individual. Some of the conversations were recreated based on the memories of those who did the talking. Though nobody's memory is perfect, I did my best to avoid embellishment. Not a single line in this book is fiction.

What follows is not a thesis. It is not an indictment—nor a defense—of anybody's actions. I draw no conclusions, nor do I pass any judgment. As you will see, there are more than enough people—people whose lives were forever changed by that bomb—with strong opinions to voice. Better to hear them than me.

To all those who agreed to share their thoughts and recollections with a complete stranger, I am forever grateful. Everyone I spoke to was both candid and sincere. I would especially like to thank the families of Marc Léger, Ainsworth Dyer, Nathan Smith, and Richard Green. Regardless of who is to blame for their deaths, it will never change who they were. By all accounts, all four were excellent soldiers, and even finer men.

Michael Friscolanti
September 2005

Acknowledgments

Many people contributed, directly or indirectly, to the completion of this book. I would like to thank my employer, CanWest Global, and all my editors at the *National Post*—past and present—who trusted a young reporter to work on this important story, including Doug Kelly, Stephen Meurice, Martin Newland, John Racovali, Mark Stevenson, Dianna Symonds, Alison Uncles, Paul Waldie, Jonathan Harris and Kenneth Whyte. Thanks also to Scott Maniquet and Jeff Wasserman, who helped me when they didn't have to. I am especially grateful to *Post* colleagues Adrian Humphreys and Stewart Bell, both of whom strongly encouraged me to write this book and were more than supportive throughout the entire process.

Many fellow journalists followed this story just as closely as I did, and some of their work is cited in this book. Thanks to Alison Auld, David Common and especially Glen McGregor of *The Ottawa Citizen*, whose tenacity kept me awake more nights than I care to remember.

On the military side, I am grateful for the co-operation and assistance of Colonel Wayne Eyre, Major Michael Taylor, Major Scott Lundy, Captain Denise Kerr, Captain Holly Apostoliuk and Captain Geoff Mundy. They were always accommodating, and always had answers to my questions.

I want to thank Don Loney, my editor at John Wiley & Sons in Toronto. Thanks also to Nicole Langlois, who copyedited the book, Mike Chan, Meghan Brousseau, Pamela Vokey and the rest of the team at Wiley Canada.

To the many, many people who agreed to speak to me for this book, thank you. I appreciate your honesty and your time.

Finally, I would like to thank all of my family and friends in Hamilton, Toronto and Sault Ste. Marie who stood behind me for nine long months as I devoted every waking second to this project. I am blessed to have you all in my life.

List of Acronyms

2 I/C – Second in Command
332 AEG – 332nd Air Expeditionary Group

AAA – Anti-Aircraft Artillery
ABCCC – Airborne Battlefield Command and Control Center
ACC – Air Component Command
ACO – Airspace Control Order
AGL – Above Ground Level
AOs – Areas of Operation
AOR – Area of Responsibility
ASOC – Air Support Operations Center
ATO – Air Tasking Order
AWACs – Airborne Warning & Control System
BOI – Board of Inquiry
BOSSMAN – The call sign of AWACS
CAOC – Coalition Air Operations Center (pronounced "Kay-ock")
CCO – Chief of Combat Operations
CFACC – Coalition Forces Air Component Commander
CFLCC – Coalition Forces Land Component Commander
CIB – Coalition Investigation Board
CINC – Commander-in-Chief
CQB – Close-Quarter Battle
DCO – Director of Combat Operations
FAC – Forward Air Controller
FEB – Flying Evaluation Board
FEBA – Forward Edge of Battle Area
FLOT – Forward Line of Troops
FSCL – Forward Support Coordination Line

GLO – Ground Liaison Officer

GOB – Ground Order of Battle

JAG – Judge Advocate General

JTF-SWA – Joint Task Force Southwest Asia

MANPADS – Man-Portable Air Defense System

MLRS – Multiple Launch Rocket System

MPC – Mission Planning Cell

NFAs – No-Fly Areas

NOTAM – Notice to Airmen

NVGs – Night Vision Goggles

OEF – Operation Enduring Freedom

ROE – Rules of Engagement

ROZs – Restricted Operating Zones

RPG – Rocket-Propelled Grenade

SAFIRE – Surface-to-Air Fire

SOP – Standard Operating Procedure

SPINS – Special Instructions (theater-specific ROE)

TCA – Terminal Control Area

TMAs – Terminal Movement Areas

TOC – Tactical Operations Center

UCMJ – Uniform Code of Military Justice

VFW – Veterans of Foreign Wars

PART I: "SHACK"

chapter one

It takes Brad McKenzie a few minutes to find him, but when he spots Joe Jasper amid the darkness, he relays the message right away. "You got to get on means," Master Corporal McKenzie says, referring to the company's VHF radio. "9B wants you right now."

Captain Jasper is in the middle of briefing members of the Canadian military's National Investigation Service, who were dispatched to the desert shortly after the explosion. But this call cannot be ignored. 9B is Major Peter Dawe, the official mouthpiece of The Old Man, Lieutenant-Colonel Pat Stogran. For Canadian troops in Afghanistan, the chain of command does not go any higher.

"We can continue this down there," Capt. Jasper says, leading investigators toward the Iltis jeep that doubles as a command post. "All the glowsticks you see are essentially either body parts or pieces of equipment. Some of those pieces of equipment are Claymores with detonators still in them, destroyed grenades, or other pieces of high explosives. So don't step on any of the light sticks. Don't kick anything."

It is just shy of 4:30 in the morning. Barely two hours have passed since a U.S. fighter pilot unleashed a 500-pound laser-guided bomb on A Company's position. Eight Canadian paratroopers are hurt. Four of their comrades are dead, their mangled bodies lying in a nearby ditch, the true horror of their condition hidden only by the night sky. Their families do not yet know they are gone. The inevitable knock on the door won't come for a few more hours.

For now, at least, Ainsworth Dyer, Richard Green, Marc Léger, and Nathan Smith are still what they have always been: proud, anonymous soldiers. Their names and faces and aspirations have not yet landed on the front page, reminding Canadians that yes, we do have a military. And no, they aren't just peacekeepers.

For now, few have heard of Harry Schmidt or Bill Umbach, either. Months will pass before the decorated F–16 pilots are charged with manslaughter and threatened with 64 years in prison. No t-shirts yet, the ones that say: "Support, don't prosecute, our American pilots." It is still long before any lawyers or generals or pundits weigh in on what happened here. Long before the finger-pointing. The excuses. The nightmares. Long before any whispers of a cover-up.

For now, all Capt. Jasper knows is that four of his men are dead—somehow bombed by fast air—and headquarters is itching to talk to him. He picks up the receiver and places it next to his ear. "Call Sign One, this is 9er Bravo," Maj. Dawe tells him. "It's time to come back. Hand the scene over to the NIS, get in your trucks, and head back to camp."

The 31-year-old captain peers over at MCpl. McKenzie—Mac—and Warrant Officer Billy Bolen, who are listening in on the conversation. They are among the 15 senior soldiers who have volunteered to stay behind and collect the corpses. "Fuck that," W/O Bolen says. "We're staying here."

He speaks for everyone. Those are fellow jumpers—fellow Canadians—lying in the sand. The least they can do is spare them the indignity of having strangers zip them into their body bags. "No, I don't think that's the best plan," Capt. Jasper radios back. "Those are our guys. We want to stay out here."

For a moment, Maj. Dawe is speechless. What the captain is saying goes against every rule in the book. Troops are not supposed to pick up their dead friends. Images like that never go away. But Pete Dave isn't about to throw some training manual in their faces. Not tonight. "Roger," he says into the radio. "Let me know when you're ready to go."

Capt. Jasper puts down the headset and walks back into the darkness, back to where he left the investigators. "So," he says, "where were we?" Joe doesn't get very far before Mac comes looking for him again. Stogran's on the other end of the radio. The Old Man.

"You *will* come in," he says to Capt. Jasper. "We're sending someone to relieve you."

"We will do that, sir," Joe answers. "But we'll stay here until the bodies are in first."

"No, you don't understand," the colonel says. "I'm not asking you. I'm telling you. You will come in. We will replace you."

"We want to stay here and recover our guys," Capt. Jasper says. "There's no need to replace us. We're all fine."

"Listen, Joe," Lt.-Col. Stogran finally pleads. "Your job is done there. You've done a good job. Come on home now."

The answer is the same. Capt. Jasper and his men are not budging, not until they bring their guys with them. All they have to do now is wait for the sun to come up.

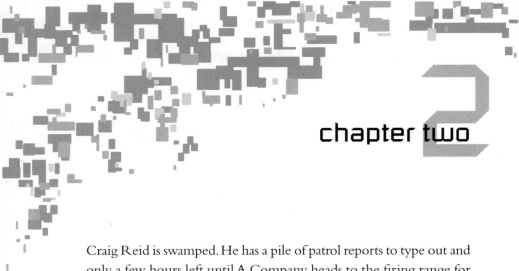

Craig Reid is swamped. He has a pile of patrol reports to type out and only a few hours left until A Company heads to the firing range for yet another long night of weapons training. The 34-year-old sergeant is penciled in to be the safety monitor for one of the shooting drills, but with the clock ticking, he already knows he won't finish his paperwork before the trucks depart for Tarnak Farm. Just the thought of it makes him sick, but Sgt. Reid has no other choice: He is going to have to ask the Company commander, Major Sean Hackett, to find a last-minute replacement.

Asking your commander for a favor is never an easy thing to do. It smacks of weakness—especially in A Company. Here, soldiers are not just soldiers. They are paratrooper commandos, trained to ambush their enemies from the sky. Instantly recognizable by their maroon berets, members of the all-volunteer Para Company have always considered themselves a little more special, a little more hardened, than their fellow infantrymen. And they have no time for excuses.

Maj. Hackett, blunt as always, tells Sgt. Reid to go find his second-in-command—his 2I/C—Capt. Joe Jasper. He's running the range tonight. Let him deal with it.

Capt. Jasper isn't exactly thrilled when Sgt. Reid breaks the news. *You have paperwork to do?* Joe doesn't have to be accommodating. As the number two man, he can tell Sgt. Reid to stick his typing up his ass and get on the fucking truck. But he doesn't. He has another idea: Go see if Marc Léger can take your spot.

It is the early afternoon of April 17, 2002, the middle of what has already been a long day for the 105 soldiers of A Company, 3rd Battalion, Princess Patricia's Canadian Light Infantry. This morning, the troops conducted yet another training drill, this time learning how to carry casualties onto American Blackhawk helicopters. Don't bang the stretcher against the fuel pod, they were told. And always load the most critically wounded last so they can be carried off first when the chopper lands back at base. It was serious stuff. You never know when you may have to rush a wounded comrade out of battle. But it was also one of those drills that is tough to do with a straight face, especially when your buddy is lying on a stretcher, playing the role of the wounded guy. How do you fight the urge to give him a friendly punch in the stomach, or "accidentally" hit his head against the chopper door?

Anything for laughs. Anything to help pass the long, sticky days in the Afghan sun, where 850 Canadian soldiers are engaged in the country's first combat mission since the Korean War. Sure, the heat and the dust storms and the "burning shit detail" are brutal, but for many, this is the deployment of a lifetime. It isn't Bosnia, Cyprus, or Rwanda. They aren't keeping the peace. This is the real thing, the chance to hunt down and kill the enemy on their own turf. September 11 is still very fresh in everyone's minds, and Canadian troops are no less anxious than their American comrades to put a bullet in some bin Laden cronies.

The Canadian Battle Group in Afghanistan is the land portion of Operation Apollo, the Liberal government's commitment to the U.S.-led war on terror. Unlike the six Canadian Navy frigates patroling the Arabian Sea, these Army troops are on the front lines of the new war. At the very front are the battalion's three rifle companies—A Company, B Company, and C Company. For a while, though, the troops doubted they would ever make it to the desert.

In November 2001, the federal government placed the Princess Patricias on 48 hours' notice to deploy. Hundreds of troops in Edmonton and Winnipeg were saying goodbye to their families, but months—and many false alarms—would pass before they left. The soldiers turned back from the airport so many times that some decided to just move back to the base. It was easier than consoling their crying wives and children, and then doing it all over again the next day because the flight had been postponed.

When they finally did board the Starlifters in early February, it was downright euphoric. As the planes approached the Kandahar Airfield, the troops were bombing up, filling their guns and vests and pockets with more ammo than they had ever carried in theater. This was a combat zone, after all, not an ice storm in Montreal.

When they landed, the Canadians fell under the operational control of Task Force Rakkasan, a 2,000-strong American army unit from the 3rd Brigade, 101st Airborne Division in Fort Campbell, Kentucky. The Rakkasans—a Japanese term that means "falling umbrellas"—already had one infantry battalion in Kandahar under the command of U.S. Colonel Frank Wiercinski. The Canadians would be his second.

Their first job was to secure a section of the airfield's perimeter, keeping a 24-hour watch on the wire fence that divides the compound from the rest of Afghanistan. It was a textbook case of hurry up and wait. For four weeks, they stared at the fence, often on little or no sleep. When they did catch a rare nap, the anti-malaria drugs had a good way of spoiling it, triggering intense dreams that were either violent or wet. A few rainstorms even rolled in—an absolute rarity in the region—filling the trenches with water and overflowing the metal drums that everyone shat in. Passing the minutes was such a chore that by the time they left The Line, some troops had managed to learn a few phrases of Pashto or Farsi, thanks to cue cards provided by the U.S. military.

"Get your hands up!" one read. "Stop or I'll shoot."

In March, the bulk of the Canadian Battle Group shipped off to Bagram for their first taste of combat—Operation Harpoon, a joint Canadian-American assault on the Tergul Ghar mountain. Their job on "The Whale" was to isolate and destroy any leftover enemy fighters who happened to flee the Shahikot Valley earlier that month during the now-infamous Operation Anaconda. Intelligence reports estimated the number of unfriendly fighters to be as high as 100. Some A Company soldiers were so excited that they high-fived one another as they climbed aboard the Chinook choppers. But after five days of destroying caves and blowing up bunkers, the mission ended without any brushes with the enemy.

There was one close call, however. Not with al-Qaeda, but with an American F-16.

In a fit of confusion, U.S. troops from 10th Mountain Division, who were attached to the Canadians for Op Harpoon, called in an air strike on a section of The Whale occupied by some of the Princess Patricias. The U.S. Brigade Tactical Operations Center was about to clear the F–16 for attack when an alert Canadian captain who just happened to overhear the radio calls yelled: "Stop! Stop! Stop!" The jet was called off seconds before unloading. A stunned U.S. Army controller turned to the captain and said, "You just saved your battalion from getting its ass bombed off."

Lt.-Col. Stogran, the commander of the Canadian battle group, was livid. In a scathing e-mail to his superiors, the colonel complained that unlike the Rakkasans, the 10th Mountain Division was "completely unprepared" to conduct the operation. "I therefore recommend that we should insist on a continued relationship with TF Rakkasan," he wrote. "I would even go so far as to suggest if this is not accepted by the coalition command that Canada should consider terminating operations in Afghanistan. Any repeat of the ad hoc nature of our last mission places our soldiers in unnecessary risk."

Lt.-Col. Stogran's soldiers did remain with the Rakkasans, and by mid-April, some of the troops are preparing for their next mission: the line. Not in Kandahar this time, but in Khowst, a coalition airfield not far from the Pakistani border. If the intel reports are right, Khowst is going to be much more intense than the soldiers' last go-round in the trenches. For more than a month, insurgents there have launched numerous after-dark hit-and-run attacks, using everything from small arms to rocket-propelled grenades. To prepare, Canadian commanders have ordered their soldiers to conduct a regimen of nighttime live-fire training drills at Tarnak Farm, a shooting range just south of the Kandahar Airfield.

Tonight is A Company's turn to fire their guns in the darkness.

"Do you mind taking my spot?" Sgt. Reid asks Marc Léger, after explaining how much paperwork he has to finish.

At 29, Léger is one of the battalion's younger sergeants, promoted from master corporal just before deploying to Afghanistan. Rank aside, everyone calls him King. King Marco. He earned the nickname a couple years ago, when Alpha Company was stationed in Bosnia on yet another peacekeeping tour. By chance, Léger's section of troops was tasked with patrolling the Livno Valley, where a few dozen Serbian refugees were returning to the rubble of the bombed-out shacks and barns they once called home.

Marc did more than just patrol. He stole food and water from the Canadian camp, scrounged building supplies from the trash heap, and harassed visiting dignitaries. He worked so hard to help rebuild the wartorn village that residents started to convince other relatives to come back home. Don't worry. The Canadians are taking care of us.

Near the end of the tour, Marc Léger convinced "his people" that they needed to elect a mayor, a spokesperson who could lobby the local aid agencies. By an overwhelming margin, the villagers voted for him. Even when he explained the intricacies of democracy—that a foreigner, especially a Canadian soldier, cannot possibly be mayor—the people once again elected Sgt. Léger. Finally, on a third ballot, they reluctantly chose a legitimate candidate. But not before appointing Marc Léger as their honorary king.

In Kandadar, King Marco is the 2I/C of A Company's supply store, tasked with making sure the troops have enough "beans and bullets." In February, while the rest of the soldiers were guarding the perimeter, the 6-foot-3 sergeant showed up every morning in the "Gut Truck" with a daily dose of food rations—and some much-needed humor. "Hot dogs!" he would often yell, to the amusement of his exhausted comrades. "Come get your cold beer!"

As he did in Bosnia, Sgt. Léger has exploited his charm. He learned very quickly that the Americans posted in Kandahar have a sweet tooth for those Canadian Army rations. Apparently the shepherd's pie—although awful in its own right—is much better than anything they have to eat. He used that to his advantage, trading case after case for much-needed supplies. At one point, his boss, Warrant Officer Billy Bolen, told him they needed a flag pole so they could hang the company colors. The one Marc brought back later that day was brand new and 20 feet long. A Company's maroon flag flies higher than any Maple Leaf in the entire Canadian camp, and it only cost Sgt. Léger a few boxes of rations.

But being a quartermaster has its drawbacks. Like when he spends a chunk of the afternoon burning shit, dousing those metal drums with diesel fuel and stirring and stirring until the crap disappears. Who could have imagined that 100 troops could produce so much human waste? Marc doesn't complain, though. Whatever the company needs, he does.

Last month, when the paratroopers got word they would be storming The Whale, he even volunteered to lead an extra weapons detachment. For five days, instead of sitting in the supply tent—or burning shit—he lugged a C-6 machine gun across the mountain.

So tonight, when Sgt. Reid asks him to fill in as a range safety officer, the answer is typical Léger. "Yeah," he says. "No problem."

★ ★ ★

As the truck he is sitting in crawls away from Kandahar Airfield, Corporal Brett Perry is busy fiddling with his C-8 machine gun, trying in vain to reattach its laser-site. It had come loose a few hours ago, when, in a typical fit of rage, he slammed his weapon against a table. Cpl. Perry is—yet again—pissed off at Master Corporal Stanley Clark, the deputy commander of his seven-man section. The two rarely see eye to eye, and everyone knows it.

"This is bullshit," Cpl. Perry says to Corporal Brian Decaire, who is riding beside him. He is angry because MCpl. Clark is demanding that the entire section do their daily P.T.—physical training—as a group. At 26, Cpl. Perry has few equals in the company when it comes to working out. His arms are nearly as thick as his legs. "We're not doing P.T. with these guys," he tells Cpl. Decaire. "They're keeping us back. We're better fit."

Cpl. Decaire is not quite as enraged as his friend. He has already found a way to squeeze in his own separate workout. Early on this morning, the 25-year-old Winnipeg native slid out of his tent and woke Corporal Ainsworth Dyer for what has become a regular pre-dawn jog. Cpl. Decaire enlisted in the Army for one reason: to be a SAR Tech, a search-and-rescue specialist. He has thought of doing nothing else since reading Robert Mason Lee's *Death and Deliverance*, the story of how, in 1991, a team of rescuers trudged through a blinding Arctic storm to reach the survivors of a CC-130 plane crash on Ellesmere Island. The only thing standing between Cpl. Decaire and his dream job are his legs. He desperately wants to shave a few seconds off his long-distance runs so he can reapply for a search-and-rescue posting after the tour. He was rejected just a few months before shipping off to Kandahar.

He could not have picked a better running coach than Cpl. Dyer, whose endurance is legendary among the company. Black, bulky, and 6-foot-3, he looks more like a tight end than a long-distance runner. But the Montreal native, the son of Jamaican immigrants, begins most of his mornings with a lengthy jog, regardless of the heavy training that might be scheduled for the rest of the day. Ains once finished Edmonton's notorious Mountain Man challenge—a 31-mile run/march/canoe race—with two stress fractures in his legs. "I wanted to see if I could do it," he said later, when someone asked why he didn't just stop. (He also slept through his alarm one year, missing the starting gun. As athletic as he is, Cpl. Dyer loves his bed.)

On the morning of April 17, he and Cpl. Decaire ran up and down the side of a runway—pistols in their holsters—until they tallied 10 kilometers. Up five times. Back five times. Cpl. Decaire finished in 51 minutes and 46 seconds, his best time yet.

Now, as Cpl. Decaire watches Cpl. Perry struggle with his gun, two Canadian-made armored Coyotes are escorting their convoy along the bumpy road that leads to Tarnak Farm. Most of A Company is along for the ride, packed into the backs of five American medium logistics vehicles that seat 18 people each. Tonight, there is a little more elbow room than usual. One section of troops was allowed to skip the exercise after a long day of patrols through the surrounding villages. A few other senior soldiers have stayed behind to learn how to fire American Mark-19 grenade launchers. The skill will come in handy when the bulk of A Company deploys north to Khowst in a couple days.

A camouflaged LSVW ambulance—light support vehicle, wheeled—is also among the convoy, as is the Iltis jeep that transports Maj. Hackett, A Company's commander. At 36, Sean Hackett is an intelligent, seasoned leader, a disciplinarian whose soft voice often hides the intensity within. Though well respected, he is not an easy man to work for. He's a bit of a micromanager, a details guy who likes to know not only what his subordinates are doing, but what his subordinates' subordinates are doing. Some of his troops joke that he has to keep a list just to keep track of all his lists.

Like the other rifle companies, Maj. Hackett's is divided into three 30-man platoons—1, 2, and 3—each with its own commander and separate weapons detachment. The platoons are further split into three smaller groups, called sections—1 Section, 2 Section, 3 Section. It makes for an intricate chain of authority, one that places young, educated platoon commanders in charge of seasoned soldiers who have much more real-life experience. To an outsider, the entire system borders on the bizarre, but it is the backbone of the Canadian military structure. New recruits can choose one of two paths. They can enlist as non-commissioned members (NCMs), beginning as privates and training to be anything from machine-gunners to mechanics. Or, if they boast good enough grades, they can join as officers. From day one, officers are trained to be leaders. They are not corporals or sergeants. They are lieutenants and colonels and, if all goes well, generals.

In A Company, none of the three platoon commanders has reached his 27th birthday. To add to the dynamic, their 2I/Cs—platoon warrants—are all high-ranking NCMs who enlisted in the Army years before their commanders could even drive a car. It is a relationship that is either perfect or terrible. There is rarely any in-between.

Lieutenant Alastair Luft and Warrant Officer Kevin Towell fit into the "perfect" category. A 24-year-old native of Kathyrn, Alberta, Lt. Luft is 3 Platoon's commander. This is his first overseas deployment. Not that long ago he was still sitting in a classroom at Royal Military College. His 2I/C is an 18-year veteran, a career paratrooper who has jumped out of an airplane more times than Lt. Luft has even seen an airplane. In between tours in Cyprus and Croatia, W/O Towell has completed every elite jumper course in the Canadian Army. He is also a qualified U.S. Army ranger, and even served a year on The Skyhawks, the Canadian Forces demonstration parachute team.

Tonight, W/O Towell is among the troops staying at camp for the Mark-19 grenade training. The plan is for him to learn the weapons system, then teach the rest of the guys tomorrow. "Listen, sir," he says to Lt. Luft, just before the trucks leave for Tarnak Farm. "Make sure the guys come back with the ammo they are supposed to have."

★   ★   ★

Lorne Ford was a 16-year-old Army cadet when he first watched one of his commanders jump out of an airplane. He was hooked. Could there possibly be a better job than that? Seventeen years later, Sergeant Ford is now one of the Para Company's most respected leaders, the top man in 3 Platoon's 3 Section. If Lt. Luft has a go-to guy, Sgt. Ford is it.

Stubborn but rarely wrong, Lorne Ford is part of the old school, a one-time member of the now-disbanded Airborne Regiment. He does nothing half-assed. During last month's assault on The Whale, he led his six men from the front. He knew it went against standard practice; section commanders are supposed to hover in the middle, poised to take charge if the lead man gets shot. But Sgt. Ford is not the type to fall back. If his men can put themselves in harm's way, so can he.

Even before The Whale, his style seemed to impress the chain of command, so much so that his section was specifically chosen to conduct a high-risk mission. If Special Forces found themselves wounded or trapped in enemy territory, Sgt. Ford's crew would be dispatched, along with a team of medics, to rescue them. Casualties were almost certain, they were told. For 10 days, Sgt. Ford prepared a painstakingly detailed set of orders. His troops knew what to do in every possible scenario. He went so far as to explain how they should react if they encountered a fallen tree on the road. But the mission never happened, and the section was eventually ordered to stand down. Sgt. Ford was disappointed, but never prouder of his men.

Sgt. Ford's 2I/C is MCpl. Clark, a 35-year-old native of Vancouver, B.C. With his skinny build and round glasses, Clark does not exactly fit the paratrooper mold. He is a capable administrator, but he's not exactly cut from the same hard-nosed cloth as Sgt. Ford. It is one of the many reasons why he often butts heads with Cpl. Perry, the physical epitome of a maroon beret.

Clark's tentmate for the tour is Rene Paquette, a 33-year-old corporal whose father fought as a Patricia in the Second World War. Though a longtime soldier with dozens of qualifications, Cpl. Paquette is not a paratrooper. And in A Company, that automatically puts you a few notches below everyone else. It doesn't seem to matter that he volunteered to leave his pregnant wife in Canada when Princess Patricia's 3rd Battalion—short of a couple dozen soldiers—asked the 2nd Battalion for volunteers. He does not wear the maroon beret, and any clout he earned over the years is essentially meaningless here. Cpl. Paquette is also not much of a fitness buff, another no-no in the Para Company. Back at 2nd Battalion headquarters in Winnipeg, he holds a support job, a coffee-and-doughnut gig. Though strong as an ox, he isn't the type to go for a six-mile run.

Two weeks ago, Cpl. Paquette spent the night calling a Manitoba hospital, waiting for word that his baby girl was born. He got to hear Breanne's first cry from the other side of the world. Tonight, as the convoy inches toward Tarnak Farm, Rene tries to steal a few minutes of sleep.

3 Section's junior man is Richard Green, a 21-year-old private from small-town Hubbards, Nova Scotia. Red-haired and skinny, Pte. Green joined the Canadian Forces straight out of high school, leaving home with a few zits and a fear of heights and coming back with a maroon beret. The guys call him "Greener," an unfortunate nickname for a soldier desperately trying to shed his image as the new guy. Ricky is probably Alpha Company's proudest paratrooper, but his age and his quiet demeanor make him an easy target for some of the older corporals. It doesn't help that he also has a low tolerance for the sun, burning almost the second he goes outside. "Sunboy."

Like the rest of 3 Platoon, Ricky Green spent most of last week at a beachfront resort in Dubai, enjoying a four-day hiatus from the tour. Forced Rest. Most of the guys drank away the break, swimming up to the poolfront bar for beer after beer after beer. Pte. Green did a bit of drinking, too, but he spent a lot of his time shopping for an engagement ring. His girlfriend, Miranda Boutilier—"Princess," as he calls her—is back at their Edmonton apartment, crossing off the days on her calendar until Ricky comes home. She doesn't know it, but her boyfriend has been showing off her new ring to the entire platoon. He plans to propose as soon as he gets back.

But that is still months away. Right now, Greener has other things to worry about, including his C-9 machine gun. It's been jamming lately.

Harry Schmidt notices the schedule the night before. Another two-plane mission into Afghanistan, another long shift of patrolling the world's newest war zone. By now, he knows the routine. Three hours out. Three hours there. Three hours back. But on April 16, 2002, as he stares at the pairings for the next day, something doesn't seem right. Flight lead: Bill Umbach. Wingman: Harry Schmidt. Wingman? *It must be a mistake*, he thinks to himself.

At 36, Harry Michael Schmidt is not accustomed to being anybody's Number Two. In America's fighter pilot universe, he is a relative superstar, a former Top Gun instructor renowned as much for his skill in the sky as his talents in the classroom. When he visits different air bases across the country, somebody always recognizes his face. He is that good.

Strangely enough, as good as he is, Major Schmidt did not appear destined for life. Growing up in St. Louis—the middle child between an older sister and a younger brother—he was the tall, athletic one, a standout in high school sports. His family called him "Augie" back then, just so nobody would confuse him with his electrician father, Harry Schmidt Sr. His mother, Joan, remembers her young son gluing together model airplanes and hanging them from his bedroom ceiling. But as a child, Harry Jr. didn't dream of being a pilot when he grew up. In fact, the main reason why he chose to even attend the U.S. Naval Academy in Maryland was because the school offered him a full scholarship to play goalie for The Mids, the varsity soccer team.

Harry excelled between the pipes, earning a selection to the NCAA all-conference team in his second year. His grades were not quite as impressive. In the academy lecture halls, where he studied mathematics and computer science, he hovered in the middle of the pack. By his senior year, he wasn't even sure what job he wanted to do once he joined the Navy full-time. He didn't want to man a sub. And he didn't want to drive a boat. Flying airplanes, he figured, would be the most fun.

The cockpit proved to be a natural fit, the perfect place for Harry to exploit the strong set of hands and split-second reflexes that God had blessed him with. He went to flight school in Pensacola, Florida, flying T-34s, then graduating to T-2 Buckeyes, where would-be fighter pilots learn the basics of formation and acrobatics. During one lesson, an instructor pilot told the rookie to merge beside his wing. Harry came in at 100 knots, stopping, almost effortlessly, six feet from his teacher's plane. The next day, the instructor jokingly warned everyone to watch out for the young pilot. "He's a psycho," he said. Of course, the nickname stuck. Harry "Psycho" Schmidt.

Despite the unfortunate call sign, Psycho's abilities were obvious. He went on to train in the A-4, learning how to pickle bombs and shoot the gun. He had a gift, and everyone knew it. He made the top of the Commodore's List, his confidence growing every day. Among the most surprised at his success were some of Harry's former classmates at the academy. *Man, you were a dumb shit at school.* He just hadn't found his element yet.

In 1990, Maj. Schmidt, then a lieutenant, was assigned to the VFA-105 "Gunslingers," where he flew the F-18 Hornet off USS *Kennedy*, then USS *Eisenhower*. His first taste of combat came over Bosnia-Herzegovina, patrolling the no-fly zone during Operation Deny Flight. Cool but conservative, Harry was an obvious choice for the Navy's élite Fighter Weapons School—Top Gun. He arrived in San Diego in 1993, into a world that will never escape its Hollywood stereotype. Tom Cruise aside, the school is nothing like the movie. No points. No trophy. Students spend as much time in the cockpit as they do in class. Every fighter pilot knows there is a missile hanging from the wing. At Top Gun, they learn how that missile works.

Even among the best of the best, Harry rose to the top. He made such an impression on his teachers that the school asked him to return in 1995 as an instructor. If you had to put a number on it, Harry Schmidt—a man who essentially chose his profession on a whim—was now among the top 1 percentile of all fighter pilots in the United States Navy. But, as his professional life soared, his personal life suffered. After seven years of marriage, he and his wife, a fellow classmate at the academy, filed for divorce. Harry was 29.

Months later, at the California gym where he worked out, he met Lisa, a Navy nurse. They went on a few dates, but, not once did Harry mention what he did for a living. He told his new friend that he simply worked on the "flight line." When she finally found out the truth, Lisa was floored. *You're a Top Gun instructor? Aren't you supposed to be cocky?* The couple eventually married.

After his instructor stint, Maj. Schmidt was once again flying for the Gunslingers. When NATO began to bomb Kosovo in 1999, Harry was among the anonymous pilots pulling the trigger. His hands killed dozens— if not hundreds—of people. After one memorable mission, an intelligence officer stopped him in the hall. "Hey," he said. "I think you killed 122 tonight." It wasn't the type of news that made Harry pump his fist in the air. He isn't motivated by body counts or bloodshed. If anything, he has—as many fighter pilots do—struggled to stomach the end result of his talent: death. You never become completely comfortable with that part of the job, but that's what it is. Part of the job. At some point, you just have to block it out of your mind and chalk it up to the greater good.

After Kosovo, Harry was selected to fill yet another élite position: the Navy's first-ever exchange instructor at the U.S. Air Force Weapons School. He had to learn a whole new aircraft—the F-16—but like everything else, it came naturally to Harry. In July 2001, near the end of his two-year posting at Nevada's Nellis Air Force Base, the public affairs newsletter published a story about him. By then, Harry Schmidt had tallied more than 100 combat missions in a fighter jet. "The first thing I noticed about combat is that everyone, no matter how cocky they are, sits down and takes notice when people are shooting at them," he told the paper. The reporter later asked him which jet he likes better—the F-18 or the F-16. "It depends on what I'm doing," Harry answered. "If I'm fighting air-to-air, I would rather be in the Hornet. It has a more capable radar and is more maneuverable. If it's an air-to-ground fight, I would definitely want the F-16. It's better at putting bombs on target."

When he made those remarks, Harry Schmidt was already well into the process of leaving the Navy. He and Lisa had made the decision a couple years earlier, not long after he came back from Kosovo. Harry was gone from the house so often in those days that Tucker, his two-year-old son, barely knew him. For a long time, he wouldn't even call him Daddy.

After Lisa gave birth to their second son, Colton, Harry sent his resumé to a number of Air National Guard units throughout the midwestern United States, hoping for a chance to settle into a job that didn't force his family to pack and move every couple years. He also started chatting with Major John Milton, one of his old instructors at Top Gun, and now a member of the 183rd Fighter Wing, an F-16 Guard unit in Springfield, Illinois. Five minutes into their first meeting, Colonel Robert J. Murphy, the wing commander, offered Harry a job as his full-time weapons officer, in charge of training and standardization for all the unit's fighter pilots. Harry accepted. It was perfect. He would still deploy, but nowhere near as often as he did in his Navy days. And Springfield was the ideal location, a short drive from his parents in Missouri and Lisa's family in Wisconsin.

It took more than a year for his teaching job to expire, but Maj. Schmidt—a trophy catch for the small unit—finally arrived in December 2001. Three months later, he and his family moved into their new home, nestled along a picturesque golf course in nearby Sherman, Illinois. Maj. Schmidt didn't even finish unpacking before he shipped off to Kuwait's Al Jaber Air Base.

His roommate for this tour is Maj. Milton, the operations officer for the Springfield unit. Along with flying his own share of sorties, John posts the flight schedule. Tonight, Maj. Schmidt asks his friend why he is slotted as the wingman for tomorrow's mission into Afghanistan. "John, what the hell?" Harry says. They talk it over for a few minutes, but in the end, the schedule stays as it is. Bill Umbach is going to lead the flight.

★ ★ ★

Most of the F-16 pilots attached to the 183rd Fighter Wing are reservists, "traditional guardsmen" who manage to squeeze in a few practice flights a month between their other full-time jobs. Air National Guard units across the United States are full of guys like that, former Air Force or Navy or Marines who still want to serve, who still want to feel the thrill of tearing through the sky at supersonic speed. Weekend warriors, as the cliché goes.

One of Springfield's part-timers is Major Bill Umbach, a 43-year-old father of two young girls whose day job is flying jumbo jets for United Airlines. He doesn't look the part of a fighter pilot. He's bald, not that tall, and he speaks in a soft twang that matches to a tee his modest personality. But, looks are deceiving. Bill Umbach has been flying fighters for two decades, inspired by his father, himself a decorated pilot who served in the Korean War. With 3,100 hours of cockpit time to his name—half of that in an F-16—Maj. Umbach has been a qualified instructor pilot almost as long as he has been a pilot.

Bill was 15, living on his family's farm in the tiny town of Havana, Illinois, when his dad first agreed to buy him a few flying lessons. By 16—even before he had a driver's license—Bill completed his first solo flight. He had clearly inherited his father's genes. After high school (where he was valedictorian) Umbach joined the Air Force Academy in Colorado, earning a degree in civil engineering before flying F-4s on active duty for seven years.

Bill Umbach probably would have stayed in the Air Force, but as he moved up the ranks he could sense an office job looming. He didn't want to fly a desk. He wanted to fly jets, so in 1990, he retired from active duty and joined the 183rd, the same hometown Guard unit where his dad had served. For more than a decade now, Maj. Umbach has split his time between commercial airliners and F-16s, sometimes flying both on the same day. He is a popular fixture in his unit, known as much for his straitlaced approach as his quick wit, which tends to emerge when the other pilots least expect it. They call him "Guido," in honor of Father Guido Sarducci, the famous *Saturday Night Live* character.

Friends and colleagues use the same words to describe Bill Umbach. Humble. Selfless. Loyal. His wife, Marlene, often jokes that she has never heard her husband say a bad word about anybody—even just to her. If anything, Bill is the social glue of the 183rd Fighter Wing. Over the years, the Umbach home has hosted countless barbecues and Super Bowl parties for fellow pilots and their families. As one of Bill's colleagues once said: "We all became part of the Umbach family."

In 1998, Bill was named commander of the 170th Fighter Squadron, the F-16 unit embedded within the Fighter Wing. It was a rare achievement for a major; squadron commander is typically a lieutenant-colonel billet. Though often considered more of a symbolic gesture than anything else—a title as opposed to a responsibility—the job was an ideal match for Maj. Umbach's meticulous personality. Bill is ultra-organized, the type of guy who lives by lists, checking things off as he goes. When he and his friends take hunting trips out of state, he not only looks up the relevant regulations, but he highlights them for the rest of the guys. In only his first year as squadron commander, Maj. Umbach helped lead his unit to an "excellent" grade in its Operational Readiness Inspection.

Scores aside, however, it was a shaky time for the squadron. Col. Murphy, the new wing commander, was cracking the discipline whip. He even forced a few pilots to retire, hoping that any other bad apples would fall in line. Morale fell, too. And it only got worse in November 1999, when a young pilot in the unit collided with his teacher during a nighttime training exercise. The instructor was forced to eject, leaving his US$20-million airplane to crash into a rural forest. An Air Force investigation into the high-profile blunder concluded that the young pilot was flying "very aggressively" during the drill, displaying an "overconfidence in his own flying abilities." Col. Murphy never let him fly again.

Two years later—December 2001—the squadron was knee-deep in preparation for its upcoming deployment to Kuwait's Ahmed Al Jaber Air Base. The pilots and their support staff knew long before 9/11 that they were heading overseas in March 2002. It was their turn in the rotation. But September 11 added a whole new level of purpose to the mission. Suddenly, it was personal.

It was also unprecedented. The 170th Fighter Squadron would be among the first to fly their F-16s into two separate combat zones during the same deployment—Operation Southern Watch, the no-fly zone in Iraq; and Operation Enduring Freedom, the war in Afghanistan. As fall turned into winter, the pilots spent hours studying binders of information relevant to both theaters. The Rules of Engagement (ROE). The SPINS (Special Instructions). Commander's Intent. When they weren't reading, they were flying, training in the latest weapons delivery system: the LITENING II targeting pod. Every pilot flew four training flights with the new pod, dropping a few practice bombs along the way.

The Kuwait mission was originally supposed to be 30 days, but by early 2002, two other Guard units were diverted to Operation Noble Eagle, the 24-hour patrols that were launched over the U.S. and Canada after the terrorist attacks. Springfield volunteered to pick up the slack—the first time since the Gulf War that an Air National Guard unit had accepted a full 90-day overseas rotation.

It is a bit of a juggle. The plan is to deploy some of the squadron's 33 pilots for 30 days, others for 45, and then invite some sister units to fill a few of the remaining spots. Air Force/Guard politics make the logistics that much more difficult. According to the rules, National Guard wing commanders can only deploy as line pilots, not as the boss. So even though Col. Murphy is overseas, he's just one of the boys. Officially, the man at the top of the Springfield chain is Lieutenant-Colonel Ralph Viets, the operations group commander. A part-timer, Ralph is responsible for 10 F-16s and 220 personnel, from pilots to mechanics. Maj. Milton, another reservist who came back to active duty after 9/11, is the ops officer, responsible for the flying side of the operation.

Bill Umbach is the squadron commander, the man technically in charge of all the fighter pilots. When his unit left for Kuwait in mid-March, Bill led the procession of F-16s as they tore down the runway at Springfield's Capital Airport.

★ ★ ★

Like most things military, the Afghanistan air war is a complex beast, a cluster of fighter jets and attack choppers and transport planes all sharing the same small sky. If orchestra is the right metaphor, then the conductor is the Coalition Air Operations Center. Headquartered at Saudi Arabia's Prince Sultan Air Base, the CAOC (pronounced "Kay-ock") is the nerve center of the air portion of Operation Enduring Freedom. A massive radar facility, the CAOC is manned by hundreds of military personnel, all under the ultimate direction of Lieutenant-General T. Michael "Buzz" Moseley, the top air force official in U.S. central command (CENTCOM). Every single mission, every single sortie into Afghanistan, is planned by CAOC staff and posted in the Air Tasking Order (ATO), a daily schedule that is filtered to flying units across the Persian Gulf.

One of those units is the 332nd Air Expeditionary Group, stationed at Al Jaber. On a constant rotation, the 332nd currently includes a Marine F/A-18 squadron, some Air Force A-10s and a search-and-rescue component. And, as of last month, Springfield's 170th Fighter Squadron. Like all the units at Al Jaber, the Illinois contingent has a Mission Planning Cell (MPC), a group of airmen and intel officers whose job is to read the CAOC's schedule and prepare briefing materials for the pilots. It is a 24-hour operation, run by a team of rotating mission planning chiefs. The chief of the chiefs is Maj. Harry Schmidt.

Mission planning is hardly an exact science, especially when it comes to Afghanistan. Ground forces are everywhere, not only at bases like the Kandahar Airfield, but hidden in remote mountains, hunting small pockets of the enemy. Finding reliable intelligence about the location of friendly troops has been a challenge, to put it mildly. A crucial reference point in that search is the Airspace Control Order (ACO), another database published by the CAOC. Updated multiple times each day, it contains detailed information about the Afghanistan skies, from No-Fly Areas (NFAs) to Terminal Movement Areas (TMAs) to Areas of Operation (AO)—the sections of Afghanistan that are under the control of coalition ground forces.

The ACO is nearly 50 pages long, impossible for an airman to fully digest before taking off on a mission. It is the MPC's job to dissect the voluminous information and pass along what's relevant. When the squadron first arrived, intel officers mapped the ACO using computer software called Task View, but a lot of the pilots said it made their onboard maps completely unusable. There was so much data—so many NFAs, TMAs, TCAs and ROZs—that the whole map was covered in tiny circles. To compensate, mission planners now typically filter out airspace restrictions that fall well below 15,000 feet, the minimum altitude that fighter jets are supposed to be flying in Afghanistan. Some in the 170th Fighter Squadron have disregarded the ACO altogether, looking instead to other briefing notes and secure websites in search of the latest intelligence.

For nearly three months now, the ACO has contained a brief entry about a ROZ—a Restricted Operating Zone—that is in effect 24 hours a day. Stretching a mile wide and up to 11,000 feet MSL (above sea level), the invisible bubble of airspace is off-limits to pilots unless they have specific permission to venture inside.

"TARNACK FARMS," the entry reads. "SMALL ARMS RANGE AT KANDAHAR. NOT CONTINUOUSLY ACTIVE. CONTACT KANDAHAR TOWER FOR STATUS."

★　★　★

It is already 10:30 in the morning by the time Harry Schmidt rolls out of bed on April 17, 2002. That was the plan. Try to sleep in. It's going to be a long night. After getting dressed, Maj. Schmidt does some laundry, then grabs a bite to eat. When he finishes his lunch, he strolls over to Al Jaber's medical clinic to pick up some Dexedrine. Go-pills, as the pilots call them. Speed.

For more than three decades, the U.S. Air Force has been prescribing dextroamphetamines as a way to keep its pilots from falling asleep in the cockpit. Countless fighters popped the little orange pills during the first Gulf War, and although the controversial program was canned in 1992, it was reinstated four years later when America started bombing the Balkans. Classified by the U.S. Food & Drug Administration as a Schedule II narcotic—a category that also includes cocaine—Dexedrine is not recommended for people who operate heavy equipment. Common side-effects include nervousness, anxiety, and euphoria. Nevertheless, the U.S. Air Force considers the drug a crucial tool in the fight against its number-one killer: fatigue. More than 100 fatal crashes have been blamed on drowsy pilots, and most happened during long, taxing missions like the one Maj. Schmidt is about to fly.

His job tonight, as wingman to Maj. Umbach, is to circle around northeastern Afghanistan for two-and-a-half hours, just in case ground forces need their help. But just getting there from Kuwait takes more than three hours, maneuvering east over the Arabian Sea and then up through

Pakistan. Throw in the flight home and any unexpected run-ins with al-Qaeda, and it makes for a pretty exhausting trip, jammed inside a cramped cockpit where the only bathroom is a tiny bag. Earlier in the war, an F-15E Strike Eagle logged a 15.5-hour mission, the base record.

A typical crew-duty day—briefings and flight-time included—is not supposed to exceed 10 hours. But for Operation Enduring Freedom, the brass has boosted the limit to 14 just so everyone has enough time to get to and from the war zone. And if you're too tired, there's always the Go-pills. A career Navy pilot, Maj. Schmidt is new to the Air Force's Go-pill program, so new that he underwent the standard testing just days before he deployed. Captain Brad Houston, a flight surgeon with the 183rd Fighter Wing, handed Maj. Schmidt a form entitled: "Informed Consent for Use of Dextroamphetamine as a 'Go-pill' in Military Operations."

"It has been explained to me and I understand that the U.S. Food & Drug Administration has not approved the use of dextroamphetamine to manage fatigue," reads the one-page document, which lists as possible side-effects insomnia, nervousness, and weight loss. "My decision to take dextroamphetamine is/will be voluntary. I understand that I am NOT being required to take the medication." Harry signed the form on March 6, then swallowed one of the pills.

The next day, Capt. Houston asked him how he felt. Did you see things? Does your chest hurt? Any other side-effects?

"No," Harry said.

Next came the No-go pill, the sedative—Ambien—that helps bring the pilots down from their jolt. Pop the Go-pill while you're still in the air; take the No-go before bed.

"Did you sleep well with it?" Capt. Houston asked the next morning.

"Yeah," Maj. Schmidt answered. "Actually I slept pretty good with it."

Harry is back at the clinic this afternoon, chatting with Captain Dawn McNaughton, the base's medical director. As she hands him a fresh supply of pills, Maj. Schmidt notices a photo on her desk, the one of her daughter. They start talking about family, about Harry's new home on the golf course, about his two young sons. Since he arrived in theater, Maj. Schmidt has been carrying American flags in the cockpit, then mailing them home after each mission. Lisa, his wife, tells Tucker and Colton that when they see the stars and stripes flapping in the wind, it is Daddy waving at them.

★ ★ ★

Bill Umbach snuck in a nap this afternoon, waking up just in time for the meeting. Most of the other pilots are here, too, listening to Maj. John Milton as he dissects a mission gone wrong.

Two days ago, Milt was the flight lead in a two-ship formation tasked with dropping a bomb on a mobile target in Iraq. After more than a month in theater, it was the fighter squadron's first chance to push the pickle button. With the targeting pod videos rolling in the background, Maj. Milton explains how he and his wingman, Mark Skibinski, agreed in advance that whoever found the target first would be the one to make the drop. His Number Two spotted it, calling "captured." After a few calls over the radio, Skibinski dropped. The bomb fell 150 feet short. Turns out he wasn't even aiming at the right target anyway. It had moved.

If the miss was embarrassing, it was made worse by the fact that Major-General Walter E. Buchanan—the commander of Joint Task Force Southwest Asia, and General Moseley's immediate deputy—happened to be visiting Al Jaber that day. He personally debriefed the mission with the pilots. Not exactly a high point for the 170th Fighter Squadron.

When the hotwash ends, Maj. Schmidt and Maj. Umbach head directly to their mass brief. They are already running a few minutes late because Maj. Milton's meeting lasted a bit longer than expected. As the flight lead for tonight's mission, Bill presents the briefing slides prepared by the Mission Planning Cell. Lieutenant-Colonel Mark Coan, the acting deputy commander of the 332nd Air Expeditionary Group, is sitting in the room with them. So is Captain Evan Cozadd, an intel officer with the 170th Fighter Squadron. They talk about the weather forecast. Wind conditions. Call signs. For this sortie, Bill will be "Coffee 51"; Harry, "Coffee 52."

Among the briefing slides is a map that depicts Afghanistan's AOs—Areas of Operation—including AO Truman, Task Force Rakkasan's turf. Another slide describes the Kandahar Airfield as a friendly divert base, just in case the pilots suddenly have to land. Kandahar is referenced a third time, this one a warning that Special Forces are still operating in the vicinity.

"100% Release Clearance," one slide reads, stressing the need to get approval before dropping a bomb.

"100% Force for Battle," reads another. "No Fratricide." The fancy term for friendly fire.

Slide 14 describes the threat level as "Medium." Underneath, a warning about MANPADS—Man-Portable Air Defense Systems, missile launchers that have been prevalent in Afghanistan since the Russians first invaded more than 20 years ago. And another warning: AAA, the common term for anti-aircraft artillery. Another slide says that up to 2,000 Taliban fighters are potentially regrouping in the region south of Kandahar, and may be equipped with new surface-to-air weapons smuggled into the country from Iran. The Taliban, the slide warns, has won allies in the region who are angry about the new government's crackdown on the illegal poppy industry.

"Don't be complacent/predictable," another slide reads.

It is just after 5 p.m. local time when Harry Schmidt and Bill Umbach climb into the step van that will drive them to their jets. Both men are wearing inflatable anti-G suits that hug their bodies like Spandex, protecting them from the forces of gravity and acceleration that go hand-in-hand with the job. A 9mm pistol is hidden in the pockets of their vests, their only line of defense should they go down in unfriendly territory. When the van reaches the planes, Harry and Bill hop out, carrying their personal helmets and the small green bags that hold their mission materials. A ladder hangs from each cockpit.

All F-16s that belong to the 170th Fighter Squadron are Block 30s, built by Lockheed Martin but stuffed with General Electric engines. They are gorgeous machines, 49-and-a-half feet long with a bubble canopy and a pen-like nose that can rip through the sky at up to 1,500 miles per hour. Even with a full load of fuel, an F-16 can withstand up to 9 Gs—nine times the force of gravity. No other fighter jet can say the same. Officially, the planes are called "Fighting Falcons," but among the pilots who fly them, "Viper" is the preferred lingo.

By 6 p.m., Harry and Bill have climbed inside their Vipers, buckling their bodies into the small seats that recline 30 degrees. Hanging from their wings—two on each side—are four 500-pound GBU-12s, Guided Bomb

Units that can be dropped on the enemy at a moment's notice. As both engines hum, each pilot conducts a last-minute check of his instruments. Everything appears to be in order. At 6:20 p.m., Maj. Umbach peels down the runway, disappearing into the Kuwaiti sky. Maj. Schmidt follows 20 seconds later. Three more hours until Afghanistan.

Not long after takeoff, the pilots receive a radio call from base. What was supposed to be their first "tanker" has fallen off the map. Tanker is the common term for KC-135s, the airplanes/gas stations that keep fighter jets airborne for so many hours. During long sorties like this one, F-16s have to hit at least three tankers. Vipers go through a lot of fuel in nine hours.

Losing your tanker is a lot like trying to find a service station along a dark, desolate highway. All you can really do is keep hoping that a sign appears in the distance. In the case of an F-16, pilots can continue flying only until their fuel gauge reaches the halfway point. After that, they have no choice but to abort the mission and turn around.

Working the radio frequencies, Harry and Bill manage to spot an alternative tanker just minutes before they reach that turning point. Relieved, they gas up, then continue on toward Afghanistan.

They will always wish they'd never found that tanker.

A team of U.S. Army Rangers is still firing away at Tarnak Farm when A Company arrives. The Canadians have the range booked for 3:30 p.m., but the Americans—running a little late—ask Capt. Jasper if they can steal an extra half-hour or so to finish up.

Sure, he says. He knows how tough it is to get time out here.

Amid the dust and rocks surrounding the captain is a slice of al-Qaeda lore. Tarnak Farm was once a key training ground for thousands of Osama bin Laden's jihadis. The terrorist leader himself spent many nights sleeping amid the dozens of mud huts that lined the south side of the compound. In 1998—three years before 9/11—the Central Intelligence Agency's "bin Laden unit" concocted a bold plan to capture the al-Qaeda chief not far from where Capt. Jasper is standing, but the covert raid was called off for fear of civilian casualties. Two years later, a remote-controlled CIA Predator drone videotaped what appeared to be the outline of a tall, bearded man inside Tarnak Farm. Intelligence agents were convinced that the lanky figure was the 6-foot-5 bin Laden. A missile strike was reportedly denied, however, because the White House wanted him alive.

By April 17, 2002, Tarnak Farm is merely a shadow of what it once was. The 80 or so "buildings" that housed bin Laden's trainees have been reduced to rubble, bombed and bombed again by U.S. fighter jets in the months after September 11. But this is hardly a playground. Landmines lingering from the Afghan-Soviet war of the 1980s are strewn across much of the 100-acre complex. Weeks earlier, one of those mines killed a U.S. soldier and wounded two others.

The surrounding desert presents its own dangers. Canadian Forces intelligence reports assess the enemy threat as high, warning that the "Kandahar region was the birthplace and spiritual centre of the Taliban" and members of the ousted regime are likely hiding in the area. Another intel report warns that aircraft coming into Kandahar "are routinely targeted by small arms fire and sometimes by RPG [Rocket-Propelled Grenade] fire." A popular tactic is to aim anti-aircraft artillery (AAA) "at a specific point in the sky in the hopes that a coalition aircraft will fly through that zone." Fortunately, the report says, "this tactic has not worked and has little likelihood of success in the future."

In recent weeks, Taliban and al-Qaeda holdouts have focused their sights on ground troops, launching a series of attacks near the airfield perimeter. In one case, a rocket landed just short of the fence. Rumors swirled around camp that it was a BM-21 attack—a 122mm Multiple Launch Rocket System (MLRS) that can hit a target 12 miles away. Canadian troops gave chase, eventually uncovering a cache of 107mm Chinese rockets. Not quite a BM-21, but with a range of five miles, dangerous just the same. All the more reason for A Company to brush up on their nighttime firing skills.

Among the first troops to see the potential of Tarnak Farm were U.S. Marines and Special Forces from the ultra-secret Task Force 11. They started practice-firing here in late 2001, shortly after the fall of the Taliban regime. Lt.-Col. Stogran, the Canadian Battle Group commander, was anxious to get his troops out here, too. When he arrived in early 2002, he actually tried to watch a few of the U.S. training sessions, but Task Force 11—the covert bunch that they were—didn't show up when they were scheduled.

When they did arrive for practice, their firing often triggered a few seconds of panic among the troops patrolling the airfield's outer wall. More than once, soldiers radioed brigade headquarters with frantic reports of gunfire just outside the gate. It sometimes took 10 minutes to convince them that what they were seeing was actually a live-fire exercise, not the enemy. In fact, on the night Canadian soldiers chased down the source of that suspected BM-21 attack, they reported a firefight a few hundred yards in front of them. It turned out to be Tarnak Farm.

As the weeks wore on, the confusion dwindled. Task Force 11, working with Lt.-Col. Stogran and his staff, actually approached the local governor for permission to use a section of Tarnak Farm for live-fire drills. The brigade also designated it a Restricted Operating Zone, and assigned a training officer to coordinate a range schedule. Every company, if they wanted, would have a fair shot at getting time at Tarnak Farm.

Capt. Jasper submitted his request almost two weeks ago. Following Standard Operating Procedures (SOPs), he handed it to the Canadian Battle Group's training officer, who then presented it at a weekly resource conference with his counterparts at Task Force Rakkasan. The U.S. brigade approved the captain's request last week, slotting A Company for April 17.

How—or if—the brigade shares that information with the Air Force is well beyond Capt. Jasper's pay scale. His only job is to make damn sure the brass in TF Rakkasan knows what his troops are doing tonight. He fills out a range checklist, indicating everything from how fast the convoy will drive (15–20 miles per hour) to the call sign of their radios (1). The paperwork also lists the weapons that the Canadians will be firing. Pistols. Shotguns. Claymore mines. C-6, C-7, C-8, and C-9 machine guns. Shoulder-mounted Carl Gustav rocket launchers.

If all goes according to plan, the troops will be back at camp by 4 a.m. local time. Not that "local time" means anything here. Like all soldiers and sailors and airmen deployed in the war on terror, the Canadians in Kandahar have their watches set to Greenwich Mean Time. Zulu Time, as it's commonly known, is four-and-a-half hours behind the clocks in Afghanistan. So even though the sun is starting to set as Capt. Jasper waits for the Americans to finish shooting, his watch has not quite reached 4 p.m.

★ ★ ★

Most of the paratroopers don't really want to be out here tonight. A lot of them are exhausted, not from the heat or the missions, but from the aggressive training schedule. The practicing never seems to end. This morning was the CASEVAC choppers. Tonight is Tarnak Farm. The troops will be lucky to catch even a couple hours of sleep before the sun comes up and the day starts all over again.

But it's not just the sleep deprivation. That goes hand in hand with the job. It's the stupid orders that have been trickling down from headquarters lately, like the one that says you can't leave your tent to take a piss without donning full battle rattle—flak jacket and helmet included. In a form of mild protest, some troops have stopped doing up the chin straps on their helmets.

About the only soldiers excited to be here tonight are the Pioneers. This is a rare chance for them to do what they do best: build things, and then blow them up. In the infantry, Pioneers are the guys you call if you find yourself caught in a booby trap or face to face with a chemical weapon. Although not quite Engineers, they are more than capable of clearing a minefield or detonating some C-4.

In Afghanistan, the Canadian Battle Group has four Pioneers at its disposal. Three of them—Master Corporal Dave Bibby, Corporal Aaron Bygrove, and Corporal Jon Bradshaw—are with the Para Company tonight, anxious to try out some new wooden pop-up targets they built a few days ago. A slight variation of the standard Figure-11s, these targets lie low to the ground, strapped down by some wire and attached to a Claymore mine. When a Pioneer hits the detonator, the wire snaps, launching the target upwards. An enemy ambush. Perfect for one of tonight's drills.

With the range set up and the sun nearly gone, Capt. Jasper gathers his troops in a semi-circle. They are standing in the administration area—the adam area, as it's often called—where the ambulance and the Iltis are parked beside a few of the camouflaged trucks that drove everyone here. Approximately 500 feet away, two huge ditches—known as wadis—intersect in almost a perfect L.

Tonight, the wadi running east to west will simulate a Close-Quarter Battle (CQB). Armed with pistols and shotguns, two to five soldiers will move along the dried-out ravine, firing at the Pioneers' pop-up targets until they reach the corral, a series of stables where bin Laden once raised his horses. "I will be the safety officer for this one," Capt. Jasper says.

In the ditch running south to north, an entire section, bolstered by a C-6 machine gun detachment, will march until they encounter an enemy soldier on the left side. When the lead man shoots down the target, the section will storm up the edge of the ravine and assume firing positions along the top. They will not leave until the Carl Gustav gunners fire six rounds at a series of old tanks a few hundred yards away. Sgt. Léger will be monitoring this one.

Marc's boss in the supply tent, W/O Billy Bolen, parked his truck in the low ground where the two wadis join together. His job tonight is to hand out the ammo that everyone will fire. And bust a few balls. The son of a paratrooper, W/O Bolen is one of the most beloved characters in the battalion, if not the entire Canadian Army. Every second word is *fuck*. Every other word is *gold*.

Before the ranges go hot, a handful of paratroopers head over to the south side of the compound to "zero" their machine guns. The Canadians have just received a new shipment of PAQ-4s, laser-sites that can be seen only with Night Vision Goggles (NVGs). They need to fire a few test rounds just to make sure the gear is lined up correctly.

For now, Pte. Green's C-9 appears to be rocking.

★ ★ ★

When the shooting begins, Corporal Jean de la Bourdonnaye walks to the back of the ambulance and brews himself a cup of coffee. His mother has been shipping him a regular load of Starbucks ever since he landed in Kandahar. All he has to do is stoke up his Whisperlite stove, boil some water, and voilà.

This is about as exciting as things get for Army medics at Tarnak Farm—or any other firing range. Maybe someone will cut his finger and need a Band-aid, or sprain an ankle running up the wadi. If not, it's a long night of nothing. Coffee is a must.

A 28-year-old Ottawa native, Cpl. de la Bourdonnaye is one of three medics attached to the Para Company. Everybody calls him DLB for short, or LFK, for "Little French Kid." Corporal Victor Speirs, one of his fellow medics, prefers the latter. Not that his nickname is any better. The troops call him Britney, in honor of the teen pop diva who bears the same last name. That the spellings are a tad different—Spears and Speirs—isn't enough to spare Vic any abuse. This nickname's a keeper.

Unlike DLB, Cpl. Speirs is not much of a coffee fan. He likes his caffeine cold and in a red can. If you see the 32-year-old without a Coke, he must be sleeping. The son of a nurse, Cpl. Speirs is very tall and very much in love with his job. About the only downside is when DLB manages to sneak his way behind the wheel of the ambulance. Much shorter than Cpl. Speirs, Little French Kid likes to drive over the bumps as fast as he can so Britney's head smacks against the roof.

A Company's lead medic is Sergeant Bill Wilson, a soft-spoken veteran of Rwanda and Somalia. Now 35, he wasn't even supposed to be in Afghanistan, but his boss asked him to fill in at the last minute after another medic got hurt. Although he had only 10 days to get ready, Sgt. Wilson was ecstatic. Everyone, after all, was trying to get a spot on this tour.

The only hiccup he encountered was at his eye doctor's office. Unable to fill Sgt. Wilson's full order of contact lenses before he shipped off, a staff member at the office promised to mail him the remainder as soon as they were ready. Lianne was true to her word, going so far as to attach a note wishing the medic a safe return. By now, the two are e-mail buddies, the first step in what will be their eventual marriage.

During live-fire exercises, the ambulance tends to be a hub of activity. It is parked in the middle of the adam area, where dozens of soldiers smoke and joke while they wait for their turn to shoot. It is also the main link between A Company and Call Sign Zero, the Canadian Tactical Operations Centre (TOC) at the Kandahar Airfield. As the Company signaler, MCpl. Brad McKenzie—Mac—spends most of his time near the amb, monitoring his radio for any updates from headquarters. The vehicle is also equipped with a large speaker, so when the back doors are swung open, as they are tonight, anyone standing nearby can hear the chatter coming from camp.

Maintaining constant communication is crucial during exercises like this. Before the firing can even begin, A Company has to tell Call Sign Zero that the troops are ready to go. Zero then asks for approval from RAK TOC, the U.S. brigade headquarters. It is a last-minute warning, just in case the paperwork slipped through the cracks or somebody happened to forget that the Canadians are going to be here tonight. Call Sign Zero is also in constant touch with the Kandahar tower, where every day air traffic controllers juggle the arrival and departure of dozens of aircraft, from C–17 cargo planes to Blackhawk helicopters. A few weeks earlier, the brigade enacted a new rule: Every unit training at Tarnak Farm must have a sentry in the tower to pass along hold-fire orders whenever a plane is about to fly over the range.

It works like this. When radar controllers in the tower spot an incoming aircraft, they advise the sentry to relay a "check fire" to Call Sign Zero. Zero passes the order to whoever is manning the radio inside the ambulance. That soldier then yells "Check Fire," prompting everyone on the range to start screaming the same thing. For good measure, the soldier with the radio also gets on a walkie-talkie and passes the message directly to Capt. Jasper and Sgt. Léger, the range safety officers. Both men have three-foot-long red glowsticks in their back pockets, which they then wave around on the slim chance that someone out here can't hear all the yelling. The entire process is repeated when the ambulance gets word of a "cancel check fire," clearing the troops to start shooting again.

On April 17, Corporal Cheyenne Laroque is A Company's man in the tower.

★ ★ ★

It is a very dark and moonless night at Tarnak Farm. If not for their night vision goggles, the Canadian troops would be able to see barely a yard in front of them. It is that black.

Flip down your NVGs, however, and it's a different story. Instantly visible are the bright pieces of glint tape plastered on everyone's uniforms—one on the left shoulder, one on the head. Everyone's helmet is also equipped with flashing infrared beacons, though only half the soldiers have theirs switched on tonight. The chopper pilots have been complaining lately that the blinking is just too overwhelming.

To keep the drills as realistic and tactical as possible, none of the trucks has its headlights on either. No flashlights allowed. And no paraflares, which troops typically use to illuminate firing ranges back home in Canada. The only artificial light anywhere near Tarnak Farm is coming from the Kandahar Airfield, three miles away, where a row of high-voltage bulbs shines on a prison holding captured al-Qaeda fighters.

The darkness has Corporal Shane Brennan a little nervous. And it takes a lot to rattle Shane Brennan. At 28, he is both cool and well spoken, his Oakley shades either on his face or resting in his blond hair. Shane is such an outgoing guy that whenever reporters venture into camp, his fellow troops always point them in the direction of media-friendly Cpl. Brennan.

But tonight, as one of 2 Platoon's Carl Gustav gunners, his job is to fire the 84mm bazooka-style rocket launcher. It is the highest-caliber weapon out here, and the only one that must be fired with the naked eye—not with NVGs. Some of the other Carl G. gunners who already went through the range have warned Cpl. Brennan that they can't see fuck-all out there. It's just too dark. Shane doesn't want to be the guy who drops a round short.

On his way to the wadi, Shane bumps into Sgt. Léger, who seems just as concerned about the pitch-black conditions. "This is fucked," Sgt. Léger tells him. "I'm going to see if we can shut this shit down. This isn't safe."

★ ★ ★

On paper, Corporal Chris Kopp is 3 Platoon's signaler. But as a certified emergency medical technician (EMT), the 25-year-old is just as comfortable applying first aid as he is working the radio. Last month, while most of the troops were watching the Canadian men's hockey team win the Olympic gold medal, he was at the scene of a car accident, saving the life of a young Afghan boy.

Tonight, the native of Westbourne, Manitoba—a town of 50—is lounging near the ambulance, not far from Corporal Ainsworth Dyer and Private Nathan Smith. The three are chatting, not about chicks or fights or terrorism, but about life in Afghanistan, about just how weird it is that they are here, sprawled out in the dirt. *Does the average Canadian have any idea we are even in this country? Or how filthy we are?*

Pte. Smith is Cpl. Dyer's number two on the C-6 machine gun. Dyer fires the weapon; Smith loads it. A 26-year-old from Porter's Lake, Nova Scotia, "Smitty" is one of the company's older privates, having dabbled in a few classes and odd jobs before enlisting at age 23. He has done pretty much everything. In high school, he played bass guitar in a rock band (*Ringworm*), got fired from Subway (he closed the store a few minutes early one night), and spent hours playing *Dungeons & Dragons* on the ping-pong table in his parents' basement. After graduation, he drove a dry-cleaning truck for a while before enrolling at Toronto's Seneca College, where he finished at the top of his class in the Underwater Skills Program. He figured he could land a gig as a commercial diver back home in Nova Scotia, but it didn't quite pan out. He headed west in search of work. That's when he enlisted.

The decision caught his parents a little by surprise. Nathan is way too laid back for the Army, they thought. But Smitty was in his element. Because of his age, the younger recruits looked up to him, and he returned the admiration by helping the slower guys clean their weapons and organize their kits into the wee hours of the morning. As he did at Seneca College, Pte. Smith went on to graduate from Battle School at the top of his class.

At his side then and now is his fiancée, Jodi Carter, a young woman he knew as a little girl back in Porter's Lake. When he was posted to the PPCLI in Edmonton, she joined him there, enrolling at the University of Alberta. She is studying to be a brain surgeon. The guys always ride him for that one. *Maybe you need brain surgery, Smitty? Your wife is a doctor-to-be, and you're out here sweating in the desert with the rest of us?*

Tonight, Smitty and Dyer—members of 3 Platoon's weapons detachment—are scheduled to go through Sgt. Léger's range three separate times, once with each of the platoon's three sections. Their commander, Master Corporal Curtis Hollister, is going with them.

As they disappear toward the ammo truck, Cpl. Kopp rolls onto his side, pulls down his balaclava, and tries to catch a few minutes of sleep, oblivious to the machine guns rattling in the distance. Dozens of troops are doing the same. Others are enjoying a cigarette, squishing anthills, and complaining.

Major Arthur Henry has been in the air for more than five hours now, manning his terminal at the back of the AWACS plane. Short for Airborne Warning & Control System, the AWACS is a radar station in the sky, a Boeing 707 jumbo jet equipped not with passenger seats and stewardesses, but with sensors and radios and all the other gadgets needed to keep track of the crowd of coalition aircraft flying over Afghanistan.

The AWACS does many things. It detects enemy aircraft, directs traffic, and pinpoints tankers. But its primary job is to be the buffer between fighter pilots in the air and U.S. ground control in Saudi Arabia. If a jet wants clearance to engage a target, the AWACS passes the request to the CAOC, which renders the final yes or no.

Maj. Henry hasn't had to make too many of those calls since arriving in theater last month from Oklahoma's Tinker Air Force Base. This is his crew's 10th mission, and with Operation Anaconda long over, very few bombs—if any—are being dropped on Afghanistan these days. About the only noteworthy call tonight came from the crew of a P-3 surveillance plane, who noticed what appeared to be a missile launch near the city of Gardez. Following standard procedure, the pilot "took a mark," pinpointing the precise latitude and longitude. CAOC officials will examine the coordinates to determine whether the shooting was friendly or foe. It could prove to be the target of a future bombing run. But not today.

Among the AWACS crew on board for tonight's mission is Tech-Sergeant Michael Carroll, a weapons director with eight years of service. He is the tanker controller, tasked with making sure coalition jets link up with the flying gas stations. To pilots, he is the voice of the AWACS. His call sign is BOSSMAN.

Sitting at the console behind him is Captain David Pepper, the crew's senior director. If the captain wants an order passed to a pilot, TSgt. Carroll repeats the exact words over the radio. It's called parroting, for obvious reasons.

Nearly 20 others are working in this mobile radar station tonight. As mission crew commander, Major Art Henry is in charge of them all. But his position of authority isn't the only thing that sets him apart. He is also the only Canadian on board, embedded with the American squadron as part of a NATO exchange program.

★   ★   ★

Sgt. Ford is going to let his 2I/C run the show tonight. The way he sees it, this is the perfect chance to make sure MCpl. Clark can assume command if he ever goes down. It's not what Cpl. Perry wants to hear. He is still fuming about the whole P.T. fiasco, and the last thing he wants to do is listen to Clark chirp orders in his ear. "Fuck," he says to himself.

Down the wadi, 2 Section is just finishing its turn on the tank stalk drill. Lt. Luft, 3 Platoon's commander, is right behind them in the ditch, watching closely as Cpl. Dyer, lying on his stomach, fires his machine gun. Ains is almost out of bullets when the yelling begins: "Check fire! Check fire!" A C-130 Hercules transport plane is coming in for a landing at Kandahar Airfield. Tarnak Farm goes cold.

For the guys on the range, few things are more frustrating than check fires. On some nights, it feels like they do far more sitting than shooting. And that only means a longer stint away from camp, away from their cots.

During the lull, Sgt. Léger leaves his wadi and strolls back to the adam area. He asks some of the guys loitering around the ambulance if they have any clue how long the check fire is going to last. Nobody knows. Sometimes 15 minutes. Sometimes 30. Sometimes longer. Before heading back, the young sergeant runs into Capt. Jasper and Maj. Hackett. He cracks a joke about how dark it is tonight. But if Sgt. Léger truly believes that his range is unsafe—as he told Cpl. Brennan about an hour ago—he doesn't say anything to his commanders. They would have listened if he did.

At 8:51 p.m. Zulu, Cpl. Laroque, A Company's sentry in the tower, cancels the check fire. In Afghanistan, it is already April 18.

★   ★   ★

Harry Schmidt and Bill Umbach have been circling northeastern Afghanistan for nearly two-and-a-half hours. Add the flight here, and they've been airborne for more than double that, strapped to tiny, cushionless seats the entire time. Maj. Schmidt has already eaten a couple power bars. About 90 minutes ago, he swallowed two five-mg Go-pills.

In Maj. Umbach's jet, a large water bottle sits on the floor. He usually brings one along for every ride, drinks it, then refills it with his urine. This isn't a road trip. No bathroom breaks here. Bill has also popped a Dexedrine tablet.

Shortly after 9 p.m. Zulu, Guido calls the AWACS. Coffee Flight's uneventful mission is over, and the Vipers need some fuel before turning back to Al Jaber. BOSSMAN tells the pilots to fly south approximately 75 nautical miles, where a tanker is waiting for them.

To get there, the F-16s must vector through some highly restricted airspace. The Rakkasans own the sky above the Kandahar Airfield, and any plane flying between 6,000 and 27,000 feet cannot venture within 30 nautical miles unless they contact radar controllers on the ground or somebody in the Kandahar tower. There's also that ROZ surrounding Tarnak Farm, the one that's been a permanent fixture in the airspace control order since January.

Neither the AWACS crew nor the pilots has any idea the ROZ exists.

★   ★   ★

Pte. Green has a lot on his mind tonight. His machine gun is on the fritz. The section has given him an M-72—a 66mm disposable anti-tank rocket—to fire at the start of the exercise. And to top it off, it is his job is to detonate a Claymore mine at the end of the drill, triggering the section's retreat from the wadi. Greener doesn't have a lot of experience with Claymores, and he doesn't want to fuck this up. That's all he needs. Another reason for Sgt. Ford to get on his case, or for Cpl. Perry and the boys to bust his balls.

When 2 Section finishes shooting, Lt. Luft walks back to the ammo truck to make sure all the guys replace what they just fired. It's exactly what Kevin Towell reminded him to do right before he left camp tonight. Sgt. Léger is also standing near the truck, briefing Sgt. Ford's men. He has scribbled the scenario on his notepad. "We have confirmed reports of Taliban extremists operating in the Tarnac Farm region," he wrote. "It is suspected that they are conducting recces of the Kandahar Airport in order to plot a terrorist act against the coalition forces. Their morale is high & their strength is estimated to be 50 pers. They are well armed & are expected to fight to the death."

With that, MCpl. Clark leads his men to the entrance of the wadi.

Twenty feet deep, the wadi is akin to a dark subway tunnel—only this tunnel is littered with rocks and weeds and lined with sand as fine as talcum powder. It goes on and on for hundreds of yards. Cpl. Paquette, clenching his C-9, walks near the front of the line, just steps from MCpl. Clark. Shielding the top half of his face are his night vision goggles, transforming the blackness of Tarnak Farm into a green haze. Like all the troops, Cpl. Paquette is in full green battle rattle. Tonight, he even slid his protective metal plate into the back of his camouflage flak jacket. He never does that when he's just going to the range.

Cpl. Decaire is a few steps back, lugging the 84mm Carl Gustav. Cpl. Perry is with him, carrying the six rounds they plan to fire. The C-6 team—Cpl. Dyer and Pte. Smith—is next in line. Similar to an M-60, the C-6 is a heavy weapon, about three feet long and weighing about 20 pounds. Cpl. Dyer, like most C-6 gunners, has his gun tied to a sling around his neck. Smitty, his loader, is hauling two belts of ammo, exactly 440 bullets. This isn't Rambo, though. The rounds are in his backpack, not wrapped around his chest. MCpl. Hollister is following Ains and Smitty. He will crouch behind them during the entire drill, shouting orders and controlling their rate of fire.

Pte. Green and Sgt. Ford are at the end of the line. The sergeant has no role in this drill, but he wants to see how well his section performs under his deputy's command. Sure, he could sit this one out, maybe catch a quick nap with the rest of the guys near the ambulance. But that's not Sgt. Ford.

The only member of 3 Section absent from the wadi is Corporal Chris Oliver. Ollie's primary weapon, the M-203 grenade launcher, is not part of tonight's drill. As the rest of his unit walks through the ditch, he lounges in the adam area.

The guys are well down the wadi by the time Lt. Luft—still sorting out 2 Section's ammo—even notices they are gone. *I'll catch up with them in a few minutes,* he figures.

★ ★ ★

Cpl. Paquette can see the wooden target at the top of the wadi. He signals a halt. But Sgt. Léger, walking beside him, orders the corporal to continue moving until the "enemy" is directly to his nine o'clock.

"Okay," Sgt. Léger says, moments later. "Contact left!"

Cpl. Paquette turns, aims his machine gun up the steep slope, and pulls the trigger. Three quick bursts. Ta ta ta. Ta ta ta. Ta ta ta.

"Target down!" someone yells.

The troops storm up the hill, their brown suede combat boots sinking into the sand with every step. At the top, nothing but wide-open desert awaits. Dyer and Smith set up their C-6 in the middle of the firing line, with Hollister crouched directly behind them. The C-9 gunners hunker down on either side—Paquette on the right; Green on the left. Clark orders the Carl G. to fall in directly beside the C-6.

"No," Cpl. Perry barks back. "I'm going right." Typical Perry. Clark says one thing; he does the opposite.

The machine-gunners unload on a few pop-up targets, every fourth or fifth round accompanied by bright red tracer fire. Cpl. Decaire kneels down, throws the Carl Gustav over his right shoulder, and waits as Cpl. Perry loads the first rocket-propelled round into the chamber. In his crosshairs is an old tank a few hundred yards away. "Standy!" Cpl. Decaire yells.

MCpl. Clark, crouched just to the left of the 84 team, relays the order to MCpl. Hollister. On his mark, the machine guns swing their fire toward the tank so Cpl. Decaire—not wearing NVGs—can use their tracer flashes to lock in on the target. At the far left of the firing line, Pte. Green lets go of his machine gun and reaches around his back for the M-72. Greener and Decaire squeeze their triggers at the same time, momentarily lighting up the night sky with two bright flashes and a massive boom.

"Son of a bitch," Sgt. Ford says. He didn't wear his earplugs tonight, and the M-72 is deafening. He turns to his left and moves a few steps away from Pte. Green.

In the adam area, Shane Brennan stands up and starts walking toward 3 Section's position. He is anxious to see if Perry and Decaire are having any more luck than he did hitting targets in the dark. He stops about 200 feet from the wadi. A perfect view. As he watches, two helicopter pilots approach the airfield from the east. They see the tracer fire in the distance, but they've been coming in and out of this region for weeks now. They know it must be Tarnak Farm. But just to be sure, one of the choppers calls the Kandahar tower to ask if the range is hot. "Yes," he is told, "it is."

★   ★   ★

Coasting toward the tanker at about 22,000 feet, the F-16s are split in a standard loose wedge formation, nearly a mile apart. Maj. Umbach is on the left; Maj. Schmidt on the right. Both men have taken off their NVGs and flicked on their overt navigation lights—a red one on the left wing, a green one on the right, and a blinking white strobe on the tail. As soon as they gas up, it's back to Kuwait. Six hours down; another three to go.

Maj. Umbach is the first to notice the flashes. He radios Maj. Schmidt, alerting him to the "fireworks" coming from the dark desert below. Because the call is not captured on tape, it is impossible to know exactly what was said. But Maj. Umbach will later insist that he radioed the AWACS, saying: "BOSSMAN, Coffee 51. We have SAFIRE (surface-to-air fire) in our present position. Are there any friendlies in the area?" Both pilots will also claim that Maj. Umbach said: "I think they are shooting at us," followed by: "I think they are pulling lead," suggesting that the weapon on the ground was tracking him.

What is certain is that both jets make a hard left turn through the night sky. Maj. Schmidt kills his lights and grabs his NVGs. Maj. Umbach reaches for his goggles, too, but unlike his Top Gun wingman, he doesn't think to turn off his headlights. Maj. Schmidt yells at him over the radio to hit the switch.

Inside the AWACS, TSgt. Carroll listens as the pilots try to determine the location of the SAFIRE flashing underneath them. They eventually ask BOSSMAN for permission to take a mark. Headset on, TSgt. Carroll forwards the request over Net 2, an internal AWACS radio that is usually manned by Capt. Pepper. But a moment ago, the captain left his station to go to the bathroom. Maj. Henry, the Canadian, answers the call for him.

"Yes," he tells TSgt. Carroll. "Go ahead and mark that."

BOSSMAN passes the approval to the F-16s, then picks up his pencil. He is ready to write down the coordinates as soon as they come in. Behind him, Maj. Henry scribbles a note in his logbook: "21:21. Coffee 51 Flight experienced SA fire."

Seventy miles away, both F-16s are now flying north toward the flashes. The jets are nearly five nautical miles apart—Maj. Umbach approaching on the left; Maj. Schmidt on the right. Tarnak Farm is almost directly between them.

Thousands of feet below, Cpl. Decaire has fired his third rocket-propelled round from the Carl Gustav. He takes the weapon off his shoulder and switches spots with Cpl. Perry, giving his loader the chance to shoot a few rounds, too. They can't help but laugh. Decaire didn't even come close to hitting the target once. Down the firing line, Pte. Green's C-9 has jammed—again. There is little he can do about it now, so he starts shuttling his ammo boxes to Cpl. Paquette, the other C-9 gunner. Someone has to fire them, or the Carl G. team won't be able to see a thing. Not that it's been much help so far.

High above, both pilots activate their cockpit voice recorders. It is exactly 9:22:38 p.m., Zulu time. A Company has been training at Tarnak Farm for more than five hours.

"Do ya got good coordinates for a mark or do you need me to roll in?" Maj. Umbach asks his wingman.

"Standy," Maj. Schmidt answers. "I'll mark it right now."

"Copy."

"I'm in from the southeast," Maj. Schmidt says, steering left and descending toward the unknown ground fire: 16,000 feet, 15,000 feet. From the belly of his jet, a pulsing infrared laser shines on the ground, visible only through the NVGs clamped on the pilots' helmets. Turning black into green, the goggles stick out from their eyes like two toilet paper rolls.

"If you get a dive toss SPI, I can take that and make it a point off of it," Maj. Umbach says, suggesting that his number two transmit the coordinates on the tip of his laser. Maj. Umbach continues north at nearly 23,000 feet, keeping the source of the flashes on his right side. Heavy breathing fills their black oxygen masks. *Hhhhhhhhhhuuuuu, huuhhhh. Hhhhhhhhhhhh-huuuuuhhhhh, hhhhhhhhhuuuhhh.*

Inside Maj. Schmidt's cockpit, a computer-generated voice—female—issues a warning: "Altitude," she says. "Altitude." His jet is approaching 10,000 feet, the "hard deck," the absolute lowest point that pilots are allowed to dip without permission. Harry immediately starts to climb: 12,000 feet, 13,000 feet.

In the AWACS, Capt. Pepper returns from the bathroom and walks over to TSgt. Carroll. "Anything happening?" the captain asks.

"Yeah," his controller answers. "We just had a SAFIRE event."

Capt. Pepper rushes back to his radar station, grabs his headset, and sits down. He plugs into OCRE 6, the UHF frequency that TSgt. Carroll is using to talk to the pilots.

At Tarnak Farm, Ainsworth Dyer and Rene Paquette spray their machine guns at a burnt-out tank downrange. Red tracer slices through the night, just enough for Brett Perry, now armed with the Carl G., to see the target. He fires. A split-second rocket flash illuminates the firing line.

Maj. Schmidt turns right, steering his Viper away from the Canadians. "Altitude," the voice says again. "Altitude." He continues to descend. 12,000 feet, 11,000 feet. "Okay, BOSSMAN," he says over the UHF. "This is, uh, Coffee 52. I've got a tally on the vicinity. Uh, request permission to lay down some, uh, 20 mike-mike."

"Standby," BOSSMAN says.

Twenty-millimeter cannons? The request catches Maj. Umbach by surprise. "Let's just make sure that it's, uh, that it's not friendlies, that's all," he tells his wingman. The call travels over VHF, a plane-to-plane frequency. Only Maj. Schmidt—not BOSSMAN—hears the transmission.

Aboard the AWACS, Maj. Henry switches his headset to a satellite stream and radios the CAOC. The F-16s are not equipped to hear these calls. "K-Mart, this is BOSSMAN," Maj. Henry says. "Coffee 51 flight has experienced SAFIRE near the city of Kandahar, requesting permission to open up with 20 millimeter. I'll try to get you a little more information. We told them to hold fire."

If Maj. Henry did order a hold fire before getting on the radio, it never reached the F-16s.

"When you get a chance, put it on the SPI, if you've got a good hack on it," Maj. Umbach says. Again, he wants his wingman to show him exactly where his laser is pointing.

Hundreds of miles away in Saudi Arabia, Major Scott Woodson answers the call from the AWACS. He turns around and relays the 20 mike-mike request to his boss, Lieutenant-Colonel Craig Fisher.

"Negative," the colonel says.

A large radar screen on the wall shows Coffee Flight in the vicinity of Kandahar. Col. Fisher picks up a phone near his desk and calls the ASOC, an Army/Air Force liaison office in Bagram, Afghanistan. The person on the other end puts him on hold. In the "Crow's Nest"—an elevated desk in the center of the CAOC floor—Colonel Charles McGuirk is answering an e-mail from CENTCOM. "Are you hearing this?" Lt.-Col. Fisher asks him.

"BOSSMAN, K-Mart," Maj. Woodson says to the AWACS. "We copy report reference Coffee. We need SAFIRE details from Coffee when able and hold fire."

In the sky, Maj. Schmidt has turned right and is now heading west, the ground fire a few miles to his right. His lead is a few miles to the north, flying almost directly over the Kandahar Airfield. Both men's eyes are racing, peering outside as they try to pinpoint the source of the unidentified flashes. Their left hands grip the throttle, their thumbs sliding across a small cursor that controls every movement of those invisible lasers. When they're not following the pulsing beams through their NVGs, they glance underneath the goggles at their targeting pod videos—grainy images captured by tiny cameras underneath their F-16s. Their breathing grows heavier. "Okay," Maj. Schmidt says over the radio. "I'm going to flow down here to the, uh, southwest."

Maj. Schmidt still hasn't heard back on his request to strafe the desert with 20mm gunfire. He starts to wonder whether he should talk to somebody else on board the AWACS, or even better, on the ground. "BOSSMAN from Coffee 52," he says. "Do you want us to push a different freq?"

At the Kandahar Airfield, a Hercules transport plane is parked on the edge of the runway, engines purring. It's ready to take off. Cpl. Laroque, A Company's sentry in the tower, passes a "check fire" to Call Sign Zero. Parked near the Herc, the crew members of a Canadian Coyote are waiting for orders to head back to Tarnak Farm. They escorted the paratroopers out there tonight, and it's almost time to bring them home. Corporal Neil Miller is huddled inside the Coyote, enjoying a brief taste of air conditioning. Over the radio, he hears Lieutenant Mark Batten—Call Sign Zero—contact Tarnak Farm.

"One, this is Zero," Lt. Batten says. "Check fire, Tarnak Farms." Nobody answers. The lieutenant will repeat the dispatch two more times, but never get a response.

At the range, Lt. Luft has finished sorting out 2 Section's ammo and is about to head down to the wadi to catch the tail end of 3 Section's drill. Cpl. Bygrove, one of the Pioneers, cuts him off just as he begins to leave. They start chatting. Neither has any idea that Maj. Umbach is pointing an invisible laser just a few feet from where they are standing.

"Check my sparkle, check my sparkle," Bill says to Harry. "See if it looks good."

Cpl. Perry pulls the trigger on another Carl G. round—a brief flash captured forever by the camera underneath Maj. Umbach's Viper. White light fills Maj. Schmidt's NVGs. He immediately slides his laser over the wadi, stopping right beside his flight lead's. "I'm contact your sparkle as well," Maj. Umbach tells him.

Inside the AWACS, TSgt. Carroll parrots the CAOC's latest order to the pilots. "Coffee 51, BOSSMAN," he says. "Hold fire. Need details on SAFIRE for K-Mart."

Maj. Schmidt's answer is immediate. "Okay, I've got a, uh, I've got some men on a road and it looks like a piece of artillery firing at us," he says. "I am rolling in in self-defense."

"BOSSMAN copies," TSgt. Carroll says.

Behind him, Maj. Henry again radios the CAOC. "He's invoking self-defense ROE on the fire," he tells Maj. Woodson. "On the road he sees artillery shooting at him. Stand by for details."

Maj. Schmidt turns north, his target approaching on the right side. "Check master arm, laser arm," Maj. Umbach reminds him. "And check you're not in mark."

"Got 'em both on," his wingman answers. "I'm in from the southwest."

Maj. Schmidt descends again: 14,000 feet, 13,000, 12,000. "Altitude," the voice says again. "Altitude." He presses his right thumb over the red button—the pickle button—on the tip of the control stick.

"Do you show 'em on a bridge?" Maj. Umbach asks him.

"Bombs away, cranking left," Maj. Schmidt answers. A dart-shaped GBU-12—500 pounds—falls off his wing, plummeting to the ground along another invisible laser beam.

At Tarnak Farm, the C-6 is out of ammo. Cpl. Paquette, hunkered down under the lip of the wadi, is the only machine-gunner firing, but he is also running low on bullets. As Rene waits for a signal from the Carl G. team, he unloads a short burst with his C-9, then counts to 10. One Mississippi. Two Mississippi. Three Mississippi.

Cpl. Perry has flipped off his helmet so he can take a closer look through the scope of the Carl Gustav. Sgt. Léger spots the safety violation and sneaks up behind him. "Perry," he says. "Put your fucking helmet on, eh."

Marc watches as the corporal takes the bazooka off his shoulder, retrieves his helmet, and buckles up the chin strap. When he gets back on his knee, Cpl. Decaire starts loading the sixth and final round into the chamber.

Pte. Green is on his knees, struggling to set up the Claymore mine. Cpl. Perry—unaware that Greener's gun jammed a few minutes ago—is screaming at him to get more tracer downrange. "We can't see fuck all!" he yells from the other side of the firing line. "I need tracer. Get your fucking gun going!"

Decaire is just about to give Perry the ready sign when he notices that the rubber ring on the end of the weapon—the piece that dampens any vibration—is loose. "Don't fuckin' pull the trigger," he warns Cpl. Perry.

In the CAOC, a crowd has gathered around the Crow's Nest, scrambling to figure out what could possibly be firing under the F-16s. Lt.-Col. Fisher—on hold with the ASOC—gives Maj. Woodson another order: Get the pilots out of there. He doesn't know that Canadians are practice-firing. He just knows that coalition troops are stationed in the region.

"BOSSMAN, K-Mart," Maj. Woodson radios back to the AWACS. "Be advised Kandahar has friendlies. You are to get Coffee 51 out of there as soon as possible." He has no idea that Maj. Schmidt's bomb is already bulleting toward Tarnak Farm.

"Check wide field of view," Maj. Umbach tells Maj. Schmidt.

"I'm fine," he says, his F-16 hitting 10,550 feet. "Laser's on."

In the AWACS, Maj. Henry answers the CAOC. "Roger," he says. "We'll get him out of there right now."

Cpl. Paquette peers over at the Carl G. Four Mississippi. Five Mississippi. MCpl. Hollister pats Ainsworth on the ankle. Good shooting. Sgt. Léger starts to climb up the hill behind them. Sgt. Ford hears a whistle and looks up at the sky.

"Shack," Maj. Schmidt says. A direct hit.

The cockpit recorders inside the F-16s have been rolling for three minutes and 23 seconds.

"BOSSMAN, BOSSMAN," Maj. Schmidt says over the radio, a cloud of smoke growing underneath him.

"Coffee 51, BOSSMAN," TSgt. Carroll says. "Disengage. Friendlies, Kandahar."

As his troops fire into the night, Maj. Hackett sits inside his jeep, reviewing some last-minute paperwork for the upcoming Khowst assignment. One of his platoon commanders, Lieutenant Jeff Peck, is lying on the hood. Joe Jasper is about to brief the next group of soldiers on the Close Quarter Battle range. More than once tonight, he has told Dave Bibby, one of the Pioneers, that there seems to be a magical connection between his drill and Sgt. Léger's. Every time the guys storm the corral, the other troops start pounding the tanks.

Near the ambulance, DLB finishes another Starbucks. Sgt. Wilson is relaxing in the front seat, reading a new book he bought during 3 Platoon's hiatus in Dubai: *Oxford Handbook of Accidents and Emergency Care.* He got a good deal on it, only 20 bucks. Behind him, Mac lounges on one of the stretchers, listening to the radio chatter. Britney slides on a polar fleece underneath his flak jacket. It's getting chilly.

Sergeant-Major Al Whitehall—the highest-ranking non-officer in the company—is directing traffic outside, making sure his troops head down to the ammo truck when it's their turn to fire. With his booming voice and bushy moustache, Whitehall is a difficult man to miss. "Come on," he says, looking at Private Norman Link. "Get up. You're next."

The bomb crashes into the ground right beside Richard Green, tearing him apart. Shrapnel and fire and a blinding white light rip through the sand, tossing aside troops who never see it coming. Even in the adam area—nearly 500 feet away—the force of the blast knocks some people over.

Capt. Jasper flops on his stomach and flips down his NVGs. All he can see is a huge ball of dust. Cpl. Bygrove hits the deck, too, yanking

Lt. Luft down with him. Chris Kopp—startled from his nap—throws on his flak jacket and helmet. He has seen the intel reports. *Did we just get hit with a BM-21?*

Somehow, Cpl. Perry manages to keep his balance. He doesn't even lose his grip on the Carl Gustav. "What the fuck was that!?" he yells. Nobody answers. The entire firing line is gone. His loader, Cpl. Decaire, isn't even beside him anymore. *Holy fuck*, Cpl. Perry thinks to himself. *I just killed everybody.*

High above, Harry Schmidt acknowledges BOSSMAN's call to disengage. It came across the airwaves eight seconds after his bomb exploded. "Copy," Maj. Schmidt says. "Uhhh, disengaging south." A tingle fills his spine.

"Coffee 51, BOSSMAN," TSgt. Carroll says to Maj. Umbach. "How copy?"

"Copy," he says. "Uhh, can you confirm that they were shooting at us?" Bill waits seven long seconds for an answer.

"Coffee 51, BOSSMAN," TSgt. Carroll finally says. "You're cleared. Self-defense. K-Mart wants you to work south. There may be friendlies, Kandahar."

On the ground, Cpl. Decaire emerges from the wadi. The blast knocked him backwards, but only a few feet. His right hand—covered in blood—is already starting to swell. It is dead quiet. People are yelling in the distance, but here, in the darkness of the ditch, Cpl. Decaire hears nothing.

"What the fuck happened?" Cpl. Perry asks him. "Was that us? Was that us?"

"No way," his friend answers. "It couldn't have been us."

Perry takes the weapon off his shoulder and shines a small red flashlight onto the Venturi lock. The safety is on. It wasn't the Carl G. Something else triggered this explosion.

Sgt. Wilson throws down his new book and jumps out of the ambulance. Neither he nor anyone else heard that "check fire" come across the radio. "DLB!" Cpl. Speirs yells. "Bring the amb to the scene!"

Britney and Sgt. Wilson grab their med bags—40 pounds worth of Tylenol, field dressings, gauze pads, and IV solution—and turn toward the billowing black smoke. "Does anyone know if this field is clear?" Cpl. Speirs yells. The quickest route to the explosion is straight across the desert, but he is not sure if the area is off-limits because of landmines. He shouts again, a little louder this time. "Does anyone know if this field is clear!"

"Follow me," Sgt.-Maj. Whitehall says. As the three men run toward the ammo truck, Maj. Hackett reaches into the ambulance and grabs the headset.

"Zero, this is One," the company commander says over the radio. "We've just been engaged by fast air."

Even from a few miles away, everyone at the airfield felt the thud of the blast. Jolted from their sleep, some guys took cover under their cots, just like they're supposed to. RAK TOC, the U.S. Army command post down the road, has already called Lt. Batten, asking what the hell the Canadians are firing down there tonight. The explosion shook their tent.

In the wadi, whatever silence there was has been replaced by the sounds of screaming men. Clicking on his headlamp, Cpl. Decaire spots Rene Paquette a few yards down the sandy hill, moaning as he struggles to catch his breath. He is vomiting blood. MCpl. Clark is stumbling nearby. The orange flash of the explosion punched him in the chest and threw him down the ravine. As he follows the screams, his mind is spinning. Did the Carl Gustav malfunction? Did guys on the other range accidentally shoot us? "I think there's guys hurt over here," he says.

Cpl. Perry finds MCpl. Hollister, whose face is red and burnt. Beside them, two men lie motionless in the sand, face down. It is pitch black. "I'm going to get the box amb 'cause those fuckers aren't here," Perry tells Clark and Decaire. He bolts south through the wadi, where he sees Sgt. Ford lying on his right side. Lorne's left leg is gushing blood, and he doesn't appear to be moving. Perry keeps running.

Near the ammo truck, Lt. Luft lifts himself off the ground and sprints toward his men, heading north along the gravel road that runs parallel to the wadi. In the darkness, he sees Cpl. Perry coming toward him. "Where is Sgt. Ford?" Lt. Luft asks him.

"I think Sgt. Ford is dead," Brett answers.

By now, Sgt. Ford can feel the dampness underneath his left leg. He reaches down, then lifts his hand back to within inches of his face. It is soaked in blood. He doesn't even notice that he can't see a thing out of his right eye. "I'm over here," he says, waving his arms in the air. "I'm hurt real bad." For a moment, he actually giggles.

Across Tarnak Farm, troops are taking cover. Capt. Jasper and the Pioneers run back to the adam area, where some soldiers, including Shane Brennan, are diving underneath the logistics trucks. A few of the drivers have turned on their headlights. "Kill the lights!" Capt. Jasper yells.

"Get out from under the fucking truck!" someone else screams. "It's coming around again! It's coming around again!"

Billy Bolen is barking the same order at some soldiers shielding themselves behind the ammo truck. It's packed with C-4. Not the place you want to be if another bomb comes sailing in. As they flee, Bolen turns the other way and sprints toward the explosion, where he can see the outline of a burning helmet lighting up a small chunk of the night. Sgt. Ford is lying nearby, halfway up the ravine. Bolen sticks a field dressing underneath the sergeant's mangled leg and continues toward the noise.

Whitehall and the medics are just seconds behind. As they sprint across the ditch, a jet roars overhead. It's Maj. Schmidt, disengaging south. "Medic!" they hear in the darkness. "Medic!" Speirs and Wilson run right past Sgt. Ford.

Aboard the AWACS plane, Maj. Henry's crew is not quite sure if the F-16s actually dropped a bomb. For some reason, nobody heard the "shack" call come over the radio. "Coffee 51, BOSSMAN," TSgt. Carroll says to the pilots. "I need coordinates when able and need to know if any rounds were fired."

"Go ahead," Maj. Umbach tells his wingman.

"Yeah, I had one bomb dropped in the vicinity of, uh, 31 24 north, point 78 65 43 point 522," Maj. Schmidt radios. "That's an estimate. Uh, if you had our general vicinity ..."

"BOSSMAN," TSgt. Carroll says. The coordinates Maj. Schmidt passed are actually five miles away from the spot he just bombed.

Both pilots continue south, the cloud of smoke growing smaller and smaller with every transmission. Maj. Schmidt has switched off his targeting pod camera. "Wow," he says.

"Coffee 51, repeat east coordinate," BOSSMAN says.

"Yeah, I'm not sure it's that accurate," Maj. Schmidt answers. "I don't, I don't have an accurate coordinate right now. Do you want me to go back and get you one?"

"BOSSMAN, negative."

"Let's go back safe," Maj. Umbach says. He takes another deep breath. "Shit."

"Yeah, they were definitely shooting at you," Maj. Schmidt tells his lead.

"It sure seemed like they were tracking around and everything and, uh, trying to lead," he answers.

"Well, we had our lights on and that wasn't helping, I don't think," Schmidt says. "I had a group of guys on a road around a gun and it did not look organized like it would be our guys."

"It seemed like it was right on a bridge," Maj. Umbach says. "That's kinda where I was at."

"Nah, not quite," his wingman answers.

"I hope that was the right thing to do," Maj. Schmidt says.

"Me too."

Norm Link is on the ground near the adam area, twitching in pain. A piece of burning shrapnel sailed all the way from the wadi and lodged in his right foot. Corporal Pete Filis helps DLB cut Norm's laces and yank off his sock. The medic applies a pressure dressing, then runs to grab the ambulance.

"What the fuck is this?" Cpl. Perry yells. Having raced all the way from the wadi, he is shocked to find so much attention being given to a wounded foot. "You've got fucking guys dead down there!" he screams, unaware that the other two medics have already reached the blast scene. "Let's get the fuck down there!"

Cpl. Filis and Corporal Kent Schmidt lift Pte. Link into the amb. Kent cocks a shotgun and tosses it to his wounded friend. "Anyone comes around here that you don't know, shoot 'em," he says. Cpl. Kopp hands his radio to a fellow soldier and jumps in the back with Pte. Link. As DLB drives away, Kopp slides on his latex gloves.

In the wadi, Bill Wilson and Vic Speirs are treating everyone they can find. Wilson spots Sgt. Léger lying in the dirt, but because of the darkness, he can't quite decipher who it is. He feels his neck for a pulse. Nothing. Under the glare of his headlamp, he notices the huge hole in Sgt. Léger's stomach. Marc is dead. Sgt. Wilson moves on.

Cpl. Speirs, armed with a tiny flashlight, finds Rene Paquette. Covered in blood and still gasping for air, his uniform is almost completely torn off. Except for the loud ringing in his ear, he can't hear a thing. Cpl. Speirs scans Rene for any other signs of damage, then climbs up the hill.

MCpl. Hollister is sitting up when Wilson finds him. The medic pulls out a pressure bandage and covers the blood on the left side of his face. He can hear Vic yelling his name from the top of the ditch.

Amid the confusion and the adrenaline, Capt. Jasper races down the wadi. He wants to link up with Sgt. Léger. As the range safety man, Marc should be able to explain what the hell happened here.

"Coffee 51, BOSSMAN," TSgt. Carroll says.

"Go ahead," Maj. Umbach answers.

"Yeah, I need type bomb dropped, result, and type of SAFIRE," he says.

"Yeah," Maj. Schmidt answers. "It was a single GBU-12 dropped. It was a direct hit on, uh, the artillery piece that was firing. Uh, as far as the SAFIRE, multiple rounds. It looked like, uh, MLRS, uh, to Coffee five-two. Five-one, what do you have on that?"

"I'd say the same," Maj. Umbach says. "It was, uh, sort of continuous fire and, uh, it appeared to be, uh, leading us as we were, uh, flying by and then as we came back around."

"Did you get a top altitude on the SAFIRE?" TSgt. Carroll asks.

"Negative. They, uh, they were burning out before here," Maj. Umbach says.

"I would estimate the top was approximately 10,000 feet," his wingman adds.

At the back of the AWACS, Maj. Henry, the Canadian, radios Maj. Woodson in the CAOC. "It appeared to be an MLRS-type firing on Coffee 52," he says. "I will get you lat/long for that, over."

"And, uh, just to let you know," Maj. Schmidt tells TSgt. Carroll, "we split in azimuth sending, uh, five-one to the south and five-two went to the northeast and, uh, one of the guns turned back around to the east, uh, firing at, uh, five-two, uh, as well."

"BOSSMAN copies. And, uh, if we get a rough, uh, longitude?"

"Yeah," Maj. Schmidt says. "I did not take a mark, uh, at the time."

"BOSSMAN copies."

Cpl. Speirs reaches for his stethoscope as he kneels beside Ainsworth

Dyer. "He's breathing!" Britney yells. He rips open Dyer's shirt and shouts his name, hoping for an answer as he searches for a beat. The sand underneath Dyer's head is soaked in blood.

Sgt. Wilson pulls two pressure bandages out of his med bag and wraps them around the top of Ainsworth's bleeding head. Capt. Jasper hands over his field dressing, too, then reaches into Dyer's pocket in search of another one. He looks down at Ainsworth's feet. The left one is gone, sheared off by a piece of the bomb. "He's dead," says Cpl. Decaire, standing nearby, flashlights beaming all around. Hollister hears him. He will never forget those words.

Surrounded, Ains takes one more deep gulp, then tilts his head to the side. Vic hears nothing in his stethoscope. As he feels Dyer's neck for a pulse, Sgt. Wilson leans forward and removes the bandages from Dyer's head. Only now, up close, does he see the extent of the damage. He puts the bandages back on. Capt. Jasper can only watch as the medics stand up and move on to somebody else.

In Saudi Arabia, a crowd lingers on the CAOC floor, still clueless about what the F-16s just attacked. Nobody knows. Lt.-Col. Fisher—still on hold with the ASOC—hangs up. His boss, Col. McGuirk, phones upstairs to the Battle Cab, a large glass room that overlooks the CAOC floor. Brigadier-General Stephen Wood, the CAOC night director, is sitting at his desk, reviewing the final plans for a landmark event the next day: Mohammed Zahir Shah, the King of Afghanistan, is flying back into the country after 29 years of exile.

"It's Coffee Flight," Col. McGuirk tells the general. "And they may have dropped."

General Wood looks over at Major Tom Smedley of the Battlefield Coordination Detachment (BCD), a U.S. Army unit embedded within the CAOC. The BCD's main job is to tell the Air Force where coalition ground troops are operating. "Is there friendlies south of Kandahar?" General Wood asks Maj. Smedley.

"Negative," he answers.

"Any activity south of Kandahar?" the general asks.

Maj. Smedley takes a moment to look at his computer.

"Negative," he says.

The headlights on the ambulance aren't very bright, but Cpl. de la Bourdonnaye can see the flashlights bobbing in the distance. Outside, Private Darren Astles is pointing the amb down the road that leads to the ammo point. A quick right, and it's a straight drive to the firing line. But DLB—dealing with a combination of the darkness and the directions—misses the turn. He throws the amb in reverse. In the back, Cpl. Kopp wishes he'd just run. It would have been faster.

In the adam area, section commanders are conducting roll calls, trying to account for each of their troops. Master Corporal Rob Coates—a certified emergency medical responder—is among the dozens of soldiers hunkered down in a large crater just behind the Iltis. Against the advice of his section commander, he bolts for the range.

Lieutenant Jay Adair and Warrant Officer Rob Jones have also taken off toward the smoke. As they run, Adair trips over something smoldering in the dirt. For a moment, he thinks it's a dead animal, maybe a sheep. Jones knows better. He drops a glowstick, then keeps sprinting.

"Is that, was that definitely the airfield that was close?" Maj. Umbach asks his wingman over the plane-to-plane frequency. BOSSMAN—unable to hear the transmission—cuts him off.

"Coffee 51, please repeat the, uh, coordinate you passed."

"Yeah," Maj. Schmidt says, answering his flight lead's question about the airfield.

"He wants the coordinate again," Maj. Umbach says.

"Yeah, I do not have the, uh, proper coordinate for that, uh, BOSS-MAN," Maj. Schmidt says.

"BOSSMAN."

"Would you estimate, I'd estimate about three miles to the south, maybe at 150," Maj. Umbach says. BOSSMAN chimes in again, this time to tell the pilots where their tanker is waiting. The Vipers still need gas.

"Yeah, BOSSMAN," Maj. Schmidt says. "Uh, there was no ROZ effective in that area tonight as far as our brief was concerned, you concur?"

Inside the AWACS, Maj. Henry calls the CAOC again. "K-Mart, this is BOSSMAN Two," he says. "Rough coordinates of bomb drop—3124/6555. If they overflew again they could give it, but we turned them away. And just confirm that you have no ROZ active at that location, over?"

Based on the incorrect coordinates—and the fact that the AWACS crew has never heard of Tarnak Farm—Capt. Pepper and Maj. Henry agree with Maj. Schmidt: there is no ROZ effective in that area.

"BOSSMAN concurs," TSgt. Carroll tells the pilots.

Only five minutes have ticked by since his bomb hit the ground, but Maj. Schmidt can already sense the scrutiny to come. "Yeah, stand by for the microscope, huh?" he tells his flight lead.

"Yeah," Bill says.

"I'm at your right side," Maj. Schmidt says.

"Roger that," Maj. Umbach answers. "I'm going cameras off."

Near the Iltis, Mac is on his knees, smoking and scribbling and talking to Zero. Reports are already trickling back about the carnage up ahead. He sends Cpl. Kent Schmidt to find out just how bad it is. Behind him, troops have taken their machine guns and set up a security perimeter. For all they know, this might still be an enemy attack.

As he maneuvers down the wadi, Chris Kopp can see Sgt. Ford's helmet. The scrim is still on fire, surrounded by twisted pieces of gear and machine guns.

"Lorne, can you hear me?" Kopp says.

"Yes," he answers, his right eye swollen shut.

"Can you take a big deep breath for me?"

"Haaaaaaa, hoooooo."

"Does that hurt?"

"No."

"Where do you hurt?"

"My leg."

The gash in the back of Sgt. Ford's thigh is massive, soaking the sand with more and more blood as the seconds pass. Cpl. Kopp digs into his pocket and pulls out a light blue tourniquet. DLB, running down the hill after parking the ambulance, kneels beside him. "Here, put this on," Cpl. Kopp tells him.

Cpl. de la Bourdonnaye is hesitant. If applied tightly enough, the belt-like device completely cuts off circulation to anything below. But for years, the Army has preached tourniquets as a last resort. They are life-savers, not limb-savers. DLB wants to try direct pressure on the wound before resorting to a measure that might leave Sgt. Ford without a leg. He grabs a bandage and sticks it under the sergeant's thigh.

By now, Master Corporal Rob Coates has arrived from the adam area. He sees Nathan. He sees another body, covered by a blanket. Rob reaches down and peels back one of the corners. Lying underneath is Ainsworth Dyer, his bandaged head sprinkled with sand. Only a few days ago, he, Ains and Greener had spent the afternoon together at a water park in Dubai. They went down the slides. Took a few photos. Dyer's booming laugh was as loud as ever. Rob slides the blanket back over his friend's face.

Down the wadi, Coates spots DLB and Kopp kneeling beside Sgt. Ford. He sprints toward them. As he helps to cut off Lorne's gear, Rob sees the blood dripping from the sergeant's swollen right eye. "I'm hurt real bad," Ford tells him. He is shaking, growing colder by the minute.

Cpl. Speirs returns to Cpl. Paquette. His coughs are uncontrollable, triggered by the blood filling in his lungs. Guided by a tiny flashlight hanging from his teeth, Speirs slices off Rene's shirt to get a better look at his chest. On his back, bruises have already started to take shape. Vic can't tell just yet, but somehow Rene Paquette was not hit with a single piece of shrapnel.

As he watches the medic scramble over top of him, Rene can barely hear a whisper, like he's watching an action movie with the mute button on. He's terrified that maybe a burst of static electricity in the dry Afghan air somehow detonated the Claymore mine strapped to his back. In the darkness, he can see a combat boot. *Why is nobody working on him?*

Cpl. Perry, back from fetching the ambulance, is still not sure who survived the explosion. He saw Marc, but he thought it was Ricky. For a while, he is convinced that Sgt. Léger is somewhere in the desert, alone and dying.

Cpl. Decaire tries to cut off Hollister's webbing, but when he reaches for his knife, his right hand is too swollen and bloody to grip the handle. He has never felt more useless. A senior officer finally tells Brian to go sit in the amb with Pte. Link.

Sgt. Wilson is everywhere. As the lead medic, his job is to triage, not necessarily treat. He can hear DLB yelling in the distance. As he runs over, another soldier stops him, pointing at Marc Léger. Wilson still doesn't know who it is.

"It's Sgt. Léger," Whitehall tells him.

"Sgt. Léger is dead," the medic says. "And so is Cpl. Dyer."

Under his headlamp, Sgt. Wilson sees Nathan Smith. He runs the other way, following DLB's voice.

More green uniforms arrive. Warrant Andy Hulan. Jones. Adair. Hackett. Bibby. Bygrove. Bradshaw. Schmidt. Filis. Some help the wounded. Others form a mini-search party. It is so dark that soldiers six feet from each other are screaming, convinced that the person they are trying to talk to is actually much farther away. Amid the flashlights, amid the panic, Billy Bolen takes charge. "If you're not involved in giving orders, then shut the fuck up!" he yells. Like Perry, Bolen also believes Marc is missing. In the confusion and the darkness, he doesn't see his friend's body lying in the sand.

Alastair Luft begins sifting through Nathan's pockets, trying to find a piece of I.D. The face he is staring at is unrecognizable, crushed by the force of the bomb. Luft eventually finds a Gerber parachute knife with a retainer band tied around the handle. He's pretty sure Ricky Green has a knife like that. This must be Greener, Luft thinks to himself. Cpl. Perry rushes up behind him. "Sir, come with me right now," he tells his platoon commander. "I can't fucking live with myself. Tell me if it was me or not."

The two men march back up the hill toward the Carl Gustav. Perry throws the 84 back on his shoulder while Luft flips open the Venturi lock and peers down the chamber. "Yeah, Brett, it's still in there," he says, referring to the round. "It didn't fire. This was not your fault." As he speaks, Lt. Luft can't help but think how lucky *he* is. He was supposed to be here when the bomb exploded. If Cpl. Bygrove hadn't stopped to talk ...

At Call Sign Zero, Lt. Batten receives another call from RAK TOC. They've been talking to the AWACS. It seems the F-16s felt threatened and released ordnance in self-defense. As Batten records the update in his logbook, A Company radios again. They need a CASEVAC chopper. It is 9:36 p.m. Zulu time—10 minutes since the explosion.

Lt. Batten leaves his post and rushes toward Pete Dawe's tent. Maj. Dawe is the operations officer for the Canadian Battle Group, the man who essentially runs Call Sign Zero. "Sir, we have a real problem," Lt. Batten says. "Guys are hurt." Maj. Dawe is already half-awake. Like nearly everyone, he heard the explosion. He throws on a t-shirt and heads for the radio room.

In Saudi Arabia, the CAOC still doesn't know what went wrong. Gen. Wood is pacing the CAOC floor, asking all his army liaison officers—including Special Forces—whether their troops are conducting any missions near Kandahar tonight. All is quiet. When the general walks back upstairs to the Battle Cab, Maj. Smedley tells him about the CASEVAC request. It's obvious now. This can't be anything else but friendly fire.

Kent Schmidt, back from his first run to the wadi, returns to the crater where most of A Company is positioned. He sits down beside Corporal Patrick Farrell and takes off his helmet. "It's fucked up," he says. "There are guys dead up there."

Capt. Jasper wants to talk to Call Sign Zero himself. As he climbs up the wadi, he sees Maj. Hackett, the company commander. "Sir," he says, grabbing his boss's arm. "I think Cpl. Dyer is dead." Scanning the scene for the first time, Maj. Hackett can see the crowd gathered around Sgt. Ford. He yells into the darkness for Sgt.-Maj. Al Whitehall. The brief he receives is difficult to stomach: at least two dead, many more injured. Among the men Maj. Hackett finds in the ditch is Sgt. Léger, whose arm is sprawled across his face, hiding his identity. As Sean lifts up the young sergeant's hand, he can't help but stare. The two men went for a run together just the other day. They talked about Marc's new dog.

Just steps away, Cpl. Speirs is hovering over Cpl. Paquette, listening to his lungs with a stethoscope. As a precaution, the medic puts Paquette on a spine board and runs to the ambulance to grab the oxygen tank. Rene can barely catch his breath. The dog tags hanging from his necklace feel like a 100-pound brick. "Get it off!" he yells. "Get it off!"

At the amb, Speirs finds Norm Link sitting in the back, his injured foot wrapped in a bandage. Brian Decaire has already gone back to the wadi to help treat the casualties. He couldn't just sit there. Norm can hear the chaos outside, the wailing and the hollering, but he can't see it. The oxygen tank isn't here, so Cpl. Speirs bolts down the hill toward Sgt. Ford. It is Vic's first glimpse of Lorne. He ran right past him a few minutes ago. "Are you using the tank?" he asks DLB, crouched over Lorne.

"No," he says.

After a quick chat with his fellow medic, Cpl. Speirs rushes back to Paquette, weaving his way through the many troops who are now sifting through the scene. He slides the oxygen mask around Rene's mouth. The bottle is good for 15 minutes.

"We're still missing people!" Billy Bolen yells behind him. "Where is Marc?"

Cpl. Kopp, wearing a headlamp, can hear the panic. He leaves DLB and Coates to help search the wadi. Lorne Ford's leg continues to pour blood, drenching the field dressings underneath his thigh. The gaping wound is covered in sand, the rest of his body littered with shrapnel. From his swollen right eye, a small streak of blood drips down his cheek. When Sgt. Wilson arrives, DLB immediately asks him for another pressure bandage, but Bill has only one left in his med bag. He used the other ones on Hollister and Dyer.

As Wilson runs back up to the ambulance to fetch more dressings, Kopp returns from his short search through the wadi. Ford's leg looks even worse than when he left. For a second time, he tells DLB to strap on a tourniquet. Anything to stop the bleeding. Wilson arrives with four more bandages, but they are no match for the wound. It's like trying to plug a fire hydrant with a bottle cap. "I'm going to apply a tourniquet," DLB says to Wilson, more asking than telling. The sergeant agrees.

Immediately, MCpl. Coates slides the blue tourniquet across the sand under the upper half of Sgt. Ford's leg. Rob leans over and tells Lorne what they are about to do. The sergeant knows what's coming. He's taken a few combat first aid courses in his time. *Okay, Lorne*, he thinks to himself. *You just lost your leg. But just keep breathing.*

He wails as Cpl. de la Bourdonnaye wrenches on the strap with all his weight. DLB's hands are slippery, so it takes him two tries before he buckles up the strap correctly. Lorne screams again. When he finishes, Cpl. Kopp takes out a black marker and writes the time on Sgt. Ford's forehead. "T 21:54." Twenty-eight minutes had elapsed since the bomb exploded.

Before he reaches Mac in the adam area, Capt. Jasper bumps into Lt. Adair. "You gotta see this," Jay tells him. "I think we've got a lot more wounded here than we think." He walks Capt. Jasper toward the lump that he tripped over a few minutes ago. It is the upper torso of a paratrooper, recognizable only by the chest hair and the intestines and the tattered pieces of green camouflage. Neither man has any idea who they are standing over.

As far as Capt. Jasper knows, he now has two confirmed deaths: Cpl. Dyer and the torso. When he reaches Mac at the Iltis, Kent Schmidt is there, too. The captain tells them to order a CASEVAC chopper. "Already done," Mac says.

"How long till it gets here?" Joe asks.

"Twenty minutes."

Mac updates Call Sign Zero on the latest casualties: one Priority 1 (gravely injured), two Priority 2s (seriously injured), and one Priority 3 (walking wounded). And two Priority 4s. They are the lowest priority—medically speaking—because they are already dead. By now, a small crowd has gathered around the radio. Everyone is stunned. Two Pri 4s? Are they reporting that correctly? Capt. Jasper picks up the headset and confirms the transmission. Two KIA, he says. Killed in Action. Maj. Dawe sends a runner to wake up Major Dan Vouriot, the Battle Group's senior medical advisor.

In the wadi, Dave Bibby finds a green wallet half-buried in the sand. Inside the flap, a photo of Ricky Green is staring back at him. All around, people are yelling that a chopper is en route. "Twenty minutes!" W/O Bolen grabs Pte. Astles and orders him to set up an LZ—a landing zone—on the west side of the wadi. He has a three-foot piece of para cord with a blue glowstick attached to one end. *When you see the chopper*, Bolen tells him, *start waving this around.*

Sgt. Ford is dipping in and out of consciousness. The pain of the tourniquet is vicious, but he wants to know how his guys are doing. How's Clark? How's Paquette? He even asks about Oliver, though he knows full well Ollie wasn't with them in the wadi tonight. How's Green? No one answers him.

DLB is debating whether to give Sgt. Ford a morphine drip to dull the pain. He whispers the idea to Cpl. Kopp, but Lorne—slipping fast—somehow hears him. His eyes suddenly open as wide as they can go. *No fucking drugs*, he says. What he wants is his Airborne coin, which he has carried with him since he joined the now-defunct parachute regiment in 1990. For some reason, he didn't bring it with him tonight.

Shivering, he tells Rob Coates to make sure someone goes in his barracks box to get it.

"Airborne!" he yells, still lying in the sand. "Airborne!"

Sgt. Wilson, running from casualty to casualty, tells Kopp to find Curtis Hollister, who is sitting up, but still dazed by a concussion. Curtis had just turned to walk away from the C-6 team when the might of the bomb hit him in the back. He rode the flames like a wave. Kopp, who has spent most of the past half-hour with Sgt. Ford, cuts off Hollister's webbing and tells him to lie down. Only now, as he wraps a brace around Curtis's neck, does he start to see dead bodies.

Right beside him, Cpl. Speirs pulls a 14-cathelon needle out of his med bag. Sgt. Wilson holds the IV line as Vic pierces the tip into Rene Paquette's right arm. Whitehall is kneeling beside them, his hand caressing Rene's forehead. The sergeant-major was in the room a couple weeks ago when Paquette was on the phone, listening to his new baby girl cry for the first time. "Come on, Rene," Whitehall tells him. "Hang in there for your new daughter." Cpl. Paquette can't hear a word.

With the sound of a chopper humming in the distance, Sgt. Wilson runs back to DLB. The corporal has tried to hook up an IV to Sgt. Ford's arm, but he missed the vein. Wilson tries, but he, too, has no luck. On the west side of the ditch—the same side where 3 Section was firing—Pte. Astles swings his blue glowstick like a lasso, marking where the chopper should touch down. Troops start to carry the stretchers up the hill toward him.

As Brett Perry helps lift Paquette off the ground, he feels a sharp pain in his left arm. Up until now, he hasn't even noticed the blood seeping through his sleeve, sliced by shrapnel. He asks Jon Bradshaw if they can switch sides. His right arm is fine.

Spotting the headlights on some of the trucks, the helicopter crew touches down near the adam area, hundreds of feet from where it's supposed to land. The UH-60 immediately takes off again, this time stopping on the opposite side of the wadi from where Astles is waving his glowstick. It's closer, but still not quite in the right spot. Rob Coates leans over Lorne's head, shielding his face from the sand kicked up by the rotor blades.

"To hell with it," Billy Bolen says. The paratroopers carry the stretchers—Ford, Paquette, and Hollister—back down the wadi and up the other side. "Don't drop me, you pricks," jokes Sgt. Ford, who is wrapped in blankets and slipping out of consciousness. Moments later, he passes out.

Screaming over the noise of the chopper, Sgt. Wilson briefs Sergeant Jamie Rath, the U.S. medic on the CASEVAC. He conducts his own quick triage, then directs the paratroopers to start loading the casualties. They just practiced this yesterday. Remember, don't hit the fuel pod. And Sgt. Ford goes on last, because he obviously has to get off first. DLB jumps on behind him. He has been with Lorne since the beginning, and he figures the American medic on board could use an extra set of hands.

Warrant Jones tells Perry and Decaire to climb on the bird, too. The order catches Sgt. Wilson off guard. For the past half-hour, he has watched both corporals apply first aid to other wounded soldiers. He had no clue they were even hurt. Strapped to a jump seat, Cpl. Decaire looks around the helicopter. He sees Brett Perry, shaking with anger. He sees medics hovered over the stretchers. He thinks about his dead friends outside, about his family back home in Winnipeg. About just how close he came. As the chopper lifts off, he starts to cry.

From the adam area, Mac and Kent Schmidt watch the helo pass overhead. As it makes a sharp right turn toward the airfield, DLB loses his balance, sliding toward the open door. He manages to grab hold of a handle on the wall at the last possible moment, but not before his head and shoulders dangle over the desert for a few long seconds.

The American CASEVAC chopper unleashes another mini-sand-storm as it lifts off toward the Kandahar Airfield. It is 10:20 p.m. Zulu; 54 minutes have elapsed since the patients lying inside were hit by a laser-guided bomb.

In the adam area, W.O. Jones gathers his platoon. There is no doubt that what happened here tonight will be the focus of an exhaustive investigation. Our job, Jones tells his troops, is to sweep the scene, dropping glowsticks beside any potential evidence. Shattered pieces of equipment. Bomb parts. Body parts. "There is a time to mourn," Jones says. "And there is a time to do our jobs." Kent Schmidt slips on a pair of latex gloves.

Like a search party sifting through a field, a few dozen soldiers form an extended line between the wadi and the adam area. They walk slowly, their eyes scanning the dark ground with each step. Within minutes, hundreds of green, yellow, and red glowsticks—each about the size of a pencil—line the desert. From the sky, it looks like a Christmas tree.

The Blackhawk chopper touches down at the airfield four minutes after leaving Tarnack Farm. Ford, Paquette, and Hollister are rushed into Charlie Med, the headquarters of the U.S. 1980th Forward Surgical Team. Doctors inject Rene with morphine. Lorne is wheeled under the spotlight for immediate surgery. Even with the tourniquet, there is no guarantee that the sergeant will wake up with his leg intact.

Brett Perry and Brian Decaire are ushered into a separate room. Brett is still fuming. His friends are dead, and he's pretty sure Sgt. Ford isn't going to make it either. He tosses a tray of medical instruments against a wall. "Get the fuck away from me!" he yells to an American doctor. "Don't fucking come near me." A nurse eventually sits down beside him, whispering—almost cooing—in his ear. Brett won't remember what she's saying, but he will never forget the soft tone of her voice. As she talks, the nurse wraps a bandage around his bleeding left arm.

Most of 2 Platoon is guarding the perimeter around the adam area, their eyes never far from the scopes of their loaded machine guns. They have not seen the damage downrange. They have only heard the rumors. Lt. Peck, their commander, returns from the wadi.

"Is anybody hurt?" he asks his troops.

"Well, I don't know what's wrong with my leg, but I've got blood all in the inside of my thigh," Cpl. Brennan says.

"What happened?"

"I don't know."

"Well, go get it checked out," Lt. Peck says.

"No, sir, I'm fine," Brennan answers. "I'll just hang out here."

At the impact site, the Pioneers are rummaging through the sand for any signs of unexploded equipment. They have a bad feeling about the Claymores. Sgt. Fords's section took at least two of the remote-controlled mines down the range tonight. If there are detonators lying around, the Pioneers want to find them before somebody accidentally steps on one, triggering another blast. As he searches, Cpl. Bradshaw steps right through the large crater left behind by Harry Schmidt's GBU-12. He is not the first to trample over it tonight; it's already starting to fill back up with sand. Jon is pretty sure that whoever investigates this mess will want to know where the bomb hit. In his butt pack, he finds just enough white tape to mark a square around the hole. Seventeen feet.

With the most serious casualties already back at camp, Sgt. Wilson, the lead medic, steps into the amb to re-examine Norm Link's foot. The metal burned through his skin, but it doesn't seem to have disrupted any circulation. He can still wiggle his toes.

"Is Brennan on that fucking ambulance yet?" someone yells in the direction of the security perimeter.

"No, I'm fine!" Shane shouts back. "I'm staying here."

"Get on that fucking ambulance. You've got to go get checked out!"

Reluctantly, Cpl. Brennan stands up and starts walking toward the logistics trucks parked in the adam area. He can see the glowsticks up ahead. Somebody must have marked a pathway, he figures. A few more steps, and Shane feels a squish under one of his combat boots. Is that a puddle? What the fuck? It hasn't rained here in months.

As he continues to maneuver through the dark, a Bison ambulance drives up behind him. It was dispatched from the airfield not long after the explosion and is heading toward the wadi—headlights blaring. On the ground, Cpl. Brennan sees a finger. A pool of blood. A piece of someone's backbone, ripped and charred and marked with a green glowstick. Shane stops moving, nauseated by what the headlights have uncovered. "Please God," he says, looking up at the sky. "Get me through this."

When he finally does reach the ditch, the medics tell Cpl. Brennan to pull down his pants so they can take a look at his leg. It's red and tender, but no cause for alarm. Before he even gets his pants back on, the Pioneers are drilling him about the Claymores. You went down the range earlier tonight, Shane. Where did you set up the mines? Cpl. Brennan can barely register what anybody's saying. He just walked through a sea of severed body parts. Fuck the Claymores. "Did you guys see what's back there?" he asks.

"There's more over here," one of the Pioneers tells him.

Shane can only shake his head as he looks down into the wadi. All around him, A Company soldiers continue to throw down glowsticks as Hackett, Jasper, and other senior troops try to nail down exactly how many of their men are dead. Even now, an hour after the bombing, the body count is uncertain.

Sgt. Wilson knows he has at least three fatalities. Nathan, Marc, and Ainsworth are in the ditch. But the lead medic can hear people talking about a possible fourth. Some of the guys point him toward an area not far from where the amb was originally parked, where, up until the explosion, he was enjoying his new book. Walking quickly, Sgt. Wilson finds a few paratroopers standing around a small silver blanket. They have covered up whatever it is that Jay Adair tripped over earlier this morning. By now, Pte. Richard Green is the only soldier unaccounted for. This must be him.

Major Shane Schreiber isn't sitting in Call Sign Zero, but he can hear the radio chatter from his command post. He is the man in charge of the Administration Company, the crew that makes sure every Canadian soldier in Afghanistan has food to eat and bullets to fire. He heard the explosion from his cot. He thought it was the forklift driver outside, unloading the latest shipment of mail.

He is listening when Maj. Hackett issues his latest update over the airwaves at 10:35 p.m. Zulu: four Pri 4s, he says. Seventy minutes after they died, four Canadian paratroopers are officially dead. Maj. Schreiber orders one of his subordinates to run down the road and wake up the NIS guys—the National Investigation Service. And get some body bags ready, he says.

Norm Link wraps his arm around Vic Speirs' shoulder as he hobbles out of A Company's ambulance. The plan is to load the rest of the walking wounded onto the newly arrived Bison amb so they can head back to camp for treatment. As Link limps aboard, Stan Clark shows up, complaining of chest pains. He was caught in the heart of the explosion, but like Perry and Decaire, he has been helping to treat casualties ever since. Wilson tells him to climb aboard. Shane Brennan is the last to get on. He sees Norm, pale and bandaged. They both shake their heads. Clark is sitting on the other side, dazed and bleeding from a gash on his chin.

"Stan, are you okay?" Shane asks.

MCpl. Clark stares straight ahead, oblivious to the question. He's seen as much as Cpl. Brennan tonight, probably more. Shane starts to cry.

Captain James MacEachern is the lead NIS man in Kandahar. He's hardly a favorite among the rank and file. NIS guys rarely are. Their main job is to investigate troops accused of breaking the rules. "We have four dead and possibly five injured," Maj. Schreiber tells Capt. MacEachern. "There's a convoy leaving in 10 minutes. I'll get you a seat."

As the captain heads down the road to headquarters, Maj. Schreiber can hear Maj. Dawe over the radio, asking A Company for some ZAP numbers. Every Canadian soldier has a four-digit ZAP, an I.D. code that commanders can pass over the radio instead of broadcasting the names of their dead and wounded. It limits the possibility of any outsiders hearing about the death before the military has a chance to properly notify the families. At exactly 11 p.m. Zulu, Capt. Jasper relays the numbers to Call Sign Zero.

"Pri 1," he says over the radio. "8 4 6 5. 2 2 4 1."

"Pri 2: 3 3 4 1."

"Pri 3: 4 7 5 0. 7 7 6 2. 6 7 2 1. 6 1 6 2. 5 6 1 7."

"Pri 4: 8 8 1 4. 1 4 9 2. 9 2 2 8. 2 2 2 5."

Maj. Schreiber can't help but hope that he doesn't know any of the guys. It's a terrible thought, but it's natural. Nobody wants his friends to die. "Do you want to know who they are?" asks his 2I/C, Captain Chris Allen. He scribbled down the digits as they came over the radio.

"I guess so," he says.

Capt. Allen passes him the list.

"What the fuck was Léger doing on the range?" Maj. Schreiber asks. "He's the storeman."

The Pioneers have found a few grenades. One is missing a pin. Already worried about the Claymores, MCpl. Bibby tells Maj. Hackett that it's probably best if the troops stop traipsing through the desert. The company commander agrees, and calls off the search. With first light just a couple hours away, Hackett's plan is to take the bulk of his troops back to camp, leaving behind the weapons detachment and a few other soldiers to secure the site until the NIS arrives.

Rob Jones doesn't like the idea of any junior troops being exposed to this scene—especially when the sun comes up. He volunteers to stay, and suggests to Maj. Hackett that he find some other senior guys to do the same, guys who have been around, who have seen their share of death. Billy Bolen volunteers. Dave Bibby talks it over with his fellow Pioneers. They'll stay, too. Hulan. Mac. Filis. Arnie Parris. Marco Favasoli. Joe Schechtel. Kyle Caldwell. And the medics, Speirs and Wilson. Maj. Hackett leaves Joe Jasper in charge.

At A Company's camp, the few paratroopers who didn't go to Tarnak Farm tonight are beginning to wander out of their tents. Not everyone heard the explosion, but some did, including Craig Reid, who had dozed off beside his computer. He still hasn't finished those reports.

With a list of names in his hand, Maj. Schreiber leaves his post down the road and walks toward the A Company lines. He knows these paratroopers as well as anybody. When they were in Bosnia two years ago, he was their commander. It's only right that they hear the news from him. "Okay, here's the deal," he says, after gathering the guys inside a tent. "There has been an accident at Tarnak Farms. I don't know what has happened, but there are four guys killed and two or three in the hospital right now." His eyes red with tears, Maj. Schreiber reads the list of casualties. Marc Léger. Ainsworth Dyer. Nathan Smith. Richard Green.

Corporal Yan Bérubé didn't hear the last two names. Ainsworth Dyer? That's his best friend, his roommate back in Edmonton. He just saw his buddy a few hours ago, right before he left for Tarnak. "Have fun on your range," Yan told him, bragging that he didn't have to go. "I'm having some Cheerios and going to bed."

"Fuck you," Dyer said.

Yan storms out of the tent and crouches behind a nearby truck, chewing on his sweater as he cries.

Sgt. Reid can't cry. He is stunned. Sgt. Léger took his spot tonight. *He was supposed to be on the range, not Marc.* Walking away from the tent, Craig falls to his knees, puking as he punches the ground. The guilt—guilt that will never fully go away—is paralyzing.

At Tarnak Farm, A Company begins to board the trucks that will take them back to camp. Out of habit, Lt. Luft conducts a roll call of his platoon. 1 Section. *Here.* 2 Section. *Here.* 3 Section. Alastair stops himself. There is no 3 Section. Except for Corporal Chris Oliver, the troops are either dead or in the medical tent.

The guys left behind watch the trucks drive away. For nearly two hours, everyone has been operating on instinct, on training. But now, all the noise, all the adrenaline, are gone. It's suddenly real. Four men are dead. Outside the amb, Wilson and Speirs are chain-smoking Korea 88s, replaying the chaos and confusion of those first few minutes. *Could we have been faster? Did we save everyone who could be saved?* There are always doubts. Bill feels shitty that he ran right past Sgt. Ford. In the darkness, he just didn't see him. Vic is thinking about Ainsworth, about those deep, gurgling breaths he took in those last few seconds. Neither medic had ever seen anything like that before, but they figure Ains was already dead by then. His body just didn't know it.

Mac has driven the Iltis down to the edge of the wadi, parking it just a few meters from the ambulance. His radio is inside. Capt. Jasper kicks the tire. *Fuckin' Americans.* By now, there's little doubt about what happened.

Some of the guys heard the jet. Some even saw it. They don't know the details yet. Nobody really does. But the Taliban doesn't have any F-16s. That was a U.S. bomb. "How could this happen to us?" Sgt. Favasoli asks Cpl. Filis. "How could this happen to coalition forces?"

Maybe the pilot didn't know we were here and just dropped a bomb to get some practice. Maybe someone called in an air strike nearby, and he just missed. Not everyone is speculating. As if it makes any difference *how* this happened. It happened, and those guys are dead. Exhausted, some of the troops are sprawled in the sand, staring at the moonless sky. Others are sitting alone, their tears hidden by the darkness. Andy Hulan pulls Billy Bolen aside. *Marc is dead*, he says. Billy still didn't know.

A few minutes before midnight, Maj. Pete Dawe, sitting in Call Sign Zero, radios back to the range. Mac answers. "Is 19 around?" Maj. Dawe asks, referring to Maj. Hackett's call sign.

"No," Mac tells him. "He's en route back to camp. But 19A is available." 19A is Capt. Jasper, who has left the Iltis to meet Capt. MacEachern and his fellow NIS investigators.

"Tell him to contact me when he can," Maj. Dawe says.

During their three-hour ferry back to Kuwait, the American pilots hear nothing. News of the bombing has already reached the highest levels in their chain of command, but the men who launched the attack still have no idea who was on the receiving end. During their rendezvous with the tanker—the one they were flying toward when this all began—Maj. Schmidt even asks one of the crew members if he saw the flashes coming from the ground. He didn't. He only saw the bomb explode.

"I don't know what I'll do if that was a friendly fire accident," Maj. Schmidt tells him before continuing on. Amid the uncertainty, he and Bill Umbach barely speak. For long stretches, the only voices they hear are the ones in their stomachs, the ones telling them to brace for the possibility that they just killed some of their own. Maj. Schmidt prays.

"I'd be interested to see if someone is waiting to meet us," Maj. Umbach finally radios to his wingman, just as the Al Jaber runway comes into view.

Colonel David C. Nichols is already on his way there. Earlier this morning, he was jolted from his sleep when the phone rang in his trailer. It was Gen. Wood, the CAOC night director, calling from Saudi Arabia. "There has been an incident involving your aircraft," the general said. "I want you to call me on a secure line." When he phoned back, Gen. Wood filled him in on what little he knew: Coffee Flight attacked coalition forces near Kandahar. Details are still sketchy, the general said, but at least one soldier is dead.

Col. Nichols got dressed, woke a few of his subordinates, and headed down the hall to the operations hub, Al Jaber's own version of central command. The incoming phone calls were furious, some demanding updates, others providing them. In between the constant ringing, the colonel eventually learned that his airmen had bombed a unit of Canadian troops near Kandahar. By the time Col. Nichols heads out to the tarmac, the body count has climbed to four.

He is devastated. In the fighter pilot universe, this is as low as it gets. Friendly fire. Blue on blue. But even amid the shock, Col. Nichols is not entirely surprised. He almost saw this one coming.

As commander of the 332nd Air Expeditionary Group, "Face"—a call sign he earned not for his good looks, but for a skiing accident that left his face scratched and bruised—is in charge of more than 2,000 men and women stationed at Al Jaber, including Springfield's 170th Fighter Squadron. When the 43-year-old first arrived in June 2001, his pilots were patrolling Operation Southern Watch, but a month after the September 11 attacks, his fleet nearly doubled with the launch of Operation Enduring Freedom. Col. Nichols himself was among the many fighter pilots who happily laid waste to Taliban and al-Qaeda targets in Afghanistan. His acting deputy commander, Lieutenant-Colonel Mark Coan, actually directed some of the bombs that demolished Tarnak Farm in the early days of the offensive.

But despite the early success, Col. Nichols was always worried that his pilots were essentially flying blind, climbing into their cockpits without any solid intelligence about the location of friendly ground forces. Among his biggest gripes was the Airspace Control Order (ACO). He openly questioned how such a voluminous document could possibly contain so little valuable information, especially when it's designed to be the CAOC's intelligence roadmap.

Then came Operation Anaconda, the cave-by-cave sweep of the Shahikot Valley in March 2002. From an air perspective, the mission was an absolute disaster, plagued by ad hoc ground control and a near-complete lack of coordination. B-52s were dropping 2,000-pound bombs, unaware that fighter jets were flying directly underneath them. In the meantime, those same fighter jets were being directed to pound the mountain with GBU-12s, in some cases right beside an unsuspecting unit of friendly forces. In one incident, two Canadian snipers watched in horror as a bomb landed just 100 feet away. Somehow, it did not explode.

To Col. Nichols, the problem was obvious: Too many people were calling for bombs, but nobody was de-conflicting the airspace. He believed each mission over the Shahikot Valley should have included a Forward Air Controller (an Air-FAC), who could talk to the troops on the ground and coordinate every strafe. It is standard procedure for Close Air Support (CAS)—the way fighter pilots are supposed to attack enemy targets that are right beside coalition forces. But in this war, the CAOC has the final say. It directs the whole show from hundreds of miles away in Saudi Arabia, via the AWACS radar planes. Col. Nichols has repeatedly complained that such centralized control leaves the fighter units in the field without all the information they need—especially information about the location of friendlies. For the most part, the colonel's complaints have fallen on deaf ears.

Finally, exactly a month before Maj. Schmidt unleashed his bomb on A Company, the CAOC gave Dave Nichols permission to host a close air support symposium, a meeting to give senior officers the chance to come together and try to fix the problems that plagued Anaconda. Slides from the March 17 get-together discussed concerns about the CAOC's "centralized execution," calling it "slow and inefficient." Units are "not getting good intel for planning purposes," one slide reads, suggesting that GLOs—ground liaison officers—be assigned to each fighter wing in theater. "CAS doctrine not being followed," another said. "Causes confusion and fog. No one on same page. Training not aligned with combat. Safety measures not taken, or understood. Hi[gh] possibility for fratricide."

Maj. Schmidt and Maj. John Milton, who had just arrived in theater, were among the pilots from the 170th who watched the symposium from the sidelines. Nobody from the CAOC showed up. A sandstorm in Saudi Arabia forced them to cancel their trip.

★ ★ ★

The morning is still black when the pilots touch down at Al Jaber, oblivious to the flurry of phone calls and e-mails their mission has triggered. As Maj. Schmidt follows Maj. Umbach to his parking spot, both men look outside, scanning the ground for anything out of the ordinary. Nobody there. Maj. Schmidt continues steering, and when he reaches his final stop, about a mile away, he radios back to his flight lead. Again, no sign of anyone bearing bad news.

Momentarily relieved, Maj. Umbach unstraps himself from his seat and flips open the canopy, free to stretch his legs and breathe fresh air for the first time in nearly 10 hours. As he steps onto his ladder, his helmet under his arm, he catches his first glimpse of Col. Nichols. The question that has been dancing through his mind the entire flight home—Did they kill friendlies?—has an answer. Commanders who meet their pilots planeside at 3:30 in the morning are not there to pat them on the back.

"Is it good news or bad news?" Maj. Umbach asks.

"Bad," Col. Nichols says. "Really bad." He tells Bill that the guys on the ground were Canadian, and that they might have been conducting a training exercise.

A training exercise? Maj. Umbach is stunned. In his 20 years as a fighter pilot he has never heard of soldiers practice-firing their weapons in a war zone. As he and Col. Nichols drive to pick up Maj. Schmidt on the other side of the base, he replays the attack over and over in his mind. He is sad, but more confused than anything. "Tell me something different," he thinks to himself. "Tell me it was just a ground battle and we hit the wrong guys. Tell me something else, because that just doesn't make sense. That is not believable."

Maj. Schmidt is already standing beside his jet when the Chevy Tahoe pulls up. Like his flight lead, Maj. Schmidt can taste the bad news. He already looks like he's been crying. When Col. Nichols provides the details—"Canadian Special Forces"—the former Top Gun instructor turns pale, physically sickened by what he's done.

Col. Nichols orders their jets impounded and secures the cockpit videos from both F-16s. He wants to debrief the flight as soon as possible, and he makes sure the two pilots do not leave his sight. No showers. No food. No opportunity for collaboration.

In an Al Jaber boardroom, Col. Nichols and his deputy, Lt.-Col. Coan, jot down some notes as they stare at the targeting pod tapes, which captured every word and every deep breath. *Permission to lay down some 20 mike-mike. Standby. Do you want us to push a different freq? Hold fire. Men on road. Piece of artillery. Rolling in in self-defense. Shack.*

Sitting with both pilots, Col. Nichols watches the videos three times before reaching a conclusion. This is a catastrophic mistake, a horrendous error made in the fog of war. But he is convinced it is not a crime. When the colonel emerges from the closed-door debrief, another telephone call is waiting for him. On the other end is his direct boss, Major-General Walter Buchanan, the commander of Joint Task Force Southwest Asia (JTF-SWA). He wants a statement from the pilots so the Air Force can issue a news release. The press—especially in Canada—is already drooling over this one.

By now, Captain Erin Wirtanen is also awake, jostled from her sleep by a phone call from Lt.-Col. Coan. He tells her to get dressed. You may have to take some statements. The base staff Judge Advocate, Capt. Wirtanen figures it must be something serious, maybe a rape. She stops by her office to grab a copy of the *Uniform Code of Military Justice*, then heads over to the ops center. She quickly learns that this is much more than a rape case. Two fighter pilots just killed four infantrymen.

Col. Nichols tells his JAG that Gen. Buchanan has already called, demanding a statement from both pilots. Capt. Wirtanen tells her boss that before he does anything else, he should read the men their rights. Tell them, she says, that they are suspected of violating Article 92—dereliction of duty. Maj. Schmidt, however, tells his commander that if this is being treated as a criminal matter, he's not going to say another word without a lawyer sitting beside him. Col. Nichols eventually offers a concession, then leads the pilots back into the briefing room.

"I am investigating the alleged *incident* of 17 April of which you are involved," Col. Nichols says, replacing the word "offense" with "incident." "I advise you that under the Provisions of Article 31 of the *Uniform Code of Military Justice* you have the right to remain silent. That is say nothing at all. Any statement you make, oral or written, may be used as evidence against you in the trial or by courts-martial or in other judicial or administrative proceedings."

The military will provide a lawyer free of charge, Col. Nichols tells them, and you can request that lawyer at any time during this interview. "Are you willing to answer questions?" he asks, a tape recording whirling on the table.

"Yes, I am," they reply, one after the other.

"Okay. Now, the first question is: 'What resulted in you feeling as though you were being threatened?' I guess the flight lead should start."

"We observed fire from the surface right near, right next to where we were flying," Maj. Umbach says. "It appeared to be coming directly at us. We maneuvered the jets. We asked BOSSMAN if he knew anything about what was going on down there and reported it. As we maneuvered the jets around, the shooting appeared to follow us. We split in two directions and it appeared to follow us, leading where we were flying. At that point, Number Two was initially going to find the location and then when they started what appeared to be tracking him, called 'defending'[2] and retaliated with a weapons release."

"Okay," Col. Nichols says, turning toward Maj. Schmidt. "Psycho?"

"From my perspective, I was flying in a loose-wedge formation," he says, estimating their altitude to be about 21,000 feet. "We've taken off our NVGs because we've been at the end of a three-hour vul [mission] in the AO and we've got our lights on. So, in the position that I could still fly and see, I'm on the inside of the formation, and, uh, my flight lead starts talking about something that looks like fireworks on the ground down underneath. At that time, I start to maneuver the jet. I execute a hard right turn away from the site, and not feeling comfortable because I see the rate of fire and the length it's going. I don't feel that I can get out of the effective range of it."

Instead, Maj. Schmidt says, his plan was to keep an eye on the fire and do his best to maneuver against it. "At that time I see that the site appears to be pointing in the lead, in the direction of my lead, since I have split from him now, in the direction that he is going in. And it looks like it's got lead pulled [tracking Maj. Umbach] and it's shooting right at him. I believe at that time I made a statement 'it's shooting at you' and I call in for a mark."

Maj. Schmidt says he then tried to mark the target with his infrared laser so he could pass the coordinates to the AWACS. "And as I spin back around, it looks like something shoots up at me so I maneuver away from it again, and as I continue back around on a right-hand turn, I see that it looks like it is still leading my Number One. At that time, we called and asked if there was any friendlies in the vicinity. We don't get a response back from BOSSMAN and now it looks like this system is tracking my Number One. So, I call in for a—that I'm in for self-defense."

"So, it all happened pretty quick?" Col. Nichols asks.

"Probably a matter of 45 seconds to a minute, would be my guess of the whole thing transpiring," Maj. Schmidt answers. "It happened right underneath us. We maneuver, I don't know, with time compression I can't estimate, it's on the tape. But, my release was mostly in regards to the continual firing in the direction of my Number One. Looked like MLRS system or BM-21 shooting. You know, who knows what kind of weapon it was at the time."

"So ... absolutely," Col. Nichols interjects. "I mean, you felt he was threatened and if you weren't going to do something he was going to get schwacked out of the sky."

"Because of the angle that I was looking at the system, I could see the launch angle and it looked, uh, the rounds were obviously propelled and burning out, in my estimation, around 10,000 feet," Maj. Schmidt continues. "And from the time I could see the round going up and seeing it burn out at about 10,000 feet, it appeared to me that it was going in front of my Number One."

"That's it," Col. Nichols says. "The problem we have is: Why don't we, as an organization, know where those friendlies are? If in fact it was a friendly unit, the problem that we have is why didn't we know that friendly unit was there and why didn't we know that friendly unit was gonna be practice-firing into the sky?"

"Were they practice-firing?" Maj. Umbach asks. "Is that what they were doing? They were not—"

"I don't know," Col. Nichols says. "I don't know what it is. That will have to be decided."

"I tried to visually search the area to see if it was a two-way battle," Maj. Umbach says. "And I tried in my mind to find any reason or any possibility that it could be friendlies. The location from the airport seemed to be where in the past they've called the enemy fire has been. I didn't see anybody retaliating on the ground. It did not appear as a ground battle. It appeared as a site—"

"Shooting?" someone in the room asks.

"Shooting at me and my wingman," he says.

"Concur," Maj. Schmidt says. "The other issue is that over the last week and a half we've been briefed that in that vicinity of Kandahar there's the highest concentration of Taliban, at least an estimation that we've been briefed of over 2,000 Taliban in that vicinity. And in our briefing this evening for intel we were also briefed that that vicinity has got a heightened state of alert, if you will, against the coalition of what is going on there due to the government that's in place and what they are trying to impose against the poppy industry. And that they are aligning with Taliban forces and expect them to be gathering weapons. And that's right off of our slides from tonight."

"So you never egressed there and came back?" Col. Nichols asks. Both men say no.

"I estimated I couldn't get away so I turned back in again to more effectively maneuver against them," Maj. Schmidt says. "I felt like I had a better chance with a tally on the system than by running tail on."

Maj. Umbach says he spent most of the time looking outside the cockpit, not staring at the tiny video screen between his legs. "When I did look in," he says, "I tried to get my pod into that area and I think what I saw was a vehicle along a road. And I could not imagine our friendly forces pulling up a vehicle three, four miles off—not directly off the end of the runway, but in the general direction of off a runway and shooting at anything but us. It just—everything made sense to me: This is somebody shooting at us. It is on the road. They are ready to run. It was just another indication that I had that set in my mind that this is, this is bad."

"There were folks standing around and I do not envision that our forces would be standing around if there was a fire fight going on," Maj. Schmidt adds. "And again, not being informed that there is a live-fire happening and here's people standing around, which is typical to what I have seen in other tapes of Taliban/al-Qaeda ops of hostiles standing around equipment and firing at it, or firing at Americans. So, when I saw that there were people in the open vice[3] bunkered or hunkered down, which is what I would anticipate for a fire fight if that's what was going on, then I would have certainly probably came off at that point and held the weapon. But again, there is no correlation to a ground fight. There's no awareness that there's a friendly force there conducting a live-fire operation into the sky. It all looks like a surface-to-air engagement from my cockpit."

Out of questions, Col. Nichols passes the floor to Capt. Wirtanen, the JAG. "What type of munitions did you think were being shot at you?" she asks. "Could you tell?"

"Well there's, uh, some sort of rocket system that could shoot into the air," Maj. Schmidt answers. "BM-21 is my best guess of what was going on. I believe the quote I said on the radio, 'it looked like some sort of MLRS,' which unfortunately, I believe I was spot on. It looked like some sort of—you can't tell at that point of the colors and what's going on. All you know is something's coming out of that thing really fast and it's going at your airplane first, then at my flight lead's airplane."

"How quick were the repetitions between the shots that you observed?"

"I probably saw a total of at least 20 ... 20 shots," Maj. Schmidt says.

"At the very least, if not more than that," Maj. Umbach adds. "Many times there'd be one coming in, another coming before the other one is burned out."

"And I probably see three, four, five in a salvo," Harry says.

"Continuous," Bill says.

"Just come out," Harry continues. "Almost adjust fire, and shoot again and I would say there was probably 15 seconds, 10 or 15 seconds between salvos."

"So three or four salvos is what you saw?" asks Col. Nichols, jumping back into the conversation.

"Well," Maj. Schmidt answers, "the initial—I did not see the initial two that my flight lead talked about. By the time I turned away and turn back, I'm seeing them coming underneath. And then I see, I probably see at least three full salvos."

"And you say you saw them burn out at around 10,000 feet?" Capt. Wirtanen asks.

"Yes."

"How high were you flying?"

"We were initially at about 22, and then when we started maneuvering, things started going downhill from there," Maj. Schmidt says. "So, I would guess, I would guess I'm at 15 to 18,000 feet."

"The motor burns out," says Col. Nichols, helping to clarify the answer for his JAG. "But the projectile is still climbing."

"Okay," she says.

"And the 10,000 feet would be an estimate as well," Maj. Umbach adds.

"It was not—it did not appear to be a low fire, in my opinion," Maj. Schmidt says.

After a long pause, Col. Nichols offers another observation: When he flew missions over Bosnia, ground forces trained at a range called Glamoc. Every fighter pilot knew it was there, and nobody was allowed to fly anywhere near it. "Glamoc Range had walls on it that you could not penetrate," he says. "You were not there. And obviously that wasn't true here. And the other thing is that we recently had communications that BM-21s in the other theater are firing at us."

Someone in the room switches off the tape recorder so everyone can watch the cockpit videos yet again. When the interview reconvenes—the length of the break is unclear—Col. Nichols asks his pilots if they've ever had trouble finding reliable intelligence about the locations of friendly ground troops in Afghanistan. "How hard and how long have you as the engaged squadron, or us as a group, been looking for this information, and is it available or not?" the colonel asks. "Ground order of battle, basically."

"It is not," Maj. Umbach answers. "I had no idea that there were friendlies there. BOSSMAN, if he had any idea, sure did not communicate that to us."

"Have we been asking?" Col. Nichols asks.

"We've been asking for this," Maj. Umbach responds.

"There was a failure tonight based on us not knowing where the friendlies were, executing a live-fire in a hostile zone and doing it in the vicinity of friendly airplanes," Maj. Schmidt says. "And I've got the inherent—actually, it's not a right, it is a responsibility—the inherent responsibility of self-defense of myself, my platform, and my flight lead."

"Absolutely," his commander says.

Harry Schmidt and Bill Umbach leave it at that. They are free to go, and for a second time, someone shuts down the tape recorder. When it's turned back on—again, the length of the lapse is unclear—Col. Nichols makes a statement of his own. He begins by applauding the pilots for making "a very good defensive maneuver."

"[They] split their airplanes apart and the wingman was convinced that the surface fire was engaging his lead," he says. "Made the quick decision and engaged the system that was shooting his flight lead, in error. The problem I see with this is we have friendly aircraft in a war zone that is unknown as to where the bad guys are and where the good guys are. There is a piece of that that could be known. We could know where the good guys are. Our guys in the airplane, our guys providing command and control for the guys in our airplanes, should have absolute confirmation where friendlies are at all times. We have been doing this mission since the 16th of October. And that has been a stated, ongoing problem from the beginning, not knowing where the friendly locations are."

His deputy commander, Lt.-Col. Coan, also reads a statement for the record, calling the bombing an "unfortunate incident."

"It reminds me of what happens a lot of times during a safety mishap board, where there is usually about four or five instances that all come together that end up equaling into some type of mishap," he says. "And I think we are going to find out in this incident that there are several factors that led to the unfortunate accident."

Outside, Maj. Schmidt and Maj. Umbach knock on the trailer door of their wing commander, Col. Bob Murphy. He is still asleep, preparing his body for another long mission scheduled for later today. The colonel listens as his men, white as ghosts, tell him what just happened. He is devastated, not only for them, but for his unit. Even now, this early in the process, he knows that the 183rd Fighter Wing will never fully recover from this one.

Col. Murphy tells both pilots to go to the medical clinic for blood tests. After filling the vials, a flight surgeon recommends that Harry and Bill try their best to get some sleep. He even offers them a No-go pill.

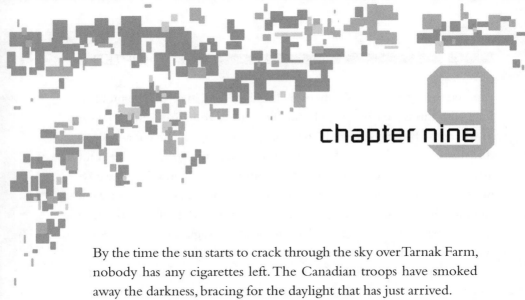

By the time the sun starts to crack through the sky over Tarnak Farm, nobody has any cigarettes left. The Canadian troops have smoked away the darkness, bracing for the daylight that has just arrived.

They are not alone. Throughout the morning, teams of American investigators joined them on the range. An EOD unit—explosives ordnance disposal—is picking up where the Pioneers left off, scanning the sand for mines and grenades. A DMART—disaster mortuary affairs response team—is also on-site. They are the forensic specialists. That they're even here is a "lucky" break. The team just happened to be in Kandahar, cleaning up after another explosion three days ago. Four American soldiers were killed while trying to blow up a cache of Taliban rockets.

The dung beetles have also arrived. Dozens of them, each one crawling toward the sprinkled remains. Canadian soldiers squish as many of the black bugs as they can, but it's impossible to get them all.

Some of the beetles are already crawling away with tiny balls of flesh. The Army has tried to prepare its troops for a day like this. There was a time when training fields would be sprayed with pieces of dead, bloodied animals, giving soldiers a small taste of the gore they may encounter on the battlefield. It seems almost laughable now, considering what the sun has uncovered this morning. Mags. A canteen. Burnt skin. Shattered pieces of machine guns. Webbing. Marc Léger's notepad.

Most of it is marked by the sea of glowsticks, but the troops who swept the desert last night didn't find everything. In the daylight, Billy Bolen stumbles upon the buckle of an A7-A strap, the kind used to tie down cargo. It's the same one Greener asked him for the other day. The young private told Billy he was losing a lot of weight, and needed something to hold up his pants.

Pete Filis finds a foot. No boot. Just a foot. As he climbs out of the ambulance, Dave Bibby nearly steps on a piece of someone's jaw.

In the wadi, an investigator snaps photos. Another is videotaping. The Canadian troops aren't allowed to go in just yet, but peering down from the edge, they can see the evidence of last night's chaos. Med bags. Tattered uniforms. Red-stained bomb parts. Footprints. Three gray blankets. Sgt. Wilson stares at the covers, hoping to see the rise and fall of a chest. He knows he won't, but he can't stop looking. He and his fellow medic, Vic Speirs, are both amazed at just how close the casualties are to one another. In the darkness, they seemed so far away.

As the lead investigator on scene, Capt. MacEachern walks through the glowsticks, taking notes and recording interviews. He has already spoken to Joe Jasper and Billy Bolen. Shortly after sunrise, he stops by one of the Coyotes, where Corporal Neil Miller is among the extra troops guarding the perimeter. When the bomb hit, Neil was back at camp, parked beside that waiting Herc on the runway. He tells Capt. MacEachern about the repeated "check fire" order he heard over the radio moments before the thud, the order that went unanswered by anyone at Tarnak Farm.

Nearby, Cpl. Filis and Cpl. Caldwell are guarding the north end of the ditch. The sun has barely risen, but it's already sweltering in Afghanistan. "Shoot any fucking dog you see coming this way," W/O Hulan tells them.

"No problem," Filis says.

★ ★ ★

For the dozens of A Company soldiers who didn't stay behind at Tarnak Farm, it is a quiet truck ride back to camp. Many are staring at the walls, their eyes swollen with tears and disbelief. Nearly everyone is smoking. Even troops who have never taken a puff in their lives have cigarettes dangling from their lips. At the Company lines, Maj. Schreiber and a small team of peer counselors are waiting for the convoy. The guys on board already know exactly what happened. They were right there when the bomb hit. But nobody knows for certain who died. Up until now, they've only heard the rumors.

Like he did earlier this morning, Maj. Schreiber gathers the rest of his former company around the long, narrow tables inside the TV Tent. For a second time, he lists off the casualties: Marc Léger. Ainsworth Dyer. Nathan Smith. Richard Green. Shane would gladly burn shit for the rest of the tour than have to do that again. It's as if he killed those guys himself.

Horrified, some of the troops ask about the wounded. With what little details he has, Maj. Schreiber does his best to update their condition. Maybe a few of you can go down and visit them, he says.

"Is there anything else?" Maj. Schreiber asks.

"What's going to fucking happen to the pilot?" someone asks.

"Look," Maj. Schreiber says, answering the question as best he can. "There is going to be an investigation. I don't know what's going to come of it, but for right now, I know we got to look after these guys, and that's the important thing. And you have to look after yourselves. Even though you may not think that this has significantly affected you psychologically, it has or it can. So I need you to go outside and talk to somebody about this. I'm not going to tell you when to do it, but there are the guys. Find somebody you trust and just do it."

Maj. Hackett and Lt. Luft have made their way to Charlie Med. Perry and Decaire are still here. Hollister is flattened by a concussion, but he's conscious and talking. Paquette is out cold, a morphine drip hooked up to his arm, an oxygen mask over his mouth. Sgt. Ford is still on the operating table, unconscious as surgeons poke away at his mangled thigh. Lt. Luft looks at the sergeant's swollen right eye and the tiny bits of shrapnel still scattered across his body. Who ever thought Lorne Ford could look so helpless?

Private Michael Frank—"Knuckles"—woke up early this morning. It was still dark. By sunrise, he sees some of the Coyotes driving back from the range, the sour looks on everyone's faces. "What's going on?" he asks, almost laughing. "Okay, who rolled the jeep?"

Pte. Frank is attached to Bravo Company, but most of his good friends are paratroopers. He first met Nathan Smith three years ago, when they were both living in "the shacks" at the Edmonton garrison. Michael came home from a bar one night and found the new guy—shoes off—passed out on the floor in front of his door. Knuckles tried to help him up, but

Nathan ran down the hall, thinking Michael was the military police. The next morning, he knocked on Nathan's door. "Are these yours?" he asked, holding Smitty's shoes.

A few months later, when both men moved down to the city's trendy Whyte Avenue neighborhood, Pte. Frank started hitching a ride to work in Nathan's dirty-red Mazda pickup truck. They'd grab Tim Hortons—two large double-doubles—and shoot the shit as they headed north toward the base. Michael learned a lot about Nathan during those half-hour rides. Like the fact he carries "an emergency twenty" deep in the bottom of his wallet, folded into a tiny square. You never know when you might need $20, he would always say.

One night, a few minutes after Nathan dropped Michael off at home, Smitty called and asked him to walk over to a nearby parking lot. His truck had broken down. Knuckles tried to hammer away at the starter with a wrench, but it just wouldn't go. Nathan had no choice but to call for a tow truck. "You got 35 cents for the phone?" he asked Michael.

"What about the emergency twenty?"

"Whoa, whoa," Nathan answered, almost offended. "This really isn't an emergency now, is it?"

A few weeks later, the two men were at the West Edmonton Mall, firing pistols at the shooting range. Nathan used the emergency twenty to buy an extra round of bullets.

It is ironic that Nathan even carries emergency cash, considering he's never been the type to worry about money. In the two years he's driven Mike to work, he's never once let him pay for gas. Pte. Frank got so frustrated by his refusals that he once snuck into Smitty's locker and stuffed $20 into the pocket of his combat jacket. Nathan was so happy—thinking that he'd put the cash in his jacket but somehow forgotten about it—that he treated Michael to lunch.

Before shipping off to Afghanistan, Nathan and Michael made a pact: If something happens to one of us, the other will bring him home. Pte. Frank's commander tells him to start packing his things. He's going back to Canada.

★ ★ ★

Captain André Gauthier is dispatched to Tarnak Farm just before 8:30 a.m. local time. A U.S. medical examiner has just officially pronounced all four soldiers dead. Capt. Gauthier, a chaplain attached to the Canadian Battle Group, will perform the last rites. By now, the sun is searing, leaving an undeniable odor in the desert air. Dung beetles continue to surface, way too many to kill.

Most of the troops follow Padre Gauthier down into the wadi, taking a knee beside each body as he administers his blessing. Many medical professionals have never seen such damage to a human body. The chaplain definitely hasn't, and neither has any of the men hovering around him. Tears in his eyes, Capt. Gauthier places his bare hand on each man's skin, leaving it there for minutes at a time as he slowly recites his prayer. He looks right at each soldier. Ains. Marc. Nathan. Ricky.

Billy Bolen is crying. Nobody has ever seen Billy cry. You wouldn't even think he knew how.

★ ★ ★

Lloyd Smith has spent his adult life working on oil tankers, most of it as a captain. On April 17, his ship returned to the Halifax harbor after yet another 30 days on the water. A month on; a month off. That's his life.

Lloyd visited his daughter today, had dinner at his sister's place. His wife, Charlotte, is going to spend the night there while he goes back to the boat. His relief is coming first thing in the morning. At Lloyd and Charlotte's home in rural Tatamagouche, RCMP officers are ringing the doorbell. They've come and gone four or five times now, bearing news they'd rather not break. The officers have no way of knowing that the Smiths are in Halifax.

Lloyd is fast asleep when the phone rings in his quarters. It's Karen, his daughter. "Jodi called," she says, crying. "She said Nathan was killed."

Shock is a meaningless word. Killed? Lloyd just saw his son in December, when Nathan and Jodi flew east for the holidays. They all ate lobster and shrimp and laughed and told stories about the kids' younger days, before they were in love and engaged to be married. Lots of good stories. Like the time 10-year-old Nathan helped his cousins burn some garbage in his uncle's backyard. His aunt asked him to throw a few large bags on the fire. Nathan stuck his head right in the barrel, watching them burn. He didn't even see the explosion. Lloyd ran out and stuffed his son's face in the pool, holding his head in the water to stifle the pain. He watched his son do a lot of crazy things over the years. The band. The jobs. Selling children's raincoats door to door. Two cracks at university. Taking a homeless guy for lunch.

After Christmas, Lloyd and Charlotte drove Nathan to the airport, waving as he and Jodi disappeared through the security gate. They knew he was going to Afghanistan, that they wouldn't see him again for a long time. But not this. Lloyd leaves the harbor and drives to his sister's house. He has to wake up his wife and tell her that their only son is dead.

Halfway across the country, in the Ottawa suburb of Stittsville, Ontario, the phone rings at Richard and Claire Léger's house. Richard answers. It's Marley, his son's wife, calling from Edmonton. A few minutes ago, a general and a padre knocked on her door. Marc is dead.

Richard punches a kitchen cupboard. Claire starts washing dishes. Anything to occupy her hands. Nothing is registering. Bombed by an American plane? Marc told his parents he was the beans and bullets guy. He burned shit most of the day. Why the hell would a U.S. jet target the Canadian supply tent?

Richard and Claire raised Marc, along with his younger brother and sister, in the small town of Lancaster, Ontario. They spent the summers playing baseball in the backyard and boating on the St. Lawrence River. When Marc was 16, his parents watched him work three jobs to buy a beat-up brown Toyota. He didn't even have his license yet. A couple years later, when the heater broke, Marc made sure a friend was always in the front seat so he could lean out the window and scrape the frost off the windshield as he drove.

Everything wasn't always peachy. Marc got in a few fights. The cops came by the house a couple times. But he was a good kid, a genuine personality. Two years ago, he married Marley, his girlfriend of nine years. The love of his life. The day before he left for Afghanistan, Marc went to an Edmonton flower shop and placed a special order: He wanted a bouquet delivered to his wife every month while he was gone. He wrote a separate card for each delivery.

★　★　★

The inevitable phone calls from the media have begun. Reporters back in Canada started to hear whispers about the incident late on the evening of April 17. The first story hit the wire just after 11 p.m. EST. An hour later, General Ray Henault, Canada's soft-spoken Chief of the Defence Staff, addresses a pack of reporters gathered at National Defence Headquarters in Ottawa. The four fallen Patricias are still lying in the sand at Tarnak Farm.

"Ladies and gentlemen, mesdames et messieurs, bonsoir," the general says. "I stand before you tonight with an announcement that certainly any chief of Defence Staff would hope to never have to make. I'm saddened, quite frankly beyond words, to inform you that several of our troops from the PPCLI Battle Group deployed to Afghanistan, as you are well aware, were involved in a tragic friendly fire accident earlier this evening.

"I regret to inform—and I know that it has been on the airwaves for the last little bit now—to inform you that four Canadian soldiers were killed and eight injured, some very seriously, when an American F-16 fighter jet released one, possibly two—we are not sure at this time—500-pound bombs on troops of the Battle Group involved in a night firing exercise on a range 14 to 15 kilometers south of the Kandahar Airfield in Afghanistan. This occurred at roughly 5:25 p.m., our time, that is Ottawa time, which of course was the middle of the night in Afghanistan.

"Now please remember that because of the nature of this incident and certainly the confusion that surrounds an incident of this case, we are just now starting to get more and more and much clearer information about exactly what happened. This is obviously, and I know you will agree, a horrible and again a tragic accident, and while I understand and acknowledge your desire for more information, it is simply too early to speculate on many of the details of this incident at this time.

"Our primary concerns, quite frankly at this point in time, are with the families of those that were killed, with the proper care and proper treatment of those who are injured and trying now to recover, with the battle group itself who had gone through a traumatic experience of its own and certainly with the proper return of our fallen comrades. The wishes of the affected families, especially those families who have now suffered a tragic loss, will be respected and we would ask you to help us honor their grief.

"Now, in addition, American and Canadian authorities will launch an investigation into this incident to obviously determine the causes and also to prevent as much as it possibly can be done, any reoccurrence of this kind. Details of this process are now being worked out as much by our staff here in Ottawa as the staff in Tampa and in the U.S. at the Pentagon. We will release those details as soon as we have them, but I don't think we will have them, in fact I know that, until tomorrow morning.

"The nature of the professions of arms is, such as it is, one in which there are inherent dangers. Those dangers are magnified by missions of this kind. This, I have to tell you, is inherent in military service. We remain committed to our duty to this campaign and will certainly continue."

"Can you give us an idea, an inkling, of how something like this could have happened in your estimation?" a journalist asks him.

"The Battle Group was conducting a regular live-fire training exercise, a nighttime live-fire training exercise in an area that is recognized as a training area," answers the general, himself a former fighter pilot. "The aircraft that are overflying and assisting operations in Afghanistan are operating on well-recognized and very well-controlled routes and under very strict control. How this sort of thing can happen is a mystery to us. That is what the investigation will determine. I can't speculate on it at this point in time. All I can say to you is that without a doubt, there was a misidentification of the Canadians and what they were doing on the ground and that was obviously the cause of this accident."

"Was this aircraft assigned to this night exercise?" another reporter asks.

"I don't know the details of all of the events surrounding this incident, but my understanding is that this aircraft was in no way supporting or involved in that particular exercise, in that training exercise on the ground in Kandahar."

"General, back on this question of misidentification, can you explain, did the American plane apparently think that these were enemy forces, enemy troops?"

"Please remember, though, that this exercise was taking place in the middle of the night," the general says, "so there is no way to visually identify from the altitudes that fighters operate. If the American fighter had acknowledged and identified these troops as Canadians or other coalition troops, I can assure you that he would not have dropped his bomb into their location. So it can only be a misidentification that caused this to occur. What the details were surrounding it and how this occurred will need to be the object of an investigation and it will be a very detailed and comprehensive one, I can assure you."

"A final question on the rules of engagement," another reporter asks. "Are aircraft operating in Afghanistan able to attack targets of opportunity without first receiving some kind of approval from ground control?"

"Aircraft are very closely controlled and therefore we can only assume that there was some measure of control in this operation. We don't know the details of that just yet and that obviously is what will form the object of our investigation."

"But normally a pilot would ask for permission to attack and get permission from the ground before attacking?"

"You are correct."

"General, was there any—was there any indication of hostile activity in the area that you are aware of, that might have caused confusion?" another journalist asks.

"There is no hostile activity in the area that I'm aware of," Gen. Henault says. "But again, the details are something that need to be determined. Those kinds of details, we have not been made privy to, but certainly my understanding is that there was no hostile activity in the area that would have created this incident. Thank you very much. Merci beaucoup et à demain."

★ ★ ★

Jocelyn Van Sloten caught a snippet of the news conference on TV. She immediately called Nadine, Yan Bérubé's girlfriend. The two have grown close since their men shipped off to Afghanistan. In fact, Jocelyn had just left Nadine's house when she caught the news. Friendly fire. Four Canadian soldiers dead.

Jocelyn drove back across town. She and Nadine tried to reassure one another, looking at some photos that Yan sent home from Kandahar the other day. Hours passed. It can't possibly be the guys. Somebody would have knocked on the door by now. It is after 2 a.m. by the time Jocelyn heads back to her Edmonton apartment. She's exhausted, but terrified, thinking of that brief phone conversation she had with Ains just a few hours ago. He called her right before getting on the truck for Tarnak Farm. He sounded down, almost like a totally different person. Jocelyn tried to make him laugh, but it didn't work. "I really miss you," he said. "I'm ready to come home."

Jocelyn met Ains five years ago at The Greenhouse, an Army bar in town. A girl wouldn't leave him alone, so he turned to the blond stranger nearby. "Do you want to dance?" he asked Jocelyn.

"No," she answered.

"Why not?"

"I don't know how."

"Too bad."

Ainsworth grabbed her hand anyway, pulling her onto the dance floor. They laughed the rest of the night. When the lights came on, Ains gave her his phone number. They talked a lot, but for the first little while, they were just friends. You can't not be Ainsworth's friend, after all. He is hilarious, with that booming Bullwinkle laugh to match. But he's also intelligent and independent, a graduate of the so-called school of life. When he was only 15 and living with his dad in Toronto's tough Regent Park neighborhood, he used to work illegally in the construction business, helping to pay the bills. Ten years later, he was still helping support his dad, sending him a chunk of his paycheck every month. He has a large tattoo of Jesus on his back.

Jocelyn and Ainsworth were good buddies for more than a year before she finally gathered the guts to tell him how she really felt. They had just watched a movie at Ains' place on base. Jocelyn babbled on forever, frightened by what he would say if she ever stopped talking. He wanted to be with her, too.

Ains met Jocelyn's parents—and her seven brothers and sisters—not long after. He was a nervous wreck, the only black man in the living room. Even if you try not to notice, you just can't. Before walking in the front door, Ains actually told Jocelyn that he was going to throw up. "Too late," she laughed. But Ains fit right in, so much so that he started dropping by Aart and Janna's house even when Jocelyn wasn't around. One day, he came by with a ring. *Keep it a secret, though,* he said. *Jocelyn doesn't know yet.* Her mother joked that she was going to have chocolate grandchildren.

On October 21, 2001, Ains and Jocelyn went to their favorite restaurant, The Silver Palace, for dinner. They'd eaten there so often that the staff didn't even take their order anymore. Szechwan beef. Wonton soup. Egg rolls. Chicken chow mein. "I can't wait to tell my mom that you're buying me this big ring," Jocelyn told him. She was just teasing, of course. The two of them had gone ring shopping the other day, but Ains, typical Ains, told her he couldn't afford it just yet. Maybe next year.

When they finished eating, Ains looked ill. "Why don't we go to the park?" he asked her. They always went for late-night walks in Rundle Park, where they would talk and people-watch and sip hot chocolate from Tim Hortons. As they walked along the big wooden footbridge that connects Rundle Park and Gold Bar Park, Ains knelt down. "You're the woman of my dreams," he told Jocelyn, pulling the ring from his pocket—the same one Jocelyn stared at in the jewelry store. She started to cry.

Before Ains shipped off to Afghanistan, they talked about who to invite, where the wedding should be. They even picked a color: blue. And a date: September 27, 2003. Two days ago, Jocelyn found the perfect dress.

She is lying in bed when the buzzer rings in her apartment. It's her mom and dad. The officers went to their house first, thinking Jocelyn still lived there. *Ains must be hurt,* Jocelyn thinks to herself. *He can't be dead. He's too strong. He's Superman.*

"Is he injured?" she asks the officers.

"Ainsworth is dead," one of them answers.

★ ★ ★

Miranda Boutilier didn't see Gen. Henault's press conference. She was cleaning the apartment. She loves her Edmonton apartment. It's not big, but it's theirs. Hers and Ricky's.

Oddly enough, Richard Green's life actually began in this city. He was born here in 1980, the only child of David Green and Doreen Young. It was a short stay, though. His parents, originally from Nova Scotia, moved back home three months later. The next few years were hardly a fairy tale.

David and Doreen never married. By the time Ricky was three, his dad had moved out of their trailer for good. Other men came and went, none for the long haul.

As he grew up, Pte. Green saw his father here and there. Not as much as he would have liked, but he still loved his dad. He loved his mom, too, living with her until he joined the Army at age 18. But if anything, Ricky was an independent kid, learning at a very young age how to look after himself. In those early years, he also spent many days and nights with his grandmother—his father's mother—Joyce Clooney. Nan spoiled him when few others did. She would never tell her other grandchildren, but he was always her favorite.

When he was 15, Richard Green met Michael "Herbie" McDonald, a retired naval officer who lived in town. He was a father figure and a friend. By high school graduation, Herbie's tales of life in the service had inspired the red-haired teenager to enlist. Ricky's grandma threw him a small party right before he shipped off for basic training.

It was during one of those early visits back to Hubbards that Miranda Boutilier, then 16, really started to notice her best friend's older cousin. They were at the local bowling alley, where Ricky was impressing pals with tales of shooting machine guns and jumping out of airplanes. He was 5-foot-9 and skinny, but toned and strong. Miranda watched him speak. He was checking her out, too.

In June 2001, the summer before Miranda started Grade 12, she moved to Edmonton to be with Ricky. They were young, just starting out. Just the two of them. Her plan was to finish high school in Edmonton, then apply to the University of Alberta. The Kandahar mission fell right in the middle of all that. If anything, Miranda was upset because Ricky was probably going to miss her senior prom. "Don't worry," he told her. "When I get back we'll rent a limo and go out on the town. It will be a special night that you won't forget." He didn't have the ring yet, but he was already planning his proposal.

Tonight, a friend calls and interrupts Miranda's cleaning. Did you hear the news? When she arrives at the base, a horde of reporters is already there. One sticks a mic in Miranda's face. She pushes it aside and continues toward the main doors, where other wives and fiancées and relatives are begging for updates. Nobody from the Army has any answers for them. Not yet.

Ricky's aunt, who also lives in Edmonton, drives Miranda back home. It is well past midnight. She grabs her teddy bear and Ricky's blanket and curls up on the couch. When the buzzer rings, she sprints down the hallway, screaming in disbelief.

★ ★ ★

Arnie Parris knows how much Ainsworth Dyer loves to sleep. They jog together all the time, and every time they do, Arnie has to drag Ains out of bed. Looking at him now, sprawled in the sand at Tarnak Farm, Sgt. Parris can't help but think that maybe he's faking it, trying to squeeze in a few more minutes of sleep.

"Come on Dyer, you bullshitter," he says quietly, gazing at his friend. "Get the fuck up. You're lazy."

About the only two black guys in the entire battalion, Arnie and Ains are tight. They talked a lot, about religion, about Dyer's dad, about Jocelyn. Arnie calls him "Ghetto Millionaire" because Ains was so good with his money. Sgt. Parris cannot stomach the thought of putting him in a body bag. He tells Marco Favasoli, a fellow sergeant, that he's going back up to the jeep. He doesn't want to remember Ainsworth this way.

Marc Léger has a trace of a smile on his face, hiding any clue that he saw what was coming. Except for the shrapnel that pierced his stomach and the tiny gash over his left eyebrow, Marc's massive frame withstood the force of the blast. Staring down at his friend, Billy Bolen is overcome with doubt. He can't forgive himself for not seeing Marc right away last night. What if we got to him sooner? Did he suffer? Months will pass before an Army doctor tells Billy what he needs to hear: Marc died instantly. There is nothing you could have done.

Jon Bradshaw crouches beside Nathan, but he does his best not to look. Put your head down. Watch what your hands are doing. Don't take in the big picture. Of the three dead Canadians lying in the wadi, Nathan took the brunt of the bomb. He was hunkered down between Ains and the crater, loading the C-6 when the blast smashed into the left side of his body. It's hard to figure out where to even pick him up. Fav, wearing latex gloves, grabs the middle of Nathan's shirt and hauls him onto the stretcher.

"Sorry, Smitty," he says.

Under the scorching sun, the troops carry Nathan to a portable X-ray machine near the ambulance. The EOD guys need to do one last scan for unexploded material. They don't want a grenade going off in the morgue. Somebody has already put Ricky's remains into one of the green plastic bags. Capt. MacEachern, the NIS investigator, has also seized that piece of jaw Dave Bibby found earlier this morning. He is pretty sure it's Pte. Green's.

At 230 pounds, Marc is the heaviest, and that's not including the flak vest he's wearing. Some of the guys are actually joking about it. *Fuck, he weighs a lot. You owe us one, buddy.* Anything to get through this. As Joe Jasper helps carry Sgt. Léger's stretcher up the hill, a wave of Marc's blood splashes on his boots.

Ainsworth's shirt is ripped open, left that way after Vic Speirs tried to find a heartbeat with his stethoscope. Pete Filis is among the guys who lift Cpl. Dyer onto the stretcher. "He used to call me a big teddy bear," Cpl. Filis says, sweating under the vicious heat. He and Vic try not to cry.

At the top of the wadi, Sgt. Wilson remains near the ambulance. As the temperature rises, he can't help but think of an old colleague, a medic who was stationed in Rwanda during the genocide. He hanged himself in 1997, overwhelmed by the death he saw there. Sgt. Wilson is pretty sure he's seen enough already today. He'll let the other guys do the lifting.

As noon approaches, the troops load all four stretchers into the back of A Company's ambulance. Two on the top. Two on the bottom. Both medics close the camouflage panels covering the red crosses on either side of the amb. It's standard operating procedure. For this drive back to camp, the ambulance is technically not an ambulance. It is a hearse.

For the next four days, forensic investigators will sweep Tarnak Farm, inch by inch, placing tiny flags beside everything they find. Yellow for unexploded ordnance. Orange for personal equipment. Pink for human remains. By the time they finish, 443 pink flags will stick out of the ground.

Since they first arrived in Afghanistan, Billy Bolen and Marc Léger have shared a tent, sleeping among boxes and boxes of Army supplies. They even have a Chuck Norris Total Gym, as if just being here isn't enough of a workout. Back from Tarnak Farm, W/O Bolen hunches over the edge of his cot, staring, teary-eyed, at Marc's stuff on the other side of the room.

"Get that shit out of here," he says to a few soldiers sitting with him. When they're done packing up, Billy slides the exercise machine over to where the other cot used to be. As much as he can't look at Marc's things, he doesn't want to see an empty space, either.

Outside, Warrant Officer Rob Jones is doing his best to make sure the paratroopers talk to somebody about what just happened. Trained to conduct what are officially known as "critical incident stress debriefs," Jones knows they have to nip this trauma in the bud. A lot of the troops don't realize it yet, but they have all been scarred in some way by what they saw last night. It's inevitable. Some of the soldiers are already talking to the peer counselors. Others are venting among themselves. *What the fuck was that pilot thinking? How could he not know we were there? And why the hell were we out there anyway, firing Carl Gustavs in the pitch black of night? We've never done that before.*

Private Simon Hughes has just been told that he's going to accompany Ricky's body back to Canada. He is the obvious choice. Simon lived with Greener and Miranda for a few weeks before they shipped off to Kandahar, and he's already heard about his friend's engagement ring a hundred times. Just before noon, Pte. Hughes sees Jon Bradshaw coming back from the range. "How bad is he?" Simon asks. He wants to know what he should tell Miranda. Jon pulls him aside, careful to make sure nobody else hears what he's about to say.

★ ★ ★

Even though it is 4 a.m., Lisa Schmidt isn't startled by the ringing telephone. When Harry is overseas, he always calls in the middle of the night. It's the best time to talk. The kids are asleep. No distractions. "Hello sweetie," Lisa says, knowing full well who is on the other end.

As her husband speaks, she barely recognizes the voice. He immediately tells her what happened. *I dropped a bomb. Four Canadians are dead.* Lying in bed, Lisa is speechless. She can only listen as Harry tells her to watch out for the boys, to brace for the possibility that reporters might start knocking on the door. Before he hangs up, Harry tells his wife how much he loves her.

Joan, Maj. Schmidt's mother, is staying in Springfield this week, visiting Lisa and the kids while Harry is away. At breakfast, her daughter-in-law breaks the news. Both women cry and pray, not just for Harry, but for the families of those dead Canadians.

★ ★ ★

Lorne Ford is half-awake by the time medics carry his stretcher onto the C-17. He's not completely coherent, though just enough to continue demanding that somebody bring him his Airborne coin. By the time the plane takes off at 11:30 a.m. Zulu—14 hours after the bombing—Lorne passes out again, dropping his cherished memento on the ground. Brett Perry picks it up.

Sgt. Ford and Cpl. Perry are among the six wounded Canadian soldiers bound for Landstuhl, Germany, and the comfort of a U.S. Army hospital. Curtis Hollister, still feeling the effects of a concussion, is also on board, as is Rene Paquette, drugged and unconscious. Norm Link, hobbling from the gash in his foot, is walking with crutches. Brian Decaire's hand is so swollen that it looks like he's wearing a baseball glove. Cpl. Jean de la Bourdonnaye—the medic who worked on Sgt. Ford with Chris Kopp and Rob Coates—is also flying to Germany. He convinced his boss to let him go.

As the plane disappears from Afghanistan airspace, an American official starts taking photos of the wounded troops. Some of Sgt. Ford. A few of Cpl. Paquette. It's common procedure for the crew to chronicle each medical extraction out of theater. Brett Perry tries to keep his mouth shut, but he just can't. "Listen, you assholes," he says. "We went to war for you. We're helping you guys and you're taking pictures of our guys while they're hurt?"

It makes for an awkward seven-hour flight.

★ ★ ★

Maurice Baril watched Gen. Henault's press conference last night, but he hasn't read the papers yet today. He was out of bed early, at the airport by 7 a.m. It's a beautiful, clear morning in Ottawa, perfect weather for a ride in his Challenger II airplane.

Baril has a cellphone clipped to his belt, but it's so loud inside the cockpit that he doesn't hear the ringing. The prime minister's office calls. The defence minister's office. The chief of the Defence Staff. His wife. They each leave a message, asking him to call back as soon as he can. When he checks his voicemail a couple hours later, he is pretty sure he knows what everyone wants to talk about.

Now 58, Maurice Baril is only eight months retired from his post as Canada's top general—the pinnacle of a four-decade military career that was both exceptional and controversial. Most Canadians know his name because of what happened in 1994, while he was working for the head of peacekeeping operations at the United Nations. Baril was on the receiving end of a now-infamous telex from fellow Canadian general Romeo Dallaire, the UN commander in Rwanda, warning of the impending "extermination" of thousands of Tutsis. General Dallaire wrote that his troops were planning to raid a Hutu arms cache in an attempt to thwart the looming massacre, but the mission was vetoed by General Baril and his superiors. When the genocide erupted three months later—leaving more than half a million people dead—some in the international community pinned the blame on Gen. Baril. He dismissed such finger-pointing as "pretty cheap," saying years later that he could have stuck a copy of the telex "on every telephone pole of New York City" and the UN still would not have intervened.

In September 1997, Prime Minister Jean Chrétien promoted the general to chief of the Defence Staff, giving him command of the Canadian military at a time when it was reeling from scandal. Mounting allegations of sexual harassment. Deep budget cuts. Some of the country's lowest-ranking soldiers were being paid so poorly that their families were forced to visit food banks. And of course, a sweeping inquiry had just concluded that senior officers, having bungled preparations for Canada's mission in Somalia, tried to cover up the March 4, 1993, shooting death of a civilian by members of the Airborne Regiment. The incident triggered the unit's eventual disbandment two years later.

It was hardly the glory days. But Gen. Baril made progress. He cracked down on sexual misconduct, opened all combat positions to women, and lobbied behind closed doors for increased defense spending. But along the way, he also caught flak from within the ranks for being a little too cozy with his political masters. In February 1999, some critics went so far as to brand him a "Liberal lapdog" when he blamed himself for Chrétien missing King Hussein's state funeral in Jordan. The prime minister was skiing in Whistler, B.C., at the time, but Gen. Baril, always the good soldier, said his staff should have had a plane ready nonetheless. "Baril the fall guy," one headline read.

Today, after listening to his voicemails, Maurice Baril knows who to call first: his wife, Huguette. *The prime minister already phoned the house looking for you,* she tells him. His next call is to Gen. Henault, the man who replaced him as Canada's top officer just a few months ago. His hunch is correct. The powers that be want him to lead the board of inquiry that will investigate yesterday's friendly fire bombing.

When Gen. Baril phones Mr. Chrétien's office, the woman on the other end asks him to call back on a landline. He hangs up and starts walking toward his truck. "Can you park the airplane back in the hangar?" the general asks one of his friends.

"What's cooking?"

"You'll find out."

Gen. Baril drives to a nearby Giant Tiger discount store, asks a clerk for change, then calls the prime minister from a payphone outside. They speak in French. When Baril tells the PM that he missed his earlier call because he was flying, Chrétien jokes that he didn't realize his old friend was "Aviateur," French for Air Force. He's not, of course. He's Army, himself a former Princess Patricia. He actually began his career in Alpha Company, the same unit that was just bombed.

Jokes aside, Chrétien is anxious for an answer now. He wants to announce Baril's appointment in the House of Commons as soon as possible. The general says yes, even though his instincts are screaming at him to hang up the phone. This can only be messy. How can a Canadian looking for the truth possibly pry into the inner workings of the U.S. military? And the mud-slinging will certainly start all over again, the people who will dredge up all that stuff about how Maurice Baril is nothing more than Jean Chrétien's pawn.

When he arrives home, Gen. Baril calls Art Eggleton, the minister of national defence. "This is a can of worms," he tells the minister.

"This is a real can of worms," Eggleton answers. "But let's see what we can do."

★ ★ ★

Brigadier-General Ivan Fenton is commander of all Canadian Army forces west of Thunder Bay, Ontario. Tens of thousands of troops. On the morning of April 18, it is his job to tell Canadians exactly who died yesterday in the Kandahar desert. While a light snow falls on the Edmonton garrison, Gen. Fenton walks outside to address the crowd of reporters. He looks as though he hasn't slept all night. "I'll just start off by saying that the priority of our effort right now is to look after the families," the general says, wearing full military fatigues and a green beret. "Our deepest sympathy is with them. We have soldiers and family members and friends with all the family members who have suffered a loss, and our focus for the next day or two is helping them get through this time.

"We have four fatalities, as you know," he continues. "They are: Sergeant Marc Léger. Corporal Ainsworth Dyer. Private Richard Green. And Private Nathan Smith." The general's deep voice fades into a whisper as he reads the last name. It takes him six long seconds to compose himself.

"All military families brace themselves, but expected or not, this is a terrible shock and we're doing everything we can to help these families," he continues. "They have our deepest sympathy, and we, across Canada, our military community, is sharing this suffering with them."

If there is such a thing, the entire nation is in mourning today. Four dead soldiers, Canada's first combat casualties since the Korean War. Flags across the country are lowered to half-mast. At the homes of the dead and the wounded, phones ring and ring and ring. Friends. Family. The prime minister. In many cases, journalists, all anxious to tell the stories of the men who were bombed on the other side of the world.

Debbie Brossoit, Cpl. Shane Brennan's mother, heard about the accident on the news this morning, but didn't know her son was alive until he called her Collingwood, Ontario, home just before 8 a.m. "I'm okay, Mom, please calm down," Shane told his mother. "Please stop crying. I love you. This is my job."

When MCpl. Curtis Hollister deployed overseas, residents in his home-town of Cupar, Saskatchewan—population 625—tied yellow ribbons around trees. Today, dozens of people have stopped by the family home to offer support. "Our hearts go out to the families of the soldiers who died," his father, Len, tells a reporter. "It's sad that they lost their lives in a training exercise."

At Alice Léger's home in Lancaster, Ontario, old friends are knocking on her door, offering their condolences for her dead grandson, the one who used to come and visit every day. She spoke to Marc on the phone last week. "He was my pal, I was his grandma," she says. "My heart is just in the water. He's gone, but I just can't imagine why. Why him? Why did it happen?"

Nobody knows. Not yet, at least. But speculation is already flying. Trigger-happy pilot. Weekend warrior. Poor training. Out-of-date equipment. On Parliament Hill, some MPs are already trying to exploit the tragedy for political points. "If ever there were any evidence needed that Canadian troops should not be in Afghanistan under United States command, we have seen the tragic evidence of that," Svend Robinson, the NDP foreign affairs critic, tells a news conference. "If Canadian troops cannot be certain that they're not going to be fired on by Americans, we have no business being there."

Joe Clark, the federal Conservative leader, takes it one step further, sug-gesting that Liberal government defense policies could be to blame. "Even in these tragic circumstances, hard questions must be asked and answered,"

Clark says, to the jeers of many fellow MPs. "War is always unpredictable, but Canadians want to know the exact circumstances that led to Canadian soldiers being killed by friendly fire. Did the arrangement whereby American commanders direct Canadian troops have any impact on the casualties? Was there any incompatibility between the communications systems of our troops on the ground and the aircraft involved in the incident? Were the Canadian troops adequately equipped?"

South of the border, journalists hammer the Pentagon and the White House for reaction to the accident. General Richard Myers, the chairman of the U.S. joint chiefs of staff, tells a media briefing that the bombing "is right up there with the worst news I've heard in my career." His boss, Defense Secretary Donald Rumsfeld, is out of the capital today, traveling, ironically enough, in the pilots' home state of Illinois. His office releases a statement. "I want to express my deep regret and sadness over the tragic accident in Afghanistan that killed and wounded a number of Canadian troops," it reads, promising a full investigation. "Our thoughts and prayers go out to them, their comrades, and their families."

Throughout the day, President George W. Bush makes a number of public appearances, but he does not mention the friendly fire incident. As the president leaves his fourth event of the day, a CBC reporter shouts a question about the bombing. "I talked to the prime minister last night and expressed my condolences," Bush says, walking away.

Later in the day, the president's office releases its own statement of condolence. "All Americans are deeply saddened by the deaths yesterday of four brave Canadian military personnel in Afghanistan—and by the injuries sustained by eight others," the press release reads. "Canada is a vital member of a mighty coalition against terrorism and hatred. It is shouldering great burdens and making tremendous sacrifices to make the world a safer place for all people. It is doing so in defense of the values that define the Canadian nation and that unite our two peoples."

★ ★ ★

It is mid-morning when the phone rings in Stephen Sargeant's office at Arizona's Luke Air Force Base. By now, Brigadier-General Sargeant has seen the news on CNN. Four dead Canadians. One of his bosses has already called. On the other end of this ringing telephone is Lieutenant-General "Buzz" Moseley, the top Air Force guy in U.S. Central Command—the man in charge of the Afghanistan air war.

Gen. Sargeant knows the voice. Back in 1996–97, when he was still a colonel, he served under then-Brigadier-General Moseley at Nevada's Nellis Air Force Base. Three years later, just before Sargeant took over as commander at Luke, Moseley—working at the time for the secretary of the Air Force—called to talk about some relevant legislative issues. This morning, Gen. Moseley tells Gen. Sargeant to start packing. He is going to lead the U.S. investigation into the friendly fire bombing. It will be a multi-national board, Moseley tells him, though it's not clear yet how many Canadians—or who—will serve with him.

When all the traveling and interviewing and analysis are done, Sargeant's job will be to submit a final report to Gen. Moseley. If the findings recommend any disciplinary action, it will be Moseley's responsibility to dish it out. In the meantime, the three-star general sends an urgent note to his subordinate commanders, urging them to review the rules of engagement with their pilots.

"There is a well-defined mechanism to ensure you and I do not engage friendly forces," his memo reads. "It is difficult to imagine a scenario, other than troops in contact, whereby we will not have time to egress the threat area, regroup, deconflict, and then engage in a well thought-out and coordinated plan that ensures success.

"I need everyone's head in the game—we cannot afford another tragic incident," his e-mail continues. "Before air crew step to the jet, they must have a solid understanding of the ground situation and the ongoing dynamics. I cannot overstate how fluid the ground environment in Afghanistan is and the challenges this creates in identifying friendly vice Taliban and al Qaeda forces.

"Friendly forces on the ground are lightly armed and working in difficult terrain against an elusive enemy. These troops have come to rely on air power when they become engaged. We need to be there and do it right in accordance with the ground commander's priorities and deconfliction plans among the many teams throughout the area."

The note ends: "Gen. Moseley sends."

★ ★ ★

All day, A Company troops have been lining up to use the phone. Everyone gets a free call, just to let their families know they're okay. Physically, at least. Cpl. Kent Schmidt phones his girlfriend, Maureen. When he's done, he makes a second call, this one to Marley Léger. He knows the phone number off by heart. It used to be his.

Kent Schmidt first met Sgt. Léger in Wainwright, Alberta, where Marc was teaching young recruits during their 16 weeks of Battle School. When Kent was later posted to the PPCLI in Edmonton, Marc would always ask how he was doing. During one chat, Léger mentioned that he and Marley had a couple rooms for rent at their place, just in case the 18-year-old was looking. He moved in during the summer of 1999.

It was like a family, and Kent was the little brother. He did dishes, mowed the lawn. They threw a lot of backyard parties, had a lot of good laughs. Schmidt only moved out last fall because he and Maureen found a place of their own.

Today, Marley is glad to hear Kent's voice. She asks him to come home with Marc's body, to be there for the funeral. According to the rules, only a sergeant can escort a sergeant home. Kent is just a corporal, but when he tells his platoon commander about Marley's request, nobody argues. Marc will have two escorts: Cpl. Schmidt and Sergeant Ken Dunn, a section commander in 2 Platoon.

By the time Kent phones, reporters are camped out at the end of Marley's driveway. It is the dirty side of daily journalism, the relentless pursuit of a quote from the grieving widow. But by late afternoon, when Marley emerges from her front door, only a few reporters are still around. Her hair in a ponytail, a friend holding onto her arm, Marley carries a picture of her gorgeous husband, smiling back in his maroon beret. She holds it up for the cameras.

"I just want everyone to know what kind of man my husband was," she says, weeping. "I think everyone should know that these soldiers were very brave and they are definitely heroes, each and every one of them. And I'm going to miss him very much, and I loved him very, very much and I'm extremely proud of the man that he is, and that he was, and what he's done for his country and for all of you."

Marley and Marc were married just a couple years ago, but they were together for more than a decade. They first met at a high school party. A few weeks later, they were a couple. It wasn't always easy. Marc traveled a lot, either overseas or on a training course. Just before Marc left for Afghanistan, Marley had a miscarriage. She was three-and-a-half months pregnant. Yesterday, around the same time Sgt. Léger agreed to take Sgt. Reid's spot at Tarnak Farm, he sent his wife an e-mail. "Boy, do I ever miss you," he wrote. "I wish I could spend more time writing you. Everyone is sharing the one computer, except all the officers, they have their own.

"I love you very much, and now that I have your address I will write as much as possible.

"Love, Marc."

In between sobs, Marley recalls how she heard the news the night before. "It was a little before 10, I believe," she says. "I hadn't been watching the news so I didn't expect it. It was the same as the movies. I mean, three men came to the door and took their berets off and said: 'There's been an accident.' And I said: 'Is he okay?' and they said: 'No.' And I said: 'Is he gone?'"

She covers her mouth for a moment, composing herself.

"And they said: 'Yes, I'm so sorry.'"

For a few minutes, Marley talks about the phone call she got from Marc on the weekend, how they talked about taking a trip when he got home, about trying again to start a family.

"Had the two of you talked about—"

Marley finishes the reporter's question. "Death?" she asks. "Yes. You always do. This time it was a little bit different. He asked if I understood why he was going. I did. I do. I understand why he had to go. He said: 'I can't let what happened continue. This is my job. It's what I'm here to do.'"

Another journalist asks if Marc's death is even harder to comprehend because it came by friendly fire. "Maybe I'm not there yet," Marley answers. "He's gone. Do I hold a grudge? No. Does it make a difference? No. He's gone. He was over there serving his country."

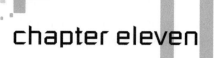

chapter eleven

Marco Favasoli wakes up early on April 19. He spent yesterday's sunrise at Tarnak Farm. This morning, he is out for a jog, making a deliberate point to nod or wave or say hello to every American he passes. It's his own little way of saying: "No hard feelings, eh."

At camp, Yan Bérubé is packing a bag for the flight back to Canada. He is going to bring his roommate home. Simon Hughes collects some of Ricky's belongings, things that Miranda will probably want. He grabs the red heart-shaped box, the one that holds the engagement ring she doesn't know about yet. Michael Frank has a Ziploc bag full of odds and ends. Nathan's maroon beret. His dog tag. His wallet, half-charred, is also in there. No sign of the emergency twenty.

By late afternoon, coalition soldiers start to gather around the runway. Thousands of them. Even Special Forces soldiers have emerged from their hiding places to pay respect to four dead Canadians. Col. Wiercinski, TF Rakkasan's commander, addresses his troops as they stand firmly at attention. "For the last several months, we've lived together, we fought together, and we will mourn together," he says, half yelling. "This will not—will not—hamper our resolve. If anything, it will strengthen our commitment. We will be stronger. We will be better. We will have them—those four brave soldiers—looking over our shoulders as we continue this fight until its end."

Bagpipes play in the distance as pallbearers, fellow jumpers, load each ice-filled silver casket into the belly of a waiting Hercules. Billy Bolen is among those carrying Marc's body on their shoulders. Troops of his rank aren't supposed to do this job, but he insisted. Once on board the airplane, soldiers drape a Canadian flag and a maroon beret over each coffin, sprinkling the top with fresh rose petals. Like a jumpmaster,

Lt.-Col. Stogran, the Canadian commander, smacks the back of each coffin. "You're okay, jumper," he says. "Have a good one. Airborne!"

The pallbearers stay on the plane until the last possible moment, crying and hugging and struggling to understand how this is even possible. Cpl. Patrick Farrell kisses his hand four times, touching each coffin as he leaves. "Take it easy, guys," he says, tears welling in his eyes. As the doors finally close, Sgt.-Maj. Al Whitehall, standing in the Kandahar darkness, salutes the plane from the runway, the last of the troops to turn and march away. Inside, six men remain with the four caskets: Yan Bérubé, Michael Frank, Ken Dunn, Kent Schmidt, Simon Hughes, and Captain John Gallo, their officer escort. Exhausted, Yan lies beside Ainsworth's coffin and falls asleep.

★ ★ ★

When Rene Paquette wakes up, one of the first people he sees through his bleary eyes is Adrienne Clarkson, the governor general of Canada. Cpl. Paquette was still unconscious the day before, when Her Excellency first stepped onto the plane to greet the wounded soldiers as they arrived in Germany. She starts talking to Rene, but nearly two days after the bombing, he still can't hear a thing. He's feeling good, though; the morphine drip is doing its job.

Lorne Ford is also awake and alert. When he first came to, he immediately started asking the nurses about the score in the Toronto Maple Leafs game. He also reached down to feel his leg. Bonus. He was convinced the doctors would have amputated it by now.

Lorne knew before he left Kandahar that Ricky was dead. He was asking about him even before the chopper whisked him away from Tarnak Farm. But today, as he lies in his hospital bed, a sickening guilt begins to overwhelm him. A member of his section was killed. On his watch. He thinks back to the weeks before they deployed, when he lambasted his guys for doing something stupid. *I don't care what you think of me*, he yelled. *My only job is to make sure you come home alive.* In his mind, he didn't do his job.

But Lorne is a realist. Even as he cries, he knows in his heart that this wasn't his fault. Somebody else pushed the pickle button, not him. Amid his own struggle, he tries to comfort Curtis Hollister, who lost two of his men, Ains and Smitty. His entire weapons detachment. "You know what, Curtis," Lorne says to his friend. "We have to get over this and deal with it right now. There is nothing we could have done. We had no control."

Brian Decaire has a cast wrapped around his right hand, an IV line in his left arm. It makes for an interesting trip to the bathroom, to say the least. The entire experience is a bit surreal, like a gong show almost. Dignitaries and generals are constantly coming and going, some expressing condolences, others apologizing. The governor general and her philosopher husband, John Ralston Saul, seem to drop in every few hours—and not just when the photographers are around. During one visit, Saul trips and falls on his ass as he tries to sit in a chair. Brian, still in soldier mode, points and laughs.

In the midst of the almost-suffocating attention, Brian answers the ringing telephone in his hospital room. It's a Canadian journalist who flew to Germany shortly after the bombing. He asks about Decaire's four dead comrades, about how the injured guys are holding up. What would you say to the guy who dropped the bomb?

"It's a shitty thing that happened and a dumb mistake by that pilot," Cpl. Decaire says. "I hope he's hurting now. There are a lot of families that are hurting. The whole battalion's hurting."

★　★　★

On April 19, the front page of every Canadian newspaper is plastered with photos of dead paratroopers. Among the tributes, damning headlines: "Pilot ignored orders," one reads. Quoting anonymous sources, numerous page-one stories report that the unnamed F-16 pilot was ordered to hold fire in the moments before the attack, but invoked self-defense after seeing what he thought was an enemy ambush. "When he saw tracer fire again, he bombed away," one source told the *National Post*.

But among the pages and pages of coverage this morning, there are no quotes from George W. Bush, no personal words of sympathy from the U.S. president to bolster the press release his office issued late yesterday. John Manley, Canada's deputy prime minister, is as diplomatic as possible when cornered by reporters. "I think it undoubtedly would have been of some comfort to the families to hear the president's own words through the media," he says before scooting into his office.

Politicking aside, things are moving quickly behind the scenes as both countries piece together their separate boards of inquiry. In Ottawa, Gen. Baril, the man who will lead Canada's investigation, walks into a packed room of journalists for the first time since he retired from the military last fall. Everyone has the same question: Will you be able to talk to the pilot who unleashed the bomb? Not even Gen. Baril knows the answer to that one just yet. "You know we're dealing with national laws and rules and regulations and tradition and everything," he says. "And would you like to see the Canadian soldiers being dragged in front of another country's board of inquiry on something that had happened that you don't know what happened?"

By late afternoon, George W. Bush is touring a Secret Service training facility in Maryland. While watching a demonstration of bomb-sniffing dogs, he suddenly turns and walks toward a group of reporters standing nearby. The president's staff has undoubtedly told him about the grumblings north of the border. "It was a terrible accident," Bush says, speaking slowly. "Parents and loved ones of the soldiers have my most heartfelt sympathy, and I wish we could bring them back.

"I appreciate so very much the sacrifices that the Canadians are making in the war against terror," he continues. "And again, I'm so sorry that this accident took place." It has been nearly two days since the men were killed.

★ ★ ★

Yan Bérubé has been sleeping for hours, curled up just inches from his best friend's coffin. He opens his eyes only moments before their plane touches down in Germany. It's a quick stop. Medical officials are going to fill the caskets with fresh ice, then re-load them onto an Airbus bound for Canada. A team of pallbearers meets them on the tarmac, as does the governor general. The wounded troops who can still walk watch silently as the bodies are carried off the Herc. They weren't in Kandahar for the send-off, so this is their first glimpse of the caskets.

In a private room in the airport, a case of beer is waiting for the paratroopers. Michael Frank and Brian Decaire, both bawling, embrace in a bear hug. Some of the guys feast on cold French fries, heaven compared to the rations they've been eating for the past eight weeks. One beer and they're buzzing. Some of the guys take a few bottles with them as they board the Airbus.

In Kandahar, Master-Corporal Dave Bibby is nearly finished writing a seven-page letter to his wife, Bonita. He tells her about what he saw in the desert, the remains, the dung beetles, the smell. He writes about picking up the corpses, how it was almost therapeutic to do that service for his fellow soldiers. "I hope this letter helps you to share what I have just gone through," he writes. "I think the fact that you want/need to know what happened has helped me. I feel closer to you and writing this down for you has helped put events in their place and sorted things out for me.

"I love you very much and cannot wait to be home in your arms again," he continues. "But I want you to know that I'm doing what I love to do and I'm where I want to be. I love you more than ever.

"Dave."

★ ★ ★

The Airbus touches down at Canadian Forces Base Trenton just before 11 a.m. on Saturday, April 20. Marc Léger's flag-draped casket is the first to be carried off, lifted by an honor guard of pallbearers and placed into a waiting black hearse. The men who flew the bodies here stand in the sun, saluting. Bagpipes play. On the other side of a chain-link fence, a few dozen Canadians have gathered to watch, to honor four men whose faces the entire country now knows. On the runway, the prime minister and the defense minister are among a quiet crowd of dignitaries. Marc's grandmother is here, too. His parents are not. They jumped on a plane to Edmonton right after the news, thinking the bodies would be taken there.

Ainsworth's silver coffin is next. Ricky. Then Nathan. By 11:30, four hearses and two limousines, led by an escort of Ontario Provincial Police motorcycles, make the turn onto Highway 401, heading west toward Toronto. A coroner there is waiting to perform official autopsies before releasing the bodies to their grieving families. When they arrive in a couple of hours, the six military escorts will refuse to leave, insisting that they be the ones to carry their friends into the morgue. They will stay in that chilly room, fighting the stench and the reality of it all to make sure these soldiers, their brothers, are treated with dignity. Some will go so far as to help lift the corpses out of those wet, plastic bags, forever scarring any fond memories they once had of these young men. As horrid as it is, they won't leave. They will sneak outside to smoke and vomit, but they will always come back. They have been ordered to accompany these soldiers all the way home—and every stop in between.

As the motorcade leaves Trenton, throngs of people line the highway, paying their respects with a wave or a cheer. Suddenly—literally overnight—the Canadian military matters again. In the coming days, the country will watch what many here have never seen: a succession of full military funerals. Thousands of strangers will wait in long, twisting lines to pay their respects to men they have never met.

In Toronto, the crowd at Ainsworth's wake will be so large that Jocelyn won't even have a moment alone with her fiancé's body. At the cemetery, her father, Aart, will tell the mourners that even in their pain, they must find it in their hearts to pray for that pilot. Aart has already written a letter to the still-anonymous airman, forgiving him for what happened.

As she flies to Halifax to meet Ricky's coffin, Miranda will find her mind playing tricks on her, her stomach filling with butterflies at the thought of seeing her man again. She will love the ring, vow to never take it off her finger. As she watches the casket come off the plane, she and Doreen Coolen, Ricky's mom, will sob and hold hands. "I love him more than life itself," Doreen will tell reporters. "I can't say how proud I am of him. This is tearing the heart out of me."

In Dartmouth, Nathan Smith will be remembered at a private ceremony, then cremated, his ashes scattered along Peggy's Cove. It's what he wanted. His father, Lloyd, will wear his captain's uniform to the ceremony, holding onto his wife as tearful strangers watch from across the street. As the weeks wear on, he will hope and pray for that phone call, the one telling him that this was all a misunderstanding, that his only son is indeed alive.

In the small town of Lancaster, Ontario—population 700—stores will close during Marc Léger's funeral. In lieu of flowers, the family will ask for donations to a new fund set up to continue "King Marco's" work in the

Livno Valley. Outside the ceremony, a television reporter will corner Yan Bérubé, asking him what he thinks of the man who dropped the bomb. "Don't put the blame on the pilot," he will say. "Those guys cover us most of the time. The reason we're there is because a bunch of retards September 11 decided to fly some planes into the World Trade Center. That's why we're there."

But the anger will come. The questions. Why hasn't the pilot apologized? Why won't he express some remorse for what happened in the sky that night? Four good men are dead. Doesn't he care?

The man steering Ainsworth's hearse down the 401 is clearly a little nervous. It's only him and Yan and a two-hour drive to Toronto. "Is it okay if I smoke?" asks Cpl. Bérubé, still in the same green army fatigues he was wearing last week.

"Sure," the driver says, rolling down the windows. Yan lights his cigarette.

"You got any tunes?" he asks.

"Sure," the driver answers. "What do you want to listen to?"

"Well," he says, gesturing to the coffin behind him, "my buddy back here likes hip-hop and techno." As people wave at the passing hearse, Yan puffs hard on his cigarette, Outkast cranked on the radio.

PART II: RECKLESS DISREGARD

chapter twelve

Maurice Baril and his Canadian board of inquiry are high above Afghanistan, flying inside the belly of a CC-130 as it barrels toward the Kandahar Airfield. Like all the troops who have come before them, the investigators are in full battle rattle, ready to engage the enemy on the slim chance that they're waiting for them on the tarmac. It has already been a long week for the board. Seven days ago, they convened for the first time, gathering in an Ottawa conference room at National Defence Headquarters. Gen. Baril began the 8 a.m. meeting with a simple question.

"What is the aim of this board?" he asked. When someone started reading the official terms of reference, the general cut him off. "What is the aim of this board?" he asked again. "How are we going to achieve success?"

During his four decades of military service, Gen. Baril has seen his share of successful boards of inquiry. And he's seen some brutal ones. His goal for this go-round is clear: Write a report that answers every possible question the grieving relatives might have. Do that, and everything else will fall into place. "If the families don't believe," Gen. Baril told the board, "the nation will not believe."

Three days later, he and his team—more than a dozen people—flew to Al Minhad Air Base, home of Camp Mirage, Canada's not-so-secret forward logistics base in the United Arab Emirates. They spent two days flipping through paperwork and preparing witness lists. They even received a quick refresher course on how to fire a 9mm pistol. They left Camp Mirage this morning, April 29, 2002.

Sitting near Gen. Baril for the short flight to Kandahar are his board's three members, the men who will help him try to figure out what went wrong that dark night over Tarnak Farm: Colonel Greg Matte, a CF-18 fighter pilot; Colonel Mark Hodgson, an Army officer whose credentials include a Master's Degree in Military Science; and Chief Warrant Officer Denis Levesque, a 32-year veteran and, like the four dead soldiers, a longtime paratrooper. Their final report is due in less than 60 days. Also on board the Herc is an assortment of experts and support staff, including a medical specialist and a legal advisor. Major Mike "Bull" Zigan, a U.S. F-16 pilot, joined the board of inquiry (BOI) just yesterday. His expertise will no doubt come in handy.

As the Herc nips the runway at Kandahar Airfield, the morning newspapers are hitting the stands back home in Canada—filled with stories and columns and photos of an unprecedented memorial service the day before. More than 16,000 people gathered at Edmonton's Skyreach Centre to say a final public goodbye to Marc Léger, Ainsworth Dyer, Richard Green, and Nathan Smith. The prime minister spoke. The governor general. Some of the wounded soldiers were even there, including Sgt. Lorne Ford, wheeled into the arena under the white covers of a hospital bed and a booming round of applause.

Amid the countless pages of coverage today is a front-page story in the *National Post*: "A real pro" airman overcome by grief, the headline reads. Unnamed sources tell the paper that the U.S. fighter pilot who dropped the bomb is heartbroken over the accident. "He's one of the greatest guys we have," one source says. "You can't imagine how he feels. I don't think your imagination can comprehend it."

For now, Harry Schmidt's identity is still a heavily guarded secret.

★ ★ ★

Brigadier-General Marc Dumais graduated from Montreal's McGill University with a degree in chemistry. An ironic footnote, considering his current posting is an exercise in just that. The general—in an unprecedented move—has been appointed co-president of the U.S. Accident Investigation Board that will also probe the friendly fire bombing. He was originally named to Gen. Baril's team, but after some closed-door negotiations, the Pentagon agreed to allow a Canadian co-president. Gen. Dumais holds the same power to interrogate witnesses as his American counterpart, Gen. Stephen Sargeant.

The appointment is nothing short of a public relations coup for the Canadian government. Art Eggleton, the defense minister, was so excited about the news that he rushed to announce it to the media before both countries even worked out the final details. If nothing else, Gen. Dumais' posting will help facilitate the exchange of evidence between the two separate boards, which have agreed to share certain pieces information, including interview transcripts and flight data. But the rules are clear: No collaboration. Both investigations will be completely independent, free to reach their own conclusions.

Gen. Dumais is not the only Canadian sitting on the American board. He is joined by Lieutenant-Colonel Marsh Simpson, an AWACS advisor; Major Dave Galea, a long-time infantryman; and Major Jason Smith, a Canadian exchange officer at the U.S. Air Force Safety Center in New Mexico. Gen. Sargeant's side of the table includes Lieutenant-Colonel Joyce Adkins, an aerospace psychologist whom he handpicked for the task; Lieutenant-Commander Kevin Protzman, a Navy fighter pilot and expert on rules of engagement; Captain Brian Turner, an F-16 pilot from Utah's Hill Air Force Base; and Lieutenant-Colonel Jeffrey Walker, the lead legal advisor. In all, 27 people sit on the American board.

They begin their work at Kuwait's Al Jaber Air Base, Building #100—not far from the runway where Harry Schmidt and Bill Umbach were told they had killed four Canadian soldiers.

★ ★ ★

"We are not questioning what you have been doing here," Gen. Baril says. "But we have no choice, because of our terms of reference, to establish the training routine based on rules and regulations and orders and everything that brought us to the incident. We are starting with you and we certainly would like to hear from you."

Gen. Baril is talking to Lt.-Col. Pat Stogran, the Canadian commander in Afghanistan—and the board of inquiry's first witness. "Okay, sir," Lt.-Col. Stogran says. "I think I probably should go back, probably back to the fall period around September 11." It was then, he tells the BOI, that the battalion was first warned about a possible deployment. Training was intense, but it wasn't until March—right before the Battle Group stormed The Whale—that the entire battalion was actually together in one place. So when the troops got off the mountain, Lt.-Col. Stogran designed a live-fire training regimen for each of his companies. It was supposed to culminate in a mock air/ground assault using Apache helicopters, but that plan eventually fell through because the Rakkasans just didn't have enough choppers to spare.

"So we decided that the focus of effort should be night training," Lt.-Col. Stogran says. "That was sort of the stage we were at as we were coming up to the night of the accident. A Company was on the range and they were doing section-level training. The other thing I might add is we had taken a step away from the traditional peacetime safety that we exercise in Canada with the red panel vests and all of this. The emphasis was, in the interest of preventing fratricide, that they would come up with realistic range safety practices that could be used in a combat scenario. So we were using flags when grenades were being thrown and companies were developing their own SOPs [standard operating procedures] to ensure that their maneuver elements would be safe and then we could use the same safety [practices] in a combat scenario. That had to carry over into nighttime training also.

"I was confident," the colonel continues. "Things were going well in terms of the ground maneuver training. We were fully capable of launching an attack if we were called upon, but this was just—as I would refer to it with the company commanders—this was our insurance policy. The more practice we could get, then the less likely that we would encounter fratricide." The irony is not lost on Lt.-Col. Stogran.

"What is your understanding of the rules and regulations of the coalition force that would allow you to train the way you wanted to train your troops, but doing it in a safe environment because of all the other pieces of weaponry that fly at will around this place?" Gen. Baril asks him.

"It was very closely coordinated with the brigade here," Lt.-Col. Stogran answers. "The brigade has responsibility for AO [area of operation] Truman and we did nothing unless it was coordinated and approved by the brigade headquarters in terms of leaving the camp."

"You have, I guess, two worries," the general says. "One was the danger that you could create to somebody else by live fire."

"Yes sir," Lt.-Col. Stogran answers.

"But how about the worry that you have, to be hurt by somebody else?"

"No," the colonel says. "It never ever entered our head in the least. AO Truman was locked up very tight in terms of command and control by the brigade and we had the Tarnak training area ... As far as other military assets either being engaged in the danger area, or possibly engaging us, there was never any worry about that because it was controled through the brigade Tactical Operations Center, the TOC, in terms of making sure that the personnel in the perimeter were aware that there was going to be live firing down at Tarnak ranges... From that perspective, we had no concern whatsoever of any sort of fratricide issue and the air component never entered into my consciousness as a threat."

"Did you have any capability to do any coordination with the air element?" Gen. Baril asks.

"None, sir. The only elements I could have had some influence on would have been the attack aviation here, but as far as the wild blue yonder, I couldn't even say if the brigade itself has coordination."

"Col. Stogran, could you please comment on your impression of the effectiveness of the medical response to this incident?" Lieutenant-Colonel Allan Darch, the board's medical advisor, asks later in the interview.

"It was outstanding, outstanding," he answers. "It saved two lives, I think, in my estimation. Dustoff [the CASEVAC chopper] was in location, the medics—well, they were our medics, but as far as the support from Charlie Med, it was seamless. They were evacuated very quickly, moved to exactly where they should be. The right guys were in surgery. That is where I spent the bulk of my time. In fact, one of the things I am having trouble living with now is I never got out to see the actual bodies on the site. By the time things started to slow down, the bodies had been evacuated, but they were very, very slick here. World class."

"Since the accident," Gen. Baril asks, "have you checked to see how it is reported to the higher air asset side that your troops are training at night?"

"No, sir, because I knew this inquiry was going on and I didn't want to appear like I was covering my tracks or anything," the colonel answers.

"We haven't done much training at all. We have been deployed on QRF [quick reaction force] tasks recently, and I just have steered right clear of anything to do with it. I haven't been out as much as I wanted to get out to the Tarnak site. As I said, I wished I had gone out there to see the bodies. I just stayed right away from it, pending the conclusion of the official investigations."

"Have you been made aware of any change in the control measures imposed to this area to prevent another accident like this?"

"No, sir. I think with the relationship that I have with the commander here, I would have been told if something would have changed. I might digress on that a little bit. When we were doing Op Harpoon, there was an occasion while we were on The Whale feature, which was our objective for the sense and sight exploitation, where an F-16 almost dropped a 500-pounder on us. At that point in time, I made it clear to Tampa that there was a problem with this."

Lt.-Col. Stogran hands the general some documents, including a copy of the curt e-mail he sent to the Florida headquarters of Canadian Joint Task Force Southwest Asia immediately after the close call with the F-16. "This Task Force standing order comes from Tampa," he says, pointing at one of the papers. "Perhaps I am just venting here, my own PTSD [post-traumatic stress disorder]. This is a standing order on negligent discharges in theater. Personally, I think the task force in Tampa should be focusing on air and ground coordination more than things of this nature. I don't think this accident would have happened had that action taken place. I think there is too much time spent focusing on public affairs."

★ ★ ★

"How would you characterize the way you portrayed the threat on the time of the 17th or around that time?" Gen. Dumais asks.

"Low threat," Evan Cozadd responds. "It was a low threat. I can't see how anybody could say it's not a low threat. I wish I could say it was a high threat. It's not."

Captain Cozadd is an intelligence officer with the 170th Fighter Squadron. He works in the Mission Planning Cell (MPC) and was among those who briefed Maj. Schmidt and Maj. Umbach before they climbed into their F–16s that night. He is also among the first witnesses to testify in front of the American accident investigation board.

"Did you brief a different level of threat that night than you'd brief the preceding briefs that you'd given?" Gen. Sargeant asks him.

"No."

"Was there any extra sense of urgency against the ground threats in your briefing?"

"No," Capt. Cozadd says. "The only thing that I can think of that might have been any different about that day as opposed to any other day, was that earlier in the day the A–10s had been engaged and directed, they had their fire directed by some ground FACs against some caves."

"Is the MLRS [multiple launch rocket system] part of your threat-of-the-day briefing?" Gen. Sargeant asks, referring to the type of weapon that Maj. Schmidt claims to have seen that night.

"We discussed that they had those systems in theater there, but is it a viable threat? Do we brief it as a viable threat? No."

"Is it a widespread system?" Gen. Sargeant asks.

"No," the captain says, "not to my knowledge."

Investigators want to know who is ultimately responsible for dissecting the ACO—the airspace control order—distributed every day by the CAOC. Capt. Cozadd explains that when he first arrived in Kuwait, a Marine counterpart showed him a "nifty" way to map the data using TaskView computer software. But when pilots told him the end product was way too congested to read, he stopped producing the maps. All he does now is download the information and put it into an electronic folder so the MPC chiefs can skim through it. "I'd like to be able to tell you, obviously, based on the fact that we've got this terrible incident, that we were all falling over ourselves to take care of that ACO," Capt. Cozadd says. "That's not the fact, okay."

"Would you find it surprising," Gen. Sargeant asks later, "if I were to tell you you were expected to have been leading the organization that was responsible for the ACO?"

"Yeah, I'd be very surprised," he answers. "Flabbergasted—and based on what, I guess, would be my question back to you." Capt. Cozadd tells investigators that he was part of the advance team that came to watch how the previous MPC—the 18th Fighter Wing from Alaska's Eielson Air Force Base—prepared its briefings. The Springfield unit essentially adopted the exact same procedures, he says.

"You mentioned the numerous various restricted areas that exist and the fact that you, in looking at the ACO, you see circles, numerous circles, numerous circles or dots within the circle, 200-yard ranges within a larger circle, and you've also mentioned that although these may not have always been formally briefed, what is your opinion of the overall awareness among the aircrew?" asks Major Jason Smith, the Canadian F-18 pilot who sits on the American board. "Do they know that there are numerous ones out there? They may not have exact SA [situational awareness] on every one of them, but what is your feeling of the overall awareness of the existence of these areas?"

"Now I think that they are aware of them, but I don't think they were aware of them before," Capt. Cozadd answers. "Frankly, I wasn't aware of them before. That's a pitiful answer, but it's the truth, you know. As I, I told you before what we would do with that ACO. And the general's telling me it was my responsibility to break out that ACO and brief it. I don't know where that's defined."

"No, that's not what the general said," Gen. Sargeant says. "What I asked was, Would you be surprised if anyone had said that you were responsible for breaking out the ACO, as a hypothetical question. How would you react to that?

"Well, if somebody asked me to do it, I would do it," he says. "Somebody now said that?"

"My question is, sitting here today, if someone were to have told you that they expected that was part of your responsibility, how would you react to that?"

"Violently," the captain says.

"That's what I was asking," says Gen. Sargeant. "And I wasn't implying anything, I was just asking how you would react to someone describing that responsibility around your name."

"I'd like to meet that person in a dark alley. You know, I take this very, very seriously, okay. I've never, obviously, I'm uncomfortable beyond belief. I apologize to you and your countrymen, all the servicemen for this incident and I'm embarrassed about it. And I feel ashamed and any pride in what we were doing over here now is shattered with this terrible incident. And, you know, we thought we were doing what we needed to do to brief and to prepare to fly a mission over there, okay. And everybody up and down the chain of command, as far as I could tell, was satisfied with the level of briefing, the level of preparation, and everything that we had done."

★ ★ ★

"It is particularly important that you are the first of our American friends and coalition partners who comes in front of me and all of us," Gen. Baril says. "I can probably speak for my country that we are just delighted with the cooperation that we are having, from your brigade commander all the way down. You sitting here is a mark of that friendship, trust, and cooperation that we have. Like you, we feel very sad about that accident because it happened between friends, coalition members. So we are very glad you are here."

Gen. Baril's warm welcome is for Captain John H. Knightstep, the U.S. soldier in charge of the Kandahar tower. An American, he is under no obligation to talk to the Canadian board of inquiry, but he has volunteered to take an oath. "My primary function here is to ensure air traffic services. As you can hear, the aircraft are flying around," he tells the BOI. "We have anywhere upwards of a hundred air movements within the Kandahar airspace on a given night."

He explains how the task force controls all the airspace—6,000 feet and below—stretching from the "bull's-eye" of the airfield to 10 nautical miles in all directions. That ring of airspace is called a terminal movement area (TMA), and any pilot who wants to fly inside is supposed to contact the tower for permission. Beyond that TMA, the captain continues, is a terminal control area (TCA), a ring of 30 nautical miles that includes all the airspace between 6,000 feet and 27,000 feet. Depicted on a piece of paper, both parts combined look like a mushroom—the TMA being the stem, the TCA the cap. All that information is included in the ACO, he says. "It gets a little complicated," Capt. Knightstep admits. "But I'll try not to lose you.

"When aircraft approaches within the 30-nautical-mile ring of our airspace, they have to contact us on a GCA [ground control approach]," he continues. "The GCA is a radar. It is a very primitive radar. It's 1950s technology. It does not tell you the type of aircraft. It does not tell you the height of aircraft. It does not tell you the tail number of the aircraft. It has no IFF [identification friend or foe] capabilities. All it does is, it is just like the old war movies where you see the blip. Before the aircraft enters that 30-nautical-mile ring, he has to call GCA to get permission to travel through.

"On the night of the incident, the 17th," the captain says, "an aircraft was spotted going through our 30-nautical-mile ring, did not ask to enter our airspace, which happens often due to so much traffic that goes around here. We had two other aircraft close to the airfield. The controller asked the aircraft to identify itself and explain its intent or its purpose or what it would like to do. The aircraft never responded.

"We had it on all our frequencies as posted here," he continues, pointing to a list he handed Gen. Baril. "That is the reason I gave you these frequencies in the front. We tried each one of those frequencies and the unidentified aircraft would not respond.

"The last I heard—and I am not sure if this is the aircraft that caused the incident because we didn't have eyes on it, we just had radar—he came in kind of close from the northern quadrant and came down toward the south and then we lost him on radar. Then that is when we heard the radio calls that there were some injured at the Tarnak Farms."

★ ★ ★

"Did he express any frustration to you not being able to drop bombs on the enemy?" Gen. Sargeant asks.

"Not at all," she answers. "He actually said the opposite and was hoping that, as long as everyone stayed safe, that's all that he was interested in."

"How'd you describe Major Schmidt's personality?"

"He's a pleasant man, easy to get along with, well liked by other people in the squadron and other people on base. My staff like him. Nice guy."

Gen. Sargeant is interviewing Captain Dawn McNaughton, the director of medical services at Al Jaber. She is the doctor who gave Maj. Schmidt his Go/No-go pills that afternoon, the doctor who chatted with him about his kids and his new house by the fairway. "Did you discuss how the mission was going at that time?" Gen. Sargeant asks.

"How his mission was going?" she replies.

"Right. Or the deployment?"

"I always just say: 'Any exciting stuff going on? Hopefully things will look up and you guys will have some fun out there.' And that's about all we did."

Gen. Sargeant asks her to elaborate.

"It seems that around here when we had active missions with operations, such as Anaconda, the pilots were in much more excited and happy moods because they were getting to do what they're trained to do out there, and actually drop bombs occasionally on the bad guys. And here, most of the time that they had been here, so far that this squadron had been here, they did a lot of flying to areas—circling in the area and flying back, so it was a lot of long missions without a lot of gratification for what they were doing. So a lot of training to fly there and fly back. So I said hopefully they would see some action 'cause that's what fighter pilots like to do."

"Did he express frustration to you at being here?" Gen. Sargeant asks later.

"Not at all."

As interested as they are in Maj. Schmidt's brief chat with his doctor, the board is here to ask Capt. McNaughton about the Go-pills. She is not qualified to prescribe the drugs, but she is allowed to distribute the orange tablets to pilots who are already cleared to take it. "Do you know what the pills are?" Gen. Sargeant asks. "What the medications are for the No-go pill?"

"The No-go pills? Yes. We have Ambien and the alternative medication is Restoril."

"And what about for the Go-pill?"

"For the Go-pill we use the dextroamphetamine, or Dexedrine."

"And what type of side-effects do the Go-pills produce?" the general asks. "Can you describe the papers that you're looking at there?"

"These are the paperwork that we give out to the pilots before they take their medications and it's for the ground testing of the Go-pills and the No-go pills. ... And the Go-pill side-effects that we brief all the pilots on are the ones that are listed on Form 2B, which include insomnia, nervousness, anxiety, appetite loss, dryness of mouth, rash, diarrhea, constipation, rapid heartbeat, heart palpitations, tremor, head-ache, and euphoria."

"Do you brief the pilots every time that you issue the Go-pills to them on the side-effects?" Gen. Sargeant asks.

"We do not," she answers. "We do not rebrief them every time that they are issued these pills. We do not."

"Did you discuss any of the side-effects with Maj. Schmidt on the day you issued them?"

"I always ask the pilot if they've had any problems with their medica-tions before issuing it," she says. "And he indicated 'no' and he was given new medication that day."

chapter thirteen

"Bringing you back here is a bit difficult, but it has to be done," Gen. Baril says, his eyes hidden by a large pair of sunglasses. "We are going to do it as quickly as we can, but we will take as long as we need to."

It is 8:30 a.m. on April 30, another scorching Kandahar morning. Maurice Baril and his Canadian board of inquiry, decked out in helmets and camouflage flak jackets, are standing at Tarnak Farm, taking their first glimpse of the desert firing range where four paratroopers were killed 13 days ago. Maj. Sean Hackett, A Company's commander, is standing in the sun with them. So is Captain Jasper, his 2I/C. They both flew in on a Chinook helicopter from Bagram, where A Company is preparing to deploy on Operation Torii, another mountain-to-mountain search for al-Qaeda and Taliban hideouts. Sean has not been back to the range since that night. The last time Joe was here, he was helping to lift his dead friends out of the ditch.

"Shall I carry on with christening the ground, sir?" Capt. Jasper asks, holding a C-8 machine gun.

"Please," Gen. Baril says.

"This is the compound known as Tarnak Farm, where Osama bin Laden trained his terrorists," the captain says, pointing south at the big mud wall. "We don't go in the compound. The compound is out of bounds basically for Canadians because it is not cleared and there is a high threat of mines and booby-traps. What we have here is not a cleared area, but a high-confidence area in that the Engineers have looked over the area for immediate threats. It has not been cleared, flailed, or mine-swept at all. I will reiterate the threat of UXO [unexploded ordnance] and mines. Just watch where you are going and don't pick up anything that you don't recognize."

Capt. Jasper leads the investigators to where the adam area was that night, where the ambulance and the Iltis and the logistics trucks were parked. "This is where the first casualties that I ran into were being treated," he says, gesturing toward the sand. "The ambulance was just a little bit farther up this way. This is where Private Link and some of the other Pri 3 casualties were first brought. They were sitting here, probably about a platoon-and-a-half worth of people, sitting behind the trucks in the administrative area.

"This is the beginning of Wadi East," he continues, pointing to the ditch where the bomb landed. "This is my ammunition point. This is where CQMSA Warrant Officer Bolen was set up with his storeman. They would issue the ammo here. Then the various dets that were doing the tank stalk or the dets that were going through my range, the close-quarters combat range, would get their ammo, bomb up, and then move off in their various serials to their range..."

Under the baking sun, Capt. Jasper leads the board members toward the start of the ditch where he conducted his drill with the Pioneers. Most of the investigators are carrying pads and a pen, scribbling the odd note as he speaks. Gen. Baril has a water bottle in his hand. "I am not going to walk you all the way down through the wadi and into the corral because it isn't really part of the incident, except to say that when the bomb hit I was walking back from the close-quarter combat lane and admitting the next group right here," the captain says. "We walked approximately to the beginning of the wadi and were just kind of heading down into the wadi when we turned, faced this direction, and I said: 'Are you guys ready to go?' and boom, the bomb hit. When the bomb hit, I was standing just over there and it hit to about my 11 o'clock, about 150 meters away."

Gen. Baril wants to know what IFF equipment—identification friend or foe—the paratroopers were wearing that night. "The normal IFF that we wear is a SOP [standard operating procedure]," Capt. Jasper says. "They would wear two glint tape markers, one on the top of the head here, one on the left shoulder. They would wear their IR [infrared] strobe like this set fast. Approximately 50 percent of the guys had IR strobes on, that I could see. As well, for the range staff we had marking, IR glowsticks stuck in the sides of our helmets. So we kind of had a big beacon of lights flashing around the range staff if you look at them in infrared." Investigators will later discover that neither the strobes nor the glint tape is visible from the altitudes that the F–16s were flying that night.

"I have one additional question," Col. Hodgson says. "In terms of the timings, you had mentioned that the close quarter was finished and you had actually turned when the actual—"

"One serial of it was," he says.

"But the fire had finished on that serial when you had turned," Col. Hodgson says. "Can you give us an idea of how many minutes that would have been?"

"The fire would have stopped in the corral once I gave them the 'stop, unload for inspection, clear weapons,'" Capt. Jasper says. "And I would give them a short debrief of their performance. On site essentially is where I did it. … Usually the debriefing and the unload would take five minutes, and then it would take about five minutes to get back here. That was basically timed perfectly with the amount of time that it took the Pioneers to set up the battle sim again."

"If I take that correctly, no rounds would have been fired here for approximately 10 minutes before the actual incident took place on the tank stalk," asks Col. Matte, the board's F–18 pilot. "Is that correct?"

"Yes, sir."

"I understand you were concentrating on your safety job," Gen. Baril says. "But during that 10 minutes that you gave the cease fire, debrief, and come back, can you remember what kind of firing activity from an intensity point of view was going on with the stalk exercise?"

"Quite heavy, sir. In fact, we had remarked a couple of times during the range between MCpl. Bibby and I that there seemed to be some kind of magical connection between the two ranges. Whenever we seemed to come out of the low ground it was perfectly timed with the Carl G. hitting the target. It was actually quite good from a battle simulation scenario because the two ranges were tied together with a tactical scenario in that we were doing one part of the clearance job while they were doing another as cutoff."

"You used the expression 'quite heavy,'" Gen. Baril says. "What does that mean to you?"

"Definitely rapid rate for the machine guns," Capt. Jasper says. "They had six rounds to expend from the Carl Gustav, plus two M-72s."

"From your vantage point over here with the goggles on," says Col. Matte, referring to NVGs, "how would the Carl Gustav rounds appear with regard to the light?"

"They would look like a big tracer round going off, like a ball of light that would go off and then explode," he says. "Explosions don't short out your goggles or anything. You could see it. It would explode. The same thing with tracer. You would be able to see the tracer go by. It would bounce off and ricochet."

"Could you describe the ricochet directions?"

"You would be able to see it better when we go up to the tank stalk area. Essentially the tank stalk is firing in this kind of direction, from the wadi toward, for the most part, that tank hull with the machine guns and the anti-tank weapons. Whatever kind of machine-gun rounds were hitting the ground or the tank hull would ricochet from there. The anti-tank rounds generally don't skip or ricochet because our gunners were pretty bang-on. They were hitting I would say at least 80 percent of the time that night."

"Did you observe with your night vision goggles on from here, let's say, the backblast flame of the Carl Gustav?" Gen. Baril asks.

"You could see clouds of dust kick off if you were looking back there."

"But you could not see the big long flame behind?"

"A flash of light, sir, a brief flash of light," Capt. Jasper says. "There's no big tongue of flame or anything. It's mostly dust that gets kicked up. It's pretty quick too. It's like a muzzle flash."

"Did I understand as well that for that particular exercise, the light fire [machine guns] would have had tracer?" Col. Matte asks, referring to the red streaks that accompany every few bullets.

"All the machine guns had tracer," Capt. Jasper says. "4B1T, which means four ball to one tracer."

"Sorry for belaboring the point," Col. Matte says. "How would the M-72 appear with your NVGs with regard to light and flame?"

"The same way," Capt. Jasper says. "A flash and you could sort of see a bit of a tracer effect as it goes to the target if you are looking at it from behind especially, and then it would explode when it got there. If you haven't seen anti-tank weapons, they are nothing like in the movies. It's mostly dust, smoke, and a very brief flash. There's no flames. There's no big balls of light or fire. It's a quick flash and mostly a big cloud of dust."

"Thank you very much," Gen. Baril says.

"What we can do now is move straight down to the wadi," Capt. Jasper says. "I will guide you up the wadi and describe the practice for the anti-tank stalk." He leads the group to the start of the northbound ditch, to the exact point where Sgt. Léger briefed 3 Section on their fictitious scenario. They continue walking through the tunnel-like ravine, the weeds and the sand much more visible than they were in the pitch black of April 17. Joe stops at the point where the paratroopers stormed up the hill.

"As you can see by all the little evidence flags, or whatever these are, markings, this is the area where it happened," the captain says. "You can see a target which was an infantry target. That was a target which would pop up basically making sure that they didn't extend too far along the range this way. It would be a pop-up target representing a sentry that would engage them. They would have to engage the sentry, take him out, and then take up a position to fire on the tanks with their tank stalk. Up closer to that target is where the anti-tank weapon and the machine gun were sited, and that's where the bomb hit. As you can see, there's nothing here now, but this area, wherever you see pink flags, was littered with broken equipment and pieces of remains.

"This is the site of the hit, right here on the white line tape," Capt. Jasper continues, pointing to the sandy hill. "The crater has been blown in a bit, but you can sort of gauge the layout. If you look toward the range here, they were laid out on the berm stretching from just past this target. This was approximately the center of the position and there was another half of the troops laid out with their machine guns and weapons along here. The Carl Gustav would have been laid halfway between the target and the crater. The machine gun which Corporal Dyer was manning, the C-6, was essentially right beside this crater. Right over here is where Corporal Dyer died.

"The night in question I was, as I said, just coming back from the corral, moving back toward the administration area to pick up the next group. I linked up the next group and was just over there looking roughly in this direction," he says, pointing almost directly north. "The plane, as I heard it, was coming from that direction over my left shoulder and going that way." He gestures from the southwest to the northeast.

"Tell me again about the direction of the plane," Gen. Baril says.

"As far as I could tell, sir, I was looking roughly in this direction, but over there. It came over my left shoulder, as I could tell, moving in this direction."

"I heard it very much," Maj. Hackett adds. "To this day I still believe that I saw a shadow cross. It was very dark and it was pretty low. Pretty low and pretty loud."

"Yes," Capt. Jasper says. "It was like an air show when they go right over your head and put on the afterburner. It was loud, fast, and low … The jet noise was an afterthought anyway, because the first thing we saw was the flash and the bang of the bomb hitting and then the jet noise. We were basically looking off in this direction when we see the big boom, flash, and the noise. My automatic instinct was that there was a range accident. I could tell right away that it was on the firing line and that it wasn't a normal Carl Gustav firing or hitting. It was too big. I thought that something had gone wrong and they had put a round right down in front of them or something. But as soon as the bomb went off and I heard the jet noise, I changed my mind as to what I assumed had happened. From that point things proceeded here pretty quickly. People reacted extremely quickly to start administering first aid."

Capt. Jasper recalls for the board how when he ran to the wadi, he saw medics kneeling beside Ainsworth. "I came over right to here," he points. "I think I actually stood in the crater, perhaps, or just off to the side right there. Corporal Dyer was right beside it. The medic was working on Corporal Dyer at that time. There were more casualties that were pretty obvious lying about on the other side of Corporal Dyer, other medics who were working on them …" Joe pauses for a moment, the memory still fresh in his mind. "… with Corporal Dyer and asked if there was anything I could do because there were already two people working on him," he continues. "I took off my webbing and gave them my field dressing. They put the field dressing on his head, but Corporal Dyer was already basically past the point of saving. That's when I talked to the senior medic on the station and he said: 'No, he's gone. I'm going to move on to the next man just on the other side of him.'"

★ ★ ★

John Milton joined the Illinois Air National Guard in 1997, giving up the Navy for his family farm and United Airlines. He has been back on active duty since shortly after 9/11, helping the 170th spin up for deployment. Two days before his Al Jaber roommate dropped a bomb on Canadian paratroopers, Maj. Milton was the flight lead on the two-plane mission that dropped on—and missed—a pre-planned target in Iraq.

"My wingman thought he had picked up the target and I cleared him to drop on that and he missed about 150 feet short," Maj. Milton says, testifying in front of the U.S. accident board.

"Okay," Gen. Sargeant says. "And then what were the circumstances that only the wingman employed?"

"That was our game plan going in. Whoever picked up the target first would call 'captured.' We would talk back and forth to determine that we had the right one in the right spot and that was the way it was briefed."

"Okay. No re-attack option?"

"No, sir."

"Due to the threat?"

"No, sir," Maj. Milton says. "After the release, my opinion looking back is like, well, that was our chance. We dropped our, employed our two weapons and when I saw where his hits were and I thought that I was in the right spot and I was not picking up the target we were looking for, I executed our option to egress."

"In the post-battle damage assessment, were his bombs in fact within 150 feet of the real target or were they just 150 feet from something?"

"The perceived target."

"Real target or perceived target?"

"There was no target there."

"There was no target there?"

"Yes, sir."

"Can you describe how you debriefed that," Gen. Sargeant asks later. "And was that debrief shared with anyone besides just the two ships that went out?"

"Yes, sir. It so happened that General Buchanan was there that day. So I got to debrief with him personally. Coming back, we went through the whole mission, the tapes were played on the 17-inch screen, the big screen up there so everybody could see it, and we went through the debrief points on that ... It was in front of everyone. I also brought everybody in the next day and said: 'Hey, here is the things that I would have done better as a flight lead or the things I learned.' And hopefully passed that on, so we have a 'lessons learned' built up and then we could press on for the next mission."

⌣

"You're an experienced pilot," Gen. Sargeant says. "You're out there and you're at night, with all the limitations and capabilities of a pod, all limitations of the Mark-one eyeball, all the limitations and capabilities of goggles and putting them on, and you find yourself in a situation where you perceive there is a SAFIRE and you perceive initially that that may be AAA [anti-aircraft artillery], and you're in an altitude block of 15,000 feet. Describe to me what your defensive reaction is going to be when you perceive that altitude of that AAA is no higher than 10,000 feet. You've got 350 knots as a start and you're at 15,000 feet. What are you going to do?"

"Is it guided, barrage?" Maj. Milton asks, referring to the type of ground fire.

"It's just AAA."

"Just AAA coming up. I'm going to—"

"And you perceive the height of that AAA to be no higher than 10,000 feet," Gen. Sargeant adds. "And your starting parameters are 350 knots, 15,000 feet, and your flight lead is up at 24,000 feet. What are you going to do?

"One G flight, sittin' in here talking ..."

"You're just driving along and you look down, you go: 'I think I see some AAA.'"

"Being here, with the information obviously that we're going after right now: Light the wick and get out of town."

"You're going down to the deck? You're going straight and level? You're going up? What are you going to do?"

"I'm going to maneuver," Maj. Milton answers. "Every five to 10 seconds, I'm going to move the airplane and I'm going to try to get away from them."

"Okay. Again, your perception is, it's not even—it's below your altitude. You're at 15 and you're cruising, and your flight lead, for some reason, is up at 24,000 feet, what are you going to do as far as altitude-wise and airspeed-wise over the next couple of minutes?"

"I'm going to get fast and separate," Maj. Milton says.

"Do you train to slow down to 260 knots and start descending down to closer to 10,000 feet where you think the top of the AAA is and hover around there?"

"No, sir, we don't train to do that."

"Do you train to roll in it from 10,000 feet with that kind of airspeed and go below 10,000 feet to engage the perceived AAA?"

"No, sir, we don't train to do that."

"How would you characterize Major Umbach and Major Schmidt in terms of their capabilities and their professionalism?" Gen. Sargeant asks later.

"Major Umbach is a good officer and a good pilot," Maj. Milton says. "His leadership style is pretty well received by the other pilots and traditionals. He's involved, but he is not a micromanager or right in there directing every move that people make. But he is aware of what's going on and involved in the decision process. Major Schmidt is a great weapons officer. There's probably just a few people on the planet that have had more training than him between his Weapons School IP [instructor pilot] tours. He is extremely professional, driven. He's been a really great asset for us; we just got him in December. And he has helped us with a lot of our training, picking up our targeting pod training, and putting the Weapons School detail into our planning and our execution. Coming out of that environment he was really up to speed, and it's been great having him."

"Given Major Schmidt's stature on the squadron," Gen. Dumais asks, "what was his attitude with respect to the rest of the members? How did he display his experience? Was he sort of a cock of the walk, or was he sort of self-effacing or did he downplay that and—"

"He's a—I wouldn't call him a cock of the walk," Maj. Milton says. "He will definitely, if he sees something that is not right, he will try to correct it, sometimes with more tact than others, as we all do. But I would say he usually handles those problems fairly well."

"Is he a humble guy?" Gen. Sargeant asks.

"I wouldn't say he's—I don't know if I would describe him as humble. But I wouldn't describe him as overly cocky or arrogant either."

★ ★ ★

It is not quite noon when Gen. Baril and his team return to the Kandahar Airfield, escorted by a patrol of Coyotes down the windy brown road that connects the base to Tarnak Farm. They still have a full day of testimony ahead of them, but before moving on to the next witness on their list, they recall Capt. Jasper and Maj. Hackett to answer some follow-up questions. Outside their temporary office, a handwritten sign hangs on the blue door: "BOARD IN PROGRESS. DO NOT DISTURB."

"You have had some time to think about everything," Chief Warrant Officer Levesque says to Maj. Hackett. "Is there anything that could have happened to stop this from happening, something you could have had on the range?"

"I have thought about that often and I still can't think of anything that we on the ground could have done, bar some of the discussion today, knowing that perhaps our IR strobes had not registered for fast air," Maj. Hackett says. "We were using them extensively for aviation and other IFF at night. If there was something that could have worked better for someone flying at that altitude to mark friendlies, I suppose it would have been something that I would have had in place prior.

"We were training in a very established range close to an airfield that was restricted airspace at the best of times, which is why we are told to check fire all the time," he continues. "In fact, we sometimes joked that Tarnak Farm was far enough away from the airfield—we were always constantly checking fire—they were looking for reasons that were a little bit too far afield. I can't think of anything that would have prevented it, bar actually canceling the activity and not going."

"I guess it is difficult to imagine how an infantry company doing, call it 'routine training,' in a well-known training area would have the capability to coordinate with unknown patterns of fast air over an operational theater," Gen. Baril says.

"Yes, pretty much," Maj. Hackett answers.

"You have your battalion that is protecting your rear," the general says. "The brigade is protecting your rear, and a whole bunch of other echelons that should protect your rear from those incidents."

★ ★ ★

Colonel Robert J. Murphy joined the Air Force Academy at 17, following his older brother into the service. Active duty for seven and a half years. With the Air National Guard for 18, including his current post as commander of Springfield's 183rd Fighter Wing, where he has more than 30 pilots and 1,200 support staff under his nose. But despite all his years in a flight suit, this tour at Al Jaber is Col. Murphy's first-ever taste of combat.

"I'd like to describe a situation for you, and I'd like you to give me your tactical rundown and how you would react to it," Gen. Sargeant asks the colonel, who has been testifying in front of the American board for more than an hour now. "You're about 20,000 feet and your flight lead is up there too, you're the wingman, and you see something on the ground that you think might be AAA. Your flight lead actually sees it first. Then you see it. You're above 20,000 feet. Could you describe your reaction to that?"

"I'd take a look and see where it's going," says Col. Murphy, who, for a commander, is a rather soft-spoken man. "Is it coming at me? Is it going somewhere else? Can you see tracers? Is it pulling lead? Do I think I'm targeted? I don't know, and again I don't know the difference between 80 millimeter, 100 millimeter, 57 millimeter, 23 millimeter. All have altitudes associated with them and a 57 could pop you up in the low 20s, 80s or above, whether they got them or not. Again—"

"What do you expect to find in OEF [Operation Enduring Freedom]?" the general asks, cutting him off.

"I would not—I'd expect the smaller calibers. I don't expect 91s and 100 millimeter out there, okay. I wouldn't doubt they've got the capability to shoot some stuff that high whether it's rockets or AAA. I don't know every piece that they got."

"And in your judgment, with your night vision goggles on, after you donned them, you think the highest height to that AAA is 10,000 feet. Now you're about 20,000. Can you describe what type of actions you're going to do in relation to the ROE [rules of engagement] you're operating under?"

"I would be reluctant to give you that analysis sitting here at zero knots and one G," Col. Murphy says, using the fighter pilot slang for life on the ground. "I think that's a question that's been probably analyzed by people post-incident that weren't there that say: 'I wouldn't have done that.' But they weren't there. They didn't have the same perception and I'll guarantee you one thing: those guys did not drop—or that person—did not drop without a thought that they were targeted. And I'm the most sorry that people died. But he did what he thought was the right thing."

"I'm not asking you to cast judgment on what one of the individuals did on that flight," Gen. Sargeant says. "What I'm asking you is, given the perception that's been read out by that pilot that did drop, saying that he thinks that an AAA was no higher than 10,000 feet and he is above 20,000 and there is a 15,000-foot floor you're operating in, and there is a 10,000-foot ROE violation floor that you will not go down below, and there's a self-defense ROE that talks about a little prioritization of what you do unless you are actively engaged yourself. And I think it says: 'You will evade, flee, leave the area.'"

"No, I don't think so," Col. Murphy says. "It says: 'Under attack you have the right and obligation for self-defense.' If you're talking post-incident where it says: 'I envision no scenario where you couldn't exit the area, coordinate, re-attack with K-Mart,' that all came out post-incident. Read the SPINS [special instructions] from 1 April. It says: 'You have the right and the obligation to self-defense.'"

"Always," Gen. Sargeant says.

"Right."

"Always," the general says again. "Nobody is questioning that."

"All right."

"But in reading the SPINS and reading the ROE—"

"Proportional force, right?" Col. Murphy says.

"Proportional force is certainly there as well," Gen. Sargeant agrees. "The other thing, in reading it several times, is you leave. If given the opportunity, you leave. If you can't, then to protect yourself and to save your airplane, you engage."

"Correct," the colonel answers. "If you think you're going to get hit by your leaving, where are you? I think that would—I would hope you wouldn't ask other people that same question—but that's your right as the board president, but I think that's speculative on somebody's part that doesn't have the same perception looking down at the ground."

"What I'm trying to ask you right now is a training question by an F-16 pilot with a lot of hours and time in fighters."

"Right."

"And that's you," Gen. Sargeant says. "And it's also me."

"Right," Col. Murphy says. "And I can't tell you. I've never been shot at. I've never seen anything that I ever thought was going to hit, and I don't know how I'm going to react. Do you? And I'm not supposed to ask you questions. But I don't really know, if I thought my wingman was going to be blown up in five seconds, what I would do."

"If you were in a low-threat environment and you know the threat when you walk out the door as briefed and you have a mentality and you have 20,000 feet is where you're roaming—to be above 15 for sure, but you happen to be roaming at 20,000—I'm asking as an F-16 pilot, reaction-wise, are you going to slow down and descend down into the envelope or are you going to keep your smash and get your altitude to be above and move away until you sort out what you have?" Gen. Sargeant asks.

"I'm going to do everything to make myself a small target and then if I still think I'm targeted I'm going take actions in self-defense, sir. I think that's justified. I will try to make myself as small a target as possible, but if I still think somebody is going to get hurt, based on what I perceive is out there—and I don't know what the perception was, whether they thought it was big AAA or they thought it was rockets launched or some type of different ordnance coming up at them, I don't know. I don't know what the Russians left necessarily there that could reach that high. And I'm not sure we all know what's out there. I think that's perception you'll probably have to ask the person that took. And again I would question the mentality that would say: 'Boy that's what I would do because I know that.' Because you're sitting here, you're not there looking out the window moving that fast and under those situations."

14

Two weeks ago, Major Art Henry was aboard an AWACS radar plane, commanding the crew that was talking to Harry Schmidt and Bill Umbach as their F-16s circled over Tarnak Farm. Tonight, he is sitting inside a room at Oman's Thumrait Air Base, where his squadron is stationed in support of Operation Enduring Freedom. Gen. Sargeant, Gen. Dumais, and their team of investigators have flown here from Kuwait to talk to him.

This is not the first time that an AWACS crew member from Oklahoma's 552nd Air Control Wing has been grilled by an Air Force accident board. In April 1994, when two F-15 fighter jets accidentally shot down a pair of U.S. Army choppers over Iraq—killing 26 people—an AWACS radar officer, Captain Jim Wang, was the lone officer dragged in front of a court-martial. It's hard to imagine that that fact hasn't crossed Maj. Henry's mind at least once over the past two weeks.

"On the first occasion when he asked for the 20mm pass, I gave 'negative,'" Maj. Henry says. He is recalling the conversation he had with TSgt. Michael Carroll, the weapons director who was speaking directly to the pilots. "I'm not sure if I said it on the first occasion or the second occasion—I said to him 'friendlies in the vicinity of Kandahar,' so it was either the first or second occasion, and I did hear him say that over the radio. And on the third occasion when we said 'definitely no,' we used words to the effect 'K-Mart directs negative.'" (Again, K-Mart is the CAOC in Saudi Arabia.)

"On the first one, did you not say 'definitely no'?" Gen. Sargeant asks.

"We said 'definitely no,' but we didn't—I'm not sure if I amplified that with friendlies—but we definitely said, on the first occasion when he asked for 20mm, pass, 'negative.'"

"Would you have expected your weapons controller then to use the word 'standby' as a denial word?" Gen. Sargeant asks.

"No, sir."

"What would you have expected him to say?"

"Negative."

"Do you find the ACO usable in building your Ground Order of Battle situational awareness?" Gen. Sargeant asks.

"No, sir. Not—from the—no, sir. The ACO, as it was written then, did not contain a lot of the small-range activities, that sort of thing. We have found that there had been bits and pieces of information that were not known to us when we go to fly."

⌣

"Who prepared the mission material based on the ACO for your missions?" Gen. Dumais asks.

"Our mission planning team here, sir," Maj. Henry answers.

"Okay, so did you personally, before every mission, go through the ACO or the changes?"

"No, sir. We came in for the brief. We are briefed on it on the airplane and then we'll review the ACO on the aircraft. On the day in question, no, I did not go through the ACO with a fine-tooth comb. I took the brief, as briefed, which was our practice."

"Did you go back, after this incident, to review the ACO on the night of 17 April?" Gen. Sargeant asks.

"We reviewed it as soon as the incident was done to see if we had missed anything," Maj. Henry answers.

"Was the ROZ [restricted operating zone] at Tarnak Farms active?" the general asks him.

"We knew nothing about Tarnak Farms."

"Was the ROZ at Tarnak Farms established?"

"Not to my knowledge," Maj. Henry says. "It was not on the ACO that we flew with and we knew nothing about it."

⌄

"Among the crew, in the discussion post-event, was there any concern that you may have given the wrong guidance or said the wrong thing?" Gen. Dumais asks.

"That's been a very—very good thing," Maj. Henry answers. "Our leadership within the squadron, our [operations] group commander and our wing commander, have been nothing but supportive. We debriefed them as soon as we landed, and we, you know, we do the natural human thing. We say: 'Gee, maybe if I hadn't said that, this wouldn't have happened.' But we looked at it hard and fast and we can't come up with a reason or a thing that we could have done differently. And to put [it] in summary, no means no. You can't actually grab the stick and control the aircraft yourself."

"In one of the debrief items—because I know that's very important to your mission in making it better—one of the things we talked about earlier was the terminology used by your weapons director to 'standby,'" Gen. Sargeant says. "Would you change that terminology?"

"If he's seeking guidance, no," Maj. Henry answers. "If he's not sure of what the guidance ought to be, then 'standby' seems to work."

"Could you have made your guidance more clear to the weapons director when he requested your approval authority to pass to the crew?"

"Actually, sir, I haven't heard the tapes so I don't know exactly what the weapons director said to the aircraft."

"I have heard the tapes," Gen. Sargeant says. "And the tapes say: 'standby.'"

"Okay, so can you ask the question again, sir?" Maj. Henry asks.

"My question is, did you make it abundantly clear to the weapons director that you did not want this crew to drop?"

"Yes, sir."

"Therefore, should the weapons director have used a more directive term than 'standby?'"

"I can only assume that the 'standby' word—did the 'standby' word come about when the initial request was, came from the F-16?" Maj. Henry asks.

"The F-16 pilot requested to lay down 20 mike-mike," Gen. Sargeant says.

"And the controller then said 'standby'?" Maj. Henry asks.

"That's correct."

"Okay. At that point in time, then he was talking to me and asking for direction and then I passed the 'negative' and I assume then that the tapes reveal that he said negative after that? Is that…"

"Yes," says Gen. Dumais, the Canadian co-president.

"In which case—if that is indeed the scenario as it occurred on the radio—then no, I believe he said the right thing because he was seeking guidance from his superior."

⌣

"What was the nature of your communication with K–Mart?" asks Lieutenant-Colonel Joyce Adkins, the board's "human factors" advisor.

"After the first 20mm attack was requested, I denied it, and then I went to K–Mart and said that Coffee 51 requested a 20mm attack. They said 'negative,' and I replied 'WILCO' [Will Comply] and I pass that on as well."

"And that was all?" Lt.-Col. Adkins asks.

"At that point in time," Maj. Henry answers.

"Until the end, okay," she says.

"And then on subsequent requests, we reported a little bit more of the detail of what was going on. I'd have to see the transcripts. I can't remember off the top of my head, but I believe I gave them a better indication that there was some type of SAFIRE event happening with Coffee 51 Flight, that it was in the vicinity of Kandahar and they also have an air picture. They can see the tracks where this guy is so they can see the relevant location, relative location of the aircraft so they would have a fair understanding where they were as well."

"So you knew they were in the vicinity of Kandahar, but you didn't know exactly where?"

"Oh, yes," he says. "I knew exactly where the aircraft were relative to Kandahar. It appears on my console, and I knew, within a mile, where they were."

"Okay, okay," Lt.-Col. Adkins says. "I thought you said that you didn't know exactly where they were?"

"Who's they?"

"Flight Coffee 51."

"I knew where Coffee was," Maj. Henry says. "I was not sure where all the ground friendlies were."

"I see, okay."

"I just knew, instinctively, that Kandahar was an area where we did not expect al-Qaeda and that there was a lot of friendlies operating in that area, so Coffee Flight—I knew exactly where they were because we have a radar display that tells us that. The ground troops, no, I'm not sure where precisely they are, nor am I sure exactly where there's enemy movement."

"So you had definitive knowledge that there were friendlies in that area?" she asks.

"No."

"You just believed or had a gut-level feeling that there were friendlies in that area?"

"Correct."

"But you indicated at the end that you told them not to fire because there were friendlies in the area?"

"That's correct."

"But that was just your belief?"

"My belief."

"So you didn't know for sure that there were or who was there or where they were?"

"No, ma'am."

"Okay. Did you ever come to have that knowledge?"

"Oh, after the fact," Maj. Henry says.

"After the fact?"

"After the fact, yes," he says. "Obviously, with the press reports and that sort of thing and obviously, being a Canadian, it was very close to my heart to find out what happened. As soon as we landed, we found out there were Canadian troops killed."

"Your first 'negative,'" Gen. Sargeant says a few minutes later. "Did that include the reason why to your director, as in friendlies?"

"I don't recall, sir."

"Would you find that a significant piece of information to pass to a fighter?"

"Yes, sir, sure would," Maj. Henry says. "I don't recall if I said it on the first occasion or the second. I do know I remember saying 'friendlies in the vicinity of Kandahar,' but I can't recall if that was the first—the 20mm request—or if that was the second request, but you're—yes, that's correct. That's a very good piece of information to know."

"Did your controller pass that on the second response?" Gen. Sargeant asks.

"You'll have to ask him, sir. I heard him say it either on the first or the second. Once again, I can't ascertain whether that went out on the frequency or not."

"Do you think that information would have made a difference to a fighter with a 2,000-pound bomb strapped to his airplane?" Gen. Sargeant asks.

"It—don't know," Maj. Henry answers.

"I'm asking you now, under oath, if a fighter pilot who was about to drop a bomb on a SAFIRE event was told there were friendlies on the ground in that vicinity, would that have made a difference to the fighter pilot's decision, in your best estimation?"

"Yes, sir, that would make a difference."

Gen. Sargeant asks Captain Brian Turner, his board's F-16 advisor, to read the cockpit voice transcript from the night of the accident. "Yes, sir," Capt. Turner says, looking at the paper. "'Okay, BOSSMAN, this is Coffee 52. I've got a tally in the vicinity, I request permission to lay down some 20 mike-mike.' BOSSMAN: 'Standby.' Coffee 51—this is on Victor [VHF, a plane-to-plane frequency that the AWACS can't hear]: 'Let's just make sure it's not friendlies, that's all.'

"Now, I'll skip down to the next Uniform [UHF] transmission," Capt. Turner says. "This is from Coffee 52: 'BOSSMAN from Coffee 52. Do you want us to push to a different freq?' BOSSMAN: 'Coffee 51, BOSSMAN. Hold fire. Need details on SAFIRE.' Coffee 52: 'Okay, I've got some men on a road and it looks like a piece of artillery firing at us. I'm rolling in in self-defense.' BOSSMAN: 'BOSSMAN copies.' The Coffee 52 transmission—'SHACK'—it does not annotate which frequency. Coffee 52: 'BOSSMAN, BOSSMAN,' and then BOSSMAN comes back: 'Coffee 51, BOSSMAN. Disengage, friendlies Kandahar.' 'Copy. Disengaging south.' BOSSMAN: 'Coffee 51, BOSSMAN. How copy?' Coffee 51: 'Copy, can you confirm that they were shooting at us?'"

"Okay, you can stop there, please," Gen. Sargeant says. "As I count, there's one denial by the word 'standby.' The next denial is a 'hold' call with no amplification as to why. The next call comes from Coffee 52 who says:

'I'm rolling in exercising my right to self-denial' *[sic]*. What would that mean to you?"

"That he felt threatened, that he was invoking his right to self-defense," Maj. Henry says.

"Is he going to expend weapons?" the general asks.

"If he's rolling in, yes."

"Therefore," Gen. Sargeant says, "what would be the appropriate response from your weapons director who you have said now on at least one occasion 'there are friendlies in Kandahar' as to the—and you have issued 'negative'—was it an appropriate response for him to come back and say 'copy'?"

"If he's invoking his right to self-defense, no," Maj. Henry says. "We can't fly the jet for him and if he's—we have no way of ascertaining how dire it is out there so if he is rolling in, my controller, I'm guessing, is letting him use his self-defense ROE."

"Would it have been more appropriate to say: 'Coffee 52, friendlies in the vicinity. Negative, negative, negative. Abort, abort, abort,' or something of that nature: 'Friendlies in the vicinity'?"

"If he gave the words 'negative' or 'hold fire' and 'friendlies in the vicinity' at least once—"

"'Friendlies in the vicinity' was never relayed in the transcript that you just heard read to you," Gen. Sargeant says.

"Okay."

"Was that a critical bit of information that needed to be passed to the crews if you did not want them to drop a bomb in the vicinity of the friendlies, in your gut check, that you knew immediately when your weapons director first asked you about 20 mike-mike expenditures?"

"That would have been an important piece of information, yes, sir," Maj. Henry says.

"Excuse me?"

"Yes, that would have been an important piece of information for him to pass: 'Negative and friendlies in the vicinity,' to consolidate that in one transmission."

★ ★ ★

"I had to go to the bathroom," Captain David Pepper says. "We were like six hours of on-station time at this point. So I ran to the back real quick. Came back up, I stood next to a tank—Sergeant Carroll was sitting tank controller. 'Anything happening?' He goes: 'Yeah, we just had a SAFIRE event.' So I ran and grabbed my headset and sat down."

Capt. Pepper was the senior director in the AWACS that night, a notch below Maj. Henry in the crew's chain of command. "So the next thing I knew is I had his frequency up and he was requesting permission to fire on, fire 20-millimeter, and I pulled out the internal net, said: 'negative,' and the MCC [Maj. Henry] is saying: 'negative' at the same time. Sergeant Carroll repeated immediately: 'negative.' We passed that up to K-Mart or Major Henry, MCC, passed that up to K-Mart that they're requesting to fire and it came back 'negative.' At this time multiple things were going on at once, but the fighters were requesting permission to engage. He said 'negative' again, 'standby, negative,' just basically telling him 'no.' Asked K-Mart. K-Mart came back: 'Negative, friendlies in the area.' We passed that off. Once again they requested to engage. We told him 'no.' Somewhere in there, either myself or the MCC said: 'Hey, self-defense is never denied.' And I told Sergeant Carroll: 'Negative, they're not cleared to engage unless self-defense.' Copy. A couple more seconds, told them to scram south. They turned around and worked south. At that point we started gathering information and we asked: 'Hey, did you drop anything?' and they said: 'Yeah, we dropped a single GBU-12, direct hit.'"

"How would you describe the state, the atmosphere in the back of that AWACS during that SAFIRE event?" Gen. Sargeant asks.

"It was really relatively straightforward, sir. I don't know, calm and we were obviously interested in what was going on, but we weren't stressed or anything like that. It's a common thing."

"You all came back fairly quickly with the 'negative,'" Gen. Sargeant says. "Both you and the mission commander both said 'negative' on the first request?"

"Yes, sir."

"Did you state a reason that you were so emphatic about a 'negative'?"

"Like we talked about earlier, sir, you're not dropping bombs without K-Mart's approval. And that is just kind of a—something I've learned, I guess, over the couple years is you're never just going to throw out dropping bombs, giving permission to drop."

"So do you know what the weapons director [TSgt. Carroll] said to the crew at that point?" Gen. Sargeant asks. "What word he used or words he used?"

"I had the frequency up, sir. I can't remember the exact words, I'm sure it was 'negative' because like I said I monitored that, it was what I told him. He's—the entire time it flowed really well. Like I said, he's very experienced, he said exactly what I told him to say. And I never had to go back and correct him. So—"

Gen. Sargeant takes out the cockpit transcript and begins reading it to Capt. Pepper. *Permission to lay down some 20 mike-mike. Standby. Do you want us to push a different freq? Hold fire. I'm rolling in in self-defense.*

"Now," Gen. Sargeant says. "You've talked about the weapons director passing your words verbatim. This is actually on tape. Does that help clarify what you heard that night that your weapons director relayed?"

"Sir, I heard the 'men on the road' and 'artillery piece,'" Capt. Pepper says. "I never heard him say 'rolling in,' and talking to Sergeant Carroll, I don't think—he's never mentioned that either. We've discussed it before, so—"

"As far as critical information to pass to the crew, is 'standby' a typical term, an accepted term for a firm denial?" the general asks.

"No, sir," the captain says. "'Standby' is 'we need to get information.' It's 'you're not cleared until we get information.'"

"Then when they come back and make another request: 'Coffee 51, BOSSMAN, hold fire. Need details for SAFIRE.' Is that a definite standard way of denying employment of weapons?"

"'Hold fire,' sir? Yes, sir."

"Was there any critical information that should have been passed by this point to the crew?" Gen. Sargeant asks.

"Pardon me, sir, which—"

"On the second denial, was there any information known up on the AWACS, amongst the AWACS crew, that should have been passed to fighters to build their situational awareness?"

"No, sir. Not that I know of."

"Was there a reason that you were emphatic about 'negative?'"

"Simply because I never give authorization to drop bombs without someone's approval," Capt. Pepper says. "I cannot—as AWACS, I cannot give anyone permission to drop bombs."

"Did you hear your mission crew coordinator [Maj. Henry], at any point up until now, discuss the reason he was saying 'negative' was because there were friendlies in the vicinity of Kandahar?"

"No, sir. He never said anything along those lines. I remember hearing that from K-Mart."

"The mission commander never spoke the word 'friendlies' in relation to his reason for saying 'negative'?"

"No, sir. We just said: 'Negative, negative, friendlies in Kandahar.' I don't know if that came from mission crew commander. I thought it came from K-Mart and then he repeated it to me. I can't remember for sure which one it came off of."

"How did you perceive the event unfolding on this SAFIRE as far as timing-wise?" Gen. Sargeant asks.

"I don't understand your question, sir."

"Was it happening slowly, very controlled, or was it happening quickly?"

"These were happening very quickly, sir."

"With a sense of urgency?"

"Not really urgency," Capt. Pepper says. "Just the requests were coming out to engage. We were passing that to K-Mart telling them 'no.'"

"Did you have a sense that these fighters were getting ready to employ ordnance?" the general asks.

"No, sir. I had the sense these fighters were getting fired upon and were very concerned about it. But I did not know they were about to employ ordnance."

"When a fighter has requested to employ ordnance twice within a very short period of time, do you think he is more worried about defending himself, or that he is about to employ ordnance?"

"Sir, I didn't have time to think about it that way," Capt. Pepper says. "I just—he was worried he was—I figured if he was defensive at that point, he was worried about his own skin, he could easily run away."

"Given the complexity of the ACO, did the thought [of] friendlies in the area ever cross your mind as a reason to say no?" the general asks.

"No, sir."

"Did anyone on that crew say the word 'friendlies' as a reason to say 'negative'?"

"As I said earlier, sir, I can't remember if that came from K–Mart or specifically the MCC," Capt. Pepper says. "My understanding was it came from K–Mart in response to one of the questions: 'Negative, friendlies in the area.' I did not have any feeling that they were friendlies. The pilots were talking about being—they were, felt very stressed at the time. They felt they were being fired upon. My initial take was, there's no way that there would be a live-fire exercise in the middle of a war zone without someone telling us, so these got to be bad guys. Especially with intel constantly briefing that there's bad guys everywhere."

⌣

"I have one more question," Gen. Dumais says, near the end of the interview. "Because the AWACS is a critical link in the command-and-control chain for this kind of operation, what do you think should be improved in your procedures to enhance the passing of critical information to the fighters in their cockpits?"

"I think the biggest thing, sir, is making sure we have the information," Capt. Pepper answers. "We had no idea that there was a live-fire exercise going on. Like I also said, there was a live-fire zone right there. If we had known that, it could have solved a lot of problems. The passing of information within AWACS went smoothly, I felt. It's a matter of how much information we have. The Special Forces guys especially out here don't want us to know pretty much anything they're doing. And that's been a bone of contention there since I got here. It's just make sure we have the information to pass."

"In hindsight," Gen. Dumais asks, "do you feel there was information on friendlies that was available, but that—or that existed and that was available—but that you did not have in your possession on board the aircraft?"

"Someone had to know that they were doing a live-fire exercise there. Whatever Army liaison officer at K–Mart that should have passed that up, or if K–Mart had it and it didn't get to us. I don't know. But I assume someone had to know that that live-fire exercise was going on. We did not."

★ ★ ★

It is approaching midnight by the time TSgt. Michael Carroll sits down with Gen. Sergeant, Gen. Dumais, and the other investigators. He was BOSSMAN on April 17, the AWACS tanker controller speaking to Harry Schmidt and Bill Umbach over the radio. "As far as I can remember, they wanted permission to use 20 mike-mike," he says. "I think I replied 'standby.' I talked to, passed that on to the mission crew commander that they wanted permission because all this coordination has to go through the CAOC down to the ground and then back up through the mission crew commander and then normally to the senior director. But since the senior director—I don't know exactly when the senior director sat down, I don't exactly know when he did, but he did sit down shortly after that. They came back from the CAOC with 'negative,' so I went on the radio and said 'negative.' Shortly after that, I can't remember exactly how it went—like I said, it was a while ago—they came over the radio and said, this was my senior director and MCC came over and said: 'Tell him hold fire, negative, friendlies at Kandahar.' And that's what I passed over the radio. I'm not sure exactly how many times I said 'negative.' It was at least two to three times: 'Negative, hold fire.'"

"Did you hear a call about them saying 'men on the road' and 'rolling in in self-defense'?" Gen. Dumais asks later.

"No, sir."

"You didn't hear that call?"

"No, sir. I remember them—I remember me passing only in self-defense, I can't remember exactly how I worded it. 'Hold fire, negative unless in self-defense.' And then—"

"But you don't recall them calling that they were going to engage because they were declaring self-defense?" Gen. Dumais asks.

"No, sir, I did not hear that."

"So you never heard the pilot declare he was going to employ under the self-defense rules?"

"No, sir."

"What was your sense of the urgency of the situation as it was unfolding?" Gen. Sargeant asks.

"My sense of urgency? For me as a tanker controller I wasn't, I was figuring it was a—we had some other SAFIRE reports before when I was strike controller, so I was just waiting for a mark. That's originally what they're supposed, go out there and mark, so my pencil was in my hand. My paper was there. I was ready to write down some coordinates so I could pass that through my senior director so they could pass it on to K-Mart."

"How about the sense of urgency or concern in mission crew commander as this particular SAFIRE was unfolding?"

"Really, everyone wasn't really that wound up," TSgt. Carroll says. "I mean, everyone was relaxed. The information flow was working well and, like I said, I was voicing exactly what was coming over on my Net 2 from the senior director."

"The senior director comm was working good?"

"Yes, sir."

"How about your sense of the urgency inside the cockpits as the radio calls were coming to you?" Gen. Dumais asks.

"It didn't seem like—it didn't seem like he was threatened in any way. I didn't really hear any urgency in his voice, anything out of the ordinary."

"Did you think he was going to drop imminently?" Gen. Sargeant asks.

"No, sir."

"Did you think he understood that you didn't want him to drop?"

"Yes, sir."

⌣

"When you went to fly that night, did you have a feel for where friendlies were in relation to Kandahar?" Gen. Sargeant asks.

"No, sir," TSgt. Carroll answers.

"Did you have a feel for where friendlies were in Afghanistan?"

"No, sir, because when they give our briefs in here, they tell of different pockets of where all the possible al-Qaeda are, but usually they can't pinpoint where all the friendly forces are at. That's why we do all of our coordination through K-Mart and they can call the different agencies and find out where all these, where all our friendlies are at."

⌣

"I'm looking at the radio call that 'men on the road' and 'artillery' and then 'I'm rolling in in self-defense' that came out of Coffee 52 and then you answered: 'BOSSMAN copies,'" Gen. Sargeant says. "Can you explain how—"

"Yeah, I can't remember," TSgt. Carroll says. "I don't remember him saying this exactly: 'Rolling in in self-defense.' I do not remember that call."

"Were other people yelling at you in the headset with information?"

"There's people calling me on Net 2, like I said, the SD and the senior director, all the coordination comes through them on Net 2. So I'm listening to them and I'm listening to the radio. So I very well have, you know—it says there that I came out and said: 'BOSSMAN copies.' Usually that's, you know, either that or just 'BOSSMAN' when they make calls to me. So, I did not hear 'in self-defense,' so—I definitely did not hear that."

"Based on the flow of the communication at this point, when would you give—just tell me your best, to your best recollection—when you were told there were: 'Negative, friendlies in the vicinity of Kandahar,' and by whom?" Gen. Sargeant asks.

"I was told when I voiced it on the radio, so whenever it was on the recording, that's when—when I find out there's friendlies in Kandahar, that's when I voiced it because that information, like I said, comes through Net 2 on the radio and whatever they voice me to say, I voiced it."

"Do you pretty much voice what the senior director or the MCC tell you to do?"

"Yes, sir. The senior director is my boss, so if he gives commands to say something, that's the way we're taught—we repeat."

"If you asked the mission crew commander about the 20 mike-mike—"

"Yes, sir."

"If he said the word 'negative,' what would you have said to the crew?" the general asks.

"What I have said to Coffee 51?"

"Yes."

"BOSSMAN, negative, negative."

Colonel David Nichols has been waiting to have this conversation. Ever since that morning on the tarmac, when he watched Harry Schmidt fall to his knee, the commander of the 332nd Air Expeditionary Group has been anxious to tell investigators why *he* thinks four Canadian soldiers are dead. Maybe now the Air Force brass will start listening to his criticisms. Maybe now his pilots will start getting some useful intel about where all the friendlies are in Afghanistan.

"How did you see the threat level in the OEF mission?" asks General Marc Dumais, the Canadian co-president of the American investigation board.

"I still say it's very high," answers Col. Nichols, who has been testifying for nearly half an hour now. "But the problem with the threat level in OEF is it's everywhere and it's nowhere at the same time."

At the beginning of the war, he says, he and his pilots took AAA fire all the time. But lately, it's been tougher to sort through the legitimate SAFIRE reports and false alarms, such as Afghanis firing in the air to celebrate a wedding. "When you put survival at the top of your list of things, then that pretty much drives your thought process," Col. Nichol continues. "So, we do have that. 'He does come home alive' is the thought process."

"Can you expand a little bit more on the survival aspect of the ROE [rules of engagement] in the commander's intent?" Gen. Dumais asks.

"Well, you always have the right to self-defense, if that's what you're getting at," Col. Nichols says. "And that stays current and I think, as war fighters in a 'bad-guy land,' that should never be taken from us or we shouldn't go is the bottom line there."

"Can you be specific in defining the self-defense ROE as written?" Gen. Sargeant asks.

"Yeah, currently as written it has to be proportional and it has to be 'no kidding' self-defense. And it's changed recently."

"What was it on 17 April?" Gen. Sargeant asks.

"You have the right of self-defense," the colonel answers. "It needs to be proportionate and you need to make sure that the self-defense is warranted, I think were the words."

"What was your first line of defense against a threat?"

"Depends on how you analyze that threat. If you think it's threatening you or anyone in your formation, you have to maneuver your airplane properly: get away. But if you can't get away, then you have to engage it."

As the questioning continues, Col. Nichols tells investigators how Operation Anaconda was a "disaster," how the Air Force was flying close air support (CAS) missions with some crews who had never been trained to drop bombs anywhere near friendly forces. The mountain was also littered with so many different ground controllers and air controllers that pilots were never sure who was actually in charge. The colonel recalls that one memorable mission when a B-52 almost unleashed a J-DAM right through his formation. And all the while, he says, nobody seemed to have a solid idea of where the ground forces were—let alone where they were going to be in a couple of hours.

"Could you ever get additional information on the Ground Order of Battle from AWACS?" Gen. Sargeant asks.

"No. No," Col. Nichols says. "We often asked."

"Was it frustrating to work with AWACS?"

"Yes."

"How would you characterize most of your operations with AWACS after Anaconda?"

"You're looking for a characterization word?" Col. Nichols asks back. "The word I would use in a scale of 'outstanding' to 'terrible' would be 'competent.'"

"You talked about the documents that your people use in mission planning and execution," Lt.-Col. Joyce Adkins says later in the interview. "And I believe that you talked about the ACO?"

"Right," Col. Nichols says.

"And I think you said that was a very important document?"

"Yes."

"What do you perceive as the opinion of your fliers of the ACO?"

"That's a good question. It's too long and too complicated, and it isn't what I call single-seat proofed or fighter-pilot proofed in that it requires prioritization, all 46 pages of it ... The user scenario for the ACO is very difficult, but Task View helps that."

"How often would you expect your fliers to read the ACO?" Lt.-Col. Adkins asks.

"Weekly."

"Weekly?"

"Yes."

"Not prior to every mission?"

"No, it's not possible," Col. Nichols says. "It's not possible."

"You did mention that there's some information that's not available," she says. "And I think one of the things that you mentioned was not available was information about ground forces. I think you said you don't know about ground forces until you get there, right?"

"Correct," he says.

"And then once you get there, how do you find out then?"

"Look out the window."

"So you have to rely on seeing them?"

"Rely on seeing them or rely on whatever you are getting out of this convoluted command-and-control network."

"On April 17th, when did you learn about the nature of the ground forces involved in that incident?" Lt.-Col. Adkins asks.

"When did I learn about them?"

"Right."

"As soon as I got the phone call from General Wood."

"General Wood called you?"

"Yeah."

"What did he say about the ground forces?"

"He said there was a friendly fire incident. 'Your guys were involved.' That's what he said, and then I came back. And our mission directors plot—they listen to the SATCOM [satellite communication] and plot everything. So then we called up the FalconView and I knew right where it was. I knew there was a small-arms range there, but the truth of the matter is I never put that small-arms range on mine. I just know what's going on in Kandahar."

"So you knew there was a small-arms range there?"

"As a guy flying GBUs around at 20,000 feet, small arms to me means nine millimeters in the side of a sand hill."

"That small-arms range was on FalconView when you pulled it up that night after General Wood called you?" Gen. Sargeant asks.

"No, it wasn't. On TaskView."

"TaskView?"

"TaskView. If you click it, it would come up on the ACO."

"So you had to click it and it would show?"

"It would—"

"And that night it did show when you looked?"

"It's in the ACO, yes," the colonel says, referring to the Restricted Operating Zone (ROZ) around Tarnak Farm. "What I did is I went to the mission materials. What we do is we save the mass brief for the execution of the ATO [air tasking order] time so the mission director—it was not in the mission materials—but when I went back over and turned on Task View, I just turned it on and 'click-click-click,' and went through the things I normally do and it was in."

"Thank you," Gen. Sargeant says.

"And when did you learn that it was a live-fire exercise, not nine millimeters?" Lt.-Col. Adkins asks.

"I learned it was a live-fire exercise from the newspaper," Col. Nichols replies.

"Not till the next day?"

"No, it was days after that. No, in fact, you are the first authoritative organization that has told me it was a live-fire exercise."

"Well, I actually don't know," Lt.-Col. Adkins says.

"It was not in the ACO?" Gen. Sargeant asks.

"No."

"It was not in the verbiage text of the ACO?"

"It was live—it [said] 'small arms range'—active from, I think, the day prior to the day after. The rule was they contacted Kandahar tower for activation to the range. That was the blurb that I had on the thing."

⌣

"What would you say are the lessons learned from this for your operation here, as a result of April 17th?" Lt.-Col. Adkins asks.

"That's a great question," Col. Nichols answers. "And the lesson learned is obviously make sure—there's really two big ones—make sure that when you are employing in self-defense that it is, in fact, self-defense. That's the first one. But goodness—I say that as an experienced guy and the commander—that is a tough thing to say out loud because, given the situation, I very well may have done the exact same thing. Others may have done the same thing. Others may have taken it differently so I don't know the answer to that, but the real lesson learned, I hope that comes out of it, is across the board from, no kidding, the CINC [commander-in-chief] perspective and especially at the component level that we are sharing information and trust among one another so that we share information and that way we can support each other. There's a lot of examples other than this where the sharing of information would have helped, and I don't think it's—I don't think anybody out there at the planner level on a land component side or a naval component side or an air component side wakes up in the morning and says: 'I'm not going to share information today.' I think what happens is they wake up and say: 'I have an operation which I am responsible for today,' so boom, like all of us, they get focused and they forget about the fact that there are special ops guys. There are air guys. There are naval guys. There are all these other pieces to this joint coalition puzzle that need to go. So I think the lesson is bigger than my organization."

⌣

"Is it safe to say that of all the pilots in the squadron, Major Schmidt, as the MPC [Mission Planning Cell] chief, would have been the most well-versed in the ACO?" Gen. Sargeant asks.

"Yes," Col. Nichols says.

"Daily changes as well as weekly?"

"Yes, sir."

"And if you were the most well-versed in the ACO, would you have the best understanding in the squadron of where the friendlies were and where the enemies were?"

"You'd think that, if where the friendlies and enemies were known or available."

"The best tool you had was the ACO in this theater?" Gen. Sargeant asks.

"Yes, sir. However, the best tool we have is now self-retrieved out of the CFLCC [Coalition Forces Land Component Commander] web page and the CENTCOM web page and by having a Marine in Camp DOHA and a—"

"But," Gen. Sargeant interrupts, "the MPC chief had all those tools available to him, had that interaction with the Marines, and Schmidt was the go-between with the Marines?"

"Yes, sir, but we were still—yes, sir." Col. Nicholos says. As he tries to elaborate, Gen. Sargeant interrupts again: "Maj. Schmidt was your main person in the 170th Fighter Squadron?"

"Yes, sir."

"And having that information and disseminating that information to the pilots?"

"Yes, sir."

"So, given the talented flier that you described earlier, he should have had the highest situational awareness?"

"Yes, sir."

"Of anyone stepping to fly that night?"

"Yes, sir."

"In the 170th Fighter Squadron?"

"Yes sir, without question," Col. Nichols says. "When I went to bed, that's what I believed. I said: 'Here's a good flight.'"

⌣

"Have you re-characterized the threat for the 170th Fighter Squadron, post 17 April?" Gen. Sargeant asks.

"Yes, we put ... re-characterized, I don't think ... my biggest concern is complacency and it still is complacency."

"I'm specifically asking about the threat on the ground to the crews," the general says. "Are you still at the 'very high' level?"

"No," Col. Nichols says. "I don't use those words. I say that the threat still exists, and that they have to be aware and that there are really three phases of an OEF mission—getting there, flying the mission, and then getting home. Those are the three phases. In flying the mission, I want them active, I want them engaged and the expression I use is—I don't know if you've heard it yet or not—but I say: 'I want their fangs out with their brain in their lap.' When the fangs touch the top of the brain, something's wrong. You're a little too aggressive, but I don't want you in there, kind of—you know how you can get on a long mission. I want you focused and if you don't feel you are focused, I want you to tell BOSSMAN that you want to leave, you need to get home."

"You mentioned self-defense earlier and making sure the pilots knew that they were really in a self-defense situation," Gen. Sargeant says. "Could you expand on that a little bit in relation to Maj. Schmidt's actions on the night of 17 April?"

"That's a tough one because you just never know what he saw out the window," Col. Nichols says. "I heard what he described. But I always make sure the guys have the right for self-defense and they carry that with them. In the process, I said: 'Make sure that it is self-defense and make sure that—'"

"Could you specifically answer my question, though, in relation to what Maj. Schmidt did that night and how he reacted from the starting point of about 22,000 feet until the time that he ended up employing his munitions?" Gen. Sargeant says. "Did he do things that exacerbated the situation, that forced him into a self-defense situation, in your professional opinion?"

"I would say yes, and it looks to me like what he was doing is he was trying to maintain awareness of whatever it was on the ground and his flight lead because they were in what I call a SADL [situational awareness data link] formation and that's the thing that maybe made him think that way because they had their lights on dim so they were flying in a data-link formation kind of a little far away from each other so, Gen. Sargeant, I could say yes, his—the maneuvering of his airplane could have exacerbated the self-defense."

"It appeared his flight lead stayed above 22,000 or thereabouts for the entire engagement, if you will, and Maj. Schmidt rapidly descended down below 10,000 feet, which is an ROE bust, as I understand it, and there was never a flight lead call," the general says. "Is that what you would expect out of a normal flight lead monitoring a wingman with NVGs available at night?"

"I don't think the flight lead had a visual on his wingman. What it looked like was—or when—my reconstruction in my mind was is the wingman got very concerned very fast about the scenario and assumed he had a little more awareness, situational awareness, than the flight lead, is what I think happened."

"Did the flight lead maintain sufficient control of that flight, in your mind?"

"I wasn't there."

"You've heard the tapes?"

"I've heard the tapes. I wasn't there. He did make some comments, some timely comments, and I don't think he had as much information as the wingman did at the time."

"Did he aggressively pursue an avenue to fill in the lack of SA?" Gen. Sargeant asks.

"Listening to the tapes, no," Col. Nichols says. "Listening to the tapes, I don't think he did. Again, though, it's difficult to say."

After more than an hour of questions, the board dismisses Col. Nichols. "You are reminded of the official nature of this interview," Lt.-Col. Walker, the board's legal advisor, tells him. "You may not discuss your testimony, our questions, or the subject matter of this investigation with anyone, without the express permission of this board, at any time before the Report of Investigation is officially released to the public. And, sir, I'm going to have to have your notes, too."

"It's just your names and that great picture I drew," Col. Nichols says, referring to a diagram he scribbled for investigators earlier in his testimony.

"The other thing I would add," Gen. Sargeant says, "since earlier you pretty much indicated this is the first type of investigation like this you're involved in, many people will ask you how it went and that sort of thing. Just friendly advice—"

"I'll tell them it was fun. How's that?"

"How about if you just say: 'I can't talk to you about it until it's released publicly.'"

"Okay," Col. Nichols says. "That's fair."

★ ★ ★

Gen. Baril and his team are in Dubai, a stopover on their way home to Ottawa, when an American military courier arrives with the first batch of data—three binders and a few CDs—compliments of Gen. Sargeant and the U.S. Air Force. Gathered in a hotel room, the Canadian board huddles around Colonel Greg Matte as he slides one of the discs into the side of his laptop computer. Nobody says a word as the targeting pod videos—the cockpit recordings from the night of the attack—flash onto the screen.

They hear the heavy breathing. *20 mike-mike. Standby. Let's just make sure it's not friendlies. Hold fire. I'm rolling in in self-defense.* They can see the wadi in the center of the grainy videos, the shadows of 3 Section nearing the end of their exercise. They see that tiny dot—Marc Léger—walking into the invisible crosshairs of a laser-guided bomb. *Shack.*

16

Colonel Charles McGuirk was sitting in the Crow's Nest on that night, at the elevated desk in the middle of the CAOC floor. It has the perfect view, 360 degrees. You can see the huge digital display on the wall, that one that shows the location of every single plane flying over Afghanistan. On all sides of the nest, dozens of radar controllers and liaison officers, headsets on, are working the radios in support of those blinking planes. If not for all the uniforms and the computers, the CAOC floor in Saudi Arabia could easily be mistaken for a noisy restaurant during the dinner rush. As Director of Combat Operations (DCO), Col. McGuirk was the senior man on the floor when Major Art Henry—the AWACS commander—called in Maj. Schmidt's request to attack the unidentified ground fire with his 20mm cannons.

"After it happened it seemed like it was probably about a 60- or 90-second evolution from the time I had visibility on what was occurring," Col. McGuirk tells the American board of investigators, who arrived in Saudi Arabia yesterday, May 4. "I was up in the Crow's Nest, actually working a CENTCOM e-mail ... The CCO [Chief of Combat Operations] at the time, Lt.-Col. Fisher, looked over at me and asked me if I was hearing this and I said 'no.' He said, whatever the call sign, is saying they are being engaged by AAA [anti-aircraft artillery]."

"Would that have been Coffee 51?" Gen. Sargeant asks.

"Coffee 51, and I did jot down some notes after the fact that I have with those kind of details, but I asked him then: 'Is he under control of the GFAC?'" Col. McGuirk says, referring to a ground forward air controller, a soldier on the ground who passes targeting coordinates to fighter pilots. "And he said 'no' and I said: 'Well, tell him to get out of there then.' And he turned and then looked back and he said: 'He has declared self-defense.' We both looked at each other in a 'not sure what that means' kind of look, and then got word that he had released a weapon. And then we just began trying to get information as to where it was, where the release was, SAFIRE details."

"On that night, would you have expected fighters to have encountered a threat that would have forced them into a defensive posture, given the altitudes and the enemy order of battle?" Gen. Sargeant asks.

"No," Col. McGuirk answers. "I would not have."

"You were fairly adamant that you said: 'Tell him to get out of there,'" says Gen. Dumais, the board's Canadian co-president.

"Yes."

"On what basis were you able to make such a prompt assessment?"

"If he's indicating he's taking AAA fire, we don't want them around that area."

"Did the ROE [rules of engagement] lay that out?" Gen. Sargeant asks.

"The ROE would allow you to engage if you know it's Taliban or al-Qaeda, if you are threatened in a self-defense deal. But you can't do it in retaliation after the fact."

"Were you aware that there was a friendly fire exercise going on in that area?" Lt.-Col. Adkins asks later.

"No, I was not aware of a friendly fire exercise going on," Col. McGuirk says.

"A live-fire exercise, to clarify the question," Gen. Sargeant says. The answer is still no.

"Would you normally be aware of that detail?" Lt.-Col. Adkins asks.

"I would say no," the colonel says. "We had limited visibility on actual training exercises that were going on, or at least my awareness of it."

"Was that data contained in the ACO, to the best of your knowledge?" Gen. Sargeant asks.

"Not with specific times," Col. McGuirk says. "And in particular, Tarnak Farms was kind of an open-ended deal to contact Kandahar tower to determine if the range was hot or not."

"So you weren't aware of that level of detail," the general says. "Who would have been aware of that?"

"I don't know of anybody in the CAOC that would have been aware, other than potentially the BCD, if they were."

★　★　★

The BCD, the Battlefield Coordination Detachment, has one overriding job: to keep Air Force staff in the CAOC up to speed on the location of friendly ground troops. Staffed with Army officers, the BCD gets its intel directly from the office of the Coalition Forces land component commander (CFLCC), the Army general who runs the Afghanistan ground war. The BCD occupies its own little corner on the CAOC floor. If anyone has a question, they just yell "BCD!" and someone runs right over. It's how Major Jacqueline Bagby spends her graveyard shift.

"Can you describe your relationship with CFLCC prior to 17 April as far as the amount of interaction that you had with them?" Gen. Sargeant asks her.

"Sir, once CFLCC-Forward got on the ground, we interact pretty much, I guess, depending on what's going on as far as missions that are out there," Maj. Bagby says. "But we get updates from them and [are] constantly getting fed information from them, and I'm calling them for updates continually throughout my shift, if that's what you're asking."

"How about with training exercises in the field—because units have to stay qualified and current—on the amount of information that you receive on live-fire training, for instance, pre- and post-17 April?"

"Sir," she answers, "Post-17 April has been more vigilantly reported probably. Before that there may have been things going on that we didn't necessarily know, ranges open and things of that nature, but I just don't remember it being an issue before."

★　★　★

"How would you rate the coordination of ground activities to the CAOC as far as announcement of ground activity?" Gen. Sargeant asks.

"Well, I, to be very honest with you, I have thought it was very good."

Brigadier-General Stephen G. Wood has spent his fair share of time inside a fighter jet: more than 3,000 hours, including 49 combat missions during Operation Desert Storm, the first Gulf War. On April 17, he was the top officer in the CAOC, sitting up in the glass Battle Cab that overlooks the main floor. If a fighter pilot wants to open fire on an unknown target, ultimate approval rests with Gen. Wood.

"Okay," Gen. Sargeant asks. "If there were a SAFIRE event reported, outside of an area that you were tasked on a mission to provide coverage for, how would you expect K-Mart [the CAOC] and BOSSMAN [the AWACS radar plane] to interact with an aircrew that calls in a SAFIRE and requests to employ [ordinance]?"

"I would tell them to withhold, to, negative on employing," Gen. Wood answers. He explains that unlike in conventional wars, there are no advancing troops in Afghanistan. No FLOT (forward line of own troops). No FEBA (forward edge of battle area). No FSCL (fire support coordination line). "You have threats," he continues. "It can be anywhere if you assume the worst case. ... We do not know who is good guy and who is bad guy. Who is friendly green, in regards to Afghani? If it's Afghani tribal-on-tribal? So, we do a very detailed vetting process inside the CAOC when we ask someone that wants, that believes they're threatened, or believes that they have seen something on the ground, with it. And this has happened very, very few times, to be honest with you, where I've ever had anyone that wanted to engage a target on the ground or reported something, because we just can't tell who is good and who is bad."

"Could you, in your own words, explain to us your understanding of this self-defense ROE?" Gen. Dumais asks later.

"Yes, I can, with it," Gen. Wood answers. "I wish I had it to speak to it to you because—"

"We will, we can bring the ROE to the table," Gen. Sargeant interjects.

"Well, the only reason I would do that to you is that, in the ROE, every word matters," Gen. Wood says.

Lt.-Col. Walker, the board's legal advisor, stands up and retrieves a copy of the rules of engagement that were in effect on the night of April 17, 2002. He places it on the table in front of Gen. Wood. "Okay," Gen. Sargeant says. "And take your time referring to the documents."

"I have a … I'm looking through here," Gen. Wood says, flipping the pages. "I don't mean to prolong this, I'm looking for it in here because I use, I pulled, extracted, the kinds of key points out of here and I'm just having a hard time finding where they're at."

"Take your time, General," Gen. Sargeant says. "We're not in a hurry."

"Here," Gen. Wood says, reading from the document. "'During continuous Enduring Freedom operations in Afghanistan, known terrorist cells, groups, individuals and Taliban military units, including military aircraft, excluding marked medical aircraft and SAM/IADS that pose a likely and identifiable threat to U.S. forces, are to be considered hostile and may be engaged and destroyed.' The reason I bring that up is because that is the one thing that allows us here to attack on the ground in an offensive manner. Now, when we talk defensive, it has to be an identifiable threat to you, okay? And then for self-protection, if you have [an] identifiable threat to you, right now, then you are obligated—if you cannot get away from it—to attack it to survive. I think that's what you're getting at, I think."

"In part," Gen. Dumais says. "And the other part is coming back to the positive control dimension you mentioned of it, the thing—"

Gen. Sargeant interrupts his Canadian counterpart. "What is the first line of defense?" he asks Gen. Wood. "What is the intent of the self-defense ROE?"

"The first thing of ROE, of self-defense, is to survive, obviously," he says. "But I think it's to get away from the threat, with it. I don't understand what you're saying here. The self-defense is to preserve, to stay alive. To keep yourself from, from getting hurt or attacked."

"Are there exact words in the ROE to describe the self-defense ROE?" Gen. Sargeant asks.

"There is, and I'm just scrambling through here," says Gen. Wood, looking back down at the documents. "Do you know exactly where it is?"

"Do you have the SPINS ROE as well?" Gen. Sargeant asks, referring to the special instructions, the theater-specific rules of engagement for Operation Enduring Freedom.

"I do not have the SPINS ROE," Gen. Wood answers. After a few more questions, the board takes a 10-minute break so Lt.-Col. Walker can fetch the SPINS for Gen. Wood to review. He opens the binder to the page entitled "Commander's Guidance." A highlighted section is waiting for the general when he walks back into the room.

"The specific question that I asked that drove us into bringing the SPINS was: What is your understanding of the self-defense ROE?" Gen. Sargeant asks.

"I think it's, my understanding of it is, the minimum, it is, it is only do what you need to, to get away or negate the attack. In other words, if you can avoid it, or someone shoots at you and you can avoid them and get out of the way and get out of the area, then that's the first thing you should do. If only as a last resort, if you cannot maneuver and get out of the way of someone attacking you, do you then return fire or engage."

"General, in this theater, what are the transient altitudes for fighters to and from the areas that they're fragged [assigned] to provide coverage over?" Gen. Sargeant asks.

"They're dictated in the ATO [air tasking order], normally, or directed by—"

"Generally, what are those altitudes?"

"Normally about 15,000 feet AGL."

"So, if a pilot perceived from a SAFIRE that there might be AAA fire, up to say 10,000 feet, and they're transiting above 15,000 feet, what would you expect that aircrew to do?"

"I would expect them to get away from the area, with it. But certainly not go down into that threat area ..."

"If a 20 mike-mike request came in from an F–16 at night, and 'standby' were given as the order, what would you expect that flight to have done?" Gen. Sargeant asks, a few minutes later.

"I would expect them to hold their fire," Gen. Wood says. "I would expect them to get away from the target area and not try to attack the target. 'Standby,' I don't know what the words were used. I should remember them, but I can't. But there was definitely, from what I've been told by controllers, there was definitely 'standby' or 'hold your fire.'"

"Let's assume that 'standby' was given."

"Okay."

"Let's just use 'standby' as the word that was given," Gen. Sargeant says. "For the aircraft—and I'm relying on some of your F-16 expertise in this questioning—that as the aircraft, the pilot observed the SAFIRE and was above the altitude that he perceived that fire going to, what would you expect him to do with his altitude and airspeed, given the situation where he's told, he observes it, is told to 'standby?' Altitude and airspeed wise, what would you expect him to do with his aircraft?"

"Climb up higher," Gen. Wood answers. "Go faster. Get out of the way. Stay out of the threat."

"Okay. Thank you."

Going back to the night of the bombing, Gen. Dumais asks Gen. Wood how long it typically takes, in urgent situations, for the CAOC to determine whether a SAFIRE report is friendly or foe. "We have LNOs quickly, on headsets, that can respond very quickly," Gen. Wood says. "We almost do, I guess, a poll of all our LNOs that represent all the different components on the ground."

"An LNO being?" Gen. Sargeant asks.

"Liaison officers ... Once you get there you'll see how close they all are so that it's—it's rapid but it's thorough. And, you have to be very detailed with it and that can take some time."

"Is part of that process for the LNOs, to check back with their land units?" Gen. Dumais asks.

"Yes, sir."

"So, we're talking minutes to several minutes?"

"Yes, but it is quicker than that because we have exercised the systems real good."

"So, just hypothetically then, if you can summarize that, what would be the time delay from the BOSSMAN call to K-Mart through the LNO back to the ground units back up through to BOSSMAN?" Gen. Dumais asks.

"I would say, to ensure that we were doing it right, at least five minutes," Gen. Wood answers. "I mean, it's, I guess what I would like to convey to you is we take that very serious."

"General, is there a Canadian LNO in the CAOC?" Gen. Sargeant asks.

"Right now, I don't think so. We have—can we stop the mike? We've had Canadians in as LNOs before, but they've been in their capacity working as a representative of the United Kingdom and that's the—"

"Would there have been," Gen. Sargeant interrupts, "an LNO that would have been in communication with the Canadian forces on the ground?"

"The way that would've been run would have been through the up-per agency, through our Battlefield Control Detachment, through our BCD."

"When you learned the correct coordinates and you had the data from MEDEVACS that were on Tarnak Farms, did your ACO data show that there were friendlies, that there were friendly activity on Tarnak Farms that night?" Gen. Sargeant asks.

"No," Gen. Wood says.

"So the ACO did not show this ground activity?"

"No."

"Should the ACO have shown it?"

"Yes."

"Was there a breakdown in coordination between that unit and their higher headquarters and the CAOC?"

"I don't know that," the general answers. "We had a breakdown be-tween at—I don't know if it was—it's between all three of those areas. If you talk, and I don't know exactly who caused it all over there, but there was breakdown."

"The Tarnak Farms ROZ was submitted early on when we first got here, based on the requirements for the ground commander," says Chief Warrant Officer 3 Rodney Merrill. "They wanted to establish an area for troops to continue to train small arms, improve their skills, keep guys current. I was asked to put it up."

It is the late afternoon of May 7. Five days after Canadian investigators left Afghanistan, their American counterparts—now collectively known as the Coalition Investigation Board (CIB)—have arrived. Among their first witnesses is CW3 Merrill, a helicopter pilot and the airspace manager for Task Force Rakkasan.

Brigade headquarters approves every single visit to the firing range, he tells the board. But rather than pass the specific times to the Air Force, CW3 Merrill created a 24-hour ROZ—a Restricted Operating Zone—around Tarnak Farm. A permanent boundary, the ROZ prohibits planes from venturing within half a mile of the range unless they fly above 11,000 feet MSL. Whether or not troops are actually firing is irrelevant. The airspace is always off-limits. The ROZ has been included in the daily ACO for nearly three months, visible on TaskView computer software as a small green circle. "SMALL ARMS RANGE AT KANDAHAR," it reads. "NOT CONTINUOUSLY ACTIVE. CONTACT KANDAHAR TOWER FOR STATUS."

"Were you aware of any previous incidents, close calls, intrusions into the ROZ prior to 17 April?" Gen. Sargeant asks.

"No, sir," CW3 Merrill responds. "I haven't been advised of any." But the ROZ has been slightly rewritten since the friendly fire bombing, he says. "It's increased in size and we had changed some verbiage based on the fact that it's now the 'Kandahar ROZ low.' So when you do fire small arms it's there, and then when we fire mortars for 24 hours ahead, we put the 'Kandahar high ROZ,' which is to 24,000 [feet] to avoid anybody even potentially flying in the area. The other statement we added was the fact that tracer fire will be visible at night during operations."

★　★　★

"I remember something hit me hard," Rene Paquette says. "I was jack-knifed in the air and I was enveloped in white. I was hovering there, it seemed like five minutes. I was wondering: 'What the hell happened?' Just beyond my fingers and my toes, I was trying to touch the ground, but for some reason, I was just floating there."

It has been three weeks since Cpl. Paquette was hit by the force of a laser-guided bomb that he didn't see coming. This morning, May 8, he is sitting inside a conference room at the University of Alberta Hospital, retelling those moments to the Canadian board of inquiry. "Reality finally came back in and it was a world of pain," he says. "There was someone to my left, there was a set of large feet to my left just beyond arm's reach. Someone was lying there and I was thinking: 'Why isn't anyone helping the guy there?' It never registered right away. I am not entirely sure what the extent of the injuries were to the deceased, but for some reason no one was helping that guy. So either, whatever ..."

"Before we ask any questions, let me assure you that those you saw motionless around you when you were down on the ground had been checked by the medic," Gen. Baril says.

"They were checked by the medics?"

"They were checked. They were the first ones to be checked and if they were not being taken care of, it is because the medic had found out what happened to them. They were not left there suffering."

"I had some questions that have been running through my mind," Cpl. Paquette says. "I know a mortar round has a killing radius of 40 meters, and this thing was a 500-pound or 250-kilogram bomb. I can't explain in my own head why I am alive and guys that were lying beside me two meters away perished so quickly. What were their injuries that they received? I wasn't hardly touched."

"It is a question that is difficult to answer, but it is the law of physics and the law of luck," Gen. Baril says. "If you are below the angle of the blast, you will survive and for those who are in the blast, it is a very heavy bomb and the effect—"

"Did it hit ground?" Rene asks. "I don't know myself, but I heard it was air-detonated."

"It hit."

"It did hit."

"It was a super-quick fuse," Gen. Baril says. "We call it a super-quick fuse. On touching, it blows."

"Do you know what it was aimed at?" Cpl. Paquette asks. "Are you aware?"

"We know where it was aimed at," the general answers. "It was aimed at the source of fire that the pilot had identified from the air."

Still struggling to hear, Rene has to lean forward a few times as the board continues its questioning. The drum in his left ear is completely blown, never to heal. What little he can hear in his right ear is mixed with a constant ringing.

"Did you get answers to all your questions?" Col. Hodgson asks at the end of the interview.

"Pretty much, I think so," he answers. "I will wait until the actual inquiry comes out. Obviously I would like to know what the pilot was thinking when he—"

"We all would," Col. Matte says.

"We all would," says Chief W/O Levesque.

★ ★ ★

Corporal Cheyenne Laroque was A Company's man in the Kandahar tower. He sat in a corner that night, wearing his headset and waiting for orders. Whenever a plane was about to land or take off, he would pass the "check fire" to Call Sign Zero, the Canadian headquarters. They would relay the message to the range, ordering the paratroopers to stop shooting while the plane flew overhead.

"Could you describe for us how the events of the friendly fire unfolded and your role in response to that incident?" Gen. Sargeant asks Cpl. Laroque.

"Well, the air traffic controllers gave me 'check fire,' gave it to Zero, and then a few minutes later they gave me a 'cancel check fire.' And then, after a while, they gave me another 'check fire.' I gave it to Zero, but they told me to 'wait out' so I gave them another 'check fire' later and then that's when we heard the explosion and the air traffic controllers were wondering what that explosion was and I didn't know what it was either."

"So the air traffic controller turned to you and said: 'Issue a check fire'?" Gen. Sargeant asks.

"Yes."

"Pretend I am Zero, if you will, and tell me the call you made."

"I said: 'Zero, this is 11 Sentry, check fire.'"

"And then what did I say back to you, if I was Zero?"

"'Zero, wait out,'" Cpl. Laroque says. "And then I called back: 'Zero to 11 Sentry, 'check fire' on Tarnak Farms.'" And then they pass it on."

"How much time passed from the 'wait out' until you were able to pass it again and get an acknowledgment from Zero?"

"Probably about three or five seconds."

"Do you know why that second 'check fire' was given?" asks another member of the board. "You said there was one earlier in the evening and then you had another 'check fire' that was given."

"Okay, the first one, there was an aircraft coming and that's why that one was given. The second one, there was another aircraft coming in and I guess it was an aircraft that was coming in at a scheduled time and that's why he gave me that 'check fire' and that's when we pretty much heard that explosion." (The second "check fire" was actually related to that outgoing Herc, not an incoming plane.)

"Could you estimate the time between the second 'check fire' and when you heard the explosion?" asks Maj. Dave Galea, the board's infantry advisor.

"Probably about five to ten minutes," Cpl. Laroque says.

After a few more questions, Gen. Dumais, the Canadian co-president, revisits the "check fire" issue. "Did you just respond to Maj. Galea that the 'check fire' had been in effect for five to 10 minutes when you heard the explosion?"

"Yes," Cpl. Laroque says. "I gave the 'check fire' and the air traffic controllers, they're the ones who give me the 'cancel check fire' and they never gave me a 'check fire' because when they gave the—correction, they never gave me a 'cancel check fire'—because when I initially gave the second one, then about five, 10 minutes later after that, that's when you heard the explosion."

★ ★ ★

"Every time we were about to shoot a round, we would say: 'All right, light up the target,'" Brian Decaire tells the Canadian investigators. "From then, Perry was about to fire the sixth round and I noticed the rubber mount at the end of the Carl Gustav came loose. Do you all know what I am talking about?"

"I know," Col. Matte says.

"Yes," Chief W/O Levesque says.

"Right at the end where all the backblast and all the shit comes out, there is a rubber mount," Cpl. Decaire continues. "That is to dampen the vibration, and if that's loose, you can give yourself a serious concussion."

"Right," Col. Matte says.

"I noticed it was loose and I was like: 'Hold on, Brett.' So I got the rubber mount back on the end and as I was messing around with it, I heard a whistling noise and I thought the round had armed. I looked toward the center of the section and all I saw was a flash of light. At first I thought Perry had fired the round accidentally. I was blown back. I wasn't blown back meters or anything, I just kind of went back from the flash and it felt like—I thought I blew off my hand first of all because all I felt was burning there. I felt like someone took a sledgehammer to it and I just had a burning sensation in my hand. Then I was blinded for a bit because there was no illumination from the moon, there was no moon. I just took a few minutes to see what the hell had just happened.

"The eeriest part of it was the silence afterwards," Brian continues, "because usually if something messed up happens, the senior NCO is like: 'What the hell was that?' But it was just the silence. A few seconds after, we heard Paquette and Hollister—we heard them in pain. I got up a few seconds later and saw the dead, saw the wounded, and did what we could. That's about it."

★ ★ ★

The tiny shrapnel wound on Shane Brennan's thigh is barely noticeable anymore. He is still in Afghanistan, and when the rest of the Canadian troops hit the Tora Bora mountains for Operation Torii, he was with them. They just returned to Kandahar yesterday.

"How would you describe the support services that your unit has received since the incident?" asks Lt.-Col. Adkins, the human factors advisor on the U.S. board.

"Support as in which way, ma'am?" Cpl. Brennan asks. "Like as in counseling or—"

"Right. Counseling or the chaplain or—"

"Personally, I have a pretty negative view about that," Shane answers. "I have got a bit of post-secondary education in psychology and a friend of the family is a psychiatrist and stuff like that too. I have some negative feelings towards it, and so do a lot of the other troops."

"In what way?" Lt.-Col. Adkins asks.

"I just think that, like I said, the only thing I'll say on that, ma'am, is that I hope that we start getting guys not being asked if they want to talk, but told they are going to talk about whatever—and to do it soon. Because being on this last mission I can say not only for myself, but for even the other men of my section and the other men that I've talked to in the platoon and the company, when we had the fast air come around almost every night—and I've never been afraid of anything in my life—and I can only say when that fast air come over by us on that mountain, I was in the fetal position in my Bivi bag and I just sit, just hope, you know, and when I poke my head up to see what flew over I could see other members of my section, they're the same."

"Well, it's a traumatic thing," she says.

"It is, ma'am," Cpl. Brennan says. "It definitely is."

"So you think that people should be directed to participate whether they want to or not?" Lt.-Col. Adkins asks, referring to peer counseling.

"I know so," Shane says. "I know so."

★ ★ ★

"The C-9 was putting down a very, very slow rate of fire and that is when there was a big flash of light," Brett Perry recalls. "The first thing I thought immediately was the Carl Gustav blew up or I had pulled the trigger or something. The first thing I did was put it down and make sure it was on safety. I looked down the tube to make sure the round was still in there, and it was still in there. I don't know where you want me to go from there, sir."

"Carry on to tell us what happened after the explosion," Gen. Baril says.

"Right after?"

"Yes."

"Decaire was, I guess, thrown back a bit. He came to me and something was wrong with his hand. I went immediately to my left, Decaire followed me up, and we started triaging everybody as soon as possible, wherever. Then I went back to the Carl G. because I was having a rough time thinking that I did this. I thought I caused everything."

He still can't shake that feeling. For nearly three weeks, Cpl. Perry has been reading about himself in the newspapers, about how he took burning shrapnel to his left arm, but still scrambled to treat some of his injured friends. Hero. But when the cameras aren't around, when nobody's stopping him on the street to say sorry or say thanks, the guilt returns. Brett Perry knows he didn't kill those guys. He knows that an F-16 Viper, not his Carl G., spilled all that blood in the sand. But somehow, Brett still believes—as he did in those first few moments—that he is to blame for all this.

"I think it is probably worthwhile to just reassure you that the Carl G., to the best of our knowledge, did not go off, that final round, the way it was found," says Col. Matte, the Canadian board's F-18 pilot.

"Yes," Cpl. Perry says. "I had gotten the platoon commander and actually grabbed him by the scruff and made him open up the Carl G. That was for my own—"

"Yes, but just to reassure you that there was no misfire," Col. Matte says.

"Right, sir."

"You did nothing wrong. In fact, I am impressed by the fact that given what had just transpired, you had the state of mind to actually check the weapon, safety it, and put it down before you carried on. So, well done."

In less than a week, Cpl. Perry will be back in Kandahar with his fellow paratroopers, wishing even harder that it was he, not the other four, who had gone home in a casket. When it's quiet, when the guilt is at its heaviest, Brett will hear Ainsworth's booming laugh in the distance, comforting him, if only for a moment.

"Let me role-play Colonel Nichols," Gen. Sargeant says.

"Uh-huh," she nods.

"And I'm about to read you your rights."

"Yes, sir."

"How would you have advised me to do that?"

Back in Kuwait for a second round of testimony, the general is interviewing Captain Erin Wirtanen, the staff judge advocate at Al Jaber Air Base. She was in the briefing room when Harry Schmidt and Bill Umbach returned from their mission. "I provided him [Col. Nichols] the rights advisement card and asked him to read it to the pilots and asked him to read it as an alleged offense of Article 92, dereliction of duty," Capt. Wirtanen replies.

"And what did I say back to you, specifically?" Gen. Sargeant asks.

"I cannot remember exact words, but the gist of the conversation was, um, Colonel Nichols said to me he did not like the word 'offense.' He preferred the word 'incident.' I believe that's the word he used ultimately and that he wanted to substitute that word, and I advised him that I didn't think that was, um, that was prudent and I thought that he should read it as is."

"So tell me what you told him, as best you can recollect," Gen. Sargeant says later.

"Um, again, sir, I can't remember exact words, but I, I know that I did advise him that he should read it as per the rights advisement card, as per Article 92."

"And what was his answer back to you?"

"He, he just didn't like the word 'offense' and he did not want to read it in that way. When I suggested that was the best course of action, then the pilots were, were there and he said: 'Let's start.'"

★　★　★

Brett Paola flew Blackhawk search-and-rescue helicopters before learning how to operate an F-16. He's been qualified as a Viper pilot for nearly three years now, all three of those spent with the 170th Fighter Squadron in Springfield, Illinois. On this deployment, Capt. Paola is one of six pilots who rotate through as chiefs in the Mission Planning Cell (MPC). He was there on April 17, compiling the briefing slides for Coffee Flight's sortie over Afghanistan. This afternoon, Gen. Sargeant hands the captain a copy of the onboard map that Maj. Schmidt and Maj. Umbach carried into their cockpits that night.

"With this map," the general asks, "can you tell me where the different areas of operations were, the different AOs, that these pilots were going to be flying into that night or that would potentially be of interest to the pilots flying up into these areas?"

"As far as—well, actually, sir, no," Capt. Paola answers. "One is because I can't remember exactly what we sent them out the door as far as intel goes, and secondly, for these maps we don't plot any kind of airspace on them because plotting airspace on a big map or on them for the whole country is not really usable in the cockpit. So what we do is we sent them out with these, like this map, for example, because there's been some activity in this area and it provides them a way to concentrate in that particular area. Also that night—and it changes nightly, I can't remember, but they'll give you certain areas that you're expected to work in, either through intel or sometimes it's on the ATO [air tasking order]."

"Uh-huh," Gen. Sargeant says. "So this was an adequate map for you to fly with when you flew missions?"

"Yes, sir. Truth be told, for me, the bigger one was actually better so I could keep an eye on the whole country of what was going on."

"Did you have the AOs marked on here anywhere?"

"No, sir."

"Could you today tell me where the Truman AO was from this mission?" Gen. Sargeant asks, referring to the Kandahar territory under the control of Task Force Rakkasan.

"No, sir," Capt. Paola says. "I couldn't."

"Would any of those AOs have meant anything to you? Let's say there was a Truman AO that kind of went like this, and I'm just drawing a relatively straightforward square around the area called 'Kandahar.'" Gen. Sargeant says, pen in hand.

"Yes, sir."

"And suppose that was labeled 'Truman.' Would that have been of use to you in the cockpit with that size?"

"An area of that size, being 60 by 60, you know, you're looking at 60 square miles, something that would, it's difficult to tell. I mean, the whole country is covered with them, whether or not I can actually use that in the cockpit. We've decided, the MP Cell decided, that you can't plot all those and have it be usable, so. Am I answering the question, sir, or not?"

"You just did," Gen. Sargeant says.

★ ★ ★

"What's your professional relationship with Captain Wirtanen?" Gen. Sargeant asks Col. Nichols. Eight days after the colonel first testified in front of the CIB, investigators have recalled him for another round of questioning.

"She's my JAG," he answers.

"Does she give you advice?"

"Yes, that's her job."

"Do you follow that advice?"

"I usually do on—Article 15s, she's very typical of a JAG, very procedural and objective, which I ask her to be. And then she will, when I discuss, like we just did an Article 15 before I came in here, when I discuss with her, she takes her side pretty firmly, so ... I listen to her. How's that? I listen to her advice."

"What training have you received regarding reading of rights to military members suspected of an offense?" Gen. Sargeant asks.

"Just a commander's course, just the local squadron commander's school and ops group commander school, they have an hour, I think, I don't know exactly how long it is, but I remember—I remember the part where they say you must read the rights and all the stuff that goes with it."

"Has your JAG ever given you advice in the past on reading anyone their rights?"

"No."

"On the night of 17 April, did Captain Wirtanen give you legal advice regarding reading the rights to the pilots of Coffee 51 and 52?"

"Yes."

"We need to take a break," Gen. Sargeant says.

After a short discussion with his legal advisors, the general sits back down at the table. "I have several more questions I'd like to ask you," he says to Col. Nichols. "But before we proceed, I'd like Lt.-Col. Walker to read you your rights. Colonel Walker ..."

"Wait, wait, wait, wait," Col. Nichols says. "If you're going to read me my rights, I don't have to answer any questions. I mean, I thought this was a board of inquiry trying to figure out what happened on the night of the accident."

"You have that right," Gen. Sargeant says. "Colonel Walker will read you your rights."

"Okay," says Col. Nichols, half laughing.

"Sir," Lt.-Col. Walker says. "We have reason to suspect you of the alleged offenses of dereliction of duty under Article 92 of the UCMJ, and non-compliance with procedural rules under Article 98 of the UCMJ. I advise you that under the provisions of Article 31 of the Uniform Code of Military Justice, you have the right to remain silent; that is, to say nothing at all. Any statement you make, oral or written, may be used as evidence against you in a trial by court-martial or in other judicial or administrative proceedings. You have the right to consult with a lawyer if you desire and to have a lawyer present during this interview. You have the right to military legal counsel free of charge. In addition to military counsel, you are entitled to civilian counsel of your own choosing, at your own expense. You may request a lawyer at any time during this interview. If you decide to answer questions without a lawyer present, you may stop the questioning at any time. Do you understand your rights?"

"I do," Col. Nichols says.

"Do you wish to remain silent or will you answer questions?"

"I wish to remain silent."

"Do you want a lawyer?"

"Yes."

★   ★   ★

Up until April 18, Jamie Key's clients could hardly be considered block-buster. A few assault cases. Drunk and disorderlies. The odd guy surfing for porn on government computers. The typical stuff that tends to slide across the desk of a U.S. Air Force area defense counsel—the military equivalent of a public defender. You take what you get.

The son of an Air Force "cost analyst," Captain James E. Key III is one of three area defense counsels stationed at Ramstein Air Base in Germany. He was sitting with Captain Mike Roderick, one of the other attorneys, when the e-mail arrived from the JAG at Al Jaber. We need lawyers for two pilots, the note said, a flight lead and a wingman. No names, no other details that went beyond what both attorneys had already heard on the news. "So which one do you want, Mike?" Capt. Key asked Capt. Roderick. They eventually flipped a coin. Jamie got the wingman.

Harry Schmidt called not long afterwards, but there was little he could say over the telephone. Almost everything about the case is classified. Even the simple fact that OEF missions are being flown out of Kuwait is still considered secret. Two weeks after that first e-mail, Jamie Key and Mike Roderick finally managed to hitch a ride to Al Jaber in the back of an Air National Guard plane that just happened to be taking off from Germany. Both men were officially listed as cargo. When they landed on May 2, Harry Schmidt was a little skeptical. Not that Jamie Key didn't seem intelligent or committed during all those phone conversations. It's just that his short frame and baby face don't really do much justice to his 31 years. *Oh my God,* Harry thought to himself. *My attorney is 12.*

Within a day, advisors working for Gen. Sargeant and Gen. Dumais laid out the ground rules for Capt. Key and Capt. Roderick. You are not allowed to interview any witnesses. You can't talk to anyone about the case. And you can't review any evidence, including the targeting pod videos.

Nobody has been charged with any crime, after all, so normal disclosure rules don't apply.

With little else to do, Capt. Key has spent the past 10 days familiarizing himself with how things work at Al Jaber. He has sat in on a few mass briefs, watched the Mission Planning Cell do its thing. And he has spent hours and hours talking to Harry, who, despite his glowing reputation and his obvious confidence, is clearly a broken man. Not only did he kill four coalition soldiers, but he is hearing whispers about the tough questions that Gen. Sargeant has been asking behind closed doors. First thing Sunday morning—May 12, 2002—it is Harry Schmidt's turn to testify in front of the Coalition Investigation Board.

"Major Schmidt, I'm Brigadier-General Steve Sargeant. I'm co-president of this Accident Investigation Board. I am currently the 56th Fighter Wing Commander at Luke Air Force Base, and I've got a background in A-10s and F-16s."

"I'm Brigadier-General Marc Dumais. I'm the Canadian co-president of this board, and I'm an air transport pilot, former pilot. I've flown mostly C-130s, about 5,500 hours of flying time."

Maj. Schmidt takes an oath, then listens as Maj. Anjilvel, one of the board's legal advisors, reads him his rights.

"We are investigating the alleged offenses of dereliction of duty under Article 92, Uniform Code of Military Justice and negligent homicide under Article 134, Uniform Code of Military Justice, of which you are suspected," she says. "You have the right to remain silent; that is, to say nothing at all. Any statement you make, oral or written, may be used as evidence against you in a trial by court-martial or in other judicial or administrative proceedings. You have the right to consult a lawyer and to have a lawyer present during this interview. You have the right to military legal counsel free of charge. In addition to military counsel, you are entitled to civilian counsel of your own choosing at your own expense. You may request a lawyer at any time during this interview. If you decide to answer questions, you may stop the questioning at any time. Major Schmidt, do you understand your rights?"

"I do."

"Do you want a lawyer?"

"Yes, I do."

"And that would be whom?"

"Captain Key."

"And are you willing to answer questions at this time?"

"No, I'm not."

"Thank you."

"Sir," Capt. Key says to Gen. Sargeant, "Maj. Schmidt has prepared some documentary evidence which we hope that the board will consider in its deliberations. We put it together in this package. As we have stated before, Maj. Schmidt is willing to consider responding to questions in writing. We note that's been denied on at least two occasions in the past. That offer is still open. However, at this point in time, Maj. Schmidt will not be making any oral statements or answering any questions."

"Maj. Schmidt, since you are giving these to the board, I will gladly take them into consideration," the general says. "But are you willing to discuss any of the significance of why you are submitting these to the board? What significance you feel—what is the significance of these slides?"

"We believe that it is contained—"

"I'm asking Maj. Schmidt," Gen. Sargeant says, cutting off Capt. Key.

"Sir," the captain says, "Maj. Schmidt cannot answer any questions. I'm sorry."

"Okay," Gen. Sargeant says. "Then I will take these and that's all."

"Thank you, sir."

"I'll take whatever he's written on here then for the board. That is all, and you're dismissed."

"Yes, sir," Capt. Key says.

The package he leaves with Gen. Sargeant is 38 pages long. It includes maps, intel slides, a written statement Harry made the morning after the bombing, and a more detailed explanation that he and his lawyer have crafted over the past few days. "I would like to say first and foremost that I sincerely regret the accident that occurred on 17 April 2002," it reads. "My heart goes out to the families of the men killed and injured in what can only be called a very tragic accident. I have replayed the events of that evening in my mind over and over again and I come to the same conclusion every time. Although what happened was extremely unfortunate, I firmly believe that I did nothing wrong. In fact, if I was in the same exact situation armed with the exact same knowledge, the outcome would be the same. I was called upon to make a perfect decision in a rapidly unfolding combat scenario, and I had to make that decision with what I now know was imperfect information."

His statement says that after Maj. Umbach noticed the "fireworks" on the ground, his lead tried to talk his eyes onto the flashes. "When I correlated that it was nearly underneath me, my flight lead then said: 'I think they are shooting at us.' My first priority was to maneuver my aircraft to avoid being predictable and switching my lights back to the covert setting. My lead continued to maneuver with lights on when he said: 'They are pulling lead' [referring to the anti-aircraft artillery technique required to shoot down an aircraft]." Harry says he yelled at Bill to turn off his lights. "After executing my initial hard turn away from the site to egress, I was uncomfortable because I saw the rate and speed of the fire and estimated that my flight lead wasn't going to be able to get out of the maximum effective range of the round. Therefore, I turned back in to provide visual mutual support and to better keep track of the site to better maneuver against it ... I felt that the rounds were still being fired in front of my flight lead and commented 'They are shooting at you.'"

Harry's written submission reveals that during the previous 10 days, pilots had been briefed about the suspected presence of "Ringbacks" in Afghanistan. A type of BM-21, Ringbacks are 122mm Multiple Launch Rocket Systems that have a range of 56,000 feet—far higher than any F-16 can fly. For years, Iraqis have been firing the exact weapon at U.S. fighter jets. "It is within the realm of probability that Taliban forces could have been using the weapon for similar purposes in ambush tactics," Maj. Schmidt writes. "I felt these projectiles posed a real and present danger to our flight. I engaged because I believed that my flight lead was at risk of being shot down. At the time, I probably could have egressed the situation myself. This, however, would have done nothing to support my flight lead, who appeared to be drawing fire. As a wingman, my primary responsibility is to provide visual, mutual support. Therefore, I felt it was my duty to remain in the area of the threat and provide that support, which I still believe was the appropriate action given the situation."

Maj. Schmidt says he asked BOSSMAN to lay down some 20 mike-mike in an attempt to "stop the gunners long enough for my flight lead and I to egress successfully. That request was denied. ... As I turned back to create some range from the site I saw another salvo being fired out of the corner of my eye. Unaided by NVGs, this salvo appeared to be shooting at me. As I continued back around in a right-hand turn, the site fired one more salvo where I thought my lead was. We asked BOSSMAN if there were any friendlies in the vicinity. BOSSMAN did not respond. Then the machine fired a salvo where I thought my lead was again. I called that I was in self-defense due to the apparent threat to my flight lead. As I rolled in, I could see the rounds going under my airplane and at that point, I had established a track with my targeting pod, using my IR pointer and the range I had created. I could see the target area for about 20 seconds before I released the bomb. There was a vehicle or two sitting on the side of a road with people standing around the weapon as it fired. I do not envision our forces would be standing around if there was a firefight going on. ... From the cockpit, it looked like a surface-to-air engagement. I then released a single instantaneously fused GBU-12. It all happened within one minute and 45 seconds."

Since he first arrived in theater, Maj. Schmidt continues, he was never once briefed about the possibility of a live-fire training exercise in Afghanistan. "One of my greatest fears came to realization tonight of not knowing where friendlies are, not knowing of their operations, ending up in the middle of a perceived firefight trying to sort it out in a short amount of time while airborne receiving fire." His statement also criticizes BOSSMAN for providing "very little assistance" during the engagement. "This is the very reason I asked if he wanted us to switch to another AWACS frequency. It seemed that the controller did not have situational awareness outside of his tanker-coordination responsibilities, nor did he seem to appreciate the gravity of the situation." And, like the pilots, BOSSMAN did not know anything about the existence of Tarnak Farm or its ROZ, let alone that Canadians were firing there at the time.

"No one in the air was aware of this ROZ because it was buried in a bloated and completely unworkable airspace control order [ACO]," Maj. Schmidt writes. "After the accident, I again reviewed the ACO for 17 April.

It is 45 pages of single-spaced type. There are 353 ACMs [airspace control measures] for us to consider. Tarnak Farms ROZ was described on page 30 as a 'small arms' range that was 'not continuously active.'" Mission planners and pilots are "forced to hunt for the proverbial needle in the haystack each time the ACO is published," he writes. "It would be next to impossible to simply try and memorize or plot the location of all possible conflicts to and from and in the vicinity of the tactical area. I know this because we tried before the accident. As the mission planning chief, I had actually started requiring the production of maps with all conflicts posted on them for in-flight use. They were discontinued after a few flights because the information on the map was too concentrated to be of any use in flight."

And even if he and Maj. Umbach did know about the ROZ, Maj. Schmidt says he is not convinced it would have prevented what happened that night. "While the term 'small arms' may be ambiguous, I cannot imagine calling what was flying up at our aircraft as small arms," he writes. "Even if I had been aware of the Tarnak Farms small-arms range, the type and trajectory of the munitions we observed would have led us to conclude that it was enemy fire, not friendly forces training on a small-arms range." Maj. Schmidt even suggests that perhaps the Canadian paratroopers did not properly alert "U.S. channels" about their training drill. Even if they did, he writes, "friendlies executing a live-fire in a hostile zone in the vicinity of friendly airplanes is unsatisfactory, adding to the fog of war."

Overall, finding reliable information about the location of friendly ground troops "has been a difficult, uphill struggle for our flyers," Maj. Schmidt writes. During the close air symposium in mid-March, which he attended, concerned participants repeatedly complained that the Air Force is failing to provide "any sort of comprehensive view of where our troops are." Many at the conference suggested that bases such as Al Jaber be assigned a ground liaison officer—a GLO—who would be armed with the latest information on Army movements and exercises. "These critical billets are still not currently filled," Maj. Schmidt says.

"The fear of fratricide was a constant, overarching concern in the unit," he continues. "We felt as if we were operating independent of, rather than in support of, ground forces. Since the accident, I have noticed a profound shift in the amount of information about ground activity flowing to our unit ... Although I am glad to see the increased flow of information, I am distressed it took a tragedy of this magnitude to spark change."

Maj. Schmidt is also distressed that he has been "shut out" of the investigative process. Because of the gag order enacted by Gen. Moseley in the days after the bombing, "I have been completely deprived of any ability to try and learn what factors contributed to the accident. I understand that I have not been charged with any sort of crime, however, I had hoped to defend my actions in this setting." His written submission also accuses the Coalition Investigation Board of refusing to allow him to testify in front of the Canadian board of inquiry, noting that the "BOI can only get copies of testimony given to the CIB. Thus, the only information the BOI will have will be filtered through whatever questions the CIB saw fit to ask witnesses. The BOI will have no opportunity to shape its own theory of the accident, effectively turning the BOI into nothing more than an arm of the CIB.

"I fear the CIB is unconcerned with what happened and is advancing some independent agenda, because I can find no other explanation as to why I have been formally shut out of the process," he continues. "I feel as if I am a suspect in a criminal investigation as opposed to a witness in an Accident Investigation Board. ... I have had a distinguished career serving this country, and I hope it will not be brought to an end because of this accident."

★ ★ ★

"I'm Major William J. Umbach. I'm the squadron commander of the 170th Fighter Squadron."

Maj. Umbach walked into the interview room as soon as his wingman left. He is accompanied by his military lawyer, Captain Mike Roderick. They both sit down and listen as Maj. Anjilvel reads Bill his rights.

"Sir, do you understand your rights?" she asks at the end.

"Yes, I do," Maj. Umbach says.

"Do you want a lawyer?"

"Yes, I do."

"And who would that be, sir?"

"Captain Roderick."

"Are you willing to answer questions?"

"No, I'm not."

"If you are not willing to answer questions," Gen. Sargeant says, "then you are dismissed."

"Yes, sir."

chapter nineteen

Lorne Ford is lying in an Edmonton hospital bed when Gen. Baril meets him for the first time. The Canadian board of inquiry originally planned to interview the sergeant last week, but he was in no shape to talk. When investigators stop by on May 14, Sgt. Ford is feeling a little better, although the future of his mangled left leg—numerous operations later—is still unclear. Doctors have braced Lorne for the possibility that they still might have to amputate the lower half, including his foot.

"I looked up into the air and it couldn't have been even three seconds later, I heard the screaming of the bomb coming in," says Sgt. Ford, a black patch covering the hole where his right eye once was. "In a split second I put two and two together. Knowing that the jet had already flown by, I figured we had just had a bomb dropped on us. Before I could even get a sentence out of my mouth, the explosion went off. The heat, the force of the explosion, the noise—everything was just incredible.

"The next thing I knew I was on my right side," Lorne continues. "And I knew that I had been hit. I didn't know how bad, but I knew I was injured. I put my left hand down towards my left leg or at least down towards that area, and I had looked down and my leg was more or less a mess. There was blood all over the place and I knew that for the amount of blood that was on my hand that it was coming out pretty fast and that I needed help pretty quick."

Sitting up in his bed, Sgt. Ford tells investigators how he started waving his hands in the air, how he heard people in the distance screaming to take cover. "I had heard one person say they didn't even know if we were under attack by Taliban, if it was an RPG [rocket-propelled grenade]. What it was, nobody knew in that first split second. At this time, I really don't have a timeframe in my mind. I don't know if I had passed out as soon as the bomb hit. I don't know if I woke up. I don't know if it was instantaneous that I was awake after the explosion, so I can't—I don't know."

He saw Perry. Decaire. Moments later, Kopp, DLB, and Coates were kneeling around him, talking about the tourniquet. "I was asking about my troops, if they were okay," Sgt. Ford recalls. "I believe I refused the morphine just so I could make sure that there was enough for my guys." He blacked out by the time the CASEVAC chopper touched down at the airfield.

"We thank you very much for your testimony in front of the board in difficult circumstances," Gen. Baril says at the end of their short chat. "We, the board—and we can't speak for all Canadians, but I will anyway—thank you for your service and wish you all the best ... Unless you have any questions, we will go back to the airport and fly back home."

"I actually have a couple," Sgt. Ford says. "Did the bomb land in the wadi? Did it land on top of the wadi, on the edge? Because of my injuries and what has happened to other personnel, and since Green, Smith, and Dyer were obviously three of the personnel that died and I know that they were directly to my right—I know exactly where they were—so I am imagining that the bomb landed pretty close to them."

"You are not imagining," Gen. Baril says. "It hit right on the lip, right on the top."

"Okay, so it hit on top."

"They figure it was about a foot-and-a-half below the top of the edge, kind of on a bit of an angle," Col. Matte adds. "You know how it is quite steep?"

"Right," Sgt. Ford says.

"It hit about a foot-and-a-half from the edge itself."

Lorne wants to know from which direction the jet made its attack run. "We are not in a position, unfortunately, and cannot confirm that yet because of what General Baril has mentioned," Col. Matte says. "But, yes, we know precisely from what direction he came. The reason for that is the sources. At this point, we don't want—"

"Have you talked to the pilot himself?" Sgt. Ford interrupts.

"Not yet," Gen. Baril says. "We are not sure if the other board has talked to them yet. It is not only a pilot. The pilot, as you may imagine, works in a big organization, command and control. So we are very careful not to single out one, but somebody pulled the trigger and released the bomb. It is much more complex than that."

★ ★ ★

Miranda Boutilier is sitting in the passenger seat of a friend's pickup truck, on the way to school on a Thursday morning. Anything to feel normal. She promised herself—and Ricky—that she wouldn't spend her days alone, locked in her bedroom with the lights off and the blinds closed.

Not that anybody would blame her if she did. Four short weeks ago, the 17-year-old was in her Edmonton apartment, cleaning and studying and hoping that Ricky would be home by her prom night. Since then, she has suffered through his wake and his funeral, the reporters and the photographers, the idiotic questions. "Do you like your new ring?" one journalist asked. She could only stare back, stunned.

Away from the cameras, she gazed at that new engagement ring, dreaming and wondering how her boyfriend would have given it to her, what he would have said. What she would have said. Amid the chaos of those first few days, one of the diamonds even fell out. She managed to catch it before the ground could swallow it.

Every day, her mailbox fills with a fresh load of letters and sympathy cards, many sent by total strangers who saw her crying face and her red hair on the 11 o'clock news. Some of the notes are from the U.S. Some are even stuffed with cash. By now, the check has arrived, too, the $100,000 life insurance payment from the policy that Ricky took out in her name. As if money dulls the disbelief, the pain of having to pack up and move out of that Edmonton apartment. Miranda's living with her parents again, back in little Lunenburg County, Nova Scotia, not far from the Hubbards bowling alley where she and Ricky first met.

This morning, as she rides along on the way to school, the pickup truck loses control, flipping over four times before sliding to a halt on Highway 3. Miranda survives, but suffers numerous compression fractures to her neck.

She will spend the next two weeks strapped to a hospital bed, dealing with the realization that after all this, after all she has endured, she will have to teach herself to walk again.

★ ★ ★

By May 16, the same day as Miranda's accident, Gen. Sargeant and his team of investigators are back in the United States, working out of an office at MacDill Air Force Base in Tampa, Florida, the home of CENTCOM. The board has already traveled to five different countries and questioned more than 60 witnesses connected to the friendly fire incident. One of their last interviews is a conference call with Chief Richard Emley. He was among the crew onboard the fuel tanker, the one that the F-16s were on their way to meet when they noticed the fireworks on the ground.

"We heard them check in with BOSSMAN, which is the AWACS controller at the time, and at that time we heard them coming towards us to get refueled and go home," Chief Emley says into the phone. "And we were still on BOSSMAN freq listening for them to come in when I heard them, the F-16s, say that they were taking ground fire and they asked BOSSMAN if they wanted them, the F-16s, to go back and get the coordinates. At that time, BOSSMAN returned and said 'yes.'"

Worried that the pilots might run out of gas, Chief Emley says, the tanker operator asked BOSSMAN if they should follow the Vipers. BOSSMAN agreed. "And while still listening on BOSSMAN freq, we heard them say that once they made the second pass, that they were still taking fire," Chief Emley recalls. "And the fighters asked if they were cleared to fire and at that time BOSSMAN said: 'No, only in self-defense.' And then—my statement said—I heard them say over BOSSMAN freq that they had armed the lasers and shortly after the 'armed the lasers' call, we heard 'bomb dropped' and we looked, I looked out and over in the cockpit saw the orange blast and heard 'shack' over the radio."

A few minutes later, the pilots banked up alongside the tanker. Chief Emley immediately noticed that a bomb was missing from Maj. Schmidt's left wing. "Over boom interphone we chatted a while," the chief says. "And his last statement to me was that he didn't know what he would do if it was a friendly accident, that he would have to live with that for the rest of his life. And then we took them back home and dropped them off."

★ ★ ★

Jocelyn Van Sloten is back at work, sitting behind the reception desk at her Edmonton dentist office. She came back two weeks ago, right after the huge memorial service at the Skyreach Centre. She couldn't afford to take any more time off. Even though she and Ains were in love and engaged and saving up for their wedding, Jocelyn was not listed on his insurance papers as a beneficiary. His dad, Paul Dyer, was.

Paul always hated that his son lived in Edmonton, so far away from the apartment they used to share, the one that Ains was still helping to pay for right up until the morning he died. Paul used to tell Jocelyn that one day, Ainsworth would move back to Toronto and live with him again. After the funeral, Paul wanted everything, even the care packages that Jocelyn had mailed to Ains in Kandahar. She asked Paul if she could keep Ainsworth's car, the Silver Grand Am, and take over the monthly payments. But Paul wanted that, too. He had the car shipped to Ontario. He didn't even have a driver's license.

Among the few things that Jocelyn did get to keep were Ainsworth's letters, including a few that continued to arrive weeks after he was killed. They were longer than usual, deeper. They will always be her favorite ones.

★ ★ ★

A boardroom is waiting for Gen. Baril and his team of investigators when they arrive at Canada's embassy in Kuwait. It is June 2. The plan is to spend the afternoon talking to Maj. Art Henry—the Canadian commander on the AWACS plane that night—then fly to Saudi Arabia, where a full tour of the CAOC is scheduled for later this week.

It has been nearly six weeks since the friendly fire incident. Maj. Henry has already been grilled once by American investigators, and he's flown a dozen missions since. But he's a Canadian. And the Canadian board of inquiry is anxious to hear his story firsthand. He flew overnight from his base in Oman to be here.

"On the night in question, you as the mission crew commander were not aware of the Tarnak Farm Restricted Operating Zone [ROZ]?" asks Col. Matte, the board's F-18 pilot.

"No," Maj. Henry says, "I was not."

"When this all transpired," Col. Matte asks later, "I take it that you would have seen their movements on your screen?"

"That's correct."

"At any time, did anyone question them as to how much longer they were going to continue orbiting? They were in the area for about six minutes before anything really serious happens where they invoke self-defense."

"At the time in question, they were en route," Maj. Henry says. "They had the SAFIRE, asked to mark, and then the situation quickly became intense and time really, from my perspective, almost stood still where we had a rapid succession of radio transmissions, command-and-control coordination issues, and the five to 10 minutes that it occurred, from my perception, went by very, very quickly."

Maj. Henry recalls how Capt. David Pepper, the senior director, was in the bathroom when TSgt. Michael Carroll—BOSSMAN—said the F-16s wanted permission to mark the target. Moments later, TSgt. Carroll informed Maj. Henry that Coffee 52 wanted to fire his 20mm cannons. "We denied that due to, I felt, an unclear ground situation," Maj. Henry tells the board. "The fire continued. From my perspective, no engagement authority had been given to the aircraft and there was a third request to engage, which we had denied. So, first, '20 millimeter engage, engage,' and then we said: 'Just get out of there. Just get out of there.' After the fact, I have come to find out that the aircraft actually did launch somewhere between our second and our third [denial of permission], dropped a GBU-12. We did not know on our aircraft from my personal knowledge and in secondhand knowledge in interviewing my senior director and my controller that that had happened. To our knowledge, the first time that we had heard that a GBU-12 had been launched is after we asked, which was well after the event."

"We don't have any recording of your net because that particular AWACs didn't have that capability?" Col. Matte asks.

"Correct."

Col. Matte refers to a log of the radio transmissions for his next question. At 21:23:43 Zulu, BOSSMAN responds "standby" in response to Maj. Schmidt's request to "lay down some 20 mike-mike." At 21:25:00—one minute and 17 seconds later—BOSSMAN orders Maj. Schmidt to hold fire. "Between the time that the request is made to lay down some 20 millimeter, and by the time that BOSSMAN comes back and basically tells them not to fire in a definitive sense is almost a minute and a half later at 21:25," Col. Matte says. "I realize that you were not monitoring OCRE 6 [radio frequency] at that point, but the senior director, I believe, was. Does that seem like an unusual delay? If it is, how could you explain that?"

"When the request came out," Maj. Henry says, "I refer to the time 21:23:34: 'permission to lay down 20 mike-mike,' and then BOSSMAN replies: 'standby.' There is a conversation which ensues on our internal net that was probably at least 30 seconds or more in length where we said: 'No.' I can't explain why there is a long period of time between that and the 21:25."

"TSgt. Carroll, we understand from previous testimony that we had from the Coalition Investigation Board, was rated as being a very experienced tactical controller," Col. Matte says.

"Yes."

"He himself attested to the fact that he was not overly excited in and around the incident and the voices of Coffee 51 didn't relay any excitement either. Yet it seems that he, for whatever reason, failed to pass on that piece of information that obviously was key. What you had mentioned was that there was friendlies in Kandahar. Is that unusual, that he would miss a key thing because he is listening on the other frequency?"

"In the case of this, the 'friendlies in Kandahar,' as I refer at time 21:26:10, by my recollection, that was the second time that he passed it. I can recall him passing it twice. I was not listening to his actual frequency, but I can hear ambient noise. In the aircraft, I can hear him transmitting. I cannot explain why it would not be on this transcript other than it may have been 'stepped on.' There is another incident where the communications were stepped on."

"I will leave it at that for now," Col. Matte says.

"What do you mean by 'stepped on'?" CWO Levesque asks.

"Oh, I'm sorry," Maj. Henry answers. "Mutual interference from radios. With multiple radios, the fighter has two radios, a VHF and a UHF radio. The VHF is used interflight usually to talk to each other. The UHF is to talk to us or external agencies. Much in the same way as a conversation if two people are talking at the same time, radios will exhibit interference if you get two conversations going at the same time or two people trying to transmit at the same time. So it can happen either (a) two people trying to transmit on the same frequency or (b), which is more likely the case, two people transmitting at the same time on separate frequencies, but the aircraft is listening to both at the same time. So a transmission on VHF [the F-16s' plane-to-plane frequency] may have blocked out a transmission on UHF [the frequency that AWACS uses to talk to the pilots]."

What Maj. Henry is suggesting to the board is that his tanker controller, TSgt. Carroll, passed a "negative" order well before the "hold fire" he voiced at 21:25:00, but it was "stepped on" by a transmission between the two pilots. In other words, the men in the F-16s—moments from unleashing a bomb on friendly forces—may never have heard the "negative" call because they were talking to each other at the exact same time. The "hold fire" order that did reach the pilots came at 21:25:00. Four seconds later, Maj. Schmidt announced that he was "rolling in in self-defense."

During the rest of the two-hour interview, Maj. Henry offers a few other compelling—and largely unsubstantiated—suggestions. He tells the board that the F-16s actually requested to open fire on the target before the cockpit recorders started rolling, well before Maj. Schmidt's request to lay down 20 mike-mike. He says that like the other AWACS crew members, he did not hear the "self-defense" call, even though a transcript from the CAOC shows that immediately after Maj. Schmidt's announcement, Maj. Henry radioed Saudi Arabia and said: "He's invoking self-defense ROE on the fire. On the road he sees artillery shooting at him." Maj. Henry also testifies that during those radio calls, the CAOC never warned him that friendlies were in Kandahar. In fact, they did, at 21:25:47—just as Maj. Schmidt's bomb fell toward the wadi.

Then, near the end of his testimony, this: "After 17 April, it came to my attention through conversations with other crews from my squadron that that F-16 unit in particular had had a history of being cavalier, wishing to engage targets at inappropriate times before 17 April," Maj. Henry says. "And that that had been debriefed in writing to our Mission Planning Team and in conversation with our Mission Planning Team, that that had been relayed to the CAOC, that the F-16 squadron had been somewhat problematic in that area."

"If that was significant enough of a point for the AWACS unit to actually submit a letter of complaint, it seems unusual that yourself as the mission crew commander would not have been apprised of that development prior to the 17th," Col. Matte says.

"It was not a letter of complaint per se," Maj. Henry responds. "We have so many debriefing issues, it is one of many, quite frankly, that we deal with on a daily basis as a result of a debrief. Problems with airspace control, problems with dealing with the U.S. Navy, problems with dealing with Pakistani airspace officials, that is all consolidated into a report, which is sent to the CAOC—the F-16 problem being one of many."

"Was this one of many notes repeated more than once to the CAOC from your AWACS unit?" Col. Matte asks.

"I don't know. At least one occasion."

"So it wasn't amplified in a letter from your commander to the CAOC?"

"No, sir."

"So it was not seen as a hugely significant event?"

"Significant among other significant events."

"The unit in question, the F-16 unit in question, do you know if they were actually involved with Op Anaconda?" Col. Matte asks.

"Unknown to me," Maj. Henry says. "I can't recall."

"When you were apprised of this after April 17 by whoever at your unit, were they able to conclusively link the pilots flying in Coffee formation to this previous incident?"

"No, sir, just the unit."

The day after Maj. Henry testifies, Gen. Baril and his team drive to the airport in Kuwait City to catch their flight to Saudi Arabia. For nearly a month now, the board has been planning this trip to the CAOC, but the Saudis still haven't approved the visas that the Canadians need to enter the kingdom. By late afternoon, an embassy official finally arrives at the airport, sprinting through the terminal with the paperwork in his hand. But he is literally minutes too late; the 4 p.m. plane has just left. There is a later flight, but it includes a stopover in Yemen. Gen. Baril decides that it's best if the board just goes home. They will have to settle for a CAOC tour by videoconference.

"The 17 April 2002 Tarnak Farms Range incident was a direct and proximate result of actions taken by the two F-16 pilots involved, Major William Umbach, call sign Coffee 51, and Major Harry Schmidt, call sign Coffee 52."

Those words—sandwiched between hundreds of pages of testimony and exhibits—are waiting for Lt.-Gen. T. Michael Moseley, the commander of the Afghanistan air war, when he arrives at work on Friday, June 7. Seven weeks and more than 70 witnesses later, the Coalition Investigation Board that Gen. Moseley appointed has reached a "clear and convincing" conclusion: Blame the pilots.

Signed by Brig.-Gen. Stephen Sargeant and his Canadian co-president, Brig.-Gen. Marc Dumais, the report is a hammering indictment of two veteran airmen: the former Top Gun instructor who rushed to attack, and the part-timer who failed to rein him in. "Both pilots of COFFEE flight demonstrated poor airmanship and judgment and a fundamental lack of flight discipline throughout the course of the incident," the final synopsis reads.

More than 70 pages, the report's summary of facts begins by noting that within days of launching Operation Enduring Freedom, "coalition air forces destroyed essentially all of the Taliban and al-Qaeda controlled air defenses, including aircraft, surface-to-air missiles, and anti-aircraft artillery [AAA]" in the country. The intense bombing runs left behind few—if any—legitimate threats that could shoot down a fighter jet flying above the imposed altitude floor of 15,000 feet. Early in the war, coalition ground troops also chased most leftover pockets of enemy forces into the mountains and border regions of Afghanistan. "As a result, traditional battle lines have not formed, with hostile forces spread throughout the country, widely interspersed with coalition and friendly Afghan ground forces," the report reads. "Due to the fluidity of this ground situation, known to soldiers and airmen as the ground order of battle, coalition commanders have instituted strict positive controls and conservative rules for the use of force by air forces operating over Afghanistan in order to prevent accidental bombing of friendly forces."

Surface-to-air fire—SAFIRE—is still common in the war zone, the report says, but standard procedures dictate that pilots mark the location with their targeting pods, then pass the coordinates to the AWACS. The OEF rules of engagement clearly state that "aircraft always have the right of self-defense against AAA," but "aircraft should NOT deliberately descend into the AAA range to engage and destroy AAA units which fire well below their altitude." Investigators say Maj. Schmidt did just that, displaying a "reckless disregard" for the strict rules in effect to prevent exactly the type of incident that occurred in the early morning hours of April 18.

Moments after the AWACS approved the F-16s to take a mark, Maj. Schmidt descended below 15,000 feet—"a serious breach of flight discipline, which reflects poor judgment"—and did not climb above the altitude floor until long after his bomb exploded. Although he needed to descend his jet as part of the technique he chose to acquire a mark, investigators say he should have selected an "alternative method" that would have kept his F-16 at a higher, safer altitude.

As he descended to just above 10,000 feet, Maj. Schmidt's reaction to the flashes in the night was to request permission to fire his 20mm cannons, an "ill-advised" tactic that the board says would have placed his jet even closer to the perceived threat. When told by the AWACS to "standby," Maj. Schmidt "appeared impatient," asking BOSSMAN if he should talk to a different controller onboard the radar plane. When ordered to "hold fire" one minute and 17 seconds later, the decorated pilot invoked self-defense, unleashing a 500-pound GBU-12 "with technical proficiency."

Not once, investigators say, did he try to leave the area or maneuver his jet in a defensive manner. And even though he claims he only dropped the bomb because he believed Maj. Umbach was under attack, Maj. Schmidt never radioed that perception to his flight lead or warned him to steer clear of the fire. "Because neither pilot stated over the radio that he was defending from the AAA, it is difficult to determine when, or if, they felt threatened," investigators concluded. "This lack of defensive maneuvering despite the post-incident description of the perceived SAFIRE does not indicate that COFFEE flight felt they were in imminent danger."

As his wingman slowed down and descended closer to the ground fire, Maj. Umbach, the leader of the two-plane mission, kept his F-16 in a wide right-hand turn, circling the target from more than five miles away and never descending below 20,000 feet. It is the flight lead's job—not the wingman's—to talk to BOSSMAN, yet when Maj. Schmidt asked for permission to lay down some 20 mike-mike, Maj. Umbach failed to step in and regain control. Instead, he cautioned Maj. Schmidt, using a jet-to-jet radio frequency, to "make sure it's not friendlies." However, Maj. Umbach never asked BOSSMAN about possible friendlies, nor did he repeat the call to his wingman when Maj. Schmidt failed to acknowledge the transmission.

"COFFEE 51 demonstrated what is commonly referred to as 'co-pilot syndrome,'" the report concludes. "As an average pilot, especially in comparison with the TOPGUN reputation of his wingman, he deferred his lead responsibilities, took a 'passive observer' role, and allowed the wingman to take actions clearly not in line with accepted procedures and in violation of the Commander's Intent and ROE." It is safe to assume that Maj. Schmidt "did not consider Major Umbach, who was reported by peers as an average pilot, as an authority or as an expert in this situation," the report says. "Thus, only a strongly authoritative call would have been likely to capture his attention. As it stands, that call did not come."

When Maj. Schmidt announced that he was rolling in in self-defense, Maj. Umbach "demonstrated his endorsement" by reminding his wingman "to check master arm, laser arm"—crucial steps in ensuring laser-guided bombs hit their targets. Yet more than three minutes after the explosion—and after BOSSMAN told the pilots to "disengage, friendlies Kandahar"—Maj. Umbach still wasn't sure if he and Maj. Schmidt were actually looking at the same target. He even asked BOSSMAN: "Can you confirm that they were shooting at us?"

"In his recorded and written statements, Major Umbach described a progression of the SAFIRE as moving from something relatively benign, to something threatening his flight, to a situation that was going bad very quickly," the report reads. "If COFFEE 51 believed his flight to be, at any point, in a threatened situation, the proper procedure would be to depart immediately to protect the aircraft and pilots for which he was responsible as flight lead."

Though self-defense is the inherent right of every pilot, the report notes that it cannot be "used as a planned work-around for solving poor tactics and decision trees. The F-16 pilot must make a conscious decision that the immediate threat outweighs the risk of fratricide." In other words, for self-defense to be a legitimate excuse, it must be absolutely necessary. "Numerous F-16 pilots interviewed by the Board stated that if they had found themselves in similar circumstances to those confronted by COFFEE flight on the evening of 17 April 2002, their immediate course of action would have been to accelerate to greater airspeed, climb in altitude, and leave the immediate area to evade and avoid the threat," the report reads. "COFFEE flight took none of these actions. Neither COFFEE 51 nor COFFEE 52, both of whom stated they believed they were being targeted at some point by the ground fire, aggressively maneuvered their aircraft in the face of what they presumably believed was a surface-to-air threat."

So how did these two pilots—so experienced and well trained—make such a catastrophic mistake? Part of the blame, investigators say, lies with Col. David C. Nichols, their commander in Kuwait. He "believed that the command and control relationship between his unit and the CAOC was dysfunctional," and "he emphatically stated that his unit was unable to obtain critically needed information on the locations and movements of friendly forces on the ground in Afghanistan." But investigators say the colonel—who appeared more interested in "being one of the boys" than being the boss—failed "to communicate these concerns to his superiors." That, "coupled with his indiscreet sharing of these concerns with subordinates, bred a climate of mistrust and led to an operational environment within his unit inconsistent with the Commander's Intent for Operation Enduring Freedom."

The biggest casualty of that "climate of mistrust" was the mission-planning process, investigators concluded. The airspace control order—the ACO—was a "critical reference for pilots in maintaining situational awareness to prevent mistaking friendly force activity for hostile actions." It included the existence of AO Truman (Task Force Rakkasan's turf) and the restricted operating zone in place over Tarnak Farm. But because Col. Nichols believed the 45-page ACO was full of "unmanageable information," the pilots under his command dismissed it as a useless tool. Officers working within the 170th Fighter Squadron's Mission Planning Cell weren't even sure whose job it was to skim through the daily ACO and make sure relevant airspace measures appeared on the pilots' onboard maps. "The resulting materials failed to provide pilots an adequate understanding of the airspace and ground restrictions published in the ACO," the report reads, "providing the COFFEE flight pilots with insufficient information to execute their assigned mission."

It is obvious, the report concludes, that Col. Nichols'"command style and the operational environment he fostered within the group was inappropriate." And unique among those stationed at Al Jaber, the colonel considered the surface-to-air threat level in Afghanistan to be "very high," while most pilots, including his acting deputy commander, described it as "low." It is impossible to know, the report says, whether that viewpoint trickled down to Maj. Schmidt, tainting his perception in the sky that night. But it is possible "that Colonel Nichols may have intentionally overstated the threat to OEF aircraft during his interview to provide some justification for COFFEE flight's aggressive reaction to the perceived threat on 17 April 2002."

Adding to the "atmosphere of complacency" at Al Jaber was a confusing chain of command within the Springfield fighter squadron. The wing commander, Col. Murphy, was deployed as a pilot, not an authority figure, but he described himself as the "detachment commander" and was "personally and fully involved in the post-incident debriefing" with Maj. Schmidt and Maj. Umbach. Lt.-Col. Ralph Viet was the operations group commander—in charge of more than 220 Springfield personnel in Kuwait—but "he viewed his role as primarily being in a monitoring capacity." Maj. Umbach was the squadron commander in charge of all the fighter pilots, but the board found that he "exercised little actual command authority." Indeed, the man actually responsible for the day-to-day activity of the pilots was Major John Milton, Harry Schmidt's roommate and the 170th operations officer. "It appeared that leadership positions in the 170 FS were filled based on rotation, or when it was time for a squadron member to have a certain duty title for career progression, with the expectation that everyone would have their opportunity," the board found. "As such, 'commander' was viewed more as a title than as a responsibility as evidenced by their 'monitoring' method of leadership. The presence of the wing's entire chain-of-command in the OEF deployment was unusual and it appeared from witness testimony that there was confusion as to exactly who was in charge in the deployed squadron environment and who had the ultimate responsibility to ensure that standards were met."

Like the F-16 pilots, the AWACS crew knew nothing about Tarnak Farm, its ROZ, or the existence of AO Truman, yet the board found that the "mission planning process provided the crew with adequate information to meet AWACS mission objectives." As soon as Maj. Schmidt requested permission to open fire, the mission crew commander, Maj. Art Henry, followed proper procedure and contacted the CAOC. "This process typically required at least five minutes and was done in a non-urgent reporting environment commensurate with this conservative" approach to dropping bombs in Afghanistan. "The timeframe in this situation was significantly compressed due to COFFEE 52's inappropriate response to the perceived SAFIRE," the report concludes. "From the time of the transmission from COFFEE that he 'had a tally in the vicinity' and was requesting permission to 'lay down some 20 mike-mike' until he released his GBU-12, only 1 minute and 57 seconds had elapsed."

That was hardly enough time for the CAOC to figure out what was firing on the ground—especially since neither pilot took a proper mark that would indicate exactly where they were looking. Nevertheless, within two minutes of hearing about Maj. Schmidt's 20 mike-mike request, the CAOC floor warned the AWACS "that there were friendlies in Kandahar and that COFFEE flight should egress the area," the report says. "Unfortunately, COFFEE 52 had already released a GBU-12" on the Canadian soldiers.

"Communications from BOSSMAN to COFFEE 52 to 'standby' and 'hold fire' prior to COFFEE 52 declaring self-defense were adequate and reasonable to the situation," investigators say. "The total time from the initial request to engage with 20mm fire until the friendlies advisory was passed from BOSSMAN to COFFEE flight was 2 minutes and 32 seconds. These rapidly accelerated time constraints caused by COFFEE 52 significantly limited the potential for the command and control procedures between the F-16s, AWACS, and the CAOC to prevent this incident."

The incident also had nothing to do with Go-pills, the board concluded. Neither pilot's use of the Dexedrine was "considered excessive or beyond what would typically be expected at their deployed location. The prescribing physicians felt that both pilots tolerated the Go/No-go-pills and managed their crew rest well prior to the incident." However, investigators did note that both pilots had complained about the grueling "24-hour nature of the operations in OEF," and that Maj. Schmidt carried the added burden of being a pilot, the chief of the Mission Planning Cell, and an expert tactician whom many junior fliers turned to for advice—"adding to the potential for chronic fatigue." In fact, an Air Force equation that measures fatigue concluded that Maj. Schmidt was performing at 91 percent "cognitive effectiveness" at the time of the incident, which is roughly the same as somebody who is about to fall asleep or has a blood alcohol level of .05 percent—the legal driving limit in some countries. "Added to this," the board wrote, "were the known challenges of the night-flying environment and limitations associated with NVGs," which "would have made light-producing events on the ground, such as weapons firing, more noticeable" and difficult to estimate.

"Prior to the identification of the perceived SAFIRE, the COFFEE flight mission had been uneventful," the board wrote. "Apart from a recent unsuccessful mission in Iraq against a mobile target that had moved, both pilots and their squadron had been flying in theater for over 30 days without experiencing an actual combat situation. The only experience the squadron had was dropping ordnance on a target that was not there. This mistake had been briefed to the JTF-SWA Commander just prior to the COFFEE flight mass brief. In addition, flying for long hours of time in a holding pattern over Afghanistan leads to boredom, increasing the level of experienced stress, the potential for complacency, and the probability of performance errors. Anxiety also impacts negatively on attention. However, during the sequence of radio transmissions recorded during the COFFEE flight, there is no indication that either of the pilots experienced a high level of anxiety."

If anything, Maj. Schmidt "appeared to channelize attention onto the ground fire to the exclusion of other important pieces of information about flight that should have directed him to select a different course of action." In their report, investigators go so far as to suggest that the former Top Gun's actions were driven "by existing supervisory and peer pressure on him to build credibility for the squadron along with his reputation as an experienced instructor pilot and an exceptionally proficient weapons officer." His stature in his new unit "likely created a perceptual set or expectancy related to encounters with SAFIRE," perhaps even leading Maj. Schmidt "to actively search for threats. In his statements, he described his mental model to some extent. He reported that he considered two scenarios when he encountered the SAFIRE; that is, it could be a ground fight between friendly and enemy forces or it could be a surface-to-air attack. Since it did not appear to be a ground fight, the only alternative in his mind was an attack on his or his wingman's aircraft."

Amid the final pages of the CIB's report—more than 26,000 words later—the board lists 11 additional "findings of significance," including recommendations for corrective action. Implement a mission-readiness inspection at units across Joint Task Force-Southwest Asia. Reinforce the importance of breaking out the ACO before every mission. Ensure that the CAOC does a more timely job of analyzing and disseminating SAFIRE reports.

"Ground forces are not required to report live-fire training or activity within the given Air Tasking Order day," reads Finding #4. "Recommendation: Establish requirements for ground forces to specifically identify and adhere to their planned periods of live-fire activity within a given Air Tasking Order."

"Ground forces are not currently represented at the Air Expeditionary Group level," the next finding says. "Recommendation: Assign Ground Liaison Officers [GLOs] to at least the group level of Expeditionary Air Force units." It is the exact same recommendation that emerged from the close air support symposium that Col. Nichols organized a month before the friendly fire bombing.

"The Airspace Control Order description of the Tarnak Farms did not encompass all types of weapons that were being fired," reads Finding #6.

"Recommendation: Ensure descriptions for live-fire training areas accurately and completely reflect the types of weapons being employed."

On the final page, Gen. Sargeant, the American co-president, submits three additional recommendations.

"I recommend appropriate disciplinary action, up to and including trial by general court-martial, against Major Harry M. Schmidt, the incident flight wingman."

"I recommend appropriate disciplinary action, up to and including trial by general court-martial, against Major William J. Umbach, the incident flight lead."

"I recommend appropriate disciplinary action, up to and including non-judicial punishment, against Colonel David C. Nichols, 332nd Air Expeditionary Group Commander."

What happens next is up to Lt.-Gen. Moseley.

21

For weeks, Canadian journalists have been poking around Springfield, Illinois, knocking on doors and filing stories and visiting the crypt of Abraham Lincoln, the capital city's favorite son. Everywhere they go, the question is always the same: Do you know the pilot who dropped the bomb? All across the city, all across the state, the families of the 183rd Fighter Wing have been visited by journalists. One showed up at John Milton's corn farm in rural Illinois. Another trampled through the flowers outside Bill Umbach's next-door neighbor's house. One even staked out a doctor's office parking lot, ambushing a flight surgeon as he walked to his SUV.

Ottawa Citizen reporter Glen McGregor is the first to knock on Harry Schmidt's door. Back from Kuwait, Harry refuses to talk about the bombing and threatens to call the police unless McGregor gets off his property. A *Citizen* photographer later snaps a shot of the crew-cut pilot as he leaves the West Side Christian Church on a Sunday morning. On Monday, June 10, the picture is plastered on the paper's front page: "F16 pilot 'haunted nightly,'" the headline reads. McGregor's story, citing several sources close to the Springfield Guard unit, is the first to identify Harry "Psycho" Schmidt as the fighter pilot who bombed and killed four Canadian soldiers. The article also quotes Captain Jamie Key, Maj. Schmidt's military lawyer, who phoned the newspaper after Harry told him about McGregor's surprise visit.

Capt. Key refused to confirm his client's name, but he assured readers that the fighter pilot "believed he was under attack" when he pressed the pickle button. "From hindsight, surely it was a mistake," Capt. Key told *The Citizen*. "But if you were to put him back in that

situation with the exact same knowledge he had that night, he would probably make the same decision he did and drop the ordnance." Capt. Key said
the past two months have been hell for his client "because he has no real
avenue to express his condolences to the families. He can't go to the press
and say he's extremely sorry, although that's exactly how he does feel. It's
something that haunts him nightly. Every time he goes to bed he knows that
he killed people on our side."

★ ★ ★

Six days after submitting its findings to Lt.-Gen. Moseley, some members
of the Coalition Investigation Board reconvene for a final meeting at
CENTCOM headquarters in Tampa. The general has sent a memo to the
co-presidents, asking them to clarify a few facts before he decides what disciplinary action, if any, to take against the F-16 pilots and their commander.
Brig.-Gen. Sargeant and Brig.-Gen. Dumais respond to the memo on June
14, writing their answers underneath each specific question.

Question: *Was the lack of specific notice disseminated to the air units of exactly
when the Tarnak Farms Range would be in use causal or substantially contributory
to the incident?*

CIB response: The CIB found this to be neither causal nor substantially
contributory to the incident.

Question: *Was the failure of the 332nd Air Expeditionary Group commander
[Col. Nichols] to ensure standardized mission planning causal to the incident?*

CIB response: While the failure by the 332nd Air Expeditionary
Group commander to ensure standardized mission planning was a substantial contributing factor, as indicated in the report, it was not causal
to the incident.

Question: *Was the 332nd Air Expeditionary Group's command environment
causal to the incident?*

CIB response: While the 332nd Air Expeditionary Group's command
environment was a substantial contributing factor, as indicated in the report,
it was not causal to the incident.

Question: *Was the ambiguous command structure of the 170th Expeditionary
Fighter Squadron causal to the incident?*

CIB response: While the ambiguous command structure of the 170th Expeditionary Fighter Squadron was a substantial contributing factor, as indicated in the report, it was not causal to the incident.

Question: *Was the lack of clear responsibility with the 332nd Air Expeditionary Group or the 170th Expeditionary Fighter Squadron routinely to check the Airspace Control Order (ACO) and disseminate important ACO information causal to the incident?*

CIB response: While lack of clear responsibility with the 332nd Air Expeditionary Group or the 170th Expeditionary Fighter Squadron routinely to check the ACO and disseminate important ACO information was a substantial contributing factor, as indicated in the report, it was not causal to the incident.

Question: *Do you conclude that environmental and situational factors were causal or substantially contributory to the incident?*

CIB response: The individual acts of the individual pilots were found to be the cause of the incident. Nevertheless, many environmental and situational factors provide context for understanding the acts or omissions of the pilots. An example of an environmental factor is the long duration of the incident sortie, resulting in pilot fatigue, as discussed in the report.

Question: *Did the ambiguous ground situation in Afghanistan and the incomplete information concerning friendly ground order of battle cause or substantially contribute to the incident?*

CIB response: The ambiguous ground situation and attendant risk of fratricide was a major reason the ROE [rules of engagement] for OEF were very restrictive. The incident pilots' failure to comply with the ROE led to a result which the restrictive ROE were designed to avoid. The CIB found the ambiguous ground situation to be neither causal nor substantially contributory to the incident.

Question: *Of what importance was the target missed by the 170th Expeditionary Fighter Squadron two days prior to the incident?*

CIB response: First, the debrief of this mission caused the incident pilots to have less time for pre-departure planning and briefing. Second, this represented a significant event for the unit and the debriefing reinforced the requirement to positively identify targets before employing. This debrief was attended by the incident pilots just minutes before their own mission mass brief and departure for their aircraft. However, the CIB found this to be neither causal nor substantially contributory to the incident.

★ ★ ★

The media's relentless pursuit of Harry Schmidt has enraged many in his adopted home of Springfield, where the 183rd Fighter Wing is as much a source of civic pride as the city's link to Abe Lincoln. Few in the Illinois capital have even met Maj. Schmidt. He just moved here a few months ago. But they don't like the idea of all these Canadian reporters harassing such a talented pilot—a patriot who volunteered to serve his country—as if he's some cold-blooded murderer. On June 13, three days after Maj. Schmidt's photo appeared on the front page of *The Ottawa Citizen*, Springfield's *State Journal-Register* swoops to his defense, publishing an editorial under the headline: "Losing focus in the fog of war."

"From fund-raisers for the affected families to sympathetic letters to the editors of various Canadian newspapers, Americans—and especially people from Springfield—have made it clear how saddened we are by this horrible mistake," the opinion piece reads. "But no one should forget this was a mistake of war. It was not a calculated attempt to injure friendly troops. It almost seems that vital distinction has been lost on some Canadians and the Canadian media, who in recent weeks have mercilessly hounded Maj. Harry Schmidt, the man they claim piloted the plane that fateful night. Canadian reporters have visited the wives and families of 183rd pilots; Maj. Schmidt has had to threaten to call the police to get reporters off his property and he was staked out at his church for a photograph that was published in some Canadian newspapers. It is a distasteful, inconsiderate, paparazzi-like pursuit of an extremely qualified and talented pilot who was serving his country and who is bound not to speak until the investigation is concluded."

The editorial notes that nearly 50 Americans have died in Afghanistan since 9/11, including more than 30 that the paper goes on to list name by name. "The death of the four Canadians was truly tragic. But we see no reason to add to that tragedy by badgering a man who may have made a mistake in the heat of battle. As the numerous deaths in this conflict prove, war is hell. It's time to get some perspective on this matter, and time for some people to remind themselves who the real enemy is."

★ ★ ★

Shortly after 5 p.m. on June 18, three days before Gen. Baril's final report is due on the desk of the chief of the Defence Staff, an Army public affairs officer walks into the downtown Ottawa office that doubles as the board's temporary headquarters. "Well, sir," he says. "You just won ten bucks."

Since he first took this job eight weeks ago, Gen. Baril has had a nagging hunch that the other board will release its findings before his team has a chance to finish their investigation. His hunch proved true. Someone in the U.S. military has leaked the CIB's report to *The New York Times*. The newspaper's wire service is already reporting some of the details, and by tomorrow morning, it will be front-page news across Canada.

Gen. Baril can already sense the fallout: If he submits his findings and recommendations a few days after the American report is already public knowledge, people will inevitably accuse him of copying, of trying to appease the U.S. by reaching the exact same conclusions. The press has already been hammering him lately, writing about the juicy contract that pays him $1,000 a day to lead this investigation. Some reports have suggested—incorrectly—that the general continues to be paid for another federal government contract while serving as president of the board.

Gen. Baril suggests an all-nighter. Work through the wee hours of the morning, then hand in the final report just as the papers hit the stands. His board members agree, assuring him that they can finish by the time the sun comes up. Gen. Baril orders his public affairs officer to read *The New York Times* article when it's posted on the Internet later tonight. *Keep the details to yourself*, he says, *but just tell me whether we absolutely need to finish by the morning.*

"A military investigation has found that an F–16 pilot mistakenly dropped a 500-pound bomb on Canadian soldiers conducting a nighttime live-fire exercise in Afghanistan in April because he did not take time to assess the threat properly before striking," reads the lead of the story. "The inquiry concluded in a classified report that the pilot, Maj. Harry Schmidt of the Illinois Air National Guard, thought he was under attack from the ground when he dropped the bomb that killed four Canadian soldiers and wounded eight. But instead of leaving the area to assess the threat and plan a possible counterstrike, as procedures dictate, Maj. Schmidt and the pilot of a second plane rushed to attack before a radar plane could confirm that they were hostile, officials said."

The article goes on to say that "the accident was all the more confounding to investigators because Major Schmidt is a seasoned former Navy pilot and instructor at the Navy's elite Top Gun weapons school." Maj. William Umbach, the flight lead, also allowed "events to spiral out of a control," the story adds. "'It's pretty cut and dried,' one anonymous official told the paper. 'They didn't follow proper procedures.'"

It is late in the evening when Gen. Baril's public affairs officer reads a version of the article online, then walks back to the BOI's offices. "You'd better can the report tonight," he tells the general.

★ ★ ★

Nobody can accuse Bill Umbach of violating the Air Force gag order hovering over Gen. Sargeant's investigation. Two months since the bombing, he still hasn't told his wife, Marlene, that he was the one flying with Harry Schmidt when he killed those Canadians.

Like everyone else, Marlene Umbach has already seen Maj. Schmidt's name in the papers. When she ran into Harry the other day, she even tried to reassure him and his wife that everything would work out for the best. By tomorrow, when she reads Bill's name in *The New York Times*, Marlene will have to start reassuring herself of the same thing.

★ ★ ★

The BOI's final report is at the printers by 6:30 Wednesday morning; on the desk of the chief of the Defence Staff by 8:00. Except for a few minor spelling errors, you wouldn't even notice it was a last-minute job. (Brian Decaire, for example, is referred to as Cpl. Declare. Billy Bolen's name is misspelled two different ways—Bolan and Boland.) In all, the final draft

217

is more than 800 pages long, including hundreds of pages of testimony transcripts and nearly 50 exhibits. At the very top of the pile is a letter to John McCallum, the minister of national defence, who recently replaced Art Eggleton in the job. Eggleton was dumped from the federal Cabinet the month before amid reports that his department had paid his ex-girlfriend $36,500 for a 14-page report on post-traumatic stress disorder.

"The Canadian Board has determined that the actions of the *Coffee 51 Flight* are the primary cause for the injuries and deaths," reads the BOI's report. "The pilot's actions were not consistent with either the expected practice for a defensive threat reaction or the existing published procedures, including the SPINS. This represented a failure of leadership, airmanship and technique.

"Even though it is reasonable to believe that the ground firing exercise at Tarnak Farm might have been perceived as enemy surface to air fire," the report continues, "a longer, more patient look from a safe altitude and range, combined with a good knowledge of the airspace and the threat in the area, should have confirmed that the event observed was neither a direct threat to their formation or enemy activity of a significant nature ... It remains a fact that highly qualified and experienced pilots, in continuous contact with an airborne controller, made the fateful decision to escalate an essentially benign but ambiguous situation to the point that a weapon was released and Canadian troops were killed."

The board concluded that both pilots, cleared by the AWACS to mark the target, approached the ground fire in a "routine fashion," appearing "calm and relaxed." Throughout the entire sequence of events, Maj. Umbach steered his jet in a wide right turn, miles away from the flashes—at one point flying directly over the Kandahar Airfield, a well-known concentration of thousands of coalition ground troops. Maj. Schmidt's "flight path over [the] same time interval is irregular, flown at a slower average speed and a lower average altitude than his lead," the report says. He insists he invoked self-defense because he thought Maj. Umbach was under attack, but "such an assessment defies the documented facts," investigators concluded. If he truly believed the other F-16 was in imminent danger, he should have "provided his lead with a directive call to take defensive action (i.e.: break L/R) or provide description of the threat direction and range." Instead, "both aircraft continued to circle the observed area and no attempts were made at creating a safe distance between what was observed on the ground and their location."

Not only were the flashes on the ground "sporadic" by the time the pilots noticed them, but the rounds were nowhere near their altitudes. The firing was surface-to-surface—not surface-to-air—and even if the weapons were aimed at the sky, the projectiles would fall far short of an F-16 flying above 15,000 feet, the minimum altitude at which fighters were supposed to be transiting (the maximum range of Ainsworth Dyer's C-6 machine gun was 10,170 feet; Brett Perry's Carl Gustav could only reach 6,720 feet; and numerous witnesses testified that any machine-gun ricochets bouncing off the tank hulls were burning out no higher than 1,000 feet).

The board concedes that "ranges and heights are very hard to evaluate" using night vision goggles, and it is "very likely that the apex of the tracers observed by *Coffee 51 Flight* appeared much higher than reality. That said, since neither aircraft took evading action, the height was still most likely well below their comfort level for observed AAA."

Tragically, while there is no doubt the pilots saw something firing into the lenses of their NVGs, the infrared strobes and the glint tape that the Canadian troops were wearing on their uniforms was not visible from so high in the sky.

Adding to the confusion that night was the fact that neither pilot—"due to poor technique"—transmitted an accurate mark to BOSSMAN, hindering "the AWACS and CAOC from potentially correlating the SAFIRE report with the night live-fire exercise being conducted at Tarnak Farm." It typically takes the CAOC at least five minutes to assess coordinates and approve a bombing run, the board concluded, but without a mark, ground control has no way of knowing exactly what the pilots are seeing. Yet even without the proper coordinates, the CAOC ordered the pilots to leave the area just two minutes after the AWACS first passed along Maj. Schmidt's request to "lay down some 20 mike-mike." Unfortunately, CAOC's order to the AWACS came as Maj. Schmidt's bomb fell toward Tarnak Farm.

"Perhaps most central to the tragedy," the report reads, "was the simple, initial fact that *Coffee 52* [Maj. Schmidt] did not recognize the observed ground fire event as a surface-to-surface training exercise, instead perceiving it as enemy surface-to-air fire. This failure of perception was the initiating factor that started the ensuing sequence of missed cues and hasty, imprudent actions that led to the premature release of the weapon."

However, the Canadian board of inquiry concluded that "as much as the F-16 pilots bear final responsibility for the fratricide incident, there existed other systemic shortcomings in air coordination and control procedures, as well as mission planning practices by the tactical flying units, that may have prevented the accident had they been corrected." Some of the "systemic shortcomings existed in the quality and nature of the coordination between ground and air forces, as well as between the CAOC and the tactical flying units. Had they been corrected, the incident might have been prevented."

Following all the proper rules, Capt. Joe Jasper, A Company's 2I/C, submitted a Tarnak Farm "Range Request Form" to the 3 PPCLI's training officer more than a week before the bombing. The Para Company's plan to fire at the former al-Qaeda compound was approved during a Task Force Rakkasan weekly resource conference. "The Range SOPs [standard operating procedures] do not delegate any responsibility to the unit [A Company] for coordination higher than the Task Force, or with the Coalition Force Air Component Command," the report reads. "This was and is, clearly a US responsibility." The Rakkasans believed they fulfilled that responsibility, establishing a ROZ—a restricted operating zone—around Tarnak Farm. The entry in the ACO did not specify exactly when soldiers would be firing, but the ROZ was effective 24 hours a day. Whether or not soldiers were actually shooting, pilots were not allowed to fly within half a mile of the compound, from the ground to 11,000 feet MSL (above sea level)—let alone drop a bomb in there without absolute approval.

"From the testimonies reviewed, it quickly became evident to the Canadian Board that AWACS and F-16 aircrew knowledge about the presence of the Tarnak Farm Range near the Kandahar Airport was lacking," the report reads. "There were a number of reasons why this was the case."

Because of the long duration of OEF flights, neither pilots nor AWACS personnel are allowed to prepare their own mission materials. Doing so would add hours to their crew duty days, violating strict rules meant to ensure that everyone gets enough rest. Instead, fliers depend on the Mission

Planning Cell (MPC) to brief them on what to expect when they reach Afghanistan. But within the 170th Fighter Squadron, nobody quite knew who was responsible for breaking out the 45-page Airspace Control Order (ACO) and ensuring that pilots were aware of things such as restricted operating zones and areas of operation. "Since everyone in the unit involved with the ACO felt the document was cumbersome and difficult to work with" and "the volume of the information is often unmanageable and can lead to confusion," all details about Afghanistan airspace "below 10,000 ft AGL was intentionally removed from the mission data given to the aircrew in order to simplify the information provided in their mass briefs and flight maps." AWACS mission planners followed a similar routine, filtering "some of the airspace coordination to make it a little bit more user friendly for the mission." In both cases, the Tarnak Farm ROZ and AO Truman were among the many measures that didn't make the cut.

Had the pilots "transmitted a complete and accurate SAFIRE report, and had either the F–16 or the AWACS aircrew known of the existence of the Tarnak Farm Multi Purpose Range Complex and its ROZ, this knowledge may have dramatically altered the decision making process, thereby precluding the fratricide incident," the BOI concluded. "It is common knowledge that ACOs and ATOs have never been easy to work with. Their size and the intricate airspace coordination that is contained within, reflect the complexity of modern airspace battle management requirements, a fact of life that has to be dealt with in modern aerial conflict. Nevertheless, it is clear that in this instance, a possibly arbitrary decision within the MPCs of disparate units to filter information led to the unintended consequence of excising critical mission data. Regrettably, such unintended oversights were not detected due to the lack of a feedback loop to ensure that key elements did not slip through the cracks."

And elements did slip through the cracks. The Army, for example, established a terminal control area (TCA), a 30-nautical-mile ring of restricted airspace around the Kandahar Airfield that it thought extended from 6,000 feet to 27,000 feet. But in reality—and in the ACO—it only reached 18,000 feet. So, on the night of April 17, when Kandahar Ground Control Approach saw the blip-blip-blip of the F–16s on their radar screen, the planes were actually above the restricted airspace and under no obligation to contact the airfield. Still, investigators said the pilots, being so close to the airport, should have surmised that the firing on the ground could be friendlies.

From the Air Force side, the pilots' local chain of command bears some responsibility for the substandard mission planning because "no process appeared to have been in place to confirm that all aircrew read and understood all applicable documents prior to mission execution." However, the report notes that "this shortfall extended as far as the CFACC organization [the Coalition Forces Air Component Command, led by Lt.-Gen. T. Michael Moseley], which did not appear to have a defined process in place to familiarize incoming aircrew with the theater organization, the existing command and control facilities, or the overall Commander's Intent." Unlike in other operations, such as the Balkans, new pilots arriving in theater were rarely given a familiarization tour of the CAOC. Such a visit, the report suggests, would "increase the individual's knowledge of the theater, his understanding of the various mechanisms in place to support him, and give the CAOC leadership the chance to reinforce the key messages such as the Commander's Intent and the ROE."

Among its recommendations, the board suggests that the CAOC initiate a mandatory briefing for all newly arrived pilots, and also periodically review the mission briefs being prepared by its units across the Gulf region. Current mission-planning procedures—within fighter units and AWACS squadrons—should also be reviewed to ensure that all fliers are properly briefed on the ACO. "More specifically," the board urges, "the way in which ROZ activation and deactivation procedures are dealt with during combat operations need to be reviewed. If such procedures are currently in place, it would appear from the evidence collected to date that their use was incomplete. The Board believes that if the procedures had been more stringently enforced, the chain of events that led to the incident at Tarnak Farm on 17 April 2002 could possibly have been avoided."

The SPINS—special instructions—for Operation Enduring Freedom should include an additional section called "COALITION FORCES RANGES IN AFGHANISTAN," which would include details about the existence and use of live-fire ranges, the board suggests. As well, the ACO "should contain a detailed list, including but not limited to timings, weapons to be used, altitude restrictions and coordinating agencies of all the live firing exercises scheduled to take place." The air tasking order (ATO), the daily schedule of missions posted by the CAOC, should also include "banners" warning pilots about every live-fire exercise scheduled that day for the Afghan theater.

"Overall, therefore, it is the conclusion of the board that both the nature and the quality of the coordination between ground and air forces surrounding the incident was revealed to be lacking. While each party had established procedures, the degree to which their mechanisms were able to exchange significant information, and more importantly, transmit this information to operational aircrew, was not sufficient to break the chain of this particular accident."

PART III: ON TRIAL

Lloyd Smith isn't exactly sure what made him put up those three white flagpoles near the side of his driveway. In hindsight, it was a combination of things rather than one specific reason. He needed to keep busy, of course. For a while, with the wake and the funeral and all the confusion, the days and the nights blended into one, leaving little time to ponder what it all meant. But as the weeks wore on, the distractions faded. Nathan is really gone.

Charlotte, Lloyd's wife, has found some smidgen of comfort in the old photos, the ones of her son back in Porter's Lake, and later, standing in his Army fatigues, proud and fearless. One of the shots, framed and displayed in their Tatamagouche living room, captures a smiling Pte. Smith crouched under the Kandahar sun, holding a rifle close to his dirty brown t-shirt. Unlike Nathan's mom, his dad never looks at the picture when he walks by. He hasn't looked at any photos since he answered that ringing telephone on his oil tanker. He just can't.

But he can stare at those skinny white poles on the front lawn, sometimes for hours. Atop the middle one, a Canadian flag flaps in the Nova Scotia wind. On one side, the Union Jack flies; on the other, the colours of Alpha Company, Nathan's unit of paratroopers. As the years pass, Lloyd will add to his homemade monument. Cement patio stones. A wooden gate near the entrance. Soon it will even include an elevated bronze plaque in honor of Private Nathan L. Smith, who died "In Defence of our Freedom." That won't seem quite right, though. His dad knows Nathan wouldn't have wanted all the attention to himself, so he'll install three more wooden plaques near the bronze one, each chiseled with the names of the other soldiers who died at Tarnak Farm: Ainsworth Dyer. Richard Green. Marc Léger. This shrine, and all the work that goes with it, will be Lloyd's temporary escape, his own solitary way of coping with what he lost that night in Afghanistan. His wife will flip through photo albums. He will tinker with his monument.

On June 28, 2002—what would have been Nathan Smith's 27th birthday—Lloyd wakes up and walks out his side door, raising all three of his new flags into the summer morning. A few journalists have stopped by to watch, not because it's Nathan's birthday, but because—as if today isn't already hard enough for the Smiths—it is also the morning that both Canada and the United States will officially release the results of their investigations into the friendly fire bombing. Considering last week's leak to *The New York Times*, what both militaries have to say is a mere formality, official confirmation of what everyone already knows: The pilots messed up.

In Ottawa, Gen. Maurice Baril releases a censored version of his board's seven-page executive summary, which concludes that "the proximate fault for the outcome of the attack lies with the two F-16 pilots." Gen. Baril tells a packed news conference that neither pilot was briefed about the Canadians training on the ground, but nevertheless the decision to drop a 500-pound bomb was "not consistent with either the expected practice for a defensive threat reaction or the existing published procedures" in place for Operation Enduring Freedom. "There is one cause of the accident in here," the retired general says. "The decision of the pilot to engage at that time was his sole responsibility and he is the cause of the accident."

In Florida, Lieutenant-General Michael DeLong, the deputy commander of U.S. CENTCOM, reads a short, two-page statement to the media. "The CIB found the cause of the friendly fire incident to be the failure of the two pilots to exercise appropriate flight discipline, which resulted in a violation of the rules of engagement and an inappropriate use of lethal force," he says. "The board further found that failings within the pilots' immediate command structures, while not causing the incident, were contributing factors." Because the 1,500-page report is still classified, and because Lt.-Gen. Moseley is still contemplating disciplinary action, Gen. DeLong refuses to discuss any other details. A few "no comments" later and the news conference is over—six minutes after it started.

Among the families left behind by Maj. Schmidt's bomb, reaction to the news is mixed, as it will often be as the years drag on. Richard Léger, Marc's dad, is relieved. All along, he worried that maybe his son, who was the range safety officer that night, accidentally made a mistake that somehow led to the bombing. It is obvious now, more than two months later, that Marc did nothing wrong.

Ainsworth's father, Paul, wants money. "Our children always helped us," he says, remembering how Ains often sent home a chunk of his paycheck. "This report can't bring back our children. Give us something to help support us. I get nothing out of it. I can only go to the place where my son is buried."

Sitting inside his home, his flags waving outside, Lloyd Smith says he just wants to make sure this never happens to anyone else. "If sending him to jail would bring my son back, I'd say do it," he says of the pilot. "But my son's death has got to mean more than that. Some good's got to come out of it."

Sgt. Lorne Ford, who almost died in that Afghan desert, has watched his mouth since landing back in Canada. His leg is still a mess, and what was once his right eye is a shiny glass orb. But he's kept quiet, hesitant to say anything out loud that would compromise the investigations. Now that they're done, all he wants is an apology, not necessarily for him, but for the families. "I would like to see them come forward," he says of Maj. Schmidt and Maj. Umbach. "It's been the way I've always been taught—if you do something wrong, you come forward and take it."

★ ★ ★

Charles William Gittins has as many courtroom sketches hanging on his office walls as he does degrees. Framed, each one larger than the last, the charcoal drawings are surrounded by an even wider array of mounted newspaper clippings and magazine articles—all written about him. A client visiting for the first time would know at least one thing for certain: This defense lawyer isn't afraid of the spotlight. Or the big bad military machine.

For more than a decade, Charlie Gittins has made a career of saving soldiers and sailors and airmen from going to jail, all while degrading and humiliating any senior officer who stands in his way. He adores the life, the high that comes with shredding generals on the witness stand, waiting to pounce when he catches one in a lie. JAGs fear him. The Pentagon hates him. And, for the most part, the press loves him, a quote-factory whose by-the-minute remarks and sometimes hyperbolic accusations only get more outrageous—and personal—as a trial unfolds.

Ironically enough, this constant pain in the military's ass is its own creation, a former Marine Corps navigator who went to law school on the government's tab. After graduating from Washington, D.C.'s Catholic University at the top of his class, Gittins, a New Jersey native, served six more years in uniform, including a stint as a deputy staff judge advocate during Operation Desert Storm. In one of his more awkward assignments, he was tasked to investigate a friendly fire incident along the Kuwaiti border, where a Marine A-6 pilot mistakenly dropped on an American Howitzer. It was tough. He was actually interrogating guys he used to fly with. In the end, he and his co-investigator concluded that the bombing was pilot error and recommended disciplinary action. The cockpit recordings were the clincher. "Burn, motherfuckers!" one of the pilots yelled as the bomb exploded.

But Charlie has always been a defense-minded guy. *Better 100 guilty men go free than one innocent man go to jail.* When he left active duty as a lieutenant-colonel, Gittins won a coveted job at the Washington, D.C., law firm of Williams & Connolly, which defended U.S. President Bill Clinton during the Whitewater scandal. His breakthrough case came in 1993, when he acted on behalf of Naval Commander Bob Stumpf, an elite F-18 Hornet pilot who was dragged before a military court of inquiry—a notch below a court-martial—for his attendance at the now-infamous 1991 Tailhook convention in Las Vegas. What was supposed to be a gathering of current and retired fighter pilots became a festival of porn and strippers that ended with more than 80 women claiming they were assaulted. Backed by Charlie Gittins, who accused the military of conducting a "witch hunt" fueled by "feminist backlash," Comm. Stumpf was eventually exonerated.

In 1998, the bombastic lawyer was again the subject of courtroom sketch artists when he represented Sergeant-Major Gene C. McKinney— the highest ranking non-officer in the U.S. Army—who was facing a court-martial on 18 counts of sexual misconduct. Six different women leveled accusations against the sergeant-major, but a jury found him guilty on only a single count of obstruction of justice. Along the way, Gittins, now working for his own private firm, toyed with the Pentagon, threatening to release the names of other top Army officers who, unlike McKinney, were allowed to retire quietly amid allegations of sexual misconduct. His bulldog style, both in and out of the courtroom, won him many new fans in the press gallery. More than anything, the reporters loved the fact that instead of driving 90 minutes from his rural Virginia home to his office in Alexandria, he flew to work every morning in the cockpit of his twin-engine Cessna. Those 22 minutes, he often boasted, are "the high point of my day."

Indeed, Charlie Gittins knows as well as any defense lawyer that the court of public opinion is sometimes more important than the court of law. He always takes time to talk to reporters, well aware that every single bit of ink puts that much more pressure on the people trying to bury his clients. "Ninety-nine times out of a hundred, sunlight disinfects," he says. "So the more people see, the better they will understand." As far as he is concerned, none of his clients is a real criminal anyway. "Military guys get in trouble once," he says. "You don't see guys repeatedly get in trouble. One time they get a court martial, and then they are going to be good guys for the rest of their lives."

His latest high-profile client was Scott Waddle, the commander of USS *Greeneville*, the Navy submarine that collided with a Japanese fishing boat off the coast of Hawaii, killing nine. The crash occurred as the crew performed an emergency surfacing drill for the viewing pleasure of more than a dozen civilian VIPs onboard. Military investigators concluded that Comm. Waddle didn't conduct a proper periscope search in advance of the maneuver. Waddle disputed the claim, but—against the advice of Charlie Gittins—he apologized directly to the victims' families and agreed to testify at a court hearing even though the Navy refused to grant him immunity. "I'd like to extend my sincere apology," he told relatives of the dead, speaking through a Japanese interpreter. "I can't ask for forgiveness. This is a burden I will carry to the grave." Comm. Waddle was allowed to retire with a full pension.

It is mid-June 2002 when Harry Schmidt first phones Charlie Gittins at his farmhouse office in Middletown, Virginia. Lang Sias—Bob Stumpf's wingman back when the Tailhook scandal erupted, and a friend of Maj.

Schmidt's from their Navy days—suggested that he give Charlie a call. During that first chat, Harry takes Gittins through the night of the attack, how he thought Bill was going to be shot down, how he had no choice but to invoke self-defense.

"You said: 'Rolling in in self-defense?'" Charlie asks him. "You swear to me, we're going to get a tape and it's going to say: 'I'm rolling in in self-defense.'"

"Yes," Harry answers.

★ ★ ★

"Moments after an American pilot dropped a bomb that accidentally killed four Canadian soldiers in Afghanistan in April, an air controller told him, 'You're cleared. Self-defense,' according to a transcript of the communication obtained by *The Washington Times*. The F-16 fighter pilot who dropped the bomb, Maj. Harry Schmidt, and his lead pilot, Maj. William Umbach, are expected to cite this clearance in their defense as the military decides whether they should face criminal charges."

Published July 18—exactly three months after the bombing—the front-page article is the first to quote Charles W. Gittins as Maj. Schmidt's lawyer. As he has so many times before, Gittins wastes no time attacking the Air Force officers who sit higher up the chain of command than his new client. "It shows that neither the air crew nor the AWACS were briefed about friendlies conducting a live-fire exercise," he says of the newly disclosed transcript. "And that's a command-and-control failure, not an air crew failure."

The article ignites a frenzy north of the border, especially in the country's newsrooms, where journalists scramble to figure out exactly what this leak means. "You're cleared. Self-defense." Did the AWACS authorize Maj. Schmidt to drop? Was the attack inevitable, even though the "you're cleared" came 30 seconds after impact? For weeks now, the powers that be have assured the country—and the soldiers' families—that the pilots are to blame. They dropped that 500-pound bomb. They killed those soldiers. But the cockpit transcript, the first piece of raw evidence to surface since the night of the attack, appears to reveal that the AWACS also has some explaining to do. Why didn't investigators release this transcript to the public? A cover-up must be brewing. Charlie Gittins certainly thinks so.

"Our aviators need to be provided the best intelligence possible, and it's clearly apparent to me—and it should be to anyone who reviews the information—that they're not being well-served," he says after *The Times* article is published, his office phone ringing all day with Canadian reporters. "It is unconscionable that general officers would stand up and accuse the pilots of being derelict when they were not provided that kind of information." In another interview, Gittins says he is "dumbfounded" that investigators hid the fact "that our guys were cleared to drop." Maj. Schmidt is "clearly remorseful and sad that people were killed and injured in the accident, but it was an accident," he says. "Now his concern is that he's going to be left holding the bag."

In Canada, at least, the sensational leak shifts the spotlight back to Gen. Maurice Baril, the Liberal lapdog, the prime minister's lackey. The man who was paid $1,000 a day to get to the bottom of all this. Did you even see this transcript? Did you know that the AWACS was in the dark about the live-fire exercise? Are you conspiring with the U.S. to hide the truth? Gen. Baril, of course, *has* seen the transcript. He knows full well that the AWACS controller said "you're cleared, self-defense" 30 seconds after the bomb exploded. He also knows that the AWACS had no clue Tarnak Farm even existed. So what? As far as he is concerned, that certainly doesn't exonerate Harry Schmidt. He should have marked the target. He should have waited for the CAOC to do its job. He should have flown away from the ground fire—not toward it. But Gen. Baril can't say that aloud, not yet, not while the U.S. is still deciding what to do with these two pilots. "It would not be either right, fair or even legal for me to say anything," the general tells one reporter. "I'd love to, though."

That's hardly enough to silence the conspiracy train. Some opposition members of parliament are already demanding a completely new investigation. "He's the wrong guy to put in charge of an inquiry that is so important to a nation, so important to the families of those killed," Leon Benoit, the Canadian Alliance Defence critic, says of Gen. Baril. "We need someone we can trust."

Editorial pages overflow with similar sentiment. "We wonder what the coalition soldiers still on the ground in Afghanistan think of this apparent cover-up," writes *The Gazette* in Montreal. "And we wonder why the Canadian government played along with it." *The Toronto Sun* says the transcript "raises questions about the integrity of the whole process. Perhaps two inquiries weren't enough." Canada's largest daily newspaper, *The Toronto Star*, goes one step further. "Bluntly put, we feel as if we've been duped," reads one of its editorials. "That the U.S. military would try to downplay its responsibility for the breakdown in vital communications that led to the tragedy should not really come as a surprise. But that our own forces may have participated in a cover-up of the facts is an appalling affront to the families of the young men who lost their lives." What is "most upsetting," *The Ottawa Citizen* writes, is that Gen. Baril "seems to have concealed pertinent facts from Canadians."

Even some of the survivors' relatives, confused by the details of the leak, are starting to wonder whether the military is pushing a lie. "I hate to say it, but it almost sounds like a cover-up," says Richard Léger, Marc's father. "They're covering up for the higher command that didn't follow their procedure and trying to blame it on the pilots. That's what it sounds like to me. I just want the truth. I don't want contradiction. I just want the truth." The truth, as Richard will learn in the coming months, will be difficult—if not impossible—to spot. It will be twisted and manipulated, spun and re-spun by lawyers and flacks and columnists and witnesses and nearly everyone else with two cents in their pockets.

★   ★   ★

The day after *The Washington Times* publishes the cockpit transcript, Bill Umbach answers the telephone at his lakefront home in Petersburg, Illinois. For weeks, reporters have been calling the house and knocking on the door, but he and Marlene, following their lawyer's instructions, have kept quiet. But on July 19, 12 weeks after those four Canadians died, Maj. Umbach doesn't hang up. He keeps talking to the journalist on the other end of the line. He wants those families up in Canada to know just how sorry he is for their loss.

"It's a tragic incident and my heart and thoughts are continuously with the families there," he tells the *National Post*. "I cannot overemphasize that, and it's been from the very beginning. It's the greatest tragedy of war and it would be my greatest hope that we do everything to try to minimize the chances of that happening again.

"I consider all of them my friends, my partners," he continues. "We are all in one force working against the bad guys. It's not us and them. Our two countries are together."

When asked if he and Maj. Schmidt are being used as scapegoats to cover up for a larger command-and-control problem, Maj. Umbach reluctantly clams up. "I wish I could answer, but I really want to stick with my lawyer's advice on that," he says. "I wish I could answer that one."

★ ★ ★

The first batch of Canadian troops lands back in Edmonton on July 28, a Sunday. As the buses roll from the airport to the garrison, hundreds of people line the streets, waving and cheering and standing near trees wrapped in yellow ribbons. In many storefront windows, hand-painted signs welcome the Princess Patricias home. Soldiers cry and laugh as they hug families they haven't seen in six months. Some stare at the beauty of their newborn babies for the first time. Marley Léger stays home, careful not to intrude on everyone's happiness. The flowers that Marc ordered before he left—one bouquet every month—are still arriving at the door. "The fact that everybody else is getting their soldier home except a few of us, it's going to be rough, very rough," she says. "I've come out of shock and come to the realization that this is reality and Marc isn't coming home. It is their day. My being there would just bring back a lot of bad memories for them. It is a day to rejoice."

★ ★ ★

John Odom was out jogging on the morning of April 18, his Walkman tuned, as it always is, to National Public Radio. If you're going to go for a run in Shreveport, Louisiana, April is probably the best time to do it. It's not too hot yet, and those famous roses are just starting to bloom. As he ran through the streets of the southern city where he was born and raised and has been fortunate enough to work for most of his 54 years, Colonel

Odom heard the news report through his earphones: Canadian troops were killed yesterday in what appears to be a friendly fire accident. He felt an immediate chill. Not because the colonel has any specific connection to Canada, but because nearly eight years ago to the day, those F-15s shot down the Blackhawk choppers in Iraq, killing 26. *You know,* he thought to himself, *April is not a good month for the United States Air Force.*

Col. Odom was part of the prosecution team that conducted the pre-trial hearing—called an Article 32—for the AWACS crew that was later charged in connection with the Blackhawk shootdown. It was, at least for now, his highest-profile case as a JAG. But it was hardly his first. Col. John S. Odom Jr. has been working as an Air Force lawyer for a long time, nearly 30 years now. A graduate of Louisiana State University's law school, his resumé includes stints at more than 50 air bases in 18 different countries, most as a reservist. For the better part of three decades, he has squeezed his part-time Air Force duties in between a successful private practice, where he specializes in personal injury and medical malpractice litigation. His firm—Jones, Odom, Davis & Politz—occupies one of the old, beautiful mansions on Shreveport's Fairfield Avenue. Except for the new elevator, the entire home, including the wooden spiral staircase in the main hallway, looks exactly the same as the day it was built.

In May 2002, a month after he heard the news on the radio, Col. Odom settled one of his largest-ever lawsuits. He had more money in his bank account than he was going to need for a long, long time. So he called his Air Force boss, Brigadier-General Charles Dunlap, the staff judge advocate in the headquarters of Air Combat Command. Odom started working part-time for the general shortly after 9/11, helping dozens of Air National Guard units mobilize for Operation Noble Eagle, the daily fighter jet patrols of Canada-U.S. airspace. He helped pilots write their wills, and when JAGs deployed overseas, the colonel was in charge of finding replacements for the bases back home. Important work, but not exactly the glamorous side of the United States Air Force.

"Look," he told Gen. Dunlap over the phone, speaking in his thick Louisiana drawl. "I've had a great year and it's only May. I'll keep doing what I'm doing, but if you come up with something and you need me full-time, you just have to call."

That call comes three months later, in mid-August 2002, when Col. Odom and his wife, Gale, are on a New York getaway, enjoying some Broadway shows and the comfort of the Waldorf-Astoria Hotel. Gen. Dunlap phones the mansion first, but Wanda, his longtime paralegal, says the colonel is out of town for the weekend. The general asks for the hotel phone number. This can't wait. He catches the Odoms right after dinner.

"You remember back in May when you called and said you could volunteer for a long tour?" Gen. Dunlap asks.

"Yes, sir," Col. Odom says, a tad shocked that the general tracked him down. "What you got?"

"Well, I think I've got a project that you might be interested in."

"What's that, sir?"

"Well, we think somebody is going to have to look at this friendly fire incident from Tarnak Farms over in Afghanistan and we think it's going to be kind of a big deal. It might be quite a chunk of time."

"Cool," Col. Odom says.

"Well, give it some thought and get back to me," Gen. Dunlap says.

"Sir, I just gave you my answer. I said cool. When do we start?"

"When are you and Gale coming home?"

"Well, we're going to be home Sunday, sir."

"Monday would be fine."

When Monday arrives, Col. Odom drives through the main gate at Shreveport's Barksdale Air Force Base. Waiting for him inside is the complete 13-volume report of the Coalition Investigation Board. For two months, the pile of paper had been sitting on the desk of Lt.-Gen. Moseley, the man who was supposed to decide whether the pilots should be disciplined. Last week, however, the Air Force brass suddenly removed Moseley from the case amid a potential conflict of interest. As the overall commander of the Afghanistan air war, he was technically in charge of the pilots when Maj. Schmidt unleashed his bomb. Probably best, the Air Force figures, if someone else decides how the pilots are punished.

Of course, many suspect the decision to dump Gen. Moseley had a lot more to do with that memo he fired off to his subordinates the day after the bombing, the one that said "it is difficult to imagine a scenario" in which the F-16s could not have flown away from the perceived threat and waited for further instructions before unleashing their attack. The e-mail was recently leaked to *The Washington Times*, adding even more pressure to an already sensitive file. The front-page article quoted Charlie Gittins, Maj. Schmidt's new lawyer. "If true," he said of Gen. Moseley's memo, "such comments would cast grave doubt on the fairness of any decision that Gen. Moseley might make in this case, as it indicates pre-disposition prior to completion of the investigation."

Whatever the reason, the case has been handed off to Lieutenant-General Bruce Carlson, the commander of the 8th Air Force. Headquartered just outside Shreveport, "The Mighty Eighth" encompasses more than 41,000 active-duty, Air National Guard and reserve personnel. Their specialty is the B-52 bomber. No Vipers here, although the boss is no stranger to fighter jets. A one-time combat pilot in the old OV-10 turboprops, Gen. Carlson also has hundreds of hours in the cockpit of an F-16.

But before the three-star general can decide what to do with America's most infamous Viper pilots, his legal staff—which now includes Col. John Odom—has some work to do. This morning, as the colonel parks his car at the base, he has no way of knowing that two more years will pass before he returns to his civilian law firm.

★ ★ ★

In law school, Gregory C. Graf specialized in the intricacies of oil and gas litigation. Never actually practiced it, though. Became a federal prosecutor instead, then a defense lawyer. When boredom set in a couple of years later, the New York native left the courtroom and joined the Air Force, flying F-4 Phantoms in Japan and Korea. "Ghost" Graf jumped back to the legal world in 1991, resigning from active duty in the cockpit and taking a job as an assistant district attorney in Colorado. He spent most of his time sending organized criminals to prison, but he never quite left the military, working as a reserve JAG in the Colorado Air National Guard for most of the next decade. In 1999—nearly nine years after he last flew a fighter jet—his unit asked him to retrain in the F-16. By the time Col. John Odom calls him in August 2002, Lt.-Col. Graf is a prominent Denver defense lawyer moonlighting as a fighter pilot at the 120th Fighter Squadron.

It is pretty obvious why Col. Odom is phoning. Ghost is one of one, a certified F-16 operator who has also prosecuted his fair share of high-profile defendants. Col. Odom wants him to fly down to Louisiana and take a look at the targeting pod videos, see if he reaches the same conclusion as Gen. Sargeant and the CIB. Lt.-Col. Graf is hesitant. In the fighter pilot universe, nobody wants Harry and Bill to be criminally charged. How can a lawyer, after all, possibly judge what a warrior does in the heat of combat? They sit at a desk all day. Ironically enough, Greg Graf even called the office of the Air Force's Judge Advocate General in the days after the bombing, volunteering to represent the pilots long before anyone knew who they were. More than anything, he wanted to make sure the brass didn't try to railroad Harry and Bill for the simple fact that they are Air National Guard—not full-time Air Force.

As reluctant as he is to help Col. Odom build a case against one of his own, Lt.-Col. Graf does want to watch those tapes. He wants to see firsthand what went wrong that night, what exactly triggered Harry Schmidt to attack the Canadians. He eventually agrees to come to Barksdale, review the evidence, and give his personal opinion—as a lawyer and a fighter pilot—about whether this case belongs in court. By the time he arrives in Shreveport, Col. Odom has already assembled an impressive team of would-be prosecutors. Among his recruits is Major James K. Floyd, widely considered one of the best Air Force trial lawyers in the entire United States military. The group's junior attorney is Captain Kate Oler, a Boston University law school graduate stationed at Bolling Air Force Base in Washington, D.C.

Greg Graf only has to watch the videos once. *Why don't they just fly away? Why is Umbach letting Schmidt take over the flight? Doesn't "hold fire" mean anything to you?* If Lt.-Col. Graf had any moral qualms about prosecuting fellow fighter pilots, they'd vanished by the time the tapes stop rolling.

★　★　★

In the military justice system, criminal charges are not so much laid as they are recommended. The official term is "preferred," and it is up to a commander or an investigator to do the preferring. Col. Odom's only job is to assess the evidence and tell his bosses what is—and what isn't—a provable case in court.

For three weeks, he and his team have drowned themselves in the final report of the Coalition Investigation Board, learning as they go about ROZs and ACOs and ROEs. They watched as Lt.-Col. Graf explained, frame by frame, just how reckless and ridiculous the pilots acted that night. By Labor Day, it seems pretty obvious to everyone in the room that what happened over Tarnak Farm was not an accident. It was a crime.

In early September, Col. Odom phones Gen. Stephen T. Sargeant, the CIB co-president who is now on temporary duty at Alabama's Maxwell Air Force Base. "Sir," he says, after a quick introduction, "you concluded that disciplinary action should be taken against these individuals, did you not?"

"I certainly did," the general answers. As they chat, Col. Odom explains that every possible charge carries a different burden of proof. Dereliction of duty. Aggravated assault. Involuntary manslaughter. The colonel wants to know if Gen. Sargeant believes his team uncovered evidence that can support all three of those charges. "Definitely," Gen. Sargeant answers.

"Well, sir," Col. Odom says. "Since you feel that way, would you be willing to sign the charge sheet as the accuser?"

"Absolutely."

It's not that simple, though. Because Maj. Schmidt and Maj. Umbach are back from Kuwait and back under the control of the Air National Guard, Col. Odom must personally ask Dr. James Roche, the secretary of the Air Force, to recall the pilots to active duty to face the charges. If the men are not recalled, the rules clearly state that they can never be punished with jail time, regardless of how the case unfolds. When he irons out that wrinkle, the colonel has to find a JAG in Alabama who can bring the charge sheet—a DD-458—over to the general's office. Odom catches Sargeant on the phone one more time, just as he's having lunch. They review the specifications of each charge one more time: Four counts each of involuntary manslaughter, one for each dead paratrooper. Eight counts of aggravated assault, one for each wounded soldier. And one count of dereliction of duty. As he eats, Brig.-Gen. Sargeant scribbles his signature on both of the documents. It is September 11, 2002.

★　★　★

Bill Umbach is flying a United Airlines jet back to Chicago on September 11—the first anniversary of the terrorist attacks—when Col. Murphy, his wing commander, calls him on his cellphone. *Be in my office tomorrow morning at 8 o'clock,* he says.

Criminal charges? For the past five months, Maj. Umbach has clung to the hope that somebody in the Air Force would come to their senses, that they would open their eyes and realize all the other command-and-control failures that triggered the accident. Obviously not. Bill Umbach, a guy who won't even badmouth people in the privacy of his own living room, is suddenly an accused killer. He calls Dave Beck, a Tennessee-based lawyer. Charlie Gittins passed along the phone number.

A former Marine pilot who flew attack helicopters and fighter jets, Dave Beck, like Charlie Gittins, is as good as they come in the niche market of civilian defense attorneys who specialize in military law. In 1987, while still working on the government's side, he prosecuted the Marine Corps' first-ever espionage trial, securing a conviction against Clayton Lonetree, a sergeant who sold secrets to the Russians while working as a security guard at Moscow's U.S. embassy. A decade later, Beck defended Captain Joseph Schweitzer, the navigator of a Marine jet that clipped the cable of a ski gondola in northern Italy, killing 20 people. Investigators accused the captain and another pilot of flying too low and too fast over the holiday resort, but Dave Beck managed to wipe out all the manslaughter charges against his client, largely because he proved that the pilots' onboard maps did not include the location of the gondola. Along the way, he made a few senior officers eat their words.

While their resumés are equally impressive, Dave Beck is the polar opposite of his friend, Charlie Gittins. At 54, he speaks softly in his southern twang, smiling and quoting Scripture as he goes. His sentences sometimes go on for so long that even he loses track of them. But no matter what he's saying, or what he forgets he's saying, he treats everyone—from janitor to general—as if they are old friends. Even if you're out to crush his client, you're going to get a warm grin and a firm handshake from Dave Beck. "He's the good cop," Gittins often jokes. "I'm the bad cop."

Dave is also a juggler, the kind of guy who answers his e-mail and cellphone while trying to vacuum and eat lunch at the same time. It's just his style. He's always been a workaholic, rarely catching more than three or four hours of sleep a night. But he always finds time for his afternoon jog, the chunk of the day when he does his best thinking. More than one total stranger has been stopped by a sweating Dave Beck, desperate for a pen and a piece of paper to jot down his latest brainstorm.

When Dave does find a rare moment to sit down and chat, the conversation almost always turns to his family. His five kids. His beloved father, a P-47 pilot in World War II who was shot down and sent to a Nazi prison camp. A motivational speaker on the side (as if he needs more work to do), Dave Beck often tells the story of Valentine's Day, 1987, when, just minutes before the FBI and the CIA and all the other secret folks were about to brief him on the espionage case, he got word that his father, the former POW, had died of a heart attack. Mom, suffering from cancer at the time, told him to stay focused on his case. It's what Dad would have wanted.

And then there's Melinda, Dave's wife of three decades, who helped him get through law school and watched, over and over again, as he left home on a deployment or a big trial overseas. She often jokes that being Dave Beck's wife for 30 years is actually the equivalent of about a 14-year marriage, considering just how often he's away from home. For the ski gondola case, he jumped on a plane to Italy the morning after his daughter's wedding. By the summer of 2002, Dave has promised Melinda that he's going to slow down, that he's going to just be a regular Tennessee lawyer. That's it. And then Bill Umbach calls.

"Do you know that they are charging those Air Force pilots in that friendly fire accident over in Afghanistan?" Dave tells his wife after hanging up the phone.

"You gotta be kidding me," she says. "How did you know?"

"Oh, I just talked to one of the pilots."

Melinda knows what's coming. "You did tell him that you promised your wife of 30-plus years that you weren't going to be involved?"

"Melinda, he's got a wife, he's got two young daughters—"

"Did you tell him or did you not?" she asks.

He didn't, of course. Dave Beck has trouble saying no to cases like this. And he knows his wife will eventually come around. By tomorrow, in fact, she'll be trolling the Internet, searching for information about Go-pills.

★ ★ ★

Charlie Gittins is vacationing in Ireland when Gen. Sargeant prefers the charges. Checking his e-mail from an Internet café in Dublin, his inbox is overloaded. His voicemail back at the office is full, too. When he eventually gets Harry on the telephone, he tells him to drive to the base and pick up the paperwork. *Don't say a word to anyone.*

CENTCOM officially announces the criminal charges on September 13, simultaneously posting a censored version of the CIB's summary of facts on its website. As planned, the Canadian Department of Defence also releases a redacted copy of the BOI's executive summary. In all, more than 130 pages of new evidence—evidence that has been under wraps since June—is suddenly in the public domain. The "reckless disregard" for the rules of engagement. The former Top Gun who twice turned his F-16 back toward the flashes, slowing to "well below tactical airspeed." The flight lead—suffering from "co-pilot syndrome"—who sat and watched as his wingman dropped the bomb. And the commander, Col. Dave Nichols, who was more interested in "being one of the boys" than making sure the boys were properly planning their missions.

Journalists seize on the Canadian report, not only because the writing is easier to comprehend, but because of the harsh words aimed at U.S. command-and-control. While stressing that "the proximate fault for the outcome of the attack lies with the two F-16 pilots," Gen. Baril and his investigators note the numerous "systemic shortcomings" in air-to-ground coordination. "Had they been corrected," the board concluded, "the incident might have been prevented." But much of the specifics remain classified, including that a 24-hour ROZ surrounded Tarnak Farm, and that neither the AWACS nor the pilots had any idea it existed. Even the segment of the cockpit transcript—the part when BOSSMAN "concurs" with Maj. Schmidt that there was "no ROZ effective in that area" tonight—is blacked out. Also erased from the public version of the BOI's final report is the fact that "unfortunately," the glint tape and infrared strobes the Canadian paratroopers were wearing that night "are not visible to high flying aircraft, such as the F-16s in this incident."

But far more significant, at least today, is the news that the Air Force has criminally charged two of its fighter pilots for a mistake they made in war. It is virtually unheard of. In fact, the last time it happened was during the Second World War, when a pilot and a navigator—convinced they were flying over Germany—bombed Zurich, Switzerland. Both men were charged with dereliction of duty, but were later cleared. This time around, the charges are much more severe. In the worst case scenario, Harry and Bill face 64 years in prison.

"It's saying: 'Put your life on the line for freedom, but if a terrible accident happens that a number of people contributed to, we'll hang you out to dry,'" Dave Beck tells one reporter. "Maj. Umbach has a distinguished record and killing friendly forces was the last thing he could have imagined. It's just a tragedy. He's served his country for a long time and he's got a family that he's obviously concerned about. I just told him to hope and pray for the best, but to prepare for the worst."

Charlie Gittins releases his own prepared statement to the press. Maj. Schmidt "regrets that Canadian troops were killed and injured," it says, but he "honestly and reasonably believed troops were directing hostile fire at he and his wingman and that his actions were required in self-defense." His client "also regrets that the Air Force has taken the unprecedented step of charging a combat aircrew involved in a combat mission criminally where those officers were required to make split-second life or death decisions without benefit of detached and calm reflection."

LEGEND >>

Umbach: Major Bill Umbach
Schmidt: Major Harry Schmidt
Fossil 22: Airborne refueling tanker
Carroll: Tech-Sergeant Michael Carroll (Bossman), stationed aboard the AWACS radar plane
Henry: Major Arthur Henry (Bossman), stationed aboard the AWACS radar plane
K-Mart: Major Scott Woodson, stationed at the Coalition Air Operations Center (ground control) in Saudi Arabia

VHF: Radio frequency that pilots use to talk to each other. Only they can hear calls on VHF.
UHF: Radio frequency that pilots use to talk to the AWACS (Bossman). Only the pilots and the AWACS crew can hear calls broadcast on UHF.
AC-1: A dedicated satellite communications circuit that the AWACS (Maj. Henry) uses to talk to the CAOC (K-Mart/Maj. Woodson). The pilots cannot hear calls made on this frequency.

THE TIME BEFORE THE TAPES COME ON >>

A series of radio calls were exchanged between Maj. Schmidt, Maj. Umbach and the AWACS radar plane before the pilots activated their on-board recorders. Because none of the transmissions was captured on tape, it is impossible to know exactly what was said, but Maj. Umbach claims that as soon as he saw the "fireworks" on the ground, he radioed the AWACS, saying: "Bossman, Coffee 51. We have SAFIRE in our present position. Are there any friendlies in the area?" Both pilots claim Maj. Umbach also said: "I think they are shooting at us," followed by: "I think they are pulling lead."

At a pre-trial hearing in January, 2003, the pilots'

lawyers suggested that their clients were "taking fire" before the tapes came on, and that they explicitly relayed that fact to Bossman. Prosecutors accused the airmen of lying in a "desperate attempt" to try to justify their "indefensible" actions.

What is clear is that at some point before the recorders start to whirl, Bossman granted the pilots permission to "mark" the target, to use their targeting pod lasers to capture the exact latitude/longitude of the unknown ground flashes. Maj. Umbach and Maj. Schmidt are attempting to take that mark when they activate their tapes at 21:22:38 Zulu.

ROLLING IN IN SELF-DEFENSE >>

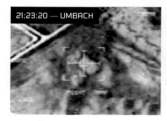
21:23:20 — UMBACH

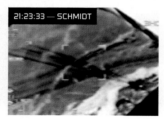
21:23:33 — SCHMIDT

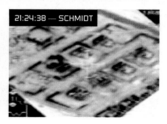
21:24:38 — SCHMIDT

Maj. Bill Umbach: (VHF) (21:22:40) Do ya got good coordinates for a mark or do you need me to roll in?
Maj. Harry Schmidt: (UHF) (21:22:42) Ah, standby. I'll mark it right now.
Umbach: (VHF) (21:22:46) Copy.
Schmidt: (UHF) (21:22:47) I'm in from the southeast.
Umbach: (VHF) (21:22:53) Alright, if you get a dive toss SPI, I can take that and make it, uh, a point off of it.
Fossil 22: (UHF) (21:23:22) Bossman, Fossil 22.
Carroll: (UHF) (21:23:27) Fossil 22, Bossman go.

Fossil 22: (UHF) (21:23:28) Uh, I suppose I might as well, uh, make a left turn and stay in Zeus until, uh, 51 is ready.
Schmidt: (UHF) (21:23:33) Okay, Bossman, uh, this is, uh, Coffee 52, I've got a tally on the vicinity. Uh, request permission to lay down some, uh, 20 mike-mike.
Carroll: (UHF) (21:23:43) Standby.
Umbach: (VHF) (21:23:45) Let's just make sure that it's, uh, that it's not friendlies, that's all.
K-Mart: (AC-1) (21:23:48) Bossman, K-Mart.

Henry: (AC-1) (21:23:49) K-Mart, this is Bossman. Coffee 51 Flight has experienced SAFIRE near the city of Kandahar, requesting permission to open up with 20 millimeter. I'll try to get you a little more information. We told them to hold fire.
Umbach: (VHF) (21:23:50) When you get a chance, put it on the SPI, if you've got a good hack on it.
Schmidt: (VHF) (21:24:38) Okay, I'm going to flow down here to the, uh, southwest.
K-Mart: (AC-1) (21:24:38) Bossman, K-Mart. We copy report reference Coffee. We need SAFIRE details from Coffee when able and hold fire.

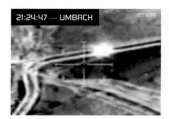

Schmidt: (UHF) (21:24:42) Bossman from Coffee 52, do you want us to push a different freq?

Umbach: (VHF) (21:24:47) Check my sparkle, check my sparkle. See if it looks good.

Umbach: (VHF) (21:24:53) Yeah, I'm contact your sparkle as well.

Henry: (21:24:56) ...over Kandahar... and we'll get more details for you.

Carroll: (UHF) (21:25:00) Coffee 51, Bossman. Hold fire, need details on SAFIRE for K-Mart.

Schmidt: (UHF) (21:25:04) Okay, I've got a, uh, I've got some men on a road and it looks like a piece of artillery firing at us. I am rolling in in self-defense.

Henry: (AC-1) (21:25:06) Roger. He's invoking self-defense ROE on the fire. On the road he sees artillery shooting at him. Standby for details.

Carroll: (UHF) (21:25:15) Bossman copies.

Umbach: (UHF) (21:25:17) Check master arm, laser arm. And check you're not in mark.

Schmidt: (UHF) (21:25:19) Got 'em both on. I'm in from the southwest.

Umbach: (VHF) (21:25:36) Do you show 'em on a bridge?

Schmidt: (UHF) (21:25:39) Bomb's away, cranking left.

K-Mart: (AC-1) (21:25:47) Bossman, K-Mart. Be advised Kandahar has friendlies. You are to get Coffee 51 out of there as soon as possible.

Umbach: (VHF) (21:25:48) Check wide field of view.

Schmidt: (UHF) (21:25:50) I'm fine.

Schmidt: (UHF) (21:25:53) Laser's on.

Henry: (AC-1) (21:25:58) Roger, we'll get them out of there right now.

Schmidt: (UHF) (21:26:00) Shack.

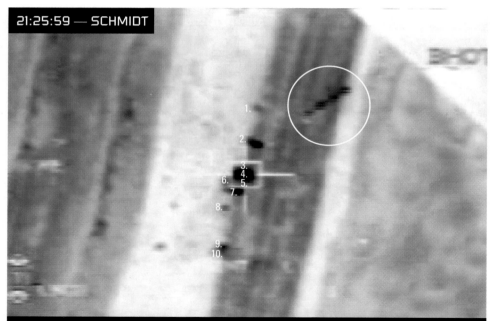

A 500-POUND LASER-GUIDED BOMB (CIRCLED), MILLISECONDS BEFORE IT LANDS ON A SECTION OF CANADIAN TROOPS CONDUCTING A LIVE-FIRE TRAINING EXERCISE IN AFGHANISTAN. BEGINNING AT THE TOP, **THE SOLDIERS ARE:** SGT. LORNE FORD (1), PTE. RICHARD GREEN (2), PTE. NATHAN SMITH (3), CPL. AINSWORTH DYER (4), MCPL. CURTIS HOLLISTER (5), SGT. MARC LÉGER (6), CPL. RENE PAQUETTE (7), MCPL. STANLEY CLARK (8), CPL. BRETT PERRY (9), CPL. BRIAN DECAIRE (10). >>

Schmidt: (UHF) (21:26:07) Bossman, Bossman.

Carroll: (UHF) (21:26:09) Coffee 51, Bossman. Disengage, friendlies Kandahar.

Schmidt: (UHF) (21:26:15). Copy, uh, disengaging south.

Carroll: (UHF) (21:26:18) Coffee 51, Bossman. How copy?

Umbach: (UHF) (21:26:20) Copy, uh, can you confirm that they were shooting at us?

Carroll: (UHF) (21:26:30) Coffee 51, Bossman. You're cleared, self-defense. K-Mart wants you to work south... there may be friendlies, Kandahar.

Umbach: (UHF) (21:26:39) Okay, One's coming back left. Steer 82.

Carroll: (UHF) (21:26:43) Coffee 51, Bossman. Scram south.

Umbach: (UHF) (21:26:47) Bossman, Coffee 51 scramming.

Carroll: (UHF) (21:26:50) Bossman.

Carroll: (UHF) (21:27:14) Coffee 51, Bossman. I need co-ordinates when able and need to know if any rounds were fired.

Umbach: (VHF) (21:27:22) Go ahead.

Schmidt: (UHF) (21:27:23) Yeah, I had, uh, one bomb dropped in the vicinity of, uh, thirty-one twenty-four north, point 78. Sixty-five, forty-three, point 522. That's an estimate, uh, if you had our general vicinity.

Carroll: (UHF) (21:27:44) Bossman.

Schmidt: (VHF) (21:27:53) Wow.

Carroll: (UHF) (21:27:54) Coffee 51, repeat east coordinate.

Schmidt: (UHF) (21:28:00) Yeah, I'm not so sure it's that accurate. I don't, I don't have an accurate coordinate right now. Do you want me to go back and get you one?

Carroll: (UHF) (21:28:06) Bossman, negative.

Umbach: (VHF) (21:28:11) Let's go back safe.

Umbach: (VHF) (21:28:19) Shit.

Schmidt: (VHF) (21:28:25) Yeah, they were definitely shooting at you.

Umbach: (VHF) (21:28:28) It sure seemed like they were tracking around and everything and, uh, trying to lead.

Schmidt: (VHF) (21:28:34) Well we had our lights on and that wasn't helping, I don't think.

Schmidt: (VHF) (21:28:41) I had a group of guys on a road around a gun and it did not look organized like it would be our guys.

Umbach: (VHF) (21:28:47) It seemed like it was right on a bridge, that's kinda where I was at.

Schmidt: (VHF) (21:28:51) Nah, not quite.

Schmidt: (VHF) (21:28:55) I hope that was the right thing to do.

Umbach: (VHF) (21:28:59) Me too.

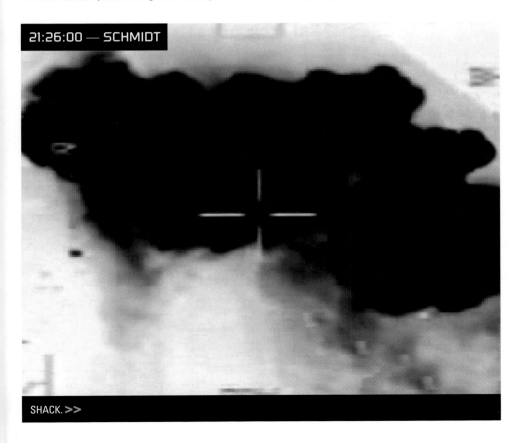

21:26:00 — SCHMIDT

SHACK. >>

Carroll: (UHF) (21:28:59) Coffee 51, Bossman.

Umbach: (UHF) (21:29:01) Go ahead.

Carroll: (UHF) (21:29:02) Yeah, need type bomb dropped, result, and type of SAFIRE.

Schmidt: (UHF) (21:29:08) Yeah, it was a single GBU-12 dropped. It was a direct hit on, uh, the artillery piece that was firing. Uh, as far as the SAFIRE, multiple rounds, it looked like a, uh, MLRS, uh to Coffee 52. 51, what do you have on that?

Umbach: (UHF) (21:29:26) I'd say the same. It was, uh, sort of continuous fire and, uh ... it appeared to be, uh, leading us as we were, uh, flying by and then as we came back around.

Carroll: (UHF) (21:29:45) Did you get a top altitude on the SAFIRE?

Henry: (AC-1) (21:29:49) It appeared to be an MLRS-type firing on Coffee 52. I will get you a lat/long for that, over.

Umbach: (UHF) (21:29:50) Negative, they, uh, they were burning out before here.

Schmidt: (UHF) (21:29:53) I would estimate the top was approximately 10,000 feet. And, uh, just to let you know, we split in azimuth, sending, uh, 51 to the south and 52 went to the northeast and, uh, one of the guns turned back around to the east, uh, firing at, uh, 52, uh, as well.

K-Mart: (AC-1) (21:30:00) K-Mart copies.

Bossman: (UHF) (21:30:14) Bossman copies and, uh, if we could get a rough, uh, longitude.

Schmidt: (UHF) (21:30:24) Yeah, I did not take a mark, uh, at the time.

Carroll: (UHF) (21:30:28) Bossman.

Umbach: (VHF) (21:30:35) Is that, was that definitely the airfield that was close...

Carroll: (UHF): (21:30:38) Coffee 51, please repeat the, uh, coordinate you passed.

Schmidt: (VHF) (21:30:40) Yeah.

Umbach: (VHF) (21:30:41) He wants the coordinate again.

Schmidt: (UHF) (21:30:44) Yeah, I do not have the, uh, proper coordinate for that, uh, Bossman.

Carroll: (UHF) (21:30:48) Bossman.

Umbach: (VHF) (21:30:51) Would you estimate, I'd estimate about 3 miles to the south maybe a 150—

Carroll: (UHF) (21:30:58) Coffee 51, Fossil 22 BRA 155/27 base plus 25, track north.

Schmidt: (UHF) (21:31:04) Yeah, Bossman, uh, there was no ROZ effective in that area tonight as far as our brief was concerned, do you concur?

Henry: (AC-1) (21:31:08) K-Mart, this is Bossman 2. Rough coordinates of bomb drop, 3124/6555. If they overflew again they could give it, but we turned them away. And just confirm that you have no ROZ active at that location, over?

Carroll: (UHF) (21:31:12) Bossman.

Carroll: (UHF) (21:31:18) Bossman concurs.

Schmidt: (VHF) (21:31:27) Yeah, standby for the microscope, huh?

Umbach: (VHF) (21:31:30) Yeah.

Schmidt: (VHF) (21:31:32) I'm at your right side.

Umbach: (VHF) (21:31:33) Roger that, I'm going cameras off.

K-Mart: (AC-1) (21:31:33) Bossman from K-Mart. That's affirmative, we copy coordinates, over.

21:27:00 — SCHMIDT

A CLOUD OF SMOKE AND CONFUSION. >>

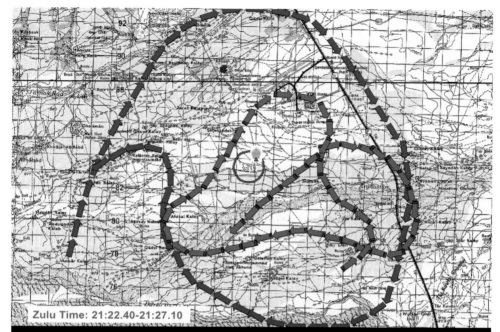

Zulu Time: 21:22.40-21:27.10

MILITARY PROSECUTORS ENTERED THIS FLIGHT PATH RECREATION AS AN EXHIBIT AT THE PILOTS' PRE-TRIAL HEARING. THE GREEN ARROWS DEPICT THE MOVEMENTS OF MAJOR HARRY SCHMIDT IN THE MINUTES BEFORE HE UNLEASHED HIS 500-POUND BOMB. THE BLUE ARROWS ARE MAJOR BILL UMBACH. >>

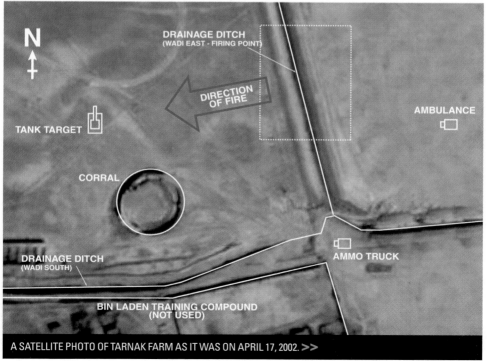

N

DRAINAGE DITCH
(WADI EAST - FIRING POINT)

DIRECTION OF FIRE

TANK TARGET

AMBULANCE

CORRAL

DRAINAGE DITCH
(WADI SOUTH)

AMMO TRUCK

BIN LADEN TRAINING COMPOUND
(NOT USED)

A SATELLITE PHOTO OF TARNAK FARM AS IT WAS ON APRIL 17, 2002. >>

SOURCE: TARNAK FARM BOARD OF INQUIRY

AMERICAN FORENSIC INVESTIGATORS SIFT THROUGH THE BOMB SCENE, DROPPING TINY PINK FLAGS BESIDE EACH PIECE OF HUMAN REMAINS. >>

AN OVERHEAD VIEW OF THE DESERT DITCH WHERE FOUR CANADIAN SOLDIERS WERE KILLED. THE WHITE TAPE INDICATES THE EXACT SPOT WHERE THE BOMB HIT. >>

THE SCATTERED DEBRIS OF A LASER-GUIDED BOMB. >>

THREE MONTHS AFTER THE FATAL BOMBING, CANADIAN TROOPS FIRE A C-6 MACHINE GUN AT TARNAK FARM. >>

THE FLASH OF AN 84MM CARL GUSTAV ANTI-TANK ROUND AT NIGHT. >>

TWO CANADIAN SOLDIERS FIRE A CARL GUSTAV IN KABUL, AFGHANISTAN. >>

23

In the military justice system, whenever criminal charges are preferred, as Gen. Sargeant did on September 11, it signals the launch of a whole new "investigation." Known as an Article 32, these investigations are often compared to civilian grand juries. Both sides, prosecutors and defense lawyers, have the chance to plead their cases in front of an investigating officer (IO)—similar to a judge—whose sole job is to recommend whether the military has a decent chance of winning the case at a full-blown court-martial.

In this case, the man making that recommendation will be Colonel Patrick Rosenow, a longtime Air Force judge, and, in his spare time, an internationally licensed basketball referee. The colonel will find himself plying both trades—analyzing complex legal statutes and standing in between bickering players—by the time this Article 32 finishes. He answers to one man: Lt.-Gen. Bruce Carlson, the boss of the 8th Air Force. When the hearing is over, Col. Rosenow will tell the three-star whether he thinks this case belongs in front of a jury. But the decision ultimately rests with Gen. Carlson. He can follow the advice. He can ignore it.

In Springfield, Illinois, most people have already made up their minds. This whole thing is a charade, a conspiracy to protect senior officers while appeasing a jilted ally. Sixty-four years in prison? Two outstanding men risk their lives for their country and you're going to toss them in jail because of a split-second mistake? A day after the Pentagon announces the charges, a grassroots effort is already underway in central Illinois to help raise money for the pilots' legal bills. At the local Veterans of Foreign Wars post, John Russo, a 71-year-old major who served in Korea, has collected $300. "No one's perfect," he says. "They're maybe not proud of what happened—I know they're not—but they both feel they were doing their duty. We're a veterans' group, and we've all been involved in one way or another in friendly fire. It happens. What kind of a message is this sending to the people going into the service? 'If anything happens, you're on your own. We don't want anything to do with you.'"

An awful message indeed, especially now, with President George W. Bush asking the American public to support a possible invasion of Iraq. You need soldiers to do that, George. Guys like Bill and Harry. If you send them to prison for doing their job, who the hell is going to want to volunteer? It's bad enough the troops have to worry about ending up in a box. But behind bars, too? Or maybe the White House isn't interested in the men and women in uniform. Maybe they're too busy trying to make Canada happy, trying to atone for the embarrassing fact that the president waited two long days to personally express his remorse about the accident. And we certainly don't want Canada mad. We need to butter them up so they come along for the Iraqi ride. What better way to do that than throw the book at those nobody fighter pilots who dropped the bomb?

"It looks to us that they have been hung out to dry," says Mike Williams, Bill Umbach's next-door neighbor. Mike is already planning a fundraising dinner, maybe with bands and a silent auction. "It looks like they're being railroaded. I don't think it's fair that he has to go hire his own private attorney to defend himself against his own government." They're having enough trouble just trying to defend themselves against all the cameras and the microphones, the constant knocking on the door by reporters desperate for Harry to say something more than "no comment." His five-year-old son, Tucker, can see the news crews approaching from the window, day after day after day. "The bad people are here again," he tells his mom and dad. The advice from their lawyers is still the same: Keep quiet. Anything you say can and will be used against you.

The city is speaking for them. Around town, volunteers hang small red bells on people's doorknobs. "Ring the Bells of Justice for our pilots!" At the VFW post, John Russo opens more letters every morning, many from aging veterans outraged that two fine airmen are being sacrificed as scapegoats to hide a much bigger problem. Most send checks: $10, $100, $1,000. "I realize things must seem bleak to you right now, but keep in mind that the entire community is behind you," one man writes to Bill Umbach. "You and Harry were serving your country and deserve a 'thank you,' not a 'screw you' from our government." A Thunderbolt pilot who flew in the Second World War sends his best wishes from Santa Rosa, California, where he and his squadron recently enjoyed a reunion. One of the guys started to "pass the hat" around the room. "We understand that no matter how careful you try, a 'friendly fire' accident can happen," he writes. "We hope our enclosed $153 check will help with a proper legal defense of the two brave pilots who were following orders into combat."

By October, a website appears on the Internet—www.183rdpilotsdefe nsefund.com. Beside each pilot's impressive military biography are photos of the men in their Air Force blues, smiling and laughing as they play with their children. Harry, Lisa, Tucker, and Colton. Bill, Marlene, Ingrid, and Ava. "The incident," the site reads, "while tragic and regrettable, was the result of a continuously changing combat environment, coupled with breakdowns in the command, control and communications structure that ultimately failed to provide information to those who needed it most—the pilots. In a misguided attempt to redress a wrong, the USAF is willing to sacrifice two loyal airmen, while denying any command and control failures." The site also pays tribute to the fallen Canadian paratroopers and their grieving families. "Our hearts are with you." At the bottom, a hyperlink encourages visitors to make a donation. Visa and Mastercard accepted.

T-shirts are for sale, too, stamped with the catchy slogan that has become Springfield's unofficial rallying cry: "Support, don't prosecute, our American pilots." People are wearing them everywhere, at the pizza parlor fundraisers and the golf tournaments and especially at the VFW post, where the envelopes keep arriving. "Good luck in your fight against the influence of political correctness, which is holding you two hostage in the country you have sworn to defend," one donor writes. "It is easy to criticize the decisions of two pilots at our desk or in the comfort of our living rooms," another note reads. "Do NOT allow the persecution of these two morally upstanding, patriotic, volunteer service members! The right to defend yourself in a war-zone should not be questioned!"

On October 5, Lisa Schmidt, Harry's wife, is on the front page of the local newspaper, the first of many, many interviews she and Marlene Umbach will grant to the American—and Canadian—media. Lisa refuses to just sit back and watch as the military machine squashes Harry into the ground. "I'll do anything to help my husband," she says. "My husband would never, ever have intentionally hurt or killed anyone." He "feels very guilty" about what happened that night in Kandahar, she says, and despite what some people might think, he "is not a monster." But as difficult as this has been for them, Lisa knows their suffering is incomparable to what those Canadian families have endured. "For us, it's been difficult, but for them it is worse," she says. "They lost their loved ones."

As the community mobilizes behind its pilots, so do the politicians, urging people to open their prayer books and their checkbooks. "These pilots have dedicated a lot of time over the years," says Raymond Poe, who occupies Springfield's seat in the Illinois House of Representatives. "In some instances, they have neglected their own families to serve our country. We should, in turn, help them." Dick Durbin, a Democratic senator from Illinois, goes one step further, suggesting that America's military brass is motivated not by justice, but by a desire to please Canada. "Whether this resulted from wrongdoing or simply an accident of war, it does not change the tragic outcome for the victims and their families," he tells *The Ottawa Citizen*. "But it will make a great deal of difference in the lives of these airmen."

Among the pilots' most vocal political allies is George Ryan, the governor of Illinois. As head of the state's National Guard, he is, at least symbolically, the pilots' commander-in-chief. "These men are not cowboys," he says. "They are Top Guns. They were not dropping bombs for the hell of it. They are patriots. They should be supported, not prosecuted." In mid-October, he invites the airmen and their wives to a private luncheon at his home, brushing aside grumblings that his hands-on involvement is a blatant conflict of interest. A week later, Ryan opens up the governor's mansion for a $50-a-plate dinner, with every penny going to the 183rd Pilots Defense Fund. By now, the bank account already contains more than $40,000.

As hundreds of guests mingle, many stopping to personally thank Bill and Harry for their service, an e-mail arrives at the governor's office from a Canadian Internet address. "If the pilots are not convicted and court-martialed," it reads, "funeral homes will have two more customers."

★　★　★

After the bombing, Rene Paquette went home to Winnipeg, to the small house he had been living in with his pregnant wife when he first volunteered to deploy with his fellow Patricias from Edmonton. He was never a paratrooper. He barely even got to know the guys in his new section before Harry Schmidt rolled in. Now back in Manitoba, Rene is hundreds of miles away from anyone who was with him that night at Tarnak Farm. Nobody who can fill in the blanks. Nobody who knows exactly what's racing through his brain.

Six months later, his ears are still borderline useless, his back a twisted, painful mess. He blacks out every once in a while. The other day, as he walked to the corner gas station to grab a cup of coffee, a sudden bolt of lightning hit the Winnipeg sky. Rene fell to his knees, landing in a puddle. For a split second, he thought it was another bomb. At night, when it's quiet, Cpl. Paquette flashes back to that ditch, to that brown suede boot he could see in the distance as the medics jabbed an IV needle into his arm. He knows the soldier wearing that boot died instantly. That's what Gen. Baril told him. But he still doesn't know who it was. As far as he can figure—and he has thought about it many times—it had to be Ains. They were crouching right beside each other on the firing line, shooting their machine guns only a couple feet apart.

In October 2002, when Queen Elizabeth visits Winnipeg, Rene and Brian Decaire and Brett Perry are among those on the guest list for dinner. Rene, because he's already in the city; the others, because they grew up here and their families are still around. It is the first time in months that Cpl. Paquette has seen the other two soldiers. They huddle near a wall, talking about the charges and the fundraisers and the looming "trial" south of the border. That was Marc's boot, Brett tells Rene. Not Ainsworth's.

★　★　★

By late October, after a few conference calls with Col. Rosenow, lawyers on both sides of the case pencil in a date for the Article 32 hearing: January 13, 2003. Behind the scenes, however, Charlie Gittins and Dave Beck are lobbying hard to make sure that court appearance never happens. Days after first reviewing a partially censored version of the CIB's complete 13 volumes, both defense attorneys write to Dr. James Roche, the secretary of the Air Force, imploring him to order a new investigation.

"Having now had the opportunity to review the Board report and the regulations under which it purports to have been conducted, we have significant concerns concerning investigator bias," their letter reads. They suggest that Lt.-Gen. T. Michael Moseley, anxious to hide the obvious communication problems plaguing his Afghanistan air war, appointed his "protégé," Brig.-Gen. Stephen Sargeant, to pin blame on the lowest common denominator: the pilots. "In the investigation report he prepared, BG Sargeant indicated that command and control failures contributed to this accident, but declined to consider them as causative," the lawyers write. "The CAOC and its deficiencies as they related to this incident—and there were a number of serious failures in command and control that could have prevented this accident had they not occurred—were the direct responsibility of LTG Moseley."

Gittins and Beck also accuse Moseley and Sargeant of ignoring rules that ensure an Air National Guard member is appointed to accident investigation boards that involve Guard jets and pilots. And what about Harry's 38-page submission to the Coalition Investigation Board? It barely warrants a mention in the final report that was released to the press. Even more troubling, the Canadian BOI notes that it was provided only a 12-page submission from Maj. Schmidt, via the CIB. Where are the other 26 pages? "It is clear that BG Sargeant had little interest in whatever the pilots in this case might have had to say, even if they were inclined to waive their rights," the letter says.

Colonel Craig A. Smith, chief of the U.S. Air Force's Military Justice Division, responds with a short, two-paragraph letter, saying "it would be inappropriate for the Secretary" to intervene while an Article 32 is pending. The hearing, he says, "will provide your clients with an appropriate forum to present your clients' concerns to an impartial investigating officer."

But the letters keep coming. "Having now had the opportunity to review the classified testimony and evidence that was collected by BG Sargeant, I am now even more firmly convinced that General Sargeant produced a biased, professionally and ethically flawed investigative report that merits investigation in its own right," Gittins writes. "Review of the transcripts, conveniently classified primarily to avoid public scrutiny, demonstrates that General Sargeant misrepresented testimony, substantially misrepresented facts when questioning witnesses, and in some cases, reached conclusions that were simply made up of whole cloth without any factual basis. Suffice it to say that the lawyers and clients who reviewed the evidence were shocked by the conclusions contained in the unclassified executive summary provided to the press and public because they were directly contrary to the evidence and testimony collected by the AIB." Gen. Sargeant's "handiwork" is not only rife with "hundreds of factual errors," but much of the classified information is being kept under wraps to "avoid uncovering a broken command and control structure." Gittins specifically cites the CIB's interview with Brig.-Gen. Stephen G. Wood, the senior officer in the CAOC that night. He displayed "a curious unfamiliarity" with the rules of engagement and needed "to be provided a copy, highlighted, for his review in order to testify about them." It is apparent, Gittins writes, that "this portion of the redacted report has not been released publicly in order to avoid embarrassment and exposure to a General Officer's unconscionable lack of knowledge about mission critical information that Major Schmidt and Major Umbach did not have the luxury to reflect upon in the stress of combat."

In his own rebuttal to Col. Smith, Dave Beck, Maj. Umbach's lawyer, says what is happening to the pilots is a "travesty," especially since neither airman was briefed about the Canadian training drill. "Astoundingly, no one in the AWACS plane on station or the CAOC was aware of this exercise," he writes. "In fact, when numerous persons on duty in the AWACS and the CAOC were asked by their superiors if friendlies were in the area while Maj. Umbach and Maj. Schmidt sought to obtain information on friendlies, they replied 'negative.'" Even more astounding, he says, is the fact that the CIB somehow concluded that the bombing had nothing at all to do with a communication breakdown. "This failure to communicate critical information is the single most important factor that could have prevented the accident," he writes to Dr. Roche. "I urge you to require General Sargeant to explain to you, and to the families of the Canadian soldiers who lost their lives, how he can reasonably assert this failure by the command was not a causative factor." In the meantime, the Canadian and U.S. governments should immediately compensate the grieving families, Beck says. "Under all the foregoing circumstances, the prosecution of Maj. Schmidt and Maj. Umbach (or even putting them through the Article 32 process) sends a chilling message to pilots and other service members on the frontline of our nation's defenses," his letter concludes. "If all the facts are made public, it also will likely have a significant adverse effect on recruitment and retention of pilots. Neither political appeasement nor a misguided attempt to downplay, ignore or cover up serious mistakes by senior officers should ever be condoned or justified."

★ ★ ★

By the time Bill Umbach walks through the door, says a few hellos, and takes off his sportsjacket, somebody is handing him a check. The 43-year-old has been doing this a lot lately, but it's pretty clear, both by his cautious smile and sweaty forehead, that he's still not completely at ease with the idea of taking people's handouts. Comfortable or not, Maj. Umbach thanks the man for his donation, even posing for a quick photo. Behind them, inside a massive airport hangar that has been transformed into a banquet hall, a crowd has gathered among hundreds of red, white, and blue balloons. Another fundraiser. Another $20-a-head chance for the people of Springfield to show how much they support their local fighter pilots.

This is definitely the most extravagant one yet. On one side of the hangar, just to the right of a gigantic American flag, are dozens of door prizes—from crystal bowls to National Football League tickets—all donated by local businesses. On the other end, past the rows of tables where people are eating pork chop sandwiches and popcorn, is a "Kids' Corner," complete with face painting, a clown, and a mini-playground. Ava, Bill's three-year-old daughter, sits patiently as an artist paints a tiny American flag on her left cheek.

On a makeshift stage—the trailer of a transport truck—band after local band perform for the crowd, mostly country music. In between songs, they urge everyone to reach a little deeper into their pockets and pull out a few more dollars for "a good cause." When the crowd is at its largest, more than 500 people at least, the man at the microphone asks for a moment of silence, a tribute to Marc Léger, Ainsworth Dyer, Richard Green, and Nathan Smith. When it's over, the raffle begins.

As people stop to check their yellow tickets for a winning number, others keep chatting. The topic is always the same. What's wrong with our government? How can it possibly justify criminally charging these two guys? And on September 11, no less! What a slap in the face. Go after some real criminals, the murderers and the child molesters. Why weren't Harry and Bill told that the paratroopers were going to be practice-firing that night? And what about that AWACS commander, Art Henry? He's Canadian. Why didn't he know that his countrymen were shooting it up at Tarnak Farm? And why is the military coming down so hard on these pilots, and not the crew of that AC-130 gunship that invoked self-defense on an Afghan wedding back in July, killing 40 locals? Isn't an Afghani's life worth the same as a Canadian's?

"There's going to be accidents, and mistakes are going to happen, but they're not looking at the whole picture," says Bob Umbach, Bill's brother. Outside his nearby farmhouse, Bob has nailed a sign to a tree: "Support, don't prosecute, our American pilots." Bill's mom, Carol, is also at the fundraiser, quiet in voice, but proudly wearing one of those t-shirts that everyone is buying. Her late husband was a fighter pilot, Bill's inspiration to climb inside a cockpit. "Of all my children, he's the one who shows his emotions the least," Mrs. Umbach says. "That's the way he deals with it, but it will be in his mind for the rest of his life."

A few steps from the stage, the wall is plastered with letters, just a sample of the hundreds that have been arriving from across the United States—and north of the border. "Not everyone in Canada wants to punish those pilots," reads one note, sent from a Toronto address. "We lost fine family men in that firing," reads another, this one from Nova Scotia. "I do not see any justifiable reason that a further two fine men be lost as well from their families."

Sixty-four years. It seems insane. These pilots aren't rapists or traitors. More than one person glancing at the door prizes dutifully points out that John Walker Lindh, the so-called American Taliban captured in Afghanistan, got only 20 years. So Harry and Bill are three times as bad as some no-good terrorist? "If they had the information beforehand, the bombing never would have happened," says Jerry Helfrich, another veteran who has volunteered untold hours to the pilots' cause. Maybe they violated protocol, he says, and maybe they even deserve to be punished. But not criminally. "We're not judging," he says. "What we're fighting against are the criminal charges."

Among the many faces at the fundraiser is Joan Schmidt, Harry's mother, who drove the 90 minutes from St. Louis to be here this afternoon. She is, and always will be, her son's fiercest advocate, calling and writing and e-mailing anyone who will listen, including the president of the United States. Nearly every day, she e-mails an update about the case to her ever-widening list of friends, supporters, and journalists. Each note is signed the same: "Harry & Joan Schmidt, proud parents of Maj. Harry Schmidt." At her home, she fills binder after binder with documents and newspaper clippings that discuss her son's case. At the front of one of the red three-ring binders are photos of the four dead paratroopers. Harry's allies. She constantly prays for their families. "They were precious lives," she says. "We want the truth to come out so it never happens to any soldier again. Never."

The one person who isn't at today's event is Harry Schmidt. He and Lisa reluctantly chose to stay home, still spooked by that threatening e-mail that landed in the governor's inbox. Some of the people who forked over $20 to get into the hangar are a tad disappointed. This is for him, after all. But most are sympathetic. Nobody should have to suffer through what the Schmidts are facing. Joan, his mom, hasn't stopped worrying. "Do you think your mom would?" she asks.

★ ★ ★

It is raining on Parliament Hill, adding a steady patter of noise and a sea of umbrellas to this year's two minutes of silence. The veterans are here, as they always are on November 11, neatly dressed in their uniforms and telling stories about those black-and-white wars, back when soldiers deployed for years, not months, and most of their friends never came home. They are joined by the widows, the sons and the daughters, the people who dutifully turn out to pay their respects on Remembrance Day, red poppies pinned on their jackets. In recent years, they've watched as the crowds dwindled, a combination of old age and a country's collective apathy. Sure, every Canadian knows what this day is all about. Sacrifices made in the name of freedom. But it's hard to fully grasp the significance of Remembrance Day when you're too young to remember.

There is clearly something different this year. Seven months ago, the whole country watched those silver caskets slowly come off the plane, Canada's first battlefield casualties in 50 years. Very few have not read at least some of the newspaper articles, the glowing tributes to Pte. Green, Pte. Smith, Cpl. Dyer, and Sgt. Léger. They mourned with the families, watching snippets of each funeral on live television. Still fresh, those images are the obvious reason for the larger crowds today, not just in Ottawa, but in cities from coast to coast. In Edmonton, nearly 5,000 people pack an indoor service at the University of Alberta, bursting into applause as Marley Léger, Marc's wife, and Jodi Carter, Nathan's fiancée, place wreaths at a cenotaph. On the other side of the country, Nathan's mom, Charlotte, does the same at a large ceremony in Halifax. "Like any other Canadian, for a long period of time we took the military for granted," says her husband, Lloyd, after the service. "But now that's changed, obviously."

In Toronto, Paul Dyer attends a gathering at his son's old high school, where a scholarship has been created in his memory. "I got up this morning in tears," he says. Ainsworth's mother, Agatha, is in Montreal, in the same modest neighborhood where she's lived since the divorce so many years ago, when Ains moved to Ontario with his dad. For a long time, she had an engagement photo of Jocelyn and her son hanging on the living room wall. She recently took it down, leaning it up against the side of her bookshelf so she won't have to stare at it anymore.

A short drive away, in the Ottawa suburb of Stittsville, Sgt. Léger's parents, Claire and Richard, attend a Remembrance Day gathering at a local elementary school. They carry a framed photo of Marc, recalling for the children how their eldest son earned the nickname King Marco. "The children brought me back, and I'm sure brought Claire back, to Marc when he was young," Richard says.

And on Parliament Hill, under the rain, Doreen Coolen latches onto Adrienne Clarkson, the governor general, sniffling as a trumpeter plays the Last Post. Seven months after Ricky died, Doreen is this year's National Silver Cross Mother, representing every Canadian mom who has lost a child in war. "He had a heart as big as Nova Scotia," Doreen says of her 21-year-old son, her only child. "Too young. Too young."

★   ★   ★

Two months until the Article 32, and Maj. Schmidt's office at the 183rd Fighter Wing is now the unofficial headquarters of the U.S. military's most recognizable defendants. Because Harry and Bill are back on active duty, they technically don't work for the National Guard anymore. They still have to report to the base every day, but about the only thing they're allowed to do is get ready for January 13. So they pass the hours poring over classified documents, searching for more damning examples of how the Air Force command and control system failed them so miserably.

By now, prosecutors have turned over copies of all the testimony and exhibits collected by the CIB. Medical data. Log books. Affidavits. Autopsy reports. Photos from the morning after, of bloodstained sand and dead bodies. Charlie Gittins has specifically instructed Harry not to look at the pictures. He doesn't need to see that.

When the pilots' lawyers fly into Springfield, they sit on Maj. Schmidt's office couch, drinking coffee and talking courtroom strategy. By now, there are six attorneys attached to the defense team. Lieutenant-Colonel Clay Moushon, the 183rd's JAG, has joined Charlie Gittins and Jamie Key on Harry's side of the table. Bill has Dave Beck and Mike Roderick and Captain Matt Scoble, another military defense attorney. Dave Beck specifically asked for someone who was willing to work 22 hours a day. Scoble put up his hand.

Not everyone at the base is thrilled about all the lawyers walking around, about the constant negative attention these two pilots have brought to the unit. Some wish Harry and Bill would just stay home and prepare their case from there. But most are onside, fearful of what this whole thing could mean to other fighter pilots flying in and out of combat. Are they going to have to worry about calling a good attorney every time they land?

As November turns into December, more evidence trickles into the newspapers, all of it favorable to the pilots' cause. *The Ottawa Citizen* reports that there was no Canadian liaison officer stationed in the CAOC that night, somebody who might have known that the Princess Patricias were at Tarnak Farm. A Canadian Defence official says the position wasn't necessary because the Edmonton troops were attached to an American Task Force, which already had a representative in the CAOC. But, Charlie Gittins insists the bombing "would not have happened" if a Canadian had been in the radar center and known about the live-fire exercise. A week later, Cpl. Cheyenne Laroque's testimony appears in the press, the interview in which he tells the CIB that he radioed a "check fire" from the Kandahar tower five to 10 minutes before the bomb hit. The "check fire" had nothing to do with the F-16s; it was ordered so a Herc could take off from the airfield. But it raises the obvious question: Did the Canadians ignore an order to stop shooting at the exact same time Maj. Umbach happened to notice the fireworks? "This," Charlie Gittins tells *The Citizen*, "is material evidence that tends to explain the cause of this accident that was unconscionably omitted" from the CIB's final report.

Next, the revelation that Cpl. Paquette fired a few bursts of his C-9 machine gun "into the sky" when he engaged that pop-up target at the top of the wadi. "It was almost directly up," he told the CIB. A few other soldiers said Stan Clark also opened fire on the wooden target. Two guns shooting wildly into the sky! The brief burst of surface-to-air bullets was over by the time the pilots even noticed 3 Section's drill. But it is still "unconscionable," Charlie Gittins says, that investigators failed to mention the skyward shooting anywhere in their final reports. Another leaked document, this one obtained by the *National Post*, reveals that regardless of which way the bullets were traveling, both F-16 pilots were wearing night vision goggles that made it "impossible to accurately estimate" the height of munitions firing on the ground below. Producing a two-dimensional view—a lot like a television screen—the NVGs are famous for the way they distort images, according to an expert report prepared for Gen. Sargeant and his Coalition

Investigation Board. Maj. Schmidt estimated that the projectiles he saw from his cockpit window were burning out at 10,000 feet, even though numerous witnesses testified that any ricochets bouncing off the tank hulls were traveling no higher than 1,000 feet. "He clearly saw something shooting," Gittins says. "The problem is that the NVGs distorted it so that he believed it was coming at his lead and he couldn't tell the distance."

And then there are the Go-pills, those little orange tablets of dextroamphetamine that the Air Force "pushes" on its pilots. Going to war on speed. True, everyone signs those voluntary consent forms, but nowhere on that paper is there any mention of what's written on the side of a Dexedrine bottle: "May impair the ability of the patient to engage in potentially hazardous activities such as operating machinery." Maybe the Air Force doesn't consider an F-16 Viper to be a heavy machine? Nobody seems too worried, after all, that the drug's well-documented side-effects include paranoid delusions, hallucinations, and violent, aggressive behavior. Just what you need when you're strapped in a cockpit, forced to make instant decisions in the heat of combat. Harry and Bill popped those pills that night. Is that why they attacked? Was Harry too trippin' to stop and think for a second that he might be on the brink of making a terrible mistake?

★   ★   ★

Greg Graf has been running into a lot of cold shoulders lately. The guys in his Denver unit, his friends, aren't exactly rooting for him on this one. Where do you get the balls to prosecute one of your own? Were you in the cockpit that night? Did you see what he saw? The lieutenant-colonel's newly found pariah status extends well beyond his home base. All across the United States, nobody who flies F-16s for a living has any interest in helping him out. He needs only one expert witness, one seasoned pilot to tell the investigating officer just how stupid Harry Schmidt was when he rolled in on those Canadians. No thanks. Not interested.

The razzing gets so bad that Lt.-Col. Graf eventually gathers a bunch of his squadron mates into a briefing room to show them the targeting pod videos. *Hhhhhhhuuuuuhhhh, hhhhhhuhhhhh. Request permission to lay down some 20 mike-mike. Standby. Let's just make sure that it's not friendlies.*

Hhhhhuuuhh, Hhhhuuuhhh. Hold fire. Okay, I've got some men on a road and it looks like a piece of artillery firing at us. I am rolling in in self-defense. Hhhh-huuuuuhhh, Hhhhuuhh. Bomb's away, cranking left. Shack. Disengage, friendlies Kandahar. Nobody bothers Col. Graf anymore.

At Barksdale, John Odom can't help but read the daily press reports about how evil and slimy the U.S. Air Force is. As far as he is concerned, if the Air Force deserves any flak, it's that it's too damn quiet. Americans always root for the underdog. Fine. But can't we at least try to refute some of this stuff that's all over the papers? Firing into the sky? The Canadians ignored a "check fire"? *I see.* So the soldiers did this to themselves. It's their fault they're dead. And what would have been the pilots' excuse if they dropped 20 minutes later, when there wasn't a "check fire" in sight? Or 20 minutes before? Or any other time in the five hours that the paratroopers were out there shooting? That's almost as absurd as the one about the Canadian liaison officer. God himself could have been stationed in the CAOC that night, and the answer still would have been the same. Hold fire. But no, the Air Force school solution is to shut up. Let the defense lawyers say what they want. Just worry about the courtroom.

★ ★ ★

If he drinks enough, if he throws enough punches outside the bar, the voices go away for a little while. But never for good. If anything, they're getting louder these days, following him, reminding him at every turn that this is all his fault, that the Carl G. on his shoulder is what really caused that explosion. Brett Perry knows how irrational that sounds. But common sense is no match for the demons circling in his head. He still hears Ainsworth's laugh, and Marc, seconds before the flash of the bomb, telling him to put his fucking helmet back on. He sees Rick, too, on his knees fiddling with the Claymore. Brett, typical Brett, was screaming at him, swearing at the young private to get more goddamned tracer on the target. It's probably the last thing Ricky heard before the bomb ripped him to pieces. Brett can't forgive himself for that. He won't forgive himself for anything.

Doctors call it post-traumatic stress disorder. Survivor's guilt. Whatever the name, it has consumed Cpl. Perry, turning this tank of a man into little more than a terrified child. The nightmares have become so horrific, so vivid, that he sleeps with the lights on now. Lately, he has even started to wonder whether that is really shrapnel lodged in his left tricep. Maybe it's actually a piece of one of the dead soldiers' bones. Maybe that man is somehow living inside him.

In between the counseling and the flashbacks, U.S. prosecutors, prepping Cpl. Perry to testify at next month's Article 32, show him the targeting pod videos. In Maj. Umbach's crosshairs, Brett sees the quick boom of the Carl Gustav—his Carl Gustav. Seconds later, Maj. Schmidt slews his invisible laser to the exact same spot on the ground. *Okay, I've got some men on a road and it looks like a piece of artillery firing at us. I am rolling in in self-defense.* It was Brett all along. The demons are right. Those guys really are dead because of me.

chapter twenty-four

Six days after ringing in the new year, Harry Schmidt eats dinner with his two young sons, kisses them goodbye, and sets off, all alone, for Barksdale Air Force Base. His Article 32, his official chance to fight back against the military, is scheduled to begin in a week. He's driving down early to meet his lawyers, to review some last-minute preparations. It's a long haul, about a 12-hour drive down through Missouri and Arkansas and into Louisiana. Harry's used to such solo exercises, having flown so many long, lonely missions over the past 15 years. At least on this journey he can stop for gas and stretch his legs.

"He was probably a nervous wreck," says his wife, Lisa, thinking of her husband's drive. "He's been a nervous wreck for nine months." Indeed, it has been an exhausting year for the Schmidts. The accident. The unprecedented charges. Fundraiser after fundraiser, shaking hands and saying thanks. The death threat. And, of course, the reporters, so quick to mention, in every single story they write, that Harry's nickname is Psycho. He must be guilty. "When you go away and actually do what you're supposed to do, and then you come home and someone says you're a criminal and they want you in jail ... It's just an unbelievable thing he's dealing with," Lisa says. "The worst fear is that Harry will be removed from our family life. The tragedy would be that our sons would not have their dad. I think of Tucker at a school event and everybody has their dad there and a little friend says: 'Tucker, where's your dad?' And he says: 'He's in jail for the rest of his life.' What will that do to my son's life?"

For months, Lisa has watched her husband prepare to defend himself while at the same time struggling to stomach the reality that his bomb killed four good men. "He's a very emotional person," Lisa says. "He cries, he hugs and kisses, he's just a very tender man. And the loss of the men—people think he's callous to that—but he struggles with it all the time." Yet she and Harry still have to listen, over and over, as strangers try to compare their plight to that of the Canadian families, as if there's some neat little equation that can calculate anguish. "They have the ultimate grief and the ultimate sorrow, and I totally acknowledge that and I'm so sorry for it," Lisa says. "There would be no hesitation for me to offer my condolences, and they'd be sincere. I don't know if they'd be received, but obviously I would tell them that I'm very sorry for the situation."

Lisa asks only that the Canadian families try to put aside what the Air Force has already told them, and listen objectively to the evidence that proves, without a doubt, that Harry is also an innocent victim in all this. "My hope is that they would choose to receive the proper information, not what has come out prior to this, because it's all been lies and misconstrued and skewed," she says. "And so if they really do want to have a proper hearing, and make a proper judgment, then they need to listen to the hearing materials and then decide what they think. And whatever they think, that's personal to them."

Marlene Umbach has thought about mailing the Canadian families a card, just to let them know that everyone here is praying for them. For months, she's been reading all the newspaper clippings. It's almost an obsession now, staring at those soldiers' photos. But everybody says no to the card idea. No competent lawyer whose client faces the possibility of 64 years in prison would ever condone something like that, something that could so easily be construed as an admission of guilt. So Marlene keeps working, telling the reporters and the talk-show hosts how the Air Force is using her husband to protect the careers of a few self-serving generals. "It's common sense to know that in every war, all the way back to the Civil War, they've had friendly fire accidents," she says. "Why are they picking this one incident to publicize and scrutinize and sensationalize? Everybody that goes to war signs on the dotted line and knows that they might die. Bill could have died that night."

But he didn't. And Marlene knows that. Somebody else died that night, four other men with wives and wives-to-be. "They all had a story," she says. "I'm one of those people who always thinks that there's somebody else who has it worse off. That's how I handle things. I would just tell them that I hope they can accept our apology one day."

Amid the media circus, Marlene sometimes wonders why Bill is facing the same music as Harry. He's not the one who pickled the bomb, after all. "It's really not worth worrying about," she says. "Bill said: 'I'm not going to get an attorney who is going to try to separate us. We were there together that night and we're going to do this together. If I get a lawyer who says one word about that, I'm just going to get a different lawyer. I'm not turning my back on Harry. We were together that night and we were a team.'"

At Springfield's VFW post, the letters and checks continue to arrive. $2,000. $5,000. "The haze of war and the pressures that come with it must not be complicated with second guessing after the fact," one reads. "Being 81 years old and a veteran of four years' service in WWII, my heart goes out to the pilots," reads another. "My only wish is I could have sent 10 times more. Love, Stan." Days away from the Article 32, the account now contains more than $165,000.

"People were asking what we were going to do with the money and we didn't want them to think that we were collecting to have a big party or something," says John Russo, the VFW commander and the man who launched the campaign back in September. "So it was decided that the appropriate place would be for it to go back to the Canadian survivors. If there's any money left over, it will go back to the Canadian families. It's a done deal."

★ ★ ★

Among the growing list of potential witnesses, defense lawyers have requested the appearance of two Air Force generals at the Article 32: Brig-Gen. Stephen T. Sargeant, the CIB co-president who preferred the criminal charges, and newly promoted Major-General Stephen G. Wood, the top man working in the CAOC that night.

The pilots' lawyers hope to grill Gen. Sargeant about his supposed cozy relationship with Lieutenant-General Michael Moseley, the commander of the Afghanistan air war and the officer who appointed Sargeant to investigate the friendly fire accident. For months, Charlie Gittins and

Dave Beck have accused Gen. Sargeant—through the media—of blaming the pilots in a sinister plot to protect Gen. Moseley and his dysfunctional CAOC from embarrassment.

Gittins and Beck plan to question Wood, then a brigadier-general, about the communications breakdown that left the CAOC completely unaware of the Canadian live-fire exercise. Gen. Wood is also expected to testify that the Canadian military, unlike the Brits and the French, did not have a liaison officer assigned to the Coalition Air Operations Center who might have known that the Princess Patricias were firing at Tarnak Farm.

But a week prior to the hearing, Colonel Patrick Rosenow, the investigating officer who will oversee the 32, rules that neither general will be available to testify. His specific reasons are unknown, but such decisions are typically based on a combination of where a potential witness is stationed and the significance of what he might have to say. To the pilots' supporters, Col. Rosenow's ruling is yet another sign of a cover-up. Why can't the pilots cross-examine the man who laid the charges? Or the man who commanded the radar center that failed to warn them about the live-fire drill? They must have something to hide.

On January 9, five days before the hearing is scheduled to begin, the pilots' lawyers ask the judge to reconsider his decision. Included in their written submission is a proffer of expected testimony from Gen. Wood, a summary of an earlier conversation between the general and the defense team at Nevada's Nellis Air Force Base. "The ACO did not show that there was a friendly activity at Tarnak Farms," the submission quotes the general as saying. "It should have. There was a breakdown between 3 PPCLI and their higher headquarters and the CAOC. I don't know if the breakdown was between all three of those areas, and I don't know exactly who caused the breakdown, but there was a breakdown. There was no indication the ROZ would be active or that there would be troops there doing anything at all."

At one point during Operation Enduring Freedom, there was a Canadian liaison officer stationed in the CAOC, Gen. Wood told the pilots' lawyers. "He came by mistake, and we made him British on paper to avoid upsetting the Saudis," the proffer reads. "The Saudis only wanted us to have British, US and French people in the CAOC. Would I have expected a Canadian LNO to know about the exercise? Maybe, maybe not."

Defense attorneys also asked the general about Go-pills. "I took a personal interest in the use of amphetamines after the media attacked us for using them in the Desert Storm," said Gen. Wood, who flew dozens of missions during the Gulf War. "I was unaware of the side effects and warnings that come with these drugs at the time of the accident. I did not know that there were side effects that were not being briefed to the pilots. Now that I know about the drug manufacturer's warnings regarding the operation of dangerous machinery, I'd ask for more information about the pills before allowing aircrews to use them."

The pilots' lawyers send Gen. Wood a copy of their proffer, hoping he will authenticate it with his signature. He refuses, concerned that "it was not entirely accurate." Instead, he crafts his own sworn affidavit. "To the best of my knowledge, no one in the CAOC knew the Canadians were at Tarnak Farms firing that night," he writes. "I know that Major [Thomas] Smedley in the Battlefield Coordination Detachment (BCD) did not know because I queried him when I heard the radio calls from BOSSMAN. I must say, however, that even if the CAOC had known that there was a live-fire exercise going on at Tarnak Farms that night, the response from the CAOC would not have been any different. The CAOC still needed more data about the location of both Coffee Flight and the perceived threat from the ground, especially in view of the fact that Kandahar was an area with more than 2,000 friendly troops on the ground." The pilots never passed along specific coordinates, alerting ground control to precisely what they were looking at. "Without a location of Coffee Flight or a mark on the perceived SAFIRE, nothing that the CAOC was told would have led us to conclude that what Coffee Flight was observing was ground fire at Tarnak Farms.

"The situation on the ground was such that you could not tell where the enemy was and where friendly forces or Afghani civilians were, in regards to the friendlies and non-friendlies in Afghanistan," Gen. Wood continues. "In my opinion, such a situation made it more important than ever for pilots to have positive target identification before dropping any weapons on the ground and have a clear understanding of current operations."

And the Go-pills? "I have never heard of any crew member complain of any adverse effects from the pills," he writes. "In my opinion, they save lives by helping to combat aircrew fatigue."

★ ★ ★

When it was first unveiled in the 1930s, Barksdale Air Force Base, at 22,000 acres, was the world's largest airfield. Built on top of the cotton fields in Bossier City, Louisiana, the base is named in honor of Lieutenant Eugene Hoy Barksdale, a decorated fighter pilot who shot down three enemy planes in the First World War. On August 11, 1926, the lieutenant was test-flying a new Douglas 0-2 observation plane over Ohio when it started to spin out of control. He tried to bail, but his parachute got tangled in one of the wings. Lt. Barksdale fell to his death.

The base that now bears his name is right next door to Shreveport, a city of historic southern mansions and dirty casinos and Cajun restaurants that you would probably never even look at if the locals didn't insist the food was so good. Like Herby K's, over on Pierre Avenue, where the dining room barely fits a dozen people but the butterfly shrimp is phenomenal. Ironically enough, Shreveport, Louisiana, was also home to one of America's only two Canadian Football League franchises, the Pirates. The team lasted all of two seasons before folding. Eight wins. Twenty-eight losses.

Shreveport's latest brush with Canada will be even more brief, but definitely not unnoticed. Television crews and newspaper writers from across North America have flown to Shreveport, to Barksdale Air Force Base, to watch two fighter pilots stand trial. All the 24-hour networks are talking about the Go-pills, about how this is all a big farce to please America's northern neighbors. Outside the local VFW post, the one just beyond Barksdale's main gate, a sign hangs near the road: "Support, don't prosecute, our American pilots." John Russo called ahead.

On Sunday, two days before the hearing begins, dozens of journalists wait in line for a quick look at the building where everything will unfold. Barksdale doesn't have a real courtroom, so the Air Force made one, placing some long tables and some black leather chairs in a white room at the far end of Building 845—a large warehouse on Logistics Lane. In more normal times, when there isn't a metal detector guarding the door, the makeshift courtroom is where deploying airmen fill out their wills. Canteens and sleeping bags are piled nearby.

Down the hall, the press will be stuffed into its own temporary room, equipped with tables, phone lines, and two large screens that will broadcast the proceedings via closed-circuit television. If the lawyers start talking about something classified, a technician can simply cut the feed. Fittingly, CNN will be shown in the meantime. Even in open session, however, the hearing will be difficult to see. One of the two cameras is in the far corner of the room, providing a perfect view of the backs of everybody's heads. The other is tacked to the ceiling directly over the witness stand, beaming a dimly lit overhead shot into the media room. Most of the time, it will be hard to even tell whether a witness's lips are moving. *National Post* columnist Christie Blatchford will later compare the quality of the feed to that of low-budget pornography.

A five-minute drive away, at the Doughtery Conference Center, relatives of the four dead soldiers have their own private room, with couches, a fridge, and a small kitchenette. They will be able to watch everything transpire without being hounded by the press, and, more importantly, without having to bump into the pilots in the warehouse bathroom. Nine months after the bombing, few of the soldiers' families have much sympathy left for Harry Schmidt or Bill Umbach. Nobody really wants to see them go to jail, but some genuine remorse would be nice. A phone call or a letter, something that shows you're actually sorry for what you did that night. They've heard wives and lawyers express their condolences, but never a direct apology from the pilots themselves.

"They don't have to do it publicly," says Richard Léger, Marc's father. "All they have to do is say it to me." He and Claire flew to Barksdale the other day. So did Marley, their son's beautiful widow, wearing Marc's wedding ring around her necklace.

Nathan's parents, Lloyd and Charlotte, will also spend the next two weeks in that room. Lloyd, as always, says he just wants to let the justice system run its course. "All I'm looking for is the accountability process," he says. "But at the same time, if the investigation warrants four counts of involuntary manslaughter—and this is people in the military who are making this judgment based on the facts presented—then so be it. If the pilots have to serve jail time, so be it."

Paul and Agatha, Ainsworth's parents, won't say a word to one another the entire time. He thinks she's an actress, crying crocodile tears for their son. She thinks he's a con artist. It's all about the insurance money, and any other handouts he can bully out of the Canadian Forces. Jocelyn couldn't come to Louisiana. As in the weeks after the funeral, she can't afford to take the time off work. She'll have to settle for reading about the hearing in the newspapers, in the articles that will appear right beside the engagement photo of her and Ains. More than one patient at the dentist's office will stare at Jocelyn behind the reception desk, stunned to realize that they're in the same room as the blond woman on the front page.

Miranda didn't come to Shreveport, either. It's been a slow recovery since the car accident back in May. She was out of the hospital in two weeks, but only because she swallowed the pain and proved to the doctors that she could walk up three stairs on her own. For months, Miranda wore a metal corrective brace around her fractured neck, enduring bouts of physiotherapy that will continue for years to come. She's back in school, though, a history major at Halifax's Mount Saint Vincent University. She wants to be at the hearing, but traveling to Louisiana would mean at least two weeks of lost classes. And Miranda is trying her best to move on with her life. She promised Ricky that.

Nobody from Pte. Green's family is here. Doreen, his mom, is at home in Nova Scotia. By the time the Article 32 begins, it will be obvious why she stayed away. Her new lawyer, Dick Murtha, is planning to file a multi-million-dollar wrongful death claim against the U.S. government.

★ ★ ★

On the flight to Shreveport, an American passenger asks Cpl. Shane Brennan why the Canadian government is prosecuting those Illinois fighter pilots. When he lands, one of the first things he sees is the big sign outside the VFW post: "Support, don't prosecute, our American pilots." At the restaurants, at the mall, everywhere he and the other paratroopers go, they get the sense they're not very welcome in this Air Force town. Selfish

Canadians. Who would protect you if the U.S. wasn't watching your back? Nobody. And now, when a couple of upstanding American fighter pilots make an honest mistake, Canadians want them locked in jail for the rest of their lives. How ungrateful can you get?

Shane is one of seven Princess Patricias penciled in as potential witnesses at the Article 32. With him on the plane to Louisiana were Capt. Joe Jasper, Sgt. Lorne Ford, MCpl. Curtis Hollister, and corporals Brian Decaire, Brett Perry, and Rene Paquette.

Col. David C. Nichols is also listed as a possible government witness, though his loyalties clearly lie on the defense side of the table. It was just a few weeks ago that the colonel even agreed to meet with prosecutors, and that was only after his own lawyer negotiated an immunity deal. No matter what he says from here on in, Col. Nichols, the pilots' commander in Kuwait, cannot be punished any further for what happened on April 17, 2002. An official letter of reprimand, which he received three months after the bombing, will be the only black mark on his record.

Signed by Maj.-Gen. Walter Buchanan, the commander of Joint Task Force Southwest Asia, the written rebuke isn't much different than what Gen. Sargeant concluded in his CIB report. You complained to your subordinates about the CAOC's alleged deficiencies, but you said nothing to your superiors. You would rather be everybody's pal than enforce discipline. You failed to ensure that missions were adequately prepared and briefed. And you violated your duty as a commander when you misread the pilots their rights, when you "arrogantly" changed the word "offense" to "incident." "You are hereby reprimanded," the letter states. "Your conduct falls woefully short of that expected of a commander."

Col. Nichols—as is his right—typed a reply to Gen. Buchanan, calling his punishment "unwarranted and obviously based on an extremely shallow understanding of the situation" that led to the bombing. "My command and leadership in no way contributed to the accident. It was evident from the arrival of the board that they were looking for someone to blame for this terrible accident."

The real problem, Col. Nichols says in his letter, "was the lack of information available to the aircrews prior to, during and after their missions." There was "limited and inadequate ground order of battle information," and the ACO "was complex and not suitable for the mission." Col. Nichols claims that he and his senior staff tried "over 100 times" to push the CAOC to provide more information about the locations of friendly ground forces, but the "staff in the CAOC always had the attitude that they were not interested in what the fighter crews that were flying in the AOR thought or had to say."

Much of the colonel's three-page letter criticizes the Air Force for the way it conducted close air support (CAS) with ground troops in Afghanistan, especially during Operation Anaconda. The mission was hampered by "the complete failure of coordination" between air and ground elements, he says. "After having exhausted all possible ways to communicate with the CAOC, I 'begged' the CAOC to let me host a CAS conference to discuss and 'fix' the problems we all lived with during Anaconda," he wrote. "I was initially met with no interest from the CAOC staff but extreme interest from everyone else involved in the operation. Eventually, the conference was sanctioned by the CAOC and had the potential to be very valuable to all involved. Of note, NO ONE FROM THE CAOC attended." It is important to also note that Maj. Schmidt and Maj. Umbach were not engaged in close air support that night. They were on their way home when they noticed the Canadians, not supporting ground troops engaged by the enemy. But Col. Nichols says the overriding worry—Where are the friendlies?—was the same during every single sortie into Afghanistan.

"There is no one in the Air Force today that understands combat operations at the Wing level and all that goes with them better than me," the letter finishes. "Each time an Aircrew takes off, I as the Commander, am personally responsible for them returning safely. This requires an intense commitment to the mission and the people performing the mission in all areas. This is what I did for the entire 13 months and that is what I was doing at the time. Thank you sir for taking the time to read this Memorandum. I hope the information can be used to make our Air Force more mission capable and better prepared for whatever comes next."

Days before the Article 32 begins, Col. Nichols requests a meeting with the Canadian soldiers at Barksdale. He wants to tell them what really happened that night. "What we need to do is move on, and you need to understand that there was nothing intentional done to harm you," he tells them. "And we believe the same, that you did everything right. And you need to know that we believe we were doing everything right." We're neighbors, Col. Nichols says. Allies. This was a horrible mistake, but a mistake that extends well beyond the two pilots. Before he leaves, he gives the paratroopers an American flag.

★ ★ ★

On Tuesday, January 14, 2003, Col. John Odom stops by a Shreveport doughnut shop to pick up some breakfast. Not just for him, but for his fellow lawyers and all the Canadian soldiers who traveled here to testify. They'll be hungry, no doubt. They're infantrymen. As he stands in line, decked out in his Air Force blues and his shiny black shoes, an elderly gentleman taps him on the shoulder.

"Sir?" Col. Odom says, a little surprised.

"Boy, I tell you what," the man tells him. "It is a crying shame what you Air Force boys are doing to those poor fighter pilots out at Barksdale."

The stranger, of course, has no idea that he just poked the lead lawyer prosecuting those poor fighter pilots. Odom is furious. He can almost feel the back of his neck turning red. But he stops himself from firing back. If this guy, who knows absolutely nothing about the evidence, can get you so riled up, you're not going to do too well when the real thing starts in a couple hours. "Well, sir," Col. Odom says back, smiling politely. "There are an awful lot of facts about that case that you might not be familiar with. It's not quite as clear as you might think."

Minutes later, as he steers his car toward the temporary courthouse, Col. Odom can see the ocean of satellite trucks in the parking lot. CNN, CBS, ABC, NBC, CBC. The hearing was supposed to start the day before, but Col. Rosenow granted a one-day postponement so the defense team could interview the Canadian soldiers. The delay seems to have made the reporters that much more anxious. They have been here since 6 a.m. That's when the bus leaves from the main gate. If you miss it, you miss it.

Nearly a dozen television cameras line the walkway that separates the lot from the warehouse's side doors. As 8 a.m. approaches, the key players begin to walk by for the first of what will be many times, each group igniting another flurry of camera flashes. As Dave Beck leads Bill and Marlene toward the door, he stops at the microphones to give a brief statement. The message is the same as always. This was a terrible accident. We need to compensate the Canadian families and fix the problems so it never happens again.

Harry Schmidt is almost oblivious to the cameras by now. They camped outside his front door. They followed him around Springfield. And now they're here, in Louisiana, capturing every step he takes from his car to the courtroom. Maj. Schmidt stares straight ahead as he passes by the lenses, holding tightly onto his wife's left hand. A few steps away, an Army sergeant stands guard in his green fatigues, a sniffer dog sitting on the grass near his feet.

chapter twenty-five

Joe Jasper has a new tattoo on the inside of his right forearm, a parachute with wings. Para Coy. He got it right after Afghanistan, right around the same time as the anti-depressants. Joe thinks often of that April morning, when he and the others defied their commanders and waited in the desert to pick up the corpses. Since landing back in Canada six months ago, his sleep has been troubled at best, interrupted almost every night by vivid dreams and sweaty fits of adrenaline. The drugs are just a temporary thing, but they help. So does the tattoo, reminding Capt. Jasper that despite the media frenzy outside, he was part of something larger, something much more significant than a routine training drill at Tarnak Farm. Those four guys didn't die because they were conducting a live-fire exercise, or because some hotshot pilot was looking for a medal. They died because they were soldiers soldiering.

But that's not the focus anymore. These days, it's all about that moonless night, about a few short minutes captured on video by a pair of F-16s. It's in the papers every morning, on the news every night. Nobody's interested in The Whale anymore, or Operation Torii, or any other Afghanistan mission that didn't occur on April 17. The lawyers don't want to ask Joe Jasper about the month he spent on The Line. They want to talk about Tarnak Farm.

"Prior to 17 April, how many times had you been to the Tarnak Farms range?" asks Col. John Odom, the lead prosecutor.

"I would not be able to quote an exact number," Capt. Jasper answers. "But between five and 10 times."

"Both daytime and nighttime?"

"Correct, sir."

Wearing his full dress uniform, Joe Jasper is the first witness to testify at the Article 32. He sits behind a small, white table, directly facing both the government lawyers and the defense team. That camera on the ceiling beams his every gesture into the media room down the hall, and to the small quarters on the other side of the base where the Canadian families are watching quietly.

Capt. Jasper explains how he submitted A Company's request for time on the range to the Canadian Battle Group's training officer. The request was approved by Task Force Rakkasan at a weekly resource meeting. The paratroopers, approximately 70 of them, arrived at the range just before sundown. They zeroed their weapons. Capt. Jasper briefed everyone on the scenario. Wadi South was the Close Quarter Battle range, his range. Wadi East was the tank–stalk drill, Sgt. Léger's drill.

"Did you have any reflective gear?" Col. Odom asks.

"Yes," the captain answers. "We had on all of the normal IFF [Identification Friend or Foe] for the brigade and what we had was the infrared strobe on the back of our helmets. We had glow tape on the top of our helmets and on our left shoulders."

"How many of the men were wearing the IR strobes on their helmets?"

"Just about everyone was wearing them, but we didn't always turn all of them on because they tended to overwhelm helicopter pilots as they came in—so many flashings. Typically, you would always have at least a couple per element, that element was a section of eight men, and typically you would have three or four on, maybe. Every second or third man would have it on."

"During the live-firing exercise that your company had on Tarnak Farms that night, had you received any 'check fire' orders?" Col. Odom asks.

"Yes, sir," Capt. Jasper answers. "We had received one earlier in the evening and one later on closer to the actual incident."

"As to the first one, did you get a 'cancel check fire'?"

"Yes, sir."

"As to the second one, did you get a 'cancel check fire'?"

"Yes, sir."

"At the time the bomb struck on 17 April, was the range in a 'check fire' status?"

"No, sir."

The questions inevitably turn to the precise moment of the explosion, a story that Joe Jasper has told and retold many times since that night. He was about to bring another group to the start of the CQB range when a cloud of fire lit up the sky to his 11 o'clock. He hit the sand. "I took a look around in my night vision goggles to see what had happened and we all, basically, just turned to each other and said: 'What the hell was that?'" he recalls. "We had a conversation and said: 'Well, it's obviously something bad.' The first thing that flashed into mind was that it might have been a range accident, and, obviously, we had to go back and sort that out. The route I had to take to get back to where the explosion obviously was, I had to take the road back to the administration area and then head north up the wadi. If I had cut straight across the desert to where they were there was some danger of not knowing exactly what the status of their range was. I didn't want to do that."

"Could you hear any aircraft?" Col. Odom asks.

"I did, actually. The sound of the aircraft seemed to go from southwest to roughly east or northeast."

"Did you have any idea of what type of air it was?"

"It most definitely sounded like fast air to me."

"Were you aware of any fast air that Taliban or al-Qaeda had?"

"No," Capt. Jasper answers. "As far as I know they didn't have any fast air."

He explains how he and Billy Bolen ran to the wadi. He saw the medics working on Cpl. Dyer. Bolen found Sgt. Ford. Brett Perry grabbed him and told him it wasn't the Carl G. They loaded casualties on the chopper. Then the sun came up.

★ ★ ★

"Capt. Jasper, good afternoon."

"Good afternoon."

"I'm Dave Beck and I wanted to tell you, as I told you yesterday—we met for the first time yesterday, is that correct?"

"Yes, it is."

"That I am sorry about what happened and sorry you have to be here because of that. You were the range training or coordinating officer for this particular exercise on April 17th, is that correct?"

"Range conducting officer is correct," Capt. Jasper says.

"You did submit the training plan for April 17th?"

"Range in motion."

"And who did you submit that to?"

"I submitted that—usually we submitted those electronically and I submitted that to the training officer and I also usually carbon copied his training staff."

"Would that be the training officer within your battalion?"

"Yes, it would be; that of the battalion or that of the training officer."

"And whether or not that information was passed to whom or to anybody, you don't have any information on that, do you?"

"To who he passed it to?"

"Yes."

"Well, he would need to take what I gave him and go to brigade with it because it was the brigade chief who needed this information for co-ordination. And he would get back to me saying, verifying we could have the range, these weapons for this practice, so on and so forth, and verify exactly what I could do with the requests that I make."

"And, as you told us yesterday, whether or not that information was ever passed or coordinated beyond the brigade to anyone else, you don't have any idea, do you?"

"No, sir."

Dave Beck, Maj. Umbach's lead defense lawyer, asks Capt. Jasper about his testimony in front of Gen. Sargeant's Coalition Investigation Board. "Did you express to them that you were concerned that things might have been done better as far as coordination and communication?"

"I was concerned that the accident happened and that there was obviously some mistakes," Capt. Jasper says.

"Did you express concern about things that might have been done better?"

"Words to that effect."

"Do you recall testifying that obviously the coordination higher than our level in response to a question: 'Do you have any worries or concerns about things that might have been done better?' Your response: 'Obviously, the coordination higher than our level.'"

"That sounds like what I said," Joe answers.

"And you also recall that you testified: 'Obviously, there is something that needs to be fixed there' with regard to coordination, communication higher than your level?"

"Words to that effect, yes, sir."

"And, in fact, do you recall testifying in response to Gen. Sargeant's question: 'What do you think happened, Captain?' Your response: 'I think there was a breakdown in communications between air to ground.' Do you recall that?"

"Not specifically, but that sounds—"

"Can I approach the witness, sir?" Beck asks Col. Rosenow.

"Sure," the IO answers.

Beck hands Capt. Jasper a copy of his testimony to the CIB. "What did you testify?" he asks.

"'I think there is a breakdown in communications between air to ground and I don't think that normally pilots flying through the area would know days when people down there are on training or not, but definitely there has got to be some more coordination as to typically what is going to a training pattern.'"

"Did Gen. Sargeant or anybody make you aware whether or not any pilots knew that Tarnak Farms was a training area or even existed before April 17th?"

"No," Capt. Jasper answers.

"Did Gen. Sargeant or anybody from the U.S. government ever make you aware that there was a symposium one month before where the same kind of concerns you expressed under oath to the board after the accident were expressed, a month before this happened?" Beck asks, referring to the Close Air Symposium that Col. Nichols convened at Al Jaber shortly after Operation Anaconda.

"No," Capt. Jasper answers. "I didn't have much contact with the U.S. government at that time."

"Does that concern you that the concerns you expressed about what happened, the communication, coordination, and that those concerns were expressed and the problem wasn't fixed?"

"I would say it concerns me if there was an accident."

"Do you agree that safety is important in conducting training any place, especially in the combat environment?" Beck asks, a few moments later.

"Yes."

"Do you agree that those concerns you expressed, coordination, communication, so that everybody knows what's going on both on the ground and the air, is very important?"

"Yes."

"Has anybody from the U.S. government told you to this day that no one from the brigade, that once the word was passed from your unit to the brigade, that that word never got passed any further?"

"Not that I recall, especially while we were over there we really didn't have any need to discuss what happened with the brigade."

Dave Beck, always polite, never abrasive, shifts his questions to the definition of "small arms." The Canadian Army considers small arms to be any weapon that fires projectiles less than 20 millimeters wide, such as the light machine guns the troops were shooting at Tarnak Farm that night. The Carl Gustav, at 84 millimeters, is definitely not a small arm.

"Has anybody from the U.S. government to this day told you how Tarnak Farms was classified with regard to what type of range it was?" Beck asks Capt. Jasper.

"If your point is that it was a small arms range, I can't recall if it was designated as such. It was the range that was designated to use all of the weapons that were out there and all the weapons that we used to template for that range."

"Certainly," Beck says. "In other words, when you put in that request for training or training plan, you indicated what weapons you were going to use and you were approved to use those?"

"Precisely," Capt. Jasper answers. "And we were already pre-approved as to what weapons can and can't be used there. So we don't ask to use weapons that we know are outside the range."

"Do you know anything about the ACO, the Air Control Order, which the commander of the Air Force has issued for pilots in the area?"

"No."

"Do you think it would be important, since for safety purposes coordination, communication is important, that people on the ground are using the same definitions and terms and information as people in the air?"

"I imagine that would be important," Capt. Jasper says.

"Did Gen. Sargeant or Gen. Dumais tell you that people, even in the AWACS, in the command center and pilots didn't know that Tarnak Farms was even there before April 17th?"

"Sir, I can't recall a conversation between the general."

"Would that concern you if you were going out for night training in a combat zone, and U.S. forces in the air controlling it in the command center, don't even know there is a training area there?"

"That would concern me because, obviously, we are close to the Kandahar Airfield, which is hard to miss," Capt. Jasper says.

"Would it also concern you if anyone could find out anything about Tarnak Farms in the Air Control Order, they would be told it is a small-arms range? By definition, Canada, we've established is 20 millimeters and below, and U.S. Army regulations define small arms as 50 caliber, so that would be about 12 millimeters. Would that concern you that you were being told you could use the range for one purpose when the U.S. Army defines small arms and put out the word that its small arms is something entirely different?"

"No, not really," Capt. Jasper answers. "Because we templated the range and not the U.S. Army. And I would imagine that whenever the Americans use the range they use their safety regulations and when we use the range we use our regulations for safety and templating. The Americans were in charge of—the brigade is in charge of coordinating all range use. So, overall, they kept an eye on what was being done with the range. For myself, I had confidence that when I went out there to train that I was well within the parameters set by my C.O. [commanding officer]."

"Set by your C.O.?"

"Set by my C.O. And, for instance, Carl Gustav wasn't small arms, that wasn't a factor that I was concerned about."

"So, it doesn't concern you that U.S. forces are being told—or if they are being told anything at all—there is nothing but small arms 12 to 20 millimeter?"

"It didn't concern me whatsoever what the American forces were being told, as long as it didn't affect safety and training."

"Do you believe that could adversely affect safety?"

"For the American troops, perhaps."

"It has been reported that Lt.-Col. Stogran indicated that a unit of 3 PPCLI in mid-March, before this incident happened, there had been an aircraft that nearly strafed them and they were called off at the last minute by a Canadian liaison," Beck says, referring to the F-16 that nearly bombed Patricias during Operation Harpoon in March.

"I had heard that," Capt. Jasper says. In fact, the captain testifies that he heard secondhand rumors about another near-miss during the assault on The Whale.

"Were there any changes put in place with either 3 PPCLI or with the Americans who were coordinating things as a result of this potentially very dangerous situation?"

"Specifically, I can't recall. But, there are several times, of course, when you are reminded to have the proper IFF deck on."

"Did you yourself do anything or do any inquiries to find out what happened in March, why it had happened and what, if anything, could be done to be sure it didn't happen again, especially if there hadn't been a Canadian liaison officer to call it off?"

"No, because we had talked about this as it came up. We knew that we always had our eye, in fact, on it, and we were dressed properly for recognition, so we didn't worry too much."

⌣

"Who ultimately approved your range request?" Charlie Gittins asks Capt. Jasper.

"I'm not sure who approved them at brigade level."

"Was it the brigade? Was the brigade a U.S. organization?"

"Yes, it was."

"Did the brigade manage the range, schedule people on the range?"

"Yes, they scheduled them."

"So, overall control for this range was the United States Army, correct?"

"Correct."

"At any time prior to conducting this range that you designed, did you read the relative regulation governing operation of the U.S. Army Fire Wing?" Gittins asks, referring to an American Army document written in 1983.

"I didn't read any U.S. Army manuals," Capt. Jasper says.

"The governing range regulation is Army Regulation 385-63. 'Policies and Procedures for Ammunition for Training, Target Practice and Combat' requires that a blinking red light be shown during night hours on a small-arms range. Was a blinking red light operating at Tarnak Farms on the night of the accident?"

"Not that I can recall."

"The regulation provides that 'the scarlet streamer during daylight hours, substituted by blinking red lights during night hours, will be displayed from a prominent point for a range complex and at all times during fire. No firing will take place unless these conditions are met.' Would it be fair to say that you cannot say whether or not those conditions were met on the night that your unit was firing?"

"I would say they weren't met. With respect to that though—"

"Thank you, sir," Gittins says. "You've answered my question."

"Could he be allowed to finish the answer?" Col. Odom interjects.

"Eventually he will be allowed to one way or another," Judge Rosenow says. "But I will allow defense to finish their examination."

Later in his testimony, when Capt. Jasper does have the chance to finish his answer, he explains that the company had placed a line of four or five red glowsticks inside the corral, as well as an infrared stick on the top of the crumbling structure. But, he says, the goal of the exercise was to practice firing weapons at night, in the dark. Lighting up the range with blinking red strobes would defeat the whole purpose. "If I had known about the regulation and was held to obey it, then I wouldn't have ignored it," Capt. Jasper says. "In this case, I don't think I ignored anything."

⌣

"Can I have IO Exhibit 5 put up on the screen, please?" Gittins asks, referring to some still photos pulled from the targeting pod videos of the F-16s. "When did you first see this photograph?"

"I believe it was with Col. Odom," Capt. Jasper responds. "I saw the video, actually, before I saw the photograph. I just saw the still, I believe, with Col. Odom."

"Now, on the still you indicated that you could identify trucks along the road, places where they were staged?"

"I can identify the place they staged on a black blob."

"Were you asked to identify that while the video was moving?"

"At which point? When?"

"At any time while you were viewing the video, were you asked to point out where different things were?"

"Yes, actually, I believe so," Capt. Jasper says.

"Were you able to do that?"

"Based on the layout of what I could see, yes."

"And that's because you had been there on the ground, correct?"

"Yes."

"And when you were pointing out these different things on this diagram, would it be fair to say that you were not maneuvering a jet, correct?"

"That would be fair to say."

"And you've also been there so you knew where the things had been to begin with, correct?"

"Correct."

"And you were not pulling Gs, were you?"

"No, I was not."

"And you were at zero knots, sitting in a chair, correct?"

"No, I was not," Capt. Jasper says.

"Were you standing?"

"Standing up."

"In the screen that you were looking at or the pictures that you were looking at, were 8 by 10 stills, correct?"

"I believe they were 8 by 10s, yes."

"They weren't moving on a three-and-a-half by three-and-a-half-inch screen, correct?"

"No, they were not."

⌣

"You were shown 5.56- and 7.62-millimeter small-arms ammunition," Gittins says, referring to the machine-gun projectiles that the Canadians were firing. "You would agree with me, would you not, that the rocket-propelled projectile of the Carl Gustav is substantially bigger than the 7.62 shell casings and pictures you were shown, correct?"

"It's 84 millimeters in diameter and quite a bit longer."

"And it has a rocket-propelled motor, correct?"

"The heat rack round does, yes."

"And you were firing that heat rack round that night, correct?"

"Yes."

"And so that would have a rocket propellant that would propel the projectile downrange, correct?"

"Yes."

"And the M-72 has a rocket motor as well, initially is launched by an explosive rocket ignition, correct?"

"Correct."

"And then it has like a tracer round downrange, correct?"

"You can see like a glowing—it looks like a tracer from behind."

"When the 7.62 machine gun was firing downrange at a rapid rate to eliminate the target, there were ricochets that you could see, correct?"

"Yes."

"And the ricochets were going up into the air, correct?"

"Correct."

⌣

"The communications between Kandahar tower, that's Cpl. Laroque in the Kandahar tower, correct?"

"Yes."

"And he is talking to the TOC [Tactical Operations Center], a radio operator in the TOC, correct?"

"Correct."

"And the person in the TOC is the person who is communicating with your command center at the range, correct?"

"The ambulance, yes."

"And it's the responsibility of Cpl. Laroque to provide to you 'check fires' through the TOC, correct?"

"Correct."

"So, if Cpl. Laroque is told 'check fire,' he is required to pass that to the TOC immediately, correct?"

"Yes."

"And then the TOC is required to report back to your unit immediately, correct?

"Yes."

"And 'check fire' is a safety command, correct?

"Yes."

Gittins asks Capt. Jasper about the "check fire order" that Cpl. Laroque radioed to the TOC—Call Sign Zero—moments before the bomb exploded, the one ordered on behalf of the outbound Herc. The one that was never acknowledged by anyone on the range. "Are you aware that Cpl. Laroque told generals Dumais and Sargeant that: 'They never gave me a 'cancel check fire' because when I initially gave the second one, and then about five to 10 minutes after that, that's when you heard the explosion and they never, the air traffic controllers never gave me a 'cancel check fire.' Are you aware of that, sir?"

"No, I wasn't aware of what testimony he gave," Capt. Jasper answers.

"You've read in the newspapers about Cpl. Laroque's testimony, have you not?" Gittins asks a few moments later.

"I had heard stuff about it," Jasper says.

"You would agree with me that it would be an embarrassing fact for your unit to have continued firing on a 'check fire,' wouldn't it?"

"I don't believe that happened."

"My question was, sir, and I will ask you to answer my question," Gittins says. "My question was: 'You would agree with me, would you not, that it would be an embarrassing safety violation for you to have been firing under a 'check fire'?"

"It could have been embarrassing, but I don't think that happened."

"It could have been embarrassing?"

"I guess so. The fact of it is—"

"Pardon me, sir," Gittins interrupts.

"It depends on from whose perspective," Capt. Jasper says.

"Well, do you think your battalion commander would expect that when a 'check fire' is given that it will be honored by a unit that you were commanded by, sir?"

"He would expect that, sir."

"If Cpl. Laroque says a 'check fire' was given to your unit five to 10 minutes before the impact of the bomb, would you agree that that would be a significant contributing factor of this accident?"

"No, I would not agree with that."

"Would you agree with me that if a 'check fire' had been given five to 10 minutes prior to this accident, that there should have been no firing going on for the five to 10 minutes immediately following the ordering of that 'check fire'?"

"That may have been true."

"May have been true?"

"If we were under 'check fire' we wouldn't have been firing."

★ ★ ★

At the end of the first day of testimony, on their way from the warehouse to the adjacent parking lot, Dave Beck and Charlie Gittins stop in front of the row of television cameras that now line the paved walkway near the side door. Both lawyers will stop here many times over the next two weeks, usually to tell reporters why the last witness is a "big fat liar." Prosecutors, prohibited from talking to the press, can only watch from the window as Beck and Gittins explain the latest way in which the Air Force is conspiring against their clients. Tonight, they hammer away at Gen. Sargeant and Gen. Dumais for failing to investigate why a blinking red light was not visible on the range. And why does the CIB report not mention anything about the simultaneous "check fire" order that came across the radio moments before the laser-guided bomb smashed into the wadi? It is obvious, they tell reporters, that Operation Enduring Freedom was plagued by poor communication. You just heard Joe Jasper himself say that the Princess Patricia's were nearly bombed—twice—before the night of April 17.

"You can fill volumes with the stuff not contained in that report that was relevant to the investigation," Gittins says of the Coalition Investigation Board. "That's criminally negligent conduct by two generals—one American, one Canadian."

In Nova Scotia, Miranda Boutilier watches the news reports about the opening day of the Article 32. Like the other Canadian families, she has been assigned an assisting officer from the U.S. Air Force to brief her on what's happening. Tonight, the two will spend hours talking on the phone, taking a break only so Miranda can throw up. She made the wrong decision. She has to be here. She has to hear for herself what those witnesses are saying. By tomorrow night, she will be on a plane bound for Shreveport.

"Sgt. Ford, would you also open the exhibit book there on the desk in front of you to Exhibit 5, page 2," Col. Odom says.

"Yes, sir," answers Lorne Ford, the first witness to take the stand on Wednesday morning. With his one good eye, he scans the booklet until he reaches an overhead photograph snapped by Maj. Schmidt's targeting pod camera. The blurry image depicts 3 Section in the wadi, hunkered down just seconds before the explosion. Each black, grainy circle is one of the paratroopers.

"Alright," Col. Odom says. "On Exhibit 5, page 2, can you identify who the person to the far right of the line is?"

"I'm assuming that north is to—which direction, sir?" Sgt. Ford asks.

"I believe north is to the left on the exhibit," the colonel answers.

"Well," Lorne says, pointing. "That would be me, sir."

★   ★   ★

"Would you state your name, rank, and Armed Force, please?" Col. Odom asks.

"I am Cpl. Rene Paquette, and I missed what the last thing was. Sorry."

"And your Armed Force?" Col. Odom repeats, raising his voice. "Are you a member of the Canadian Forces?"

"I am a member of the Canadian Forces with the 2nd Battalion, Princess Patricia's Canadian Light Infantry."

"And where is the 2nd Battalion of the PPCLI located?"

"I am stationed out of Winnipeg, Manitoba, Canada."

"Cpl. Paquette, how old are you today?"

"I am 33."

"How long have you been in the service in the Canadian Forces?"

"I joined the military in December of '91."

"Just by way of introduction, as a result of your injuries on the 17th of April, have you been rendered partially deaf?"

"I have lost substantial hearing, yes," he says. "I cannot hear out of my left side and I have a 20 percent hearing loss in my right side."

"So that if I pitch my voice more loudly than would be normal, it is so you can hear," Col. Odom says. "If you do not hear one of my questions, or the question of any of the other counsel in the room, would you just let us know and we'll be glad to speak up."

"I understand."

Cpl. Paquette recalls for Judge Rosenow how he volunteered to join the 3rd Battalion for the Afghanistan tour, even though it meant deploying with total strangers instead of the troops he had served with for years in Winnipeg. He was attached to A Company for barely a month when he marched down that wadi, fired a few bursts of his C-9 at the pop-up target, and stormed up the ravine with the rest of his section. "Just as that very last moment before the bomb struck, I heard Decaire and Perry give the ready," Cpl. Paquette says. "So I glanced over, I rolled my head over toward them, basically for a second just to see any official signal from them and it was at that moment, just as I turned my head, I heard a split-second whistle and there was the flash behind me and I felt the impact."

"What happened to you after the blast, Corporal?"

"When the explosion hit me it felt like I was hit by a truck," Rene says. "It flattened me to the ground and then literally bounced me and flung me into the air. I remember being in the air for what seemed like 15 minutes. I was enveloped in a white light. I could see the ground just beyond my hands and my feet and it didn't occur to me, all I could think about was: 'Why couldn't I touch the ground?' And it was at that time thoughts started going through my head about what could possibly have happened and it was then that I started thinking about probably I got caught in the back blast of the 84. And then I started wondering: Maybe the static from the 84 triggered my Claymore, which detonated? And at that time I thought maybe I had fragged my own section. And then thoughts kept on returning to my family and my child that was born just almost two weeks to the hour before the incident, and I basically—I asked and I said: 'Please give me a chance to at least see my children, or my child, my family.' And it was at that time I woke up in the dark. I wasn't lying where I was when the bomb hit. I knew I had been thrown somewhere. It was pitch dark. It sounded like someone basically rang my bell. The ringing in my ears was quite tremendous, I couldn't hear anything. I tried to sit up and call for a medic because I wasn't sure if anyone was even aware that I was injured at that time. If I was caught in the backblast maybe it occurred without anyone realizing that I had been injured and it was at that time I realized I couldn't call for a medic, my chest was filling up with blood at that time. I was having a lot of difficulty breathing, let alone calling out for help and when I sat up, I fell back over. My equilibrium was gone. I had severe vertigo and it was at that time I thought, I mean, this is probably it and then luckily, it seemed like an eternity, but I finally saw a flashlight in the dark and then there was another time that I saw a medic and he rushed to my help."

"How were you ultimately removed from the range?" Col. Odom asks.

"Sorry, what was that?" Cpl. Paquette asks, struggling to hear.

"How were you ultimately removed from the range?"

"A Blackhawk MEDEVAC chopper arrived and they placed me, or my fellow troops, and basically placed me onto a spine board and I was carried up the hill and loaded onto a chopper."

"What is the general nature of your injuries, Cpl. Paquette?"

"I suffered, obviously, ruptured eardrums, both my eardrums are ruptured. Hearing loss, with vertigo. I had pulmonary contusions to my lungs. At that time bruised ribs, some minor flesh burns, and later on as the medications started to decrease I noticed that the pain in my back also increased and at that time I discovered that my back took quite a jarring from the throw as well."

"Are you back with the 2nd Battalion now?"

"Yes, I am."

"And what are your duties now?"

"I'm in Ops and Training."

"Thank you, Cpl. Paquette, that's all the questions I have."

"Good morning, Cpl. Paquette," Charlie Gittins says. "How are you doing today?"

"Fine, sir."

"Very good. Let me express my condolences to the loss of your fellow Canadian Forces soldiers and apologize for the injuries that you suffered in this accident."

"Thank you."

"I want to take you back to the night of the range," Gittins says. "You had an armored escort to the range that night, correct?"

"I am not aware. I know we traveled as a convoy, but I was just in the back of one of the trucks. It was night and I was kind of sleepy, I wasn't really paying attention."

"Well, you always treated the threat level over in that area as a high threat level, correct?"

"There's always a possibility," Cpl. Paquette says.

"Any time you went outside of your base you would be in full combat gear, correct?"

"Correct."

"Prior to the night of 17 April when you engaged in this tank stalk exercise, you had not done any anti-tank weapons training at Tarnak Farms, correct?"

"We had, but not by night."

"Not at night. So this would have been the first use of the 84, the M-72, and tracer fire at night on that range by your unit, correct?"

"We had used the 72s by night before, but it was the first, I believe, with the 84," Paquette says, referring to the Carl Gustav.

"First night," Gittins says. "And that was the first anti-tank exercise that you had done at night, correct?"

"Correct. That *I* had done."

"When you were moving up the wadi you fired on a pop-up target. The nomenclature, I think you said it was a 'something-11' target."

"Figure 11."

"And that was a hard cardboard target, correct?"

"Correct."

"That was not a plywood target, and your bullets, if they impacted it, would go through, correct?"

"Obviously."

"There was no berm or other terrain feature that was set up to absorb the rounds that went through that target, correct?"

"There was no need for a—"

"Well," Gittins says, cutting him off, "my question was: 'Was there one?'"

"There was not."

"So when your rounds were fired at 45 degrees, as you testified, the rounds that went through it continued into the air, correct?"

"They would have."

"And the rounds that would have missed it, if any, would have not been slowed in any way and would have continued straight up into the air, correct, at 45 degrees, which was what you shot, correct?"

"Correct."

"Now," Gittins says, a few moments later, "the tactical scenario called for machine guns to engage, to light up, illuminate the tank target for the 84 millimeter and the M-72s, correct?"

"Correct."

"And they would be firing in rapid fire at a metal object, that being an armored tank, downrange target, correct?"

"Correct."

"And so when the rounds hit the target they would fly into the air as ricochets and you could see those ricochets even without your night vision goggles, correct?"

"Yes, there were some ricochets."

"And you could also see when the weapon impacted in the tank a bright flash, correct?"

"Well, not really," Cpl. Paquette says.

"And that's because the mark, there was—they were having difficulty hitting the tank, correct? The Carl Gustav gunners?"

"They were having some difficulty, sir."

"Do you remember how many hits they had of the five that they shot?"

"I don't recall."

"Do you remember telling me the other day that you didn't think they hit it at all?"

"I don't remember that."

"Okay. Do you remember telling me that you believed that the rounds were hitting short?"

"The 84 was hitting short?"

"Correct."

"I don't remember saying that. They could have been."

"You don't really have a good sense of the time, do you?" Gittins asks.

"No. When—in a scenario like that, with live-fire occurring, time seems to work in strange ways."

"In fact you told me the other day when we talked in the defense offices that you thought time was compressed. Everything seemed like it took a lot longer, correct?"

"Correct."

"And in fact, you just testified that when you were actually moved by the explosion of the bomb it felt like you were in the air for 15 minutes, correct?"

"Correct."

"But you know that that is not true, right?"

"Obviously not."

★ ★ ★

Brett Perry has rarely left his hotel room since landing in Shreveport a few days ago. While the other Canadian troops have at least toured the city, Brett has stayed by himself, drinking beer and listening to the voices in his head. They keep telling him about the targeting pod video, about the flash of that fifth Carl G. round—his round—that prompted Maj. Schmidt to roll in. *You're the reason everyone is here in Louisiana. You did this.*

This morning, as he sits down in the witness chair, Brett glares across the hearing room, locking eyes with Harry Schmidt. He and some of the other paratroopers made a pact that they would stare him down. For what feels like an hour, Brett gazes at the Top Gun pilot, doing his very best to be the old Brett Perry, the one who would never back down from anyone—especially some asshole who hurt his friends. Harry Schmidt stares back.

"What happened after Decaire fired his three rounds?" Col. Odom asks.

"We switched around," Cpl. Perry says. "I became the Number One and he became the Number Two loader, sir."

"How many rounds did you fire that night?"

"Two rounds, sir."

"Was the rate of fire for your two rounds any different than the rate of fire had been for the first three rounds?"

"The first two rounds were basically the same rate of fire, sir, however, the third round we encountered a problem with the Carl Gustav, sir."

"Did you ever get that third round off?" Col. Odom asks.

"No I didn't, sir."

"What was the problem that you had with the 84 millimeter?"

"Cpl. Decaire had just told me that he had a problem loading and he told me to just wait out because he had to reload the round, sir."

"Alright, what happened before you fired the last round with the Carl Gustav?"

"In between that time, Sgt. Léger had come over to me and told me to put my helmet on. It is common practice for us not to wear helmets when we are firing that round because you cannot get your head close enough in to the Carl Gustav, but he had come over to me and told me to put that on, so I put the Carl G. down, put my helmet on, picked it back up. That's when Cpl. Decaire told me there was a problem. He was trying to sort it out and then there was a violent explosion to my left, sir."

"When Cpl. Decaire was firing the Carl G., how many of the machine guns were firing?"

"I believe it was the C-6 was firing, sir, as well as the C-9."

"Now when you took over as the gunner on the Carl G., how many of the machine guns were firing?"

"Both of the machine guns were still firing, sir, however, on the—after I fired my second round, the gun team reported that they were out of ammo. And I also had heard Cpl. Paquette say he's running low on ammo, sir."

"What thoughts did you have about that?"

"I didn't know how I was going to acquire that target, sir, because as soon as I heard that, I knew I was pretty much in a bit of trouble because it would have been hard for me to acquire the target, sir."

"So when you were trying to acquire the target to fire the sixth round, there was only Paquette firing?"

"Yes, sir."

"Do you have any feel for how long it was after you fired the fifth round from the Carl G. and before the bomb impacted?"

"I would say a few minutes, sir."

"Do you have a good feel for the entire duration of the exercise from when Paquette engaged the pop-up target to when the bomb hit?"

"Roughly 10 to 15 minutes, sir."

"What happened when the bomb impacted, Corporal?"

"When the bomb impacted by me, the reaction was that I was the one that did it because I had a high-powered weapon," Cpl. Perry says. "I don't know how, I just thought that I had caused this accident. I checked to see if the weapon was on safe[ty]. It was on safe[ty] and in my mind I knew, I still figured that I did it, sir."

"What did you do?"

"Cpl. Decaire got blown down the wadi a bit. The concussion never hit me. He came to me and I asked him to check to see if, you know, we did that, and he said he couldn't because his hand was pretty much all bloody and that he couldn't open the Venturi lock. He put down the weapon. I proceeded to my left with Cpl. Decaire. We did a triage on all the guys. At that point, I just didn't know what to do because I thought I had killed guys. I came upon three bodies. We knew that we couldn't help them. Cpl. Decaire stayed back. MCpl. Clark was in a pretty bad way. He rung his bell pretty good and I did a little bit of first aid on MCpl. Hollister there. I gave him my triangle bandage. I proceeded to my left to go get help. Ran into my platoon commander. I grabbed him, I said to open up the Venturi lock right now on the Carl G. because I think I killed some guys. He went over, he couldn't really open it, so I opened it, got the round out and made sure it was unloaded. Then I knew it wasn't me that did this."

"Did you ever find another body?" Col. Odom asks.

"Yes I did, sir," he says. "I tripped over Pte. Green. He was quite some ways down the wadi, sir."

"And he was dead when you found him?"

"Yes, sir."

"And you said you found three bodies there at the impact site. Was that Léger, Dyer, and Smith?

"Yes, sir."

"At any time that night did you ever see any of the Canadian soldiers firing to the east?" Col. Odom asks, a few moments later.

"No, sir."

"Did you ever see anyone tracking an aircraft with any of the weapons out there?"

"Absolutely not, sir."

Capt. Jamie Key, Maj. Schmidt's military lawyer, and Capt. Mike Roderick, Maj. Umbach's, both take a turn cross-examining Cpl. Perry. Their questions are brief, but they peck away at Brett's doubts, feeding the demons. Cpl. Perry, did you say you weren't wearing a helmet that night? Can you tell me what Canadian Army regulation says it's okay to not wear a helmet during a live-fire exercise? Cpl. Perry, you told the CIB just weeks after the bombing that the Carl Gustav was firing every one or two minutes. Today, months later, you say it was every two or three minutes. Cpl. Perry, you told the CIB that Cpl. Paquette *and* MCpl. Clark fired at the wooden pop-up target at the start of the exercise. Now you say it was just Paquette? Is there something you're not telling us?

By the time the lawyers are done with him, Cpl. Perry is dizzy, overwhelmed, yet again, with guilt. Tonight, as he does most nights, he'll go back to his hotel room and get shitfaced. A Canadian Army padre will stop and visit, another in a long line of people who will try, but fail, to convince Brett Perry that this is not his fault.

★ ★ ★

"You and I were able to speak for the first time on Monday of this week," Capt. Key says to Cpl. Brian Decaire.

"Yes, sir."

"And during that time you told me that you thought that the time between the Carl Gustav fires was about 30 to 60 seconds?"

"Approximately."

"Now, I ask you, in hindsight, if you would have wanted the pilots, the Air Force pilots, to know that you were down there, you said you would have wanted them to know?"

"In hindsight," Cpl. Decaire says.

"I also asked if you had an opinion about what should happen in this case," Capt. Key says. "Do you remember what you told me?"

"Objection," Col. Odom says. "I'm not sure if the witness's opinion as to what should be the disposition of American charges is relevant."

"You know, that is an interesting question because I was wondering if it was ever going to come up," Col. Rosenow says. "And what occurs to me is that normally, obviously, and in my role as a military judge you wouldn't even think about asking that question in front of a jury, or in front of sitting members. My problem is that one of the things I'm supposed to consider is all those factors that go toward a disposition. So, in fairness, I think I probably am going to consider the answer. You know, I'll decide how much weight to give it, but I do think it's probably within those factors that an IO can consider and should consider in recommending disposition. So I'm going to allow you to ask the question and I will consider the answer."

"Yes, sir," Capt. Key says, turning back toward Cpl. Decaire. "Once again, do you remember what you told me?"

"I told you it was up to the courts."

"You remember what you told me when I asked if you cared if the charges were dismissed at the end of this hearing?"

"Of course I care."

"Isn't it true that on Monday you told me you didn't care?"

"I don't recall, actually."

"Let me see if I can jog your memory. Do you remember telling me that even though the Air Force may be required to consider your opinion, you didn't have one because you weren't going to take these two pilots' lives in your hands?"

"Yes, I did say that," Cpl. Decaire says.

"No further questions. Thank you."

★ ★ ★

A few steps from the hearing room, down another long hallway, lawyers for both sides have been assigned temporary offices to use during breaks in the hearing. They aren't far from the room where the pilots' families are watching the proceedings via closed-circuit TV. During one of today's recesses—the second day of the Article 32—Col. Odom leaves his office and walks back toward the only door that leads to the hearing room. He arrives at the exact same time as Harry Schmidt and Charlie Gittins.

"Maj. Schmidt, I haven't had a chance to introduce myself," the lead prosecutor says, extending his right hand. "We've never spoken. I'm John Odom."

Maj. Schmidt looks down at the outstretched fingers, flops his arms to his side and stands at attention—just like any good major should when addressed by a full colonel. "Are you telling me you're not going to shake my hand?" Col. Odom says, a little stunned.

"Sir, yes, sir," Maj. Schmidt answers, staring straight ahead.

"You just don't get it, do you?" Gittins tells the colonel. "He's a warfighter and you're trying to put him in jail for doing his job. I think you'll find most fighter pilots feel that way."

"Fuck you," Odom says, walking past them through the door.

★ ★ ★

"Can you discuss with us the Time sensitive targeting [TST] cell there in the CAOC?" Col. Odom asks.

"You have to have a coordinate so everybody can talk on the same template as to geography in space," says Colonel Lawrence Stutzriem. "We have to do a couple things. We have to positively identify it, that's going to be through some types of intelligence, reconnaissance surveillance means. We have to make sure that it is a legal target, complies with the ROE. We then need to make sure that there is not—if we attack it—there's not going to be unnecessary collateral damage, or collateral damage outside the bounds of what may be acceptable at the time. And then, finally, and probably the most important thing is we need to go through a deconfliction of forces that are on the ground and that would include all the ground operating elements, special operations, Army, Marines, coalition on the ground. It could include other government agencies. It could include NGOs operating in country. You know, press convoys we may know about. So that deconfliction is the last piece that says we know, we positively ID'd this as enemy. It's a legal target. Collateral damage is good, we deconflicted, make sure that we're not going to do any damage to any friendlies."

"By mid–April of 2002, was there much time sensitive targeting approval being given by the CAOC?" Col. Odom asks.

"No," Col. Stutzriem says. "None whatsoever. During that time probably before this incident and after this incident there was just very little activity whatsoever in Afghanistan."

"Would three minutes be a normal time for a time sensitive targeting approval process?"

"No, no."

"If you had no mark, if you had no fixed location, would you be able to do the time sensitive targeting process?"

"Impossible."

When Maj. Schmidt pressed the pickle button, Col. Stutzriem—"Stutz" —was sitting up in the CAOC Battle Cab, about 20 feet away from his boss, General Stephen Wood, the man in charge of the Coalition Air Operations Center that night. Because Gen. Wood was deemed unavailable for the hearing, Stutz, who was stationed in Saudi Arabia for a year, will be the most senior CAOC official to take the witness stand at the Article 32.

"Col. Stutzriem," Col. Odom says. "I want to play the communications between the beginning of the engagement, or when the tapes were turned on by the aircrew members, and I want you to listen through the time that Coffee 52 radios that he is rolling in in self-defense. And what I want you to listen for is whether or not there are any radio calls that if relayed to the CAOC, would have given you sufficient information to do a time sensitive targeting deconfliction process in the time that the tape runs, okay?"

"I understand," he answers.

Lights dimmed, a white screen beside the witness stand depicts both pilots' targeting pod videos. From the speakers, their tape-recorded voices and deep breaths fill the quiet hearing room. *Do ya got good coordinates for a mark? I've got a tally in the vicinity. Request permission to lay down some 20 mike-mike. Standby. Let's just make sure that it's not friendlies. Hhhhhhh-huuuuuuuhhhhhhhh, hhhhhhhhhuuuuuuhhhh. Do you want us to push a different freq? Hhhuhhhhh. Check my sparkle, check my sparkle. I've got some men on a road and it looks like a piece of artillery firing at us. I am rolling in in self-defense. Check master arm, laser arm. Bomb's away, cranking left. Laser's on. Shack. Disengage, friendlies Kandahar.*

On the other side of the base, Richard Léger, Marc's father, is not watching the cockpit footage with the rest of the Canadian families. He knows that that tiny dot walking into the crosshairs is his eldest son, fresh from telling Brett Perry to put on his helmet. The video, the last moments of his son's life, will be played and replayed countless more times in the coming days, and every time, Richard will stand up and leave the room.

"Col. Stutzriem, in the portion of IO Exhibit 79 that you just heard, did you ever hear information that would have enabled the CAOC to begin the time sensitive targeting process?" Col. Odom asks.

"No. The aircrew was in complete control of the situation. Although they have certainly the SA [situational awareness] of the coordinates there from the beginning of that, but there is no indication, seeing this, there is nothing the CAOC can do for them at this point until they say what they are looking at, where they're at."

"What was the commander's intent with regard to fratricide as stated by the command authority?" Col. Odom asks a few moments later.

"Zero," Col. Stutzriem says. "Pretty simple."

"Whose responsibility, ultimately, is it to know what's in the Airspace Control Order?"

"The aircrew."

"The actual airmen flying the aircraft?"

"That's correct."

"In the entire time that Operation Enduring Freedom has been in being, have you lost any manned fixed-wing aircraft to AAA in Afghanistan?"

"No."

chapter twenty-seven

During two full days of testimony, not a single witness has said anything about Go-pills. Hard to believe, considering what all the newspapers are writing. To the average reader, this is a case about pilots on speed, about the U.S. Air Force secretly forcing its crews to ingest dangerous drugs while failing to warn them about the hazardous side-effects. Nausea. Aggressiveness. Euphoria. It's what all the U.S. networks are talking about, what the 24-hour news tickers flash across the TV screen every couple of minutes. Fighter pilots are going to war hopped up on speed. Four Canadian soldiers are dead because of a little orange pill.

The Air Force has endured so much bad press lately that on the third day of the hearing—Thursday, January 16—reporters walking off the early morning bus outside the warehouse are met by Colonel Pete Demitry, a fighter pilot/doctor. A Dexedrine expert, Col. Demitry is not here to testify. He was dispatched to Barksdale by the Air Force Surgeon-General's Office solely to tell the journalists that they've got it all wrong, that the Go-pills are a "life insurance policy," not a liability. "Fatigue kills," the colonel says, not speed. Pilots have popped the stimulant for decades, he tells scrum after scrum, and not one single accident has ever been linked to the drugs. And no one is forced to take them. It's totally voluntary.

Down the hall, in the room where the real hearing is unfolding, Colonel Larry Stutzriem retakes the stand. Dave Beck, Maj. Umbach's lead lawyer, begins what will be hours of cross-examination.

"What does TST mean?" he asks.

"Time sensitive targeting," Col. Stutzriem replies.

"As I recall, your testimony was that two to three minutes was not sufficient time to get enough information in the CAOC to react for a request for TST, is that correct?"

"That's correct. The TST time period could go from minutes to hours. That's to complete the entire process from initial finding of something to its destruction, and then an assessment of that destruction."

"Were the pilots who were operating in Operation Enduring Freedom ever told in any manner that it could take up to several hours for TST?"

"Those who participated, or oriented toward the theater, or observed, I'm sure, experienced it, debriefed it. As far as a document, or a formal transmittal that said to expect a certain amount of time was dependent upon, once again, the target, the parameters in trying to get through the destruction and the assessment of the target."

"But the testimony you gave about the time that it may take, that was not passed to the pilots in anything in writing or briefings that you are aware of, was it?"

"Not to my—I don't know. Not to my knowledge."

"And TST is a system separate and apart from self-defense, is that correct?"

"Yes, sir."

"TST has no application to self-defense, does it?"

"That's correct."

"Under the standing rules of engagement, a pilot has the right and obligation to react in self-defense whenever, in the pilot's judgment, he believes he or his wingman is in imminent danger, immediate destruction. Is that correct?"

"Yes," Col. Stutzriem says. "It is a statement in the ROE that says nothing in the ROE precludes a pilot's right to self-defense. There is also further discussion that self-defense is not intended to be something of revenge or—so it truly needs to be categorized a bonafide reasonable judgment of self-defense."

"And it says, not only in the unclassified standing rules of engagement, that it is a judgment call based on the pilot, the information he has, it's a decision he has to make. Is that correct?"

"That is correct."

"Would a 'standby' ever override a pilot's right and obligation to react in self-defense if, in the pilot's judgment, he believes he or his wingman is in immediate danger of being shot down?"

"A 'standby'?"

"A 'standby' from anybody?" Beck repeats, alluding to the radio call from the AWACS in response to Maj. Schmidt's request to fire his 20mm cannons.

"No," Col. Stutzriem says. "It should be included in his decision-making process as to new information coming in to assess the situation."

"And in a combat situation, do you agree that it's critical that pilots, before they take off, receive all available information that would be pertinent to the mission, particularly to where friendly forces may be in a combat area?"

"All information relevant to the conduct of the mission should be given, taken, studied, absorbed by the pilot before going out to fly."

"And would you agree that prior to April 17th, the ground forces were not required to report live-fire training or activity within the given air tasking order day, and you and Col. Odom talked a good bit yesterday about the ATO day. Would you agree that live-fire training was not—that information was not provided?"

"Actually, yes sir, it was," Col. Stutzriem says. "In the ACO the entry was that that entry was effective 24 hours during that ATO cycle. The note is saying that it would be intermittently active, or could be intermittently active. So the ROZ that was established, Restricted Operating Zone, was effective for a full 24-hour period."

"Let me ask you the question again," Beck says. "The question is, would you agree—and this is one of the findings in the unclassified version of the CIB report by Gen. Sargeant. Here's the question: Would you agree that ground forces were not, prior to April 17th, required to report live-fire training or activity within the given air tasking order day?"

"They were not required to, what, provide to the CAOC, is that what you're asking me, or—"

"They weren't required to report it. That's the finding of Gen. Sargeant in his board. I've read it verbatim, finding number four."

"I really can't tell you. I know that they were not required to report it to the CAOC."

"Can you show me, based on your response, in the ATO or ACO, where it was noted that the Canadian Forces would be conducting a live-fire training exercise anywhere in the area of operations?"

"Yes, sir," Col. Stutzriem says. "Not by Canadian, but by the fact that it was effective and could be intermittent throughout that 24-hour period."

"There was nothing to tell the pilots that anybody would be conducting live-fire training, was there?"

"No—well, the entry, once again, says that it is effective for 24 hours and could be intermittently active during that period—"

"Does it say effective 24 hours, or does it say 'small arms range, not continuously active'?" Beck asks.

"No, it says under the effect block, the line, it says effective 05:00 to 04:59, that's the entire ATO day, and then in the notes it says it could be intermittently active."

"Do you know of any pilots who were operating in OEF prior to April 17th who were aware of Tarnak Farms?"

"Tarnak Farms as a ROZ?" Stutz asks back.

"As a ROZ or a training area, who were even aware of Tarnak Farms. Do you know of any pilots who were aware of it?"

"From day one of the war we attacked Tarnak Farms early on so all those pilots would be aware it was on the target list in the first week of the war."

"Let's say from March until April 16th," Beck says.

"Yes, sir. It was in the ACO each day, Airspace Control Order. It's on the map."

"Was the ACO workable, in your opinion?"

"Yes, sir, it was. Can you explain workable?"

"Was it ever reported to you that the pilots, that the commanders believed that it was unworkable?"

"The ACO was difficult to—I mean, it took time to get through."

"Objection," Charlie Gittins says. "Non-responsive."

"Overruled," Col. Rosenow answers.

"It took time to get through the—about 40-some pages," Col. Stutzriem continues. "As a result we downloaded it on the net. You could download it in a document file and in another file that can be imported into Falcon View, but—and therefore could be sorted to the convenience of whatever you want to look for in it."

"But the question for pilots who are getting ready to go out and fly, do you know of one pilot, can you name me one pilot who, between March and April 16th of 2002, had any idea of Tarnak Farms?" Beck asks.

"I'm a pilot. I understood it. I know, you know, by name—"

"Pilots who were flying in the operation?"

"I can't give you a name," the colonel says. "I mean, I would assume every pilot who had read the ACO knew Tarnak Farms was there, but—"

"Well, since the accident occurred, after it occurred, did you do anything to find out whether knowledge of Tarnak Farms was generally known, or specifically known by anybody?"

"We ensured that it was in the ACO and that we reviewed. Was it clear enough? Was the ACO entry readable? And that was our communications medium for Tarnak Farms."

"But sir," Beck says. "The question is: Did you do anything to find out if whatever was in that ACO—buried in it—or what you thought was sufficient, was known by any pilots who were operating in the theater?"

"Only by retransmitting the ACO with that entry in it. Our communications vehicles, ATO, ACO, and SPINS were our primary means to communicate with the units."

⌣

"Do you agree that in a combat environment, like OEF, to the greatest extent possible, pilots in the air, and even operators on the ground, should have the best information available or possible to get on the ground order of battle, where our friendlies are in particular?" Beck asks.

"If it is available, yes, sir," Col. Stutzriem responds. "Whether—I assume we'll get into this—whether it is relevant to this is what needs to be pursued."

"Did you say if it is available before you said that about if it's relevant?"

"If it's determinable. Let me say that the nature of the war for this period, the entire war in Afghanistan, the difficulty, it wasn't a linear battlefield, and I know you're a former Marine and I'm an airman so I'm a little out of my bounds here. I just know a little bit about the ground operation. But you know, there wasn't a defined FEBA, forward edge of battle area, or forward line of troops. There weren't these lines drawn as to where the good guys and bad guys are. The bad guys often went from being on the good team to being on the bad team based upon a various given date. And then on the ground, not having these lines of battle, you have many—almost a Swiss cheese going on, little nucleus of friendly troops, small enclaves, all over this. Then you have the Afghanistan forces. You've got Dan Rather and Geraldo Rivera. You've got Greenpeace and shots. You've got medical teams. You've got deliveries of food and that kind of thing. So the reason the CAOC, or CENTCOM, retained such strict control over engaging surface targets was because it was difficult at any given time. For example, Coffee [Flight] goes out the door with a—if they could have had a perfect definition of where the friendlies and enemies were, it is going to change before long, with the long routes they flew once they get in theater."

"And when it changes, should updates be provided?"

"Well, it changes, but you don't know."

"But if you do know that it changes, or if there is information that is available, based on all of those things you just said, because of difficulties in good and bad forces, and difficulty, if you do know precisely where your good forces are, that should be made available, shouldn't it?"

"Well, no, not necessarily, because the operating procedures allow, or help the aircrew to stay above and away," Col. Stutzriem says. "The rigid structure that prohibited them delivering munitions, to go back to this elaborate process and not allow an aircrew, an aircrew could not, even if he saw the tank with the enemy signature on it, could not drop on it."

"Could they drop if their self-defense is determined to be necessary?"

"If self-defense is a legitimate call, yes."

"And sir, are you aware that post-April 17th, because of what happened and because of information that wasn't available to the pilots then, that after April 17th, the locations of friendlies doing live-fire training exercise was made known to everyone, wasn't it?"

"I don't know that to be a fact, but I assume that, you say that."

"But if that is a fact, that could have been done before April 17th, couldn't it?"

"As far as that range is concerned, yes."

"As far as any—"

"They were already written in the ROZs, the four ROZs where the training occurred. If there was—"

"Sir, I do have to object," Dave Beck says to Col. Rosenow. "It's non-responsive to the question. The question was specifically of where live-fire training was, not about ROZs, and I'm trying—"

"Live-fire training was in the ACO prior to April 17th," Col. Stutzriem interrupts.

"Sir, can you show me one place where it said Canadians were doing live-fire training?" Beck asks.

"Not by nationality."

"Can you show me where anybody was doing live-fire training exercises on April 17th?"

"The ACO says that throughout that period at Whale and Tarnak Farms you could have live-fire training."

"Your Honor, I object," Beck says again. "That's totally non-responsive. But since you've said that—"

"It is somewhat responsive," Col. Rosenow says. "But I think what counsel is really asking is versus anything saying this area may be intermittent for training, including arms training from 01 for a 24-hour period, he's asking: Are you aware of anything where it says they are actually, during this two- or three-hour block, people will be firing?"

"There is nothing that says, in the ACO, that Canadians would be firing at specific times," Col. Stutzriem says. "It's a blanket—may not be, whatever the wording was, continuously active, but could obviously be—the ROZ being active it could happen at any time. Not by nationality, not by specific time."

⌣

"Did anybody from the CAOC, any member of the CAOC attend the Close Air Support Symposium in March of 2002?" Beck asks, referring to the post-Anaconda conference that Col. Nichols hosted at Al Jaber.

"We had the chief of safety, the CENTAF, actually from CENTAF—"

"Was he a member of CAOC?"

"He was a member of the CENTAF team so he worked for the CFACC."

"Was he from the CAOC?"

"No, he wasn't working in the CAOC."

"So the question was, did anyone from CAOC go to the Close Air Support Symposium?"

"We were scheduled to go," Col. Stutzriem says. "We were on the agenda. The airplane broke the day before."

"Objection," Gittins says. "Non-responsive."

"No, that is responsive," Col. Rosenow says.

"Was there only one aircraft that CAOC had access to, to go to the symposium?" Beck asks.

"The C-21, and we had a C-130 was the next available aircraft. Dust storms closed PSAB [Prince Sultan Air Base]. The guys waited on the aircraft for a couple of hours the next morning of the conference."

"Do you recall when you and I discussed, like you said, about a month ago?"

"Yes."

"Did you tell me it was a dust storm problem the next day, or did you tell me there was some kind of diplomatic clearance problem?"

"No, the ability to get aircraft in and out of Saudi, other aircraft. For example, to get a—say I called the Navy and said could you fly an aircraft into PSAB to get us out of here, that would result in a diplomatic clearance approval request, which would take perhaps days or weeks to obtain from the Saudis."

"Was anything done to try to tell the Saudis: 'Hey, there's some important things that need to be discussed, can we get an aircraft and fly down'?"

"Well, we thought we had the 130 set up the next morning and obviously, the weather—we couldn't have gotten any aircraft out there."

⌣

"Sir, are you married to Candice Stutzriem?" Charlie Gittins asks.

"That's correct," Col. Stutzriem says.

"Are you aware that she posted an e-mail that was read by the *O'Reilly Factor* last night?" Gittins asks, referring to Fox Network talk-show host Bill O'Reilly.

"Yes, I am," he answers. The e-mail, which Gittins submits as an exhibit, reads: "There's nothing more serious than breach of combat discipline. If these pilots are allowed to walk, no battlefield misconduct would ever be prosecuted.'"

"Did you help her compose that e-mail?" Charlie asks.

"No, I did not."

"Do you have a copy of it?"

"I do not, and I did not know she did it until last night. She called me, after the fact."

"Sir, how many hours do you have in the F-16 fighter?"

"She loves me, you know," Col. Stutzriem says. "I think she was concerned and sent that in an—"

"Okay," Col. Rosenow interrupts. "These hearings can go either a little bit on the formal side or the informal side. I think this cross-examination may be more toward the formal side, which means that the rules are fairly tight. Wait for him to finish his question. The question will be answerable, and just answer it. And if there is more information that needs to be looked at, I have the option of asking questions. Col. Odom and Mr. Beck have another option, too. So we'll just play it that way."

"Sir, I believe you testified earlier that you have no—you've never served in combat?" Charlie Gittins asks, a few minutes later.

"That's correct, I have not."

"Would it be fair to say, sir, that you've never served in ground combat either?"

"Not in ground combat either."

"You've never seen shots fired at you, in the air, or on the ground?"

"No, I have not. Well, I've taken ground fire, but not as a ground—I was overseas once and had taken fire on the ground, but it was not as a combatant, no."

"In the comfort of the prosecutor's office and this room, you have reviewed what happened to Maj. Schmidt and Maj. Umbach on the night of 17 April, correct, sir?"

"That's correct, yes, sir."

"And it's clear there that there was a 'fog of war' situation, isn't it?"

"I can't tell you, it doesn't appear there's—it seems fairly straightforward and vanilla. I didn't see any fog of war. I mean, there's levels, or continuum of fog of war. I am sure there was some fog, but I didn't see some serious problem with what was depicted."

"Can we play Exhibit 79?" Gittins asks. He wants the colonel to watch the targeting pod videos. "I want you to answer again my question after you've seen that in its entirety, please."

20 mike-mike. Standby. Let's just make sure that it's, uh, that's it not friendlies. Hhhhuuuuhhhh, hhhhuhhh. Hold fire. I'm rolling in in self-defense. Bomb's away, cranking left. Shack.

"I did not see fog at all," Col. Stutzriem says. "I saw a lot of procedural problems that—I mean, we can talk about—"

"Okay, but your answer is you didn't find that to be fog of war?" Col. Rosenow asks.

"No."

"So the answer to my question, sir, was no?" Gittins repeats. "Is that the answer to the question, that you don't believe that there was a fog of war situation?"

"I don't have evidence on that of a lot of fog, as far as communications, confusion."

"Did you hear at the very end of the audio, sir," Gittins asks, "where Maj. Schmidt, Coffee 52, asks: 'Yeah, BOSSMAN, there was no ROZ effective in that area tonight as far as our brief was concerned. You concur?' The airborne command-and-control asset provided for the pilots responds: 'BOSSMAN concurs.' Now, it would appear that the command-and-control asset that was designed to provide pilots real-time information had no better information than the pilots that night. Correct, sir?"

"This is after the bomb impact. You would have to say—"

"Did you understand my question, sir?"

"Did he give coordinates to BOSSMAN?"

"Did you understand my question, sir?"

"No, I need to understand—I mean, obviously what you just read is true, yes, but—"

"Okay," Judge Rosenow says, interrupting again. "Then that's—it may seem too obvious to you, but the question he was just asking was: Was the transcript he just read accurate?"

"I trust what you just read is accurate," Stutz says.

"You indicated earlier, I think you talked about bubbles on a map," Gittins says.

"Well—"

"Sir, the prosecutor will give you all the time in the world to answer the questions you want to answer, but I'd like you to answer mine today. You've previously testified about bubbles on a map, how it was friendlies all over the place?"

"No, I said the mixture of friendlies and enemy were not in a classic shape as you would expect in a conventional war where we might see in Iraq or somewhere else, that they were interspersed among each other."

"But you knew where the friendlies were who were assigned to the base at Kandahar, sir?"

"Not all the players, not necessarily, at any given time where they might be," Col. Stutzriem says. "In general, the bulk of the forces were at Kandahar, in garrison, at the internment facility, but there could be at any time patrols, other Special Ops going on that would be moving."

"But the Kandahar Airfield and the Tarnak Farms range complex did not have a restricted fire area, or no-fire area, correct?"

"A ROZ and Terminal Control Area around the airport," the colonel answers.

"My question again, sir, was there was no restricted fire area or no-fire area overlaid over the Tarnak Farms range complex, nor the Kandahar Airfield, correct, sir?"

"There were not."

"Thank you, sir. An aircrew that believes that they are, that they are being immediately engaged and in danger of being shot down has the right and obligation of self-defense, correct, sir?"

"They have the right to—I don't know about obligation, but they have a right to self-defense."

"Are you unaware that the ROE calls for the right and obligation for self-defense?" Gittins asks.

"I don't know. I trust that's what it says if you've read the ROE."

"You talked about liaison officers when you described the CAOC the other day. And I don't want to get into any of the specifics, but there was no Canadian liaison in the CAOC on the night of 17 April, correct?"

"I can't recall. I wouldn't be able to—I think the report would tell you that."

"Are you familiar with the Canadian officer who was at one time assigned to the CAOC while you were the deputy director, sir?"

"I met several Canadians while I was there," Col. Stutzriem says. "They came in early on and then later on."

"I'm going to ask you my question again, sir," Gittins says. "Are you aware of Canadian officers who were assigned to the CAOC as watch standers, liaison officers, while you were the deputy director of the CAOC, sir?"

"I'm aware that Canadians were there. Whether they were assigned for temporary duty, I couldn't tell you."

"Were they credentialed as Canadians, sir?"

"No, no, they were not. Let me say this, I can't answer that question. I don't know, I don't know."

"Do you know if documents were produced that falsely indicated the Canadian liaison officer was from another country?"

"No, I don't know that."

"You don't know that?"

"No," Col. Stutzriem says. "And I find that—"

"Nonetheless, a moment ago you just told me that you were aware that they were credentialed as other than Canadians."

"No, I did not say that. Let me restate that answer. I am not sure what Canadians were assigned who—and I certainly have no idea, or understanding or knowledge of why a Canadian would come in credentialed in some other way. But I don't know that to be a fact, or have happened, or rumored."

⌣

"Did Col. Coan [the acting 332nd deputy commander] and/or Col. Nichols discuss with you, or complain to you, that they were provided limited and inadequate ground order of battle information, particularly with respect to friendlies?" Gittins asks Col. Stutzriem.

"I think throughout the war—and you're asking me at any time, throughout the war, everybody wanted to have a better-defined view of where friendlies and enemy were. It was an ongoing struggle, based on once again what I said, the nature of movements, not having defined lines, many static enclaves. Yes, not just Nichols, even in the CAOC everybody would want to know, have a better fidelity of where the friendlies and enemy were. Of course, once again, that's why the processes we had, we get up-to-the-minute finding of a small geographic location fairly quickly where friendlies and enemy were, as long as that process was used, which it wasn't in this particular incident."

"So the answer to my question, which was: Did Col. Nichols and/or Colonel Coan discuss with you their concerns about the location of friendly forces, your answer to that question would be yes?"

"I assume so," Col. Stutzriem says. "I can't give you a specific time, date, but I would assume it was in the discussions with many people all the time."

"So it was an ongoing issue throughout the operations, correct?"

"It would be an ongoing challenge in any war in any theater, yes, sir."

"Can you tell me why no ground liaison officer [GLO] who would provide information on friendly order of battle was provided to the 332nd AEG?" Gittins asks a few moments later.

"I can't tell you why, whether it was manning caps, positions, I don't know. The GLO doesn't necessarily have any better ability to obtain that information, so I can't tell you why, or why not a GLO was not appointed there."

"Let's—just to be clear, a GLO is a ground liaison officer, correct?"

"Yes."

"And that is a person who comes from the land commander's command, correct?"

"That's correct."

"And his job in the wing is to interface between the wing and the ground—the land component commander on friendly order of battle, correct?"

"Yes."

"And to provide deconfliction between air assets and ground assets, correct?"

"Yes, but not in a command-and-control sense."

"Not in a command-and-control sense, but in an informational sense, correct, sir?"

"That could—yes."

"And Air Force doctrine provides for a ground liaison officer to be assigned?"

"Not required," the colonel says. "But it is part of the vernacular game book, yes."

"So there were choices made about staffing the 332nd, correct?" Gittins asks.

"Choices—somebody chose whether to fill that position or not. I don't even know if a position existed at Jaber, I can't tell you that."

"Did you ever have any conversations with Col. Nichols himself about having a GLO, ground liaison officer, assigned to his unit to assist him in deconfliction of friendly forces from his aircraft, sir?"

"We may have."

"So you don't remember, sir?"

"There was a desire to have—"

"My question was—"

"—more interface across the theater."

"Hold it," Col. Rosenow says.

"He either did or he didn't," Gittins says. "Or he didn't remember, sir."

"I believe he said he did," Col. Odom interjects.

"He said he may have."

"I tell you what," Col. Rosenow says. "Let me ask. Do you remember talking to Col. Nichols about getting a GLO out in Col. Nichols' group?"

"Specifically, no," Col. Stutzriem answers. "We may have very well."

"I understand," the judge says. "You talked to a number of people about issues like that?"

"Yes."

"You talked to a number of units about wanting more information?"

"Yes."

"Okay."

"So what did you do to try to satisfy the need for a GLO at the 332nd AEG?" Gittins asks.

"I don't recall the specific request. I do know that—I can't tell you. I don't recall."

"Would you agree with me that having a ground liaison officer is Air Force doctrine?"

"Once again, it's doctrinal, it's not a requirement. You don't have to have one. I mean, it's a great idea. If the manpower is available in theater, or the manpower is available to provide those positions."

⌣

After lunch, Col. Odom questions Col. Stutzriem for a second time. "If an airfield was listed in the mission brief as a divert airfield, would you think that was an indication of the area around that airfield was friendly or enemy?" Col. Odom asks.

"Friendly."

"Do you have any knowledge that Coffee Flight, on the evening of 17 April, were in support of coalition troops in contact? Did you hear anything on the radio that would have indicated that they were vectored for support of troops in combat?"

"No. We know that on that night there was no activity so the answer is no."

"Would it be a violation of a Restricted Operating Zone for an aircraft to toss a GBU-12 down into the Restricted Operating Zone?" Col. Odom asks.

"Before contacting a control agency?" Col. Stutzriem says. "Yes."

★　★　★

Apart from the pilots themselves, few people are closer to this case than Major John Milton. He was Harry Schmidt's roommate in Kuwait, the operations officer for the 170th Fighter Squadron during its deployment overseas. He posted the flight schedule, the one that slotted Bill as the flight lead and Harry as the wingman—the schedule that Harry complained about the night before he took off for Afghanistan. Maj. Milton was also the flight lead during that sortie in Iraq, when his wingman dropped—and missed—two days before Maj. Schmidt rolled in on the Canadians.

A close friend of both pilots, Maj. Milton has stood by his squadron mates. He defended them in front of Gen. Sargeant and his team of investigators. He has cooperated with their lawyers. Yet this afternoon, in a somewhat questionable move, prosecutors call Maj. Milton to testify on behalf of the government. They are hoping that he will be their expert witness, the experienced fighter pilot who will tell Judge Rosenow why Maj. Schmidt and Maj. Umbach—his close buddies—are the ones to blame for what happened on April 17.

"Would you agree with me that both Maj. Schmidt and Maj. Umbach, both of them were volunteers for their country?" asks Lt.-Col. Greg Graf, the prosecutor/fighter pilot. He has already met with Maj. Milton behind closed doors.

"Yes, sir," Maj. Milton answers.

"Nobody drafted them to serve their country?"

"No."

"And nobody made them go to southwest Asia to fight for their country?"

"No, they're volunteers."

"With the exception of what happened in this incident—let's take that out of your frame of reference. With the exception of that, would you say that they've been exemplary officers?"

"Absolutely."

"Are they friends of yours?"

"Yes."

"Is it fair to say that you want a good outcome for them in this?"

"I am biased toward them because they are good friends of mine," Maj. Milton says. "Actually, they're brothers-at-arms."

"And that's commendable," Col. Graf says. "Would you agree with me that it's a good thing that the country is very suspicious of this side of the table?"

"Yes."

"And you agree that it's a good thing that we're giving them the benefit of the doubt, at least in public opinion so far?"

"Yes."

"You, right now, are part of the Illinois Air National Guard, correct?"

"That's correct."

"While you were in southwest Asia, were you on active federal military duty?"

"We were on Title 10 orders. It depended on the amount of time the individuals were over there. The specifics on that, and the ins and outs, I can't regurgitate exactly, but we were basically reporting to the 332nd AEG."

"Since you have been an active duty pilot, as well as a Guard pilot, is the Guard any less professional than the active duty forces?" asks Col. Graf, a fellow Guardsman.

"No, sir."

"Any less credible than the active duty force?"

"No. In some cases, we're more capable."

"And do you think this particular incident that we're here to talk about had anything to do with either of these two people being members of the Air National Guard as opposed to the active duty Air Force component?"

"No."

"Many people will think of the Air National Guard as the 'weekend warriors.' Do Air National Guard F-16 pilots have the same basic monthly minimum requirements as their active duty counterparts?"

"The way I understand it is they're basically the same," Maj. Milton answers.

"Is there any way you could continue to be proficient in the F-16 just showing up on drill weekends?"

"Absolutely not."

⌣

"I'd like to talk to you a little bit about fratricide," Col. Graf says, referring to the official term for 'friendly fire.' "You know what that term means?"

"Yes, sir."

"In your normal training operations, does the F-16 community place a low emphasis or a high emphasis on training to prevent fratricide?"

"High emphasis."

"In your mission objectives for both your air-to-air and air-to-ground, what percentage of fratricide was typically allowed? How many friendlies were you allowed to kill on a training sortie?"

"Zero," Maj. Milton answers.

"In fighter squadrons, both active duty, Navy, Marine Corps, active duty Air Force, Guard and Reserve, do fighter pilots bet on a lot of things?"

"Yes."

"Alright. When you go out to the bombing range, do you usually bet on who gets the best scores on the bombs?"

"Yes, we do."

"How about when you screw up?" Col. Graf asks. "Do you usually penalize people money?"

"You will pay a fine of some sort," Maj. Milton says. "Usually monetary."

"In your squadron standards, right in your officially published squadron standards on the last page, did you have a list of all the various fines assessed?"

"Yes, we did."

"What was the fine assessed for a friendly kill?"

"I believe it was $35."

"Objection," Charlie Gittins says. "That's in training, sir. That's beyond the pale."

"Okay," Col. Rosenow says. "Well, I will tell you it's of marginal— if it's to establish the point that the squadron discouraged fratricide, I think it's probably established by lots of other things, and common sense as much as anything else."

"A couple of definitions I'd like to go through with you real quick," Col. Graf says to the witness. "Would you just quickly define for the investigating officer what a FEBA is."

"Forward Edge of Battle Area."

"And would you describe to the investigating officer where the FEBA was in Afghanistan during the period of time that you were there?"

"There was no FEBA in Afghanistan."

"Could you describe for the investigating officer what a FLOT is?"

"Forward Line of Troops."

"And was there a FLOT in Afghanistan?"

"Not in the normal sense, no."

"Would you explain to him what the FSCL is?"

"Fire Support Coordination Line."

"And was there a fire support coordination line in Afghanistan?"

"No, sir."

"Why wouldn't you have those types of lines of demarcation between enemy and friendly troops in Afghanistan?"

"Those terms, typically, are for a linear battlefield, so to speak, where you have actual lines of troops and are taking territory," Maj. Milton says.

"In this war you have pockets of good guys with lots of big pockets of bad guys around."

"Was the existence of the pockets of the good guys interspersed between the bad guys one of the driving forces behind the creation of the SPINS and the rules of engagement?"

"Yes. I would assume that's why they were set up."

"And would you agree that part of the commander's intent was to avoid fratricide?"

"Yes."

"And that was one of the reasons the rules of engagement and the SPINS were set up the way they were?"

"Yes."

"Would a reasonably prudent fighter pilot be more cautious about dropping ordnance in an area where he didn't know where the good guys were from the bad guys?" Col. Graf asks. "Would he be more cautious or less cautious?"

"You're always cautious when you're releasing ordnance," Maj. Milton answers.

"You're always cautious when you're releasing ordnance," Col. Graf agrees. "But how about when you don't know where the good guys are? More cautious or less cautious?"

"More cautious."

"As the head of the MPC [Mission Planning Cell], was Maj. Schmidt—or should Maj. Schmidt have been aware that there was no FEBA, FLOT, or FSCL?"

"We all knew that, sir."

"Okay. And Maj. Schmidt has indicated on numerous occasions to you, has he not, and to other people, that he was concerned that he didn't know where all the friendlies were in Afghanistan, correct?"

"We all were."

"And would that have been a reason to be more cautious before dropping ordnance in an area where you weren't sure?"

"Yes."

"Let's talk about taking a mark in the F-16," Col. Graf says. "Let's go through some of the mechanisms. When I use the phrase 'taking a mark,' you will understand what I'm talking about?"

"Yes," Maj. Milton says.

"Is that a method in which you can find the coordinates of a particular location on the ground?"

"Yes."

Maj. Milton explains that inside each cockpit is an Up-Front control, a series of numbered keys that resemble the buttons of a telephone—0 through 9. Seven is the "mark button." If a pilot presses 7 once, the plane instantly records an "overfly mark," capturing the exact latitude and longitude of the point on the ground directly underneath the jet. It is one of five ways to take a mark with the F-16. Another option, Maj. Milton explains, is a targeting pod mark. A small cursor-like device on the upper portion of the throttle allows a pilot to move the LITENING II targeting pod laser with his left thumb. When the laser hits the point on the ground that a pilot wants to mark, he can punch "7, 7, enter" onto the keypad and the coordinates are automatically saved.

After a few more minutes of technical questions and acronym definitions, Col. Graf queues Coffee Flight's targeting pod videos. Maj. Milton has seen them before, first with defense lawyers back in Springfield, and the other day with prosecutors.

"Right now," Col. Graf says, pointing to a frame captured moments after the tapes start rolling, "would you agree with me that Maj. Schmidt has his targeting pod pretty close to the area where he's eventually going to drop the bomb on the Canadian soldiers? If this is the area that he was indicating he was going to mark, what should he do right now to get those coordinates of where those soldiers are?"

"He would slew over them," Maj. Milton says, referring to the targeting laser. "Block it or track it with the pod, and then hit the '7' key twice and then 'enter.'"

A tech-sergeant working the video feed presses the play button. *Hhhhhhhhhhuuuuuhhhhhh, hhhhhhhuuuuuuhhhh. Hhhuuuhhhh, hhhhhhhhuuuuuuuuuhhhhh. Okay BOSSMAN, uh, this is Coffee 52. I've got a tally on the vicinity. Uh, request permission to lay down some, uh, 20 mike-mike. Standby. Let's just make sure that it's, uh, that it's not friendlies, that's all.*

"There are a couple of transmissions that I'm confused about and maybe you can help me out with them," Col. Graf says.

"Okay," Maj. Milton answers.

"You indicated before that you don't practice night high-angle strafe, is that correct?" he asks, alluding to Maj. Schmidt's request to fire his 20mm cannons.

"That's correct."

"If you have laser-guided bombs on board, which would be the preferred method of attacking a site? Using laser-guided bombs, which is something you practice quite frequently, or rolling in at night with night vision goggles on high-angle strafe?"

"It depends on the effects that you want to have," Maj. Milton says. "Are you trying to kill or suppress it?"

"So you would say it was tactically sound to use a method of attack that you don't practice? Is that your testimony?"

"I'm not saying it's tactically sound. I'm saying that sounds like an option that he was trying to use."

"And when Maj. Umbach said: 'Let's just make sure it's not friendlies is all,' was he the flight leader at that time?"

"He was the flight lead responsible at that time, yes."

"And did you hear any response from Maj. Schmidt?"

"I don't believe I did."

"When a flight leader gives some type of directions to you are you supposed to respond, as the Number Two man?"

"Yes."

"And Maj. Schmidt did not respond, did he?"

"I did not hear it, no."

"Would you explain to me why," Col. Graf says, a few moments later, "if somebody was perceiving AAA [anti-aircraft artillery] coming up at them—"

"Objection," Charlie Gittins says. "That is mischaracterization of the evidence." The defense team, of course, has argued since the night of the accident that Maj. Schmidt saw what he believed to be a rocket-propelled weapon—a Ringback, perhaps—not anti-aircraft artillery.

"Stop," Col. Rosenow says. "I'm going to allow him to ask what is basically a hypothetical question."

Col. Graf, a seasoned trial lawyer, humors Charlie Gittins. "Would you explain to me why," he says to Maj. Milton, "if somebody thought there was either *rockets* or AAA being fired at them, why they would suspect that that would be friendlies?"

"No, I would see no reason why you would suspect it to be friendlies."

"Would you agree with me, then, that at this point in time Maj. Umbach isn't sure, because he's asking Maj. Schmidt to make sure they're not friendlies?"

"That's what it sounds like, yes."

"And you would agree with me, then, at this point in time, at least, the fire on the ground does not appear to be AAA then, because if it was AAA or rockets being fired at them it would have to be enemy, wouldn't it?"

"Correct."

"Go ahead and play the tape."

When you get a chance, put it on the SPI, if you've got a good hack on it. Hhhhhhhuhhhh, hhhuuuuuuuuuhhh. Hhhhhhuuuuuuhhhh, hhhhhhhhhhhhhh-hhuuuhh.

"Okay," Col. Graf says. "If there was a lot of ground fire going on now, would it be difficult to locate that with your night vision goggles? Would that be something difficult to locate?"

"You would think not," Maj. Milton says.

"Well, if it wouldn't be difficult to locate, would you explain to me why, at least up to this point in time, Maj. Schmidt has been unable to get his targeting pod on this area where allegedly there's the appearance of ground-to-air fire—"

"Objection," Gittins says. "It's argumentative."

"Go ahead and answer the question, if you can think of an answer to it," Col. Rosenow says.

"The only thing I can think of—I'm not in his airplane and I don't know what he's seeing outside, nor do I really know what he's doing at that time, where his eyes are looking. I mean, I'm looking at a small piece of the pie of all of the information he has at that time, so I don't have an explanation."

Col. Graf points back to the targeting pod videos. "One of the things that a lot of people might say is we don't want to Monday morning quarterback Maj. Schmidt here, do you agree with me?" he asks.

"Yes."

"But is it fair to say that after every mission that you've ever flown, you've debriefed the ride?"

"Yes."

"Well, we're going to debrief this, okay?"

"Okay."

"Go ahead and play it," Col. Graf says.

Okay, I'm going to, uh, flow down here to the, uh, southwest. Hhhuuh, hhhh-huuuuuuhhhh. Hhhhhhuuuuuuuhhhhhhhhhh, hhhhhhuuhhhh. BOSSMAN from Coffee 52, do you want us to push a different freq?

"Now," Col. Graf says, "Coffee 52 is asking BOSSMAN to push a different freq. What does that mean?"

"He wants to go to another frequency to communicate with BOSS-MAN," Maj. Milton says.

"Is that something that a wingman should be doing, or a flight lead—making that type of request?"

"Typically, that's a flight lead call."

"Is that a defensive call?"

"No."

"Based on any of the cockpit communications that you've heard up to this point in time, has anybody indicated that they are defending against AAA, rockets, or surface-to-air missile?"

"I've not heard any."

"Does the tone of the voice of any of these pilots indicate to you that they are engaged by any type of AAA, SAMs, or rockets? Does it indicate that to you?"

"I'm not going to be able to tell that off the tone of voice," Maj. Milton says.

Hhhhuhhh, hhhhhhhhhh. Check my sparkle, check my sparkle. See if it looks good.

"What does 'check my sparkle, check my sparkle' mean?" Col. Graf asks.

"That means he has his IR pointer/marker and he is marking that point and is telling his wingman to look out there and find it."

"A moment ago, before the 'check my sparkle' call, Maj. Schmidt was not on this location where he's eventually going to drop the bomb. He's away from it, is he not?"

"That's correct," Maj. Milton says.

"And it was Maj. Umbach who directed him to direct his attention to this spot, correct?"

"Correct."

"Would that indicate to you that Maj. Umbach had this location before Maj. Schmidt had this location?" Col. Graf asks. Maj. Milton nods his head up and down. "Can you explain to the investigating officer why, if there was a great amount of fire from here, Maj. Schmidt, as a Fighter Weapons School graduate and instructor pilot, would be unable to find this location on his own?"

"Objection," Gittins says. "Calls for speculation."

"Is there an answer to that that you know of?" Col. Rosenow asks the witness.

"Sir," Maj. Milton says. "I wasn't there that night, nor in that mission. So that's a question you would have to ask—"

"So you don't have an answer?" Col. Rosenow interrupts.

"No, sir."

"Okay."

"If there was a great deal of fire from this particular area," Col. Graf continues, "should Maj. Schmidt have been able to find that area on his own?"

"That is a—you should be able to make that assumption, but again, I don't know what he's looking at or seeing."

Hhhhuuuuhhh, hhhhuuuuuuuuuuuhhhhhhhh. Coffee 51, hold fire. Need details on SAFIRE for K-Mart. Okay, I've got a, uh, I've got some men on a road and it looks like a piece of artillery firing at us. I am rolling in in self-defense. BOSSMAN copies. Check master arm, laser arm. And check you're not in mark.

"Who just said: 'Check master arm, laser arm'?" Col. Graf asks.

"Maj. Umbach."

"Did Maj. Umbach passively clear Maj. Schmidt to make this attack?"

"It sounds like it is clearance, I would say. It's not a direct 'you are clear,' but it sounds as if he is telling him to go ahead and continue."

"Could Maj. Schmidt have directed—or Maj. Umbach directed Maj. Schmidt to break off his attack?"

"Objection," Gittins says. "Calls for speculation."

"You can answer the question," Judge Rosenow says.

"He could tell him to leave—to break off his attack," Maj. Milton says. "But he's already invoked self-defense at this point."

"Well, that raises a question that I have for you," Col. Graf continues. "Would you tell me whether or not, since this accident has occurred, have you had an opportunity to talk with Maj. Schmidt about this incident?"

"Yes."

"And he's given you his side of the story quite a number of times, has he not?"

"We've talked through it, yes."

"And has his story, so to speak, remained consistent throughout?"

"Yes."

"At this point in time did he tell you that he didn't feel threatened, but that he thought Maj. Umbach was being threatened?"

"My understanding is he thinks that Maj. Umbach is the one who was being threatened."

"Could you explain to me, if you know why, if he thought Maj. Umbach was the one who was being attacked, why he didn't tell Maj. Umbach to jink?" Col. Graf asks again.

"I can't speculate on that," Maj. Milton answers.

Hhhhhuuuuuhhhhhhhhh, huuuuhhhh. Hhhuuuhh, hhhhhhh. Do you show 'em on a bridge? Bomb's away, cranking left. Hhhhuuuuhhhh, hhhhhuuuuuhhhh. Check wide field of view. I'm fine. Laser's on. Shack. Hhhhuuhh, huuhh. BOSSMAN, BOSSMAN. Coffee 51, BOSSMAN. Disengage, friendlies Kandahar.

28

Every day this week, testimony at the Article 32 has continued well past sundown. The Louisiana sky is always dark when Charlie Gittins and Dave Beck walk outside for their nightly press conferences. And it is still dark early the next morning when the media bus pulls away from Barksdale's front gate. The next day always begins again at 8 a.m. sharp, regardless of how long yesterday lasted.

The grueling schedule is starting to show, not necessarily on the folks in uniform, but on the faces of the Canadian families living on the other side of the B-52 base. For days, they have sat on those couches, watching, crying, as lawyers and witnesses spend hours deconstructing, frame by nauseous frame, the final seconds of their boys' lives. Many leave the room when the tapes start rolling. Watching them die once is more than enough. The Dyers, Paul and Agatha, are still coping with the revelation that Ainsworth, unlike the others, did not die instantly. He lay there on his back, gasping for a few last breaths of air before tilting his head to the side. "I could just see him there as if he was right in front of me," Paul tells one reporter. "The air was just going out of his body. I hope he didn't suffer too much."

This morning—Friday, January 17, 2003—Major John Milton is back in the hearing room for 8 a.m., his second day on the stand. He and Col. Graf go through the cockpit videos yet again, discussing how far the two jets are from the perceived target in the minutes before Maj. Schmidt invokes self-defense. Maj. Umbach keeps his plane above 21,000 feet, at one point steering more than seven nautical miles away from the flashes. Maj. Schmidt descends, then climbs, twice turning his jet back toward the ground fire: 3.4 nautical miles away, 4.3 nautical miles away.

"Let me ask you as a fighter pilot," Col. Graf says. "If you were at a slant range of six miles away, at 21,756 feet, would you roll in from that position or would you leave?"

"If I felt like my wingman was being shot at, or I was, I would roll in from there," Maj. Milton says. "You are in parameters to do that if you are calling self-defense. You're going hypothetical. If I think that I need to do that to survive or for my wingman to survive, I would."

"Is it your testimony under oath that if you were flying a jet, being fired at by AAA, and you were at 21,750 feet AGL [above ground level], and 4.8 nautical miles—is it your testimony that the proper procedure or the procedure you would employ would be to attack the site rather than leaving the site?"

"Objection," Gittins says. "Misleading. You've got to characterize AAA. There are multiple threats of AAA."

"With the AAA threats that you knew existed in Afghanistan at the time or had been briefed on, what would you have done?" Col. Graf asks. "Under oath, would you please tell the investigating officer?"

"Objection," Gittins says again. "Calls for speculation."

"No," Judge Rosenow says. "He's asking what you would have done."

"Objection," Gittins says. "He can't possibly answer that without the sensory inputs, sir."

"Well, I'll let the witness answer whether or not he can answer the question," Col. Rosenow says.

"Sir, you have two options—" Maj. Milton continues.

"I would ask that you answer the question," Col. Graf interrupts.

"I am answering the question," Milton shoots back. "And this isn't a yes or no answer, and I'll tell you why it's not a yes or no answer. We know what the result of this is. I mean, you sit here and you're asking me to put myself back in that position, knowing what the result is. At that time, in their minds, they thought that they were defensive—"

"You're basing that on what they told you," Col. Graf says. "Would you please—"

"Hold it. Hold it. Hold it. Hold it," Judge Rosenow interrupts.

"Could you please let me answer the question?" Maj. Milton says. "I know it's not what you want, but I will give you my answer. In their mindset right now, they are being fired on by a threat system. They think, and they believe, that they're in danger and they need to invoke self-defense. I wasn't in that situation. Sitting here right now, I really don't know how I would handle that, particularly with the fact that we're sitting here in an Article 32, looking at what these guys did in combat. And we are going through all of the minutiae on everything they did in a tactical situation, where there is not one defined, clear answer."

On the other side of the base, Lloyd Smith can't help but feel sorry for John Milton. It is obvious, at least to Nathan's father, that Milton doesn't want to rat out his buddies. Like most soldiers would, he's protecting his own.

"Did either Maj. Schmidt or Maj. Umbach just say to you: 'You know, I made a mistake and that judgment was based on the effects of Go-pills that I may have taken'?" Col. Graf asks later.

"We never discussed that specifically."

"Let me ask you a little bit about your squadron policy on Go-pills. Were you ever tested for Go-pills?"

"Yes."

"Was that testing voluntary?"

"Yes. Actually, I didn't ask the question. They were going to test them and I did."

"Did you test?"

"Yes."

"Did you recognize whether or not you suffered any adverse effects?"

"I did not."

"Once you were tested, did anybody ever tell you you had to take Go-pills?"

"No."

★ ★ ★

Charlie Gittins is the first of the defense lawyers to "cross-examine" Maj. Milton. "Sir," he says. "You have served with Maj. Schmidt both in the Navy and in the National Guard?"

"Yes. He came through as a student of mine while I was an instructor at Fighter Weapons School and then at Springfield."

"Were you instructors together at the Navy Fighter Weapons School?"

"We had just missed each other."

"In the time that you've known Maj. Schmidt, would you characterize him as professional?

"Yes."

"You've also had the opportunity to get to know him personally, correct?"

"Yes."

"How would you characterize his integrity?"

"Impeccable."

"Would you believe him if he told you something?"

"Yes."

"Do you think he would lie about an incident like this?"

"No."

"Yesterday, the prosecutor asked you, absent this accident, do you think Maj. Schmidt is still an exemplary officer."

"Yes."

"Including this accident, do you still think he is an exemplary officer?"

"Yes."

"Would you agree with me that combat is stressful?"

"Yes."

"Have you ever been shot at?"

"Yes."

"Is it scary?"

"Yes."

"Have you ever trained to see rocket-propelled munitions with night vision goggles?"

"No."

"Are you aware that Hill Air Force Base, Utah, is trying to do a training program for their pilots and to show them what different munitions look like at night on night vision goggles?"

"I was not aware."

"Do you think that would be good training?"

"Yes."

"Did you ever have any of that kind of training before you went overseas?"

"No."

"You've seen that tape for God knows how many hours now and you've heard the comm one, correct?"

"Yes."

"Would you agree with me that what you see there is a fog of war situation?"

"Yes."

"Why do you say that?"

"It is not characteristic of what I would normally hear from Maj. Schmidt or Maj. Umbach."

"Had they had the full information about ground scheme maneuver or ground locations, do you think they would have dropped a bomb in that location?"

"No."

"Had you been briefed that ground units would be conducting live-fire training exercises in the areas where you were going to be flying in combat?"

"No."

"Would you consider that to be an unusual event?"

"Yes."

"In the United States, if you were going to be flying near ranges, would you expect that to be a NOTAM?"

"Yes."

"And a NOTAM is a Notice to Airmen, which specifically provides information about altitudes of fires, types of fires, and the specific hours when the firing is going to take place, correct?"

"That's correct."

"I just want to ask you, based on your experience, if you were to have reported to the AWACS command-and-control platform that you were taking ground fire, would you have expected a two-minute-and-49-second lapse before the AWACS communicated that fact to the Coalition Air Operations Center?" Gittins asks. He is referring to Major Art Henry's log book from the AWACS, which states that at 21:21:00—before the pilots activated their onboard recorders—"Coffee 51 Flight experienced SA fire." Maj. Henry did not radio the CAOC until 21:23:49, after Maj. Schmidt requested permission to lay down some 20 mike-mike.

"Would you consider that, as a weapons and tactics instructor in the United States Navy Fighter Weapons School, would you consider that to be an acceptable timeline?" Gittins asks.

"No," Maj. Milton says.

"When Maj. Schmidt—you heard on the tapes that Maj. Schmidt asked BOSSMAN: 'Do you want me to push a different freq?' Does that sound to you that he is speaking in an imperative tone?"

"He is talking like he wants a different freq. He is not getting the information he is wanting."

"In your conversations with Maj. Schmidt, he has colorfully described why he made that call, hasn't he?"

"Yes."

"That's because he was not getting the square root of a four-letter word, correct?"

"That's correct."

"And that was a concern to him and that's why he wanted to go talk to someone who actually knew what was going on, correct?"

"That's correct."

⌣

"Yesterday, the prosecutor told you, before we spent eight hours reviewing the tape, that he was going to debrief the video, correct?"

"Yes."

"Have you ever participated in a debrief in which you did not have the ability to talk to the pilot?"

"No."

"So that really wasn't a debrief. That was actually a Monday morning quarterback, wasn't it?" Gittins asks.

"That would not be considered a debrief," Maj. Milton says. "That would be more of a Monday morning quarterback."

"It's important when you debrief that you see what was happening, but also why that happened from the pilot's mind, correct?"

"That's correct."

"In fact, we sat here at zero knots and one G yesterday and spent eight hours reviewing an event that happened very rapidly, correct?"

"That's correct."

"I would like you to give me a sense—there are a lot of tasks going on in that cockpit of that airplane while Maj. Schmidt is flying it, correct?"

"That's correct."

"That video that we see on this screen, at least three feet across each of the multi-function display screens, those are actually four inches by four inches, correct?"

"That's correct."

"And in addition to looking at those multi-function displays, a pilot's most important sensor is looking outside, correct?"

"That's correct."

"And also flying his airplane, trying to maintain position on his lead, trying to maintain communications, correct?"

"Correct."

"Would you characterize the situation that Maj. Schmidt found himself in as a high task-loading environment?"

"Yes."

⌣

"We talked about the 20-millimeter gun yesterday. In having conversed with Maj. Schmidt, he indicated to you he didn't intend to shoot the target to kill it; he wanted to suppress it, correct?"

"That's correct."

"And was that consistent with your understanding of firing warning shots in order to try to egress?"

"After discussing it with him, I could see where, yes, that would be consistent."

Charlie Gittins hands Maj. Milton a page from his squadron's training package. "Does it depict a 30-degree strafing round by guns?"

"Yes," Maj. Milton says.

"So you could do a strafing run at night, if you are aware of how to do it, correct?"

"Yes."

"I mean, that's a technique you can use in the F–16, isn't it?"

"It's a technique. It's not prohibited."

"In fact, if you are not actually trying to destroy the target you could just roll and put the gun on the target, shoot a couple of BBs downrange and that would probably, hopefully, get the attention of the bad guys and have them stop firing, correct?"

"It could."

"The situation that Maj. Schmidt and Maj. Umbach were in, that wasn't training, was it?"

"No."

"That was a real-world combat mission, correct?"

"That's correct."

Gittins shifts his questions to the G reading on Maj. Schmidt's Fighting Falcon. It recorded a 4.7 G turn before the tapes were activated, when both pilots initially steered away from the fireworks that Maj. Umbach noticed on the ground. "Would a 4.7 G turn with four bombs and two tanks be an aggressive maneuver?" he asks Maj. Milton.

"Yes."

"Would that be indicative of a defensive maneuver?"

"Yes."

"Maj. Umbach had a similar—I believe he had a 3.7 maximum G reading. Would that also indicate a relatively hard turn?"

"Yes."

"And flying around in these OEF missions, were you basically shuttling bombs back and forth from Kuwait, you didn't normally maneuver so that you put three or four Gs on the aircraft, did you?"

"No."

"So those high G indications indicate that there must have been some defensive maneuvering at some point, correct?"

"That's correct."

"And you don't know what the actual communications were between Maj. Schmidt and Maj. Umbach prior to that tape being activated, do you?"

"No, I do not."

"But knowing Maj. Schmidt, you can be sure that they were communicating what each other were doing at the time, correct?"

"Yes."

"When Maj. Schmidt says: 'I have a tally in the vicinity,' he wasn't using euphemism for Taliban, was he?"

"No."

"Tally is code word or a word that you use, a brevity word that is common to aircrews, correct?"

"Correct."

"And what it means is I have what I believe to be bad guys in sight, correct?"

"Something in sight, correct," Maj. Milton says.

"And it usually means something bad, right? Bad guys?"

"Yes."

"And that's right out of 3-1, isn't it?" Gittins asks, referring to the standard F–16 tactics manual.

"Yes, it is."

"You've seen the weapon firing on the video from Maj. Umbach's tape?" he asks, alluding to the fifth round from Brett Perry's Carl Gustav.

"Yes."

"Does that appear to be small arms to you?"

"No."

"You never saw anything like that when you were flying over Afghanistan, did you?"

"No, I did not."

⌣

"Knowing Maj. Schmidt and Maj. Umbach, do you think that either of them went out there to drop a bomb that night?" Gittins asks.

"No," Maj. Milton answers.

"You wouldn't characterize Maj. Schmidt or Maj. Umbach as cowboys, would you?"

"No."

"In fact, they are highly skilled, professional officers, correct?"

"Yes."

"You would characterize the ACO you were provided by the CAOC as unworkable, would you not?"

"Yes, I would."

"And that was supposedly the document that was to provide pilots with information, correct?"

"That's correct."

⌣

"When you were voluntarily tested, as you said for the adverse effects of the Schedule II amphetamines that you were provided by the flight surgeon, was any performance testing done of those drugs on you that determined how they would affect your judgment or your perception?" Gittins asks.

"No," Maj. Milton says.

"In fact, the testing was nothing more than: Did you get sick? Did your heart rate increase or whatever, correct?"

"That's correct."

"It was simply to determine whether or not you tolerate the medication, correct?"

"That's correct."

"Would it be fair to say that the work schedule at Jaber Air Base caused people to be fatigued?"

"It was demanding, yes."

"Were people tired?"

"I would say tired would probably be a good way to say it, yeah. We were doing several missions and we were working very hard."

"In fact, you were flying daily missions into Operation Southern Watch and then after a certain period of time you would fly night missions into Afghanistan—that's the 10-hour round trip missions we're talking about?"

"Depending on what the OSW schedule was, sometimes that would also be at night."

"I believe you testified in response to the investigating officer's question that you believe under the circumstances, with the information the pilots had and did not have, Maj. Schmidt's employment of deadly force was reasonable under the circumstances, correct?"

"Yes," Maj. Milton answers.

"Do you think Maj. Schmidt and Maj. Umbach should be prosecuted?"

"Not in this forum, no."

"Do you believe that anything you've seen on the videos and the communications constitutes a criminal dereliction of duty?"

"No."

⌣

"Maj. Milton, can anybody sitting at zero knots and one G ever say precisely what they may have done under the stress of combat?" Dave Beck asks, standing up after Charlie Gittins finishes his questions.

"No," he answers.

"Is that why it's important that you don't just look at the HUD [Heads-up Display] tapes—stop, start, stop, start—that you have to put yourselves in the position of the pilots who were flying the mission? You have to know the perceptions, the abilities of the pilots who were flying the mission?"

"In order to do a debrief you need to have what their inputs are so you know what they are thinking at the time while you are looking at a fairly small piece of the pie."

"And if you don't," Beck says, "it can be misleading, not to be intentionally misleading?"

"You can gain any number of results from doing that."

"Having seen what you've seen, heard what you've heard, what you saw happen, you can't say that you or any other pilot would not have done exactly the same thing that those two did under those circumstances?"

"No, I cannot, sir."

"There has been testimony from an Air Force colonel who was in the CAOC, who said: 'I assume every pilot who read the orders knew that Tarnak Farms was there.' Did you know of Tarnak Farms before April 17th?"

"No, I did not."

"How many missions did you fly?"

"Four."

"Do you know of any pilots who were in theater—you've talked to other pilots—do you know of any pilots that knew that Tarnak Farms was there?"

"No."

"As a pilot, you've been an instructor, you've been in the Navy, you've been in the Air Force. Is a pilot that you know of anywhere in any school ever taught to expect that there would be a live-fire night training exercise at a combat zone?" Beck asks.

"No."

"The ACO says: 'Tarnak Farms, small arms range is not continuously active.' Does that give you any clue that there would be Canadians, British, or any other forces on the ground firing much larger than small arms at any time?"

"It doesn't give me any information at all."

"So if that officer," Beck says, referring to Col. Stutzriem, "testified that those warnings in a multi-page, 40-something page ACO—that you've already testified was unworkable—put pilots everywhere on notice that there would be live-fire training there, what would you say to that response?"

"I would tell you that would be inaccurate," Maj. Milton says.

"If you you had known that there was live-fire training going on—because part of what the investigating officer has to do is look into a pilot's mens rea, and that is a legal term. If you had been told that friendly forces were doing live-fire training at night, which you have never been trained, is that something that you would have noted?"

"Yes."

"If you had seen flashing red lights blinking, would that have given you some clue that there may have been training going on?"

"Yes."

⌣

"Perception, is that important for a pilot?" Beck asks.

"Yes."

"Is judgment important for a fighter pilot?"

"Yes."

"Is reaction time important for a fighter pilot?"

"Yes."

"Did anybody in the Air Force ever tell you that the drugs they were giving you—the speed, the amphetamines they were giving you—could adversely affect all of those three things?"

"No," Maj. Milton says.

"If they had've, would you have wanted more information?"

"I assume I would have, yes."

"That's all I have," Beck says, sitting down.

"Let me ask some questions before we start a round of redirect," Judge Rosenow says. "Did you take some of the pills when you went to fly?"

"Yes, sir, on those missions."

"Did you ever notice any effect on your judgment?"

"I did not, sir, no."

"Around the squadron, did anybody ever complain about the effects of the pills or say: 'You know, they make me feel ...'? Any complaints at all about the effects the pills may have had on their judgment or anything?"

"I was never in those conversations," Maj. Milton says. "No, I never heard those conversations."

"So, but for whatever reason, you never heard anybody complaining or discussing: 'Gee, this is a problem'?"

"No."

Judge Rosenow hands the witness back to prosecutors.

"When you saw Maj. Schmidt doing all the talking to the controlling agency, are you saying that that was not a breach of flight discipline?" Col. Graf asks.

"Yes, I am," Maj. Milton answers.

"And when Maj. Schmidt was told to 'hold fire' and he rolled in in self-defense, it's your testimony, under oath, that that was not a breach of flight discipline?"

"It's my testimony, under oath, that that was his right and obligation for self-defense."

"You were asked whether or not these two individuals should be prosecuted, and you indicated no," Col. Graf says, a few moments later.

"Correct," Maj. Milton says.

"You said not in this forum, do you recall that?"

"I do."

"Tell the investigating officer what you think the appropriate disposition would be, first for Maj. Umbach and second for Maj. Schmidt."

"I guess my comment on this is the forum we're doing here isn't doing anything to fix the problem in this type of theater. This should be a safety investigation. Let's find out what caused the problem and let's go and fix the problem. As far as disciplinary, that's way above my pay grade and I don't even want to comment on that. But we're not doing anything to address how we're going to fight these types of wars in an asymmetric battlefield, and that's the things I think we need to take from this and I think it comes down to communication."

★ ★ ★

As far as government witnesses go, John Milton was a bona fide flop. In the end, when the questions came, he defended his friends. But without a neutral expert witness in the entire country willing to testify against two fellow fighter pilots, prosecutors have little choice but to stick to the same strategy. The next witness they call is Lieutenant-Colonel Ralph Viets, another member of the 183rd Fighter Wing, another friend of both Harry and Bill.

"Before we go into some of the testimony, I want to ask you, in your conversations with me for this, have you been in any way treated anything other than fair?" Lt.-Col. Graf asks.

"No," answers Lt.-Col. Viets.

"Have I ever attempted to intimidate you in any way?"

"No."

"Have I, in fact, given you an opportunity to get me to ask you questions that will be helpful to your friends from your unit?"

"Yes."

A 20-year veteran, Lt.-Col. Viets has spent his entire career flying F-16s, most of it as a member of the Illinois Air National Guard. On paper, at least, he was the Springfield unit's highest-ranking officer in Kuwait, though Gen. Sargeant and his CIB later criticized him for doing little actual leading. Viets himself said his main role at Al Jaber was to "just sit back and monitor."

Do ya got good coordinates for a mark or do ya need me to roll in? Hh-huuuuuhh. Ah, standby. I'll mark it right now. Hhhhhuuuuhhh. I'm in from the southeast. Hhhhuuhhhhhhhhhh, huuuuuuhhhhhhhhhh.

"As a Fighter Weapons School graduate with previous combat experience, do you think someone with that level of experience should know how to take a targeting pod mark?" Col. Graf asks, referring to Maj. Schmidt.

"Yes," Col. Viets answers.

"And have you seen anything up to this point in time that would indicate to you that he has in fact hit the mark button?"

"No."

Okay, BOSSMAN, this is, uh, Coffee 52. I've got a tally on the vicinity. I, ah, request permission to lay down some, uh, 20 mike-mike. Standby. Huuhhh. Let's just make sure that it's, uh, that it's not friendlies, that's all.

"Is there any reason why, at this point in time, he couldn't exit the area, that you know of, based on what you're seeing right now?" Col. Graf asks. "Based on what you're seeing right now—"

"Without looking at these four videos going—"

"—do you know of anything that you're seeing—"

"Objection," Gittins says.

"No," Judge Rosenow says. "I think it's a fair question based on—"

"But the witness was in the middle of his answer, sir," Gittins interrupts.

"Do you understand the question?" Col. Rosenow asks Col. Viets.

"I do, sir, but I don't think it's a fair question."

"Well, in a second I'll even ask it," the judge says. "The counsel is entitled to ask questions. Based just narrowly on what you've seen up to now, is that the question?"

"Yes," Col. Graf says. "Could he have left this area right now?"

"He could have, yes," Col. Viets says.

As he continues to testify, the questions shift to the mystery chunk of time before the pilots activated their onboard recorders at 21:22:38. It is impossible to know for certain exactly what was said between the moment Maj. Umbach noticed the fireworks and the instant the tapes came on—or even how much time passed. One minute? Two minutes? Five minutes? Whatever the duration, both men insist that Maj. Umbach told his wingman: "I think they are shooting at us" as both jets turned hard to the left. Maj. Umbach also claims that he asked AWACS if there were any friendlies in the area, but received no answer.

"In the time frame before the cameras came on, I think that they were acting in a defensive posture," Col. Viets says. "In that posture—"

"Just so I'm clear," Judge Rosenow interrupts, "that's based on your discussions with them?"

"Right. Because they talked earlier about before the cameras came on we were actually in defensive—"

"So the way that you know—I'm just—there's no tapes of any of that because the tapes weren't running?"

"That's correct."

"So the only way you can say, well, my judgment on what happened before the tapes and your source of that information was from talking to them?"

"Yes, sir."

"Okay, that's fine."

"But I think it pertains to why you're seeing some of the stuff we're seeing," Col. Viets continues. "They got in a defensive posture and in thinking that Maj. Umbach was defensive, when that happens, there is an immediate role change from now. The wingman in this case could almost—the call, I think, from Maj. Umbach, I'm not sure because it's been a while since I've heard, was: 'I think they're shooting at me,' so he's in defensive posture so that makes Maj. Schmidt more or less a—to take care of the threat, if you will. Maj. Umbach's defensive, so Maj. Schmidt would be reasoning more for the comm being—wanting to talk to BOSSMAN to carry out the running of: 'Hey, I need to get coordinates' and stuff like that. That role swap, it's automatic in any engagement. So until, you know, we've got a role swap back, it's not that uncommon to hear the wingman, in this case, doing what he did, thinking that the flight lead, Maj. Umbach, was in a defensive posture."

"I'll give you a number here—21,660 feet AGL [above ground level]," Col. Graf says. "Is that above or below the anticipated threats in Afghanistan?"

"Well, it—you know, when we say 'anticipated threats' there was always the potential. When you talk about threats, you know, you can brief what you think is out there, but anytime you see fire coming up, there's still going to be a 'what is it?' Yes, the threat has been as X,Y, Z, but I don't care who you are, if you see AAA—I don't care, muzzle load, there's always going to be the thought that 'I could be in that envelope,' and until proven otherwise, that is a very capable threat coming at me … I don't think any of us sitting here are going to accept that when they see something coming up at them that I'm safe. I'm going to get to do whatever I can until I prove that that threat is what has been briefed to me. That threat is small arms, that threat is whatever, X, Y, Z. So I think any fighter pilot is that way. You always assume the adversary is more capable and then we can always back down, but we can't step up after that missile, after that bullet, is a factor to yourself or the flight. I know that's not what maybe you wanted, but I think that's what our thought process—and that's what I think these two guys were going at, they were: Worst case scenario, and then we'll go back from there."

⌣

"Your squadron was briefed at or near the time when you reported, when you arrived in the theater, about the execution and torture of Petty Officer Roberts, were you not?" Charlie Gittins asks.

"Correct," Col. Viets says. A U.S. Navy Seal, Neil Roberts fell out of a Chinook helicopter on March 4, 2002, when it came under enemy fire atop Afghanistan's Takur Ghar mountain. Alone and wounded, Roberts was eventually executed, shot in the head by an al-Qaeda fighter. Though later discredited, rumors swirled that the Navy Seal was tortured and mutilated. By the time the 170th Fighter Squadron deployed to Kuwait, pilots were being briefed that P/O Roberts was disemboweled before he died.

"What was the feeling about, by the squadron, about the potential for being shot down in Afghanistan?" Gittins asks.

"Well, obviously that, if you were shot down you weren't going to make it out," Col. Viets says.

"And that's because of the torture that exemplified what the treatment of Americans would be if they were found on the ground?"

"Exactly."

"Would that have been a concern to you, to have to jump out over hostile territory?"

"Yes."

"Would you be concerned if your wingman were required to jump out of an aircraft over Afghanistan?"

"Yes."

"The main thing I want to know is your expert opinion, as an experienced fighter pilot, career F-16 flier," Judge Rosenow says. "From what you saw, they would have been acting as reasonable fighter pilots if they were proceeding under the assumption that they were within a threat footprint?"

"Yes."

"Normally, I think the obligation is if you can get out, get out."

"Right."

"However, if trying to get out is going to put you at more risk, you can roll in?"

"Right."

"Would taking that action in this case, based on everything you see, be a reasonable response?"

"Yes."

"Did you ever take any of the pills to help you stay alert during the long missions?"

"Yes, sir."

"Did they ever have any impact that you noticed on your judgment?"

"You know, I never really put in a time—"

"I know that you never really put in a crucible to really put it to the test, but my question is just: Did you ever notice it to affect your judgment?"

"No."

"Did you ever hear anybody around the squadron complain about it?"

"We really didn't talk about it a lot. It was almost—I tried not taking it and realized that I had to take it to, because of the duration of the mission and body clock, if you will."

"All right, so you tried a couple and it just worked better to take them?"

"I tried initially not taking them."

"Right, that's what I mean."

"Right, not taking them. And then coming back from Afghanistan I actually fell asleep in the cockpit, so it was a must to take them, for the duration."

★ ★ ★

Lt.-Col. Craig Fisher was working on the CAOC floor that night, the chief of Combat Operations (CCO). In the minutes before the bombing, when nobody seemed to know precisely what was happening, the chain of communication went like this: The F-16s over Kandahar to TSgt. Michael Carroll in the AWACS to Maj. Art Henry in the back of the AWACS to Maj. Scott Woodson in the CAOC to Lt.-Col. Craig Fisher in the CAOC to Col. Charles McGuirk in the Crow's Nest. And back.

"What was the first communication that was relayed to you regarding Coffee 52 that night, having anything to do with this incident?" Col. Graf asks Col. Fisher.

"The first call was from AWACS. I don't know verbatim what it was, but it was essentially 'Coffee has AAA in the vicinity of Kandahar, requesting to employ 20mm—20 mike-mike.'"

"And would you again tell the investigating officer what your response to that was?"

"My response was: 'No, need SAFIRE information' was the relayed call back up through AWACS."

"What happened next in the CAOC after you made that decision?"

"After that call was made I looked up at the display to see where, exactly, Coffee Flight was on the display. I picked up the land-line communications and contacted the ASOC [the Air Support Operations Center, an Army/Air Force liaison office in Bagram] to ask if they had any information on what was going on in the vicinity of Kandahar and if they could contact Kandahar tower. They didn't have any immediate information and were checking into that one. Somewhere in this time I turned to the DCO, Col. McGuirk, and asked him if he was hearing this on the radio."

"And why did you ask him that?"

"It was very unusual for someone to request 20mm—to employ ordnance, period."

"And what was his response?"

"His response, either there or shortly thereafter, was looking around at where they are and saying: 'Get 'em out of there.'"

"And what did you do next, then?"

"Shortly thereafter the radio call came out that they were employing ordnance in self-defense."

"When Coffee 52 requested permission to employ the 20-millimeter gun, did that message begin the TST [Time Sensitive Targeting] process in the CAOC?"

"No, it did not begin the process. It initiated us finding out that there was something significant going on, but we had very little information at that point. That's why we requested more SAFIRE; what altitude, what caliber, what location? All we had was 'vicinity of Kandahar.'"

"Based on what you've seen and heard, including the entire tape and also the comments made by the pilots after they had dropped, is there anything that you have seen in the evidence presented to you in those tapes that would lead you to believe that Coffee 51 or Coffee 52 were at all defensive on April 17th, 2002?"

"I do not see anything that indicated that they were defensive in the tapes I've seen."

"Based on your experience, do you believe that the actions taken by Coffee 51 and 52 were appropriate?"

"No, I do not believe they were appropriate," Col. Fisher says.

"After April 17th, if there were live-fire training exercises going on in the combat zone, CAOC knew about it, pilots were briefed, and everybody was made aware of that fact, is that correct?" Dave Beck asks, beginning his cross-examination.

"To the best ability they could, yes," Col. Fisher says.

"And as you told Capt. Key and Capt. Scoble and me, that's information that really the Army should have been providing—the ground forces should have been providing to the Air Force even before April 17th, if you have live-fire training going on by friendly forces in the combat zone?"

"I would think that would be logical."

"Do you know why the Army wasn't giving the information that they should have been giving, before April 17th?

"No, I do not."

"Did you or anyone else that you know of in the CAOC know about Tarnak Farms before April 17th?" Beck asks.

"Not that they were conducting fires. That there was a range I think was probably not known. No, I did not know."

"When you first became aware of this evolving," Beck asks a few minutes later, "I think you responded to Col. Graf you heard: 'vicinity of Kandahar,' correct?"

"Correct."

"And you immediately, in your job, picked up a phone and called Kandahar?"

"I looked on the screen, which was not very accurate in pinpointing where they were, and called my counterparts."

"But you knew from the screen they were in that general area, and the call you got was 'vicinity of Kandahar'?"

"Yes, sir."

"And I don't want to talk about the type of phone, but you picked up communications and called Kandahar?"

"I did not have a number for Kandahar," Col. Fisher says. "I called the ASOC, which is the component of the CAOC which the Air Force liaisons with the Army."

"And basically—well you would agree that four or five minutes in a combat environment is an eternity?"

"Yes, sir, I would agree with that."

"And when you asked, you trying to do your job, you basically were—I won't say 'put on hold,' but you sat there and for five minutes nobody gave you any information?"

"I asked if they knew of anything. I think there was a response that they didn't know anything. I requested that they contact Kandahar tower because I thought that would be a place that would have good visibility of what's going on around Kandahar."

"And you were put on hold and didn't get any response for five minutes or more?"

"Yes. I don't know that I ever got a response. I hung up the phone to continue on with the mission."

"Were you ever taught at Fighter Weapons School or in any of the training you ever went to, to expect friendly forces to be firing at a combat zone—I'm sorry, not to be firing, but to be training—live-fire training in a combat zone?"

"No."

"Have you ever debriefed a flight without talking to the pilot?" Charlie Gittins asks the witness.

"That would not be the normal thing to do. You've got all the fliers in the debrief."

"That would be extraordinary, wouldn't it?"

"Yes."

"When you debriefed this flight with the prosecutor here today, were you ever shown the statements made by the pilots when they landed, under oath, to their commanders?"

"No, I have not read those."

"Did you ask to see them?"

"No, I did not."

"Was any reason given to you why the prosecutor in this case, who is charged with finding justice, would not provide you with information provided by the pilots relative to their thought processes, sir?"

"There was some information provided on their testimony but, no, I don't know—"

"And in fact, in the questioning by the prosecutor, he just wanted you to focus on the tapes that you were shown here today, correct?"

"He asked me my opinion of what I saw occurring in those tapes," Col. Fisher answers.

"Just on the tapes, correct?"

"That is correct."

"And the same thing with Maj. Umbach. Maj. Umbach gave a sworn statement when he landed. Were you ever shown that statement, sir?"

"No, I was not."

"Were you aware that Maj. Schmidt provided a 38-page submission to the Coalition Investigative Board that explained what he knew, and it had attachments with what he knew and why he believed what he did was right?"

"No, I was not."

"Would that have informed your opinions in this case, do you think, sir?"

"It may have."

"Can you think of any reason why you would not want to read

everything that a pilot provided regarding his thought processes in an accident like this?"

"No, I would like to read them."

"Well, why didn't you ask for them, then, sir?"

"On the same side I wanted to remain somewhat neutral in opinions."

"Really?" Gittins asks. "How could you give a neutral opinion if you don't have all the information that the pilot provided relevant to the accident, sir?"

"I am providing a piece of the information for the judge to hopefully make those determinations."

"Did you know these statements existed, even?"

"I knew they made a statement, but I didn't know how long or in what detail."

"So, I tell you what, counsel," Judge Rosenow interrupts. "Why don't we stop and give this witness a chance to look at those documents, and we can ask if this changes his opinions on anything. So, we'll take a brief recess."

Charlie Gittins agrees, but asks permission to finish his last few questions before Col. Fisher flips through the statements. "What did you tell the communicator in the CAOC when you received the first word about laying down 20-millimeter cannon fire?" he asks.

"I testified I said 'negative.'"

"No, here today."

"I said: 'No, give me a SAFIRE report. Where are you? What's going on?'"

"Okay. That was your testimony here today, correct?"

"Yes."

"Did you give a sworn statement to Brig.-Gen. Sargeant in which you told Gen. Sargeant at the time, and I'll read your answer: 'Sir, on that night it was a little while after 21:00 Zulu, in my memory. I was sitting at a position which is right behind the DDO, the defensive duty officer [Maj. Woodson, the CAOC officer talking to the AWACS]. The radio call came out over the SATCOM frequency from BOSSMAN, the AWACS, saying that Coffee Flight had received an AAA and was requesting to return 20-millimeter fire. My response was immediately 'negative.' I told him—I told the DDO to relay 'negative' and have him get out of the area and file a SAFIRE report.' Do you remember giving that testimony, sir?"

"Yes."

"You didn't say that you told Coffee Flight to get out of the area here today, did you?"

"No."

"Were you provided an opportunity to read your testimony after you listened to your tape-recorded conversations?"

"No, I was not."

"Did you read your testimony after you listened to the tape-recorded conversations?"

"I reviewed my testimony today."

"Okay. You will agree with me that the testimony you gave to Brig.-Gen. Sargeant was closer in time than the testimony you gave here today, correct?"

"That is correct."

"And to be clear, you were working for Gen. Wood on the night in the CAOC, and you are working for him today, correct?"

"Yes."

"If you told the communicator in the CAOC to tell Coffee Flight to get out of there, is there any reason that you can provide to us today that that would not have been relayed to Coffee Flight?"

"No."

"So were you wrong on the date you gave your statement or are you wrong today about what you said, sir?"

"I do not know. I testified then to the best of what I knew."

"When you testified before Brig.-Gen. Sargeant, did you know that there were tape recordings made of the communications in the CAOC?"

"Yes."

"You did?"

"Yes."

"Are you sure of that, sir?"

"Yes, I was the one who found that tape and had it secured."

"Did you listen to it?"

"Not until—I think I heard part of it much later."

"You also made some handwritten notes that were provided to the Coalition Investigative Board, correct?"

"That is correct."

"Were those virtually contemporaneous notes?"

"Please elaborate. What do you mean?"

"Well, were they made at or near the time when you, when this incident was taking place?"

"Yes."

"In your notes, your statement says: 'CCO denied request, told to pass SAFIRE and get out of the area.' Did you actually tell Coffee Flight to get out of the area? Did you pass that on, sir?"

"That was my statement. I made a statement: 'No, do not fire. Need SAFIRE,' and I picked up the phone to find out what was going on in Kandahar."

"Yes, sir, but my question was—"

"I do not remember."

"Would it refresh your recollection to look at the document, sir?"

"I've seen the document. It would not change my testimony."

"Are you concerned, sir, that you may have some criminal liability for failure and dereliction of duty or false prior statements?"

"No, I'm not concerned about that."

"Is that because you're helping the prosecution, sir?"

"No, it's because I don't think I'm derelict in duty nor am I providing—"

"On the night of the incident," Gittins interrupts, "in response to the 20-millimeter call, you stated you denied request, told to pass SAFIRE and get out of the area. Is that a true statement, sir?"

"To the best of my memory at the time, it was."

"But it's not now, is it?"

"I do not know whether that piece of the puzzle was stated then. Like you said, the statement that was made then was much closer to the incident."

"Okay, and you gave that statement under oath to Gen. Sargeant, and you made it on a document that you provided that was supposedly to document what happened that night, isn't that true, sir?"

"That is correct."

It is after 6:30 p.m. when Judge Rosenow orders a recess so Col. Fisher can read the pilots' sworn statements. It takes the colonel a little more than half an hour to skim through the pages. *I think they are shooting us ... They are pulling lead ... They are shooting at you ... Intel was warning us about Ringbacks, 122-mm Multiple Launch Rocket Systems capable of firing up to 56,000 feet ... I believed that my flight lead was at risk of being shot down ... I probably could have egressed the situation myself ... This, however, would have done nothing to support my flight lead, who appeared to be drawing fire ... We asked BOSSMAN if there were any friendlies in the vicinity; BOSSMAN did not respond ... No one in the air was aware of this ROZ because it was buried in a bloated and completely unworkable Airspace Control Order ... One of my greatest fears came to realization tonight of not knowing where friendlies are, not knowing of their operations, ending up in the middle of a perceived firefight trying to sort it out in a short amount of time while airborne receiving fire.*

"Col. Fisher, I'm going to ask you some questions and I want you to take as a predicate all of the things that you've seen on the various video and digital media about the flight on April 17th," Judge Rosenow says. "I would also include all the things now that you've read from the various statements that Maj. Schmidt and Maj. Umbach made about the events that happened that night, and put all of that into the mix together and assume that all of that is exactly what happened. In your professional opinion, based on all of that, let me just as a beginning, do you believe there were any significant departures from flight discipline?"

"No, sir," he answers. "I'm not seeing significant—there are some key points of interest, but—"

"Okay, what are the key points, just very briefly?"

"Going below the altitude deck [15,000 feet AGL] is a significant event that would need to be looked into as to what you were doing while you were below that. And, I would still be interested, sir, and it seems like they were in this target area for a long period of time."

"Okay. Again, taking as a predicate all of the things I reminded you of before, at any point do you believe that they were outside of the threat envelope and then re-entered the threat envelope?"

"Yes, sir."

"And do you believe that at any point they opted to roll in instead of departing the threat area?"

"Yes, sir. That is the question I am looking at as far as—looking at the tapes and the testimony, it seems there are periods of times where they were not immediately, at that time, under a defensive situation, where they had an opportunity to leave."

"So do you believe that the rules of engagement at that point would have required that they either stay out of the threat envelope, or it would have been better for them to depart the threat envelope rather than engaging the threat?"

"Yes, sir, I think it would have been better for them to leave."

"Okay, and again, this is based on everything, including the statements that you've reviewed?"

"Yes, sir."

"Do you believe that the actions they took were inconsistent with the actions that would have been taken by reasonably prudent fighter pilots of their experience?"

"It's a difficult question," Col. Fisher says. "With their training and experience, I think that most would have found a way to leave."

"Most?"

"A reasonable and prudent one, yes, sir."

⌣

"Do you believe that when you were witnessing the tapes and Maj. Schmidt had descended to approximately 10,000—somewhere between 10,000 and 11,000 feet—and when his airspeed had descended to approximately 237 knots calibrated airspeed, in consideration of the statements that they perceived they were in a threat envelope, do you believe he maintained a tactically acceptable airspeed during this encounter?" Col. Graf asks.

"No, I do not."

"If there was a perceived threat of BM-21s in the area, do you believe that they maintained a tactically safe distance from that alleged perceived threat?"

"No," Col. Fisher says. "Based on the ranges I saw in this particular brief, I would stay farther away or higher."

"Based on their claim of the perceived threat, in your opinion, do you believe that they maneuvered their aircrafts in tactically acceptable manners?"

"No. From what I see on the tape, and the threat, I don't see tactical maneuvering to defend."

"In light of the stated perceived threat, based on their statements, do you believe that they made the appropriate defensive or engaged radio calls?"

"The testimony indicates that there was a call of 'defensive' prior to the tape coming on, but the testimony does not continue beyond that initial call. I would expect much more comm to be on the airway if somebody was in a defensive situation and was reacting."

"If there had been a defensive call in that period before they turned their tapes on, would it have been tactically acceptable to remain in the area around Tarnak Farms if, at some point subsequent to it, they no longer were defensive?"

"No," Col. Fisher says.

"Based on the altitudes that you witnessed Coffee 52 descend to, do you believe that he complied with the restrictions set forth in the ROE or the SPINS? And, please don't say any classified number."

"As a factual answer, no. He descended below the altitude."

"At any point in time, based on when you were in the CAOC or based on what you heard, did it ever appear that there was a proper SAFIRE report produced by Coffee 51 or Coffee 52?"

"No."

⌣

"Have you ever seen rocket-propelled munitions while you were flying?" Charlie Gittins asks.

"No," says Col. Fisher, who has flown more than 100 hours of combat in an F-16.

"Have you ever seen rocket-propelled munitions under night vision goggles?"

"No."

"At Fighter Weapons School were you aware of any training syllabus in which pilots are shown rocket-propelled munitions?"

"No."

"You would agree with me, would you not, sir, that reactions in combat are judgment calls, correct?"

"Yes."

"You do what you need to do to survive, correct?"

"Yes."

"I'm going to ask you a little bit about fighter doctrine, sir. You've acknowledged that Maj. Umbach's testimony and Maj. Schmidt's testimony indicates that Maj. Umbach believed he was being fired at and that he was being led by surface-to-air fire, correct?"

"At one point, yes."

"Okay. At that point, Maj. Umbach is in a defensive situation, correct?"

"Yes."

"A defensive maneuver by both aircraft would be appropriate at that time, correct?"

"Yes."

"And if Maj. Schmidt is the defending fighter—I'm sorry, Maj. Umbach is the defending fighter, Maj. Schmidt is the supporting fighter, correct?"

"Yes."

"The supporting fighter should assume comm outside the flight, isn't that true?" Col. Fisher doesn't answer. "I can show you the 3-1 if you'd like to review it, sir," Gittins says.

"That is one of his roles, is to maintain outside communications and situational awareness."

"And the defending fighter and the supporting fighter, they have their roles and they remain in those roles until there's a change of status call that is made, isn't that true, sir?"

"Yes."

"Okay. And I believe it's your testimony that you never heard Maj. Umbach make a call that he was no longer defending, correct?"

"I never heard a call that stated defensive, but it was in the testimony, other than right prior to releasing."

"Okay. Maj. Umbach never made a call on the tape that indicated he was no longer defending, correct, sir?"

"Correct."

"Okay. And for the supporting fighter, you must assume that the defending fighter is defending until he tells you differently, correct?"

"Yes. But, I would anticipate additional information."

"You would anticipate it, but by doctrine in the 3-1, you're the defending fighter until you actually change status and you have to make a radio call to change status, correct?"

"The normal comm is: the engaged in a defensive role, and a supporting fighter," Col. Fisher says. "Yes, once the call is made that you are in that position, you, as the supporting fighter, do what you can to support him, get his eyes on the threat, whatever is required, but those roles are maintained until there's a change."

"Okay. And if you are the supporting fighter, unless your lead tells you to egress, the defending fighter says 'egress,' you remain and support your flight lead, is that not true, sir?"

"Yes."

"So unless Maj. Umbach made a radio call, indicating that he was no longer engaged, Maj. Schmidt was appropriately remaining in the area, providing support to his flight lead, isn't that true, sir, by your own doctrine?"

"I—positionally, he should remain visual and around the fight, but his role as a supporting fighter is to provide information on what the threat is and what's going on."

"And Maj. Schmidt appeared to be trying to obtain that information by using his weapons system, including his pod, correct, sir?"

"There's a lot of discussion about sparkles and marks—"

"My question is, sir, and I'm going to ask you to answer it."

"Okay."

"What you saw on that video appears to show Maj. Schmidt trying to find, with his pod, the target area and provide information to his flight lead. Do you disagree with that, sir?"

"I do not disagree."

"So under the circumstances, unless there's been a change, Maj. Schmidt was taking appropriate action to support his flight lead. Do you disagree with that?"

"No, I do not."

"So until Maj. Schmidt invoked self-defense, and you read his statement—he believed his lead, his flight lead, was being engaged by the object on the road, correct?" Gittins asks later.

"Yes, that's what he believed."

"And, he swore under oath that that was what happened, correct?"

"Yes."

"And you heard it on the tape when he was talking to Maj. Umbach afterward, correct?"

"Yes."

"Before he rolled in, in self-defense, did you ever hear a change of Maj. Umbach's status from defending?"

"I never heard the defending call, but I never heard a statement changing that status."

"Okay. But you did read Maj. Umbach's statement that indicated he was defending, correct?"

"I read his statement."

"And it is a true statement that a pilot always has the right and obligation of self-defense, correct?"

"Yes."

"And Maj. Schmidt honestly and reasonably believed, under those circumstances, that Maj. Umbach was being engaged and he needed to roll in in self-defense, correct?"

"That is his testimony."

"Do you have a reason to believe that he wasn't being truthful, sir?"

"No. He is invoking self-defense, and that was a situation that he saw. From what I read in his testimony, I agree that there was a statement in there of being defensive. When I listened to the tape—you about extraneous comm, I hear comm between the two on sparkles and marks that does not normally support a defensive posture."

"But communication needs to be directive, descriptive, and what else?"

"Informative."

"Okay. There was no directive communication, directing Maj. Schmidt to leave the area, was there?"

"No."

"There was no descriptive communication or directive communication, indicating that Maj. Umbach was no longer engaged, correct?"

"Correct."

"So when Maj. Schmidt, remaining in the area because he was supporting his flight lead, rolled in in self-defense when he believed Maj. Umbach was under fire, he acted within the ROE, did he not?"

"As phrased, correct. Yes."

"In light of the doctrine we've just discussed, is it your testimony, having read Maj. Schmidt's rationale, that his actions were unreasonable under the circumstances?"

"I would not do the same actions," Col. Fisher says.

"My question was to you, sir: Are you testifying that Maj. Schmidt's actions, under the circumstances, given the information you've now read, were unreasonable?"

"I'm thinking on that one. Based on the testimony and what I saw on the tape, I do not feel that that was his only option."

"My question was—you will agree with me that the heat of combat is a very difficult situation, won't you?"

"Yes, I will."

"And some people may react to it one way and other people may react to it another way, correct?"

"Correct."

"It's a matter of judgment, correct?"

"Yes."

"It's a matter of courage, correct?"

"Yes."

"It's a matter of training, correct?"

"Correct."

"And now, I ask you again, sir, given the range of things that can go into that decision-making process, are you testifying that under the circumstances, as Maj. Schmidt has completely explained them, that he acted unreasonably under the circumstances?"

"Hold it," Judge Rosenow says.

"I'm going to object for the following reason," Col. Graf says. "Through the line of questioning from counsel, he's been making statements which he has stated as a fact that Maj. Umbach had called defensive, and then—"

"Okay," Col. Rosenow says, "and I think I understand where you're going. Your problem is that the questions all assume that everything in those statements is true. Right?"

"It assumes that everything in Maj. Schmidt's is true, and it actually contradicts Maj. Umbach's, because Maj. Umbach's statement says—"

"Objection," says. Lieutenant-Colonel Clay Moushon, one of Maj. Schmidt's two military lawyers.

"Well, we're not even talking about considering it as substantive evidence," Col. Rosenow says. "My only point here is we've had a lot of predicate questions. 'If this is true, then what about that?' And I allowed for all of you to ask it, and I'm going to allow them to ask it. ... If he wants to ask: 'Assuming that everything in those statements that you've read is true, what is your opinion?' That's a legitimate question that I can take the answer to."

"From what I've read," Col. Fisher says, "that there was a defensive call, that the roles did not change, and that there was a perception that his lead was being actively engaged by this threat system, it would not be unreasonable to engage it."

"That's all I have, sir," Gittins says.

⌣

"You looked at the materials and now we've asked you to change the predicate from just what you saw on the tape to include the information that you have about what Maj. Schmidt and Maj. Umbach said out of court, and we're telling you to consider those things and put those into the mix," Judge Rosenow says to Col. Fisher. "And do I understand now that your testimony is that, based on all of that, you would not say that their conduct is unreasonable, if you include the whole mix?"

"If you take all of the suppositions that we went through; the sequence of events with a defensive person with a threat range reaching out to the range stated—"

"Right, with the specific piece of equipment we talked about," he says, referring to an MLRS.

"Yes, sir, and the sequence of events that led up to the, the whole sequence of events to put him in that position, I would say it may not be unreasonable."

"And other experienced fighter pilots with similar training and experience might have done the same thing?"

"Might have done the same thing," Col. Fisher says.

★ ★ ★

Outside the warehouse, in front of the microphones, Charlie Gittins calls on the president of the United States to step in and put an end to this nonsense. A senior CAOC official—a supposed government witness—has just conceded that the pilots' actions might have been reasonable after all. "If it's not unreasonable," Gittins tells reporters, "it's not a crime."

"The key government witness just testified under oath that he cannot say that anything that was done was not reasonable under the circumstances," Dave Beck says. "There should be no prosecution in this case. There never should have been. They need to go back to the Canadian families and offer condolences and offer compensation and tell them that they're going to fix the problems."

chapter twenty-nine

Between last night and early this morning, President George W. Bush did not intervene to stop the hearing. By 8 a.m., as they have all week, Marlene Umbach and Lisa Schmidt stride past the now-familiar row of cameras, gripping their husbands' hands until they reach the warehouse. Later in the afternoon, during a brief break in testimony, both women walk back outside, coaxed by a few journalists, to stand behind the microphones. The question is always the same: As difficult as this is for you, what about those Canadian families? What can you say to comfort the relatives who have listened, over and over, to your husbands' deep breathing on those cockpit videos?

Lisa Schmidt, petite and blond, says she thinks often of what she would say to Marley Léger. "When I envision it with Marley, even though I don't know her, I would say that I'm sorry Marc is gone and that I will always keep her in my prayers," she tells reporters, her soft voice barely a whisper. "I laid next to my husband last night. I knew that she wasn't laying next to hers."

Wearing a red sweater emblazoned with a U.S. flag, Marlene admits that there is little she can say to comfort those families. "They still won't have a happy ending," she says. "It's hard for everybody—the Canadian families, the soldiers that were there, Bill and Harry, us, our kids." But if the families want to, if it is something that will help them grieve, Marlene says she is more than willing to sit down and talk. "I don't want to throw myself on them," she says.

A face-to-face meeting never will materialize. The tears, that video, are more than enough to stomach.

★   ★   ★

Colonel David Nichols has been in Louisiana for more than a week now, waiting for prosecutors to call him as a witness. By Saturday, Col. Odom and his team decide not to bother. The last thing they need is more testimony from another friend of the pilots.

But defense lawyers—and the press corps—are anxious to hear what the colonel has to say. Up until now, he has been cast as both inept and beloved, a commander who—depending on the source—either contributed to the tragedy or tried desperately to prevent it. When he hears that the government isn't going to call Col. Nichols, Charlie Gittins puts him on the stand instead—the first and only witness that the defense side will summon during the entire Article 32.

"As the commander of the 332nd Air Expeditionary Group, who was your first commander over there?" Gittins asks.

"I worked directly for the commander of the Joint Task Force Southwest Asia," Col. Nichols answers.

"And who was that?"

"It changed from Gen. [Gary] Dylewski to Gen. [Walter] Buchanan."

"And what was your contact with Gen. [Chuck] Wald?"

"Gen. Wald was the CENTAF commander and he was their commanders. When Gen. Wald—Gen. Wald was responsible for the AF forward functions of the units deployed and he was the person who hired me for that job. Then when he became the CFACC, it was a little unclear, but everybody knew they worked for Gen. Wald, [that] was very clear."

"The CFACC, that—"

"The Coalition Forces Air Component Commander."

"So, below Gen. Franks, who was the commander overall, he would be the air component commander?"

"Yes, sir."

"And Gen. Wald, did you have contact with Gen. Wald about your missions?"

"Gen. Wald would make his presence known, I think, on every base nearly every day via a direct phone call, via his aide, via input of some kind, but he was a very active, engaged commander."

"So would it be fair to say that while Gen. Wald was commander of the CFACC, you had good cognitivity with your overall commander?"

"Yes, and if there was a question, I could ask him or one of his personal staff and it would be clarified quickly, not always in your favor, but clarified, which is fine."

"Did Gen. Wald give up command, at some point, and was he replaced?"

"Yes, he was."

"And who replaced him?"

"Gen. Moseley."

"If you would, could you characterize the difference, if any, between your interfaces with the Coalition air component commander after the change?"

"It was significantly different," Col. Nichols says. "Gen. Moseley commanded with a different style. We, as commanders in the field, did not hear from him very often."

"So you didn't have personal interface, you weren't able to personally interface with him on the same basis that you had with the previous commander?" Gittins asks.

"No."

⌄

"What, if any, difficulty did you have obtaining information on the friendly ground order of battle?"

"It was, basically, non-existent," Col. Nichols says.

"Did you make your concerns known to your superiors in the Coalition Air Operations Center?"

"Yes, I did."

"And what, if anything, changed over time?"

"I believe they tried, but they had difficulty getting that information also, but that wasn't my concern. My concern was that my guy stepping out the door needed to know where they were and that was one of my biggest concerns in every OEF mission—is where the friendlies are, where the enemy is and really what the ground commander's intent is, what he is trying to do. Especially if we're doing close air support, you're supposed to know what the ground commander is doing by what we're trained."

⌄

"In the conversations about rules of engagement, what, if any, examples did you provide to the aircrew about using self-defense in the case of a wingman who was perceived to be taking fire?"

"That's a standard. That's an obligation. If you perceive someone in your flight to be in jeopardy, then you need to eliminate that jeopardy. You need to do what you need to do to make sure the member of your flight survives the scenario."

"Sir, during the time that the 170th checked in, did you also brief the 170th about—without any classified details—did you also provide a briefing about what happened to Petty Officer Roberts, the Navy Seal who fell out of the back of a helicopter during operations in Afghanistan?"

"'Yeah, we got rumors and some official mail, yes,' Col. Nichols says.

"Without going into specific details—"

"He didn't have a good experience before he died."

"Was that provided to aircrew to emphasize to them the danger of the area in Afghanistan?"

"Yes."

"Sir, how would you characterize the ACO, the Airspace Control Order that was provided on a daily basis to your unit?"

"It was inclusive, complex, and very difficult to use for lots of reasons. Normally, we had to sit down with units and explain to them what the abbreviations meant and all that. It was very, very thick and you had to go through it yourself and pull out what we call the 'gouge'—it's a Navy term. Those things are important."

"Would it be possible for an aircrew that was going to fly one of these 10-hour plus missions in a 14-hour crew day to personally go through the entire ACO?"

"No way," Col. Nichols says. "If he or she has prioritized there they have misprioritized their time."

"Did you yourself review the ACO on a regular basis?"

"Yes."

"Did you ever become aware of a range called Tarnak Farms range?"

"I did."

"And what was your understanding about that range, sir?"

"I remember reading it and just going through it. Then, after the accident, I went 'holy smokes' and went back and read what it was. But when I read it, you know, I would ask the mission director, as the commander I'm trying to keep up. I would turn that page, I read it, and in my mind I was counting on my mind to register significant events. It didn't register. I just knew it was there."

"Did you know about it because you had previously bombed it?" Gittins asks.

"Yeah, Col. [Mark] Coan [his acting deputy] was actually responsible for—he as an Air FAC [Forward Air Controller] worked for, I think, it was five-and-a-half hours one day and that was one of the flanks of his operation where he and a bunch of Ground FACs took over Kandahar."

"So the name 'Tarnak Farms,' it had been provided to you by the nature of the operations that had previously been conducted?"

"It had surfaced and then gone away, and then I saw it in there. I just knew that it was south of Kandahar and insignificant to the things that we were doing, in my mind."

"What understanding did you have that they would be firing live ordnance at night there?"

"I couldn't believe it," Col. Nichols says.

"Why is that, sir?"

"It's just unsafe. My previous experience in Bosnia is a range called Glomach. It has a small impact area and early on, whenever Glomach was going to be active, there was a huge airspace control measure put in place that AWACS vectored you around. But it became that you never could go through Glomach even if you were out of gas. I just assumed that—and assume is a bad thing to do, as we have learned—but I just believed that if there was going to be any live firing other than pistols, in my mind that there would be a large airspace control measure put in place and airplanes would not be let going through there, surface to infinity. Anytime there is anything that is going to be shooting on the ground, airplanes don't fly over."

"What, if any, changes did the Coalition air component commander make to procedures about live ranges after the accident on 17 April?" Gittins asks later.

"He made sure that there were processes in place and active airspace control measures that airplanes avoided."

"In fact, he required that NOTAMs be published, correct?"

"Yes."

"Is a NOTAM a common word understood by most pilots?"

"Yes. Notice to Airmen. It's what we live by. You can be going someplace and the airfield that you are to land at can be NOTAM closed, and, of course, you wouldn't go there if that were the case."

"Was there any reason to your knowledge that NOTAMs could not have been provided to aircrew about friendly live-firing ranges before the 17th of April?" Gittins asks.

"No."

⌣

"Take me through the process, if you will, about the extension of the crew duty day for night missions as flown in Operation Enduring Freedom from 10 hours to 14 hours?"

"I don't know the exact timelines," Col. Nichols says. "I know early on when the Strike Eagles left and came back, we were able to listen to the missions, the satellite communications. We realized that this particular flight was going to be gone much longer and it was dark. So we called the CAOC and told them that these guys were going to be airborne longer and, basically, the word back we got was: 'Make it happen.'"

"Sir, when, if at all, to your knowledge was the 14-hour crew day approved by the commander of the Air Combat Command?"

"I assumed that the fact that it was—and, again, there is that word—but I assumed the fact that our take-off and landing times and the tremendous successes that the various weapons systems were having was briefed at all levels, that it was obvious to everybody that, in fact, we were flying some long missions. And I felt that they were expecting me to manage that risk, which we did. I think we managed that risk very well."

⌣

"Did you meet the aircrew when they landed?"

"Yes."

"If you would, sir, can you tell me the reaction—did you tell the crew what happened when they had landed?"

"Yes. The commander doesn't go meet you in the middle of the night."

"What, if anything, was Maj. Schmidt's reaction when you told him what had happened?"

"He became physically ill. I mean, you could just feel it and just saw it."

"How about Maj. Umbach?"

"The same."

Col. Nichols explains how he and the pilots debriefed the mission, watching the tapes behind closed doors before recording an official statement. "Did they explain to you what they believed had happened?" Gittins asks.

"Yes."

"When they explained to you what they believed had happened, did they appear sincere to you?"

"Yes."

"Did you understand what they were saying?"

"Yes."

"Having reviewed the tapes and talked to the pilots when, if at all, did you believe they acted unreasonably in what they did?"

"No."

"Thereafter, were you tasked to obtain statements from the two pilots?"

"Yes."

"What were you told and by whom, sir?"

"Gen. Buchanan was rightfully concerned that we needed to find out—he had faith in Maj. Schmidt and Maj. Umbach that they believed they were doing the right thing, so he wanted a statement from them telling what happened that he could use for media purposes. I don't exactly remember how he told me that."

"Would it have happened by a telephone call?"

"Yes."

"So he directed you to obtain a statement so that it could be released to the media?"

"Yes."

"Did he give you any direction about how you were supposed to do that?"

"No."

"Did he give you any indication that he wanted the pilots read their rights?"

"I think that came through the JAG side."

"Did you have any reason to believe at the time that Maj. Schmidt or Maj. Umbach, having reviewed the tapes by now and debriefed the pilots in a tactical debrief, did you have any reason to believe that they had committed a crime?"

"No."

"Did you obtain statements from Maj. Schmidt and Maj. Umbach?"

"Yes."

"Were they sworn to their statements?"

"Yeah, I read them their rights, but as everyone knows I modified the rights statement with one word."

"What was the modification you made to the rights sworn statements?"

"I changed the word 'offense' to 'incident.'"

"Between what you read, saw on the tapes, and what the pilots told you, what, if any, opinion did you have about whether they acted reasonably and within the ROE?" Gittins asks.

"I believed with what they knew at the time and what they saw, what they did was not unreasonable."

"Was it within the sphere of reactions that you would expect of experienced fighter pilots?"

"Yes."

"Prior to the day of the accident did you have a visit—to Kuwait—by Gen. Hornburg, the ACC [air component command] commander?"

"Yes."

"What was the purpose of his visit, if you recall?"

"I believe he was doing what a good commander does and visit the troops, concerns and showing his support in the operation. He is a very experienced aviator having had a job similar to mine and on up the command. He was doing what I think a good general officer does and goes out and visits the gang and showed his support."

"Did you have a conversation with Gen. Hornburg where you were asked by Gen. Hornburg if you had any problems?"

"Yes."

"What, if anything, did you tell Gen. Hornburg?"

"I told him that there were communications difficulties with the CAOC."

"What, if anything, was his reaction to that?"

"He made a phone call in front of me."

"Was there anyone present when you had that conversation with him?"

"Yes."

"Could you describe what the nature of that person would be?"

"We were in—I believe we were in a hardened Suburban driving around on Ahmed Al Jaber Air Base. I believe the ACC/DO was in the car. I know Army Brigadier-General [Thomas] Csrnko was in the car and I don't remember the names of the other two people."

"Did you describe specifically the communication problems you were having with the CAOC?"

"It was a brief conversation that he initiated and I just said that I was having trouble expressing my concerns; 'I think they're not listening to us,' is what I said."

"And that related to the fact that you weren't being provided information about friendly ground forces and close air support, et cetera?"

"Yes, and the airspace specifically in Operation Anaconda."

"What was Gen. Hornburg's reaction and what did he do?"

"He made a phone call."

"How would you characterize the nature of that phone call? Was he animated?"

"He seemed a little angry."

"Do you know who he called?"

"I don't. I think he attempted to call the component air commander, but I'm not sure."

"Did you get a phone call later that night after Gen. Hornburg had talked to whomever he talked to?"

"No, I did not."

"You weren't told that Gen. Moseley was trying to fire you because you went behind his back to the ACC Commander?"

"That happened the next day."

"So it was the next day that you got that phone call?"

"I don't know exactly when that happened."

"It did happen?"

"Yes," Col. Nichols says.

⌣

"What, if any, opinion do you have about this situation, what happened with Maj. Schmidt and Maj. Umbach, regarding the fog of war?" Gittins asks.

"Tremendous fog of war because there was no way there should be any friendly forces shooting things that we didn't know about. You can't imagine that there, in the middle of the night, an exchange or weapons that actually proceeded vertically in a combat zone while you're flying. It's—to me, until then, it was unimaginable."

"Yes, sir."

"If there was, in fact, going to be, I would know about it."

⌣

"Subsequent to the accident, did you serve on an awards board in Abu Dhabi?" Gittins asks.

"Yes," Col. Nichols answers.

"Did you have an opportunity to have a social interaction with General Stephen Wood?"

"Yes."

"And that's the same General Stephen Wood who was the CAOC operations director on the night of the accident?"

"Yes."

"What, if anything, did he say to you about his interactions on that night?"

"I don't remember the exact words that he said, but I think we expressed mutually that we hoped that all the causes of the incident would get fixed, that there was lot of information-exchanging problems at all levels and I think that was the nature of it. We both hoped that this would never, ever happen again and that we could fix the problem."

"Did he candidly advise you that he thought his career was over as a result of this?"

"I don't remember explicitly, but I think he did express that concern."

"To your knowledge, was he subsequently promoted?"

"He is a major-general now, and he was a brigadier-general, I believe, then."

"Sir, as the commander who was in charge of 332nd AEG on the night of this accident, do you have any opinion about Maj. Schmidt's future utility as an Air Force or Air National Guard pilot?"

"Yes, I do."

"If you would share that opinion with the investigating officer, what do you think Maj. Schmidt can do for the Air Force and for the Air National Guard?"

"I think prior to the incident on 17 April, he is one of the best F-16 pilots that I have witnessed. Watching his tapes and watching him brief and debrief, his conduct in the Mission Planning Cell and the respect, which is very important in our business, that other fighter pilots have for him, of all the systems, not just because of his experience in the F-18 and A-10. I believe that this experience can help us get through this transformational era that we're in. Guys like him can lead the fight with credibility and we need to ensure that things like this [don't] happen. This is why. I was there. The system works. It defends us. And for the right of everybody that has to pull a trigger or drop a bomb in the future, it is essential that they have confidence in our service and our leadership across the board, that command and organizations will remain behind them and he can be proof of that as we step out and we sort through the answers here. I believe that to be the same of Maj. Umbach."

"Sir," Charlie Gittins says. "Do you think Maj. Schmidt and Maj. Umbach should be prosecuted criminally for the accident on the 17 April 2002?"

"No."

"That's all I have, sir."

⌣

"Do you believe that what they did, the actions they took, were the actions of reasonably prudent pilots under the same or similar circumstances?" Dave Beck asks Col. Nichols.

"Yes. The span of activities is very large and combat aviation is not a science. It's an art of which we build scientific building blocks to accomplish the skill level that these two were at and the span of reasonable responses is relatively large, so yes."

"In the same or similar circumstances, different pilots may do different things depending on what they see, not only on a HUD tape but what they see outside the aircraft, is that correct?"

"Correct."

"And you need to consider all of that, don't you?"

"Yes."

"And you yourself have had combat situations where to be defensive you've reacted differently, depending on what you saw and understood at the time, is that correct?"

"Yes."

"Again, based on what you know these two knew—that is, Maj. Umbach and Maj. Schmidt—based on the intelligence briefs that they had, without discussing what they are, based on information and lack of information, you believe what they did was reasonable under the circumstances?"

"Yes."

"You do not believe that anything they did was reckless or unreasonable under the circumstances, do you?"

"No."

"Prior to April 17th, how many times had you expressed concerns to the command about lack of information available to pilots and aircrew?"

"We expressed it a lot in many different ways, but the people in the Air Combat Command had a very difficult process working with the Joint Force Headquarters and the other component commands that were in the process, and that—I can't skip them. I have to go to them and I had my intel people, I had the major level, the lieutenant-colonel level, the captain level. I tried every way I could. I think everybody was grasping for information."

"Was the concern about lack of information to aircrews, lack of information to them before the flight, during the flight, or even after they came back from the flight?"

"All of the above," Col. Nichols says. "I wanted them to know where friendlies were and what they were doing. I wanted to know where the bad guys were and what they were doing. I wanted to know their capabilities."

"Why were you particularly concerned about lack of information with regard to friendlies?"

"I was afraid something like this would happen."

"Did you make that known to your superiors?"

"Yes."

⌣

"Did anybody to your knowledge from the CAOC attend the CAS [Close Air Support] symposium?"

"No one assigned to the CAOC staff did. There was the CENTAF safety officer, Colonel Dan Constantini, there."

"Did he come there specifically for that or did he happen to be there?"

"He happened to be there doing his safety responsibilities."

"The concerns that you had, and I'm not going to go into them because the investigating officer has them, but the concerns that you expressed and slides that were discussed in the CAS symposium, did they only apply to an operation in a combat situation or did they apply to OEF, specifically what happened on April 17th?"

"It was across the board. We were hoping that we could establish procedures and processes and understanding it's an asymmetric—we were hoping we could establish processes that aircrew members, that staff members, aircraft controllers, Ground FACs, the C flight could agree upon to enhance the process of executing this mission across the board."

⌣

Greg Graf is the first on the prosecution side to cross-examine Col. Nichols. "You had earlier testified that you believed that the actions taken by Maj. Schmidt and Maj. Umbach were reasonable, do you recall that testimony?"

"Yes."

"Did you base that opinion on whether or not they had taken Go-pills or No-go pills or was that your opinion regardless?"

"My opinion regardless."

"And based on what you saw in the video, do you base that opinion—do you base that opinion based on what you saw on the targeting pod and the heads-up displays and what you were told by the pilots, or do you base that because they told you it had no effect on them?"

"The reference to the No-go pills?"

"Yes."

"I base that on the fact that I believe in the Air Force program that they have gone through the necessary wickets whatever those, I'm not a doctor, and it was provided by my service that they're good. It should have no effect except to keep you awake when needed."

"I don't want to phrase this in a way that anybody thinks I'm making light of this, but based on what you saw, even if they were as high as a kite, you still think what they did was tactically sound?"

"Yes."

"By the way," Col. Graf says, "did either pilot ever tell you that they thought they were affected by Go/No-go pills?"

"Not that I recall."

⌣

"Issuing authority to engage a ground contact would normally be something you would get from the CAOC, correct?" Col. Graf asks.

"Yes."

"Unless there is a Ground FAC or an Air FAC in the vicinity?"

"Yes."

"And to the best of your knowledge with that being Coffee, it was not operating under the authority or in conjunction with an Air FAC or a Ground FAC, correct?"

"No."

"So the only release authority that could allow them to do this would have been the CAOC, correct?"

"Yes."

"And the somewhat cumbersome and lengthy process of the AWACS having to transmit that to the CAOC, the CAOC making a decision in getting back, caused some delays, correct?"

"Yes."

"Now during that period of time, and I know we're Monday morning quarterbacking, but while Maj. Schmidt and Maj. Umbach were waiting for clearance to engage the target, would that have been, based on what you saw, would that have been an opportunity for them to get out of the immediate threat area and set up for a first-run attack?"

"That is a course of action they could have taken, yes."

Col. Graf takes Col. Nichols back to the very beginning of the engagement, when the pilots took off their NVGs, flipped on their exterior lights, and headed toward FOSSIL 22, the refueling tanker. "Turning your lights on would make you more easily seen by potential enemies?" he asks.

"Yes," Col. Nichols answers.

"And they're on their way to FOSSIL 22. If their goggles are off and they see some surface-to-air fire or surface fire, since they don't have their goggles on they don't have that illusion. They see that, at that point in time to make a SAFIRE report—a proper SAFIRE report—would have been, for example, surface-to-air fire, three miles south of Kandahar and then an elevation of how high the tracers were going. The time, information like that, would have all been in a proper SAFIRE report, is that correct?"

"Yes."

"During this period of time where there was extremely tight control, you don't know of any other incidents where an aircrew then decided to engage those SAFIREs, correct?"

"Correct."

"And it would be your testimony that your problem is that they should have went on to FOSSIL 22 instead of going and sticking their nose into an area where they might become defensive, correct?"

"They could have gone on to FOSSIL 22," Col. Nichols says. "It's one of the choices that they had."

"And you would agree that if they perceived surface-to-air fire they were not supposed to put themselves in a position where they might become defensive, correct?"

"Correct."

⌣

"I'm not going to go in tit-for-tat with every question," Dave Beck tells Col. Nichols. "But now you've seen the tapes, you've talked to the pilots, you have to know the pilots, you have to know what they've said, based on everything you have seen and heard and you've been asked repeatedly, again and again, there is nothing that either of those two pilots did, Maj. Umbach or Maj. Schmidt, that you yourself or any other reasonable F-16 pilot may not have done—may have done yourselves under the same or similar circumstances, is that correct, sir?"

"That's true."

★ ★ ★

The U.S. Air Force has been losing the public relations battle since day one. Hands down. A long week later, the satellite trucks are still here, lining the parking lot beside the makeshift courthouse. The cameras aren't allowed to film the hearing, but they are certainly not desperate for sound bites. In interview after interview, the pilots' lawyers and their growing posse of supporters have been more than willing to tell the country what's really happening at Barksdale Air Force Base, the cover-up that is so obvious to everyone but the four prosecutors. Joan Schmidt, Harry's tireless mother, recently showed up in Louisiana, proclaiming her son's innocence to the cameras. Bob Umbach, Bill's brother, has also done the satellite truck junket. John Russo, too.

Inside, Charlie Gittins pounces on government witnesses, tossing pens and firing objection after objection. During many recesses, he turns left down the hallway to visit the press room, just in case some of the hacks didn't notice how he just destroyed that person's credibility. Sometimes, he passes out documents, like his client's "Fitness Reports" from the past four years. "Schmidt is the finest combination of officership and tactical skill!" one reads. "World-class tactician, patriot, born warrior-leader. Groom him for fighter command now!" He is a "solid gold performer," a "pure superstar." What gives you the right to question the actions of a pure superstar?

The Air Force is trying, in its own subtle way, to score a few points in the court of public opinion. There was Col. Demitry, the Go-pills pusher. Two full-colonel fighter pilots were also deployed to the media center, answering technical questions about how to deliver a laser-guided bomb.

(Read: How not to do what Maj. Schmidt did.) Amid the spinfests, prosecutors have remained quiet, prohibited from saying a single word outside the hearing room. As hard as it is to sit back and watch the hourly defense press briefings, their job is to present the evidence to Col. Rosenow—not to living rooms across North America.

But even that isn't going as well as planned. Maj. Milton: I might have done the same thing. Lt.-Col. Viets: Dropping the bomb was a reasonable move. Lt.-Col. Fisher: The pilots' actions were not unreasonable. Col. Nichols: I might have done the same thing. Everyone: I had never heard of Tarnak Farm before April 17, 2002.

On Sunday afternoon, the first day off since the hearing began, John Odom picks up his telephone and calls Randolph Air Force Base in Texas. An operator patches him through to the home of General Stephen T. Sargeant, the American co-president of the Coalition Investigation Board.

"I wondered when you'd call," Gen. Sargeant tells the colonel.

"Can you tell the investigating officer what position you served in in the CAOC?" asks Maj. James Floyd, one of the prosecutors.

"The name of the position was the defensive duty officer, DDO for short," answers Maj. Marshall Scott Woodson III. Commonly known as "The Voice of the CAOC," the DDO speaks directly to the AWACS planes flying in theater. On April 17, 2002, when Maj. Art Henry called Saudi Arabia with Harry Schmidt's request to open fire, he was speaking to Maj. Woodson—Call Sign K-Mart.

The first witness to testify when the hearing reconvenes Monday morning, Maj. Woodson sits and listens as prosecutors play a never-before-released recording of the satellite radio calls exchanged between the AWACS and the CAOC as the F-16s circled over Tarnak Farm. Maj. Schmidt and Maj. Umbach could not hear these transmissions from inside their cockpits.

K-Mart, this is BOSSMAN. Coffee 51 Flight has experienced SAFIRE near the city of Kandahar, requesting permission to open up with 20-mm. I'll try to get you a little more information. We told them to hold fire.

BOSSMAN, K-Mart. We copy report reference Coffee. We need SAFIRE details from Coffee when able and hold fire.

Roger. He's invoking self-defense ROE on the fire. On the road he sees artillery shooting at him. Standby for details.

BOSSMAN, K-Mart, be advised Kandahar has friendlies. You are to get Coffee 51 out of there as soon as possible.

Maj. Schmidt's bomb is already plummeting toward the wadi. *Roger, we'll get him out of there right now.* Shack.

"After the 17th of April, were you interviewed by the Coalition Investigation Board?" Maj. Floyd asks.

"I was, yes," Maj. Woodson answers.

"And approximately how long was that after the 17th of April?"

"It was early May. It was about three weeks, approximately."

"Were you provided an opportunity to review your testimony that you gave before the Coalition Investigation Board?"

"Yes. And to the extent that there might be some inconsistencies between what you told that board and what is actually on the tape, I'd like you to tell the investigating officer, in front of Gen. Sargeant and the board, were you saying things to intentionally mislead them or anything like that?"

"No."

"What were you giving them at the time?"

"I was giving them my recollection off the top of my head."

"And you said that approximately three weeks passed between this incident and when the Coalition Investigation Board happened?"

"Right. It was about three weeks, roughly. And I had been in the CAOC every night since the, in between the incident and the board interview, a whole lot of nights, a whole lot of hours, and thousands of radio calls."

"What would you have more confidence in, in terms of what actually happened: what's on the tape or your recollection when you were testifying at the proceeding?"

"What's on the tape."

Maj. Floyd has figured out the defense team's strategy. Witness after witness, they have tried to expose inconsistencies between what the officers told Gen. Sargeant and Gen. Dumais and what actually occurred that night. As expected, Lt.-Col. Clay Moushon, one of Maj. Schmidt's lawyers, begins his cross-examination with a copy of Maj. Woodson's testimony to the CIB. He told the board that as soon as the 20 mike–mike call came over the radio, Lt.-Col. Craig Fisher—the chief of combat operations and his direct boss— told him to pass along a "hold fire" *and* an order to get the pilots out of the area. As evident in the transcript, the call to "get Coffee 51 out of there as soon as possible" did not occur until after BOSSMAN's second transmission, after Maj. Schmidt announced he was rolling in in self-defense.

"Isn't it true that when you were asked this issue before the Coalition Board, your testimony before the Coalition Board was that upon the first call from AWACS to K-Mart, Col. Fisher told you to respond: 'Denied, get them out of the area'?"

"Okay, if that's what it says."

"Is that your recollection of what was said?"

"It's been nine months since then, so—or eight months or whatever. But if that's what it says, then that's what I said."

"And if Col. Fisher had told you on the first call to tell BOSSMAN to get Coffee 51 and 52 out of the area, then that was the transmission you should have passed from K-Mart to BOSSMAN?"

"Right. I believe I passed whatever he asked me to pass, because he was listening. And if I made a mistake or said something he didn't want me to say or not said something he wanted me to say, then at that point he would have said something otherwise."

"Maj. Woodson, at any time during the evening of April 17th prior to the bomb being dropped by Coffee 52, did you ever know that friendly Canadian forces were actually on the ground?"

"No."

⌣

"Maj. Woodson, when you were asked to give information to BOSS-MAN, did you give that information to BOSSMAN?" Maj. Floyd, the prosecutor, asks.

"Yes."

"By Col. Fisher? Regardless of what the sequence is? I mean, do you trust the sequence on the tapes as being accurate?"

"Yes."

★ ★ ★

Maj. Art Henry, the Canadian exchange officer who commanded the AWACS crew that night, is at Barksdale Air Force Base today. So is Capt. David Pepper, the AWACS senior director who just happened to be in the bathroom when Bill Umbach noticed the fireworks. Both men flew to Louisiana on the assumption that they would have to testify, that they would have to endure another grilling similar to the one that Gen. Sargeant and Gen. Dumais put them through a couple weeks after the bombing. But by Monday afternoon, prosecutors decide to call only one witness who was on board the radar plane: TSgt. Michael Carroll, the man who was speaking directly to the F-16s.

"That night I was sitting as tanker controller," TSgt. Carroll says. "Before that I was sitting strike controller and it just varies on the different aircraft you're talking to. That night I was sitting in the tanker controller, which involves keeping track of all your tankers out there and what tanker tracks they're in out there, what their fuel load is, and how much time they have available out there."

"Is the tanker controller position and the strike controller position essentially different names under the weapons director?" Maj. Floyd asks.

"Yes, sir."

"So you would switch back and forth to either role?"

"I would switch back and I'm over there switching every four missions, I believe."

TSgt. Carroll recalls how the pilots called him shortly after their on-call mission finished. They needed gas, so he vectored them toward a tanker—FOSSIL 22—approximately 70 nautical miles south of their position. A few minutes later, the pilots were reporting SAFIRE and asking for permission to take a mark.

"Did Coffee Flight ever give you any indication that they were defensive?" Maj. Floyd asks. "In other words, that they were being shot at?"

"Not that I recall, no."

"Would you expect that you would recall, if you heard a defensive call or that they were being shot at, that you would remember that?"

"Yes, sir."

"Up until Coffee Flight's request to employ 20 mike-mike, was there anything significant about what they had reported to you?"

"Not that I remember, no."

"Had you received SAFIRE reports before or were you aware of those?"

"Yeah, I think we had received one or two since we had been in theater."

"And were those reports fairly common?"

"Pretty common, I mean when you heard on the ground—you know, even our flight deck had reported some SAFIRE events."

"The request to employ 20 mike-mike, is that what got your attention?"

"That caught my attention, yes, sir."

"You sat up and started to get excited about that?"

"Yes, sir."

"Do you ever recall Coffee 51 or 52—again, off of the transcript portion that you've heard of the audio—ever ask you specifically if there were any friendlies in the area of the SAFIRE event that they had reported?"

"No."

"And, again, would that be something that if they would ask: 'Hey, are there friendlies in the area,' would you recall that?"

"Yes, sir."

"And again, do you ever recall them asking you if there were friendlies in the area prior to them requesting to engage?"

"No, sir."

"Or after their request to engage, do you recall them asking if there were friendlies in the area?"

"No, sir."

⌣

"Did you know there were friendlies around Kandahar?" asks Capt. Roderick, one of Maj. Umbach's military attorneys.

"At the time, no, sir."

"Did you know there was an ROZ around that area?"

"Did I know there was an ROZ around Kandahar? No, sir."

"And did you have the ACO onboard?"

"Yes, sir."

"The information regarding where the friendly ground forces were to you was virtually non-existent, is that correct?"

"Yeah, exact positions—yeah, was non-existent, yes, sir."

"Had you known about the live-fire exercise that night, would you have told the Coffee Flight?"

"Yes, sir."

"Should you have had that information as command control AWACS?"

"I think it would have been good to have that information, yes, sir."

⌣

"You did testify before the board," Capt. Jamie Key says. "Was it about two weeks after this all happened?"

"Yes, sir," TSgt. Carroll says.

"Is it safe to say your memory was probably a little bit better back then?"

"Probably."

"Do you remember testifying there that Coffee 51 contacted you saying that they were taking fire?" Capt. Key asks, referring to the unknown period of time before the tapes came on.

"I don't remember that now. I mean, I can imagine, I don't know, I guess the call when they were saying they were in self-defense, I guess that is probably what I was talking about."

"I'm talking about the initial call, the first call they made to you after you took control of the aircraft."

"Okay. I'd like to tell you that I remember, but I don't."

"That's fine. But you did determine, as best you can remember, that they thought something was shooting up in the air?"

"Yes, sir."

"Do you remember testifying in front of the board that they came back and started giving you position information, but you didn't think it was very clear?"

"Yeah, I remember them giving position information and we passed it, but it seemed like nothing was actually ever clear exactly where the SAFIRE was."

"But," Capt. Key says, moments later, "you told us you could tell exactly where Coffee Flight was."

"Yes, sir."

"I can't remember exactly what I had on my scope, whether I would have had Kandahar on there or not. So I don't remember."

⌣

"Would it be safe to say that as an AWACS crew member, you're pretty much as good as the information you get?" Capt. Key asks.

"Yes, sir."

"And, at the base root of the information that you have about what's going on in the air comes from the CAOC?"

"Yes, sir."

"Is that the reason why, later on in the transcript, that when Coffee said that they didn't know about any active Restricted Operating Zones, you concurred?"

"Right," TSgt. Carroll answers. "I remember the call, and I asked Capt. Pepper and Maj. Henry at the time, over Net 2, if they knew about anything and they said: 'tell them negative' and that we agreed. So I went out and told them that."

When it's his turn again, Maj. Floyd revisits the "taking fire" issue. Prosecutors don't believe for a second that the pilots ever said they were being shot at before they activated their recorders. To them, it is an all-too-convenient story, considering there is no recording to back it up. "Nowhere on that tape up until there is a request for 20 mike-mike and there is 'rolling in in self-defense,' there is no indication that they are under attack prior to that, is there?" Maj. Floyd asks.

"Not that I recall, no," TSgt. Carroll answers.

"And during the time off the tape, after they had checked in for their tanker and they called a SAFIRE report, you were never under the impression from any words that they were speaking to you that they were under attack?"

"Not that I recall, no."

"And you would recall that?"

"I would think I would recall that, yes, sir."

"I mean you would remember if something like—"

"I would remember something like that."

"And they never said prior to the self-defense or whatever you took that to mean—you never heard the words that they were defensive?"

"No."

★ ★ ★

When Col. Odom announces his next witness, the entire defense table erupts. Gen. Sargeant! The pilots' attorneys wanted to put the CIB president on the stand all along, but they were told he was unavailable, way too busy with his other Air Force duties to come to Louisiana. Yet now, when the government needs him, he suddenly has some free time on his hands.

Defense lawyers demand to know what fresh insights the general can possibly offer. He led the investigation that pinned the blame on the pilots. He preferred the criminal charges. It's no secret what he's going to say: Harry and Bill were reckless. "This is not justice," Dave Beck tells the judge. "This is ridiculous."

However, amid all the yelling, Col. Odom suggests that Gen. Sargeant does indeed have something new to add, something that wasn't contained in his lengthy report: He believes the pilots—or at least Maj. Schmidt— were so fixated on dropping a bomb that they falsely invoked self-defense to override the "hold fire" order. In other words, Psycho Schmidt was itching for a fight, and nothing the AWACS had to say was going to stop him. "He will state his opinion, that it appeared to him as setting up an attack and using self-defense as a pretext to launch an attack and violate the rules of engagement," Col. Odom tells Col. Rosenow.

"He's going to come in and testify it was murder!" Charlie Gittins shouts back, throwing his pen onto the table. After a few more interruptions, Col. Rosenow eventually rules that there is nothing in the law that prohibits Gen. Sargeant from taking the stand. Col. Odom is free to call his witness.

For those who have followed this case closely, who have spent the past week watching the closed-circuit feed, Gen. Sargeant's sudden appearance is the stuff of Hollywood courtroom drama. For two months, he did the grilling, intimidating dozens of witnesses as co-president of the Coalition Investigation Board. The roles are now reversed. For the next two-and-a-half days, the improbably named Gen. Sargeant will be on the receiving end of the questions.

But not yet. Col. Odom asks Judge Rosenow for a recess so he can interview the one-star general in advance of his testimony. Again, defense lawyers are outraged. "We've worked like galley slaves up to this point, sir," Gittins objects. "I mean, why are we stopping working like galley slaves because the government is in trouble?"

"Now that is the third time Mr. Gittins has made a cheap-shot remark and I'm tired of them," Col. Odom says.

"Stop it, both of you," Judge Rosenow says, his skill as a basketball referee starting to show.

"We've been in court for 10 hours already—" Col. Odom says.

"Stop, I'm not done," Judge Rosenow says. "Here's what we're going to do, alright. I know it's been a long day. I know it's been a long day for everybody. Defense, really, I know you don't want to have him testify at all, but I'm getting the sense from the defense you'd really like the overnight to prep for cross?"

"Yes, sir," Gittins says.

"All right. Here's what we'll do. I'm going to ask you to come back at—I'll give you an hour and a half to two hours to prep. The prep shouldn't take that long."

"Wait a minute," Col. Odom says. "Then if we start in two hours from now, it's 8 o'clock, and I'm supposed to start a direct examination of a general officer witness and go an hour and a half until 9:30, so that we're in crew rest. I mean, a 13-hour courtroom day? Judge, that's just not fair."

"Go-pills, sir," Gittins says.

"That's not particularly funny," Col. Rosenow says.

"I know it isn't, sir."

"It's about the only humor to that defense," Col. Odom says.

In the end, Judge Rosenow leaves the decision to the witness, Gen. Sargeant. "How are you, as far as freshness, feeling about trying to do an evening session this evening?"

"Given the amount of sleep that I had and the travel time to get here yesterday, et cetera, I would like to waive an evening session if possible and come back tomorrow." Done.

Standing on the walkway outside, Dave Beck and Charlie Gittins brag to the cameras that their opponents are clearly desperate. Every prosecution witness has been a catastrophic bust, conceding that Maj. Schmidt and Maj. Umbach acted within reason during those few minutes over Tarnak Farm. "After the government's case is in the toilet, they go and find the general who preferred the charges to call him to testify about his opinions in a report that is absolutely among the worst products that have ever been produced in military history," Gittins says.

But as outraged as they are by Gen. Sargeant's surprise appearance, it is the type of twist that both lawyers—especially Charlie Gittins—live for. It is the chance to embarrass a general officer, to prove what they've been saying all along: Gen. Moseley, the commander of the Afghanistan air war, appointed his toady, Gen. Sargeant, to fix blame on the pilots. "By the time you hear Gen. Sargeant finish," Gittins says, "you will be convinced that this is a big railroad job."

chapter thirty-one

"When you attended the Fighter Weapons School as a student, I believe you were a distinguished graduate of the Weapons School?" Col. Odom asks.

"That's correct," Gen. Sargeant answers.

"In the vernacular of the fighter pilot community, you are yourself a Patch Wearer, correct?"

"I am."

"Sir, briefly, the United States Air Force Fighter Weapons School at Nellis Air Force Base in Nevada was where you served as commandant, is that correct?"

"That's correct."

"Would it be fair to say that you have debriefed literally thousands of missions, either your own or those of students or of student pilots that you were training?"

"Yes," Gen. Sargeant says.

This would typically be the point in the day when prosecutors queue up the targeting pod videos for another frame-by-frame dissection. But with the general on the stand, Col. Odom introduces a new exhibit, a one-page PowerPoint presentation depicting an overhead map of Kandahar. Near the top of the black-and-white map is the airfield, the home base of TF Rakkasan. In the center of the page, marked by a small red circle, is the invisible ROZ—the Restricted Operating Zone—that was in place over Tarnak Farm. A tiny red triangle inside the hoop pinpoints the exact spot where 3 Section was hunkered in the sand.

As the PowerPoint rolls, two colored arrows appear on the bottom of the page, both heading north. On the left, a blue one. Maj. Umbach's jet. On the right, Maj. Schmidt, colored green.

Do ya got good coordinates for a mark, or do ya need me to roll in? Ah, standby. I'll mark it right now. Copy. I'm in from the southeast.

As the audio rolls, arrows continue to appear, one after the other, like footprints in the mud, depicting the precise flight paths of both F-16s. The blue arrows, Maj. Umbach, continue north. The green, Maj. Schmidt, veer left, steering directly toward the red circle in the middle of the page.

All right, if you get a dive toss SPI, I can take that and make it a point off of it. Hhhuuhhhh, hhhhhhhhhhhhhhuuuhhhh. Hhhhuuhh, hhuhh.

The green arrows, inching toward Tarnak Farm, veer right. *Okay, BOSSMAN. This is Coffee 52. I've got a tally on the vicinity. I, ah, request permission to lay down some, uh, 20 mike-mike. Standby. Let's just make sure that it's, uh, that's it not friendlies, that's all.*

Maj. Schmidt continues his right turn, flying his Viper east away from the flashes. On the other side of the page, the blue arrows remain in a wide right turn, more than six miles away from the unknown fireworks. At one point, the blue footprints pass right overtop of the Kandahar Airfield.

When you get a chance put it on the SPI, if you've got a good hack on it. Hhhuhhhhh, hhhuhhh. Hhhuhh, hhhhhhhhhhhhhhhhhhhuuuh.

Maj. Schmidt straightens out his right turn. The green arrows are now pointing west—back toward Tarnak Farm. *Okay, I'm going to flow down here to the, uh, southwest. BOSSMAN from Coffee 52. Do you want us to push a different freq? Check my sparkles, check my sparkles. See if it looks good.*

By now, Maj. Umbach's blue arrows have combined to form a wide semi-circle, never getting closer than five nautical miles from the firing range. The green arrows—Maj. Schmidt's—resemble the number 9. Left toward the ground fire, right away from it, then back underneath. He is 3.3 nautical miles south of the Carl Gustav, flying at more than 13,000 feet, when his flight lead asks him to check his sparkles.

Coffee 51, BOSSMAN. Hold fire. Need details on SAFIRE for K-Mart. Okay, I've got a, uh, I've got some men on a road and it looks like a piece of artillery firing at us. I am rolling in in self-defense. The green arrows turn right one more time, heading northeast, Tarnak Farm approaching on the right. Maj. Umbach's F-16—the jet Maj. Schmidt is rolling in to protect—is nearly seven nautical miles away from the men on the road, flying at approximately 22,000 feet.

Check master arm, laser arm. And check you're not in mark. Got 'em both on. I'm in from the southwest. Do you show 'em on a bridge? Bomb's away, cranking left. Check wide field of view. I'm fine. Laser's on. Shack.

It is a chilling exhibit. You can't see the tiny dots in the wadi, or the GBU–12 crashing into Pte. Green. But what is left, the arrow-shaped footprints, reveal just how differently—drastically differently—each pilot reacted to the ground fire. While Maj. Umbach's jet remained in a wide right turn the entire time, far away from the target, Maj. Schmidt left behind a zig-zagged trail of green arrows, left, then right, then right again, descending, climbing, slowing down, speeding up.

"When the tapes begin and the initial positioning of the aircrews is shown, is either Coffee 51 or Coffee 52 in any kind of threat envelope?" Col. Odom asks Gen. Sargeant.

"At this point, no."

"Would it have been possible for them to simply continue on in flight?"

"Yes, and I would like to further explain if I may." Both jets, the general says, were above 20,000 feet when Maj. Umbach first saw the fireworks. It also appears that Bill took an "overfly mark," capturing the coordinates directly underneath his F–16 at around the same time as the tapes came on. "Those coordinates do not plot out in the Tarnak Farms area, but they are not grossly far from it," Gen. Sargeant says. "At that point, since sighting a SAFIRE, they could have in fact continued on to the tanker and passed what information that they did, since there was a large known concentration of coalition forces at Kandahar."

"The entire time you have listened," Col. Odom asks later, "what, if any, defensive calls do you hear?"

"I hear no defensive calls between the fighters. I hear no defensive calls, or calls for help from the controlling agencies to the fighters, and I hear no call from any party on the ground through a controlling agency asking for help."

"Is that significant to you?"

"Yes, it is."

"And for what reason?"

"It is significant to me if we are trying to establish self-defense as the reason for dropping the bomb on the Tarnak Farms that evening, then

I would expect, with my experience, that there would have been communication between the two fighters. There would have been a sense of urgency expressed through the communication and there would have been evidence throughout this tape and the other tapes that this hearing has had available to them, the other processes like this, to demonstrate the maneuvering, to have seen maneuvering that would have reflected defensive-type maneuvering. If in fact there was a problem with communication, there still should have been evidence of defensive maneuvering."

"With regard to Maj. Umbach—he was the flight lead—would you explain to the investigating officer what violations of his duties as flight lead you noted in your review of the tapes concerning Maj. Umbach's performance?"

"Well," Gen. Sargeant says, "if you'll look at the still picture now, you'll see the proximity that 52 gets to that known SAFIRE area and puts himself in jeopardy." Maj. Schmidt dips his jet well below the 15,000-foot altitude floor mandated by the rules of engagement, and at one point, he almost descends below 10,000 feet—a maneuver that is prohibited without clearance from higher authorities. "What I find striking, in listening back to the tape, is that there is no challenge and response going on. When Maj. Umbach makes a statement, for instance—a very important statement—about… 'let's just make sure there's no friendlies at all,' there's no response from the wingman, 52."

"What would you expect the flight lead to do when he gave a call such as that and received nothing back?" Col. Odom asks.

"Then I would expect him to challenge the wingman and make sure that he heard that and take steps to ensure that in fact there were no friendlies. And the way they would do that is amongst themselves, plus using the controlling agency that they had available that night, AWACS." Later, Maj. Umbach asked Maj. Schmidt: "Do you show 'em on a bridge?" Again, his wingman didn't answer. "It is common technique between pilots to ensure that what they are looking at is the same," Gen. Sargeant says. "And if there's no response there when you are about to drop a bomb, a live bomb, the flight lead has a responsibility to query and make sure that is indeed the target that he wants his wingman to drop a bomb on…That lack of challenge and response 'on a bridge' is very important because in the communication that follows this attack, then Maj. Schmidt actually says 'not quite' in response to the description again given by Maj. Umbach as to where that target was."

"What does that lead you to conclude?" Col. Odom asks. "The interplay 'not quite'?"

"That in fact Maj. Schmidt had control of the situation and was directing where that bomb was going to go."

"In any of the plane-to-plane chatter, did you hear any change of lead?"

"I hear no change in lead," the general says. "I hear no declaration of defensive. I hear no declaration from one airplane to the other to go defensive in any reaction to a perceived threat from the ground."

"What responsibility would the flight lead have to make sure his wingman was compliant with the ROE and the SPINS?"

"He has the ultimate responsibility for his flight, and ensuring that his wingman stays out of the threat envelope is very important because the SPINS and the ROE are there to not only, not only prevent fratricide, which is an over-arching goal. Those SPINS and ROE are also to preserve the lives of our airmen and their assets that they are flying, their air vehicles. And so he has the responsibility to take his wingman out and bring his wingman back."

$\smile$

"Gen. Sargeant, with regard to the airmanship of Maj. Schmidt that night, did you find deficiencies in his handling of his airplane as well from your review of the tapes and the investigation?" Col. Odom asks.

"Yes, I did," the one-star general says. "As you can see from the green arrows on the diagram here, Maj. Schmidt now flies toward the area where they believe the SAFIRE to be occurring, and as he's doing that, he does two things that are very important—three things. One, he's closing the range, the slant range, down to that unknown activity that is going on, other than a SAFIRE at this point. He is descending in his altitude, which further puts him into an envelope, a threat envelope. And during this time he will allow his airspeed to bleed down from tactical airspeed to a very vulnerable airspeed, putting himself and his airplane potentially into harm's way if in fact there is a threat there." As evident in the diagram, Gen. Sargeant says, Maj. Schmidt had numerous opportunities to simply fly away from ground fire. "But he sets himself up to continue back into the threat envelope again and further putting himself and his aircraft at risk, in violation of the SPINS and the ROE and, in my opinion, this is a reckless disregard for the SPINS and the ROE."

"When he went up over the top of that turn out to the east, that's when his airspeed bled down to about 237 knots, is that correct?" Col. Odom asks, referring to the point when Harry asks to lay down some 20 mike-mike.

"That is correct."

"Is it your testimony that that is a tactically unsafe airspeed in any environment?"

"In fact, it is."

"When he made the turn to the right, when he made the turn out to the east, what could he have simply done?"

"He could have accelerated and begun a climb back out of the envelope that he had put himself in now, which was low and slow. He should have accelerated out of this fight."

"When Coffee 52 flows on down to the east and then makes the turn back to the west, that would be along that bottom track of green arrows that I'm indicating with the laser pointer," Col. Odom says. "Do you see where I'm pointing, sir?"

"Yes, I do."

"When he makes that turn back to the west, what is he doing?"

"He's now apparently setting himself back up, setting himself up in relation to that SAFIRE event on the ground, putting himself back into the threat envelope," Gen. Sargeant says. "He is putting himself back in, inside of the range that he had already established at this point in an attempt to maneuver in relation to that target and it appears that he is—is continuing to maneuver her to set himself up to attack this target."

"When Maj. Schmidt is at the point I've got indicated, the farthest eastern point, the farthest southern point, could he have simply kept on going to the south?"

"Yes."

"Should he have done so?"

"Yes, he should have."

"When he re-engaged and went back to the west, did he violate the SPINS and the ROE?"

"Yes, he did."

★ ★ ★

It is just after lunch on Tuesday, January 21, when Dave Beck first notices the five-line footnote near the end of the Coalition Investigation Board's executive summary: "Under 10 U.S.C. [United States Code] 2254(d) any opinion of the investigators as to the cause of, or the factors contributing to, the incident set forth in the investigation report may not be considered as evidence in any civil or criminal proceeding arising from such incidents." *Wait a second*, Beck thinks to himself. If that's the case, then Gen. Sargeant has no business being anywhere near that witness stand. It says right in the CIB report—a report that the general wrote and signed—that "any opinion of the investigators" cannot be used as evidence in court.

"Sir, could I note a strong objection?" Beck asks, reading the clause to Col. Rosenow. "Sir, I think we need to break because I believe we've violated the law by having any of his testimony."

"Is this the first time anybody has looked at this statute?" the judge asks.

"Yes," Beck answers.

The unexpected discovery is serious enough that Col. Rosenow orders a recess so he can examine the statute. "General," he says to the witness, "I'm really sorry, but we've got to make sure that we stay within the confines of the law. There's been a statute cited that's apparently in play that no one has raised until now. And like everything, we're all bound by the law and we've got to make sure we follow it."

"Absolutely," Gen. Sargeant says.

When Col. Rosenow reconvenes the hearing, he explains that Title 10, Section 2254, of the United States Code governs military AIBs—Accident Investigation Boards. The defense contends that Gen. Sargeant's Coalition Investigation Board was originally an AIB, and should therefore fall under the same jurisdiction of Title 10, Section 2254. Prosecutors argue that the board was actually a friendly fire investigation, a completely different beast ordered under the provisions of Department of Defense Instruction Number 6055.7, paragraphs E4.6 and E4.7.

"The normal process for an Article 32 hearing is if some side has an objection to evidence, the investigating officer notes the objection, brings the evidence into the hearing, receives the written objections after the fact by the parties, and then makes a determination of what to do with it," Col. Rosenow says. "I'm going to run this 32 like the rules I believe require me to run it, which is you have an objection under 2254. I'm going to consider that objection. I'll consider both your written submissions at the end of the evidence. I'll look at it and if I think 2254 and the law requires me not to consider it, I won't consider it. And I'm used to doing that. I've got enough cases under my belt as a judge so that if I grant a motion to suppress, that evidence is gone. I have absolutely no problem doing that at all." In other words, Col. Rosenow will continue to listen to what Gen. Sargeant has to say. But weeks from now, when he's crafting his final report for the commander of the 8th Air Force, he may decide that the defense team was right all along, and that the general's testimony is inadmissible.

But while solving one problem, the decision creates another. "Sir," says Capt. Matt Scoble, one of Maj. Umbach's military attorneys, "I've spoken with the chief circuit defense counsel of the Central Circuit. I have related to him my concerns that eliciting this sort of evidence would be an ethical violation. He concurs. And he's running up his chain as we speak. But until I get an advisory opinion, both from my chain of command and from my state bar, I don't feel like I can proceed."

"How long would it take you to get an advisory opinion from the bar?"

"I don't know, sir."

"Alright, who else?" Col. Rosenow asks. "Capt. Key?"

"Sir, I'd like the opportunity to contact my CCDC and ask him."

"You've not had a chance to talk to him yet?"

"No, sir, I've not," he says. "I was trying to research this issue."

"Col. Moushon and Capt. Roderick, are you okay?"

"Sir," Capt. Roderick says, "speaking for me, I don't feel comfortable with it at all."

"Well, I mean, do you want to go?"

"Will I stay?" the captain says back. "Yes, I'll stay."

"Well," the judge says, "I understand that you're not signing on to saying: 'Oh yes, Mr. Investigating Officer, I think you're doing the right thing.' I'm just asking, are you in the same position as Capt. Scoble where you believe you have to leave?"

"Not yet, because I still haven't heard from my state bar association," Capt. Roderick says. "And I would like to contact them."

Before Col. Rosenow orders another recess so the defense team can make some phone calls, Col. Odom tells the judge that he just talked to Lt.-Col. Jeffrey K. Walker, the legal advisor who worked on the CIB. "He said that paragraph is not supposed to be there," Col. Odom tells the judge. "It was a typographical error to have had it there. They use, as a guide for the manner in which the report is formatted, AIBs. But friendly fire is not an AIB. I might suggest to the investigating officer that it would be helpful, if you think we could move things along, it might be helpful—"

"But do I hear you saying you want to litigate this right now?" Col. Rosenow interrupts.

"Well, what I'm saying is we could take testimony from Lt.-Col. Walker—"

"Then you want to litigate it now?" the judge interrupts again. "I mean, the normal process is I don't rule on it, and that's what the rule is. The rule is that I don't rule on this stuff. I'm not supposed to."

"But normally we don't have all of the defense counsel, except the two civilian defense counsel, threatening to leave," Col. Odom points out.

"Well," Charlie Gittins chimes in, "I'm not particularly comfortable with this either, sir."

"Well, now we'll just add everybody," Col. Odom says, clearly flustered by the legal wrangling that has overshadowed his star witness.

"Well, he's not trying to leave, though," Judge Rosenow says. "Capt. Key, you go talk to your CCDC. We'll take a recess, and I'll consider what Col. Odom is saying."

"And I'll also point out, sir," Gittins says, "that Lt.-Col. Walker is being processed for an award that was initiated by Gen. Sargeant. So I'm not sure he would be an unbiased—"

"It sounds to me like you want to litigate this right away," Col. Rosenow says.

"I don't want to litigate it, sir, but I'll tell you—"

"Alright, fine. And we're not going to. We're in recess."

A few phone calls later, Col. Rosenow calls the hearing back to order. Everyone is back inside the hearing room, including Gen. Sargeant. "Given my ruling, we're going to proceed on now to further examination," Judge Rosenow says. "And I note that all counsel are sitting here: Capt. Key, Capt. Scoble, and Capt. Roderick. I take it from your presence here that you're ready to proceed on, at least through direct. Is that right?" All three nod their heads in agreement.

★   ★   ★

"Gen. Sargeant," Col. Odom says. "From your review of the tapes, did you find this to be a rapidly unfolding situation?"

"No, but I would like to elaborate on my answer. No, in that there was nothing in the tapes that showed me a sense of urgency that would force this situation to be rapidly drawing to the conclusion that it did."

"Do you believe that a reasonably prudent fighter pilot would have left the area as opposed to engage?"

"Yes."

"To your knowledge, Gen. Sargeant, in all of the sorties that have been flown in Operation Enduring Freedom, has any other emergent SAFIRE call ever been attacked, other than the Canadians on the night of April 17th?"

"No."

"Thank you, sir," Col. Odom says. "I'll pass the witness."

Cross-examination begins the next morning, 8 o'clock sharp.

★   ★   ★

For two days, Charlie Gittins has been bragging to the journalists, bracing them for the climactic moment in which he "destroys" Gen. Sargeant on the witness stand. "Wait until I'm through with him," is the oft-repeated phrase. You will finally understand the huge scope of this cover-up, how Gen. Sargeant and Gen. Moseley conspired to make sure the pilots took the fall—regardless of what the evidence said. Wednesday morning, as he strolls into the hearing room, Gittins looks downright giddy.

"Sir, I'd like to go a little bit into your background," he says to Gen. Sargeant. "You've testified that you have about 3,200 total aircraft hours?"

"That's correct." The general explains that more than half of those hours were spent in an F-16; the rest in A-10s. Not a single minute of that time, however, was flown in a war zone. In all his years as a fighter pilot, Gen. Sargeant has never been in combat.

"Would it be fair to say you have no hours of targeting pod time?" Gittins asks.

"That is correct," Gen. Sargeant answers.

"And since you have no time with the targeting pod, I would assume, also, that you're not qualified with the pod?"

"I was not qualified with the pod. I actually, in the front seat of an F-16, manipulated the pod with an instructor pilot on board, but was not qualified with the pod."

"My question was: Were you qualified?"

"No."

"Sir, how many hours do you have under night vision goggles?"

"A total of less than 10 hours under night vision goggles."

"The trial counsel, yesterday, asked you about being a Patch Wearer. That means you are a Fighter Weapons School graduate, sir, is that correct?"

"That is correct."

"You were a Patch Wearer in the A-10 aircraft, correct?"

"I earned my patch when I was qualified in the A-10 and continued to fulfill weapons officer duties in the F-16."

"Yes, sir," Gittins says. "You earned your Fighter Weapons School patch in the A-10, correct?"

"Yes."

"Yesterday, you answered in response to questions by Col. Odom that you, at the Fighter Weapons School, were a full-up instructor pilot at the Fighter Weapons School. Were you a full-up instructor pilot at the Fighter Weapons School in the F-16, sir?"

"No."

"Sir, have you ever flown with the LITENING pod, the same pod that was on the Coffee 51 and 52 flight on the incident night?"

"I did not."

"And so if you have never flown with that, I would also assume you've not trained in the pod?"

"I have not."

⌣

"When did you learn for the first time that you would be assigned as the investigating officer for the accident?"

"I learned that I would actually be assigned about mid-morning after the incident occurred in April."

"The day after?"

"Right. Once the—and again, depending on the time zone, etc., after the incident had happened and started running on CNN. So it was the next morning my time, in Arizona, when that data was out. I received a phone call that said I might be. And then, mid-morning, I received a call that said I was going to be the board president."

"And who called you, sir?"

"The first call I received was from Lt.-Gen. [John D.] Hopper."

"And what, if any, relationship did you have with Lt.-Gen. Hopper at the time?"

"Lt.-Gen. Hopper is the vice commander of Air Education and Training Command. I was a wing commander in Air Education and Training Command at that time."

"Had you received any calls prior to that, that gave you a heads-up that you might be tapped to be in charge of this investigation?"

"No, I did not."

"And who called to tell you, finally, that you had been confirmed as the president of the board?"

"That call came from Lt.-Gen. Moseley."

"Sir, with respect to Lt.-Gen. Moseley, had you been assigned with him on prior occasions?"

"I had been assigned under Gen. Moseley one time in the past, from a part of 1996 and part of 1997."

"Okay, you were assigned under him from 1996 to 1997. And what was your job?"

"My job was commandant of the United States Air Force Weapons School."

"And what was his job?"

"He was commander of the 57th Wing."

"Was that the first time you were assigned together, sir?"

"Yes."

"Were you assigned together at Homestead Air Force Base?"

"No."

"When you were assigned in 1996 and 1997 with Lt.-Gen. Moseley, who I assume then was not a lieutenant-general?"

"That's correct."

"Did you socialize with him and his family?"

"Yes."

"On how many occasions, sir?"

"That was as frequent as wing commanders invite their group commanders or equivalents to join in with them for social events, and an occasional impromptu saying hello with other people from time to time."

"Just to make sure I understand," Gittins says. "As frequent as a wing commander would socialize with his subordinate commanders?"

"Correct."

"That would be in kind of a semi-professional setting, hails and farewells? That kind of thing?"

"That sort of thing plus occasionally around some holidays or big events that were coming up in the wing like an Operational Readiness Inspection or that sort of thing, where a wing commander and spouse would invite subordinate commanders and spouses to their home or to a setting like an officers' club."

"And the occasional other events? Those would be purely social events? No military aspect to that?"

"Well, for instance, after the operational readiness inspection—it comes to mind—we gathered up some of the Weapons School instructors and we decided to knock on General and Mrs. Moseley's door on a Friday evening and celebrate the outcome of the ORI, operational readiness inspection."

"So you felt comfortable enough with Gen. Moseley that you could go over and knock on his door unannounced?" Gittins asks.

"Yes," Gen. Sargeant answers.

"Did you and your wife, for example, ever go out to the movies with Gen. Moseley and his wife?"

"No."

"Out to dinner with them?"

"We did not go out to dinner with General and Mrs. Moseley, just the two of us. We may have—no, as a matter of fact, never just the two of us."

"On how many occasions would you say you would have done it when it wasn't just the two of you, but there may have been some other people present?"

"It goes back to the question you asked earlier about the semi-professional, if you will, social exchange amongst professional officers at their home or at the officers' club having dinner, either in a buffet type of thing, or we may have brought a dish, along with 10 or 12 other couples, or where the Moseleys may have served a meal and partook with all the others."

"Sir, your official Air Force biography indicates you also served in Washington, D.C."

"Yes."

"Gen. Moseley was serving in Washington, D.C., at the same time, was he not?"

"I would have to look, but I think he may have been. He was, in fact, during one of my assignments. I do know he was in Washington when I was in the Pentagon. He was at, I believe it was the National War College, occupying a position there."

"While you were assigned in the Pentagon and he was at the National War College, did you socialize with him in any way?"

"I did not."

"Were you also assigned, on a separate occasion, to the White House?"

"I was."

"And at the time you were assigned to the White House, Gen. Moseley was assigned to Legislative Liaison?"

"Yes, I believe that's true."

"Would you have had frequent/infrequent contact with Gen. Moseley during that period?"

"Number one, it would have been infrequent," Gen. Sargeant says. "And there were no social occasions during that time. And when I say infrequent, it may have actually been if I had bumped into him in the hallway of the Pentagon. I was there very infrequently during that time, but it would have been a pleasantry exchange of 'Hello sir' and on about my business. I do know, before I went out to my job at Luke Air Force Base, he actually gave me a phone call to talk to me about a couple of legislative issues on a purely professional basis before I went to Luke Air Force Base."

"Now," Gittins says a few minutes later. "On the morning when you were called to confirm, or the afternoon that you were called to confirm that you were going to be the president of the AIB in this case, or the CIB, Lt.-Gen. Moseley called you at your home?"

"No, he did not."

"At your office?"

"I was in my office."

"And can you tell me about that conversation, sir?"

"He called me, and to the best of my recollection he said that it looked like that I was going to be the board president and that I should get my things in order to plan to assemble my board in his AOR [area of responsibility] and that I would see him over in the AOR at some point, more than likely. But I was to assemble my board and go over to the AOR, get what we needed to do in the AOR done, and then plan to return to Tampa just as soon as we had gathered the data that we had, and work on putting the report together at CENTCOM headquarters."

"He said all of that on the phone?"

"Yes, he did."

"Okay, just checking, sir. When he said to assemble your board, did he indicate to you the membership of that board in any way?"

"Yes, he did, in very vague terms. He said that with this particular board, it looked like we were going to—we as a country were going to involve another with members actually working on the board and that there would be a co-board president. Some of those details were still being worked [out], but it looked like that was going to occur, and that there would be representation from the different services, as well, since this was a CENTCOM, joint theater issue."

"Did he tell you the names of anybody who might serve on the board with you?"

"I think the only names he may have mentioned at that time would have been Brig.-Gen. Marc Dumais, who served as the co-board president from Canada. And I don't believe he mentioned any other names. He told me that Air Combat Command's Judge Advocate General's office would be getting in touch with me. And I don't believe he mentioned any of the names associated with that office."

Gen. Sargeant explains how he specifically asked that Lt.-Col. Joyce Adkins be appointed to his board as the human factors specialist. He also handpicked Capt. Brian Turner, an F-16 pilot he personally nominated to attend the Air Force Fighter Weapons School. "How did it come to be that you didn't have an Air National Guard member?" Charlie Gittins asks.

"I wanted to have a member of the Guard or Reserve on this board," the general says. "And as we looked at the makeup, as this board was growing in number, and the specialties that we had filled, I passed to [Lt.-Col. Walker, the legal advisor] that I would like a maintenance officer in the mid-field grade range or high company grade; captain, or a major primarily, or I would take a lieutenant-colonel if they couldn't come up with a captain or a major. And it was to fill that maintenance specialty. The names and positions that were passed back through ACC did not meet that qualification. I re-stated it. And over a couple of days as we were assembling to get ready to travel, continued to push back to Lt.-Col. Walker to work this issue. And at one point a colonel wing commander, and I believe it was from a wing in Texas, was offered up. And I said I do not want to take another senior officer to go do this, that what we need is a maintenance officer and I'd like to have the Guard or the Reserves represented in that function. And a name was never put forth."

"So there was no captain or major or lieutenant-colonel in the Guard in the United States available to serve on this board, sir? Is that the result that you came to?"

"No. The conclusion I came to is that neither the Guard nor the Reserve wanted to offer up a captain, major, or lieutenant-colonel maintenance officer to serve on this board."

"And would you agree with me, sir, that colonels generally have more experience than captains, majors, and lieutenant-colonels?"

"Yes, I would agree that they have more overall experience. I would not agree that they have the most up-to-date technical knowledge at the time, much like bringing Capt. Turner, a current, serving weapons officer, who is working the nuts and bolts of many different issues and technical problems."

"On Sunday a couple of days ago, you were called at 14:00 by Col. Odom, correct?"

"Yes, it was in that range of about an hour, plus or minus an hour."

"Prior to 13:00/14:00/15:00 on Sunday, whatever time it was, you had not been asked to testify in this case, correct?"

"That is correct. I had not been asked."

"The first time you found out you were going to testify was on Sunday when Col. Odom called you, correct?"

"Yes."

"And when he called you he told you that he needed a credible expert in the F-16, correct?"

"Yes."

"And that's why he was calling you—because he needed a credible expert in F-16 tactics, correct, sir?"

"Yes, that was part of it," Gen. Sargeant answers. "He was calling me because I was the board president and this was my report of two months' worth of investigation, as well as being a credible F-16 pilot."

"Did he tell you that he intended to put the board report into evidence?"

"No, he did not."

"When you talked to Col. Odom, Col. Odom also reviewed with you some of the testimony that had been taken in this hearing, correct?"

"Yes."

"He advised you that a number of pilots had come in and testified under oath that they believed that the actions of Maj. Schmidt and Maj. Umbach were not unreasonable under the circumstances, correct?"

Gen. Sargeant doesn't answer.

"And if he didn't use those words, sir, please correct me and tell me the words he did use."

"No, he did not use those words. And it was more along the lines that pilots had been in here and talked about the events that occurred and what had gone on, and did not have the same depth of background that I had on it—that they hadn't said that what they did was not reasonable."

"And did he tell you in fact that one of those witnesses was Lt.-Col. Fisher?"

"Yes."

"In your report, you refer to Lt.-Col. Fisher as an expert, do you not, sir?"

"I do."

"So he told you that an expert that you relied on in writing your report testified that Maj. Schmidt's and Maj. Umbach's actions were reasonable under the circumstances, correct?"

"He did not go into all of the various specifics on that," Gen. Sargeant answers. "He did say that Lt.-Col. Fisher had been in here and had gone through questioning and testimony, etc."

"Did he tell you, sir, that Col. Fisher's testimony changed after he was provided the opportunity to read Maj. Schmidt's and Maj. Umbach's statement, and all the other information available to the CIB, regarding what they said to the CIB?"

"No, he did not."

⌣

"Sir, your testimony yesterday was that you believe Maj. Schmidt and Maj. Umbach acted recklessly, correct?"

"Yes."

"In fact, it is your belief that Maj. Schmidt intentionally circumvented the ROE in order to drop the bomb, correct?"

"Yes," Gen. Sargeant says. "I believe that could be one of the reasons why he did what he did."

"Well, you're here to provide your opinions, sir, and it is your opinion that Maj. Schmidt intentionally violated the ROE to drop a bomb on unknown people?"

"It is my belief that he intentionally violated the ROE, and then that resulted in dropping the bomb that evening."

"He intentionally violated the ROE," Gittins repeats. "So, is it your testimony, sir, that you did not believe that Maj. Schmidt, in his mind, believed self-defense was required?" Harry Schmidt leans closer, staring at Gen. Sargeant as he chooses his words.

"Did you understand my question, sir?" Gittins asks.

"Would you state it again, please?" the general asks. Harry keeps staring.

"I will be pleased to do so, sir," Gittins says. "Is it your testimony that you believe Maj. Schmidt did not believe he needed to exercise self-defense at the time he dropped the bomb?"

"No, at that time he may have in fact felt that. But my premise is, and what my opinion is, and based upon the investigation I conducted, is that he never ever had to be in that position. And there is the possibility that he invoked self-defense after the emergency 'hold fire' to circumvent that order."

"Well let me ask you, sir—"

"And he was reckless in getting to that position," Gen. Sargeant adds.

"Okay, I'm going to ask you my question, sir," Gittins says. "I'm sure the prosecutor will give you an opportunity to say what you want to say, but I want you to answer my questions. Do you understand that?"

"Yes."

"I want to be very specific about this. You believe that Maj. Schmidt, at the time he dropped the bomb, did in fact believe he was required, as he testified and swore, to exercise self-defense in defense of a wingman, correct?"

"Yes."

"Okay. So you do not disbelieve that Maj. Schmidt, at the time he dropped the bomb, had a reasonable belief that his actions were required to protect his wingman?"

"Could you please state that without so many double-negatives?" Gen. Sargeant asks.

"Yes, sir. At the time Maj. Schmidt dropped the bomb, you do not disagree that he reasonably believed that he needed to exercise self-defense on behalf of his wingman, as he has testified?"

"Objection to the form of the question," Col. Odom interrupts. "I mean, I know we're not supposed to do that, but that's another double-negative."

"I can ask it a different way, sir, and I'll be pleased to do that," Gittins says to the judge.

"Well, let me take my shot and you're always going to be welcome to follow up," Col. Rosenow says. "Don't let me put words in your mouth, sir, and I'm sure you won't, but I understand that you believe that the most fundamental—what I think you termed yesterday was a reckless disregard for the ROE—was the initial turn around to get back into the mix at all, to turn back toward the threat instead of just pressing on toward the tanker?"

"Yes, that's the first point," Gen. Sargeant says. "And then throughout this exhibit we just saw where there were other turn points and opportunities to leave the area, he continued along the same track of reckless disregard for that ROE and SPINS, designed to protect and prevent fratricide, as well as to protect the airmen and the aircraft they are operating."

"Okay, I understand that," Judge Rosenow says. "Now, once he has elected to turn back in, and he didn't take advantage of—or didn't split or scram like he should have maybe under the ROE as far as your testimony is concerned. At the point he's dropping bombs he's actually decided—at the point he's saying: 'I'm rolling in in self-defense, I'm going in,' and then he lets the bomb go, if you just cull everything else out, and once he's in that position, do you believe that he's being reckless in exercising that part? I mean, I understand you can certainly say: 'He shouldn't have been in there in the first place, shouldn't have gone into the mix, and violated the ROE to get in there,' but once he's in there, if you disregard why he got in there, what's your opinion as to his actions, vis-à-vis a reasonable fighter pilot of his experience and training in actually rolling in and dropping the bomb?"

"My opinion is there, that at that point that he has arrived at now, at this end game, that he believed he was doing this—he could have believed he was doing this in self-defense, as he testified and put in writing."

"All right. And the next part of my question is, again, separating out how he got in there, if a reasonable fighter pilot, with his knowledge, training, and experience otherwise found himself in that position, would that have been a reckless disregard of the ROE? Again, we're talking a snapshot at that point, disregarding how he got in there. Once he got in there, do you believe that to drop the bomb was in reckless disregard of the ROE?"

MEMBERS OF ALPHA COMPANY, 3RD BATTALION, PRINCESS PATRICIA'S CANADIAN LIGHT INFANTRY STAND AT ATTENTION AFTER LOADING THE REMAINS OF THEIR FOUR DEAD COMRADES ONTO A C-17 AT THE KANDAHAR AIRFIELD. APRIL 19, 2002. >>

STANDING AT TARNAK FARM, CAPT. JOE JASPER, LEFT, BRIEFS MEMBERS OF THE CANADIAN BOARD OF INQUIRY, INCLUDING COL. MARK HODGSON, CENTER, AND GEN. (RETIRED) MAURICE BARIL, RIGHT. APRIL 30, 2002. >>

CPL. AINSWORTH DYER, LEFT, AND ALPHA COMPANY'S COMMANDER, MAJ. SEAN HACKETT. AINS BET SOME OF HIS FELLOW SOLDIERS THAT HE COULD EAT THE ENTIRE CAN OF TUNA IN HIS HAND. HE LOST. >>

CPL. AINSWORTH DYER AND HIS FIANCÉE, JOCELYN VAN SLOTEN. >>

PTE. NATHAN SMITH, LEFT, AND CPL. AINSWORTH DYER, LESS THAN A MONTH BEFORE THEY WERE KILLED AT TARNAK FARM. >>

PTE. NATHAN SMITH UNDER THE KANDAHAR SUN. >>

SGT. MARC LÉGER BURNING HUMAN FECES AT THE CANADIAN CAMP IN AFGHANISTAN. >>

SGT. MARC LÉGER IN AUSTRIA.
SEPTEMBER 2001. >>

PTE. RICHARD GREEN WEARING THE MAROON
BERET OF THE PARA COMPANY. >>

TOP LEFT: CPL. BRIAN DECAIRE WAS AMONG THE EIGHT CANADIAN SOLDIERS WHO WERE WOUNDED IN THE EXPLOSION. >>

TOP RIGHT: CPL. CHRIS KOPP, LEFT, AND MCPL. ROB COATES. BOTH WERE COMMENDED BY THE CANADIAN FORCES FOR THE FIRST AID THEY ADMINISTERED IN THE MOMENTS AFTER THE EXPLOSION. >>

LEFT: CPL. BRETT PERRY, WHO WAS INJURED IN THE BOMBING, WAS FIRING THE CARL GUSTAV THAT MAJ. HARRY SCHMIDT MISTOOK FOR ENEMY FIRE. APRIL 2005. >>

TOP LEFT: CPL. RENE PAQUETTE, WHO WAS BADLY WOUNDED IN THE BLAST, PLAYS WITH HIS THREE-YEAR-OLD DAUGHTER, BREANNE. FEBRUARY 2005. >>
BOTTOM LEFT: ALPHA COMPANY'S THREE MEDICS WERE ALL COMMENDED FOR THEIR ACTIONS IN THE DESERT THAT NIGHT. FROM LEFT, CPL. VICTOR SPEIRS, CPL. JEAN DE LA BOURDONNAYE, AND SGT. BILL WILSON. >>
TOP RIGHT: W/O BILLY BOLEN WAS A COMPANY'S QUARTERMASTER AND A REVERED LEADER. >>

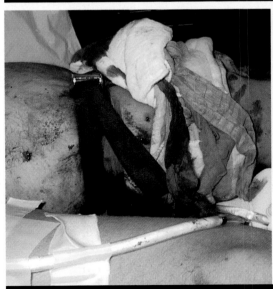

ABOVE: OF ALL THE TROOPS WHO SURVIVED THE BOMBING, SGT. LORNE FORD WAS THE MOST CRITICALLY WOUNDED. FELLOW SOLDIERS STRAPPED A TOURNIQUET AROUND HIS SHRAPNEL-TORN LEFT THIGH, STEMMING THE BLEEDING UNTIL A CASEVAC CHOPPER ARRIVED. >>

THE ABOVE TWO PHOTOS ARE COURTESY OF THE CANADIAN DEPARTMENT OF NATIONAL DEFENCE

LEFT: A NAVY PILOT AT THE TIME, HARRY SCHMIDT PREPARES FOR A FLIGHT AT NEVADA'S NELLIS AIR FORCE BASE IN JULY 2001. NINE MONTHS LATER, AS A MEMBER OF THE ILLINOIS AIR NATIONAL GUARD, "PSYCHO" SCHMIDT DROPPED A BOMB ON CANADIAN SOLDIERS IN KANDAHAR, KILLING FOUR AND WOUNDING EIGHT. >>

BELOW: MAJ. HARRY SCHMIDT AND HIS WIFE, LISA, WALK PAST A SEA OF REPORTERS ON THEIR WAY TO A PRE-TRIAL HEARING AT LOUISIANA'S BARKSDALE AIR FORCE BASE. JANUARY 2003.

PHOTO BY: TONY GUTIERREZ (ASSOCIATED PRESS)

PHOTO BY: JESSICA LEIGH, *THE SHREVEPORT TIMES* (ASSOCIATED PRESS)

TOP: MAJ. BILL UMBACH, CENTER, WAS THE FLIGHT LEAD ON THE NIGHT OF THE BOMBING. HE AND HIS WIFE, MARLENE, WATCH AS HIS LAWYER, DAVE BECK, SPEAKS TO REPORTERS AT BARKS- DALE AIR FORCE BASE. JANUARY 15, 2003. >>

LEFT: COL. PATRICK ROSENOW, THE JUDGE WHO PRESIDED OVER THE PILOTS' PRE-TRIAL HEARING, EXAMINES THE INSIDE OF AN F-16 FIGHTING FALCON. COL. ROBERT J. MURPHY, THE PILOTS' WING COM- MANDER, ANSWERS QUESTIONS FROM THE EDGE OF THE COCKPIT. JANUARY 23, 2003. >>

LEFT: COL. JOHN S. ODOM, JR. WAS THE LEAD PROSECUTOR ON THE FRIENDLY FIRE FILE. >>

RIGHT: CHARLES W. GITTINS, MAJ. HARRY SCHMIDT'S CIVILIAN LAWYER, ACCUSED THE U.S. AIR FORCE OF PINNING THE BLAME ON HIS CLIENT TO HIDE ITS DYSFUNCTIONAL COMMAND AND CONTROL SYSTEM. >>

COL. DAVID C. NICHOLS WAS THE PILOTS' COMMANDER DURING OPERATION ENDURING FREEDOM. INVESTIGATORS CRITICIZED HIS LEADERSHIP STYLE, SAYING HE WAS MORE INTERESTED IN BEING "ONE OF THE BOYS" THAN AN EFFECTIVE BOSS. >>

THE GENERALS, FROM LEFT: LT.-GEN. MARC DUMAIS, THE CANADIAN CO-PRESIDENT OF THE COALITION INVESTIGATION BOARD (PHOTO COURTESY OF DND); MAJ.-GEN. STEPHEN T. SARGEANT, THE AMERICAN CO-PRESIDENT OF THE CIB; GEN. BRUCE CARLSON, THE FORMER 8TH AIR FORCE COMMANDER WHO SIGNED THE PILOTS' LETTERS OF REPRIMAND; GEN. T. MICHAEL MOSELEY, THE COMMANDER OF THE AFGHANISTAN AIR WAR AT THE TIME OF THE BOMBING; AND LT.-GEN. STEPHEN G. WOOD, THE TOP OFFICER IN THE CAOC ON THE NIGHT THE CANADIANS WERE KILLED (ALL U.S. PHOTOS COURTESY OF AIR FORCE LINK). >>

"Disregarding the altitude, disregarding the track, disregarding all the things you said to disregard, and based on his post–incident testimony of self-defense—"

"And about the threat envelopes he believed existed," Col. Rosenow adds.

"And about that envelope, then no, I do not say that particular part was reckless. But I do stand by everything that all those violations that led up to that point, this should have never occurred because he should have never been in that situation, given the situation that was presented that evening."

"Yes, I understand, sir," Col. Rosenow says. "And we were laying a lot of predicates that I wasn't assuming you were signing onto. So, I understand your answer to my question."

⌣

"Yesterday," Charlie Gittins says to the general, "you testified in response to trial counsel's questions that you saw no evidence of defensive maneuvering, correct?"

"That's correct."

"Sir, given your qualifications as an F-16 pilot, would a 4.7 G turn with two tanks, triple ejector racks, four bombs, two missiles and rails, be an indication of a defensive turn?" Gittins asks, referring to the left turn Maj. Schmidt made before the tapes came on.

"No, it would not necessarily, all by itself, be an indication of a responsive directive turn when in that kind of configuration [one] would be performing up to five Gs for a safe escape maneuver," Gen. Sargeant says. "And if it was truly a defensive maneuver, then you would be expecting someone, if they felt truly threatened, to do things like get rid of the tanks, for instance, and exceed those Gs up to the G limits of the airplane, which without the documents in front of me I would think it would be about five-and-a-half Gs with that configuration."

"Actually we heard some testimony it was 5.2," Gittins says. "Is it your testimony that 4.7 Gs would not be a defensive reaction, even if it wasn't the maximum defensive reaction?"

"No, 4.7 could be a portion of a defensive reaction."

"That would be some evidence, wouldn't you agree, sir, of a defensive maneuver?"

"No, I would not agree with that necessarily."

"That fact alone would not, is that your testimony? That fact alone would not indicate a defensive maneuver?"

"Yes."

"However, you did have Maj. Schmidt's sworn statement and his testimony to his commander in which he indicated that his first maneuver was a hard defensive turn, correct?"

"In his testimony he indicates he makes a hard turn," the general says.

"So in combination with Maj. Schmidt's testimony and the objective data on the HUD, which was recovered after the accident, there is support from Maj. Schmidt's testimony that his first maneuver was a hard defensive maneuver, correct?"

"There is evidence that he made a turn at 4.7 Gs."

"Yes, sir. But he characterized it as a defensive turn, correct?"

"If we're going to do this to answer that and answer it accurately, then I think we would need to pull out the line-by-line, word-by-word testimony, matched up against something like the Exhibit 90 that was put together, or the 4 by 4."

"Sir," Gittins says, "you were asked to come here and testify as a government expert witness. Are you testifying that you're not prepared to do so?"

"No."

"So my question is, sir, Maj. Schmidt provided you with a sworn statement. In performing this investigation you, in fact, did read that statement, did you not?"

"I did."

"And in fact, before you came here to give the testimony that you've given here today, you considered that testimony, did you not?"

"I did."

"Maj. Schmidt testified that he executed a hard turn that is supported by a 4.7 G maximum loading on the G meter in his aircraft. That is evidence of a hard defensive turn, is it not?"

"It is evidence of a 4.7 G turn."

"Sir, did you find any evidence in your investigations that Maj. Schmidt is a liar?"

"No."

"In fact, every person you asked, who knew Maj. Schmidt, told you he was a professional, isn't that true, sir?"

"Yes."

"That he was a truthful person and they believed what he said, correct, sir?"

"Yes, they did not indicate to me that they did not have reason to believe him."

"You also testified that you do not believe there was any sense of urgency in the voices on the tape, correct?"

"That's correct."

"You interviewed Capt. Pepper who was the AWACS senior director who was talking to Maj. Schmidt, didn't you, sir?" Gittins asks. (In fact, Capt. Pepper was not talking to Maj. Schmidt, but he was listening to the radio calls between the pilots and TSgt. Carroll.) "Capt. Pepper testified that he believed, in his opinion, based on his experience, Maj. Schmidt sounded like somebody who felt he was being fired on, didn't he?"

"I have not reviewed Capt. Pepper's testimony prior—"

"Sir, I'll provide it to you, but my question was: Do you believe, as an expert witness who has been called here to testify here today, that you need to review documents to give your expert opinions?"

"No, but if you're asking me to parse words in written statements that I've not had a chance to study for individual words at that point 10 months ago or so, then I would like to review those documents, as is my right to do so."

"Yes, sir, and I'm sure trial counsel will give you that opportunity. The question you asked Capt. Pepper: 'Did you get a sense of urgency as this SAFIRE started to develop that, in fact, one of those members, Coffee 52, was getting anxious to employ ordnance?' Answer: 'No, sir. I felt he was getting shot at and he was concerned about it.' So even in response to your question, which was a leading question, Capt. Pepper told you that he believed Maj. Schmidt felt he was being shot at by the inflection in his voice, didn't he, sir?"

"Yes, although he did not say by the inflection in his voice."

"Capt. Pepper: 'Like I said, I felt that he was very worried that he was getting shot at. He did not feel that they were just kind of shooting in the area; they were leading him.' So he felt concern for his well-being. Capt. Pepper also told you that, correct, sir?"

"Yes."

"Capt. Pepper is an air controller who has served in combat areas before, isn't that true, sir?"

"For that specific answer, I would have to go back and tell you he had hours accumulated in this theater for sure as a senior director."

"Capt. Pepper, who was a senior director, testified that he believed the communication was clear and concise, 3–1 standards he can't specifically say, but the communication quote: 'I felt [the comm] was clear and in this theater that's all we go for sometimes, but things get really weird.' So he didn't have any trouble understanding what Maj. Schmidt was saying, did he?"

"No, according to his answer there."

⌣

"Yesterday, you testified that Maj. Schmidt was in a position to disengage, didn't you?" Gittins asks.

"Yes, I did."

"Maj. Schmidt was not entitled to disengage unless he was directed by his leader to disengage, and they disengaged together, isn't that true, sir?"

"Yes, that could be part of a total answer in context."

"Yes, sir. The doctrine of mutual support requires that a wingman not leave his lead, correct?"

"Yes, except in very specific situations."

"And this was not one of them, was it, sir?"

"No."

"So although, in the hypothetical sense, Maj. Schmidt could have departed, unless he was told by his flight lead to depart, he was not entitled to do so. He had to remain and support his flight lead, isn't that true, sir?"

"Yes, but in my testimony yesterday I referred to specific points along the way on this diagram and so, again, in context is what needs to be—"

"Yes, sir," Gittins interrupts. "But in no place on that diagram that you talked about yesterday could Maj. Schmidt disengage unless he had direction from his flight lead to do so, correct, sir?"

"Correct, unless he felt he had to do something in self-defense."

"Do you mean if [Maj. Schmidt] went in self-defense, he needed to disengage, that's the one place he could, but he had to tell his wingman?"

"He has the inherent right to actually make a decision and do something, and inform his leader that, in fact, he is doing that and why," Gen. Sargeant says. "He is leaving the formation because he's got some sort of activity going on."

"You would agree with me that if you are within a threat envelope that you must keep that potential threat in sight, wouldn't you, sir?"

"Yes, if you are working in relation to that threat. In most cases you would want to keep it in sight. There are times, though, that you would not need to keep it in sight and you would want to distance yourself from it."

"Yes, sir," Gittins says. "The threat that Maj. Schmidt, without speaking about what those parameters are, the threat that Maj. Schmidt told you, in his statement to the board, is that he believed was engaging him, he was well within that threat at all times during this engagement, correct, sir?"

"Yes, in the threat that he defines."

"The visual signature that Maj. Schmidt described about the threat is consistent with the weapon he believed he was being engaged by, isn't that true, sir?"

"In fact, it is not," Gen. Sargeant says. "And I would like to, if possible, present something that would actually refute that claim since you asked me about it."

"Well, I'm sure that the trial counsel will give you that opportunity," Gittins says. "Maj. Schmidt described seeing rocket-propelled projectiles, did he not, sir?"

"Yes."

"There is no place in your report where you actually used the words 'rocket-propelled projectiles,' is there, sir?"

"No, not specifically that," the general answers. "There is—we described a system."

"You described a system, but you also characterized it as AAA [anti-aircraft artillery], correct?" Gittins asks. Gen. Sargeant doesn't answer. "Throughout your report you characterized it as AAA, do you not, sir?"

"Throughout the report we've characterized the threat as AAA, that is correct," he says. "But we also referred to a weapon system in relation to what Maj. Schmidt talked about as the threat that he described."

"And the projectiles that were actually being fired on the range that night was rocket-propelled munitions, correct, sir?" Gittins asks, referring to the 84mm Carl Gustav.

"Yes, in part there were rocket-propelled munitions."

⌣

"Sir, with respect to the live-fire exercise that was ongoing on Tarnak Farms, AWACS was unaware that there was a live-fire going on, correct?"

"Yes."

"The CAOC was unaware that a live-fire exercise was going on, correct?"

"Yes."

"And not a single pilot that you talked to from the 332nd AEG believed that a live-fire exercise would be conducted in a combat zone, did they, sir?"

"The part that I can tell you is that they did not know it was going on," Gen. Sargeant says. "I can't tell you that I asked that specific question and got a specific answer to that question that you just posed."

"You found nobody on the AWACS who was controlling Coffee Flight and no one at the 170th that was aware that live-fire exercises were ongoing in Afghanistan, correct, sir?"

"I did not find someone of the groups you just mentioned who knew that ROZ was active with live-firing that night."

"Sir, you found that ground forces were not required to report live-fire training or activity within the given air tasking order day and you concluded that that was neither causal nor substantially contributing to the 17 April 2002 incident, correct?"

"That's correct."

"Sir, is it your testimony that if pilots had been informed that there was a live-fire training exercise going on near Kandahar that this accident would still have happened?"

"Your question is—these specific pilots at that specific time?" Gen. Sargeant asks back.

"Well, sir—"

"I'm asking the question back to you for clarification."

"Do you believe that with Maj. Schmidt's experience and Maj. Umbach's experience, that had they been briefed on a live-fire exercise two miles or three miles south of Kandahar, that this accident still would have occurred?" Gittins asks.

"Objection," Col. Odom says. "Calls for pure speculation."

"It goes to credibility of the witness, sir, given his opinions," Gittins says.

"Do you have an opinion?" Judge Rosenow asks the general. "Normally, I don't allow witnesses to say what they think is in the state of mind of other folks, unless they have a—"

"I didn't ask him that, sir," Gittins interrupts. "I didn't ask him about state of mind. I asked if this accident would have occurred."

"Well, it's implicit in there," Col. Rosenow says. "But I'll ask the witness to answer the question."

"I do not know, taking this question out of context," Gen. Sargeant says.

"So the answer is: You don't know whether it would have happened or not?"

"I do not know," the general answers.

"Sir, you're aware that immediately after this accident a NOTAM [Notice to Airmen] process was put in place that required live-fire exercises to be notified to all pilots, isn't that true?" Gittins asks.

"The specifics of those live-fires is to the time the ranges would be activated, went into place. The ranges, the live-fire range areas under ROZs, had been available to the pilots prior to this and on this day."

"So, in answer to my question, NOTAMs was required after this accident, were they not?"

"Yes."

"And that's a similar process to what you would expect and have found as a pilot in the United States Air Force for live-fire training that is ongoing in the United States, correct, sir?"

"Yes."

"Is there any reason that you can think of, sir, that NOTAMs could not have been used prior to the 17th of April?"

"Yes, and the reason is that the procedures only called for the ground forces to notify and establish ROZs and they could put the exact full time that any activity might be going on in there and they were not required to pass the specific times of when the activity would occur and—"

"Sir," Gittins interrupts. "My question was: Are you aware of a reason why NOTAMs could not have been utilized before the 17th of April?"

"No, for no reason beyond what I've just described."

"Sir, there is no reason why NOTAMs could not have been used prior to the 17th of April, just like they are in the United States, correct, sir?"

"Yes."

"Sir, you also found that the ground forces were not currently represented at the Air Expeditionary Group level. That finding indicates that there was some problem of obtaining friendly fire ground location, is that accurate?"

"No, you're adding to it," Gen. Sargeant says. "What we said in the report was that the addition of a ground liaison officer [GLO] would help the units to more fully understand the Ground Order of Battle."

"There wasn't a ground liaison officer at the 332nd, correct?"

"Correct."

"The job of a ground liaison officer is to interface with the ground commander's representatives to identify and locate friendly positions, correct?"

"Yes, that is one of the duties."

"The GLO would also highlight ground scheme maneuvering and concept of operations, isn't that true, sir?"

"Yes."

"And that would be for aircrew, correct?"

"Yes."

⌣

"Sir, you would agree with me, would you not, that combat is stressful—even though you don't have any combat time—you agree with me, would you not, that combat is stressful time?"

"Yes."

"And would you also agree with me that for a person to believe they are being shot at is a stressful event?"

"Yes."

"And would you also agree that not everyone reacts the same under that same kind of stress?"

"Yes."

"And there are a range of reactions that a person may have when they are shot at, would you agree?"

"Yes. And you're talking there on the reaction to stress of a range of responses?"

"Yes, sir. Would you agree with me that when you were asked to testify about the ROE, you took some time to read the ROE and the SPINS, correct, sir?"

"Yes," Gen. Sargeant says. "I reviewed that portion and obtained the document to bring in."

"Maj. Schmidt and Maj. Umbach would not have had the luxury of reading and studying under the circumstances they found themselves in, correct, sir?"

"No, that is not true. They were, in fact, in-briefed to the theater and then that was a requirement of each individual combatant to stay abreast of the SPINS and the ROE."

"Yes, sir. Did you understand my question, sir?"

"Objection, sir," Col. Odom says. "He answered the question."

"I'm afraid he didn't," Gittins says. "My client didn't have the opportunity to review and study on the SPINS while he believed he was under attack, correct, sir?"

"No, in his airplane, at that time, he did not have the chance to go back and review the SPINS and the ROE that he was operating under."

"He was required to make decisions in a very stressful time, correct?"

"Yes."

"And he was required to do so with the information he had at his fingertips, correct?"

"Yes."

"And the information he didn't have, such as the fact that there was live-fire exercise at the Tarnak Farms range, correct?"

"Yes."

Dave Beck has chatted with Stephen Sargeant before. They met in a room here at Barksdale, not long after the general's surprise appearance. The law provides all defense lawyers the chance to question government witnesses in advance of their testimony. The pilots' other attorneys were also at the closed-door meeting, but Dave did most of the talking. He usually does. He is the "good cop," the one with a knack for making even his client's worst enemies feel comfortable.

But today, when it is his turn to cross-examine Gen. Sargeant, Maj. Umbach's lawyer is brief. "Sir," he says to Gen. Sargeant, "if Lt.-Col. Dave Beck was back in the Marine Corps and I was doing an investigation, be it a safety investigation or an AIB, I would have an absolute duty to do a fair, thorough, impartial investigation to gather all the facts?"

"Yes," the general answers.

"And that's an absolute duty that has to be done?"

"Yes."

"Does a commander have a duty to ensure the safety of his troops?" Beck asks, a few moments later.

"Yes."

"And if a commander is made aware [by] members in his unit that there are things going on, and that if they're not corrected it's going to increase the risk of fratricide, I would have an absolute duty to look into that, wouldn't I, sir?"

"Yes, you have a duty to look into it."

"And if I did not, and if the very things I was warned about then happened and members of my unit got killed, I would be responsible, wouldn't I?"

"Yes, in the context that you were talking about, a hypothetical example."

⌣

"During the time that you were president of the CIB, did you have any contact with Gen. Moseley after the board went into session?" Beck asks.

"Yes, I had contact with Gen. Moseley at CENTCOM."

"On how many occasions did you have contact with Gen. Moseley?"

"There was one contact with him. We briefed him as the CENTAF commander, as we were fairly far along in the report, to give him a briefing on our findings and conclusions at that time."

"Had you completed the board's work at that time?"

"No, in fact, that caveat we made to him, but that this was fairly far along in the process."

"Do you think it was proper for you to contact Gen. Moseley to discuss where you were in the report when you had not completed the work on the report?"

"I did not contact Gen. Moseley."

"How did you come in contact with him? I thought that's what you said."

"Well, maybe I misunderstood your question. You asked if it was appropriate for me to contact him. I did not contact him. I briefed him when it was requested by CENTAF commander along with the entire board present."

"How many occasions, if any, other than that did you have? Did you have any communication with Gen. Moseley during the time that you were president of the CIB?"

"There was communication via classified e-mail in the form of updates to the board progress that were going to CENTCOM as a request by CENTCOM, and Gen. Moseley saw those requests as well."

"Did he respond to those e-mails, the updates that were being provided?"

"The response to the updates would have been, as I recall, 'thanks' or 'got it' and that sort of thing."

"Did you have any telephone conversations or any communications other than e-mail with Gen. Moseley during the time period that you served as president on the CIB?"

"Yes."

"How many times did you have telephone conversations with him?"

"My sense is that there may have been four to six actual phone calls."

"What was the subject of those phone calls?"

"The subject of those phone calls were items of significance that I as a board president, working for a convening authority, thought that he should be aware of prior to the end of the report coming out. For instance, the fact that the airspace coordination order was not posted, if you will, on a highly visible large map or other means in some of the units. And, based on what happened, I felt it was important enough to notify him of that so that he then as the commander could decide what he needed to do about that."

"So you were discussing with Gen. Moseley then the progress of the report and the findings that you believed that you were coming to?"

"No. To be very specific, I was discussing those things that were going on in his theater as a responsible commander that I thought he needed to be apprised of, even before this report came out so that others would understand. For instance—well, I gave you a 'for instance.'"

"That would include then, though based on your job, the things you were finding in determining as your investigation went on, is that correct, sir?"

"Yes."

"Do you have copies of the e-mails to and from Gen. Moseley?"

"No, I do not."

"Did anybody on the government team ask you to provide those e-mails at any time during the course since charges have been preferred?"

"Yes. I was asked to provide and SIPRNET e-mails, and I did a search for those and there were none. In accordance with proper procedures, the classified SIPRNET hard drives that were used during that period of time were wiped clean."

$\smile$

When it is his turn again, Col. Odom revisits Gen. Sargeant's alleged cozy relationship with Gen. Moseley. "At any time and in any way did Lt.-Gen. Moseley attempt to influence your findings or recommendations or conclusions in any way?"

"No," Gen. Sargeant answers.

"Objection," Gittins says. "Leading."

"Overruled."

"Did any other general officer in the United States Air Force or any branch of the United States Department of Defense contact you in an effort to influence your conclusions, findings, or recommendations?" Col. Odom continues.

"No."

chapter thirty-two

Col. Bob Murphy flew the Viper to Louisiana, a 45-minute ride from Springfield's 183rd Fighter Wing to Barksdale Air Force Base. Though surrounded, almost swallowed, by the big B-52 bombers that dominate the tarmac here, the glossy gray jet is an obvious jewel amid its bulkier cousins. Even parked, engines off, the F-16 sweats speed and sophistication and arrogance. It is as elegant as a killing machine can be, each perfect curve twisting toward the dagger-like nose that rips through the air at six miles a minute.

"I think it would be best if you sat in the seat, sir," Col. Murphy tells Judge Rosenow. After eight days of testimony, the Article 32 is in the midst of a brief field trip to the other side of the base. The defense team wants the investigating officer to slide inside the cockpit, to experience with his own eyes and long legs the cramped quarters and the symphony of switches and sticks and screens. Col. Murphy, the pilots' commanding officer in Springfield, leads the brief tour.

"Here are the night vision goggles you've been hearing about," he tells the judge. "They sit on top of your helmet and then they flip down to come in front of your eyes." He explains how a pilot can peer underneath the "nogs" to look at the sea of instruments inside the jet.

"Do you want me to get in?" Col. Rosenow asks, standing on the ladder that leads to the cockpit.

"Yes, sir," Col. Murphy says. "Just step in the seat with your right foot. Put your left foot in on the seat and then slide your right foot in the knee holes. You are tall enough to be uncomfortable but—"

"That's fine," the judge says, climbing in under the Thursday morning sun.

Snug inside, he sees what Harry Schmidt saw. The throttle. The targeting pod cursor. The red pickle button. Mark, mark, enter. In between his knees, two tiny green-tinted screens—four inches by four inches. Nowhere near as large as those videos that have been projected, hour after hour, on the big white screen in the hearing room. The difference is clearly not lost on Judge Rosenow. "The main thing for me is the significance, the size of the multi-function displays and the size of the HUD," he says.

Two minutes after lowering himself in, the judge steps out of the jet, walking with Col. Murphy to the starboard side. Murph shows the colonel where the fuel tank would have been, where the missiles typically hang from the bottom of the wing. "That pylon would have had two 500-pound laser-guided bombs on that," Col. Murphy says. "Two missiles, two bombs, two tanks."

"All right," Col. Rosenow says. "Questions from counsel or either side?" Nobody has any. "Col. Murphy, thanks a lot."

★ ★ ★

The Air Force folks at Barksdale have done their best to make things comfortable for the Canadian families. Private rooms, a cozy, secluded place to watch the hearing. Parents and spouses have been free to cry and swear and vent far away from the cameras, surrounded only by the few people on earth who know exactly what they're feeling.

There have been a few laughs, too. Like the dinner they had with the Canadian soldiers, when Brian Decaire found that long hair in his crocodile gumbo. He complained to the manager, hoping at the very least for a free meal. The boss fired the waitress instead—and still charged Brian for the gumbo. During lulls in the hearing, the families have also been escorted, a few at a time, to Barksdale's A-10 training center. Today is Miranda's turn to be strapped inside the Thunderbird simulator. Not long after takeoff, she crashes. Charlotte, Nathan's mom, somehow manages to land her plane on the grass beside the runway.

Both women are still giggling when they walk back inside the viewing room on Thursday afternoon, January 23. On the screen in front of them, standing, is Maj. Bill Umbach, holding a piece of white paper. For two weeks, the families have seen little more than the back of Bill's bald head. Now, without any advanced warning, he is looking directly at them, his eyes locking with theirs through the distant lens of a video camera.

"Sgt. Marc Léger," he says, speaking slowly and loudly. Nobody in the room says a word. "Cpl. Ainsworth Dyer. Pte. Nathan Smith. Pte. Richard Green. Sgt. Lorne Ford. MCpl. Curtis Hollister. MCpl. Stanley Clark. Cpl. Rene Paquette. Cpl. Brett Perry. Cpl. Brian Decaire. Cpl. Shane Brennan. Pte. Norman Link. I want to address your family and friends."

In the media room, where tape recorders are strictly prohibited, the only sound is the rat-tat-tat of fingers on keyboards. Nobody wants to get this wrong. "I fear that any words of mine will be weak, because nothing that anyone can do can undo what has happened," Maj. Umbach continues. "I know that I will never understand the depth of your grief. I also know that those who were lost and injured were good men, who loved their country and heard the call of duty to preserve freedom for all of us. They have earned the highest praise: They were patriots, they were true heroes. Know that my family and I hold you all in our hearts. I pray that God will help you in your anguish." Bill does not stutter once. He has clearly prepared himself for this very moment.

"Since the 17th of April, not a day has passed that I have not thought of that night, in the sky, in the darkness, and all that has happened since. I deeply regret that this terrible and tragic accident has occurred. Maj. Schmidt and I were doing our best to protect ourselves in a situation where we honestly believed we were under attack. I hope and pray for your understanding and forgiveness, and that all of the factors that contributed to this tragedy will be made known and fixed so that neither pilots, nor their brave brothers in arms on the ground, are ever in this situation again. If I could turn back time, I would. But since I cannot, I want you to know that I am truly sorry."

With that, Bill Umbach returns to his chair, oblivious to the sobbing that his blunt, sincere words have triggered on the other side of the base. As he sits down, Maj. Schmidt stands up, carrying two pieces of paper to the front of the hearing room. His large hands—hands that have steered through subsonic speed, that have pickled bombs and taken lives—are shaking. He begins to read.

"Col. Rosenow, I would like to say, first and foremost, that I sincerely regret the accident that occurred on 17 April, 2002," he says. "My heart goes out to the families of the men killed and injured in what can only be described as a tragic accident in the fog of war. The accident was truly unfortunate, and I am sorry that it happened. I was called upon to make a perfect decision in a rapidly unfolding combat environment. I had to make that decision with what I now know ..." Harry pauses, losing his spot amid the shaking sheet of paper. "Excuse me," he says, finding where he left off. "I had to make that decision with what I now know, with the acuity of 20-20 hindsight, was imperfect information."

He speaks quickly, never lifting his head. "On the night of the accident, I was flying as wingman in a loose wedge formation. We were flying at 21,000 feet, and we were descending for rendezvous with the tanker. We had taken off our NVGs because we were at the end of the three-hour period of vulnerability in the area of operation. We had visible lights on. I was on the right side of the formation and my flight lead, Coffee 51, commented that he had saw something that looked like fireworks on the right side of the formation. When I first saw the source of the rocket-propelled projectiles, it was nearly underneath me. My flight lead said: 'I think they are shooting at us,' and we reacted defensively by turning hard to avoid being predictable."

As he wrote in his statement the day after the bombing, Maj. Schmidt says he switched off his overt lights and flipped down his NVGs. "My lead called over the radio that 'they are pulling lead,' which indicated to me that my lead was defensive and defending," he continues. "I made a call to get 'tapes on.' I also noticed, after my initial maneuver, that my lead still had his overt lights on, so I told him to get his lights off. After initially turning hard away from the threat, I was uncomfortable with the rate and speed of fire I was observing visually, and estimated that my flight lead wasn't going to be able to get out of the maximum effective range of the rounds. Therefore, I turned to the beam to better assess the threat and to provide mutual support to my flight lead.

"My perception was that we had been ambushed, as we had been briefed that Taliban were expected to use ambush tactics in and around Kandahar," Maj. Schmidt continues. "I believed that the projectiles posed a real and present danger to our flight and specifically to my flight lead. I attempted to use warning shots to suppress the threat, but I was denied by BOSSMAN. I finally communicated to BOSSMAN that I was engaging in self-defense because I believed my flight lead was at risk of being shot down. I believed at the time that my flight lead's transmission to 'check master arm, check laser arm,' indicated he concurred with my decision that the situation required self-defense. While I was assigned to the 332nd Aerospace Expeditionary Group, I was never alerted to the possibility of live-fire training being conducted in a war zone. Further, at no time prior to our mission on 17 April, 2002, were we briefed of a live-fire exercise at Tarnak Farms or in the vicinity of Kandahar. Nor were we ever advised while airborne by the AWACS command and control platform, or any calls on the Guard frequency, that there was a live-fire exercise ongoing anywhere in the war zone. Because such an event in a combat arena would have been so unusual and unexpected, information about such training would be the type of information we would note so that we could avoid it. This lack of information is the one link in the chain, which if corrected, would surely have avoided this accident. I believed at the time I was acting in accordance with my training, the JCF standing rules of engagement, the OEF SPINS on self-defense, and the ROE briefing provided by my group commander when I reported into the theater.

"Finally," Maj. Schmidt says, "I would like to tell the families of Sgt. Léger, Cpl. Dyer, Pte. Green, and Pte. Smith, that I am deeply sorry for what happened on the 17th of April." Harry pauses again, stifling the urge to break down. "I will always regret what happened that night. Next, I apologize to each of the men I wounded: Sgt. Ford, MCpl. Clark, MCpl. Hollister, Cpl. Paquette, Cpl. Decaire, Cpl. Perry, Cpl. Brennan, and Pte. Link. I think about the men who were killed and the men who were injured. As a family man myself with a wife and two young boys, I can only imagine how difficult it is for them and their families to grapple with the fact these men volunteered to serve their country and were killed in a wartime accident. I sincerely want them to know that my heart goes out to them and that I am truly sorry for their loss." Harry Schmidt walks back to his seat.

Legally speaking, what he and Maj. Umbach just read were unsworn statements, not testimony under oath. The slight difference means that prosecutors—as much as they would love to—are not allowed to cross-examine either of the pilots. Nine days, 19 witnesses, and more than 160 exhibits later, the Article 32 is suddenly over. Like that night over Tarnak Farm, Harry Schmidt has the last word.

In the faraway room with the leather couches and the kitchenette, the Canadian families continue to cry, hugging and wiping their tired eyes with Kleenex. Finally, nine long months after the horrifying news and the unthinkable funerals, the pilots have personally apologized. It is what the families have wanted all along. Forget the 64 years or the stupid t-shirts. Just say sorry.

Of course, in cases like this, it's never that simple. As grateful as they are for what they've just heard, some in the room are more outraged than they have ever been. Was that supposed to be an apology that Maj. Schmidt just read? It sounded more like a laundry list of excuses than heartfelt remorse. He's sorry that the accident happened. He's sorry for our loss. But is he sorry for what *he* did? Is he sorry that *he* pickled the bomb? Some of the relatives venture outside the building, where reporters are already waiting. "Maj. Umbach touched me in a place I didn't even think was reachable at this point," says a tearful Miranda, Ricky Green's red-haired fiancée. "Maj. Schmidt didn't hit that part of my heart."

"Maj. Umbach, I felt, was very sincere," says Claire Léger, her arm around Ainsworth's mother, Agatha. "Maj. Schmidt, I have to say, I felt he was offering a defense of himself first. I know his job's on the line, but those are our sons' lives on the line; I'm sorry." There will always be friendly fire, she says. "But this was more than that. It was as if someone was probably trying to get a medal."

It is exactly 5 p.m. when Mrs. Dyer tries to speak. As it does every day at this time, the sky at Barksdale Air Force Base fills with the sound of *The Star-Spangled Banner*. "Maj. Umbach, he break my heart," Agatha says in her thick Caribbean accent. "I really feel he meant what he said. He really touch me. But I don't have no remorse about Maj. Schmidt. He was trying to defend himself before he tell us he was sorry."

Marley Léger is the last of the relatives to address the cameras. She is used to this drill by now, having confronted, on that very first day, the reporters huddled at the end of her Edmonton driveway. Nearly a year later, she is still, to many Canadians, the symbol of this tragedy, a strong, beautiful woman who has never once been vindictive or vengeful. Many strangers have shaped their opinions of this whole mess based on what Marley says. Who, after all, would know better than she? Even the pilots' wives, when they ponder what they would ever say to the soldiers' families, think about saying it to Marley Léger.

"I would just like to say thank you," she says, her sunglasses propped on the top of her long hair. "I appreciate your apologies and they are accepted. They are very much appreciated and very much needed." Of course, the reporters don't leave it at that. Do you believe Maj. Schmidt was as sincere as his flight lead? "It was Maj. Umbach who really got me deep inside," she eventually concedes, wiping away tears. But she is equally grateful for what Maj. Schmidt had to say. "I accept his apology as well."

chapter thirty-three

The metal detector is gone. So are the big white screens and the satellite dishes and the horde of Air Force public affairs officers flown in from across the United States. The Canadian families are already in the clouds, flying back to Ottawa and Edmonton and Toronto and Tatamagouche, back to a routine of remembering and waiting. Though exhausted, they leave Shreveport with what they came here to find: the truth. Or at least one version of it. "This put it together for me," Miranda says. "It made more sense."

Indeed, everyone will make their own sense of what they saw on those television screens, the fuzzy videos and the unexpected apologies. Miranda will go back to Halifax, back to class. Lloyd will tend to his flags. Richard Léger, for the first time in months, is somewhat at peace, as content as a man in his place can be. He knows exactly what happened to his son. Finally. Richard's wife knows, too, but as the weeks wear on, she will remember little else except Maj. Schmidt's trembling hands. She always tried to give those pilots the benefit of the doubt, just like Marc would have. Not anymore, not after that "declaration of excuses" disguised as an apology.

On Friday, the Schmidts and the Umbachs pack their cars for the 12-hour drive north to Illinois. Lisa and Marlene have read the papers. They know what some of the Canadians are saying about yesterday's apologies. By this point, they're not even surprised. For months, the media has made this a story about "us versus them," a debate over who the real victims are. Bill and Harry said they were sorry. They meant it. If some people can't forgive, well, that's their decision. "I don't think anyone can ask anyone to accept their apology," Lisa Schmidt says. "But Harry has a very huge heart, and he wouldn't apologize if it wasn't sincere."

"This is 10 times worse on them than it is on us," Marlene says. "I hope some day that they can forgive them both, but that may never happen."

★ ★ ★

Ricky Green's mom started thinking about suing the U.S. Air Force back in June, back before anyone even knew who Harry Schmidt was. She has talked it over, many times, with Michael McDonald—Herbie—the man who inspired her son to enlist in the Army. He's all for it. Arthur Coolen, Doreen's husband, isn't. All this talk about compensation and "making things right" has made Ricky's stepdad a little uneasy.

By the time the Article 32 is over, the Coolens' marriage is crumbling. Art didn't go with his wife to Ottawa for the Remembrance Day ceremony. Herbie did. Doreen suspects that Art is seeing another woman. He thinks she's money-hungry. On a cold February night, another nasty argument turns physical, broken up only by a visit from the RCMP. Art and Doreen are both arrested and charged with assault, led away by police from their new home in Simms Settlement, the one Doreen bought with some of Ricky's life insurance money. The Mounties eventually drop the assault charges after neither agrees to testify against the other.

Almost two weeks later, right before Valentine's Day, Doreen's lawyers—Dick Murtha and Walter Bansley—officially file their wrongful death claim against the U.S. military, demanding cash for the "senseless and unnecessary death of a brother comrade in arms." Not quite a lawsuit, the claim seeks compensation under the Foreign Claims Act, a U.S. statute that allows soldiers and their families—both American and allied—to seek redress in the case of injury or death. "Needless to say, Private Green's family has suffered immensely from his untimely and tragic death," reads the notice of claim. "Accordingly, I trust and sincerely hope that we may endeavor to promptly process this claim in order to spare our clients any further unnecessary anguish."

There isn't a dollar figure yet, but there will be. At least US$1.85 million—$1.45 million for Ricky's estate, $350,000 for his mother, and $50,000 for Herbie, the soldier's so-called "foster father." Art isn't named on the papers. By the summer, Doreen will file for divorce, citing "no possibility of reconciliation."

It is not the only relationship Doreen will lose. Others who loved Ricky Green—Miranda included—are disgusted by her quest for compensation. Blood money, they call it. "If the road was lined with a million dollars, unless Ricky was at the end of it, I would have nothing to do with it," says Joyce Clooney, the soldier's paternal grandmother. "There is nothing that is going to replace Ricky."

The looming "lawsuit" is enough to convince David Green—Ricky's natural father—to speak out. Since April 17, David has been portrayed in the press as the absentee father, the man who left his son when he was three years old and never came back. It's not totally inaccurate. David was barely around when Ricky was young, living the life of a bachelor in western Canada. But things got better. He eventually moved back to Nova Scotia and reconnected with his son. Ricky always called him "Dad." Where does Herbie get the nerve to call himself a foster father? "I know Ricky, and I know he wouldn't be angry at those pilots," David tells one reporter. "He knew the situation he was going into. I can feel it. I can feel it. He was over there to do good for the world, and so were the pilots." Ricky, David says, would "want to be remembered for what he died for."

Even at the Edmonton garrison, many fellow paratroopers are a little disappointed in Pte. Green's mother. She obviously never understood what her son was doing over in Afghanistan in the first place. Some soldiers go so far as to warn their own families to never—ever—do the same thing.

Doreen is not immune to the criticism. It hurts, especially coming from Miranda, the love of her son's life. When that silver coffin landed in Halifax, the two women held each other's hands, crying as the bagpipe played. They don't speak to each other anymore. But Doreen does her best not to dwell on that. She knows she is doing the right thing. She knows Ricky would want his mother to be looked after. "Walk a mile in my shoes," she often says. "And then judge me."

★   ★   ★

The Uniform Code of Military Justice doesn't place any timelines on the work of investigating officers. If he wanted, Col. Patrick Rosenow could take the rest of his career to complete his report for Lt.-Gen. Bruce

Carlson. Considering how much evidence he has to ponder, you could hardly blame him if he really did take that long. Hundreds of thousands of words of testimony. Almost 200 exhibits. Motions. Objections. And more objections.

Unlike a trial, Article 32s do not always end with closing arguments read to the judge. In some cases, both sides are given the chance to present a post-hearing brief, a written synopsis of why the investigating officer should rule in their favor. In yet another odd twist of military law, the prosecution and the defense are allowed to read each other's submissions, then write a second brief that refutes what the other guys mentioned the first time around. More paperwork for Col. Rosenow.

"We respectfully assert that the evidence demonstrates that no criminal offense has been committed by Major Harry Schmidt and that the Investigating Officer should recommend to the Convening Authority that criminal charges in this case should be dismissed," reads the brief signed by Charlie Gittins, Clay Moushon, and Jamie Key. At 26 pages, Maj. Schmidt's submission is nearly identical to the one written by Maj. Umbach's lawyers. As they have since the beginning, the entire defense team presents a unified front.

"In order to reach a conclusion whether Major Schmidt acted culpably negligently under the circumstances, the fact-finder must necessarily evaluate the information provided to Major Schmidt, the information he would have expected to have, and, importantly, the information that he was not provided," the submission reads. "The testimony and evidence admitted at the Article 32 hearing clearly established a breakdown in the command and control process, leaving Major Schmidt and Major Umbach without critical information that would have informed their conduct and changed the outcome on the night of 17 April 2002."

The defense argues that in order for Judge Rosenow to conclude what a "reasonable fighter pilot" would have done, he must consider that Harry and Bill were "squeezed into an anti-G suit" and sitting in a "cramped and cushionless ejection seat" for more than six hours when they suddenly noticed the ground fire. They had heard about the Navy SEAL who was allegedly tortured and killed when he fell out of a chopper. They were warned about the emergence of Ringback multiple rocket launchers in

Afghanistan. But they were never briefed about the Canadian live-fire exercise. If fact, they were never even told—not once—that ground forces *might* conduct such training. "A pilot with no reason to believe that friendly forces were engaged in night live-fire training underneath his flight path reasonably could mistake the firing of Carl Gustav rocket-propelled munitions for the firing of MLRS firing in an anti-aircraft mode, exactly as Major Schmidt and Major Umbach did," the defense argues.

The CAOC didn't know about the live-fire exercise. Neither did the AWACS. Even minutes after the bombing, when Maj. Schmidt asked the AWACS to confirm that "there was no ROZ effective in that area tonight as far as our brief was concerned," BOSSMAN concurred. It wasn't until days after the explosion that the CAOC decided it might be a good idea to issue NOTAMs—Notices to Airmen—that warn pilots about daily live-fire drills. Why not do that before April 17? "Without being provided any information that aircrews flying a combat mission in a 'hot' war zone might encounter a night live-fire exercise conducted by friendly forces on the ground, there was no reason that any reasonable combat pilot, and particularly Major Schmidt or Major Umbach, would even have suspected such a possibility when confronted with rocket-propelled munitions that appeared aimed at their aircraft."

When they did see the munitions, both pilots steered away from the target, so hard that Maj. Schmidt's F-16 recorded a 4.7 G turn—just shy of the maximum Gs a pilot can pull in a Viper carrying four laser-guided bombs, two external fuel tanks, triple ejector racks, and two AIM-9 missiles. Over the next few minutes, both men received "precious little useful information" from the AWACS or the CAOC. In fact, the defense team reiterates its claim that the targeting pod videos—which span three minutes and 23 seconds from the instant they were switched on to the moment the bomb explodes—reveal only a small slice of what was said over the radios that night. The pilots insist that before the recorders were activated at 21:22:38, they told the AWACS they were taking fire in the vicinity of Kandahar. TSgt. Carroll—BOSSMAN—testified that there were "a couple of minutes" of unrecorded radio calls between the moment the pilots saw the fireworks and when AWACS cleared them to mark the SAFIRE. That permission came at 21:21:00—one minute and 38 seconds before the tapes came on—according to a log written at the time by Major Art Henry, the AWACS mission crew commander.

Defense lawyers note that a log book belonging to Maj. Scott Woodson, the voice of the CAOC, says the first call from the AWACS actually arrived in Saudi Arabia at 21:20:00—two minutes and 38 seconds before the tapes came on. Add the "couple of minutes" of previous radio chatter that TSgt. Carroll testified about, and that leaves open the possibility that nearly five minutes ticked by before the pilots ever switched on the tape recorders. If Maj. Woodson's log is correct, the defense maintains, it is even more damaging to the government's case because it proves that the CAOC took nearly six minutes from the first call about the SAFIRE (21:20:00) to tell the AWACS to "get COFFEE 51 out of there as soon as possible" (21:25:47). That call, of course, came seconds too late. Maj. Schmidt's bomb was already away.

"No witness was able to explain why—if 'everyone' knew there were 'thousands' of Americans in or around Kandahar, according to the Government representatives, it took CAOC five minutes and 47 seconds to come to the conclusion that such information might be useful to COFFEE flight," the brief reads.

Even if the CAOC log is completely inaccurate, and the Coalition Air Operations Center received the 20 mike-mike call only at 21:23:49, the defense team says command and control still deserves the blame. For one, why did it take Maj. Henry two minutes and 49 seconds—21:21:00 until 21:23:49—to tell the CAOC that the F-16s were supposedly taking fire? Secondly, the pilots' lawyers note that officials in Saudi Arabia could see Coffee Flight's exact position on a digital radar screen. It was obvious to anyone in the room that the F-16s were near Kandahar. So why did it take the CAOC until 21:25:47—nearly two minutes after Maj. Henry's call—to come back and tell the AWACS that Kandahar had friendlies? Maj. Schmidt's lawyers go so far as to suggest that some CAOC officials "have a great deal of self-interest in not being implicated as being derelict in their own duties. This explains why—despite the clear evidence that the CAOC had approximately six minutes' notice of the SAFIRE event—all CAOC witnesses who testified did their best to minimize the reaction time available to the CAOC."

It is indisputable, the defense team says, that the HUD and targeting pod videos "do not provide the entire story because they were not activated until well after the incident began." They also fail to reveal anything other than what was playing on those tiny screens at the time of the engagement. They don't show what the pilots saw outside their cockpits, through NVGs that are famous for creating "misperceptions and illusions." And they don't provide any insight into what Bill and Harry were thinking from second to second. "Every pilot indicated that a review of those videos alone was insufficient to form accurate opinions," the submission reads. "The Government witnesses who were willing to offer opinions based upon the sum of the information they had been provided, including information from Major Schmidt and Major Umbach, indicated that they believed Major Schmidt and Major Umbach should have respected the system they perceived was engaging them and acted reasonably under the circumstances." The defense brief notes "that even Brig.-Gen. Sargeant conceded that Major Schmidt did not act unreasonably to engage the target once he found himself in the position immediately before bomb drop, believing his flight lead was being engaged by a MLRS artillery system modified for surface to air engagements." The CIB co-president also "conceded that Major Schmidt was required to remain with his flight lead and not simply 'bug out.' This concession by the Government's key witness—who was added to the mix at the '11th hour' in a desperate effort to bolster a sagging case—obviated any legal basis for recommending that the charges of manslaughter, negligent homicide or aggravated assault be referred to trial."

Military prosecutors—and Gen. Sargeant before them—have accused the pilots of displaying a "reckless disregard" for the rules of engagement by moving closer to the unidentified target instead of simply turning around and flying away. In their final brief, the defense points to Section 5 of the OEF special instructions. "Relevant here is the direction that, when a hostile act is in progress, 'the right exists to use proportional force, including armed force, in self-defense by all necessary means available to deter or neutralize the potential attacker or, if necessary, to destroy the threat,'" they write. "Notably absent from the rules is any reference to a requirement to 'turn and burn' or vacate the area in response to 'hostile act' or 'hostile intent.'" In fact, "every witness who testified at the Article 32 hearing testified, correctly, that the inherent right and obligation of self-defense cannot be overruled—the right to self-defense overrides even an emergency 'hold fire' command."

Maj. Schmidt originally asked permission to fire 20mm "warning shots to diffuse the situation," but that request was met with a "decidedly unhelpful 'standby' from the AWACS." When he invoked self-defense 90 seconds later, he did not, as the government alleges, deliberately descend to attack a weapons system firing well below his altitude. He believed he and Maj. Umbach were being ambushed by an MLRS-type system "that already possessed a great range and altitude *advantage*" on their jets. "Even if Major Schmidt was objectively wrong in his assessment, his honest and reasonable belief under the circumstances, that his wingman was being targeted and engaged by a significant life-threatening weapons system, justified his use of whatever force and whatever maneuvers he believed were required in order to neutralize that threat. It is simply asking too much to ask a pilot engaged in a combat mission to wait until rounds begin to actually impact his or her flight lead's aircraft before taking action in self-defense. Those seconds of indecision are seconds that will cost lives." Even the AWACS controller, albeit 30 seconds after the bomb exploded, reminded the pilots of their inherent right to self-defense. "You're cleared," TSgt. Carroll said. "Self-defense."

The conduct of the Canadian paratroopers also added to the fog of war, the pilots' lawyers allege. "While it is not the intent of the defense to 'blame' the soldiers of 3 PPCLI for the accident, it is nonetheless undeniable and relevant to consider the errors and omissions by the Canadians that contributed to this mishap as these errors and omissions had a direct and palpable effect on the decision-making of Major Schmidt and Major Umbach." Cpl. Paquette—and perhaps MCpl. Clark—fired their machine guns skyward at the pop-up target. There was no "blinking red light" on the range that night, an alleged breach of a U.S. Army regulation written in 1983. The ACO categorized Tarnak Farm as a "small arms range," but at 84 millimeters, the Carl G. can hardly be considered small arms. And then there is the whole "check fire" issue, the fact that Cpl. Laroque, A Company's man in the tower, testified that he ordered the range to go cold five to 10 minutes before the bomb exploded—an order that never reached the range. "The errors and omissions of the Canadians, while not the direct cause of the accident of 17 April 2002, were substantial contributing factors that must be considered in deciding whether or not Major Schmidt acted negligently."

So must the Go-pills. Those little orange tablets are known to trigger hallucinations, paranoia, and anxiety, yet the Air Force pushed them on their pilots as a "counter-fatigue measure"—an off-label use of the drug that is not even approved by the FDA. "To the extent that the Government claims that Major Schmidt somehow was 'negligent' and the Investigating Officer agrees, we respectfully submit that the effects of the prescribed medication and their effects under the stress of combat and the belief he and his flight lead had been engaged by enemy surface-to-air rocket fire cannot be excluded as the cause of these judgment errors," the defense brief reads. The Air Force has never tested how pilots react to the pills in the cockpit, let alone in combat. "It is impossible to ascribe such negligence to Major Schmidt rather than to the effects of the military issued drugs, and he should not be held criminally liable for the results of the alleged negligence, to the extent there was any involved in this case."

Near the end of their submissions, lawyers for Maj. Schmidt and Maj. Umbach argue that what happened on April 17 was a "tragic but inevitable part of warfare," another in a long line of friendly fire accidents that dates as far back as war itself. George Washington was nearly killed by his comrades during the French and Indian War. Soldiers accidentally killing their own was so common in both world wars that the exact number of casualties is impossible to calculate. Even as technology advanced, little improved. During the first Gulf War, at least 25 percent of all combat deaths were chalked up to friendly fire, including nine British soldiers who were killed when a pair of U.S. Air Force A-10s—convinced they were flying over an Iraqi armored column—fired Maverick missiles at their convoy. The Brits had fluorescent markers on the tops of their trucks, but it wasn't enough to stop the American pilots. "Perhaps the most infamous friendly fire accident occurred after the war during a routine patrol of the northern Iraq no-fly zone," the defense brief says. "In a grave foreshadowing of the events of 17 April 2002, poor Army-Air Force communications and command and control failures led two U.S. F-15s to shoot down two Army Blackhawk helicopters. Twenty-six people from four countries were killed. Only one person had charges referred—AWACS controller Capt. Wang. He was acquitted at trial."

Operation Enduring Freedom, the defense says, was rife with its own incidents of friendly fire—long before April 17. In December 2001, three U.S. Special Forces soldiers and seven anti-Taliban Afghans were killed when a B-52 dropped a 2,000-pound bomb on their formation. The mistake nearly killed Hamid Karzai, who would go on to become Afghanistan's prime minister. No criminal charges. Three months later, during Anaconda, an AC-130 was granted clearance to engage what the crew believed was an enemy convoy. Again, it turned out to be Special Forces. One soldier, Chief Warrant Officer Stanley Harriman, was killed. No disciplinary action. In yet another high-profile blunder, an AC-130 gunship opened fire on an Afghan wedding in July 2002, killing at least 34 civilians (the Afghan government reported 48 dead and 117 wounded). It seems the crew mistook celebratory gunfire for anti-aircraft artillery. Nobody was charged. "There are a number of reasons why the criminal realm has historically been seen as an inappropriate forum to deal with friendly fire accidents," the defense team writes. "For one, they are—by definition—*accidents*. Accidents involving people who are involved in one of the most stressful endeavors known to man: bearing arms against an enemy. The reality of warfare is simple: mistakes cannot be avoided. A criminal prosecution will never change that fact."

Both defense submissions conclude with almost the exact same words, urging Col. Rosenow to recommend that Lt.-Gen. Bruce Carlson dismiss all the charges. "While any unnecessary loss of life or injury to friendly military forces in combat is unfortunate, 'friendly fire' accidents are a fact of life in military operations where the 'trigger pullers' are fallible humans. Like most accidents, this one was preventable and was the culmination of a series of honest mistakes by many good people. Prosecution under these circumstances will have a chilling and potentially deadly effect for future military personnel; rather than acting whether in self-defense or aggressively in other combat situations, military personnel may hesitate to act out of fear they may make a mistake and be subject to 'arm-chair quarterbacking' after the fact and prosecution by a court-martial. If any military member loses his or her life because of such hesitation in the future, this process will be directly responsible for that death. If the United States is going to send Americans into combat where they may lose their own lives, those Americans must be empowered to make honest, split-second life or death decisions without fear of being criminally prosecuted."

★   ★   ★

Col. Odom and his team of prosecutors do not have to prove that the pilots are guilty beyond a reasonable doubt. Not yet, at least. At the Article 32 stage, they are only obliged to present a *prima facie* case, to convince the investigating officer not that the accused should be tossed in jail, but that the evidence warrants further review at a court-martial. It is a much lower burden of proof.

In meticulous, plain language so often used by prosecutors, government lawyers argue that the two-week hearing uncovered more than enough *prima facie* evidence to support each criminal charge: four counts of involuntary manslaughter, eight counts of aggravated assault, and one count of dereliction of duty. In order to prove manslaughter and assault, the government must show that the pilots acted with culpable negligence, that their actions in the sky were not only careless, but were "accompanied by a gross, reckless, wanton or deliberate disregard for the foreseeable results to others."

There is no shortage of proof, prosecutors write. The pilots dropped their bomb within three miles of a friendly airbase, in a completely different area of operation—AO Truman—than the one they were assigned to fly over that night. Moments before his wingman rolled in, Maj. Umbach even steered his F-16 right over the bright lights of the Kandahar Airfield, home to thousands of coalition troops. As the smoke billowed from Tarnak Farm, Bill already had an inkling that his wingman made a mistake. "Was that definitely the airfield?" he asked over the radio.

There is no doubt, prosecutors say, that pilots flying OEF missions were frustrated with the lack of up-to-date intelligence on the location of coalition ground troops. It was a constant struggle. But that is hardly enough to vindicate Harry Schmidt and Bill Umbach. If anything, it makes their defense that much more hollow. "Simply put, if there was not sufficient information about GOB [ground order of battle], and friendly and enemy forces were difficult to distinguish, COFFEE Flight should have been more cautious, not less, before employing ordnance. Their failure to exercise the appropriate level of caution is just another example of their deliberate disregard for the foreseeable results to others."

Minutes after the explosion, "we receive rare insight into the thought processes of the two pilots," prosecutors continue. Maj. Schmidt: *I hope that was the right thing to do.* Maj. Umbach: *Me too.* "Those words speak volumes, and indicate neither pilot was sure that they were actually in a defensive situation. That question certainly should have been answered *before* dropping a 500-pound laser-guided bomb on a group of men within three miles of the Kandahar airfield."

The government's 45-page brief goes on to list the many reasons why both pilots were allegedly derelict in their duties. Maj. Schmidt: You flew too low. You flew too slow. You failed to relay a proper SAFIRE report. You usurped your flight lead, taking over the job of talking to the AWACS. You didn't make any defensive radio calls. You failed to answer Maj. Umbach when he said: "Let's just make sure it's not friendlies, is all." Maj. Umbach: You failed to demand that Maj. Schmidt acknowledge your order to make sure it wasn't friendlies. You didn't regain control of the flight when your wingman began talking to BOSSMAN. You failed to ensure that Harry followed the "hold fire" call from the AWACS. You let Maj. Schmidt descend below the 15,000-foot altitude floor. You didn't mark the target. You allowed Maj. Schmidt to drop a bomb without proper clearance.

The heart of the pilots' case is that Maj. Schmidt invoked self-defense because he believed his flight lead was on the brink of being shot out of the sky. That's nonsense, prosecutors say. There is no evidence whatsoever that Maj. Schmidt ever believed "that death or grievous bodily harm was about to be wrongfully inflicted" on Maj. Umbach. If he did, why didn't he warn Bill over the radio or urge him to jink his jet? "There is ample evidence that Maj. Schmidt's decision to employ a laser-guided bomb was not based on self-defense of himself or defense of Maj. Umbach. Rather, the evidence suggests that Maj. Schmidt reacted aggressively to a perceived target of opportunity—not a threat to either F-16—and that he took matters into his own hands to employ ordnance after being repeatedly denied permission to drop by a proper command and control authority. In reality, using the self-defense 'trump card' of the ROEs, Maj. Schmidt, aided by Maj. Umbach, executed a quickly formulated, ill-conceived, un-authorized and unnecessary attack on a friendly position. The actions of the accused were reckless in the extreme and criminal in their result."

Even more outrageous, prosecutors say, is the invention of the so-called Time before the Tapes Came on, the unknown span of seconds in which the F-16 pilots claim they told BOSSMAN they were taking fire. "This desperate attempt to live in the off-tape world is necessary because the ac-tions of the accused on the tapes speak for themselves and are indefensible," the brief alleges. Prosecutors note that the first call recorded on tape is from a calm Maj. Umbach, asking his wingman: "Do ya got good coordinates for a mark or do ya need me to roll in?" If Maj. Umbach was truly worried that someone on the ground was shooting at their jets before the tapes were activated, why would he consider rolling in to take a mark? "The evidence is clear that neither pilot felt threatened. In fact, the evidence leads to the conclusion that Maj. Schmidt went back to the suspected site looking for a fight."

Okay BOSSMAN, uh, this is Coffee 52. I've got a tally in the vicinity. I, ah, request permission to lay down some, uh, 20 mike-mike (21:23:33). "This radio call is the most telling evidence regarding Maj. Schmidt's state of mind and his perception of a threat, or lack thereof, to either himself or his flight lead," prosecutors argue. If he was indeed defensive, he would not need BOSSMAN's permission to open fire.

Standby (21:23:43). If the pilots truly felt threatened, they should have left the area at that moment. In fact, Maj. Schmidt's F-16 is already fly-ing east—away from the target—when the AWACS tells him to standby. "However, he then turned back toward the Canadians' position while waiting for permission to engage from AWACS. Flying back toward a per-ceived target is inconsistent with being threatened. Maj. Schmidt's actions are entirely consistent with a desire to engage and attack the target."

Let's just make sure that it's, uh, that it's not friendlies, is all (21:23:45). This, prosecutors say, is "a rare demonstration of situational awareness during the engagement." It is clear that Maj. Umbach, the flight lead, had doubts about who was firing underneath them. Is it friend or foe? "This statement is completely inconsistent with Maj. Umbach feeling threatened."

BOSSMAN from Coffee 52. Do you want us to push a different freq? (21:24:42) "This radio call from Maj. Schmidt is further telling evidence of Maj. Schmidt's state of mind and his level of impatience with the controlling agency," the brief suggests. "First, he continued to wait for permission to fire, which was not required if he truly felt threatened or if he believed his flight lead was threatened. The statement is also strongly indicative of frustration or impatience with waiting for permission from AWACS to fire his 20 millimeter cannon. In other words, 'What's taking so long? Who else can I talk to—besides the tanker controller who obviously has no clue about what I'm trying to do? Who can I speak with who will give me permission to fire?'"

Coffee 51, BOSSMAN. Hold fire. Need details on SAFIRE for K-Mart (21:25:00). Hold fire: an emergency order to stop shooting, which includes the destruction of all missiles in flight. "Based on his training, experience, and familiarity with the ROEs, Maj. Schmidt knew that the only way around this directive from AWACS was to invoke self-defense. He therefore played the 'trump card' of the ROEs—he invoked self-defense so he could proceed with the attack he had been setting up for over 90 seconds. What was it about 'hold fire' that Maj. Schmidt could have found confusing or hard to understand?"

Okay, I've got some men on a road and it looks like a piece of artillery firing at us. I am rolling in in self-defense (21:25:04). By now, Maj. Schmidt has asked for permission to strafe the target, been told to "standby," been reminded to "make sure it's not friendlies," asked to change radio frequencies, and finally, ordered to hold his fire. "The 'hold fire' command was the last straw for Maj. Schmidt," prosecutors argue. "His declaration of self-defense, which came only seconds after the AWACS transmitted 'hold fire,' was nothing more than a pretext to engage a target of opportunity."

Government lawyers contend that even from a strictly legal standpoint, Maj. Schmidt's claim of self-defense is not enough to save him from criminal charges. According to U.S. military law, a person can only claim defense of another—as Maj. Schmidt did, supposedly to protect his flight lead—if the person he is defending is entitled to use deadly force under the same circumstances. "When Maj. Schmidt declared he was rolling in in self-defense, Maj. Umbach was nearly seven miles away, cruising leisurely at 23,000 feet—well out of the range of any known SAFIRE threat in Afghanistan. Since Maj. Umbach was clearly not threatened or entitled to use deadly force at that time, neither was Maj. Schmidt." The self-defense claim is even more ridiculous because Maj. Schmidt—by his "own misconduct"—flew his Viper closer to the unknown ground fire. "The situation over Tarnak Farms may have seemed to Maj. Schmidt to have grown more dangerous, but that misperception only resulted from his having been somewhere he was not supposed to be in the first place. One cannot impermissibly fly into a perceived threat zone in violation of the SPINS, when there was absolutely no valid reason to do so, then claim that an application of deadly force was in self-defense." In other words, Maj. Schmidt was already guilty of negligence long before he ever pushed the pickle button.

But why? Why would two reputable, well-trained fighter pilots—including one of the best in the entire country—do something so stupid? Prosecutors have their suspicions. "All of the legal analysis is now completed and the time has come for straight talk about what happened over Kandahar, Afghanistan on 17 April 2002," they write. Harry Schmidt was the man, a former Top Gun instructor recruited by the Springfield unit "to show them all how to do it." They waited two years for Psycho to arrive, and he played a key role in getting the 170th Fighter Squadron ready for Kuwait. But when they arrived in theater, little happened. For more than a month, the unit flew long missions in and out of Afghanistan and Iraq, hauling bombs back and forth—but never dropping any. Finally, on April 15, John Milton and Mark Skibinski were sent to northern Iraq to bomb a pre-planned target. They missed.

During the Article 32, Maj. Milton "painfully attempted to downplay the significance of the earlier mission," prosecutors say. "However, the incident was a major gaffe on the part of the 170th EFS." Maj. Milton, the flight lead, personally debriefed Maj.-Gen. Buchanan, the JTF-SWA commander who just happened to be in Kuwait that day. News of the embarrassing mis-hit spread across the entire theater of operations. Even fighter pilots back home in the United States heard about the miss. "There is no doubt that this incident was on Maj. Schmidt's mind just two days later on 17

April 2002," prosecutors allege. "When Maj. Schmidt and Maj. Umbach observed what they perceived to be SAFIRE on the way to their tanker, they were presented with what they perceived to be a target of opportunity. If the forces on the ground at Tarnak Farms had been enemy forces instead of Canadians, a 'shack' would have gone a long way in restoring the unit's tarnished reputation from the previous OSW debacle." Simply put, Maj. Schmidt was desperate to "score a win" for the squadron.

"Overlooking the rather obvious facts that no one on the ground or in the air was calling for fire support from COFFEE Flight, Maj. Schmidt abandoned his flight lead and proceeded to make a series of low, slow turns to try and find and engage an unknown target on the ground. Even Maj. Schmidt's amazing explanation of why he asked for permission to initially engage with his 20 millimeter cannon ('to get them to keep their heads down') makes no sense: it would have been just as deadly if a 20 millimeter cannon shell had hit the people on the ground as if the GBU–12 had hit them. Without positive target identification or GFAC control, any delivery of firepower in close proximity to known concentrations of friendly troops constitutes a wanton and reckless disregard for human life.

"The fact that the two pilots were absolutely wrong cannot be over-looked," prosecutors conclude. "No one was shooting at them. These cases are not about some hypothetical defense involving 'go pills' which has absolutely no basis in fact. This case is not about what the CAOC or the AWACS knew about what was happening on the ground at Tarnak Farms. Rather, these cases are about accountability for two pilots who violated the rules, went where they were not supposed to go, did what they were not supposed to do, failed to do what they were supposed to do (take a mark on the suspected SAFIRE and depart the area), disregarded 'standby' and 'hold fire' orders and, using the ROEs as a pretext to cover Maj. Schmidt's uncontrollable impatience, flew an unauthorized attack mission with disastrous results."

★ ★ ★

"The Government's assertions are fanciful, reckless, entirely devoid of evidentiary support, and nothing short of a slur on the professionalism of all

Air Force pilots," the defense team writes. "The Government provided no evidence whatsoever to indicate that Major Schmidt experienced or communicated any angst about the mission flown by the 170th in OSW two days prior. The Government presented no evidence of any circumstance that would have remotely caused Major Schmidt to abandon the professionalism he has demonstrated uniformly throughout his military career."

In their response to the prosecution's post-hearing brief, Maj. Schmidt's lawyers accuse Col. Odom and his team of presenting a "cowardly" claim that is "entirely fiction, created from whole cloth and unsupported by any evidence of record." To suggest that Harry and Bill were out to "score a win" would mean they are both bold-faced liars who concocted a cover story moments after the explosion—and have stuck to it ever since. Where is the proof? Where is the evidence that shows the pilots even cared about what happened in Iraq, let alone that it fueled their conduct that night? "This claim is simply a desperate, yet imaginative, act to create a concern that the (lack of) evidence demonstrated never existed," the defense brief reads.

If Maj. Schmidt really did want to "score a win" for the unit, why did he even turn on his cockpit tape recorder—and then remind Maj. Umbach to do the same? And what about Capt. Pepper, the AWACS senior director? He told Gen. Sargeant that the tone of the pilots' voices was that of two men who "were getting fired upon and were very concerned about it," not reckless fighters itching to drop a bomb. It is important to remember, the defense brief says, that Maj. Schmidt's story has been the same since just minutes after the bombing, when—with the recorders whirling—he first told the AWACS that the unknown fire appeared to be coming from an MLRS-type system.

Specifics aside, the pilots' lawyers say the larger issue remains irrefutable: Maj. Schmidt legitimately acted in defense of his flight lead. Pilots do not have to be grazed by the enemy before retaliating, and even if they misjudge the actual danger—as Maj. Schmidt did—it does not make the self-defense claim moot. "The SPINS do not require a pilot to wait until the rounds begin to impact around him before engaging in self-defense," the lawyers write. "The purpose of the ROE and SPINS are to protect American service members and their military equipment. The Government's effort to dilute the right of self-defense and make service members engage in legal evaluations in the heat of combat demonstrates the fundamental flaw in permitting lawyers and other non-combatants to evaluate the split-second judgments of warriors engaged in a combat mission."

★ ★ ★

"The Investigating Officer should ask what a reasonable man would have done that night over Kandahar," prosecutors write in their final reply. "Would he have stayed inside a perceived threat zone without taking any defensive actions of any kind for over four and a half minutes, flying ever lower and slower repeatedly in the direction of the alleged threat, or would he have flown away to a position of safety? Would the reasonable man have totally ignored a radio call to be sure the target below was not friendlies, or would he have taken extra precautions to positively identify the target as hostile before attacking? Would the reasonable man have relied on perceptions of fire acquired through NVGs, which that same reasonable man knew presented distorted views of images? Would a reasonable man have dropped a weapon in close proximity to an airfield which was the known location of thousands of coalition friendly troops without ground forward air controller (FAC) or airborne FAC positive target approval? Or would the reasonable man have simply continued flying at over 20,000 feet, noted the location of the perceived fire and reported it, and continued on to his tanker rendezvous?"

The answer, at least to prosecutors, is obvious: the pilots should have flown away. At 360 knots—six miles per minute—the F-16s could have scrammed well beyond the range of any known or imagined threat during the time period they circled over Tarnak Farm. "Air Force fighter pilots are trained to maintain their composure under the most extreme stress, to use logic and good judgment and to have, above all, concern for human life," prosecutors write. "They are trained to a reasonable man standard. The fact that flight operations in Afghanistan brought about stress related to combat is not surprising. However, stress provides no excuse whatsoever for the failures by Majors Schmidt and Umbach to maintain the high standards of conduct expected of Air Force fighter pilots, chief among which is positive target identification and avoidance of fratricide."

★ ★ ★

The final document submitted to Col. Rosenow—Exhibit 183—is a motion from the defense team. They want prosecutors to hand over all travel orders and vouchers issued to the Canadian families who flew to Barksdale for the hearing. They argue that if this case ever does reach trial, the documents could serve to disqualify some relatives from taking the witness stand on the grounds that their testimony was "purchased."

34

Afghanistan is a semi-forgotten war by the time Patrick Rosenow begins to write his recommendations for the commander of the 8th Air Force. It has been nearly 18 months since American troops ousted the Taliban; almost a year since Harry Schmidt's last mission in the cockpit of an F-16. Iraq is the focus now. Saddam Hussein.

Colin Powell, the U.S. secretary of state, has already appeared in front of the United Nations Security Council, holding a tiny vial of white powder and warning that Iraq has enough anthrax to "fill tens upon tens upon tens of thousands" more. Weapons of mass destruction. By March, international diplomacy is no match for the Bush administration. The president vows, again and again, that he will invade Iraq and disarm its dictator—with or without U.N. approval. America, he repeatedly says, can no longer afford to wait for the mushroom cloud before confronting its enemies. Not after September 11.

Behind the scenes, the White House continues to build its "coalition of the willing," a contingent of nations in favor of a U.S.-led invasion. Ethiopia. Latvia. Poland. Australia. Britain. Noticeably absent from the list of more than 30 countries is Canada. For months, as their southern neighbor beat the drums of war, Canada's Liberal government remained perched on the proverbial fence. We are willing to commit troops, Ottawa says, but not unless the U.N. Security Council sanctions the war. Many in Washington feel snubbed by the conditional support of their so-called closest ally.

In the backrooms of the United Nations, Canadian officials try to spearhead a compromise between the U.S., Britain, and the anti-war nations of the Security Council, including France, China, and Russia. They fail. By March 17, 2003, it is obvious that no U.N. resolution will either stop—or condone—the ousting of Saddam Hussein. Thousands of U.S. and British soldiers are already gathered on the Iraqi border, waiting for orders. Their Canadian counterparts will not be joining them. "Over the last few weeks, the Security Council has been unable to agree on a new resolution authorizing military action," Jean Chrétien, the prime minister, tells the House of Commons. "Canada worked very hard to find a compromise to bridge the gap in the Security Council. Unfortunately, we were not successful."

Hours later, George W. Bush offers a public ultimatum to Saddam and his two sons: Leave Iraq within 48 hours, and spare your country from war. They don't, and on Wednesday, March 19—two hours after the deadline expires—the president addresses his nation from the Oval Office. Stealth fighter jets and Navy ships are already launching cruise missiles and laser-guided bombs into Baghdad. Shock and awe. "To all of the men and women of the United States Armed Forces now in the Middle East, the peace of a troubled world and the hopes of an oppressed people now depend on you," President Bush says. "That trust is well placed. The enemies you confront will come to know your skill and bravery. The people you liberate will witness the honorable and decent spirit of the American military."

★ ★ ★

By the next morning, the first full day of Operation Iraqi Freedom, fighter pilots are hammering Saddam's country with bombs. *Shack.* On the all-day news networks, cameras capture the beauty of the explosions, the clouds of smoke and fire and the flawless precision of it all. There is no other story in the world today. After months of talk, the United States is finally attacking Iraq.

Amid the unrelenting coverage, the public affairs office at Louisiana's Barksdale Air Force Base issues a one-page press release. Col. Rosenow has made his recommendation to Lt.-Gen. Bruce Carlson: Drop the charges. The timing of the announcement isn't lost on anyone. Not only is it buried underneath the biggest news story of the year, but it comes just days after Canada confirmed that its soldiers won't be joining their American allies in Baghdad. The speculation is inevitable. Is this Canada's punishment? You didn't support us, so we're not going to prosecute those fighter pilots anymore? Many wonder aloud whether Harry and Bill really were political pawns all along, a goodwill offering to earn Canada's support for the Iraqi war.

The short news release—seven sentences—says little to suggest otherwise. "In his report, Colonel Rosenow concluded there was sufficient evidence to charge each accused and try him by court-martial," it reads. "However, he asserted that the interests of good order and discipline could adequately be addressed by sanctions other than trial by court-martial." Those sanctions, the judge says, could include an administrative hearing, where punishment can range from forfeiture of pay to a letter of reprimand. No jail time.

What is not released to the media is Col. Rosenow's actual decision, his 42-page explanation of exactly why he made the recommendation he did. It is a thorough, if not dizzying, examination of legal niceties and burdens of proof—undoubtedly pondered long before Jean Chrétien ever stood up in the House of Commons. His conclusion is simple: The government can present a strong case that the pilots acted recklessly that night over Tarnak Farm, but probably not strong enough to secure a guilty verdict beyond a reasonable doubt. That fine line between conviction and acquittal ultimately hinges on the expert testimony of fellow fighter pilots—testimony that is hardly unanimous. Some condone what Harry and Bill did. Others don't. Whose side a jury would believe, Judge Rosenow writes, is simply "too close to call."

The colonel's report to the general begins with a lengthy summary of not only what happened that night, but what happened before and after. The Top Gun who left the Navy to join the Guard. The squadron commander who led his Springfield pilots to Kuwait. The ACO that was impossible to plot across an onboard map. *Shack*. Gen. Sargeant. Criminal charges. The Article 32. The request for all travel vouchers given to the Canadian families. Col. Rosenow turned that one down. "Certainly, a trial judge would allow counsel to ask a witness who paid for their travel," he writes. "Vouchers aren't necessary to do that. Moreover, in my view if any relatives eventually appear at trial, their testimony will have been 'purchased' not by the promise of a free trip, but by the death and suffering of their loved ones."

If this case contains a single undisputed fact, it is this: Coffee Flight intentionally dropped a bomb on Tarnak Farm with the expectation that it would kill the people there. The government claims the self-defense call was a ruse, a pretext to hit a target of opportunity and restore the honor of the 170th after a botched mission two days earlier. The defense claims the pilots had no choice but to engage, convinced that they were ambushed by a rocket-propelled weapons system that could fire well beyond the altitude they were flying. Before even assessing which claim is valid, Col. Rosenow tells Lt.-Gen. Carlson that he has "reservations" about the wording of the involuntary manslaughter (culpably negligent homicide) charge.

"From a technical perspective, the facts of this case do not clearly 'fit' a charge of culpably negligent homicide," he writes. "Culpable negligent homicide contemplates cases in which the accused did not intend to kill the victim, but rather had a gross, reckless, wanton, or deliberate disregard for the foreseeable results to the victim." Dangling a person out of a window, for example, or giving a drunk friend the keys to your car. It is negligent behavior, but not necessarily meant to kill. "In contrast," Col. Rosenow writes, "Coffee Flight intended to kill the men at Tarnak Farms."

The judge tells Gen. Carlson that he was unable to find a single case in which an accused planned to kill the victim, but was still convicted of culpable negligent homicide. In fact, the U.S. military's senior court of appeals has ruled that the charge cannot be raised when a death is intended. From a purely legal standpoint, the appropriate charge in this case—considering the prosecutors' pretext theory—should probably be murder. "However, murder appears to be, at least on its face, a harsh charge in light of all of the facts in this case," Judge Rosenow writes. "Nonetheless, the defense could object at trial (or on appeal) that culpable negligent homicide does not apply in the case and move for the charge to be dismissed. I believe that a trial judge would probably deny such a motion and that evidence of intent would satisfy a requirement for 'culpable negligence.' Nonetheless, the issue is far from clear and there is a significant risk that the charge could be dismissed at trial or overturned on appeal."

That aside, Col. Rosenow continues his report on the assumption that all the charges—involuntary manslaughter, aggravated assault, and dereliction of duty—would remain the same come trial. "The defense presented, through witnesses and documents, evidence about the actions of third parties before and after the bombing," Judge Rosenow tells the general. Why wasn't the range marked with a blinking red light? Did the Canadians ignore a "check fire" order? The Carl Gustav isn't small arms. Why didn't the AWACS know about the live-fire exercise? Or the CAOC? Fighter units struggled to find intel on the location of friendly ground forces. Why didn't the 332nd AEG have a ground liaison officer—a GLO—who could have provided that information? Why didn't someone from the CAOC attend Col. Nichols' symposium?

None of those questions, Col. Rosenow writes, is enough to save the pilots from blame. "It is possible for the conduct of two or more persons to contribute, each as a proximate or direct cause, to the death of another," he writes. "If the accused's conduct is a proximate or direct cause of the victim's death, he will not be relieved of criminal responsibility just because some other person's conduct was also a proximate or direct cause of the death. An accused is, however, relieved of criminal responsibility for the death of the victim if the death was the result of some unforeseeable independent intervening cause that did not involve the accused. Obviously, the deaths were the natural and probable result of Coffee Flight's actions over Kandahar. Therefore, even if the acts of the third parties or Canadians were somehow negligent, Coffee Flight would still be criminally liable. None of the conduct offered by the defense rose to an unforeseeable independent cause intervening between Coffee Flight's actions and the deaths.

"The defense submits that the third party actions should also be considered for the effect they may have had on Coffee Flight's decisions," Col. Rosenow continues. "That is true, but only to the extent the accused knew about them. For example, I do not think anyone will suggest Coffee Flight was thinking about the specific US Army regulatory guidance on small arms firing ranges. Thus, the fact that there were rocket-propelled munitions would be relevant. That they do not fit the definition of small arms is not. Similarly, the only way a check fire order to the Canadians would be relevant would be if Coffee Flight had known about it, and therefore assumed the fire they saw was not coming from the Canadians. Obviously that is not the case, since they did not even know the Canadians were there. The implication that Coffee Flight dropped the bomb (and are now under charges) because the Canadians were negligent is consistent with a common courtroom strategy to victimize the accused and accuse the victim. It is an appropriate litigation tactic when supported by the evidence and the law. It is not so supported in this case, and I would expect a trial judge to exclude such evidence."

It would be pertinent, the judge says, for a jury to hear that nobody in the AWACS or the CAOC knew about the live-fire exercise, but the reason they didn't know is irrelevant to the specific charges both pilots face. "In other words," he tells the general, "the court should hear everything about the stage upon which the accused acted. How that stage came to be set and whether there was negligence or fault in the setting of that stage is not relevant to the assessment of their actions at that time and place, given what they knew. Consequently, the vast majority of the evidence offered at the hearing by the defense about the negligence, failure to follow regulations, or inaction of other parties would be inadmissible during a trial phase on guilt or innocence."

What will be admissible, Judge Rosenow says, is evidence about the Go-pills. "Their use was certainly sanctioned, if not strongly encouraged," he writes. "It would seem unfair to order pilots to fly long missions, provide them stimulants to fend off fatigue, and then hold them responsible if the stimulant affected their judgment." At trial, the defense will undoubtedly call expert witnesses who will testify that Dexedrine's well-known side-effects could have clouded the pilots' judgment. "They will point to their clients' outstanding records and character for judgment and airmanship. They will argue that if there was a significant departure from that character, it must have been due to the go-pills. Ultimately, I believe the go-pills had no effect on Coffee Flight's judgment. Nonetheless, the pills raise an additional issue and could give court members an excuse to acquit in what may really be jury nullification."

Even if prosecutors manage to prove—beyond a reasonable doubt—that the drug had absolutely no effect on the pilots, other hurdles await. "Eventually, this case devolves into three basic questions," Col. Rosenow writes. "Were the accused reasonable in perceiving that they were threatened by a rocket-based system? Were they reasonable in turning, descending and decelerating instead of departing? Once, low and slow, were they reasonable in dropping the bomb?" The government's circumstantial case for guilt is "solid," the judge writes, "but fairly complex and by no means immune to defense rebuttal." In the end, jurors—hesitant to put themselves in the shoes of an F–16 pilot—would form their opinions according to the testimony of fellow fighter pilots. At the Article 32, five F–16 pilots took the stand.

Maj. John Milton: A reasonable fighter pilot could have believed he was trapped in a threat envelope and had no choice but to drop a bomb. It was Maj. Schmidt's right to roll in in self-defense, even after the "hold fire" order.

Lt.-Col. Ralph Viets: Rolling in would be a reasonable response because Maj. Schmidt was reasonable to believe that he was already in the threat envelope of a rocket-based weapons system.

Col. David C. Nichols: A reasonably prudent F–16 pilot might have done the same thing. "Combat aviation is not a science. It's an art."

Lt.-Col. Craig Fisher: There were no "significant departures from flight discipline." A reasonable fighter pilot would have egressed the area, but that doesn't mean Maj. Schmidt and Maj. Umbach were reckless.

Gen. Stephen T. Sargeant: A reasonable pilot never would have believed that the fire on the ground was a threat to his flight. And even if he did, turning, descending, and decelerating was an unreasonable reaction. However, disregarding all the alleged reckless maneuvers Maj. Schmidt made to reach the spot where he invoked self-defense, dropping a bomb at that instant was not unreasonable. In other words, if Maj. Schmidt suddenly woke up at 14,000 feet and four nautical miles away from the mystery fire, it would be reasonable to drop a bomb in self-defense.

"The importance of Colonel Nichols, Major Milton, and Lt Col Viets' testimony cannot be over emphasized," Col. Rosenow writes. "Of course, their relationship with the accused might make their testimony less credible. On the other hand, they were the most familiar with the actual situation facing Coffee Flight, and with the information Coffee Flight would have received about the extended threats. Lt Col Fisher and General Sargeant found the real culpability in the accused's failure to stay out of range, not the bombing itself. Essentially, they say that a reasonable F–16 pilot would have never been in the position to have to engage in self-defense. I found all the witnesses to be credible and trying their best to tell the truth as they believed it to be. That they reach different conclusions from the same predicates says more about the difficult issues involved than their honesty." (Of note, Col. Rosenow did not rule on the thorny issue of whether or not Gen. Sargeant should have been allowed to testify at the Article 32. He simply highlighted the objection for Gen. Carlson, saying that if there is a trial, prosecutors will probably be able to find another expert witness with the same opinion as the CIB president.)

"I think that a court may believe that Coffee Flight did not act reasonably in determining they were threatened by what may have been a rocket-based system," Col. Rosenow continues. "However, I think it is unlikely that they would find that was proven beyond a reasonable doubt. Similarly, given the good character evidence and expert testimony that Coffee Flight was in fact entitled to use self-defense, I do not believe a court will find beyond a reasonable doubt, on the strength of circumstantial evidence alone, that Major Schmidt honestly knew self-defense didn't apply and intentionally violated the ROEs/SPINs. Finally, I believe that a court will be very hesitant to hold Major Umbach criminally liable for negligently leading Coffee Flight. It is clear that he essentially yielded *de facto* flight lead responsibility to Major Schmidt. However, given Major Schmidt's credentials and background as a surface to air threat expert and squadron weapons officer, court members without personal experience as fighter pilots may not find it unreasonable that Major Umbach let Major Schmidt take the lead."

Whatever the charge, Judge Rosenow says, securing a conviction would mean having to "substantially impeach and discredit the testimony of Colonel Nichols, Major Milton, and Lt Col Viets." A daunting task, indeed, considering that it was the prosecution team that put two of those witnesses—Milton and Viets—on the stand in the first place. To win at trial, government lawyers would now have to convince a jury to ignore the testimony of people they once relied on as their own expert witnesses.

"The difficulty of proving a case and probability of securing a conviction is not the only factor to consider in making the referral decision," Col. Rosenow tells Lt.-Gen. Carlson. "Society recognizes a number of reasons for the prosecution and punishment of those who violate the law. The purpose of deterring the accused from repeating their offenses or protecting society from them would be equally served by taking administrative action to ensure they will not be placed in the same situation again. The purpose of deterring others who know of their prosecution from committing the same or similar acts may well have been sufficiently served by the wide exposure this hearing has received. It is true that the purposes of general retribution and the expression of societal outrage might well be more fully served in prosecution. Nonetheless, the deaths and injuries of the allies who stood by our side in defense of freedom will be made neither less tragic nor more meaningful with the prosecution of Coffee Flight. Nor would a court-martial serve any purpose as a truth finding tool. The CIB and this hearing have examined the bombing from every conceivable perspective."

Col. Rosenow believes "there is almost no chance that a court would find beyond a reasonable doubt" that the pilots used self-defense as a ruse to "score a win" for the unit. Prosecutors could still present a strong case that neither pilot had any reason to fear a rocket-based system, and even if they did, that they acted unreasonably by not flying away. "However, three experienced F-16 pilots (two squadron mates of the accused from the same deployment and the commander of the deployed group) will counter the circumstantial case and expert opinions by testifying that Coffee Flight acted reasonably. The defense will also offer extensive character evidence and argue that if the accused did act out of that character, the go-pills must have been responsible. I believe it is unlikely that a court, confronted with the blanket approval and endorsement of Coffee Flight's actions by the three F-16 pilots and the good character evidence, will find the government has proven any of the offenses beyond a reasonable doubt. In sum, the favorable testimony of those pilots makes the case too close to call for the imposition of criminal liability in a combat situation."

Dismiss the charges, Col. Rosenow tells the general. "There is a wide range of alternatives available to address the failures of leadership, airmanship, judgment, and discipline that resulted in the bombing at Tarnak Farms," he writes. "In recognition of their relative culpability, I suggest you consider administrative remedies as to Major Umbach and administrative or non-judicial remedies as to Major Schmidt. In my view, those will be sufficient to adequately address the interests of good order and discipline, the circumstances of these accused, and the welfare of society."

★　★　★

The brief Air Force news release reminds everyone that the final say still belongs to the commander of the 8th Air Force. If he wants, the three-star general can toss aside the judge's advice and send the pilots to a court-martial. It is completely up to him, and like Col. Rosenow, he is under no deadline to decide.

Stunned by the colonel's recommendation—and the suspect timing of it all—few of the Canadian relatives have any delusions about what Gen. Carlson will do next. He'll follow the advice. Case closed. "It's a gross injustice," Claire Léger says. "There is something wrong with this. My God, they killed four young soldiers and they get away scot-free. They're going to get a slap on the wrist and that's all." For a while there, Claire believed the U.S. military machine actually gave a damn about those four Canadian soldiers. An exhaustive investigation. Criminal charges. Sixty-four years. And now, after all that, nothing. "They have to get some punishment," says a tearful Paul Dyer, Ainsworth's father. "I am punished right now because my son cannot call."

In Ottawa, government officials have little to say. Canada–U.S. relations are bad enough these days without somebody sticking their nose in the American justice system. John McCallum, the defence minister, says what the federal government has been saying along: Our hearts are with the families. Lt.-Col. Pat Stogran, the man who commanded the Canadian Battle Group in Afghanistan, is less diplomatic. "Clearly there was testimony that indicated that procedures were violated in this and I lost four very good world-class soldiers," he says. "Proving beyond a reasonable doubt would be a difficult thing, but that's not to suggest that parties aren't guilty."

From his office in rural Virginia, Charlie Gittins e-mails a prepared statement to the many reporters who have covered this case from the beginning. "Major Schmidt was impressed with the thorough analysis contained in that report and satisfied that Col Rosenow provided a fair, balanced and unbiased review of the evidence," he says. "Major Schmidt also welcomes and accepts the Investigating Officer's recommendation that charges be dismissed—a clear recognition that Major Schmidt's actions and judgments in the stress of a combat mission, while he perceived his flight was taking surface to air fire, should not be categorized as 'criminal.' On behalf of Major Schmidt, we, his defense counsel, believe that this recommendation, if followed by the Convening Authority, will have a salutary effect on combat pilots who now are being required to make similar judgments in the war in Iraq and who should be empowered to make honest judgments without fear that they could face trial by court-martial for making a mistake in combat."

Craig Reid figured the cemetery would be easy enough to find. In a small town like Lancaster, Ontario, there are only so many places a graveyard can be. But now that he's here, steering his car through the streets, Sgt. Reid isn't having any luck. About all he can see is a man sitting on his front porch, enjoying the shade.

"Do you know where the nearest cemetery is?" Craig asks.

"Yeah," the man answers, pointing back toward Highway 401. "It's right over there. Who are you looking for?"

"Sergeant Marc Léger," Craig says. "Do you know him?"

"Oh yeah. Everybody in this town knew him."

It has been more than a year since the bombing, more than a year since Craig Reid asked Marc Léger to fill in for him as the range safety officer. At times, the survivor's guilt has been suffocating. Craig is absolutely convinced that he deserves to be dead, not Marc. He feels so responsible for what happened to Sgt. Léger that he doesn't even have the courage to tell Marley, or Marc's parents, that *he* should have been the one standing in the ditch that night. Craig has been diagnosed with PTSD. He is getting help, including regular sessions with an army psychologist. But he needs to do this. He needs to come here.

Not exactly sure where Marc is buried, Sgt. Reid walks through the small cemetery, row by row, reading the names as he goes. It is after 7 p.m., a hot, humid evening in southeastern Ontario, when he notices the PPCLI crest on one of the headstones. Sgt. Marc Léger.

Craig, wearing blue jeans and a t-shirt, sits on the grass, talking to the grave as if Marc were answering. At one point, he stands up and walks back to his car, returning with a couple bottles of beer. He twists them both open, leaning one against the headstone. In between sips, in between tears, Craig Reid tells Marc how badly everyone misses him, how sorry he is that he asked him to do his job. How guilty he feels. Craig even cracks a joke about the noise from the nearby highway. So much for resting in peace.

Before he leaves, Craig Reid grabs an empty Tim Hortons cup from the front of his car. Marc always loved their coffee. In fact, the day Sgt. Léger left for Op Apollo, he stopped at the drive-thru and picked up two: one for him, and one for MCpl. Brad McKenzie, who was already in Afghanistan. For two days, Marc carried that coffee on the plane, making sure it didn't spill. It was a bit old by the time he reached Kandahar, but Mac couldn't have been happier to see it. Tonight, Sgt. Reid leaves the cup on the grass, salutes the headstone, and walks away.

Every April 18 and every November 11, Craig Reid, now posted in Ottawa, will drive two hours to visit Marc's grave in Lancaster. He will always bring along two beers.

36

In Bill's case, at least, Gen. Bruce Carlson agrees with the advice that has been sitting on his desk for the past 12 weeks. No court-martial. On June 16, 2003—nine months after the Air Force slapped Maj. Umbach with 13 criminal offenses—the general quietly rips up the charge sheet. In its place, he slides into Bill's military file a five-paragraph letter of reprimand, a verbal rebuke that will stand as Maj. Umbach's only punishment for what happened that night over Tarnak Farm. He escapes without any trace of a criminal record, without a prison sentence or even a fine.

"Two detailed and thorough investigations have now consistently revealed that on 17 April 2002 near Kandahar, Afghanistan, you ab-dicated your command responsibilities as the lead pilot of Coffee Flight, a two-ship flight of F-16 aircraft," the letter reads. "When your flight requested permission from the controlling agency to mark the source of what the flight suspected to be enemy surface-to-air fire, the Airborne Warning and Control System (AWACS) aircraft gave you permission to mark the target. Rather than take a mark, however, your wingman requested permission to engage this unidentified target with his 20 millimeter cannon. In response, the AWACS instructed Coffee Flight to 'standby.' Faced with these circumstances, you should have directed Coffee Flight to mark the target, report the mark to the controlling agency through the AWACS and egress the area without delay to an unquestionably safe distance to wait for further informa-tion or instructions. Instead, you allowed your wingman to usurp your control over the flight and rather than direct him away from the area, you gave him no direction and allowed him to loiter in the area for an extended period of time.

"Moreover," the letter continues, "you failed to ensure that the target your wingman requested permission to fire upon was not friendly. Despite your obvious concerns about the potential for friendly forces in the area—as evidenced by your radio call to your wingman, 'Let's just make sure that it's not friendlies, is all'—you failed to follow up on this concern by contacting the AWACS to confirm that the suspected target was not friendly forces. You also failed to direct your wingman to acknowledge your radio call warning him of the possibility of friendly forces on the ground below. Additionally, you failed to direct your wingman away from the source of the suspected surface-to-air fire until you received confirmation that the target was not friendly. Ultimately, your wingman declared self-defense and dropped a laser-guided bomb on friendly forces that were conducting a nighttime live-fire exercise. The consequences were both tragic and avoidable.

"You are hereby reprimanded," Gen. Carlson concludes. "Your failure to exercise command responsibility resulted in an unacceptable breakdown of flight discipline in combat. You failed to maintain control of your flight and, as a result, undermined a very sophisticated and reliable command and control system, consisting of the Air Operations Center, the Airborne Warning and Control System, and highly disciplined pilots, all of whom must work together in an integrated fashion to achieve combat goals and avoid friendly fire casualties. I expect much more from someone with your training and experience."

Bill Umbach was going to retire in a couple years anyway. The letter of reprimand just speeds up the inevitable. Within days, the Air Force will approve Bill's request to collect his military pension and return to his full-time job at United Airlines. But before he walked away, Maj. Umbach asked Gen. Carlson, through their respective lawyers, for a meeting. The general didn't have to say yes, but he did.

Sitting in his Barksdale office, Bruce Carlson remained largely silent as Bill tried to explain the inaccuracies in his letter of reprimand. *The same thing would have happened no matter who was flying that mission,* Maj. Umbach told him. The general listened politely, but with Maj. Schmidt's case still looming, he barely said a word. And he didn't change a word, either. The LOR stands.

★ ★ ★

The Air Force announces Harry Schmidt's fate on June 19, three days after his flight lead receives his letter of reprimand. As he did with Bill, Gen. Carlson follows Col. Rosenow's advice and opts not to forward the charges to a court-martial. Instead, the three-star offers Harry the chance to explain his actions in front of him—face to face. Known as an Article 15, such hearings allow commanders to punish alleged criminal offenses in a non-judicial setting. No judge. No jury. Just the general.

If Maj. Schmidt accepts the offer, Gen. Carlson promises to drop the manslaughter and assault charges and examine just two counts of dereliction of duty—that you failed to ensure your target was legitimate, and that you failed to follow orders to "standby" and "make sure it's not friendlies." Though still a criminal hearing, an Article 15 offers considerably lighter penalties than a full court-martial. Even if Gen. Carlson finds Maj. Schmidt guilty, the maximum sentence he can impose is a small forfeiture of pay and 30 days' house arrest.

In a completely separate move, Gen. Carlson also recommends that the Air Force convene an independent Flying Evaluation Board (FEB) to re-examine the cockpit videos from the night of the accident. Independent of the Article 15, the FEB would have the authority to decide whether Maj. Schmidt deserves ever again to climb inside the cockpit of a fighter jet.

Lumped together with the Article 15, the general's announcement is a confusing development, yet another emotional twist that neither side of the case is completely pleased to hear. The Canadian families wanted a court-martial. Maj. Schmidt wanted vindication. Gen. Carlson gives them something in between: two criminal charges of dereliction of duty that cannot be punished with jail time. "It opens up a whole road that is difficult and long again," a tired Lisa Schmidt says. "It's definitely not an outcome we were hoping for. We hoped that Gen. Carlson would drop the charges and compensate the Canadian families for their loss and injuries and allow us to move on."

Instead, the Schmidts find themselves faced with a daunting decision. They can accept the Article 15, knowing that Harry will almost certainly walk out of the general's office with a black mark on his record. Or he can refuse, daring the Air Force to try him at an all-or-nothing court-martial. It is a risky proposition. Demanding a trial would not only put jail time back on the table, but there would be nothing to stop the Air Force from referring all the charges to a court-martial—not just the two counts of dereliction. It could mean the difference between six months in prison and 64 years.

But there is an upside. The Air Force might be so stunned by a demand for court-martial that it simply backs down and forgets the whole thing. And even if Gen. Carlson does call Maj. Schmidt's bluff, a trial would still provide the once-elite fighter pilot with what he craves more than anything else: The chance to clear his name. Harry has five days to make a move.

As the hours pass, speculation mounts. Will he risk it? Will he really dare the Air Force to put him on trial? Or will Maj. Schmidt take his pro-verbial slap on the wrist—and the criminal label that goes with it—and walk away? His lawyers aren't saying. But they're hinting. "Because of all that has gone on and basically the personal indignities he has felt, he very well may be the kind of person who is going to say: 'I am not going to lay down,'" Capt. Jamie Key says.

The day after Gen. Carlson's announcement, Charlie Gittins rattles off an e-mail to reporters. Subject line: AIR FORCE LIES. In it, he accuses the military of trying to mislead "the press and the public" by suggesting that the general has "dropped" the manslaughter and assault charges against Maj. Schmidt. The truth, Gittins says, is that Gen. Carlson is dangling the more se-rious offenses like a "Sword of Damocles over Major Schmidt's head," ready to use if the pilot does not "play ball" and accept non-judicial punishment for the dereliction charges. "The Air Force has been disingenuous to you and the public," the e-mail concludes. "You need to tell the public the truth, not repeat Air Force spin like happened yesterday. Please feel free to call me."

Later that afternoon, Bill Umbach answers the phone at his home in Petersburg, Illinois. It's another reporter, of course. Bill—suddenly immune to any further punishment—agrees to answer a few questions. Would you ever want to sit down and talk to the Canadian families? "I am willing to do that if that's what they want," he answers. "I realize that this doesn't bring anybody back and it doesn't take away any of the wounds that were suffered by the injured. I realize that there was never going to be anything that we could do to fix that. That part, unfortunately, is painfully, painfully permanent."

★ ★ ★

459

Harry's decision is due to the general by 2 p.m. on Wednesday, June 25. His lawyers had hoped for a five-day extension, but their request was denied. With less than 48 hours to go, Psycho still hasn't made up his mind. His mother, Joan, doesn't even know which way her son is leaning. Charlie Gittins knows what *he* would do. "I want him to fight, but that's not my choice," he tells one reporter. "He's his own man and he wants to do what's right. He's not going to listen to me, or anybody."

The clincher comes on Tuesday, just hours from the due date. It seems that Air Force officials in Washington have quietly suspended Maj. Schmidt's flight pay, a salary bonus that pilots pocket based on their years of experience in the cockpit. Even more outrageous, the suspension was backdated to September 2002, which means Harry potentially owes the Air Force nearly $8,000 worth of flight pay that he never should have received in the first place. If Maj. Schmidt wasn't sure what to do, he is now.

On Wednesday afternoon, Col. John Odom is waiting near the JAG fax machine at Barksdale Air Force Base. He has already called Wanda, his paralegal, to tell her that he's finally going to show his face at the office. Reschedule all those postponed depositions, he told her. I'll be back at my desk by the first week of July.

The cover sheet slides through the fax first. 183rd Fighter Wing. Underneath, an Air Force Form 3070. Maj. Schmidt has initialed the middle of the page, directly beside the box that says: "I demand trial by court-martial." Col. Odom barely has time to react before another sheet spits through the machine. It's a prepared statement, also signed by Harry M. Schmidt. "The actions taken by 8th AF/CC [Gen. Carlson] in the past several days clearly indicate that imposition of punishment in my case is a foregone conclusion," it reads.

Harry's surprise statement cites a recent memo that Gen. Carlson sent to Air Force headquarters, recommending a Flying Evaluation Board as the appropriate way to evaluate "Major Schmidt's lack of judgment" and "violation of flying regulations and procedures" on April 17, 2002. "No other rational conclusion is possible from that statement except that 8th AF/CC has prejudged my case and pre-determined my guilt," Maj. Schmidt writes. "This conclusion is buttressed by the content of the letters issued to Major Umbach, which conclude that we both acted inappropriately by engaging in, among other things, '*an unacceptable breakdown of flight discipline in combat.*'"

Maj. Schmidt is equally outraged that Gen. Carlson intends to consider the entire Article 32 report, including every exhibit, as part of his deliberations. "This would result in 8th AF/CC's consideration of BGen Sargeant's error-filled and biased CIB report and testimony which was admitted in the Article 32 hearing in violation of federal law, notwithstanding the Investigating Officer's conclusion to the contrary," the statement reads. "My acceptance of Article 15 under such circumstances may constitute a waiver of that issue for purposes of further review.

"Finally," Maj. Schmidt concludes, "the action taken to suspend me from flight status without advising me of that fact and to falsely backdate the date of that action in my flight records to September 2002 indicates an unacceptable punitive intent *toward my family* as that action will have an immediate and practical effect on my wife and two children resulting in receipt of no pay to my family for a significant period. When coupled with the unreasonable denial of my reasonable request for additional time in which to consider this matter thoughtfully with my family, it is clear that I cannot and will not receive a full and fair hearing as required by Article 15, UCMJ and AFI 51-202. Therefore, I am compelled to refuse punishment under Article 15, UCMJ, and demand trial by court-martial."

By this point, the families of the four dead soldiers aren't even sure how to react. For more than a year, they have endured a legal rollercoaster that has often left them more confused than comforted. Most wanted a trial, something to hold those pilots accountable. They didn't get it. But now, because of Harry Schmidt's unwillingness to back down, a trial date suddenly looms. "It's just like starting from day one again," says Doreen Coolen, Pte. Green's mom. "He's a coward as far as I'm concerned. Everybody should be held accountable for their own actions and he won't speak up and take the blame for anything. He wants to blame everyone but himself."

Joan Schmidt has heard it all before, how her son is an arrogant jerk who refuses to admit that he might have actually made a mistake. Today, she just wants those Canadian families to know that Harry is doing all of this for them. "Those people are looking for justice, and I'm right behind them in line," she says. "They're first. They've lost loved ones in this. They want to know the truth. They want to have some justice here. I want to tell them my son's giving them an opportunity for that. He's sacrificing himself right now to get that information public. I hope the Canadian families realize that this is what he's doing."

Gen. Carlson barely flinches when he reads Maj. Schmidt's fax. If he wants a trial, so be it. Col. Odom picks up the phone and calls Wanda back. Don't reschedule those depositions just yet.

★ ★ ★

Five days after demanding a court-martial, Harry wins the first round of his gamble. In yet another short press release from Barksdale, Gen. Carlson announces that Maj. Schmidt will stand trial on just a single count of dereliction of duty. Even if he's found guilty, the harshest punishment he faces is six months in prison.

The news release offers no explanation for the general's choice, though it is widely assumed that he simply followed Col. Rosenow's original warning that the outcome would be "too close to call." Charlie Gittins says the decision proves what he has been saying along: What happened over Tarnak Farm was never a crime. "Everybody understood—or should have understood—that it was a mistake and it had no criminal component to it whatsoever," he says. "We're down to the government trying to do something because Harry has called their bluff."

chapter thirty-seven

The newspapers didn't rush out to cover these ceremonies. They're little more than a handshake and a thank-you, a few minutes of re-nown stamped on a white piece of paper. Not quite the drama of a high-stakes court-martial.

Brian Decaire and Brett Perry each got one, a Mention in Dispatch for their "outstanding professionalism and humanitarianism" so many months ago. They were both wounded and bleeding, but rushing to treat other casualties until Rob Jones finally told them to jump on the chopper with the rest of the stretchers.

Warrant Jones was awarded his own pin, a Chief of the Defence Staff Commendation for what he did in the wadi and in the days after, organizing the peer counselors and the stress debriefs. Billy Bolen earned the same certificate. So did Maurice Baril, for his "professionalism and dedication to duty" while leading the Canadian board of inquiry, and Marc Dumais, for his "dedication in determining the facts behind the bombing" as co-president of the CIB. Three other soldiers who helped organize the national memorial service in Edmonton were also honored with CDS Commendations.

Among the troops who were actually at Tarnak Farm, some were presented the less-prestigious Deputy Chief of the Defence Staff Commendation. The Pioneers—Dave Bibby, Aaron Bygrove, and Jon Bradshaw—were applauded for staying behind and search-ing the sand for unexploded ordnance. Chris Kopp and Rob Coates, who helped save Sgt. Ford, were given the same, though both were originally nominated to receive a much higher honor. The med-ics—Bill Wilson, Vic Speirs and Jean de la Bourdonnaye—were also written up for a medal, but they, too, were ultimately handed DCDS

Commendations. Vic framed his certificate, even though "Speirs" is spelled wrong. Somebody mixed up the "e" and the "i."

Joe Jasper, the captain who disobeyed his commanders and later led the men who picked up the corpses, received his DCDS Commendation in June 2003. "Your unfaltering leadership and devotion to duty inspired those under your command in a very traumatic situation," his certificate reads. "Your actions on that tragic night reflect considerable credit upon yourself and upon the Canadian Forces."

Seven other paratroopers stayed at the range that morning, waiting for the sun to come up. Brad McKenzie. Marco Favasoli. Pete Filis. Kyle Caldwell. Andy Hulan. Arnie Parris. And Joe Schechtel. None was ever recognized by the Canadian army.

★   ★   ★

Joan Schmidt spends the bulk of her days talking about Harry. She's been doing it for more than a year now. Senators. Reporters. Colonels. Political aides of every stripe. They've all chatted with Mrs. Schmidt, listening online or on the phone as she explains the many tentacles of the cover-up that has swallowed her son. Her electronic address list expands every day, each e-mail signed the same: Joan and Harry Schmidt, proud parents of Maj. Harry Schmidt.

When she is not professing her son's innocence, Joan Schmidt is doing all she can to derail the careers of the men she believes are truly responsible for what happened at Tarnak Farm. Her target these days is Lt.-Gen. Moseley, the commander of the Afghanistan air war. The three-star was recently tapped as the Air Force's next vice-chief of staff. From her home in St. Louis, Mrs. Schmidt is lobbying hard to block the promotion.

Over the past few weeks, she has personally spoken to nearly every member of the U.S. Senate's Armed Services Committee, telling them why Gen. Moseley—not her son—should be facing criminal charges. He was warned, she says, that Operation Enduring Freedom was rife with shoddy air-to-ground coordination but did little to fix it. And then, the day after the F-16s bombed the Canadians, he sent that memo to his subordinates saying "it is difficult to imagine a scenario" in which the pilots just couldn't fly away instead of dropping a bomb. Gen. Moseley fingered the culprits before the investigations even began. What else was Gen. Sargeant supposed to conclude? "He twisted and contrived to scapegoat these two pilots," Mrs. Schmidt says. "They have created a can of worms that's so smelly that they don't know what to do with the smell."

The stench, however, is not enough to sway even a single member of the Armed Services Committee. They unanimously rubberstamp Gen. Moseley's promotion. The U.S. Senate does the same.

★ ★ ★

Harry Schmidt's first court appearance at Barksdale Air Force Base is a mere formality, a 45-minute get-to-know-you session with Colonel Mary Boone, the judge who will oversee the trial. It is July 30, 2003, more than 15 months since Maj. Schmidt called "shack" over the radio, and five weeks since he dared the Air Force to meet him in this room. His lawyers and the lawyers hoping to put him in jail talk mostly about timelines, agreeing to return in three months to set a trial date. Judge Boone gives prosecutors two weeks to produce a witness and exhibit list. The defense has a month to file any requests for discovery.

Outside the base, Charlie Gittins says he will ask the government to hand over all the documented details of more than a dozen other friendly fire accidents that occurred in recent years, including what went wrong in July 2002 when an AC-130 gunship opened fire on that Afghan wedding, killing dozens of civilians. "We believe that the people who were involved in those accidents may be potential witnesses in Harry's case to illuminate and explain the 'fog of war' and the information that's required to get to pilots," he says.

It is hardly the only request the defense team will file. As summer fades into fall, Maj. Schmidt's lawyers submit motion after motion after motion. They want the case dismissed because Lt.-Gen. Carlson is "biased and prejudiced" against Maj. Schmidt. They want a new Article 32, in part because the military denied Charlie Gittins, a civilian lawyer, a "secret" security clearance the first time around. They want the public to be allowed to sit in the courtroom, not watch the proceedings on closed-circuit TV.

They want the autopsy report of Petty Officer Roberts, the Navy SEAL who was killed by Al-Qaeda fighters after falling out of his chopper. They want CENTCOM's final report into the friendly fire death of Stanley Harriman, the chief warrant officer who was shot and killed by an American AC-130 during Operation Anaconda.

In a somewhat bizarre move, the defense team even demands that Maj. Schmidt be tried on all the original charges—manslaughter and assault included—because the government has provided no guarantee that once the dereliction trial is over, the military won't drag him back into court to answer for the other allegations.

As the paperwork piles up, prosecutors continue to travel the country, interviewing potential witnesses. They talk to some of Maj. Schmidt's former students, to the young crew chief who met Harry planeside that night, who saw tears trickling down his face as he lifted off his helmet. Their witness list grows with every trip. By October, they add another name: Maj. Bill Umbach.

The addition catches even Bill by surprise. He's been out of the public spotlight for a few months now, back to flying Boeing 777s over the Atlantic Ocean. He seldom speaks to Harry Schmidt these days—not that they were great friends to begin with—but he clearly has no intention of testifying on behalf of the government. "If the prosecution is trying to use me against him, I don't think it's going to take place," he tells one reporter. "I don't think I'm going to help the prosecution's case."

★ ★ ★

The Bronze Star is the U.S. military's fourth-highest award for bravery, created in 1944 to honor "heroic or meritorious" acts by soldiers engaged in combat. The definition has since expanded to include foreign troops fighting alongside the United States, though the prestigious award—a five-pointed star hanging from a red, white, and blue ribbon—is still scarcely given to anyone outside the U.S.

Paul Cellucci, America's ambassador to Canada, oversees one of the rare ceremonies on December 8, 2003. Standing amid hundreds of soldiers at the Edmonton garrison, the outspoken Cellucci pins the Bronze Star on

26 members of the Canadian Battle Group who served with the Rakkasans in Kandahar. The recipients include Col. Pat Stogran, the Canadian commander in Afghanistan; Maj. Stephen Borland, the colonel's 2I/C; Maj. Sean Hackett, A Company's commander; Master Warrant Officer Al Whitehall, the Para Company's sergeant-major; and Major Peter Dawe, the operations officer who was at Call Sign Zero on April 17, urging Joe Jasper to come back to base.

In an even rarer honor, the U.S. ambassador also awards four posthumous Bronze Stars to the paratroopers killed at Tarnak Farm. Surviving relatives accept the stars on their behalf. "The medal, to me, represents Marc's ultimate sacrifice," says Sgt. Léger's wife, Marley. "He died fighting for what we believe in. I don't think you can get any braver than that."

Not all of the Canadian families traveled to Edmonton. Claire Léger, Marc's mother, says the ceremony smells of "damage control." Not just for the bombing, but for the fallout over Canada's decision to sit out the war in Iraq. Cellucci lambasted the Canadian government for that one. Now he's pinning medals on their soldiers.

Doreen Coolen is still demanding compensation from the Pentagon, but she did fly out west to receive the award. So did Paul Dyer, Ainsworth's father. "It doesn't change anything," he tells reporters. "My son is under the earth."

None of the eight soldiers wounded by Harry Schmidt's bomb is awarded a Bronze Star. But most of them are here, including Cpl. Brett Perry, standing at attention as his senior officers accept their medals. Almost two years after the bombing, the demons still surround him, feeding his post-traumatic stress disorder. *That pilot meant to bomb you, but he missed.* Every day, Brett used to walk past the small memorial hanging in the main hallway of the 3rd Battalion headquarters, the plaque with the photos of Marc, Ains, Smitty, and Ricky. He doesn't any more. He recently transferred back to his hometown of Winnipeg. "It was good for me to leave that unit," he says.

★ ★ ★

A week after the Bronze Star ceremony, Judge Mary Boone denies a pile of defense motions, including Harry Schmidt's request for the details of other friendly fire accidents. "The defense has not shown any relevance these reports might have to the findings in this case," the judge writes in her ruling. "What particular ROEs the accused was operating under and his frame of mind are the pivotal considerations of any court."

Charlie Gittins is not the least bit surprised by the decision. "The problem the Air Force doesn't want to have shown is that there is a systematic command and control system problem that has resulted in hundreds of these accidents," he says. Unfazed, the motions keep coming. Gittins and the other defense lawyers want access to a secure "Go-pills" website maintained by the Air Force surgeon general. They want a copy of a videotape that allegedly depicts Gen. John Jumper, the Air Force chief of staff, telling cadets at the academy that the pilots will be "held accountable." And they want all memos and e-mails about the bombing that were exchanged between senior Air Force officials in the two months before Harry and Bill were criminally charged—evidence they say could prove that Maj. Schmidt is a victim of "unlawful command influence."

As the motions multiply, they only get more personal. At one point, defense lawyers demand that the judge disqualify Col. Odom as the lead prosecutor for demonstrating "a clear lack of ethics." Among a list of allegations, they accuse the colonel of grandstanding during a presentation he made at a JAG conference days after the Article 32, playing the cockpit videos for the crowd and stopping at the point long after the bombing when Maj. Schmidt says to Maj. Umbach: *Stand by for the microscope.* "At this point," the defense motion alleges, "Colonel Odom turned off the video and audio and stated to the gathering of judge advocates in a boastful and manner full of himself: 'Well, Maj. Schmidt, I *am* the microscope.'"

Defense attorneys also accuse Col. Odom of interviewing members of the 183rd Fighter Wing without telling them who he was. He allegedly told them he was a "JAG from Barksdale," not the attorney prosecuting Maj. Schmidt. "Military personnel facing prosecution should be confident that they will not face a prosecutor who 'plays fast and loose' with the truth," the motion concludes. "A prosecutor who cannot be trusted to be candid has no place in the system and no place in this prosecution. Accordingly, an appropriate sanction in this case is to disqualify Colonel Odom from further participation in the prosecution of Major Schmidt."

On the same day—December 29, 2003—the defense team asks Judge Boone to order the release of all internal U.S. military documents that discuss why 30 Princess Patricias, including Marc, Ainsworth, Richard, and Nathan, were awarded Bronze Stars. They are concerned that some Canadian troops might have been rewarded for "prior testimony," even though none of the six Canadian soldiers who took the witness stand at the Article 32 was awarded a medal. "That Bronze Star medals were awarded wholesale to Canadian members of a single unit but not other foreign units of the coalition may be relevant to an issue of bias and improper inducement by the government," the defense motion reads.

★ ★ ★

By the new year, 2004, Doreen Coolen's divorce is almost official. All that's left is a little more paperwork, and a small change to the headstone perched over Ricky's Nova Scotia gravesite. She's going to remove Arthur's name altogether, and beside "Doreen," she plans to scratch out "Coolen" and replace it with "Young," her maiden name. "Never say 'it's written in stone' to me," Doreen says.

Pte. Green's mom spends many of her days alone, doing her best to avoid the people who won't stop accusing her of going after "blood money." For the most part, she's living off Ricky's life insurance, the $100,000 check that arrived weeks after the bomb. "Every day of my life I look around and I say I own this and I own that," she says. "But you know what? I don't care about any of it. Nothing. I'd give it all in a second to have Ricky back."

In the meantime, Doreen's lawyers continue to try to convince the other families to add their names to the wrongful death claim. Dick Murtha calls and writes and calls again, reminding the Légers and the Smiths and the Dyers that once the two-year anniversary arrives in April, the statute of limitations expires. If you want to sue, you have to do it now. *Think what you could do with the money. A scholarship fund, perhaps. Bring some meaning to their senseless deaths.*

"We realize that discussing the claims issue may still be difficult for you, and we are sensitive to the fact that you are continuing to cope with your tragic loss," Murtha writes to Richard and Claire Léger, urging them to come aboard. "Any restitution received from whatever source we are able to reach could enable you to establish a trust or foundation to honor the memory of Richard or possibly, provide educational funds for another member of your family."

Richard Léger writes back. "My son's name is Marc!" he says. "In your position, facts should be distinct and not appear as hearsay or copied! I cannot emphasize my feelings towards your lack of professionalism shown in this letter. I cannot believe that you have any sincere feelings toward our families." Neither the Légers, nor any of the other Canadian relatives, will add their names to the claim.

★ ★ ★

Harry Schmidt's trial is scheduled to begin on March 1, 2004, eight months after he challenged the Air Force to face him in court. Judge Boone has spent much of that time pondering—and in most cases, denying—discovery requests filed by the defense. Another motions hearing is set for January 26 at Barksdale, but days before all the lawyers show up, Charlie Gittins asks for a delay. His client, still an avid soccer player, broke his leg and tore an Achilles tendon during an indoor pick-up game. The 38-year-old needs surgery, and is expected to be off his feet for a few weeks.

Col. Boone agrees to put off the motions hearing while Harry recovers, setting aside March 1—the day the trial was supposed to begin—as a make-up date. The actual court-martial will now start April 5, less than two weeks before the second anniversary of the bombing. But the new timeline triggers yet another round of objections. Capt. Key, Harry's military lawyer, is also assigned to another high-profile case, defending Senior Airman Ahmad al-Halabi, an Air Force translator stationed at Guantanamo Bay, Cuba, who is charged with espionage. A preliminary hearing in the al-Halabi case is scheduled for the two weeks right before Harry's trial—leaving Capt. Key one day to travel to Louisiana for last-minute preparations. "I cannot cite a specific number of hours I've worked on [Maj. Schmidt's] case," Capt. Key writes to the judge, "but I submit it has been far, far too many to see me roll into town about 36 hours prior to the start of trial."

In his objection, Capt. Key notes that the Air Force "is entirely willing to take as much time necessary to investigate, ponder and prepare its case, with absolutely no concern for the defense's ability to do the same." Gen. Sargeant took two months to finish his investigation. Col. Odom and the prosecutors were analyzing the CIB report long before charges were preferred, and long before the defense ever saw the complete findings. Gen. Carlson spent three months pondering Col. Rosenow's recommendation, but gave Maj. Schmidt just five days to decide his next move. And now, Capt. Key argues, the government is willing to sacrifice Maj. Schmidt's "right to counsel and judicial fairness for the purpose of administrative expediency."

Capt. Key's is not the only defense motion seeking a further delay. Charlie Gittins has filed a brief with the U.S. Air Force Court of Criminal Appeals, asking that the looming trial be stayed until the military grants him a "secret" security clearance. Sixteen months after taking over as Maj. Schmidt's lead attorney, Gittins still has to ask prosecutors to approve the release of every single classified document he wishes to view—a process he says gives the government the unfair advantage of knowing what issues he hopes to exploit come trial. It also leaves the entire defense team grappling with another bizarre dilemma: Maj. Schmidt can discuss classified information that he knows—such as details about his tactical training—with his two Air Force lawyers, but not with Charlie Gittins.

"The government is trying to control how we defend Maj. Schmidt," Gittins says. "They want to know what we know and they are not entitled to know what we know. This is all about control." He notes that some civilian lawyers representing terror suspects at Guantanamo Bay have been granted unrestricted access to classified material. "While a defense counsel for an al-Qaeda detainee gets a security clearance, I don't," he says. "On its face, it's absurd."

The appeals court does not go that far, but it does agree to postpone the trial—yet again—in order to properly examine the issue. The April 5 court date will have to wait.

★ ★ ★

Not everyone was in favor of the idea. There were the traditionalists, the people who pointed out that every other footbridge in Edmonton is named after the location where it stands. Others worried that if the city renamed the structure after Ainsworth Dyer, it would be a slap in the face to countless other Canadian soldiers—including Marc, Nathan, and Ricky—who ever died serving their country. Some locals even questioned whether Edmonton has any business bestowing such a huge honor on a man who was born in Montreal and raised in Toronto.

But the Van Slotens ignored the naysayers. For months, they lobbied city officials and raised money to clean up the north end of the Rundle Park footbridge, the one where Ains knelt down on that cold October night and asked Jocelyn to be his wife. The family planted trees, installed a bench, and continued to pester until the mayor and his executive committee finally agreed to their idea.

On April 17, 2004—exactly two years after she lost Ains—Jocelyn and her family join a crowd of more than 200 people to officially dedicate the brown wooden bridge to Cpl. Dyer. "I knew Ains for many years, though I feel it can never have been long enough," Jocelyn says. "I want people to look at this memorial and think of Ains, but I also want them to think of other soldiers. It takes very special people to be in the military and risk their lives."

Near the bench, attached to an enormous gray boulder, a bronze plaque explains the story behind the newly named Ainsworth Dyer Memorial Bridge. "Ains proposed to his beloved fiancée Jocelyn Van Sloten on this bridge, playfully threatening to throw her in the river if she didn't say yes!" it reads. "He was a mountain of a man who truly made your heart dance."

Paul Dyer, Ainsworth's father, is not at the ceremony. He is at home in Brampton, Ontario, in the suburban condominium he recently bought with some of his son's life insurance money. Paul has little contact with his past any more. He doesn't speak to Jocelyn, the woman who would have been his daughter-in-law. And he doesn't speak to Agatha, his ex-wife. She doesn't even know Paul's new phone number.

"He's greedy," Agatha says, sitting at her kitchen table in Montreal. "To me, I lost a son. To Paul, it's about the money." Indeed, Paul got all the money, hundreds of thousands of dollars' worth of insurance payments. At one point, he even threatened to sue the Canadian Forces unless it agreed to pay him the salary his son would have received if he was still alive. He lost that fight. "Paul is a con artist," Agatha says. "He treated us really bad. He didn't give nobody a cent. I'm not asking Paul for anything. But he is our child, and we should grieve together. We should mourn together."

A big-screen TV sits near the front door of Paul's fourth-floor condo, right underneath a large photo of Ains and the Canadian flag that once covered his coffin. Most of the furniture is new, including the loveseat by the window that he's sitting on tonight. "It might look good," he says, tearfully. "But it's not good, because there isn't a day that tears don't come down my eyes. I love him too much."

Even though he would trade it all away to bring back his son, Paul makes no apologies for the money he continues to receive. "I am his beneficiary," he says. "I'm the only one on his papers. His mother is not on his papers." And neither is Jocelyn. "I sent him to church. I sent him to school. I do everything for him."

★ ★ ★

Harry Schmidt's court-martial has been in limbo for more than three months, postponed and postponed again by the legal wrangling over Charlie Gittins' security clearance. In April, the U.S. Air Force Court of Criminal Appeals rejected his request, ruling that the flamboyant lawyer "has no constitutional right to unrestricted discovery." The current process—asking prosecutors for specific classified documents—is fair and adequate, the court ruled.

As they promised they would, Maj. Schmidt's lawyers immediately ask the U.S. Court of Appeals for the Armed Forces—the American military's highest court—to overturn the judgment. Another delay. "People who just want to see the trial happen may view this as some sort of dilatory tactic of the defense," Jamie Key says. "But if you think about the importance of your defense attorneys being able to investigate a person's case without having to let the prosecutor know everything you're doing and everything you're looking at, this is a very significant point."

By June 7, 2004, the point is moot. Amid all the appeals, Charlie Gittins managed to obtain a "secret" security clearance in his capacity as a Marine Corps reservist. Once again, Judge Boone is free to schedule a start date for Maj. Schmidt's trial.

chapter thirty-eight

Nearly a full year has passed since Harry Schmidt demanded a court-martial. Colonel Greg Graf spent a good chunk of that year overseas, serving as the chief of staff for Task Force-West, an amphibious unit of fighter pilots and army troops deployed as part of Operation Iraqi Freedom. The colonel was supposed to ship out back in January 2003, but at the last moment, the powers that be gave the job to somebody else so that he could stay in Louisiana for the Article 32.

It was a frustrating point in his career. Col. Graf wanted that command position. He wanted to be in Iraq when the U.S. ousted Saddam Hussein. Not only did he lose that chance, but he lost it doing a job that essentially made him an outcast. Fellow fighter pilots wanted nothing to do with him, disgusted that he had the nerve to help prosecute two of his own.

But months later, when he finally did reach Iraq, things had changed. Col. Graf was no longer the pariah. Some of the same F-16 pilots who wouldn't speak to him when Harry and Bill were facing 64 years in prison were suddenly lining up to talk. Many were insulted that a man whose bomb killed four coalition soldiers turned down an Article 15. "The scene had changed dramatically after the war," Col. Graf recalls now. "Enough guys had been around to say: 'That was so horrible. We're offended by his lack of willingness to take responsibility.' There would have been no problem having witnesses. In fact, people were coming out of the woodwork."

When he returned from Iraq, amid all the motions and objections, Col. Graf even called one of the defense lawyers to warn him about all the expert combat pilots willing to testify against Maj. Schmidt. "Crème de la crème," he says. Guys who were actually fired at by the same rocket-based weapon that Harry claims he saw that night. Guys who are convinced that his reaction was all wrong.

As the months passed, Col. John Odom also kept in touch with the defense team, reminding Lt.-Col. Clay Moushon, one of Maj. Schmidt's military lawyers, that Gen. Carlson is still willing to give Harry a fair shake at an Article 15. By May 2004, Maj. Schmidt begins to listen. His stance is no different. He still believes that he acted reasonably that night, that the Air Force failed to tell him the one crucial piece of information that would have prevented the accident: Canadians are training on the ground.

But Harry also knows that he could still lose this trial. There is still the chance that a jury won't see it his way, that he'll be jailed and discharged from the military, leaving his wife and two young sons without an income. And even if he wins, there will undoubtedly be years' worth of appeals. His children could be in high school by the time this finally ends.

An Article 15 would eliminate that possibility. Regardless of the outcome, Harry's 17 years in the service—and the pension that goes with it—will not vanish, ensuring his family's financial future. And he will not go to jail. Tired, and still recovering from his broken leg, Maj. Schmidt's choice seems obvious. "We were going to fight it tooth and nail," Charlie Gittins recalls. "We were fighting to win. And Harry and Lisa said: 'You know, if we can keep the flight pay, I don't care if I fly. We'll throw in the towel.'"

Nearly 12 months after Maj. Schmidt first refused an Article 15, his lawyers begin to negotiate a deal that will put his case back in front of Gen. Carlson. Prosecutors want Harry to accept a non-flying job with the Air National Guard, ensuring that he never again climbs into an F-16. Defense lawyers agree, but they want Maj. Schmidt to continue receiving his flight pay, even though he won't be doing any flying.

On June 24, 2004—364 days after Maj. Schmidt refused the original Article 15—the Air Force announces his decision to scrap the court-martial and accept the non-judicial route. Flooded with phone calls, Gittins stresses to reporters that the change of venue is not an admission of guilt. Harry will still vigorously fight the dereliction charge, only in a different setting where the stakes are much lower. "Over the past year, Gen. Carlson's staff repeatedly has told us that the offer was still on the table, that Harry would get a fair hearing and that there was no bias," he says. "You hear that over and over and over and over, and I think Harry finally decided: 'I'm going to take the general at his word.'"

★   ★   ★

Maj. Schmidt meets Gen. Carlson in his Barksdale office on July 1. Canada Day. Lisa, his wife, walks him through the door, as does his trio of lawyers, Charlie Gittins, Jamie Key, and Clay Moushon. The general has one person at his side: Colonel Rich Harding, his staff judge advocate. When Lisa leaves, the meeting begins.

It is not unusual for a commander overseeing an Article 15 to keep a defendant standing at attention for the entire proceeding. But Gen. Carlson offers Harry a seat, then begins taking notes as the pilot explains why he dropped that bomb. The rocket-propelled projectiles that appeared to be aimed at Bill's jet. The Ringbacks. The inherent right of self-defense.

Because the one-hour hearing is not open to the public, it is unclear exactly what Harry tells the general. But before they leave, his lawyers also hand Bruce Carlson a 68-page brief that outlines their case. "Early allegations and insinuations in this case that Maj. Schmidt was some sort of rogue pilot trolling the Afghan skies looking for something—anything—to drop a bomb on have been proven to be as absurd in fact as they were when they were first uttered," it reads. "Instead, investigation has shown that on [17] April 2002, Maj. Schmidt stepped not only into his plane, but into a situation populated by information gaps, substandard practices, systems inadequate to timely respond to his calls for assistance, misguided operational priorities and, in some cases, outright negligence."

The brief also includes an affidavit written by Lieutenant-Colonel Michael Loida, a fighter pilot whom Gen. Carlson assigned to help the defense team prepare for trial. His submission concludes that the accident happened not because of a reckless pilot, but because nobody on the Air Force side had any clue the Canadians were shooting. "With no knowledge of friendly live fire training being conducted," he writes, "it was a reasonable option for him to declare self-defense, in accordance with the ROE and to neutralize the perceived threat."

After the hearing, Gittins tells a small group of reporters gathered at the base that "the general was very attentive" to their evidence and listened carefully as Harry told his side of the story. "He explained exactly what he did and why he did it."

A St. Louis newspaper will later report that Maj. Schmidt declined to salute the three-star general when he arrived at the office and again when he left. The story will spark another round of he-said, she-said, including a sworn declaration from Maj. Schmidt. "I saluted Lt.-Gen. Carlson and sounded off: 'Maj. Schmidt reporting as ordered, sir,'" he will write.

Gen. Carlson will even grant a rare telephone interview to the *Post-Dispatch* reporter who broke the original story, confirming his version of events. "He performed no military courtesies."

★ ★ ★

Col. Odom and the rest of the prosecutors technically aren't prosecutors any more. They were relieved of their duties as soon as Maj. Schmidt recanted his demand for a trial. As of now, they're just like all the other JAGs working under Gen. Carlson.

Their last official duty on the Schmidt file is to review Harry's presentation to the general, then tell the 8th Air Force commander whether any of the evidence is convincing enough to alter the government's longstanding position. Not surprisingly, it isn't. Gen. Carlson agrees, and indicates to his legal team that he wants Harry Schmidt punished for dereliction of duty.

Col. Odom just happens to have a draft letter of reprimand saved on his computer. He's been working on it for a little while now. It is essentially a summary of what would have been his closing arguments had the case made it to trial. He forwards a copy to Gen. Carlson. "I have drafted hundreds of letters of reprimand for commanders to sign," Col. Odom will later say. "It is the only one I ever had sent back to me, slid back across the table, and he said: 'It's not strong enough.'"

A few days and a few edits later, Gen. Carlson has a reprimand on his desk—609 scathing words—to which he is prepared to attach his signature. Along with the letter, the general slaps Maj. Schmidt with a fine: One half of one month's pay for two months. US$5,672. A tad more than $1,400 for each dead paratrooper.

A copy of the letter is forwarded to Harry Schmidt—and the media—on the afternoon of July 6, 2004.

"You are hereby reprimanded," it reads. "You flagrantly disregarded a direct order from the controlling agency, exercised a total lack of basic flight discipline over your aircraft, and blatantly ignored the applicable rules of engagement and special instructions. Your willful misconduct directly caused the most egregious consequences imaginable, the deaths of four coalition soldiers and injury to eight others. The victims of your callous misbehavior were from one of our staunch allies in Operation ENDURING FREEDOM and were your comrades-in-arms.

"You acted shamefully on 17 April 2002 over Tarnak Farms, Afghanistan, exhibiting arrogance and a lack of flight discipline," the rebuke continues. "When your flight lead warned you to 'make sure it's not friendlies' and the Airborne Warning and Control System aircraft controller directed you to 'stand by' and later to 'hold fire,' you should have marked the location with your targeting pod. Thereafter, if you believed, as you stated, you and your leader were threatened, you should have taken a series of evasive actions and remained at a safe distance to await further instructions from AWACS. Instead, you closed on the target and blatantly disobeyed the direction to 'hold fire.' Your failure to follow that order is inexcusable. I do not believe you acted in defense of Major Umbach or yourself. Your actions indicate that you used your self-defense declaration as a pretext to strike a target, which you rashly decided was an enemy firing position, and about which you had exhausted your patience in waiting for clearance from the Combined Air Operations Center to engage. You used the inherent right of self-defense as an excuse to wage your own war."

Gen. Carlson says that during the Article 15, "I was astounded that you portrayed yourself as a victim of the disciplinary process without expressing heartfelt remorse over the deaths and injuries you caused to the members of the Canadian Forces. In fact, you were obviously angry that the United States Air Force had dared to question your actions during the 17 April 2002 tragedy. Far from providing any defense for your actions, the written materials you presented to me at the hearing only served to illustrate the degree to which you lacked flight discipline as a wingman of COFFEE Flight on 17 April 2002.

"Through your arrogance," the letter continues, "you undermined one of the most sophisticated weapons systems in the world, consisting of the Combined Air Operations Center, the Airborne Warning and Control System, and highly disciplined pilots, all of whom must work together in an integrated fashion to achieve combat goals. The United States Air Force is a major contributor to military victories over our Nation's enemies because our pilots possess superior flight discipline. However, your actions on the night of 17 April 2002 demonstrate an astonishing lack of flight discipline. You were blessed with an aptitude for aviation, your nation provided you the best aviation training on the planet, and you acquired combat expertise in previous armed conflicts. However, by your gross poor judgment, you ignored your training and your duty to exercise flight discipline, and the result was tragic. I have no faith in your abilities to perform in a combat environment."

The general's final paragraph is the most hammering, a personal attack not on Harry Schmidt the pilot, but on Harry Schmidt the man. "I am concerned about more than your poor airmanship," he concludes. "I am also greatly concerned about your officership and judgment. Our Air Force core values stress 'integrity first.' Following the engagement in question, you lied about the reasons why you engaged the target after you were directed to hold fire and then you sought to blame others. You had the right to remain silent, but not the right to lie. In short, the final casualty of the engagement over Kandahar on 17 April 2002 was your integrity."

It is what the relatives of the dead Canadians have been waiting more than two years to hear. For many, the actual punishment is not exactly satisfying. A paltry fine and a letter. But the words are as damning as any judgment can be, official confirmation of what they've been thinking all along. Finally. "If I had to put it on paper, that's exactly what I would have said," says Marley Léger, Marc's widow. "The biggest thing for me is that Gen. Carlson acknowledged what I have been feeling for a long time—that Maj. Schmidt doesn't seem to have remorse."

Psycho will never fly an American fighter jet again. For most of the Canadian relatives, that is punishment enough. Even Paul Dyer, who once demanded that the pilots be dragged in front of a firing squad, says he can live with the reprimand. But he is still waiting for a personal apology. "I would talk to him like a human," he says of Maj. Schmidt, "if he had the heart to call."

Charlie Gittins is livid. "If it weren't so pathetic it would be humorous," he says of the general's letter. "It's like he didn't even pay attention. It shows how morally bankrupt the process was. Gen. Carlson's findings amount to a finding that Harry committed murder, which is just ridiculous." Where is the evidence? He was charged with dereliction of duty, not homicide. It is "a joke," Gittins says, "a fantasy," another attempt "to appease Canadians" and deflect the blame from the senior officers whose Afghanistan air war was an obvious disaster from day one. "By placing the blame at the lowest possible level, the lowest ranked American in the chain, the Air Force has protected the criminal negligence of its general officer corps."

★ ★ ★

The morning after he receives his reprimand, Harry Schmidt goes golfing. From the course, he calls Charlie Gittins, instructing him to start working on an appeal. It is the obvious next move. Harry, after all, doesn't believe a single word of that letter. He nearly laughed when he got it, amazed that Gen. Carlson would sign his name to such an unrealistic—and politically motivated—conclusion.

Amid word of the appeal, Harry's lawyers also threaten to sue the U.S. Air Force for violating Maj. Schmidt's privacy rights. Military letters of reprimand are typically in-house documents, stored far away from public view. Gittins wants to know why the Air Force has plastered his client's damning letter all over the Internet. "We believe that their conduct was intentional and malicious and we intend to seek redress," he says. "Maj. Schmidt is entitled to money damages, including his attorney's fees."

Harry's lawyers never do file a lawsuit, but they do submit an appeal to the LOR on July 15. In non-judicial proceedings, defendants have the right to ask their commander's commander to overturn a punishment. In this case, Lt.-Gen. Carlson's boss is Gen. Hal M. Hornburg, the commander of Air Combat Command.

"It is with disbelief and exasperation that we respond to the reprimand issued Major Schmidt," reads the 12-page appeal. "Frankly, when we reviewed the reprimand we became convinced that the Commander neither read the written submissions we provided to the Commander nor authored the reprimand. The wild allegations in the reprimand are not rooted in any evidence ever adduced in this two-plus year process and belie a desire to mount a public relations campaign rather than actually attempt to see justice done. The Commander wrote that Major Schmidt's integrity was 'the final casualty' of the 17 April 2002 accident. Sir Winston Churchill's famous quote, however, is that truth is the first casualty, and Major Schmidt's case was no different (Churchill also said, 'In time of war, the truth is so precious it must be attended by a bodyguard of lies'). The Air Force core values were mugged before Brig Gen Sargeant's investigation even began, and this process still has not been able to breathe life into anything resembling integrity."

The Air Force's decision to release the reprimand to the press before Maj. Schmidt even had a chance to read it "is ample evidence that this reprimand was not written for Major Schmidt—it was plainly written for the media and the Air Force's external audiences," the appeal reads. "We could not in good conscience advise Major Schmidt to take it seriously—simply, it is a *cartoon*, not to be taken seriously by anyone who has actually read the evidence."

Gen. Carlson accuses Maj. Schmidt of portraying himself as "a victim of the disciplinary process" during his personal presentation. That allegation "is not just inaccurate," defense lawyers say, "it is completely false." Maj. Schmidt told the general "that he found it unacceptable that he had been pre-judged by many Air Force leaders who were not involved in the investigation," but not once did he mention the disciplinary action taken against him. "We—Major Schmidt's defense counsel—did sharply criticize, with good reason, the ineffective command and control tools in the theater, to wit, the combined air operations center (CAOC) and the airborne warning and control system (AWACS). Major Schmidt, however, never leveled any such accusation, although he should have, with good reason."

The defense team notes that Maj. Schmidt asked to have his Article 15 open to the public, but Gen. Carlson refused. "By closing the hearing, the Commander gained the ability to 'spin' the presentation any way the Commander wanted in the media, an opportunity of which the Commander took great advantage. Major Schmidt sought to allow the public to draw its own conclusions from his presentation and explanation, but as has been the case from the outset, the Air Force command has shown a practiced avoidance and aversion to any critical public scrutiny of the facts and factors that actually led to the accident. It is only because of our vigorous defense that the public even has an inkling of the dishonorable Government tactics employed in this case."

The "most outrageous claim," the defense contends, is that Harry used self-defense as an excuse to wage his own war. If true, Maj. Schmidt committed unpremeditated murder, "a charge that the Air Force lacked the courage to prefer; a charge for which Major Schmidt was not notified prior to the imposition of Article 15 punishment that he was required to defend; and, a charge so outrageous on its face that no Air Force official, including the Commander himself, has had the moral courage to make on the record or directly to Major Schmidt to his face. Importantly in this regard, the few timid technical questions the Commander chose to ask of Major Schmidt during the Article 15 hearing clearly were not intended to elicit any evidence supporting these outrageous and false accusations, or illuminate what would possess a highly trained combat aviator and instructor pilot to act in the manner alleged in the reprimand. One would think that if the Commander truly harbored such concerns that a member of his command was a lying murderer, he might have at least inquired about the concerns. Highlighting the absurdity and lack of integrity of these allegations is the fact that throughout two years of investigation these accusations have never before surfaced until now. Brig Gen Sargeant's report did not include them; and when Brig Gen Sargeant was specifically asked by Mr. Gittins at the Article 32, in the presence of Major Schmidt, whether he claimed Major Schmidt declared self-defense 'as a pretext,' Brig Gen Sargeant denied he was making such a claim. The only person associated in any way with the case who has made this reckless assertion, up to now, is Col John Odom, the 'Special Prosecutor' who has spent two years of Government time, money and military pay litigating this one case (with little success) and who provided neither evidence nor testimony in any proceeding, particularly the Article 15 hearing."

Nobody has ever called Maj. Schmidt a liar or questioned his professionalism and integrity, the appeal continues. "Every witness who has ever testified" said it was reasonable for Harry to believe that Maj. Umbach was being targeted by rocket-propelled munitions. Any suggestion that he is a liar is "supported by the same quantum of evidence as the claim that the moon is made of green cheese."

Maj. Schmidt's lawyers take particular issue with Gen. Carlson's claim that Harry ignored Bill's warning to "make sure it's not friendlies." It was not an order, they say. It was "a hortatory statement directed to no one in particular." In the letter of reprimand he gave Maj. Umbach, Gen. Carlson himself criticizes Bill for giving Harry "no direction" while they circled over Tarnak Farm. How can the general now accuse Harry of ignoring Bill's warnings when he's already accused Bill of not providing any? "If Major Schmidt's flight lead never gave him any direction, as the Commander's reprimand of Major Umbach clearly states, then Major Schmidt could not possibly be guilty of violating those directions that were never given."

And what about Lt.-Col. Loida, the consultant Gen. Carlson appointed to the defense team? He interviewed Harry alone—without his lawyers—and "concluded that the accident was the product of the failure to notify the theater command and control system of the live-fire training conducted by the Canadians," the appeal says. "The question we must ask, sir, is if the Commander thought Lt Col Loida competent to evaluate the case in the first place, why did the Commander fail to credit his uncontradicted and unbiased evidence?

"Sir, it may be convenient and easy to portray the 17 April 2002 accident as the product of two 'cowboy' aviators out looking for a cheap thrill, but that superficial analysis is both naive and intellectually dishonest," the appeal continues. "Responsibility for failures and shortcomings start at the top of the command structure. When command procedures fail, it is incumbent upon the command structure to stand up and accept responsibility for those failures. ... In today's military, however, as examples of careerism increasingly drown out examples of leadership, there is a growing tendency to find the lowest person on the totem pole and focus all the responsibility at that level while turning a blind eye to any responsibility higher up the chain. Years ago, practices and training were adjusted in response to mission failures. In this case, however, Maj Schmidt was punished and nothing at all has been done to avoid the problem from recurring."

Although the defense lawyers did not raise this issue with Gen. Carlson, their appeal also attacks Gen. T. Michael Moseley. They note that Moseley's recent promotion will soon make him Gen. Carlson's immediate commander, a fact that they claim could have influenced Carlson's decision in this case. Gen. Moseley, of course, said the day after the bombing that "it is impossible to imagine a scenario" in which the pilots believed they had to drop. He imposed the gag order during the investigation. He appointed Brig.-Gen. Sargeant to head the CIB. And, defense lawyers allege, he ignored warnings that crucial jobs—such as a ground liaison officers (GLOs) at Al Jaber—were not being filled. "Pilots are trained to fight wars using the doctrine written and approved by their commanders and employed daily in exercises and simulations, yet Gen Moseley elected to take a less-costly, non-doctrinal approach and no one, certainly not Gen Moseley, has scrutinized the impact of the doctrinal deviation on this accident," the appeal reads. "His appointed accident investigation board president, remarkably, could find no fault with the CAOC and AWACS being completely unaware of the live-fire exercise or even the existence of the firing range. Nor could Brig Gen Sargeant find anything wrong with the fact the CAOC could not provide any information to help the pilots evaluate the situation that the AWACS flew Majors Schmidt and Umbach into, even though the CAOC was tasked with tracking only *two* tactical fighter flights over Afghanistan that night. We now have to question whether or not the Commander's reprimand is just another step in the ongoing process of shielding Gen Moseley from scrutiny in this case."

Maj. Schmidt's lawyers even question whether Gen. Hornburg—the man they are appealing to—is "in a position to act as a neutral and detached appellate authority, where he is reviewing a case in which his own conduct and decisions likely contributed to the accident." Hornburg is the same general who visited Col. Nichols at Al Jaber a month before the accident, the one who called Gen. Moseley on his cellphone after

Nichols complained that the CAOC wasn't listening to his concerns about Operation Anaconda. Nichols also testified that he told Gen. Hornburg that his pilots had no choice but to violate the Air Force's 10-hour maximum work-day in order to fly those long missions to Afghanistan. It was also Gen. Hornburg, the defense alleges, who "ultimately" sanctioned the use of Go-pills, which affected Maj. Schmidt's "judgment by causing him to misperceive the duration of the firing he observed and to act more quickly than he otherwise would have acted without the drugs."

The simple fact remains that Gen. Carlson was not in the cockpit that night, did not know what threats the pilots were briefed about, and was "in no position to 'look out the window' and see what Major Schmidt observed while fatigued, under the influence of Air Force drugs, and wearing Night Vision Goggles (for five hours)," the defense writes. Gen. Carlson's letter suggests that he would have steered his jet away from the flashes. But if his flight lead was later "shot down, tortured, raped and slaughtered—what would the Commander tell her parents? Would the Commander expect to be court-martialed or otherwise punished and excoriated? And what would the Commander say in the Commander's defense? No Medal of Honor has ever been awarded to someone who ran away from danger rather than confront it."

This case, the appeal concludes, "has always been about the acuity of hindsight, focused solely on *outcome*, when it should have been examined *prospectively* from the point of view of a reasonable person under the same circumstances, as is prescribed in self-defense doctrine. Had Major Schmidt been correct about the perceived threat and neutralized it after it had engaged Major Umbach, there is little doubt that he would have been decorated for his valor. That his judgment and evaluation of the threat proved wrong and were punished because, with the practiced acuity of hindsight, others who weren't called upon to make the decision in combat were able to postulate alternatives that might have avoided this accident, demonstrates that punishment under these circumstances is based on a legally incorrect standard and is based not on fact, doctrine and reason, but solely on the effect such punishment would have on USAF public relations and on the public sensibilities of the citizen of a needed ally in the Global War on Terrorism."

Gen. Hornburg takes less than three weeks to consider Maj. Schmidt's appeal. Denied. An Air Force press release announces the ruling on August 3, 2004. "Gen. Hornburg's decision," it reads, "brings nonjudicial punishment proceedings on this issue to a close."

PART IV: AFTERMATH

chapter thirty-nine

Brett Perry has a game plan for this interview. We're going to talk, then he's going to stop by the driving range and hit some golf balls. It's an improvement. Up until a few months ago, he would hit the bottle after meeting with a reporter. But that was before December 2004, before that drunken night when he was sprawled underneath his toilet, puking so hard he could barely catch his breath. Rock bottom, as he now describes it.

"I was thinking: 'All the stuff I've done, all these people that know me, and I could choke right now on my own vomit,'" Brett recalls. "And that's how people will remember me." He could see the headline: *Soldier wounded in friendly fire attack dies in drunken haze.* "I said to myself: 'What am I doing?' If I was spared, why am I throwing my life away like this? Okay, I've got problems, but why throw it away?"

At 28, Brett Perry is a massive man. Standing beside him, you can't help but think that if he saw that bomb coming, he could have snatched it from the sky and snapped it over his knee. His voice, however, is an odd match. He speaks softly, almost in a whisper, as he recalls that night in the bathroom, and everything else that led up to that moment. "I wanted to be replaced with those guys, and I still feel that today," he says of his four dead comrades. "I wish it would have been me instead of them. That pilot was trying to engage me and he missed me and hit them instead. It makes me feel responsible, and I still feel that. It's a hard thing to deal with."

Over the years, Brett has had to look at those Canadian families, convinced that they were staring back at him, blaming him, wondering why he is still alive and their sons are dead. He had to listen to those voices in his head. Ainsworth's laugh. Marc telling him to put his helmet back on. *Your Carl Gustav killed everyone.* And he's had to live with his last words to Pte. Green, the screaming and the swearing seconds before the explosion. "I can talk to a doctor, I can talk to my wife or anything like that, and you can always say: 'Oh, don't worry about it,'" Brett says. "But when you go through something like that and you actually do something or you're hard on someone and something happens..." He pauses for a moment. "I was hard on all the new guys."

Now a master-corporal, Brett is based in Winnipeg, where he trains Canadian Air Force officers—including pilots—in weapons tactics. "I give 'em a good go," he laughs. He recently married his longtime girlfriend, Andrea, and this fall they are planning to move to nearby Shilo, Manitoba, home of the 2nd Battalion of Princess Patricia's Canadian Light Infantry. Brett is going back to the Army. "I'm totally ready to give back to the battalion," he says. "They took care of me. They didn't turn their back on me, even when I was having problems."

Those problems, those demons, still haunt Brett Perry. They always will. But he insists that things are better these days, that that night beside the toilet was the motivation he needed. He's come to realize that in some strange way, what happened in that Afghanistan ditch taught him a lesson. "It's a horrible thing that happened to us, but it helped me realize a lot of stuff about other people, about leadership, about myself," he says. "I'm going to stop shaking my fist at the sky. I'm going to focus on what I have now, not what I could have had or what was there once. I'll be alright."

He has also turned to God, not just to help him endure, but to help him forgive. "I'm trying," says Perry, recently baptized as a Pentecostal Christian. "I struggle with my faith because of it. I struggle with my life because of it." But as hard as he tries, he still can't quite forgive Harry Schmidt. Not yet, at least.

"I've never been contacted or been told 'I'm sorry' or been told anything," he says. "I have no respect for him and I feel he's a murderer. I've said that many times and I'll say it again. I feel he's a murderer and I think that he got away with murder."

★　★　★

Two months after Gen. Carlson signed Harry Schmidt's letter of reprimand, Paul Dyer passed away. Sick and alone, Ainsworth's father died of a ruptured esophagus while sitting at home in his Brampton condominium. Neighbours called 911 as soon as they noticed the smell. Paul had been dead for at least a week by the time anyone even realized.

★ ★ ★

Brian Decaire is a SAR tech now, a search and rescue specialist based in Winnipeg. He spends his days parachuting and mountain climbing and scuba diving. Getting paid to do his hobbies. Admittedly, his biggest weakness is still long-distance running, just like it was when he first started jogging with Cpl. Dyer along the Kandahar runway.

Brian's memories of that night at Tarnak Farm have faded over the years, so much so that he recently began to write his recollections in a notepad. When people ask him about the bombing—and many people still do—he simply takes out his journal and begins to read.

The pages recall the instant swelling of his shrapnel-filled hand. The eerie silence that followed the explosion, a silence quickly replaced by "these agonizing sounds, sounds I cannot describe." The bodies. The blood. "It's more than just almost being killed," Brian says, reading from the book. "I mean, big deal. People come close to death every day and people die tragic deaths every day. The people that love them probably hurt just as much and are just as angry whether the son is killed by a drunk driver or by a 500-pound laser-guided bomb dropped by an F-16."

Decaire was the other Carl Gustav gunner that night, the corporal who loaded the round that lit up Maj. Schmidt's night vision goggles. For more than three years, he has watched Brett Perry, his close friend, agonize over that single shot. They still get together all the time, and they still talk about it. Brian, like everyone else, has done his best to reassure his buddy that it's not his fault. "I don't know why guys do feel guilt," he says. "That was just the physics of the night."

★ ★ ★

Aart and Janna Van Sloten earn their living just steps from their bedroom, in a small bakery attached to their Edmonton home. The family-owned shop specializes in one thing: wedding cakes. Many of Janna's most elaborate creations are on display inside the small store, as is a sign thanking people for their donations to the Ainsworth Dyer Memorial Bridge fund.

Four years ago, Ains walked into this bakery with an engagement ring and walked out with the blessing of Jocelyn's parents. No doubt his cake would have come from here. Tonight, in the family kitchen down the hall, Jocelyn and her parents sit around the table, remembering. Remembering how street-smart Ains was, how much he loved to stand in the background and people-watch. Remembering how comical he was, how he once threatened to take off all his clothes and walk down the street naked if Jocelyn didn't wipe that frown off her face. Remembering the last time she saw him, when she dropped him off at the base the morning he left for Kandahar. They sat in the car for a little while. Ains started singing.

As she tells her stories, Jocelyn never once shows any signs of crying. "I have my bad days," she says. "I definitely have my bad days. But I'm more thankful for the time that we had together. Though it was a short time, it changed me forever. And I wouldn't take it back, I wouldn't change anything. I learned a lot from Ains, and I think I'm a better person for knowing him."

Jocelyn stopped speaking to Ainsworth's parents a long time ago. Just like Ains always was, she found herself stuck in the middle, struggling to play the fence while neither seemed to think about the hell she was going through. She's not the least bit bitter about all the money Paul got. Money's not going to change the fact that her fiancé is dead. She's just heartbroken that with Paul gone and Agatha in Montreal, there's nobody in Toronto to visit Ainsworth's grave.

But Jocelyn will always have the bridge, the plaque that she and her family fought so hard to hang in the park. She still hopes to have children one day, children she can bring to that bridge. Children who will know how much she loved Ainsworth Dyer. "It's not something you get over," she says. "It will never be something I'll get over. It is something that you learn to live with, you cope with. It will be a part of me forever."

★ ★ ★

The Canadian Army has declared Rene Paquette "3B." In a nutshell, it means he is medically unqualified to do anything. The vertigo, his hearing loss, and the injuries to his back and his knee have combined to cut short his military career. By 2007, Cpl. Paquette will have no choice but to leave the service.

The battalion isn't exactly throwing him out on the street. He will still pocket his full salary for six months, then 75 percent for the next two years. In the meantime, the government will pay him to go to school and apprentice as an electrician. The rules also say that Rene, because of the circumstances surrounding his medical discharge, will be a priority hire, at the top of the list when the government goes looking for an electrician. Chances are good that Cpl. Paquette will one day end up back at Canadian Forces Base Shilo, wearing coveralls instead of fatigues.

He hopes that happens. He and his wife, Lauren, have already built a house nearby. Breanne, the daughter he almost never met, is nearly four years old now. But even around her, Rene has to be careful. Once, as they played together on the floor, the vertigo kicked in and daddy blacked out. An ambulance had to come to the house. "There's not a day that goes by that there isn't something," he says. "If it's not my knees aching, it's my back. Or I have an ear infection, headaches, you name it. There is always something, or a combination of everything."

For a long time, he hated Harry Schmidt. At the Paquette residence, "Schmidt" even became a curse word, something you said if you stubbed your toe. But as time passed, so did the hatred. "To me, he's just a joke now," Rene says.

"It drives me batty that I see things happening in the world and I hear about, potentially, the battalion going to Africa or the Middle East or somewhere, and it just kills me that they're going somewhere without me," he says. "The only thing I ever strived towards or dreamt growing up was being in the military. That was my life. That's my whole being. I'm a soldier as far as I'm concerned, and that's how I define myself. And he has essentially taken that away."

★ ★ ★

In the winter, Lloyd Smith shovels the snow off the patio stones that lead to his flags. Not all of it. Just enough for a pathway, just enough so he can reach the white poles in the morning.

Flags aside, Lloyd and Charlotte's home in Tatamagouche, Nova Scotia, is filled with memories of Nathan. It's not the house he grew up in—where his band practiced in the basement—but it's the one where he proposed to Jodi a few years ago. It's also where the Smiths spent that Christmas before Kandahar. Lloyd still breaks down when he thinks of that drive to the airport, watching Nathan disappear through the security gates. "I do this all the time," he says, wiping his eyes. "I'll do it until I die."

Even at their lowest moments, Nathan's parents have always been rational. They never craved revenge. They never demanded that the pilots be thrown in jail. "What are you going to get out of that?" Lloyd asks, sitting at his kitchen table. "They've got wives and families they've got to care for as well. To me, the outcome was adequate. He's not going to fly again, and I don't think he should, because I think he is the type of guy that could repeat that mistake."

And it was the pilots' mistake, Lloyd says. Nobody else's. He has heard all the accusations about the AWACS and the CAOC and the bumbling generals and the quiet cover-up. "That's baloney," he says. "These guys were at fault from day one."

I ask Lloyd whether he ever gave Harry and Bill the benefit of the doubt, that friendly fire and the "fog of war" are the inevitable price of combat. Did you ever consider that Nathan could have accidentally killed an ally during the assault on The Whale? He thinks for a moment before answering. "I know this of my son," Lloyd says. "If he did make a mistake like that, he would own up to it. That's the type of person he was."

After 37 years on the water, Lloyd recently retired from his job as an oil tanker captain. He appreciates what he has. His wife. His daughter. His granddaughter. He even finds some comfort in the fact that his son's death, at least for a short while, reopened Canada's eyes to its military. "If you could change it all, I'd take him back in a blink of an eye, even part of him," he says. "But they have made changes. Their lives will not be in vain. Changes will come out of this."

One thing will always stay the same. "Hardly a day goes by that I don't weep just a little," Lloyd says. "We have to live it every day until we die. The legal process is over, but the pain and suffering stays with you. We're just at the stage now where we're living with what is inevitable. It ain't going to go back to the way it was. You can't change what's happened and there is no surprise phone call."

★   ★   ★

Most of the photographs Alastair Luft snapped in Kandahar were damaged in the flood that hit his basement a while back. They're still legible, though. Shots of the camp. Shots of The Whale. Shots of Tarnak Farm. Now a captain, Luft was just 24 years old when he deployed to Afghanistan as 3 Platoon's commander. Of the four soldiers killed by Harry Schmidt's bomb, three of them—Nathan, Ains, and Ricky—were his responsibility. Like most of the troops who were there that night, Alastair still shoulders his own sense of guilt, the feeling that he could have done more for his guys.

As he flips through his wrinkled photos, he recalls how he followed 2 Section down the wadi, watching them fire at the tank targets downrange. When they were done, he went with them to the ammo truck, just as Kevin Towell, his platoon warrant, reminded him to do earlier that night. Later, when Luft tried to catch up with 3 Section—Lorne's section— Aaron Bygrove cut him off. They were shooting the shit when the bomb exploded. "As a platoon commander, I should have been with them," he says now.

He has other regrets, like when he believed—amid the confusion— that Nathan was Ricky. "When the actual event was happening, I felt like I was kind of being overtaken by the chaos, by all the stuff that was going on," he recalls. "I always felt bad that I didn't have better clarity of what I was doing. I got absorbed by the events a little bit. If the O.C. had come up and asked me what the situation was there, I had no idea what the overall situation was."

Alastair takes some solace in knowing that nothing he did—or didn't do—changed anything. Those four guys were dead by the time he got there. But in the days after, he and Kevin Towell, his older and wiser 2I/C, spent hours replaying the events, both wrought with regret that they weren't in the ditch with their troops. Kevin wasn't even at Tarnak Farm that night. He stayed at camp for the Mark-19 grenade training. But that only added to the survivor's guilt. *I should have gone to the range.*

On May 7, 2005, W/O Kevin Towell was driving his truck along a New Brunswick highway when it struck the median and rolled over, tossing him out the side. He died two days later.

★   ★   ★

The U.S. government refused to pay Richard Green's mother the compensation she demanded. The denial arrived in a short, two-page letter signed by Colonel R. Eric Rissling, a senior official in the Air Force Legal Services Agency. The colonel wrote that "after a thorough review," it was clear that the Foreign Claims Act does not apply to soldiers killed in combat.

"Although the Canadian forces may not have been involved in combat at the time of the incident, the determining factor is whether the actions of the United States forces, directly or indirectly, were part of combat activities," the letter reads. "Certainly, the US forces in this situation were engaging in activities related to combat." The only exception to that rule, Col. Rissling notes, is if a plane experiences "an accident or malfunction" while "preparing for, going to or returning" from combat. "Even if one assumes, *arguendo*, that the incident occurred while returning from a combat mission, there was no malfunction or accident with regard to the aircraft or its ordnance," he writes. "Here, the aircraft performed exactly as expected."

Doreen's lawyers had also asked the secretary of the Air Force to consider awarding an *ex-gratia* payment, a gesture of goodwill as opposed to something the military is legally bound to do. "Although the Air Force sincerely regrets the casualties resulting from this incident, the Secretary, after careful consideration, has declined to make such payments," the letter concludes. "Private Green's death was incident to his military service in a formally designated combat zone, and combat-related."

Ricky's mom now goes by her maiden name, Young. She still lives in the rural Nova Scotia region where her son is buried, but she continues to keep to herself. She has a hard time trusting people these days. So many have turned against her. But Doreen says she will continue her fight, even if that means taking the case to a U.S. court.

"It's taken its toll on me," she says. "But the more they want to deny a person what is rightfully theirs, the more I am going to dig my heels in. And if it's the last breath I take, I'll fight it.

"I just don't care anymore what people think," she continues. "I know what my son would have wanted and I know how he was concerned about having somebody here to look after me should he get killed. We're all entitled to our own opinions, but walk a mile in my shoes, then judge me."

★ ★ ★

"I'm not going to be running any marathons, that's for sure," Lorne Ford jokes. "But I don't think I've changed an iota since before the accident. Guys will tell you, I can still be a prick. I am still confident in my abilities."

Sitting at 3rd Battalion headquarters in Edmonton, Sgt. Ford is wearing a pair of maroon shorts, exposing the huge hole in the back of his left thigh. Years later, Lorne still has no feeling whatsoever in the bottom of his foot. For a long time—despite his pleas—the doctors wouldn't allow him to strap on a parachute, worried that his leg wouldn't be able to withstand the landing. In recent months, however, the Army let him try a couple of jumps into the water. They went so well that the docs are thinking about giving him the okay to try the real thing. "I think it's strong enough, without a doubt, that I could jump on land," Sgt. Ford says.

But no matter how strong his leg gets, Lorne will never again be a full-time paratrooper. The injuries he sustained at Tarnak Farm were simply too severe. These days, he limps into work, where his main job is to book training exercises for the guys who do jump. He is not angry, though. Sgt. Ford has never been the type to feel sorry for himself. "It shouldn't have happened in that situation, but there's nothing I can do," he says. "I've got to get on with my life, and there's positive things in my life that I've got to look forward to. You can't dwell on the past."

Lorne Ford has told the story a thousand times. The whistle. The flash of light. Waking up on his right side. The tourniquet. But he always shifts the focus away from himself, quick to praise the three men who saved his life: Chris Kopp, Rob Coates and Jean de la Bourdonnaye. "I can't explain it, but there's a connection," he says. "I see them, and I'm very happy to see them."

Sgt. Ford has fought through his own feelings of guilt since the bombing. Richard Green was attached to his section, a soldier under his direct command. "There is always going to be that feeling of having lost a member of your section that will never go away," he says. "I'm not over it. But I've dealt with it as best I can. I kept telling myself that I had nothing to do with it. It wasn't my fault. It was some other idiot's fucking decision."

Like some of the Canadian families, Sgt. Ford harbors no bitterness toward Maj. Umbach. He showed genuine remorse, Lorne says, and he chose to quietly retire rather than drag out the legal process. "Schmidt, the arrogant prick, didn't feel like he did anything wrong and he stuck to his guns. And if he's that type of man, you know what, what goes around comes around. It will come back to him. If he really thinks he did nothing wrong, then he's an idiot. And he showed no remorse. I have no respect for the man. I wouldn't fucking piss on him if he was on fire."

But Lorne Ford doesn't spend his days thinking about that. Harry Schmidt is the least of his concerns. When he does think about that night, it's always about Marc, Nathan, Ains, and Rick. "I always think I'm over it, but when I'm talking about it like this, it hurts just the same," he says. "It's obviously hard to deal with, but as long as the four guys are always remembered, they were amazing troops, fantastic in the field in everything they did, in every single way. And that's what I want to get across. I don't want nothing written about me. As long as everybody knows that they did everything that they were expected by their leaders. They did their job as soldiers. If everybody took their cue from those four, our Army would just be all that better."

★ ★ ★

Five Alpha Company soldiers were honored by the Canadian military for the First Aid they administered in the darkness of the wadi. Bill Wilson. Vic Speirs. Jean de la Bourdonnaye. Chris Kopp. And Rob Coates. All five received a Deputy Chief of the Defence Staff Commendation, which is about as low as an official award gets in the Canadian military. Though none of them would ever say it, many of their fellow soldiers believe the men were shortchanged, that they deserved much more recognition for the work they did that night. *They got fucked*, is how some describe it.

It is a touchy issue. Awards always are. What makes one soldier worthy of a Bronze Star, while another warrants a tiny gold pin and a firm handshake? Nobody is suggesting that those five men deserve a Bronze Star, but the obvious question lingers: If their actions don't deserve some sort of medal, what does?

Whatever the answer, none of them spends too much time worrying about it. They wish those guys were still alive. A medal isn't going to change that. "We were doing our job," MCpl. Coates says. "We just happened to be there at the shitty time and we did the best we could do." Rob still thinks about the explosion, about lifting the blanket off of Ainsworth's face, then helping to treat Sgt. Ford. "It's pretty important to me, what happened that night. And I'm glad that I could help, because there is no way I could have just sat back and let other people take care of it. It's not my nature at all."

His best friend, Cpl. Kopp, was outstanding that night. He scrambled with Coates and DLB to stabilize Sgt. Ford. It was Kopp who urged the others to wrap that blue tourniquet around Lorne's thigh—a decision that not only saved the sergeant's leg, but probably saved his life. Chris is now a SAR Tech, based in Winnipeg. "There were people that stayed away that wanted no part of it," he says, recalling those first few moments after the bombing. "There were some people contributing to the chaos and the panic. And there were some people that were getting things done."

Bill Wilson was one of the people getting things done. As Alpha Company's lead medic, he did the triaging, making sure everyone who needed help was getting it. As awful as it was, that night will always be—professionally speaking, at least—a defining moment for Bill Wilson, who is now a warrant officer. When he teaches a class to younger army medics, Tarnak Farm almost always comes up. "The call for 'medics' was everywhere, it seemed," he recalls, speaking softly. "I learned this earlier on in my career: It can either be organized or unorganized chaos. There is no other way to explain chaos. But trying to control that chaos, I think we had a lot of luck and a lot of training on our side."

Of the three medics on scene, none received more official praise than Cpl. de la Bourdonnaye. Gen. Baril's board of inquiry credited him—and him alone—with saving Sgt. Ford's life. But Jean, now a master-corporal, is not the type to gloat. He knows that the others did an amazing job, too. "We did what we could for the guys who were living," he says. "The ones we were able to save, we saved." Jean keeps his DCDS Commendation in a drawer, not on his wall. "At the end of the day, I know what I did, and I know what the three of us did," he says of his fellow medics. "To me, that is more important than any medals."

Vic Speirs does have his certificate hanging in his Edmonton home. His last name is still spelled wrong. He told the military about the typo, but nobody has bothered to print him a new one yet. "It was pretty much automatic pilot that night," he recalls. "When you eat, you don't have to think about cutting your food and putting your fork to your mouth because it is something you've done so many times. And trauma medicine is the same way. If you've practiced it enough and you're comfortable enough with your skills, you don't have to stop to think about what you should do or what you shouldn't do. You just do it."

But there was a slight difference that night, Vic says. "As much as I love trauma medicine, doing trauma medicine on your friends sucks."

★ ★ ★

The Outback diner and general store is on the main strip in Hubbards, Nova Scotia, just down the street from the bowling alley where a young Miranda Boutilier first noticed Ricky Green. "I saw him as everything," she says, sipping a coffee. "One person once asked me to describe him, and I told them to look up every nice word in the dictionary, and that's him."

Though she is now 21, Miranda still looks every bit the part of the 17-year-old redhead whose crying face made all the newspapers back in April 2002. But looks, of course, are deceiving. This Miranda is much more aware, much more mature. She has endured pain that most people never will, and if anything, it has only made her stronger.

She recalls, with a smile, how happy Ricky was that she followed him to Edmonton. They were starting a life together. He bought a Honda Civic. Ains dropped by the apartment once. *So you're the Miranda he keeps talking about.* "It was really just him and I," she says. "It would have been the biggest regret of my life if I hadn't gone out there."

She's also glad that she decided to go to the Article 32. Watching those tapes was horrific, but it was exactly what she needed. She needed to be around people who knew how empty she felt. She needed to be there when the pilots spoke. "It came down to who could say sorry," she says. "All I was looking for was a sincere apology. I got that from Umbach. I did not get that from Schmidt."

Miranda has slowly packed away most of Ricky's things. She gave his army clothes to his dad, David. She kept the diamond engagement ring for herself, but she doesn't wear it on her finger anymore. At 21, Miranda is moving on. Her new boyfriend understands that Rick will always be a part of her life. "I'll never love Ricky any less," she says. "He was my first love, and he will always be my first love. He would want nothing but the best for me."

★   ★   ★

Shane Brennan is not a corporal anymore. He's a constable, a recent addition to the Edmonton police force. He still drops by the battalion headquarters every once in a while, just to say hello. It's a bond that you never quite break.

A few months back, some of Shane's fellow police officers clued in to the fact that he is the same Shane Brennan they saw on the news, the one who was bombed by that F-16. Trying their best not to be rude, they asked him about it. Shane, never shy, told them his story. He tells it again today, about the shrapnel in his leg, about the charred body parts he stepped on as he walked toward the ambulance. He never finishes the story without his eyes turning red. This time is no different.

What *is* different is that today, Shane recalls those conversations he had with Marc Léger less than an hour before he died. He says Marc complained that the anti-tank drill wasn't safe, that it was way too dark to be firing the Carl Gustav. Over the years, Shane has kept those conversations to himself. He never told Gen. Sargeant and the CIB. And he never told Col. Odom and the prosecutors.

"He told me himself—before he gave me my orders of what was going on and before my ammo allotment—he told me: 'This is retarded. We've got to get this fucking shut down,'" Shane says. He says Sgt. Léger was worried that one of the gunners, unable to see, would drop a round short, maybe even frag the rest of the troops on the line.

Shane doesn't want to be misunderstood. He's not making an excuse for the pilots. Sgt. Léger was worried that guys on the ground couldn't see where they were shooting—not that they would be mistaken by an F-16. But for Shane, it's been that much harder to stomach what happened, knowing that Sgt. Léger told him that he wanted the range closed down. "I don't think we should have been out there firing a Carl Gustav without any kind of illumination," Shane says now. "I understand being tactical, but where do you draw the line between being tactical and being ineffective? I agree at some point in time you should throw the safety flags out the fucking window, because how are you supposed to learn in a real combat environment? Who is to say we run out of paraflares and there is a tank being driven by one of those Taliban or al-Qaeda personnel and you need to take that out? What are you going to do? I see things from both sides of the fence. But it could have been safer. We have the equipment."

★ ★ ★

Harry Schmidt's letter of reprimand, typed and framed, is on display on the fireplace mantel in Richard and Claire Léger's living room. *Shameful. Arrogant. Inexcusable. You waged your own war.* Beside the letter is a photo of their son, Marc, holding a parachute and wearing his maroon beret.

"He thinks he walks on water," Richard says of Maj. Schmidt. "All he wanted, as far as I'm concerned, was a medal to press on his chest. That's all he was looking for. He wanted to be the hero."

Beside the fireplace, scattered on the floor, are piles of newspaper articles and magazine clippings, each one about the friendly fire bombing. There are dozens of letters, too, many written by strangers who felt compelled to tell Marc's parents how sorry they were. There's also a note from

Gen. Bruce Carlson, delivered to the Légers' Stittsville home a month after he signed Maj. Schmidt's letter of reprimand.

"I cannot begin to tell you how sorry we all are that your son's death was caused by the actions of a US Air Force pilot," the general wrote. "I know you are extremely proud to have such a fine young man as your son and that losing him has been devastating. As you know, I have recently concluded disciplinary proceedings against the pilot who was principally responsible for this tragedy. I regret that I was unable to apologize to you earlier while the disciplinary proceedings were pending. I know that it does nothing to ease the pain of your loss, but I want you to know that the Air Force, as an institution, has learned valuable lessons from this horrific tragedy, and that we will do our level best to ensure nothing like this ever happens again."

Richard and Claire waited a long time for that apology. They've heard Bill Umbach say sorry. Now they've heard the Air Force. They're still waiting for Harry Schmidt. "We're not vengeful people," Claire says. Indeed, neither she nor her husband ever insisted that the pilots go to prison. They wanted their wings. And they wanted an apology. "It would have went a long way," she says. "He came across so arrogant that it turned us off. He got us so pissed off against him."

Never more so than at the Article 32, when Maj. Schmidt stood up to read what Claire now calls his "declaration of excuses." Her eyes well with tears as she remembers how angry she was that afternoon. "That's not an apology," she says. "And I was never going to accept it as such."

★ ★ ★

"Those guys have become larger than life, and deservedly so," Sean Hackett says. "They stand for so much more. They stand for the ultimate in professionalism. They were lost in the line of duty. They were lost fighting alongside their friends. They were lost fighting for something worthwhile."

Maj. Hackett is no longer A Company's commander. He is based in Kingston, Ontario, these days, far away from most of the troops he deployed with to Kandahar in the winter of 2002. Nearly four years later, Sean's memories of that night have fused into a few vignettes, a few moments in time that don't quite connect any more. But he'll never forget the sound of the explosion, or Capt. Jasper grabbing his arm, telling him that Cpl. Dyer is dead. He will always remember kneeling beside Sgt. Léger, and later, helping to lift Sgt. Ford's stretcher onto the chopper. "I can't live with the fact that we lost soldiers there," Sean says, speaking in the deep, quiet tone that his troops came to know so well. "It is something that I'll take to the grave. But I can perhaps, as a professional military officer, live with the details of the letter of reprimand. It's hammering. It's a very strong indictment of an individual's actions. And from my perspective, that's all I could have hoped for. The Air Force has lost confidence in this pilot's ability to fly in combat."

Maj. Hackett still struggles to squeeze some kind of meaning, some kind of silver lining, out of what happened at Tarnak Farm. The country certainly noticed its military again, even if only for a while. Canadians realized that their soldiers don't just hand out fruit packages or stand in between people who don't like each other. They are trained for combat. "It needs to be part of the national consciousness," Maj. Hackett says. "It needs to be part of the national understanding. It needs to be part of our own military's understanding. They should never forget that we can go and we can do these types of things."

Up until now, Sean Hackett has never heard that Sgt. Léger apparently complained that it was too dark to be firing a Carl Gustav. Marc definitely didn't say anything to him that night. "If he had had a legitimate concern, then he certainly would have been heard," he says.

We now know, of course, that it was the rocket-propelled Carl Gustav that caught Maj. Schmidt's attention. In hindsight, if the Canadians hadn't brought that weapon to the range, those four soldiers might still be alive. Sean, like many others, has thought about that possibility. "I guess it's all a question of: 'How much of a fatalist are you in terms of your outlook?' There are so many unfortunate realities that surround this affair," he says. "Was it necessary to fire the Carl G.? Perhaps not. But it's one of those friggin' weird things that you just can't plan for. Ultimately, you throw it back at old Maj. Schmidt and you look at the letter of reprimand he received for doing what he did. He had no business being there and doing what he did."

★ ★ ★

"It isn't something that ever goes away," Joe Jasper says. "You don't forget about it. It's an image burned in your brain."

There was a time when Joe thought of that image every day, of lifting those bodies out of the sand. The memory isn't as consuming anymore. Some days even pass without a thought of Tarnak Farm. But the image always comes back. "I've definitely changed," Capt. Jasper says. "You can't live through something like that and have it not change you. But I think I'm healthy and still willing and able to do the job."

Joe's job has taken him to Kamloops, British Columbia, to the post of operations officer for the Rocky Mountain Rangers. For a long time, his opinions of the pilots changed from day to day, usually depending on the latest headline or the number of beers he drank. He and Sgt. Ford used to talk about the case all the time, until they finally got sick of thinking about it. "They died unfairly, maybe unnecessarily," Capt. Jasper says. "But not in vain. Their deaths were not meaningless. One of us could have stepped on a mine at Tarnak Farm. One of us could have stepped on a mine in any number of the places we had been in Afghanistan. In the end, you're coming home in a box. You meant something to the people that you were there with, the people that you left behind."

Joe has no regrets. He doesn't regret disobeying his commanders when they told him to come back to camp. And he doesn't regret the way he operated that range. He filled out all the proper paperwork. The Rakkasans knew that A Company was going to be there that night. They knew what weapons—including the Carl Gustav—his guys would be firing. It certainly wasn't Joe's job to call the Air Force and let them know. "Everything we'd done was safe and was reviewed in detail by the CO and RAK 6 and they were all fine with it, so we went ahead."

The conversation inevitably turns to his testimony at the Article 32, to the blinking red lights that defense lawyers claimed he failed to set up that night. Joe says the manual that Charlie Gittins quoted, the one written in 1983, was never part of Task Force Rakkasan's range-operating procedures. "It wasn't what was in place for us," he says. "In a war zone, when you're training for war, trying to check some book that was written for training in the Cold War era—in the '80s—it just doesn't apply."

And it certainly doesn't vindicate Harry Schmidt, Capt. Jasper says. He should have known that he was flying right beside the Kandahar Airfield, the home base of thousands of coalition troops. And even if he didn't know that Tarnak Farm was surrounded by a ROZ, he should have known that it fell within the boundaries of AO Truman, Rakkasan's territory. "I don't think he's lying when he says he thinks he's being shot at," Capt. Jasper says. "I think when he looked out his window—through his goggles or on the TV screen—he saw a little flash flash flash or whatever, and thought: 'That's SAFIRE, I'm going to roll, self-defense.' He used self-defense to score, to get one on the enemy."

As much as Tarnak Farm has impacted his life, Joe Jasper tries to keep perspective. He is not oblivious to the fact that since April 17, 2002, hundreds of other soldiers have died in Afghanistan and Iraq—many by friendly fire. "I think the Americans are our best friends in the world, whether we like it or not," he says. "There is no American bashing when their helicopters are rescuing our wounded. There is no American bashing when they are flying us into combat and covering our ass. They were there when we needed them."

★ ★ ★

During the Afghanistan tour, part of Marc Léger's job was to resupply sections deployed on missions around Kandahar. He used body bags, stuffing them with ammo, toilet paper, batteries, field dressings, and anything else the troops might need. The plastic bags were the obvious choice, not only because they are waterproof, but because they can be chucked out the door of a hovering chopper.

When he returned home from Op Apollo, Billy Bolen began to develop a new supply bag, inspired by Sgt. Léger's, but new and improved. This one has handles, and can hold up to 450 pounds of equipment when clipped to a parachute. The Canadian army is still testing Billy's idea, but it's been getting good reviews. He already has a name for it: Load Delivery Ground System. Léger. Dyer. Green. Smith.

"When I actually looked at Marc, that fucked me up big time," Bolen says, recalling that morning in the wadi. "Marc was the one that fucked me up the most." He looked so unscathed, as if the bomb barely touched him. For months, Bolen worried that maybe he and the other soldiers didn't do enough for Sgt. Léger, that they left him in the dark to die. Billy himself ran right past Marc's body numerous times in those frantic first moments. He knows now that there is nothing he could have done.

"I think about it all the time," he says. "I'm not stressed by it. I don't think I have PTSD or anything like that. But some days, I think about it, I close my eyes and can see that picture of the four guys. It's a memory that won't go away."

It is a memory that will always be a part of the men who stayed behind at Tarnak Farm. Some, rightfully so, have no interest in talking about it, especially to a journalist who wasn't there. Others have done their best to pull something, anything, out of it. "It's hard coming face to face with someone else's mortality like that, because inevitably you're coming face to face with your own as well," Marco Favasoli says. "But in the end, I think it actually gave me a bit of closure."

For weeks, Pete Filis thought about his friends' faces every night before he fell asleep. Years later, he still wonders whether any of them saw it coming, or felt a thing. "I still think about it quite often," he says. "Every time I look up on the wall across the hallway I think about it."

When he's not at the battalion, Brad McKenzie still bounces at the Edmonton raves with Yan Bérubé and some of the other troops who used to work the door with Ainsworth Dyer. He's not proud of staying behind that morning, but he's glad he did. As hard as it was, he knows that those soldiers were recovered with dignity, with respect. "The details previous to that get foggy," he says. "But I'll never forget that part."

"If anything, it was almost therapeutic," Dave Bibby says. "It was almost better that we stayed than if we hadn't because I know for a fact I did everything possible that I could have done. There is no 'I should have' or 'if only I had.' I did, and we were there from start to finish. It felt good to bring them home."

Dave's fellow Pioneer, Jon Bradshaw, recalls how he tried not to stare. Do the job, but don't take in the big picture. "Once dawn kicked in, it turned into a matter of pride," he says. "Only your brothers will carry you home." He tells the story with a nervous laugh, his defense mechanism kicking in. "Time dulls the wounds. If you'd asked me this two years ago I probably wouldn't have been able to talk," he says. "I'm not adversely affected. I'm not stressed. I don't like the 'post-traumatic stress' people that have gone because a lot of them haven't done anything very stressful compared to what I have done. I am always going to compare everyone else who goes down with that to what I've done, and I know that most of them haven't done anything close."

Jon didn't spend much time following the criminal case. Whatever happened, it was never going to change what he saw in the ditch. "The Americans do it all the time to their own," he says of friendly fire. "The fact that it was our guys this time is the only difference."

Rob Jones didn't follow the headlines, either. "It's not going to bring your buddies back," he says. On the rare occasions when he does talk about Tarnak Farm, it's only with a few of his closest friends, people he can trust. That's the way he deals with it. "We all have crosses to bear," he says. "It's not a quick fix or a pill. A lot of guys will be carrying this with them for the rest of their lives."

Billy Bolen is certainly one of them. But as much as that night and the next morning have become a permanent nick in his memory, he holds no grudge against either pilot. "I've got nothing to say to them, good or bad," he says. "They've got to live with the guilt. That's enough of a crutch."

In the summer of 2005, Springfield's 183rd Fighter Wing cut the ribbon on a new, $9 million facility. Three stories, and three years in the making, the building boasts an auditorium, a dining hall, and offices for everyone from the chaplain to the wing commander. The grand opening, however, was bittersweet. Days earlier, the base learned that it will soon lose all of its F-16s.

Springfield's 15 fighter jets—including the one Harry Schmidt flew that night—will be transferred to Fort Wayne, Indiana, signaling the end of the 170th fighter squadron. The move is just one small piece of a massive Pentagon plan to consolidate military bases across the United States, saving taxpayers billions of dollars. Local politicians are still fighting the exodus, claiming it will cost Springfield's economy hundreds of jobs, but the transfer appears all but inevitable. By 2007, the 183rd Fighter Wing will likely be little more than an engine repair shop.

Whatever is left, Col. Bob Murphy will not be the man in charge. A year before all the changes were announced, the Illinois Air National Guard decided not to renew his contract as the wing commander. After three decades in uniform, he is looking for another job. "It lets the unit move forward," he says. "It takes a while. I don't think it's recovered yet."

Technically speaking, Col. Murphy wasn't the boss while the squadron was in Kuwait. He was just another pilot. But the colonel isn't one for technicalities. Regardless of what the paperwork said, Harry and Bill were still his men, representing the unit that he commanded. "It was a giant disappointment to me," he says of the accident. "I feel responsible. I was part of something that took somebody's life, an innocent life. That's not easy. It hasn't been easy dealing with that."

He is still dealing with it. Even now, Col. Murphy says he is not sure what really happened that night. "I've got two different reports," he says. "I've got the Air Force saying: 'Hey, these guys are lying.' And then I've got these guys saying: 'This is what we perceived and this is what we did.' The truth isn't out there yet, and I can't tell you."

It is obvious, he says, that Gen. Sargeant didn't tell the whole truth. Col. Murphy still can't fathom how the CIB concluded that the bombing had absolutely nothing to do with the fact that the Army did not have to tell the Air Force about specific live-fire exercises. "I never would have guessed that anybody on the ground would be shooting rocket-propelled ordnance at night for practice," he says, sipping an early morning coffee inside a Springfield café. "If you had given me a quiz and said: 'Col. Murphy, is this true or false, that these guys are going to be out here practicing in the middle of Afghanistan,' I would have said: 'No, they won't.'"

The Coalition Air Operations Center deserves at least some of the blame for that breakdown, the colonel says. "Everything took the heat off the CAOC," he says of Gen. Sargeant's report. "I've lost a lot of confidence in the Air Force. I've served 31 years in the Air Force and I didn't think I'd ever be in the position that I didn't necessarily think the Air Force put out the right information."

Nevertheless, Col. Murphy also believes that both pilots need to answer for *their* mistakes. There was a lot of dead space on the radio, he says. Maj. Umbach, as the flight lead, should have pressed the AWACS harder for more information. He should have demanded that Maj. Schmidt answer some of his calls. *Let's just make sure that it's not friendlies, that's all. Do you show 'em on a bridge?* In hindsight, he says Maj. Umbach probably should have told his wingman to fly away. "I think they could have left," he says. "I do. Without being at undue risk, I think they probably could have left, even if it had been rockets because I don't think they're that accurate. If they get their lights off and they wiggle around a bit and get out of there, I think they could have."

Maj. Schmidt was hardly perfect, either, Col. Murphy says. Like everyone, the former Top Gun instructor knew full well how fluid the ground situation was in Afghanistan, how difficult it was to distinguish friend from foe. He should have been more patient. "I thought the decision was pretty quick," Col. Murphy says. "I wish he would have taken more time before he dropped that bomb."

But that doesn't make Harry a liar, Col. Murphy says. He might have been aggressive. He might have rushed to attack. But in the end, he was the only person sitting in that F–16. Only he knows what he saw. "It's what's going through their mind that matters to me at that point," he says. "And I can't put myself in that position in the cockpit for seven hours, having taken a Go-pill, flying over something, and all of a sudden 'bam!' it's right there. But I think if he would have taken another minute, he probably would have got a better answer from somebody."

Indeed, 30 seconds after Maj. Schmidt pushed the pickle button, and nine seconds after his bomb hit the wadi, TSgt. Carroll told the pilots to "disengage, friendlies Kandahar."

Col. Murphy is still bitter that the Air Force didn't leave it up to him to discipline his pilots. "We got trapped in lawyers," he says now. If it was his decision, the colonel says he would have cleared Maj. Umbach to retire and ordered Maj. Schmidt to appear in front of a Flying Evaluation Board. Chances are good that the final result would have been exactly the same, without anybody—the pilots, the Canadian families, or the Air Force—having to endure such a long legal process. "They dropped the bomb," Col. Murphy says. "You have the flight lead that allowed his wingman to drop a bomb, and you've got the guy that dropped a bomb. The ultimate responsibility has got to come back to him, but along the way, you say: 'Why did they drop that bomb?' And I'm not sure we ever got the right answer."

★ ★ ★

Except for the heavily armed soldiers standing guard at the front gate, the National War College in Washington, D.C., looks a lot like any other American institute of higher learning. It is housed inside the historic Theodore Roosevelt Hall, a 100-year-old brown brick building that overlooks the Potomac River. For generations, officers and cabinet ministers and other would-be leaders have sat in the lecture halls here at Fort McNair, learning the intricacies of national security and military planning. Today, mandatory courses include "Fundamentals of Strategic Logic" and "Military Thought and the Essence of War."

Col. David Nichols teaches some of those classes. He has been a professor here for almost three years now, having been transferred to the college shortly after leaving his command post at Al Jaber. These days, "Face" wears a shirt and tie to work just as often as his Air Force blues. In a few months, the colonel won't wear his uniform at all. After 24 years in the service, he is preparing to retire. "You sign up to be disposable," he says, sitting in one of the school's classrooms. "You do your best, but you are always disposable."

The Air Force all but disposed of Dave Nichols on April 17, 2002. He was the defective commander, the leader who allegedly bred a "climate of mistrust" between his pilots and the powers that be. He was hammered by Gen. Sargeant, slapped with a letter of reprimand, and denied numerous awards—including two Distinguished Flying Crosses—that he earned in Kuwait. In the years since, the colonel has watched many friends pass him on the promotion ladder. The man who relieved him at Al Jaber is even a brigadier-general now. "The military world turned against them," he says of Harry Schmidt and Bill Umbach. "They were damaged goods. If you touched them, you were bad. And that's wrong. I didn't believe that. These are great Americans and they are good people and I was their commander and I'll stand behind them as long as I have to."

Col. Nichols still believes the roots of what happened that night can be traced back to the calamity that was Operation Anaconda. The communication gaps that plagued that mission have been well documented, even by the Air Force itself. At the close air symposium he hosted a month before the Canadians were killed, participants warned of impending fratricide. They wanted better intel. They wanted ground liaison officers assigned to the fighter wings. Of course, as everyone now knows, nobody from the CAOC attended the conference. "Had the CAOC participated in this meeting, I feel the 17 April accident might have been prevented," Col. Nichols says now.

Harry and Bill weren't flying close air support that night. They were on their way home—not assisting troops in contact—when Maj. Schmidt dropped his bomb. Nevertheless, Col. Nichols says the problems discussed at his meeting applied to every single sortie into Afghanistan. The issue was always the same: The people in the planes knew very little about what was happening below. "The translation is the desire for what's happening on the ground," he says. "That gets transposed at the operational level, high-tactical level, to the units flying in the airspace." In other words, if CAOC officials came to the meeting, Col. Nichols says they might have gone back to Saudi Arabia with an urgent understanding of just how broken the command-and-control system was—and how badly it needed to be fixed.

"Did I read the ACO cover to cover every day?" Col. Nichols asks, referring to the CAOC's Airspace Control Order. "No. I couldn't. I would still be there. It was not a useful document." Not only was the Tarnak Farm ROZ buried within the pages, but it wasn't even accurately described. "Small arms range," it said. Col. Nichols believes a warning about the live-fire exercise should have been announced in a banner on the first page of the air tasking order, or posted in a NOTAM—a Notice to Airmen. "The perspective that I had as an expeditionary group commander was: 'If there was going to be an active range inside the AOR, of course we would know.' And then the perspective that the sergeant that is shooting on the ground is: 'If I'm going to shoot this, of course they know.' It is just beyond belief that it wouldn't be known."

The pilots didn't know. The AWACS didn't know. The CAOC didn't know. At the Article 32, every witness testified that they had never heard of Tarnak Farm. Even before the bombing, Col. Nichols says pilots were reporting SAFIRE from the same location. Intelligence officers determined some of the firing to be possible enemy; others possible friendly. "Some of these probables or unknowns were in the vicinity of Tarnak Farms," he says. "So you're looking at an intel analysis of a friendly range that can't conclude what it is. Unbelievable."

Col. Nichols has heard the devil's advocate response many times: If pilots were so worried about not knowing where the friendlies were, shouldn't they have been more cautious about dropping a bomb on an unidentified target? "If you're in a combat zone declared hostile where there is incidents of people dying—helicopter crews that are tortured—and you see what you believe is an unfriendly act, and you see what you believe is an enemy force, and you ask the controlling agencies for information and they do not know anything, your conclusion is to protect yourself and other friendly forces," he answers. "Do you act in self-defense or not? The answer for our scenario today is: 'Yes, we don't want you to act, because it was friendly.' But in the year 2002, where we had command and control capabilities that are rivaled by no one, you would never imagine there would be so much unknown."

Col. Nichols picks up a felt marker and begins to scribble on the white board in the classroom, explaining the steps Maj. Schmidt took to reach his decision. "They marched in there getting more information on a declared surface-to-air-fire event, and now he feels that his flight lead is in jeopardy," he says, drawing on the board. "He believed in his heart that that weapons system knew his flight lead was there." It didn't help, the colonel says, that Maj. Umbach left his lights on longer than his wingman. "Harry is concerned that Bill's level of situational awareness isn't as high, so Harry takes over the flight."

Col. Nichols agrees that the pilots could have left the area instead of dropping a bomb, but once they were cleared by the AWACS to take a mark, the situation rapidly turned into what they honestly thought was an ambush. "If you believe that it's enemy, and you believe that the enemy knows you are there and is threatening your flight, then you are going to take action, as you should, as you are supposed to by law," he says. "Was it aggressiveness on Harry's part? Was Harry a cowboy? I come down on the 'no' side of that answer. No, he wasn't."

At 46, Dave Nichols is a charismatic man, well-spoken and self-assured. Up until three years ago, he never imagined that a lawyer would have to do some of his talking for him. Those days are long gone, but he remains close friends with Chuck Allen, the attorney who negotiated his immunity deal. Chuck is also here today, sitting in on this interview. "I cannot tell you what I would do if I was Harry," Col. Nichols says. "I cannot answer that question. And anybody who says they can I think is not being truthful with themselves."

Just weeks from retirement, Dave says he doesn't blame the bombing on any one person—including Gen. Moseley. In fact, he recently sat down with the four-star, face to face, to clear up some of the animosity between them. "He was focused at the level of war that he needed to be focused at,"

Col. Nichols says now. "He was trusting those below him to be focused at their level, and I think his staff may have let him down a little bit."

In the end, Col. Nichols says this case was never about Go-pills. It was never about the limitations of NVGs or a botched mission in Iraq or the fact that he changed the word "offense" to "incident." It was about a massive communications breakdown, a "cultural divide" between the Army and the Air Force. "The blame doesn't lie anywhere," he says. "That corporal, he followed every procedure he was told to follow. But someplace, that cultural divide didn't enable the air headquarters and the land headquarters to communicate the necessary information about the active range in the combat zone."

He believes things are changing for the better. Wartime coordination between the two services has drastically improved, in large part, Col. Nichols believes, because of what happened at Tarnak Farm. "I'll just be blunt," he says. "I think there were some people who were worried they would get blamed with a mistake also. So it got put to the lowest common denominator, and I was on the side of the pilots, so me and the two pilots are the persons to take the blame for the mistake. Is it okay? Yes, I think it's okay. Good resulted from all of this. Unfortunately, there are dead soldiers from Canada."

It is an interesting perspective. What Col. Nichols is saying is that, unlike in the civilian world, the military holds people accountable for mistakes, even if the mistake isn't their fault. In this case, the mistake was that four paratroopers were killed. It doesn't matter that Harry and Bill did nothing wrong in the sky that night, he says. They—and by association, him—still have to be punished. "If you really drag it out, the system worked," Col. Nichols says. "It worked. Harry and Bill were punished for a mistake. Bill was going to retire anyway. I'm eventually going to retire anyway. The system works. The guys and gals flying airplanes today know that they will be supported by their command chain. They know they won't go to jail for making a mistake."

Col. Nichols says he only hopes the Canadian families understand that those men didn't die in vain, that their deaths have forced the U.S. military to improve the way each service talks to the other. He is even willing to come to Canada and tell them that in person. "Everybody was doing their best," he says. "The cause of the problem is very large and there isn't one person that was out there causing the problem. There is no criminal activity. This cultural divide was let to happen. We have learned from it. We have learned a lot from it. So I think in the end, there has been some progress made. And you know, maybe it was important that we protected the careers of these great leaders that we have out there."

★ ★ ★

"Do I believe for a second that they ever felt threatened? I do not believe that. I never will. Everything that they did is completely inconsistent with that premise. And anybody who says otherwise is either living in a fantasy land or their perceptions are so skewed by what they want to believe."

Gregory Graf is now a full colonel, the director of operations for the Colorado Air National Guard. It is as high up the chain of command as a part-timer like him can go. In his other life, the colonel runs a private law firm in Denver, defending clients instead of prosecuting them. Last year, he was awarded a Bronze Star for his service in Operation Iraqi Freedom. "I answered tons of e-mails and went to tons of meetings," he says. "I was certainly no hero."

Though modest about his medal, the colonel doesn't mince words when the topic turns to Harry Schmidt. "All of the rules that were in place should have stopped this incident," he says. "This was one guy's idiocy. Everything I know leads me to believe that he was an honorable guy, hard-working and a very talented pilot prior to this incident. And everything that I've seen since this incident makes me believe that he has had a complete breakdown in integrity to the extent that I don't want to have anything to do with the man."

During the Article 32, Col. Graf and his fellow prosecutors could only watch as Charlie Gittins and Dave Beck spoke to the cameras outside. He listened to their explanations. The Go-pills. The NVGs. The long missions. The AWACS. The CAOC. He actually admired how hard both defense lawyers fought for their clients. In fact, Col. Graf admits that it's exactly what he would have done had he been assigned to the other side of the table. Shift the blame. "But does that mean it's a credible defense?" he asks. "No."

Col. Graf says it is absolutely irrelevant that nobody in the Air Force knew anything about Tarnak Farm or the Canadian training drill. The right order still came in plenty of time: Hold fire. "I would not blame the CAOC or [Maj. Art] Henry or anybody in the AWACS, because the idea that somebody is going to drop without authority, it's so far out of reality that I'm sure Henry didn't have his panties all tied in a knot worrying that something was going to happen," he says. "If you are a Fighter Weapons School graduate then you know that even with all what we refer to as 'time-sensitive targeting' training, if you think you're going to get clearance to drop on a target five miles away from your divert base within two or three minutes, then you've done more than take Go-pills. You've probably been smoking a few joints on the flight out there."

The argument that still baffles Col. Graf the most is the Ringback defense, the suggestion that the pilots were ambushed by a rocket-propelled weapon with a much greater range than typical anti-aircraft artillery. Those pilots were flying at 20,000 feet in the middle of the night. From the ground, an F-16 at that altitude isn't even visible during the *day*, he says. "I don't need rules of engagement to tell me that if somebody is shooting at me, I need to get out of the way," he says. "And if he could tell that it was rockets as opposed to AAA, then he should have felt even more secure because that Multiple Rocket Launch System was the biggest farce known to man. That was the brainchild of Saddam Hussein and his bag of idiots. That was just a stab in the dark. The only person that you are going to hurt with that Multiple Rocket Launch System were the poor suckers on the ground 60 miles away when those things fall to the ground. That whole argument is so incredible and so preposterous that I've never even spent more than 10 seconds of brain time dealing with that. Anybody who says it's not preposterous is a liar."

But as adamant as he is about Maj. Schmidt's guilt, Col. Graf admits that the Article 32 did not exactly go prosecutors' way. He accepts some of the blame for that. He was preparing for his Iraqi tour—the deployment that was later canceled so he could stay on the case—at the same time as he was scrambling to find an expert witness willing to testify against Harry and Bill. Because the government side never found that witness, Col. Graf says it might have been a better strategy to simply submit Gen. Sargeant's report to Judge Rosenow and not call a single witness. It wouldn't have made for a very dramatic hearing, but he believes the CIB conclusions contained more than enough probable cause for Judge Rosenow to refer the case to a court-martial. "There was not a single person who came in who was qualified as an expert whose sole job it was to interpret that tape," Col. Graf says now. "That was not presented. And if you are going to put on the whole horse and pony show, in my mind, then you put that witness on. If you're not going to get one of those witnesses and put them on, then you tone down the whole act."

The government settled for something in between: Lt.-Col. Ralph Viets and Maj. John Milton. That, Col. Graf knows now, was a huge mistake. It was their testimony that ultimately swayed Col. Rosenow to recommend against a court-martial. "I relied on the integrity of the people from their unit, that if I asked them a question they would give me a straight answer," he says. "It didn't quite work the way I thought it would." Nearly three years later, Col. Graf says he is still offended by the testimony of those Springfield witnesses. "In my opinion, there was a total lack of integrity, and if any of those guys applied in my unit, I would do everything I could to keep them out," he says. "If they got hired, I would quit. I wouldn't want them to get gas on my air strip."

Col. Graf isn't consumed by this case. He has more than enough on his plate without thinking of Tarnak Farm. His law firm. His family. Flying jets. But every once in a while, something happens, something to reinforce just how little he respects Maj. Schmidt. In April 2005, for example, Col. Graf read an interesting article in the latest edition of *Chicago Magazine*, an article called "Harry Schmidt's War."

In his first-ever interview since the bombing, Maj. Schmidt explained, among other things, that he was the Number Two plane that night, unable to simply fly away because Maj. Umbach, the flight lead, never gave that order. "I was the wingman," he told the magazine. "I was not in charge of making decisions. It was 'Shut up, hang on, and say, Yes, sir.' I was the lowest person on the totem pole. I was, in effect, along for the ride."

"Every time he does stuff like that, every time I start to feel sorry for him, I think he's a giant asshole," Col. Graf says. "It was the most disingenuous, untruthful, arrogant thing to say. Instead of just standing up and being a man, as far as I'm concerned, he's a pussy. And he didn't get half of what he had coming to him."

Maj. Schmidt's suggestion is not exactly new. Charlie Gittins raised the argument at the Article 32, grilling Gen. Sargeant until he finally conceded that Harry was not entitled to leave the area without Maj. Umbach. But Col. Graf says the suggestion is still ridiculous. "If you're going to use that as your excuse, then your job as the wingman is to be in formation," he says. "That means you are going to be somewhere either slightly aft and to the outside of your flight lead or directly line abreast to your flight lead. And he wasn't anywhere close to that. He was doing his own thing. When I look at what Umbach did, the way he flew his profile was exactly what you were supposed to do. He was where he was supposed to be, flying at the altitude you were supposed to be flying at, and working the targeting pod in the manner that you are supposed to work that targeting pod—to get the mark and stay away from the perceived threat. He was doing what he was supposed to be doing and Schmidt was—I have no idea what that clown act was."

If anything, Col. Graf says Bill Umbach should be the one pointing fingers. Maj. Schmidt not only murdered those four Canadians, he says, but he murdered his flight lead's career. "Umbach is an honorable guy," he says. "He's a gentleman, and he was truly sorry for his role in not controlling Harry Schmidt. There is no doubt in my mind about it. You can tell that this has sucked the life out of him. He's been punished more than enough by this whole thing. Harry Schmidt has not gotten a tenth of what he deserves."

★ ★ ★

John Milton is now a lieutenant-colonel. He is also commander of the 170th Fighter Squadron, the same job that once belonged to Bill Umbach. In late-2004, Lt.-Col. Milton led the Springfield unit back to Kuwait's Al Jaber Air Base, this time in support of Operation Iraqi Freedom. The pilots pickled a lot more bombs this time around.

But that was not the only difference between April 2002 and October 2004. "Every time we took off, we had a briefing by a ground liaison officer," John says. "They knew every unit, where they were, when they were moving and if there was anything going to be happening. You name it."

Lt.-Col. Milton still runs the family corn farm in central Illinois, the same farm that lured him from the Navy and his job as a Top Gun instructor. In 2007, when the jets leave Springfield for good, John is probably going to retire from the Guard and drive his tractor full-time. "It guts you," he says, recalling the instant he heard about the friendly fire bombing. "I can't even come close to defining it."

For a while, the incident defined him. He was Harry Schmidt's roommate, the flight lead whose wingman missed that now-infamous target two days earlier. Lt.-Col. Milton is the first to admit that debriefing the botched mission with Maj.-Gen. Buchanan was "not pleasant," but he insists it was not embarrassing. If anything, he says, the general looked at the miss as an indication of just how smart the enemy was. "It was a difficult, small, mobile target," John says. "This particular thing that we were going after had been gone after several times before. This was not the first miss on it."

Milt talked to his roommate about the mission, about how pissed off he was that the squadron blew its first chance to hit a target. "Nobody likes to fail," he says. But it is laughable, he says, that anyone would honestly believe that Maj. Schmidt was extra anxious to make things right. "I don't think that had anything to do with it."

It has been nearly three years since government lawyers called John Milton to the witness stand at the Article 32. Since then, prosecutors have repeatedly criticized his testimony, suggesting that he chose to defend his friends rather than tell the truth. Lt.-Col. Milton says he stands by his every word, and that he would have said the exact same thing even if he had never met Harry Schmidt or Bill Umbach. "Unless you're there, how do [you] make a real judgment, particulary if you think you're being fired on?" he asks. "Obviously, it was a mistake. They misperceived what was happening. But I don't have any doubt that what they are saying is true."

That doesn't mean the pilots were perfect, he says. They both made mistakes. For one, the radio communication from both jets definitely could have been better. "I don't think you can say: 'They shouldn't have done this,'" he says. "Graf tried to put it in a debrief format. If you are debriefing it, yeah, there would be several things you would look at. I'm sure Harry has several things that he would do differently—if it were a training mission. But it's not. The thing you also have to put in your mind is what they think they were seeing versus what they were seeing. Perception is reality at that time, and I don't think you ever have 100 percent situational awareness on what is being shot at you."

(Lt.-Col. Ralph Viets, the other fighter pilot from the 183rd who testified in Louisiana, declined to be interviewed at length for this book. But like Lt.-Col. Milton, he says he stands by his testimony.)

John would rather not say whether he believes Harry and Bill should still be flying for the U.S. military. It's not his decision, so why stew over it? But he did say that he is still stunned that his friends were criminally charged. The Air Force could have learned a lot from this mistake, he says. Instead, it chose to focus on only one link in the accident chain. "Anything that happens that is this horrific for everyone—particularly the guys on the ground, who we're supporting—we need to look at how we're doing business and see how we can fix it," he says. "Obviously, this wasn't the first friendly fire, and unfortunately, it hasn't been the last. But if you're going to make an investigation and make some hard-core recommendations, I was hoping that it would be more helpful in helping us fight the next battle similar to this."

★ ★ ★

In the months leading up to what was supposed to be Maj. Schmidt's court-martial, the U.S. Air Force considered John Odom as a potential candidate for brigadier-general. It never happened. A military selection panel decided against the promotion. In January 2005, as all colonels must do after 30 years of service, John Odom reluctantly retired from the Air Force.

At 57, he is back at his private practice, back at the Shreveport mansion/law firm that he disappeared from in August 2002. Col. Odom spends his days on the second floor, in a corner office that was originally built as a bedroom. The walls that surround his cluttered desk are barely visible, lined with paintings of dogs and forests and other natural settings. "Whatever Maj. Schmidt perceived I can't speak to because I wasn't inside his head at that moment," he says. "But let's give him that he really did think he was getting shot at. Every reaction he made was wrong, wrong, wrong, against the rules and wrong."

It has been a year since Col. Odom was paid to prosecute Harry Schmidt. All of his Tarnak Farm files are packed away in boxes, stacked in the corner of a walk-in closet at the side of his office. He has other clients, other looming lawsuits, to occupy his time. But the colonel still thinks about the friendly fire case. Not every day, but often enough. "If an officer will not accept responsibility for his actions, then it is incumbent on the system to impose accountability on him for his actions," he says. "It is as simple as that. If he had just said: 'I take responsibility for this. This is my error, and I will live with this every day for the rest of my life.' Instead, he decided to do the media circus. He decided to do the whole show. Okay, pal, you want to fight like that, we're bigger than you are. We can stand up there and we can take everything you can throw at us and we'll still be there tomorrow."

Col. Odom still shakes his head when he thinks of some of the defense motions that were filed over the years. The travel vouchers. The Bronze Stars. Prosecutorial misconduct. "If you tell me a stink was made by Mr. Gittins, I'm going to tell you it was a red herring," Col. Odom says. "I'm sorry. I'm just locked into that mode. Charlie Gittins would come up with anything he could to deflect attention away from the fact that the thumb on the end of the right hand on the end of the right arm that was attached to the torso of the guy who pickled off the weapon that killed the guys was Harry Schmidt. There is no way around it. It didn't, in the ultimate, have anything to do with Gen. Moseley or Gen. Wood or Gen. Sargeant or Gen. Dumais or John Odom or anybody else. It had to do with Harry Schmidt. And it was Gittins' best effort to keep everybody from ever keying on that and it was my job to focus everybody's attention on it. Quit trying to blame everybody else. I don't care about everybody else. I care about you, Maj. Schmidt."

The entire case, Col. Odom still insists, begins and ends with the cockpit videos. The voices are calm. No defensive calls. No defensive reactions. Maj. Schmidt slows down. He dives lower, putting his jet even closer to the perceived threat. *Request permission to lay down some 20 mike-mike.* "If you have to ask permission to drop a weapon, you aren't really in self-defense," Col. Odom says. "You're setting up an attack." He laughs when reminded of Maj. Schmidt's supposed rationale: warning shots. "You have an unidentified target on the ground and all you want to do is unleash some lethal 20 millimeter depleted uranium slugs? 'Oh, I didn't mean to kill ya. I just meant to warn ya. I wanted you to put your head down.'"

No mark. No patience. No fixed-wing aircraft ever shot down during Operation Enduring Freedom. No indication whatsoever that either pilot ever felt threatened, Col. Odom says. *I've got some men on a road and it looks like a piece of artillery firing at us. I am rolling in in self-defense.* "It was like he was dictating the first paragraph of his air medal," the colonel says. "Well, you'd better be right, and he wasn't."

Everything else is just empty defense spin, he says. Blinking red lights. Check fires. Charges preferred on September 11 (Col. Odom, by the way, insists that was a fluke, a coincidence that he didn't even notice until defense lawyers started complaining about it to the media). The Time Before the Tapes Came on. A political cover-up to appease Canada. "It didn't make a particle of difference who the dead guys were. Does anybody realistically think that the convening authority in this case, Lt.-Gen. Bruce Carlson, was ever contacted by anybody from the State Department who said: 'Hey General, this is really sensitive. Come up with some kind of charges against these guys to placate the government of Canada.' Well, that didn't happen. Does anybody think that Gen. Sargeant, after having spent a couple months investigating this and authoring this report, that Steve Sargeant thought: 'Well, I spent a lot of time with some of those nice Canadian guys and gee, maybe I ought to reach this conclusion just to placate Gen. Dumais.' Those ideas are just absurd. We did what we did because Schmidt and Umbach broke the rules. And because of their breaking of the rules, people died and were injured who should not have died or been injured. It's as simple as that. They could have been from Burundi for all I care."

The list of "red herrings" goes on and on. Shooting into the air. Capt. Pepper in the pooper. Go-pills. "Nobody in what I'm going to call the real Air Force—as opposed to the mythical Schmidt Air Force—there was nobody in the real Air Force who wanted Go-pills to be any kind of issue in this deal because they didn't want to lose the program," he says. "They save lives." No Canadian liaison officer in the CAOC. An unworkable ACO. "I don't think there were any problems with the ACO," the colonel says. "Except for this incident, we didn't seem to have any other problems.

Everybody else in Operation Enduring Freedom seemed to deal with it except Maj. Schmidt and Maj. Umbach."

Perhaps the stinkiest fish of all, Col. Odom says, was the spin attached to Col. Nichols' Close Air Support symposium. Yes, pilots did get together to talk about Operation Anaconda. And yes, there were warnings about fratricide. "But this was not a Close Air Support mission," he says. "It had nothing to do with Close Air Support. There were no troops in contact. There was no one on the ground calling for assistance. And there was no airborne person vectoring them down to deliver ordnance." The pilots were on their way back to base.

Procedures did change after the bombing. Days later, for example, the CAOC issued a notice to airmen that warned pilots about the Tarnak range. "Taking corrective action, you're damned if you do, you're damned if you don't," Col. Odom says. "Did we want it to happen again? Of course not. Did we maybe emphasize for a few days thereafter: 'Hey, no kidding, there is a firing range right out there at Kandahar'? Yes. Was it necessary that they do that beforehand? No."

It is crucial to understand that Afghanistan was an extremely tight weapons war, he says. Every pilot knew—or should have known—that the confusing ground situation was precisely the reason why the CAOC insisted on having the final say on every single bomb. All this talk about not knowing where the friendlies were only bolsters the case *against* the pilots, Col. Odom says. If they were truly worried about fratricide, then Harry Schmidt and Bill Umbach should have been that much more careful. "These guys were flying these incredibly long, dull missions," he says. "They took off knowing that unless something happened on the ground, they were going to bore holes in the sky for three hours on station, then they had a three-hour ride home. Was it hard work? Good God, yes, it was hard work. Am I in awe of their ability to go do that and keep their attention level high? Yes, I really am. But are they supposed to go on the way home and drop a bomb in somebody else's area of operations without anybody on the ground screaming: 'Help, help?' No, you ain't supposed to do that."

Years later, Col. Odom is adamant that he could not have done his job any better. His team of prosecutors convinced Col. Rosenow that there was more than enough probable cause to refer the case to a court-martial.

That the judge opted for non-judicial punishment had more to do with "good order and discipline" than any lack of evidence. Really, the only thing that still puzzles Col. Odom is why Maj. Schmidt turned down Gen. Carlson's original offer of an Article 15. "Because of his lawyers' advice and his hard-headedness, he just prolongs the agony for everybody for another year," he says. "What did it avail him between June of 2003 and June of 2004, when he finally changed his mind? What good did he do himself, or did that simply give Mr. Gittins the opportunity to bill him God only knows how many tens of thousands of dollars? Who made money on this deal? Well, it sure wasn't Harry Schmidt. I look at that 183rd Pilots' Defense Fund as the Charles Gittins Protective and Benevolence Fund. I think it was [a] very poor legal [decision] to turn the Article 15 down."

But an even larger question still remains: If Maj. Schmidt was indeed reckless, what triggered that recklessness? What prompted such a gifted fighter pilot to act so irrationally? Col. Odom is still convinced that the missed target in Iraq fueled Maj. Schmidt's mindset that night. Harry saw those flashes from Tarnak Farm as a target of opportunity, he says, a chance to restore the unit's pride. "We spent 14 years training him," he says. "He was as highly trained as a man can be, and he was very good at what he did. Make no mistake about that. He was superb at what he did. But he lost focus on what his job was."

★ ★ ★

"If what the government says is true about Harry, he's a pretty bad guy," Charlie Gittins says. "But I got to know him. I'm convinced it was just a friggin' accident. It was a completely defendable case. And then we start scratching the surface and you go: 'Ooh, there are some real problems here, and it isn't with Harry.'"

Maj. Schmidt's lead attorney is sitting behind the desk in his Virginia office, wearing blue jeans and a gray shirt. Lying in his lap is a tiny brown puppy, an adorable new pet that he and his wife brought home just the other day. "We're thinking of naming it 'Sargeant,'" Gittins jokes. Though he knows he can't prove it, Charlie is still convinced that Michael Moseley and Stephen Sargeant conspired to hang Harry and Bill before the CIB ever interviewed a single witness. The CAOC—under the ultimate control of Gen. Moseley—didn't know anything about the Canadian training drill. Bottom line, Gittins says. "As far as the aviators go, if the CAOC doesn't know about it, there is no possibility that the aviators can know about it."

Without that crucial piece of information, Gittins says Maj. Schmidt did everything "exactly by the book." If he holds any blame, it's that he was simply too talented a fighter pilot. "Too well trained, and you know what, that is not his problem," Charlie says. "He got trained by the Navy and the Air Force and he did exactly what his training told him to do. If he was a less-confident guy, maybe he wouldn't have pulled the trigger. But he went right down the rules of engagement and then he engaged. If he was not so certain of: 'I know what that is. It's a rocket-propelled munition. I've seen that they're using them against Americans. I know they've been used in Iraq. It looks like they're shooting at Bill. I want to fire 20 mike-mike warning shots. I'm not allowed to do that. It fired again. Goddamn it, I got to kill it.' He went right through the rules of engagement."

Throughout the Article 32, Maj. Schmidt and Maj. Umbach presented a joint defense, insisting that U.S. command and control essentially set them up to fail that night. No GLOs in the fighter units. No clue about Tarnak Farm. "Coordination between the Air Force side and the ground side is at the general officer level," he says. "The guys who fucked this up all got promoted, every single one of them."

But even Charlie Gittins knows it's not that simple. He himself argued at the hearing that his client could not have left the area because his flight lead never told him to. "Bill's in charge," Gittins says today. "[Harry] just can't take over the flight and say: 'We're out of here.' And he just can't leave without Bill. So he's waiting for Bill to do something. Meanwhile, this thing keeps shooting." Maj. Schmidt did not usurp control of the mission, Gittins says. If anything, he was waiting for an order that never came. "He is maneuvering his airplane to keep it in a position to attack," he says. "He's always being in a position to support his flight lead. The thing is shooting. He needs to be in a position where he can defend."

"He won't say it," Charlie says of Harry, "but I think if he had been leading the flight, this doesn't happen. If he would have seen it, he would have identified what it was and maybe would have done something different."

Like what? "Leave," Gittins says.

Though never one to hide his thoughts, Charlie will not go so far as to blame Maj. Umbach. "I'm not going to shit on Bill," he says. "I'm just not going to do it. It is a sure thing that the accident wouldn't have happened had the AWACS or the CAOC known that there was live-fire going on. That's the thing that causes the accident."

Time-sensitive targeting. Taking a mark. Tight weapons war. The Kandahar Airfield was a few miles away. All those things are irrelevant, Gittins says, when you honestly believe you're taking fire from the enemy. The Air Force officers who condemned Harry and Bill—including Col. Odom—have never been shot at in a combat zone. "I think he is a buffoon," Gittins says of the government's lead prosecutor. "I don't think he understood. First of all, he's not a tactical guy. He's a lawyer all his life. He's never sat in a plane and been scared. And I've never flown in combat, but I've sat in airplanes and I've been real scared in airplanes. It's real easy from your air-conditioned office at Barksdale to say somebody else did something wrong. He just doesn't get it, and he never did. He wasn't prepared for the Article 32. He looked like a buffoon at the Article 32. All his witnesses turned into our witnesses. I can't take him seriously. That's all there is to it."

The government's theories were ludicrous, Gittins says. Bringing honor back to the squadron. Self-defense as a pre-text. The Time Before the Tapes Came on. "I wish they would have had the tapes," Gittins says. "And if this was really a pretext case, why would they even turn them on? They didn't have to do that. The only reason they're on is because Harry told Bill to turn his on. Bill never would have remembered." Gittins says before Gen. Sargeant testified at the Article 32—when the defense team had the chance to question him in private behind closed doors—he even asked the CIB president if he believed that Harry used self-defense as a ruse to intentionally kill people on the ground. Gen. Sargeant said yes, Gittins says. But later, when he took the witness stand, Sargeant did not go quite that far. "Of all the people involved in this case, we know that Sargeant isn't a truthful person, because he changed his story from one day to the next," he says. The only guy that I believe actually ever told the truth in this whole thing is sitting next to me—Harry Schmidt. And you know what? At the end of the day, he knows he has his integrity."

As he pets his puppy, the conversation shifts to the Canadian families. Regardless of who is to blame, those four men are still dead. If Maj. Schmidt truly believed that he was the only person telling the truth, why not reach out to those relatives right away? Some of them might have even sympathized with Harry and Bill. "We could have done it differently," Gittins says. "Maybe we would. I don't know. The magnitude of the charges that he was charged with made it not really very smart to do that. And here's the other thing: As he sits here today, if he was put in that situation again, he drops the bomb again. Families would want to hear: 'I wouldn't do it again.' And I'm sorry, but that's not the way Harry feels."

The defense team always said the Canadian relatives should be compensated, Charlie says. His job was to defend Harry Schmidt, and nothing more. "I told my wife: You cannot live worrying about what other people think of you," he says. "At the end of the day, I am the one who has to look at myself in the mirror and go: 'I did okay.' If my client likes me, he thinks I did a good job for him, I'm okay."

Charlie makes no apologies for the statement Maj. Schmidt read at the Article 32. He makes no apologies for the money he earned while working on this case, much of it provided by the 183rd Pilots' Defense Fund. The fund is now closed. In the end, Maj. Schmidt even had to reach into his own pocket to pay some of his legal bills. "I got paid a fair wage, but not as much as I would have gotten if I would have done it hourly," Gittins says. "People pay me to do what I do. I'm not apologizing for it."

And he certainly makes no apologies for what his client did in the sky that night. "I don't think you ever should prosecute somebody because they made a wrong judgment in the heat of the moment," he says. "Nobody's ever really thought about the other side. What if this really was Taliban shooting at Bill and he didn't do anything and Bill got shot down, and Bill got carved up like Petty Officer Roberts and got sent home in pieces to his wife? How does Harry look at Bill's wife and say: 'I should have done something, but I didn't.' I can't even think of anything worse than that. If we lose one guy because somebody failed to act, that's wrong. That's criminally negligent. That's the crime."

"At the end of the day, I think what says the most about the case is that Harry doesn't feel reprimanded, and he doesn't feel the reprimand has anything to do with what his conduct was," Gittins continues. "So if your purpose is to punish someone, they have completely failed because Harry doesn't accept that as an accurate judgment. It's a piece of paper that the Air Force jammed down his throat, and he doesn't believe it's true."

Maj. Schmidt did everything a fighter pilot should have done in that situation, Gittins says. Looking back, if he did do something wrong, it was done long before he climbed into his F-16. "Harry's mistake was not putting his foot down the night before," Charlie says. "His 'spidey sense' was going off the night before when he was not the flight lead. He knew this was a mistake."

★ ★ ★

In September 2005, Gen. T. Michael Moseley, the ultimate boss of the Afghanistan air war, was promoted to chief of staff of the U.S. Air Force. As the service's top officer, he commands more than 700,000 personnel, answering directly to Gen. Richard B. Myers, the chairman of the Joint Chiefs of Staff. Gen. Moseley declined to be interviewed for this book.

Bruce Carlson, the 8th Air Force commander who signed the letters of reprimand that were handed to both pilots, was recently promoted to a four-star general. He now serves as the commander of a U.S. Air Force research and development branch at Ohio's Wright-Patterson Air Force Base. Gen. Carlson declined to be interviewed for this book.

Stephen G. Wood, the senior officer in the CAOC on the night of the bombing, has been promoted twice since April 17, 2002. Now a lieutenant-general, he currently serves as the deputy chief of staff for plans and programs in the Washington, D.C., headquarters of the U.S. Air Force. Lt.-Gen. Wood declined to be interviewed for this book.

Stephen T. Sargeant, the American co-president of the Coalition Investigation Board, and the man who signed both pilots' charge sheets, is now a major-general. He is stationed at Yongsan Army Garrison in South Korea, where he serves as deputy chief of staff for the United Nations Command (UNC). His primary job is to lead general officer talks between UNC and the North Korean army. Maj.-Gen. Sargeant declined to be interviewed for this book.

Marc Dumais, the Canadian co-president of the CIB, is now a lieutenant-general. In April 2005, he was appointed deputy chief of the Defence Staff, responsible for the planning and conduct of all Canadian Forces operations. Lt.-Gen. Dumais declined to be interviewed for this book.

Gen. Maurice Baril, the president of the Canadian Board of Inquiry, continues to do consulting work for the federal government, promoting the Ottawa Convention on Landmines to countries that have not yet signed the accord. It was the same job he was doing when the prime minister asked him to lead the friendly fire investigation. Nearly four years later, Gen. Baril insists that he received "absolutely zero" political pressure from either the Canadian government or the American military. "We were totally open to anything that could have happened," he says, sitting in his Ottawa living room.

Gen. Baril knows that much has been made about the apparent differences between his board's report and that of the CIB. Among other things, his team found "systemic shortcomings" in the "quality and nature of the coordination between ground and air forces, as well as between the CAOC and the tactical flying units. Had they been corrected, the incident might have been prevented." But Gen. Baril says the blame still falls squarely on the pilots because they knew that every bombing run required absolute clearance from the CAOC. "Nobody was to engage anything because of this possible confusion until somebody said: 'Yup, we've got troops,' or, 'We don't, so go ahead,'" Gen. Baril says. "The process to find out, anywhere in Afghanistan, if there was friendly troops was in place."

The general says he and his investigators tried to give Maj. Schmidt the benefit of the doubt, but after watching the cockpit videos, it was impossible to see how the former Top Gun possibly felt threatened. "What we had was so bloody obvious," he says. "We were hitting a dead end all the time. We could not give him confusion."

Maj. Schmidt was clearly a talented pilot, Gen. Baril says. He didn't take off that night hoping to kill friendly forces. He just had a very bad case of judgment. "They had procedures in place that would—should—have prevented the accident, if it would have been followed," he says. "The pilots did not have to attack. That is our firm conclusion, and they decided on their own to attack and we couldn't find a reason why."

★ ★ ★

A year after the Air Force closed its file on Bill Umbach, Dave Beck got sick. For months, he was in and out of the hospital, where doctors and specialists scratched their heads trying to figure out what was wrong. His blood pressure plummeted. Mysterious rashes started to appear on his body. At times, his memory even faded. Most mornings, Dave was lucky to get out of bed without falling over.

He recently returned to the office, though he is under strict doctor's orders to take it easy. No more 18-hour days. No more waking up at 3 a.m. to get a head start on everyone else. He is trying his best to obey, but on some days, the old Dave Beck sneaks through. "I barely got any sleep last night," he says over a recent breakfast. A new case, a new client, has his mind racing.

"To this day, have they gotten compensation?" he asks of the Canadian families. "It's a disgrace. That should have been one of the first things done. And the second is you send somebody over who has combat experience to do the investigation. Why would you send somebody with no combat experience? The reason is obvious."

When it comes to Bill Umbach, Dave Beck's defense has always been straightforward. Generals were warned about communication flaws. They did nothing to fix it. Harry and Bill took off without all the information they needed. And then, when something went wrong, the military tried to wash its hands of the blame. "I know Canada was upset, and rightfully so," he says. "Why the heck did Bush wait so long to apologize? Why did nobody offer compensation? Why did the U.S. government almost immediately come out and say: 'The pilots, the pilots, the pilots.' Bill Umbach and Harry Schmidt should not have been put through a criminal process. It was an accident. It was a tragedy. There were a lot of contributing factors by senior people that put them and the Canadian troops under circumstances they should not have been."

In between bites of his omelette, Dave lists some of those contributing factors. Ridiculously long missions. Fatigue. Ringback rocket launchers in Afghanistan. A bumbling CAOC. No GLOs. "The communication and lack thereof is huge," he says. "Who is responsible for that? Gen. Moseley is, and those under his command. It is irrefutable that nobody who flew knew about Tarnak Farms in general or what was going on that night. That is inexcusable. That is dereliction of duty by definition."

Do Bill and Harry belong somewhere on that list of contributing factors? "No," Dave says. "Other than they were there."

Of all the factors, one still bothers Dave Beck more than all the others: Go-pills. Not only were the drugs never tested in combat, but the Air Force never studied the long-term side-effects of pilots up on speed, down on Ambien. "That's reckless," he says. "If you try to throw everything at Bill and Harry—if you throw out all of the stuff Moseley and them overlooked, which you can't, but even if you could—the key elements of the charges against them is they exercised poor judgment, they reacted too quickly, and didn't wait long enough. Well, when the drug manufacturer says these are the hazards, how dare you give them drugs that say this can cause these effects, and then you charge them with doing those things. If you gave them drugs that can cause the things that you charged them with, then you're a conspirator and primarily responsible."

Dave Beck isn't suggesting that those Canadian soldiers would still be alive if Harry and Bill didn't ingest Dexedrine that night. But that possibility cannot be ruled out, he says. "I don't know, and I don't think anybody honestly can say. But you have to look at contributing factors, that is a contributing factor. That is something that should have been investigated and stopped."

Dave Beck read that *Chicago Magazine* article, the one in which Harry said he was just the wingman "along for the ride." He wasn't quite sure what to make of the remarks. "It was an accident. It was a tragedy. Bill Umbach and Harry Schmidt should not have been put through a criminal process," Dave says. "To the extent somebody says that 'it never would have happened had Harry been the flight lead,' look at the tapes, listen to the tapes, both recorded and other, and draw your own conclusions. I'm not drawing any conclusions. I just say that's absolute utter bullshit. But I don't cuss, so I'd say that's absolute utter crap."

chapter forty-one

Bill Umbach walked away from the Air National Guard with a letter of reprimand and a pension. When he cleaned out his locker, he also took home his personalized helmet, the gray one with "Guido" written on the side. He hasn't worn it—in the sky, at least—since that night. He had a chance. The Guard offered him one last ride in the back seat of an F-16, a final goodbye of sorts. But he declined. "I think I'll remember the one I had," he says.

He has remembered it. Over and over and over. He has watched those videos. He has listened to his voice. And to this day, after all the second-guessing and Monday morning quarterbacking, Maj. Umbach is still convinced that neither he nor Harry Schmidt did anything wrong. "In my mind and my heart, I wish that this had never happened," he says. "But taking Harry and I out of there, I don't think it would have changed it."

Simply put, Bill Umbach has always been portrayed as the "good pilot," the one who expressed sincere remorse, who stood up at the Article 32 and said he was truly sorry. At the very least, the Canadian families commended him for retiring quietly when the opportunity arose. All of that is undeniable. Bill does feel genuine sorrow for the relatives left behind by that bomb. He and his family still pray for them. But that doesn't mean that Maj. Umbach believes he made a mistake. Not at all. "These families have been lied to," he says. "The Air Force has come and put their arm around them and let them cry on their shoulder, and the Air Force has told them how sorry we are, but we've got the problem. 'We've got them, and we'll take care of them.' They've been lied to, and that's it."

Maj. Umbach doesn't have a beef with the radio communications that night, whether it was him or Harry or the AWACS or the CAOC. It's not about this many minutes or that many seconds. It's about what everybody knew, or in this case, what everybody didn't know. "There is no way in the world that you could have planned for a bigger goof-up than this," he says. "You could not have intentionally told people: 'Look, we want this screw-up to happen, so you're not going to say anything about this, you're not going to say anything about that, you guys are going to do this.' You could not have planned a bigger screw-up. No way."

Nobody in the Air Force had any idea what the Canadians were doing that night. Period. The Para Company went through all the proper channels, yet the CAOC still didn't know that those soldiers would be firing away at Tarnak Farm. Nobody on the air side had even *heard* of Tarnak Farm before April 17. "I don't know where the screw-up was because this investigation was a hoax," Maj. Umbach says. "It was not there to prevent this from ever happening again. And that's sad. Four guys died, eight guys got injured, needlessly—absolutely needlessly. We can't afford that kind of simple, simple mistake."

Bill Umbach still suspects that what happened to him and his wingman had a lot more to do with politics than justice. There was the sensitive issue of Canada–U.S. relations, the fact that President Bush waited so long to express any public remorse. There was the well-known rivalry between the Guard and the Air Force. The active duty, Maj. Umbach says, rarely misses a chance to make the part-timers look bad. And of course, there was also the looming war in Iraq. The White House needed allies. Admitting that the CAOC was a dysfunctional mess wouldn't have made for the best recruitment poster. "You don't want to point the finger and say it's the whole system, the whole string of events, from the bomb release that Harry did to the three-star general," Maj. Umbach says. "If you say that there is just so many screw-ups that you can't count them all, you lose public confidence and you can't get another country to go into Iraq."

Bill is not trying to shift attention away from his own actions that night. He has nothing to hide, he says, nothing to be ashamed of. Despite what Gen. Sargeant said, he doesn't believe for a second that he came down with a sudden case of "co-pilot syndrome." He remembers the fireworks. He remembers—before the tapes came on—telling BOSSMAN: "We have SAFIRE in our present position. Are there any friendlies in the area?" As he turned his jet, he says he told Maj. Schmidt: "I think they are shooting at us," followed moments later by "I think they are pulling lead." AWACS eventually granted them permission to mark the unknown fire.

Maj. Umbach says he did see the bright lights of the Kandahar Airfield, the home base of thousands of coalition troops. Investigators said that alone should have made the pilots more hesitant about dropping. Maj. Umbach disagrees. At the time, he says he thought the firing might have been the Taliban trying to ambush planes coming in for a landing. "It's definitely something shooting," he explains. "Is it a ground-to-ground battle? Is it a ground-to-air battle at some other airplane or somebody going into Kandahar? Or three, is it ground-to-air going at us?" It was none of those, of course. But not once, Maj. Umbach says, had his unit been warned about even the possibility of troops conducting live-fire exercises—let alone at that spot at that time.

Maj. Schmidt asked permission to lay down his 20 mike-mike. "The instant I heard it, I thought: 'That's a little bit of a strange call,'" Maj. Umbach says now. "In hindsight, it was a great idea. We've got bullets, we've got bombs, we've got missiles. It was the least lethal thing that we had, and at that range, it would have been fairly non-lethal."

Maj. Umbach knows that the government pointed to the "20 mike-mike" call as proof that he lost control of the flight to his much more talented wingman. You are the flight lead. Why is Harry talking to BOSS-MAN? The answer, Bill says, is simple: His wingman doesn't want to clog the radio. "Harry knows I can't and would not give him authorization," he says of the request to open fire. "He knows that. We have the same intel, we know what the ROEs are. So that becomes a wasted call to me. You make one radio call. You're saving radio air time so that when they come back and say: 'This is friendlies' or 'This is enemies,' we're not talking on the radio blocking him out."

Let's just make sure that it's, uh, that it's not friendlies, that's all. So much has been made of that call. It was the order that Harry refused to follow. It was the order that Bill failed to follow up on. Today, Maj. Umbach insists that the now-infamous transmission was never meant to be an order. It was supposed to be broadcast on UHF so the AWACS crew could also hear him. Only much later did he realize that he flipped the wrong switch on the radio, leaving only Harry to hear the call. "We can't land, raise the canopy, and go out and check I.D.," Bill says. "It's just a last-ditch hope that: 'Hey, is there anybody here that sees anything that would say this is friendly?' Because I don't, and obviously [Maj. Schmidt] doesn't."

As the incident rapidly unfolded, Maj. Umbach says he became "fully convinced" that the enemy was shooting at him and his wingman. He saw the rocket rounds, but he couldn't tell where they were burning out. "It went through my mind that I could get shot down," he says.

That, Bill insists, is why he was not the least bit surprised when he heard Harry invoke self-defense. It wasn't a sudden reaction, a sinister scheme to score a win. They had already seen numerous flashes by that point—rounds that they honestly believed were being aimed at them. "'Hold fire' doesn't ever mean that you can't act in self-defense," Maj. Umbach says. "So the fact that AWACS said it, and then four seconds later he's rolling in in self-defense, I'm not concerned about that." And even if Bill didn't agree with the decision, he says there is nothing he could have done to stop it. All fighter pilots have the right to defend themselves.

"When I look back and listen to the tapes and relive what I'm seeing, what I'm trying to find out and what's going on, it would happen again," Maj. Umbach says. "You put anybody up there with something that looks very convincingly like it's shooting at you, the reaction is pretty cut and dried. That is addressed in the rules of engagement and the special instructions, and what we did falls right in line with everything that is outlined there."

Bill has heard it many times before: Why not just leave? Why stick around if you think you're being shot at? For one, Maj. Umbach says he believed the F-16s were under a direct order from the CAOC, via the AWACS, to get more information on the SAFIRE. If they simply flew away, they would have been derelict in their duty. Bill also says that there was not a single word in the entire ROE or SPINS that said pilots should leave if they encounter a threat. The rules changed *after* the accident, after Gen. Moseley proclaimed that he "could not imagine a scenario" in which the pilots could not have egressed while waiting for further direction. But on

April 17, 2002, the rules of engagement contained no such guidance, Maj. Umbach says. "That is a lie that came out in the investigation."

It is not the only lie, he says. Gen. Sargeant repeatedly accused Maj. Schmidt of descending toward the anti-aircraft artillery (AAA), putting his jet "recklessly" closer to the alleged threat. "That's a good phrase that he uses," Maj. Umbach says. "But this wasn't Triple-A." It was a rocket. "We are already well within the threat envelope."

What Maj. Umbach is saying is that even if he did want to leave, he is not sure he could have. The threat appeared to be that grave. "Turning and running, like Odom said—'We could have just turned, run, lit the afterburners and got out of there'—that's really, really stupid," Bill says. "I don't know what else to say. That doesn't cut it."

Many others don't see it that way. In Bill's letter of reprimand, Gen. Carlson said Maj. Umbach should have directed his wingman to "egress the area without delay to an unquestionably safe distance." At the Article 32, Charlie Gittins repeatedly suggested that Harry was essentially stuck over Tarnak Farm, waiting for Maj. Umbach to give the word. He is still saying that today. And, in his own statement to the CIB, Maj. Schmidt conceded that he "probably could have egressed the situation," but remained in the area to support his lead. "I was the wingman," Harry later told *Chicago Magazine*. "I was not in charge of making decisions."

Bill Umbach doesn't believe any of that. He was ordered to get a mark, and that's what he was doing. Even if he wanted to leave, he didn't believe it was safe to do so. Maj. Schmidt said the exact same thing to Col. Nichols right after he landed: "I estimated I couldn't get away so I turned back in again to more effectively maneuver against them," Harry said. "I felt like I had a better chance with a tally on the system than by running tail on."

The bottom line, Maj. Umbach says, is that if someone had another suggestion, he would have listened. "If somebody's got a better idea, it's their job and responsibility to mention that," he says. "It doesn't mean that you as the flight lead have to do what it is, but you bring it up." And that goes for everyone, he says. AWACS. Maj. Schmidt. Anybody. "In a case like this, if Harry, as an individual, thought: 'Ooh man, maybe we ought to just get out of here,' he would say something like: 'Two recommends we bug out south,' or something like that."

Harry Schmidt was a Top Gun, an élite in the world's most élite profession. Bill Umbach was a United Airlines pilot, a part-time Guardsman. Unfair or not, it is an unavoidable fact of this case. The weaker pilot—at least on paper—was in charge of one of the best in the business. No one will ever know for certain if that scheduling decision contributed to what happened hours later. Investigators said Harry, arrogant and aggressive, took over the flight because he didn't like what his lead was doing. The Air Force, and others, accused Bill of buckling under the pressure, failing to give the order to egress. The stereotypes certainly fit: trigger-happy Top Gun; stammering airline pilot.

But that is all they are, Maj. Umbach says. Stereotypes. He was just as qualified to be a Number One as Harry. Not only was he a 20-year veteran, but he had already flown the lead jet into Afghanistan numerous times before April 17. He made all the right calls that night, the same calls, Bill says, that any other flight lead would have made. "Through the official channels, I got a letter of reprimand that said a bunch of stuff, and that's the grand total that's come out of this thing for me," he says. "And I can refute, without any doubt, everything that is in there—every single item that is in there—as being not true, misdirected, and inappropriate. It's not true."

I ask Bill if he blames Harry for the abrupt end to his military career. It was Harry's bomb, after all. Maj. Umbach says Maj. Schmidt bears as much responsibility as he does: none. "I felt that he did what he thought he had to as a fighter pilot, and it would have been the same for any other guy that would have been on my wing that night," he says. "So whether he was my wingman or whether I was on the ground and he was the flight lead that night and had our most junior, inexperienced wingman on his wing, when I see all the facts that I know, I don't see anything that he did wrong. I don't disagree with what he did."

Harry and Bill are not close friends. They don't golf together or drop in at each other's houses. But there are no hard feelings, Maj. Umbach says. If they bump into one another, they talk. "I don't think there is any animosity. If this had never happened, he and I, I don't think we would necessarily be hanging out any more or any less than we do."

Bill Umbach lives just outside of Springfield, in a gorgeous home that overlooks a quiet lake attached to his backyard. It has been a long time since a reporter snooped around the driveway or trampled on his neighbor's flowers. "I've had a lot of training, been a lot of places, and been through a lot of stuff, but you don't get any training for that," he says. "You don't get any preparation for it. So once you're in it, you're in it." He's out of it now, or at least as far out as he will ever be. But he knows that no matter how many years pass, he will always be that guy, one of the two U.S. fighter pilots criminally charged for killing four Canadian paratroopers. Bill even has his own Rubbermaid container full of newspaper clippings and letters. His two young daughters may have questions one day, so he's keeping the box for them.

"I would be wasting my time if I was trying to convince everybody who ever heard of it that, 'Hey guys, you've got to believe me, this is what was really happening,'" Bill says. "It comes to the point where you just say: 'Sorry it happened.'"

He knows, in his own mind, that he did everything he could that night. He knows that Harry did everything right. He can't say the same for the U.S. Air Force, especially Gen. Stephen Sargeant. "It's unfortunate, because I think so highly of the Air Force and the military," Maj. Umbach says. "The Air Force has core values, and I don't think he stands for them. I think he had his mind made up before he stepped on the ground in Kuwait."

"If you can't schedule a planned training exercise at a given point, and do that without fear from your own friendly troops, then we need to be out of the service," Bill continues. "We're better than that. The whole coalition is."

In the end, Maj. Umbach says it wasn't him or his wife or his children who bore the brunt of Gen. Sargeant's "lies." It was, and still is, the Canadian families. He is still alive. Those four men are dead, and their loved ones, he says, still haven't been told why. Yet in the same breath, Bill says that if the relatives and the soldiers and anyone else want to direct their anger at him, he is more than willing to accept it. "If it brings them the smallest bit of comfort to say: 'At least I know that it was those two guys and those two guys are not flying so that won't happen again,' if it brings them comfort, then I'm okay with it," he says. "If the families or the injured or the friends of these people, or the people in the chain of command on the Air Force side or the chain of command on the Canadian side—if somebody says this is a big screw-up and blame is the right word, and the blame goes to these two guys, okay, if it makes you feel better. If you think your system is better because of that, or if it makes you sleep better at night, or if it will give you some sort of peace, I'll take it."

Maj. Umbach still flies the international routes for United. Sometimes, on his way to Asia, he passes over top of Canada. His stomach churns whenever he does. "War is grossly ugly, always. And this—any friendly fire incident—is the bottom of it all. I try to imagine my girls in a war and being killed by their own side, their own troops. I cannot imagine anything worse." He says he will always be willing to sit down and talk to the Canadian families, but only if they want to. "It's not something I feel that I'm going to, every year, say: 'Hey, now do you want to talk to me?' It's an offer there to them, not for me."

I ask Bill Umbach if he takes any comfort in what the families have said about him. In their eyes, he is the sincere pilot, the one who sounded as if he actually felt sorry for what happened. Some have even forgiven him. "It's the lesser of two evils," Maj. Umbach says. "I just am who I am." If he has been cast in a better light than Maj. Schmidt, Bill knows why. It was those statements at the Article 32. "That is just what I decided to say," he says. "I think Harry—and perhaps his attorney more so than Harry, I don't know—also thought there is stuff that hasn't come out, that hasn't been said, that he needs to say so it's out there. The problem is then it becomes interpreted as: 'You're making excuses.'"

That is not necessarily fair, Bill says. "These families, from the first day they met or knew anything about Harry, had been told nothing good about him. He's a father, has two kids, and goes to church, but he has been painted." *Evil. Callous. The reason why.* "It would be great if those families knew that, you know what, I'm a good guy," Maj. Umbach says. "But I think they would find out that Harry is a good guy, too."

chapter forty-two

Harry Schmidt is a logistics officer at the 183rd Fighter Wing. A glorified scheduler, as he calls it. When the squadron deploys, it is his job to move all the equipment and all the people. He also organizes training sessions for the fighter pilots, training sessions that he can only watch from the ground. He will do this job until he retires in 2007. "I'm just waiting," he says. "I'm just putting in time."

At the mall, at the grocery store, strangers still stop him and ask if he is Harry Schmidt, the man they saw in the newspaper every day, the man they supported with a donation to the 183rd Pilots' Defense Fund. He always says yes, and thanks them for their help. Even now, Harry says he still hasn't met a single person in Springfield with a bad word to say. "You are put in a life-and-death situation," he says. "What are you going to do?"

Maj. Schmidt was hesitant to be interviewed for this book. He changed his mind more than once, thinking that maybe the time has come to simply let it all be. At this point, what can the monster—the lying murderer—possibly say to make things right? There were other reasons. In January 2005, the Guard once again cut his flight pay, the bonus he and his lawyers claimed to have negotiated as part of his plea bargain. The military insisted that the bonus was never part of the deal. For months, Maj. Schmidt fought the issue, in the press and in the halls of power, until the Illinois Air National Guard finally relented. He will pocket his flight pay until he retires.

The fight was draining, one final slap in the face from the U.S. government. But in August, after the dispute was finally settled, Harry agreed to a series of telephone interviews. He knows that some people hate him. He knows that no matter what comes out of his mouth, many of those people will still hate him. But he also knows that he didn't take off that night looking for blood. The system failed, he says, not just Harry Schmidt. "I have never, ever been afraid of the truth," he says. "I don't keep track of any lies that I've told between now and then to keep my story consistent, because the truth is the truth."

The truth, he says, goes back to the night before the mission, when he saw the flight schedule. He was the most experienced pilot in the squadron, and he wasn't comfortable with the idea of flying on anybody's wing. His worries grew after Maj. Umbach's briefing. Intel warned that Taliban fighters might have acquired new surface-to-air weapons from the Iranians, and were allegedly regrouping in the region southeast of Kandahar. But Maj. Schmidt says his flight lead's briefing discussed nothing tactical, not even what the pilots should do once they reached Afghanistan. "Now I'm sitting there in the step van going: 'Okay, I could cancel and say fuck it, we're not ready to fly,'" Maj. Schmidt says. "But guess what? There are Americans that may be dying on the ground in six hours."

The sortie was largely uneventful. They refueled numerous times. They flew to Bagram to see the A-10s. When the AWACS vectored them toward their final tanker, both pilots flipped up their NVGs and switched on their outside lights. Maj. Schmidt says it was the first time he ever flew over Kandahar. The fact that Task Force Rakkasan owned the neighborhood never even entered his mind, he says. "I am under the assumption that AWACS is trained and clearing us through all these AOs, because that is what 'AB-Triple-C' does." ABCCC is short for Airborne Battlefield Command and Control Center. Housed inside a Hercules C-130, the crew of an ABCCC speaks directly to units on the ground, typically through the Air Support Operations Centers (ASOCs) spread throughout a combat zone. Its key capability is analyzing rapidly emerging ground targets. ABCCCs were retired shortly before Operation Enduring Freedom, replaced by the AWACS. "AWACS is just sitting there picking their nose waiting for the CAOC to tell them what to do," Maj. Schmidt says.

Maj. Umbach saw the fireworks. The first glimpse Maj. Schmidt caught was through his naked eye. Both jets turned hard to the left. Harry put his NVGs back on and turned off his lights, yelling at Bill to do the same. "I think they are pulling lead," Harry remembers Bill saying. "I think they're shooting at us." By that point, Maj. Schmidt says he was "a pig in space," slowed down to a crawl by the 4.7 G turn he just made. Not wanting to light the afterburner—a move that would have made his F–16 an instant target—he says he dipped his nose, picking up speed by descending. He says Maj. Umbach radioed the AWACS, telling the crew that they were "taking fire at our present position." Bill also asked if there were friendlies in the area, Maj. Schmidt says, but received no answer from BOSSMAN. What they did receive was permission to mark the target. None of those calls, of course, was captured on tape.

Despite Gen. Sargeant's conclusions, Maj. Schmidt says he and his flight lead never turned back toward the target. The firing appeared directly underneath them the entire time. "We don't fly by and then 15 miles south turn back to come do this," he says. "That's the whole bullshit. The government never had any idea what we really did." By the time the tapes were activated, both pilots were flying north, Tarnak Farm directly between them. Maj. Schmidt was on the right; Maj. Umbach on the left. By then, Maj. Schmidt says he believed his flight lead was defending against the ground fire, but continuing to maneuver while trying to take a mark. "In my mind, they've got him," he says. Harry descended nearly 5,000 feet, heading straight toward the flashes. The government said he was reckless, itching for a fight. He says his quick descent was simply another attempt to gain airspeed without hitting his afterburner. "If I light the can, now they see me and know where I am," he says.

Moments later, Maj. Schmidt did light the can, just as he turned his jet east away from Tarnak Farm. At that instant, he says he saw another rocket-propelled round go off behind him. He thought his afterburner gave him away, so he asked permission to lay down some 20 mike-mike. Warning shots. "That is in accordance with the commander of the Joint Chiefs of Staff," he says. AWACS told him to "standby."

Maj. Schmidt says he heard Bill's call to "make sure it's not friendlies." Investigators and prosecutors accused him of blatantly ignoring those words, but Harry says he did exactly what he was supposed to. He assumed his flight lead made that call on UHF, the frequency that AWACS could hear. He had no way of knowing at the time that it only went out on VHF, the plane-to-plane radio. "That's a big picture call," Maj. Schmidt says.

"That's to be announced to the world. So I shut up. I don't say anything. Unless you can provide that information, you shut up."

Maj. Schmidt made a wide right turn, eventually circling back toward the ground fire. Maj. Umbach was a few miles north, flying almost directly over the Kandahar Airfield. Maj. Schmidt says as he waited for BOSSMAN to answer Bill's "friendlies" call, he slewed his targeting pod over the Tarnak Farm compound, the huts and buildings that were off-limits to ground troops. "Now it is in my mind that this place is where bad guys are, because it's been bombed and the bad guys may be coming back to get something or be using it as a staging ground," Maj. Schmidt says. Were you thinking that at that exact moment? "Oh yeah," he says. "Oh yeah."

Seconds later, he asked BOSSMAN if he wanted them "to push a different freq." Harry says he was not being impatient, hoping that a different controller would give him the okay to drop. He was, as fighter pilots say, trying to "feed the chicken." He heard Bill's question—assuming that the AWACS did, too—and was pushing BOSSMAN for an answer. "Who are you talking to? I want to be on that line. I want a conference call." Gen. Sargeant maintained that Harry took over the flight. "I don't say I'm taking control because I'm not telling Bill what to do," Maj. Schmidt says. "I didn't say 'egress.' I didn't say 'anchor.' I'm trying to get the right information to everybody to make the decision."

When Maj. Umbach told him to "check my sparkle, check my sparkle," Maj. Schmidt says he saw the flash of the fifth Carl G. round. It lit up his NVGs. He moved his infrared laser to the same spot on the wadi, right over 3 Section's position. At the time, Maj. Schmidt was flying west, Tarnak Farm a little more than three miles to the north. Maj. Umbach, having flown a wide semi-circle around the target, was now almost directly behind his wingman, nearly five miles away from the Canadians.

Coffee 51, BOSSMAN. Hold fire, need details on SAFIRE for K-Mart.

Okay, I've got, uh, I've got some men on a road and it looks like a piece of artillery firing at us. I am rolling in in self-defense.

The Air Force accused Maj. Schmidt of using self-defense as a ruse, a ploy to trump the "hold fire" and attack a target of opportunity. But Harry says when he heard the "hold fire" call, his mind focused not on the order, but on what came next. *Need details on SAFIRE for K-Mart.* He says the fact that the AWACS called it a SAFIRE—surface-to-air fire—only bolstered his fear that he was seeing the enemy. BOSSMAN didn't say: *Hold fire, we're checking for friendlies,* or *Hold fire, there's a training exercise at Kandahar.* "What comes out on the radio is: 'Hold fire, I need to fill out my administrative log,'" Maj. Schmidt says. "And I don't mean to be flippant about it, but I'm seeing supersonic rocket-propelled projectiles going towards my wingman."

What Maj. Schmidt says next is even more intriguing. In the moments before he invoked self-defense, he says he saw a source of light, perhaps another airplane, off to the southwest of his F-16. Unaware that Maj. Umbach was now behind him, he says he was certain at the time that the light outside his window was Bill's airplane. When the Carl G. fired, he says the round appeared to be headed in exactly that direction. In other words, Harry Schmidt invoked self-defense to protect Bill Umbach, only to realize later that he wasn't even looking at Bill Umbach at the time.

I ask Maj. Schmidt why nobody has ever heard that version of events until now. "There was no way to get it into evidence at the Article 32," he answers. "Is it relevant? Yeah. But am I sure? I don't know. To this day, am I sure? I don't know. I could have seen a star, and in night vision goggles, the twinkling of a star can look like an airplane. It's just one of those things."

So you invoked self-defense on behalf of Maj. Umbach, thinking he was somewhere that he wasn't? "Probably," Maj. Schmidt says. "I'm looking out the window and I see what I think is Bill."

But hindsight, Harry says, was not one of the weapons he had with him that night. It is easy to nitpick everything he did, second by second, by looking at a tiny video in slow-motion. But he saw what he saw: rocket-propelled rounds aimed at what he thought was his flight lead. "In accordance with the rules of engagement, that demonstrates a hostile act," he says. "The crux of the issue is I'm witnessing a hostile act. Obviously, I made an incorrect decision regarding the application of force in self-defense, but if you look at the indicators that go up to that point, is there anything in the AWACS comm that tells me anything different?" Even the AWACS, he says, gave him tacit approval to drop. "'You're cleared, self-defense,'" he says, alluding to TSgt. Carroll's call 30 seconds after the explosion. "Is that a powerful statement or what? They do not know that friendlies are there, even though the bomb hit the ground seconds before that.

'You're cleared, self-defense.' Wow. That might take a smidgen of the burden off of Harry Schmidt. There is at least a whole AWACS crew involved in that comment."

Radio calls aside, Maj. Schmidt points out that even if he did misjudge where Maj. Umbach was, Bill himself has said numerous times that he believed he was going to be shot down that night. "So, you know, there's two of us that were there," Harry says. "I don't know what else to say at that point. If I'm a criminal for doing that, then I guess I'm a criminal."

Harry Schmidt speaks like a man who knows he is right. He is not abrasive or condescending, but he is confident. He knows every angle of his case, and every argument that the critics have thrown his way. "I could have destroyed 90 percent of what they were saying, and then I would have been more than happy to take the other 10 percent into court," he says now. "Steve Sargeant and his report: garbage."

He has an explanation for all his actions, all the allegations that everyone said pointed to his guilt. Were you trying to atone for the unit's screw-up in Iraq? "We don't do that," he says.

Why not take a mark? He tried, he says, but the firing stopped when he stuck his laser near the wadi. Besides, he says, the AWACS crew could clearly see the F-16s on their radar screens. "We gave them: 'We're taking fire at our present position.' Do you think you could generate something out of that? They knew exactly where we were."

Why not warn Bill to jink? "He saw it," he says of the ground fire. "The only reason you're going to clutter up the radio is if he is 'no joy,' which means he doesn't see it. Well, he's the guy that saw it."

Why didn't you fly away? "I'm waiting for a decision to be made," he says. A wingman should never abandon his flight lead.

Though forever linked, Harry Schmidt and Bill Umbach have not spoken to one another in almost a year. There is no doubt that Harry still wonders what might have been had his jet been slotted as the flight lead that night. But at this point, so many years later, he says he is not interested in speculating. "It may have changed," he says. "I don't know. I don't want to second-guess any of that. Mine is not to wonder why. Mine is just to do and die. That's my creed. That's what I do. When they publish the flight schedule, it's an order."

I ask him if he holds a grudge against Maj. Umbach. "I think Bill's a nice guy," Harry says.

Are you where you are today because of Bill Umbach? "I think Bill's a nice guy," he says again.

Maj. Schmidt prefers to dwell on the bigger picture, the "stage" on which he and Maj. Umbach were left to fail. Both men swallowed Go-pills that night. Harry popped two of the 5-mg tablets just two hours before the bombing. He says he felt a jolt. "You're kind of racing," he says. "Remember when you're in high school and you've got in the car and you've got a great song going and your hands are tapping on everything. That's kind of like what it feels like. You're high." Maj. Schmidt says he will never know for sure whether the Dexedrine clouded his judgment. He still believes he did everything right, but time, he says, definitely felt compressed. "I thought the whole thing lasted about 45 seconds, and it turns out to be three or four minutes."

The way he sees it, he had a stellar career in the Navy, never once popping a pill during a mission. As soon as he transferred to the Air Force, where speed is part of the routine, he dropped a bomb that killed four Canadians. "For 3,005 hours, I might have made a couple bad decisions along the way, but nothing that catastrophic," he says. "Then give me some amphetamines, and we're going to question the decision he made somewhere between hour 3,005 and 3,006."

As far as this case goes, the Go-pills will always be the intangible. It is impossible to know what effect—if any—they really had on the pilots. But what is certain, Maj. Schmidt says, is the string of communication breakdowns that left him and Bill without all the information they needed. A voluminous ACO. No ground liaison officers in the flying units. A CAOC and an AWACS that knew nothing about the Canadian training exercise. A disaster waiting to happen. "We were flying around Afghanistan like a bunch of streakers at college," Maj. Schmidt says. "There were no safe passage routes. There were no: 'Hey, weave your way through this to avoid AOs or to avoid hot areas.' It was a train wreck of everybody going everywhere." The Air Force, he says, was ignoring its own doctrine—a failure that goes all the way up to Gen. Moseley. "He had the horsepower and the authority to institute the architecture," Maj. Schmidt says. "The bottom line is he said: 'Yes sir, we can do this,' but we couldn't."

And then, after the bombing, the Air Force suddenly realized that its muddled command-and-control system was going to be open to third-party scrutiny—just as the war in Iraq was about to break. A cover-up, Maj. Schmidt believes, was the only way the military could protect its dysfunctional CAOC. "I think I'm a victim of the fact that it was an international accident," Harry says. "I don't want to put the 'Canadian' label on it, because I don't want to make it a 'me versus you' thing. I think it might have been the same way if it had been French, or if it would have been Danish. And part of that is because the international community was invited to participate in the investigation."

If those were American troops in the wadi, the Pentagon could have kept the whole thing relatively quiet, Maj. Schmidt says. But throw Canada into the mix, and the U.S. had two options: admit that the CAOC was severely flawed, or find a scapegoat. "You're going to put America's command-and-control structure of war on trial?" Maj. Schmidt asks. "It's not gonna happen." So the military went after him and Bill. It didn't help that the president was also trying to build his "coalition of the willing" at the exact same time. "I wouldn't be surprised if this goes to the White House," Maj. Schmidt says. "They're trying to build their coalition for Iraq, and they go: 'Hey, I think we could get some momentum here from the Canadians if we show them how valuable they are to us.' I went and visited enough politicians trying to discuss the issue and trying to get some leverage. I talked to enough of them to see how they operate, and it would not surprise me in the least bit that some White House staffer came up with this, and went: 'Okay, here's how we manipulate people and the system.' They actually saw this as an opportunity."

Of course, even Maj. Schmidt admits that he has not an ounce of evidence to prove that allegation. But he says the signs are all there. He was the lowest person on the totem pole. The military took months to grant his lawyer a security clearance. They asked numerous generals, including Stephen Sargeant, to testify at the Article 32. They were all deemed unavailable—until prosecutors needed one of them. And since April 17, 2002, the American military has endured at least two dozen friendly fire accidents, some at the hands of people who declared self-defense. Nobody else has been criminally charged. "My situation is not unique as far as the accident is concerned," he says. "The circumstances are what's unique, and that's what ended up burying me. They didn't want to fix the problem. They wanted to fix the blame."

Exhibit A, he says, is his letter of reprimand. *Callous. Gross poor judgment. No faith in your abilities. Wage your own war.* Every word is a lie, Maj. Schmidt says. "It was written for the Air Force to wash its hands of the issue. And if you read it, if I am guilty of any of that, why am I not in jail? And I'll challenge the Air Force to that. If I am guilty of any of that, why am I not in jail?"

Harry Schmidt is not in jail. He is in Springfield, in the same house on the golf course that he and his family moved into days before he deployed to Kuwait. He was 36 back then. He recently turned 40. At work, he spends his days flying a desk. It is almost unimaginable, considering where he was four years ago. Maj. Schmidt was the star recruit, a prized addition to a unit that waited months and months for him to arrive. Now he is counting down the days until he leaves, filling the meantime with paperwork. Every once in a while, however, a fellow fighter pilot stops by his desk, asking him to come to the video room and debrief his ride. Despite everything that has happened, most of the guys still respect Harry's fighter pilot brain. "This could have been used as an incredible tool, a teaching tool for people," he says of the bombing. "Here I am, an experienced instructor. I could have developed something to bring this out as far as debriefing in mistakes that were made across the board. If you're going to tell me that I was guilty of dereliction of duty that night, okay, I will stand in line with all the other people who were guilty of dereliction of duty."

"The bottom line is I pushed the button," he continues. "So if you want to look at the fault, I'm the one that did this. However, if you backtrack to the point of why I did this, I did this in accordance with the rules of engagement and the command-and-control structure that I was working under."

Harry is well aware that what he just said is the exact reason why the Canadian families despise him so much. They want him to accept responsibility, and he simply can't do it. He is sorry that those men are dead, but not sorry for what he did. "Am I sorry that I pushed the button that night?" he says. "Well, I don't know. If I had waited five more seconds, I might be looking at Marlene and their two kids going: 'Gosh, I'm sorry I didn't do something different.' That is such a fine line."

If Harry is sorry for anything, it is that the Air Force has repeatedly lied to the Canadian families. To this day, he says, nobody has told those widows and parents the truth about why their men are dead. "I feel terrible for them, because I really think they've been duped," Maj. Schmidt says. "I think if I were fed what they were fed, I'd imagine my opinion would be the same." And Harry has heard all the opinions. *Monster. Coward. Murderer. Remorseless prick.* Looking back, Maj. Schmidt doesn't believe there was anything he could have done to change people's minds. From day one, the Air Force made him out to be the bad guy, a target for the families' anger. "I wish the issue of the accident in general was handled just as that—as an accident," he says. "And then I think we would have all been able to talk and discuss it as civil human beings as opposed to being adversarial."

Instead, the incident became a criminal matter. Harry's lawyers told him not to say a word to anyone, let alone the Canadian families. "I've already been given the 'shut up and color' order, which begs the question: where do you go from there?" he says now. "In our legal system, don't say anything." As awful as he felt for the families of the four dead paratroopers, Maj. Schmidt says he had no choice but to keep quiet. He had to think about his own family, his wife and two young sons. He wasn't going to do anything that jeopardized his fight to stay out of jail. "I don't know where I would have come forward," he says. "If you get on the tube and you make a public apology, you're going to see that at your court-martial, and they're going to show it to the jury and go: 'See.'"

The longer he stayed quiet, the more he was criticized. By the time the Article 32 began, Maj. Schmidt was a hated man, a Top Gun cowboy with a heart of stone. His cold stare, captured every morning by news photographers, only fueled that perception. He doesn't begrudge the families for feeling that way. They needed something—anything—to blame. "You can't calculate that," he says of their loss. "I can't even imagine that. But as far as me personally, up to the point of the Article 32, I felt that wall was insurmountable. What am I going to do at that point? I couldn't go talk to them face to face. What was I going to do? And that again is, I think, part of the

Air Force's issue of how they handled this thing. They created a scapegoat or monster—scapegoat seems appropriate—to shunt the blame."

I ask Harry if he could have reached out sooner, perhaps sent a note to the families expressing his sorrow and his sincere hope that they find what he insists is the truth. "I think that would have helped, but you wonder if they would have believed you at that point," he says. "In the big scheme of things, you're combating the Pentagon P.A. wheel." That wheel, he says, had already leaked his name to the press, giving the families their token villain. "They've built their plan, their structure."

It was against that backdrop that Harry stood up in the courtroom to read his statement. It was never meant to be an apology, he says now. It was solely for the benefit of Judge Rosenow, a play-by-play of why he did what he did in the sky that night. For the soldiers' families, it was a huge punch in the face, a litany of excuses void of any genuine remorse. "If the Air Force and the Canadian families wanted it to be a soap opera, then everybody should have told me that," Maj. Schmidt says. "I don't regret the statement because I am acting in the legal framework that I have been put in. If it was the public forum for an apology, then I guess I should have done something different. But it wasn't."

"It's not that I'm just some machine that goes out there and has no regard for what happened," he continues. "At that point, that was not the time. And then, when you get everybody yelling at you and crucifying you—okay, when is the time? Is there a time?"

It is a question Harry has pondered countless times. When he says he thinks about those families every day, his voice sounds sincere. He has endured his own demons since April 17, 2002. He has looked to God. He has looked to his wife. And he has looked to his lawyers. The answer is always the same. "I just don't think that I can breach the walls of Jericho," Maj. Schmidt says of the families. "It's a double-edged sword in that whatever healing they have had to that point, do you want to undo it and revisit whatever anger is there? I feel that whatever I tell them or explain to them is not going to make a difference, and that's frustrating, because I think that would let a lot of us let the issue go."

Is it not worth trying? Regardless of how you think they might react, don't you believe that some of those relatives would want to hear from you?

"That goes back to the balance of: is it worth reopening those wounds?" Maj. Schmidt says. "I can't balance that for them. I don't know where that is for them. Could I? Yeah, I could. But it would be pretty presumptuous of me to all of a sudden waltz into their lives and go: 'Hey, regardless of where you are in the healing process, I'm going to rip your heartstrings back out.' So I would think that at this point, we're better off to leave sleeping dogs to lie. The dust has settled. Am I happy about it? No. But I don't think the ball is in my court.

"I'm not going to come and invade their lives," he continues. "I think I've already caused enough disturbance in their lives, but if they want to come and talk to me, I would be more than happy to chat with them. And if they called me and said: 'Hey Harry, would you come talk to me?' I would even come to Canada to go talk to them. At this point, through this whole process—which has been abnormal at best—if they want to talk, I'll talk."

If that never happens, Maj. Schmidt only hopes that the families will one day realize that although he pulled the trigger, he is not the reason why those soldiers are dead. "I can tell them that I'm terribly sorry that the accident happened," he says. "I can't even begin to feel their pain. I can somewhat understand it, having fought in a couple of different conflicts. I understand the magnitude of human loss. I don't take it lightly, and I just truly hope that in their heart of hearts they understand that it was an accident, that it was nothing malicious. There was no glory involved in that. There is no glory in war. Glory is what historians make of war-time acts. You don't think of that while you're there in the heat of the moment."

On Remembrance Day, Craig Reid will get in his car and drive down Highway 401 toward Lancaster, Ont. He doesn't need directions anymore. He has been to the cemetery more than enough times now to find it on his own. When he gets there, Sgt. Reid will grab two beers from his trunk—one for him, one for Marc—and take a seat on the grass.

"I dodged a bullet, and I know I did," Sgt. Reid says. "Marc is dead because I couldn't do what was asked of me that night. Had I gone and done the RSO job that night, like Capt. Joe Jasper or Maj. Sean Hackett asked me to, I would be dead today, and I know that. There is absolutely nothing that anybody could say to me right now that would change my thoughts on that."

Though his mind will never change, the survivor's guilt has slowly diminished over the years. As much as anyone can, Sgt. Reid has learned to live with what happened on April 17, 2002. Last year, he and his wife, Colleen, had their first child, a baby girl. "Every time I see my little girl and I see her doing what little girls do, I am just so thankful that I am alive," Craig says, crying through his words. "It's such a painful thing that I'm struggling with and trying to deal with."

His visits to Marc's grave have helped. At the very least, they give him another chance to say sorry. Another chance to say thank you. "Life is not always fair," Sgt. Reid says. "If Tarnak Farm could prove anything to me, it's that you could be here one minute and gone the next. It's that quick. It's that fucking easy. You can be taken from this earth at the drop of a hat or the snap of a finger. Greener and Marc and Smitty and Dyer didn't see it coming."

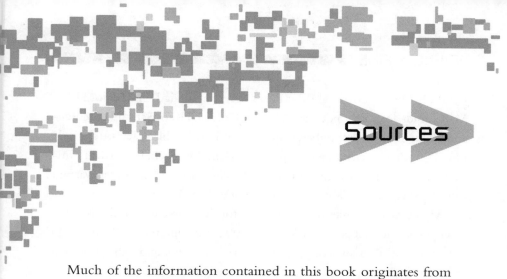

Sources

Much of the information contained in this book originates from thousands of pages of sworn testimony and exhibits, some of it classified. Over the years, numerous sources have provided me with documents that, to this day, are still considered secret by both the U.S. Air Force and the Canadian Department of National Defence. For obvious reasons, those sources remain anonymous.

Between April 18, 2002 and September 18, 2005, I also conducted hundreds of on-the-record interviews, both as a journalist at the *National Post* and in connection with this book. To the many people who lived this story and agreed to share their recollections with a complete stranger, I am forever grateful. Those people include:

Captain Jay Adair, Chuck Allen, General (retired) Maurice Baril, David L. Beck, Corporal Yan Bérubé, Sergeant Dave Bibby, Master Warrant Officer Billy Bolen, Miranda Boutilier, Master Corporal Jon Bradshaw, Shane Brennan, Master Corporal Rob Coates, Major Pete Dawe, Corporal Brian Decaire, Master Corporal Jean de la Bourdonnaye, Sergeant Tom Duke, Paul Dyer, Master Corporal Patrick Farrell, Sergeant Marco Favasoli, Kevin Ferguson, Corporal Pete Filis, Sergeant Lorne Ford, Corporal Michael Frank, Charles W. Gittins, Colonel Gregory C. Graf, Major Sean Hackett, Captain Joseph M. Jasper, Warrant Officer Rob Jones, Major James E. Key III, Corporal Chris Kopp, Claire Léger, Richard Léger, Captain Alastair Luft, Colonel Greg Matte, Master Corporal Brad McKenzie, Master Corporal Neil Miller, Lieutenant-Colonel John A. Milton, Colonel (retired) Robert J. Murphy, Colonel (retired) David C. Nichols, Colonel (retired) John S. Odom Jr., Corporal Rene Paquette, Sergeant Arnie Parris, Captain

Jeff Peck, Master Corporal Brett Perry, Sergeant Craig Reid, Major Harry M. Schmidt, Joan Schmidt, Lisa Schmidt, Corporal Kent Schmidt, Lieutenant-Colonel Shane Schreiber, Captain Matthew Scoble, Charlotte Smith, Lloyd Smith, Corporal Victor Speirs, Marlene Umbach, Major Bill Umbach, Aart Van Sloten, Janna Van Sloten, Jocelyn Van Sloten, Master Warrant Officer Al Whitehall, Warrant Officer Bill Wilson, Doreen Young.

My primary sources of information for this book are hundreds of interviews conducted between April 18, 2002 and September 18, 2005, and my review of thousands of pages of sworn testimony and exhibits, much of it classified.

chapter 1

Capt. James MacEachern, "Investigators Invest. Synopsis into Fratercide at Tarnak Fams 17 Apr 02," April 24, 2002. CLASSIFIED.

Interview notes: M.W.O. Billy Bolen, MCpl. Brad McKenzie, Capt. Joe Jasper, MCpl. Neil Miller, Maj. Pete Dawe.

chapter 2

Capt. Bryan Hynes, "BG SITREP as of 171800Z to 181800Z Mar 02— SECRET," March 19, 2002, Exhibit 1, Tarnak Farm Board of Inquiry. (*"I therefore recommend…in unnecessary risk."*)

Interview notes: Sgt. Craig Reid, Maj. Sean Hackett, Capt. Joe Jasper, M.W.O. Billy Bolen, MCpl. Brett Perry, Cpl. Brian Decaire, Capt. Alastair Luft, Sgt. Lorne Ford, Cpl. Rene Paquette, Miranda Boutilier, W.O. Rob Jones, Maj. Shane Schreiber.

Sean Naylor, *Not a Good Day to Die: The Untold Story of Operation Anaconda*, Berkley Books, 2005. (Naylor discusses the origins and deployment of Task Force Rakkasan)

Sworn testimony of Capt. Bryan Hynes, Tarnak Farm Board of Inquiry, April 29, 2002, CLASSIFIED. (Capt. Hynes discusses the near-miss during Operation Harpoon, when an American F-16 nearly bombed a unit of Canadian soldiers in March, 2002)

chapter 3

1st Lieutenant Allen Herritage, "TOPGUN: Navy pilot assists Weapons School," *Bullseye*, July 20, 2001. (*"The first thing…shooting at them."* / *"It depends on…bombs on target."*)

Coalition Investigation Board, "Summary of Facts: Tarnak Farms Friendly Fire Incident near Kandahar, Afghanistan," June 7, 2002.

Interview notes: Maj. Harry Schmidt, Lisa Schmidt, Maj. Bill Umbach, Marlene Umbach, Col. Robert J. Murphy, Col. David C. Nichols, Lt.-Col. John A. Milton, Joan Schmidt.

Jon Bonné, "'Go-pills': A war on drugs?" MSNBC, January 9, 2003. ("although the controversial…bombing the Balkans." / "a crucial tool…on drowsy pilots.")

Sworn testimony of Capt. Brad Houston, Coalition Investigation Board, April 30, 2002. CLASSIFIED.

Sworn testimony of Capt. Dawn P. McNaughton, Coalition Investigation Board, April 29, 2002. CLASSIFIED.

Sworn testimony of Maj. John A. Milton, Coalition Investigation Board, April 30, 2002. CLASSIFIED.

Sworn testimony of Lt.-Col. Mark Coan, Coalition Investigation Board, May 11, 2002. CLASSIFIED.

chapter 4

Interview Notes: Capt. Joe Jasper, Cpl. Shane Brennan, Sgt. Dave Bibby, Cpl. Jon Bradshaw, Cpl. Rene Paquette, Cpl. Jean De La Bourdonnaye, Cpl. Vic Speirs, W.O. Bill Wilson, MCpl. Brad McKenzie, Cpl. Chris Kopp, Lloyd Smith, Kevin Ferguson.

National Defence Command Centre, "Current Intelligence Report, NDCC-2 Op Apollo Support Team," January 29, 2002. ("at a specific...in the future.")

National Defence Command Centre, "Current Intelligence Report, NDCC-2 Op Apollo Support Team," March 12, 2002. ("Kandahar region was...of the Taliban.")

Steve Coll, "A secret hunt unravels in Afghanistan," Washington Post, February 22, 2004. (Coll recounts how the CIA tried to capture Osama bin Laden at Tarnak Farm)

Sworn testimony of Capt. Timothy Walshaw, Tarnak Farm Board of Inquiry, April 30, 2002, CLASSIFIED. (Capt. Walshaw discusses the 107-mm Chinese rockets that Canadian troops discovered outside the Kandahar Airfield)

Sworn testimony of Lt.-Col. Pat Stogran, Tarnak Farm Board of Inquiry, April 29, 2002, CLASSIFIED. (Lt.-Col. Stogran discusses how his staff worked with U.S. Army Rangers from Task Force 11 to secure local approval to use Tarnak Farm as a training range)

chapter 5

Interview notes: MCpl. Brett Perry, Capt. Alastair Luft, W.O. Bill Wilson, Cpl. Rene Paquette, Cpl. Brian Decaire, Sgt. Lorne Ford, Maj. Bill Umbach, Maj. Harry Schmidt, MCpl. Neil Miller, Cpl. Vic Speirs.

Maj. Arthur Henry, "Chronological Narrative of Significant Events," April 17, 2002, SECRET, Exhibit 43, Tarnak Farm Board of Inquiry.

Sgt. Marc Léger, "Seven-page excerpt from Field Message Pad," April 17, 2002, Exhibit 35, Tarnak Farm Board of Inquiry. ("We have confirmed...to the death.")

Sworn testimony of Maj. Arthur Henry, Coalition Investigation Board, May 1, 2002. CLASSIFIED.

Sworn testimony of Maj. Arthur Henry, Tarnak Farm Board of Inquiry, June 2, 2002. CLASSIFIED.

Sworn testimony of Maj. Trevor A. O'Day, Coalition Investigation Board, May 16, 2002. CLASSIFIED. (Maj. O'Day discusses how he and another helicopter pilot radioed the Kandahar Tower on April 17, just to be sure that the ground fire they were seeing was Tarnak Farm)

Sworn testimony of Lt.-Col. Craig Fisher, Article 32 hearing, January 17, 2003, Barksdale Air Force Base, La.

Sworn testimony of TSgt. Michael Carroll, Coalition Investigation Board, May 1, 2002. CLASSIFIED.

U.S. Air Force, "Heads–Up Display and Targeting Pod Tapes from Coffee 51 and Coffee 52," April 17, 2002, Exhibit 79, Article 32 Hearing, Barksdale Air Force Base, La.

chapter 6

Department of National Defence, "Battalion Comd. Duty Ops Log (3 PPCLI) starting from Serial 140 through to and including Serial 268," April 17, 2002, Exhibit 30, Tarnak Farm Board of Inquiry.

Department of National Defence, "Battalion Comd. Net Call Sign Zero (3 PPCLI) starting with Serial entry 333 through to and including Serial 625," April 17, 2002, Exhibit 31, Tarnak Farm Board of Inquiry.

Interview notes: Maj. Sean Hackett, Capt. Jeff Peck, MCpl. Brett Perry, Capt. Alastair Luft, W.O. Bill Wilson, Cpl. Rene Paquette, Cpl. Brian Decaire, Sgt. Lorne Ford, Maj. Bill Umbach, Maj. Harry Schmidt, MCpl. Neil Miller, Cpl. Vic Speirs, M.W.O. Al Whitehall, Cpl. Chris Kopp, MCpl. Rob Coates, Cpl. Jean De La Bourdonnaye, Capt. Jay Adair, W.O. Rob Jones, Sgt. Dave Bibby, Cpl. Jon Bradshaw, Cpl. Pete Filis, Cpl. Kent Schmidt, Maj. Pete Dawe.

Sworn testimony of Lt. Mark Batten, Tarnak Farm Board of Inquiry, May 1, 2002. CLASSIFIED.

Sworn testimony of Pte. Darren Astles, Tarnak Farm Board of Inquiry, May 1, 2002. CLASSIFIED.

Sworn testimony of Sgt. Bill Wilson, Tarnak Farm Board of Inquiry, April 30, 2002. CLASSIFIED.

Sworn testimony of MCpl. Stanley Clark, Coalition Investigation Board, May 8, 2002. CLASSIFIED.

Sworn testimony of Lt.-Col. Craig Fisher, Article 32 hearing, January 17, 2003, Barksdale Air Force Base, La.

Sworn testimony of Col. Charles H. McGuirk, Coalition Investigation Board, May 5, 2002. CLASSIFIED.

Sworn testimony of Maj. Marshall Scott Woodson III, Article 32 hearing, January 20, 2003, Barksdale Air Force Base, La.

Sworn testimony of Brig.-Gen. Stephen G. Wood, Coalition Investigation Board, April 29, 2002. CLASSIFIED.

Sworn testimony of Maj. Thomas J. Smedley, Coalition Investigation Board, May 5, 2002. CLASSIFIED.

U.S. Air Force, "Heads-Up Display and Targeting Pod Tapes from Coffee 51 and Coffee 52," April 17, 2002, Exhibit 79, Article 32 Hearing, Barksdale Air Force Base, La.

chapter 7

Capt. Joe Jasper, "Statement of Events—17 Apr 02," April 25, 2002, Exhibit 6, Tarnak Farm Board of Inquiry.

Department of National Defence, "Battalion Comd. Net Call Sign Zero (3 PPCLI) starting with Serial entry 333 through to and including Serial 625," April 17, 2002, Exhibit 31, Tarnak Farm Board of Inquiry.

Interview notes: MCpl. Rob Coates, W.O. Rob Jones, MCpl. Brett Perry, Cpl. Brian Decaire, Cpl. Shane Brennan, Capt. Jeff Peck, Cpl. Jon Bradshaw, W.O. Bill Wilson, Maj. Shane Schreiber, MCpl. Vic Speirs, Sgt. Dave Bibby, Maj. Sean Hackett, Sgt. Craig Reid, Cpl. Yan Bérubé, Capt. Alastair Luft, MCpl. Brad McKenzie, Sgt. Marco Favasoli, Cpl. Pete Filis, M.W.O. Billy Bolen, Sgt. Arnie Parris, Maj. Pete Dawe.

chapter 8

Coalition Investigation Board, "Verbatim Testimony of Maj. Harry Schmidt and Maj. Bill Umbach," April 18, 2002, Tab S-6.1—6.12. CLASSIFIED.

Interview notes: Maj. Harry Schmidt, Maj. Bill Umbach, Col. David C. Nichols, Col. Robert J. Murphy.

Stephen Thorne, "Three friendly fire incidents almost cost Canadian lives before tragedy," Canadian Press, January 19, 2003. (Thorne's article describes the incident in which two Canadian snipers were nearly bombed during Operation Anaconda)

Sworn testimony of Capt. Erin Wirtanen, Coalition Investigation Board, May 11, 2002. CLASSIFIED.

Sworn testimony of Chief Richard K. Emley, Coalition Investigation Board, May 16, 2002. CLASSIFIED. (*"I don't know…friendly fire accident."*)

Sworn testimony of Col. David C. Nichols, Article 32 hearing, January 18, 2003. Barksdale Air Force Base, La.

Sworn testimony of Col. David C. Nichols, Coalition Investigation Board, May 3, 2002 & May 11, 2002. CLASSIFIED.

332nd Air Expeditionary Group, "Operation Enduring Freedom CAS Symposium," 10 pages of slides, March 17, 2002, Exhibit 83, Article 32 hearing, Barksdale Air Force Base, La.

chapter 9
David Roath, "Search and Recovery Site Investigation, Tarnak Farm live fire range fratricide incident," U.S. Disaster Mortuary Affairs Response Team, Exhibit 34, Tarnak Farm Board of Inquiry. CLASSIFIED.

Department of National Defence, "Canadian Forces Briefing—Gen. Raymond Henault—Death of four soldiers in Afghanistan," April 18, 2002.

Interview notes: Cpl. Vic Speirs, MCpl. Brad McKenzie, Sgt. Dave Bibby, M.W.O. Billy Bolen, Cpl. Pete Filis, Maj. Shane Schreiber, Maj. Sean Hackett, Capt. Alastair Luft, Cpl. Michael Frank, Lloyd Smith, Richard Léger, Claire Léger, Jocelyn Van Sloten, Aart Van Sloten, Janna Van Sloten, Miranda Boutilier, Sgt. Arnie Parris, Sgt. Marco Favasoli, W.O. Bill Wilson.

chapter 10
Aaron Sands and Gary Dimmock, "Death in the dark desert: How a training exercise in Afghanistan became a disaster for Canada," *The Ottawa Citizen*, April 19, 2002. (*"I'm okay mom…is my job."* / *"Our hearts go…a training exercise."*)

Edited Hansard, "37th Parliament, 1st Session," House of Commons, April 18, 2002. (*"War is always…troops adequately equipped?"*)

Interview notes: M.W.O. Billy Bolen, Sgt. Craig Reid, W.O. Rob Jones, Cpl. Jon Bradshaw, Lisa Schmidt, Sgt. Lorne Ford, MCpl. Brett Perry, Cpl. Jean de la Bourdonnaye, Cpl. Brian Decaire, Gen. (retired) Maurice Baril, Alice Léger, Cpl. Kent Schmidt.

Julie O'Neill, "Baril defends role in Rwanda massacre," *National Post*, June 23, 2001. (*"pretty cheap."* / *"on every telephone…New York City."*)

Robert Fife and Sheldon Alberts, "Pilot ignored orders: sources," *National Post*, April 19, 2002. (*"If ever there…business being there."*)

Robert Remington, "I said, 'Is he OK?' and they said, 'No': Marley Léger says her husband died a hero in Kandahar," *National Post*, April 19, 2002. (*"I just want…serving his country."*)

Ron Corbett, "A soldier's story: Part One," *The Ottawa Citizen*, November 24, 2002. (*"I wish I…Love, Marc."*)

Rowan Scarborough, "'Friendly fire' judge's memo assailed; General criticized actions that led to deaths of Canadians," *The Washington Times*, July 30, 2002. (Scarborough's article cites various passages from the memo that Lt.-Gen. T. Michael Moseley sent to his subordinate commanders the day after the bombing)

Sworn testimony of Brig.-Gen. Stephen T. Sargeant, Article 32 hearing, January 21-22, 2003. Barksdale Air Force Base, La.

The White House, "Statement by the President," April 18, 2002. (*"All Americans are…our two peoples."*)

United States Department of Defense, "Rumsfeld Statement on Friendly fire incident near Kandahar," April 18, 2002. (*"I want to…and their families."*)

William Walker and Allan Thompson, "PM promises answers in bomb deaths of Canadian troops," *The Toronto Star*, April 19, 2002. (*"is right up…in my career."*)

chapter 11

David Halton, "Bush's Condolences," CBC News, April 19, 2002. (*"It was a…accident took place."*)

Department of National Defence, "Minister of National Defence Art Eggle-ton and General (ret'd) Maurice Baril participate in a briefing on the Board of Inquiry," April 19, 2002. (*"You know we're...know what happened?"*)

Garth Pritchard, "Canadians in Afghanistan: Friendly Fire," Fearon Productions Inc., 2002. (*"For the last...until its end."*)

Graeme Hamilton and Sheldon Alberts, "Survivor lambastes U.S. pilot: Baril vows full inquiry," *National Post*, April 20, 2002. (*"It's a shitty...whole battalion's hurting." / "I think it...through the media."*)

Interview notes: Sgt. Marco Favasoli, Cpl. Yan Bérubé, Pte. Michael Frank, MCpl. Patrick Farrell, Cpl. Rene Paquette, Sgt. Lorne Ford, Cpl. Brian Decaire, Sgt. Dave Bibby, Jocelyn Van Sloten, Aart Van Sloten, Miranda Boutilier, Lloyd Smith, MCpl. Brett Perry.

Peter Murphy, "Two more soldiers buried today," *CTV News*, April 24, 2002. (*"Don't put the...why we're there."*)

Richard Foot and Michael Friscolanti, "Nova Scotia shrouds 2 soldiers in sorrow," *National Post*, April 22, 2002. (*"I love him...out of me."*)

Robert Fife and Sheldon Alberts, "Pilot ignored orders: sources," *National Post*, April 19, 2002. (*"When he saw...he bombed away."*)

Stephen Thorne, "'You're OK, jumper. Have a good one': Emotional send-off for four dead paratroopers in Kandahar," Canadian Press, April 19, 2002. (Thorne, who was in Kandahar at the time of the bombing, describes the sombre ceremony in which the four dead paratroopers were loaded onto a plane and flown out of Afghanistan)

chapter 12

Interview notes: Gen. Maurice Baril.

Michael Friscolanti, "'A real pro' airman overcome by grief," *National Post*, April 29, 2002. (*"He's one of...can comprehend it."*)

Sworn testimony of Capt. Dawn P. McNaughton, Coalition Investigation Board, April 29, 2002. CLASSIFIED.

Sworn testimony of Capt. Evan H. Cozadd, Coalition Investigation Board, April 28, 2002. CLASSIFIED.

Sworn testimony of Capt. John H. Knightstep, Tarnak Farm Board of Inquiry, April 29, 2002. CLASSIFIED.

Sworn testimony of Lt.-Col. Pat Stogran, Tarnak Farm Board of Inquiry, April 29, 2002. CLASSIFIED.

chapter 13

Interview notes: Capt. Joe Jasper.

Mike Blanchfield, "Baril tours site of soldiers' deaths: 'We walked the ground, saw what they saw,' general reveals," *The Ottawa Citizen*, May 1, 2002. (*"BOARD IN PROGRESS. DO NOT DISTURB."*)

Sworn testimony of Capt. Joe Jasper and Maj. Sean Hackett, Tarnak Farm Board of Inquiry, April 30, 2002. CLASSIFIED.

Sworn testimony of Col. Robert J. Murphy, Coalition Investigation Board, April 30, 2002. CLASSIFIED.

Sworn testimony of Maj. John A. Milton, Coalition Investigation Board, April 30, 2002. CLASSIFIED.

chapter 14

Sworn testimony of Maj. Arthur Henry, Coalition Investigation Board, May 1, 2002. CLASSIFIED.

Sworn testimony of Capt. David Pepper, Coalition Investigation Board, May 1, 2002. CLASSIFIED.

Sworn testimony of TSgt. Michael Carroll, Coalition Investigation Board, May 1, 2002. CLASSIFIED.

chapter 15

Interview notes: Col. David C. Nichols, Gen. Maurice Baril, Col. Greg Matte.

Sworn testimony of Col. David C. Nichols, Coalition Investigation Board, May 3, 2002. CLASSIFIED.

chapter 16

Sworn testimony of Col. Charles H. McGuirk, Coalition Investigation Board, May 5, 2002. CLASSIFIED.

Sworn testimony of Maj. Jacqueline Bagby, Coalition Investigation Board, May 5, 2002. CLASSIFIED.

Sworn testimony of Brig.-Gen. Stephen G. Wood, Coalition Investigation Board, April 29, 2002. CLASSIFIED.

chapter 17

Interview notes: MCpl. Brett Perry.

Sworn testimony of Chief Warrant Officer 3 Rodney Merrill, Coalition Investigation Board, May 7, 2002. CLASSIFIED.

Sworn testimony of Cpl. Brett Perry, Tarnak Farm Board of Inquiry, May 8, 2002. CLASSIFIED.

Sworn testimony of Cpl. Brian Decaire, Tarnak Farm Board of Inquiry, May 8, 2002. CLASSIFIED.

Sworn testimony of Cpl. Cheyenne Laroque, Coalition Investigation Board, May 8, 2002. CLASSIFIED.

Sworn testimony of Cpl. Rene Paquette, Tarnak Farm Board of Inquiry, May 8, 2002. CLASSIFIED.

Sworn testimony of Cpl. Shane Brennan, Coalition Investigation Board, May 8, 2002. CLASSIFIED.

chapter 18

Interview notes: Capt. Jamie Key.

Maj. Harry M. Schmidt, "Written Submission from Maj. Schmidt to CIB," Tab U, Coalition Investigation Board final report, Exhibit 54, Article 32 hearing, Barksdale Air Force Base, La.

Sworn testimony of Capt. Erin Wirtanen, Coalition Investigation Board, May 11, 2002. CLASSIFIED.

Sworn testimony of Capt. Brett Paola, Coalition Investigation Board, May 11, 2002. CLASSIFIED.

Sworn testimony of Col. David C. Nichols, Coalition Investigation Board, May 11, 2002. CLASSIFIED.

Sworn testimony of Maj. Harry M. Schmidt, Coalition Investigation Board, May 12, 2002. CLASSIFIED.

Sworn testimony of Maj. William J. Umbach, Coalition Investigation Board, May 12, 2002. CLASSIFIED.

chapter 19

Interview notes: Sgt. Lorne Ford, Miranda Boutilier, Jocelyn Van Sloten, Gen. Maurice Baril.

Sworn testimony of Maj. Arthur Henry, Tarnak Farm Board of Inquiry, June 2, 2002. CLASSIFIED.

Sworn testimony of Sgt. Lorne Ford, Tarnak Farm Board of Inquiry, May 14, 2002. CLASSIFIED.

Sworn testimony of Chief Richard K. Emley, Coalition Investigation Board, May 16, 2002. CLASSIFIED.

chapter 20
Coalition Investigation Board, "Summary of Facts: Tarnak Farms Friendly Fire Incident near Kandahar, Afghanistan," June 7, 2002.

Glen McGregor, "'Go-pills' clouded F16 pilots' judgment: lawyers," *The Ottawa Citizen*, November 10, 2002. (*"blood alcohol level…in some countries."*)

chapter 21
Brig.-Gen. Marc Dumais and Brig.-Gen. Stephen Sargeant, "Addendum to the statement of opinion, Coalition Investigation Board," June 14, 2002.

Editorial, "Losing focus in the fog of war," *Springfield State Journal-Register*, June 13, 2002. (*"From fund-raisers for…real enemy is."*)

Eric Schmitt, "Inquiry on Canadians' deaths says U.S. pilots broke rules," *New York Times News Service*, June 18, 2002. (*"A military investigation…follow proper procedures."*)

Glen McGregor, "F16 pilot 'haunted nightly': Lawyer says pilot feels sorrow, not guilt," *The Ottawa Citizen*, June 10, 2002. (McGregor's story, the first to identify the pilot who bombed the Canadian soldiers, includes numerous comments from Maj. Harry Schmidt's military lawyer, Capt. James E. Key III.)

Interview notes: Gen. Maurice Baril, Maj. Bill Umbach.

Tarnak Farm Board of Inquiry, "Tarnak Farm Board of Inquiry, Final Report," June 19, 2002. SECRET.

chapter 22

Adrian Humphreys and Sheldon Alberts, "Pilots accused of reckless disregard," *National Post*, September 14, 2002. (*"It's saying: 'Put…for the worst."*)

Ajay Bhardwaj, "A wife's grief lingers," *The Edmonton Sun*, July 28, 2002. (*"The fact that…isn't coming home."*)

Allan Thompson, "Findings classified, Baril says," *The Toronto Star*, July 20, 2002. (*"It would not…love to, though."*)

Associated Press, "Commander of sub in fatal collision offers tearful apology to families," March 10, 2001. (*"I'd like to…to the grave."*)

Canadian Press, "Military report a relief for grieving families," June 29, 2002. (*"I would like…and take it."*)

Editorial, "A cover-up higher up?" *Montreal Gazette*, July 20, 2002. (*"We wonder what…along with it."*)

Editorial, "Our troops deserve the whole story," *The Toronto Sun*, July 20, 2002. (*"raises questions about…inquiries weren't enough."*)

Editorial, "Reveal the truth in U.S. bombing," *The Toronto Star*, July 20, 2002. (*"Bluntly put, we…lost their lives."*)

Editorial, "Unfriendly investigation," *The Ottawa Citizen*, July 20, 2002. (*"most upsetting…facts from Canadians."*)

Glen McGregor, "Overhaul friendly-fire inquiry: MP," *The Ottawa Citizen*, July 20, 2002. (*"He's the wrong…we can trust."*)

Interview notes: Lloyd Smith, Charlotte Smith, Richard Léger, Charles W. Gittins, Gen. Maurice Baril, Col. John S. Odom Jr., Col. Gregory C. Graf, Dave Beck.

Larry Johnsrude, "Pilots may never fly another mission: Families relieved no fault found with Canadians," *The Edmonton Journal*, June 29, 2002. (*"If sending him…out of it."*)

Michael Friscolanti, "F-16 pilot 'cleared to drop bomb," *National Post*, July 19, 2002. (*"It is unconscionable…kind of information." / "clearly remorseful and…holding the bag."*)

Michael Friscolanti, "U.S. pilot sorry for bombing 'partners': Airman speaks out on Canadian deaths," *National Post*, July 20, 2002. (*"It's a tragic…answer that one."*)

Ron Corbett and Keith Gerein, "Fanfare greets returning soldiers: Thousands line motorcade route decorated with yellow ribbons," *Vancouver Sun*, July 29, 2002. (*"It is their…day to rejoice."*)

Rowan Scarborough, "Controller 'cleared' U.S. pilots after friendly fire," *The Washington Times*, July 18, 2002. (*"If true, such…of the investigation."*)

Rowan Scarborough, "'Friendly fire' judge's memo assailed; General criticized actions that led to deaths of Canadians," *The Washington Times*, July 30, 2002.

Rowan Scarborough, "Tailhook 'injustice' righted," *The Washington Times*, July 31, 2002. (*"witchhunt" / feminist backlash."*)

Tarnak Farm Board of Inquiry, "Tarnak Farm Board of Inquiry, Final Report," June 19, 2002. SECRET.

Tim Naumetz and Glen McGregor, "U.S. pilots 'direct cause' of Canadian soldiers' deaths," *The Ottawa Citizen*, June 29, 2002. (*"The decision of…of the pilot."*)

William Walker, "'Friendly fire pilots may face military hearing," *The Toronto Star*, June 29, 2002. (*"Our children always…help support us."*)

William Walker, "'You're cleared. Self-defence'; Lawyer says transcript vindicates F–16 pilot blamed in deaths," *The Toronto Star*, July 19, 2002. (*"dumbfounded…cleared to drop."* / *"I hate to…want the truth."*)

chapter 23

Charles W. Gittins and David L. Beck, "Letter to the Honorable James G. Roche, Secretary of the Air Force, re: Objection to Coalition Investigative Board report and request for appointment of new investigative board on grounds of material failure to comply with Air Force regulation," October 11, 2002.

Charles W. Gittins, "Re: Major Schmidt and Major Umbach," November 4, 2002.

Col. Craig A. Smith, "Response to Charles W. Gittins and David L. Beck," October 29, 2002.

David L. Beck, "Re: U.S. v. Major William J. Umbach," November 11, 2002.

Glen McGregor, "F16 pilots receive death threats: RCMP, FBI hunt Canadian who e-mailed warning to Illinois governor," *The Ottawa Citizen*, November 3, 2002. (*"If the pilots…two more customers."*)

Glen McGregor, "Friendly fire trial intended to appease Canada: senator," *The Ottawa Citizen*, October 30, 2002. (*"Whether this resulted…of these airmen."*)

Glen McGregor, "Governor opens mansion to help pilots," *The Ottawa Citizen*, October 18, 2002. (*"These men are…supported, not prosecuted."*)

Glen McGregor, "No 'liaison' to warn F16 pilots," *The Ottawa Citizen*, November 8, 2002. (*"…would not have happened…"*)

Glen McGregor, "Princess Pats were warned: Stop firing: U.S. pilot's lawyer says missed ceasefire order led to deaths," *The Ottawa Citizen*, November 19, 2002. (*"This is material…was unconscionably omitted."*)

Graham Hughes, "Marc Leger's parents share memories with schoolchildren," *The Ottawa Citizen*, November 12, 2002. (*"The children brought…he was young."*)

Interview notes: Cpl. Rene Paquette, Col. Robert Murphy, Charles W. Gittins, Col. John S. Odom, Col. Gregory C. Graf, MCpl. Brett Perry.

Maureen Murray, "Solemn ceremonies hit home," *The Toronto Star*, November 12, 2002. (*"I got up…morning in tears."*)

Michael Friscolanti, "Americans rally around charged pilots: Legal fund set up," *National Post*, September 16, 2002. (*"No one's perfect…do with you."* / *"It looks to…his own government."*)

Michael Friscolanti, "He 'is not a monster,' wife of U.S. pilot says," *National Post*, October 7, 2002. (*"I'll do anything…their loved ones."* / *"These pilots have…turn, help them."*)

Michael Friscolanti, "New transcript reveals soldiers fired into air: Contradicts report prepared by investigators," *National Post*, November 27, 2002. (*"unconscionable"*)

Michael Friscolanti, "Pilots blame night goggles in deaths," *National Post*, November 30, 2002. (*"He clearly saw…tell the distance."*)

Michael Friscolanti, "'Not all of us want pilots punished': Canadians counted among supporters of U.S. airmen in friendly fire deaths," *National Post*, November 11, 2002. (*"There's going to…the whole picture."* / *"Of all my…of his life."* / *"If they had…the criminal charges."* / *"They were precious…soldier again. Never."*)

Rachel Bloomer, "Thousands pay respects: Ceremonies across the city remember veterans, war dead," *The Halifax Daily News*, November 12, 2002. (*"Like any other…that's changed, obviously."*)

The letters cited in this chapter are contained in a bound scrapbook entitled: "The People Speak, Letters to Major Harry Schmidt and Major Bill Umbach," Monterey Products, 2003.

chapter 24

Bill Gertz and Rowan Scarborough, "Friendly punishment," *The Washington Times*, January 17, 2003. (*"You are hereby…of a commander."*)

Col. David C. Nichols, "Memorandum for Major General Walter E. Buchanan III; Subject: Written Matters in Response to LOR," July 22, 2002.

David L. Beck, Capt. Matthew Roderick, Capt. Matthew Scoble, "Proffer of Expected Testimony of Maj.-Gen. Steven G. Wood," January 9, 2003, Exhibit 137, Article 32 hearing, Barksdale Air Force Base, La.

Interview notes: Lisa Schmidt, Marlene Umbach, John Russo, Jocelyn Van Sloten, Lloyd Smith, Richard Léger, Claire Léger, Miranda Boutilier, Cpl. Shane Brennan, Col. David C. Nichols, Col. John S. Odom, Maj. Harry Schmidt.

Maj.-Gen. Stephen G. Wood, "Affidavit of Maj Gen Stephen G. Wood," February 24, 2003, Exhibit 182, Article 32 hearing, Barksdale Air Force Base, La.

Michael Friscolanti, "Pilots feel forgotten by military," *National Post*, January 11, 2003. (*"He was probably…for nine months."* / *"It's common sense…scrutinize and sensationalize."* / *"They don't have…it to me."*)

chapter 25

Interview notes: Capt. Joe Jasper, Miranda Boutilier.

Sworn testimony of Capt. Joseph M. Jasper, Article 32 hearing, January 14, 2003, Barksdale Air Force Base, La.

Michael Friscolanti, "Officer: 'I didn't know the American regulations,'" *National Post*, January 15, 2003. (*"You can fill…American, one Canadian."*)

chapter 26

Interview notes: Col. John S. Odom, Charles W. Gittins, Maj. Harry Schmidt,

Sworn testimony of Col. Lawrence Stutzriem, Article 32 hearing, January 15, 2003, Barksdale Air Force Base, La.

Sworn testimony of Cpl. Brett Perry, Article 32 hearing, January 15, 2003, Barksdale Air Force Base, La.

Sworn testimony of Cpl. Brian Decaire, Article 32 hearing, January 15, 2003, Barksdale Air Force Base, La.

Sworn testimony of Cpl. Rene Paquette, Article 32 hearing, January 15, 2003, Barksdale Air Force Base, La.

Sworn testimony of Sgt. Lorne Ford, Article 32 hearing, January 15, 2003, Barksdale Air Force Base, La.

chapter 27

Sworn testimony of Col. Lawrence Stutzriem, Article 32 hearing, January 16, 2003, Barksdale Air Force Base, La.

Sworn testimony of Maj. John A. Milton, Article 32 hearing, January 16, 2003, Barksdale Air Force Base, La.

chapter 28

Glen McGregor, "F16 pilots' decision to bomb 'not unreasonable': witness," *The Ottawa Citizen*, January 18, 2003. (*"If it's not…not a crime."*)

Michael Friscolanti, "Bombing was reasonable, says air force official," *National Post*, January 18, 2003. (*"The key government…fix the problems."*)

Sean Naylor, *Not a Good Day to Die: The Untold Story of Operation Anaconda*, Berkley Books, 2005. (Naylor recounts the truth about what happened to P.O. Neil Roberts).

Sworn testimony of Maj. John A. Milton, Article 32 hearing, January 16–17, 2003. Barksdale Air Force Base, La.

Sworn testimony of Lt.-Col. Ralph Viets, Article 32 hearing, January 17, 2003. Barksdale Air Force Base, La.

Sworn testimony of Lt.-Col. Craig H. Fisher, Article 32 hearing, January 17, 2003. Barksdale Air Force Base, La.

William Walker, "The truth has to come out; A U.S. military hearing on the 'friendly fire' deaths of four Canadian soldiers plays out on two stages," *The Toronto Star*, January 19, 2003. (*"I could just…suffer too much."*)

chapter 29

Glen McGregor, "'I lay next to my husband last night. I knew she wasn't laying next to hers,'" *The Ottawa Citizen*, January 19, 2003. (*"When I envision…next to hers." / "They still won't…myself on them."*)

Sworn testimony of Col. David C. Nichols, Article 32 hearing, January 18, 2003. Barksdale Air Force Base, La.

chapter 30

Alison Auld, "Explosive exchange at friendly fire hearing," *Canadian Press*, January 20, 2003. (*"After the government's…in military history."*)

Glen McGregor, "Defence lawyers object to hearing witness," *The Ottawa Citizen*, January 21, 2003. (*"This is not…this is ridiculous."*)

Michael Friscolanti, "Deadly tragedy almost averted, hearing told," *National Post*, January 21, 2003. (*"By the time...big railroad job."*)

Miro Cernetig, "General to say self-defence was pretext," *The Globe and Mail*, January 21, 2003. (*"He will state...rules of engagement."* / *"He's going to...it was murder!"*)

Sworn testimony of Maj. Marshall Scott Woodson III, Article 32 hearing, January 20, 2003, Barksdale Air Force Base, La.

Sworn testimony of TSgt. Michael Carroll, Article 32 hearing, January 20, 2003, Barksdale Air Force Base, La.

chapter 31

Exhibit 90, "PowerPoint recreation," Coalition Investigation Board, June, 2002.

Sworn testimony of Brig.-Gen. Stephen T. Sargeant, Article 32 hearing, January 21-22, 2003. Barksdale Air Force Base, La.

chapter 32

Michael Friscolanti, "Umbach wins more sympathy than Schmidt," *National Post*, January 24, 2003. (*"Maj. Umbach touched...of my heart."* / *"Maj. Umbach I...line; I'm sorry."* / *"Maj. Umbach, he...he was sorry."* / *"I would just...apology as well."*)

Sworn testimony of Col. Robert Murphy, Article 32 hearing, January 23, 2003, Barksdale Air Force Base, La.

Unsworn statement of Maj. Bill J. Umbach, Article 32 hearing, January 23, 2003, Barksdale Air Force Base, La.

Unsworn statement of Maj. Harry M. Schmidt, Article 32 hearing, January 23, 2003, Barksdale Air Force Base, La.

chapter 33

Canadian Press, "Suit splits family of dead soldier," January 12, 2003. (*"want to be…he died for."*)

Charles W. Gittins, Lt.-Col. Clayton W. Moushon, Capt. James E. Key III, "Article 32 Hearing Revised Defense Post-Hearing Brief," February 28, 2003.

Charles W. Gittins, Lt.-Col. Clayton W. Moushon, Capt. James E. Key III, "Article 32 Hearing Defense Post-Hearing Reply Brief," March, 2003.

Clifford Krauss, "Canadian families split on fate of U.S. pilots," *New York Times News Service*, February 8, 2003. (*"I know Ricky…were the pilots."*)

Col. John S. Odom Jr., Lt.-Col. Gregory C. Graf, Maj. James K. Floyd, Capt. Katherine E. Oler, "Post-Hearing Memorandum on behalf of the United States," February 24, 2003.

Col. John S. Odom Jr., Lt.-Col. Gregory C. Graf, Maj. James K. Floyd, Capt. Katherine E. Oler, "Reply Memorandum on behalf of the United States to the Accused's Post-Hearing Briefs," March 7, 2003.

Exhibit 183, "Request for family member travel vouchers," Article 32 hearing, January 8, 2003.

Michael Friscolanti, "U.S. pilots return home to await fate," *National Post*, January 25, 2003. (*"This put it…made more sense."* / *"I don't think…it wasn't sincere."* / *"This is ten…may never happen."*)

chapter 34

Col. Patrick Rosenow, "Article 32 recommendations," March, 2003.
Michael Friscolanti, "No friendly fire trial," *National Post*, March 21, 2003. (*"It's a gross…and that's all."* / *"They have to…son cannot call."* / *"Clearly there was…parties aren't guilty."*)

The Associated Press, "Text of Bush's speech," March 19, 2003. (*"To all of...the American military.."*)

Tim Harper, "Bravos greet Chretien," *The Toronto Star*, March 18, 2003. (*"Over the last...were not successful."*)

U.S. Air Force press release, "Article 32 Recommendations," March 20, 2003.

chapter 35
Interview notes: Sgt. Craig Reid.

chapter 36
Glen McGregor, "A friendly fire pilot's agonizing choice," *The Ottawa Citizen*, June 24, 2003. (*"I want him...me, or anybody."*)

Lt.-Gen. Bruce Carlson, "Memorandum for Major William J. Umbach, Subject: Letter of Reprimand," June 16, 2003.

Michael Friscolanti, "A decision no one is celebrating," *National Post*, June 20, 2003. (*"It opens up...to move on."*)

Michael Friscolanti, "Friendly fire pilots face lesser penalties," *National Post*, June 20, 2003. (*"Because of all...to lay down."*)

Michael Friscolanti, "Friendly fire pilot wants to meet families," *National Post*, June 21, 2003. (*"I am willing...painfully, painfully permanent."*)

Michael Friscolanti, "U.S. pilot takes gamble in bid to clear his name," *National Post*, June 26, 2003. (*"He's a coward...everybody but himself."* / *"Those people are...what he's doing."*)

Michael Friscolanti, "Friendly fire pilot faces one charge: Maximum 6 months in jail," *National Post*, July 2, 2003. (*"Everybody understood—or... called their bluff."*)

chapter 37

Canadian Press Newswire, "3rd Battalion Princess Patricia's Battle Group honoured by Canada and U.S.," December, 8, 2003. (*"It was good…leave that unit."*)

Capt. James E. Key III, "United States v. Harry M. Schmidt—Objection to Scheduling Decisions Made in 27 January 2004 R.C.M. 802 Conference," January 28, 2004.

CBC News, "U.S. awards medals to Canadian soldiers," December 9, 2003. (*"The medal, to…braver than that." / "It doesn't change…under the earth."*)

Charles W. Gittins, Lt.-Col. Clayton W. Moushon, Capt. James E. Key III, "Motion for appropriate relief, United States v. Harry M. Schmidt," November 24, 2003.

Charles W. Gittins, Lt.-Col. Clayton W. Moushon, Capt. James E. Key III, "Motion to dismiss, United States v. Harry M. Schmidt," November 24, 2003.

Charles W. Gittins, Lt.-Col. Clayton W. Moushon, Capt. James E. Key III, "Motion for appropriate relief, United States v. Harry M. Schmidt," December 29, 2003.

Charles W. Gittins, Lt.-Col. Clayton W. Moushon, Capt. James E. Key III, "Petition for extraordinary relief in the nature of a writ of mandamus and for a stay of court-martial," United States Air Force Court of Criminal Appeals, January 7, 2004.

Col. Mary Boone, "Memorandum for all Counsel, Subject: Motions—U.S. v. Schmidt," December 15, 2003.

Glen McGregor, "Friendly fire pilot on list to testify against wingman," *The Ottawa Citizen*, October 10, 2003. (*"If the prosecution…the prosecution's case."*)

Interview notes: Doreen Coolen, Paul Dyer, Agatha Dyer, Jocelyn Van Sloten, Joan Schmidt.

Jessica Leeder, "Two years to the day, memorial a reality," *Edmonton Journal*, April 18, 2004. (*"I knew Ains…risk their lives."*)

Michael Friscolanti, "Maj. Schmidt fights to clear name; boss getting promotion," *National Post*, July 31, 2003. (*"He twisted and…these two pilots." / "We believe that…get to pilots."*)

Michael Friscolanti, "U.S. won't have to reveal other friendly fire events," *National Post*, December 18, 2003. (*"The problem the…of these accidents."*)

Michael Friscolanti, "Bombing's toll continues," *National Post*, April 17, 2004. (*"Every day of…have Ricky back." / "Paul is a…should mourn together." / "It might look…him too much."*)

Michael Friscolanti, "U.S. pilot's court-martial in limbo," *National Post*, January 9, 2004. (*"The government is…all about control." / "While a defense… face, it's absurd."*)

Michael Friscolanti, "Schmidt has 'no right' to see air force secrets," *National Post*, April 3, 2004. (*"People who just…very significant point."*)

Richard A. Murtha's letter to Richard and Claire Léger, April 6, 2004.

Richard Leger's letter to Richard A. Murtha, April 8, 2004.

chapter 38

Charles W. Gittins, Lt.-Col. Clayton W. Moushon, Capt. James E. Key III, "Memorandum for 18 AF/CC, Appeal of Nonjudicial punishment—Maj Harry M. Schmidt," July 15, 2004.

Harry Levins, "Officer disputes that he refused to salute," *St. Louis Post-Dispatch*, August 6, 2004.

Interview notes: Col. Gregory C. Graf, Charles W. Gittins, Col. John S. Odom, Maj. Harry Schmidt.

Josh White, "Air Force pilot fined $5,672 for attacking Canadians," *Washington Post*, July 7, 2004. (*"By placing the…general officer corps."*)

Max Maudie, "Fine for soldiers' deaths," *The Calgary Sun*, July 7, 2004. (*"The biggest thing…to have remorse."*)

Michael Friscolanti, "Friendly fire pilot avoids court-martial," *National Post*, June 25, 2004. (*"Over the past…at his word."*)

Michael Friscolanti, "Pilot 'acted shamefully': U.S. general. Schmidt guilty, fined US$5,672 for killing Canadian soldiers," *National Post*, July 7, 2004. (*"If I had…would have said." / "I would talk…heart to call." / "If it weren't…is just ridiculous."*)

Rowan Scarborough, "Friendly fire pilot blames poor chain of command," *The Washington Times*, July 6, 2004. (*"Early allegations…cases, outright negligence." / "With no knowledge…the perceived threat."*)

The Associated Press, "American pilot to sue air force," July 8, 2004. (*"We believe that…his attorney's fees."*)

The Associated Press, "Pilot accused in bombing of Canadians defends himself before 3-star general," July 1, 2004. (*"He explained exactly…he did it."*)

chapter 39

Col. R. Eric Rissling, "Claims of the Estate of Richard Green, Doreen Coolen and Michael McDonald, Air Force Claim Nos. JACT 04-13, 04-14, and 04-15, respectively," December 15, 2004.

Dale Anne Freed, "Fallen soldier's father dead," *The Toronto Star*, October 2, 2004.

Interview notes: MCpl. Brett Perry, Cpl. Brian Decaire, Aart Van Sloten, Janna Van Sloten, Jocelyn Van Sloten, Cpl. Rene Paquette, Lloyd Smith, Charlotte Smith, Capt. Alastair Luft, Doreen Young, Sgt. Lorne Ford, MCpl. Rob Coates, Cpl. Chris Kopp, Cpl. Victor Speirs, W.O. Bill Wilson, MCpl. Jean de la Bourdonnaye, Miranda Boutilier, Shane Brennan, Richard Léger, Claire Léger, Maj. Sean Hackett, Capt. Joe Jasper, M.W.O. Billy Bolen, Sgt. Marco Favasoli, Cpl. Pete Filis, MCpl. Brad McKenzie, Sgt. Dave Bibby, MCpl. Jon Bradshaw, W.O. Rob Jones.

Lt.-Gen. Bruce Carlson's letter to Richard and Claire Léger, August 16, 2004.

chapter 40

Bryan Smith, "Harry Schmidt's War," *Chicago Magazine*, April 2005. (*"I was the...for the ride."*)

Interview notes: Col. Robert J. Murphy, Col. David C. Nichols, Col. Gregory C. Graf, Lt.-Col. John A. Milton, Lt.-Col. Ralph Viets, Col. John S. Odom, Charles W. Gittins, Gen. Maurice Baril, David L. Beck.

chapter 41

Interview notes: Bill Umbach, Marlene Umbach.

Coalition Investigation Board, "Verbatim Testimony of Maj. Harry Schmidt and Maj. Bill Umbach," April 18, 2002, Tab S-6.1—6.12. CLASSIFIED.

chapter 42

Interview notes: Maj. Harry Schmidt

chapter 43

Interview notes: Sgt. Craig Reid

Index